McGraw-Hill Reader

McGraw-Hill, Inc.
New York | St. Louis | San Francisco
Auckland | Bogotá | Caracas
Hamburg | Lisbon | London
Madrid | Mexico | Milan
Montreal | New Delhi | Paris
San Juan | São Paulo | Singapore
Sydney | Tokyo | Toronto

GILBERT H. MULLER
The City University of New York
LaGuardia

The
McGraw-Hill
Reader

Fourth Edition

The McGraw-Hill Reader

1 2 3 4 5 6 7 8 9 0 DOC DOC 9 5 4 3 2 1 0

ISBN 0-07-044028-X

This book was set in Palatino by Waldman Graphics, Inc.
The editors were Lesley Denton and James R. Belser;
the production supervisor was Janelle S. Travers.
The cover was designed by Karen K. Quigley.
R. R. Donnelley & Sons Company was printer and binder.

Acknowledgments appear on pages 660-665,
and on this page by reference.

Library of Congress Cataloging-in-Publication Data

The McGraw-Hill reader / [edited by] Gilbert H. Muller.—4th ed.
   p.   cm.
  Includes index.
  ISBN 0-07-044028-X
  1. College readers.   2. English language—Rhetoric.   I. Muller,
Gilbert H., (date).
PE1417.M44   1991
808'.0427—dc20   90-13270

About the Author

Gilbert H. Muller, who received a Ph.D. in English and American Literature from Stanford University, is currently professor of English at the LaGuardia campus of the City University of New York. He has also taught at Stanford, Vassar, and several universities overseas. Dr. Muller is the author of the award-winning *Nightmares and Visions: Flannery O'Connor and the Catholic Grotesque, Chester Himes,* and other critical studies. His essays and reviews have appeared in *The New York Times, The New Republic, The Nation, The Sewanee Review, The Georgia Review,* and elsewhere. He is also a noted author and editor of textbooks in English and composition, including *The Short Prose Reader* with Harvey Wiener and, with John Williams, *The McGraw-Hill Introduction to Literature.* Among Dr. Muller's awards are a National Endowment for the Humanities Fellowship, a Fulbright Fellowship, and a Mellon Fellowship.

To

Parisa and Darius
My favorite readers

Contents

1 Personal Narrative 1

2 The Sense of Place 51

3   Manners and Morals **99**

4   Education **136**

5   Human Development and Behavior **191**

6   Social Processes and Institutions 230

7   Business and Economics 299

8   Language, Writing, and Communication 350

9   Literature, Media, and the Arts 404

10   Philosophy and Ethics 455

11   Religious Thought and Experience 491

12 Mathematics, Science, and Technology 536

13 Civilization 589

Contents of Essays by Rhetorical Mode

Narration

Description

Illustration

Comparison and Contrast

Analogy

Definition

Classification

Process Analysis

Causal Analysis

Argument and Persuasion

Logic

Humor, Irony, and Satire

Preface

The fourth edition of *The McGraw-Hill Reader* preserves the form and spirit of earlier editions. It continues to present the finest classic and contemporary essays for today's college students. Addressing the continuing national interest in core liberal arts programs, this text offers students and teachers a full range of prose models important to writing courses, reading sequences, and key undergraduate disciplines. All the selections, consisting of complete essays, chapters, and self-contained sections of chapters, have been selected for their significance, vitality, and technical precision. With its high caliber of material, its consistent humanistic emphases, and its clear organization, *The McGraw-Hill Reader* is lively, sophisticated, and eminently usable for college composition and reading programs.

The organization of *The McGraw-Hill Reader* is one of its most significant features. Composed of thirteen chapters, the text embraces all major modes of writing and most disciplines that college students encounter as undergraduates. Chapters 1 to 3 provide students with prose models largely of a personal, experiential, narrative, descriptive, or reflective nature—essays that enhance the acquisition of basic language skills. Following chapters cover core liberal arts disciplines, including education, the social sciences, business and economics, the humanities, and the sciences, and they culminate in a final interdisciplinary chapter on civilization that is integral to the scope and method of *The McGraw-Hill Reader*. While reinforcing earlier modes of writing presented in the text, these disciplinary chapters offer prose models that provide practice in techniques of analysis, criticism, argumentation, and persuasion. As an integrated text, *The McGraw-Hill Reader* seeks to reconcile expressive and abstract varieties of thought in order to treat the total reading and writing process. An alternate table of contents, listing carefully selected essays in each of twelve rhetorical categories, adds to the flexibility of the text.

A second distinct advantage of *The McGraw-Hill Reader*, perhaps the primary one for teachers who prefer to create their own approaches to composition and reading courses, is the wide range of material and the varied constituencies represented in the text. The essays in this book have been selected carefully to embrace a rich international assortment of authors, to achieve balance among constituencies, to cover major historical periods, and to provide prose models and styles for class analysis, discussion, and imitation. The authors in this text—whether Plato or Maya Angelou, Swift or Joan Didion—have high visibility as writers and thinkers of value. Some of these authors are represented by two or three essays. All the authors—writing from such vantage points as literature, journalism, anthropology, sociology, art history, biology, and philosophy—presuppose that ideas exist in the world, that we should be alert to them, and that we should be able to deal with them in our own discourse. Because the selections extend from very simple esaays to the most abstract and complex modes of prose, teachers and students will be able to use *The McGraw-Hill Reader* at virtually all levels of a program. Above all, teachers can develop their own sequence of essays that will contribute not only to their students' reading and writing proficiency but also to growing intellectual power.

The third major strength of *The McGraw-Hill Reader* is the uniform apparatus that has been designed for every essay. Much can be learned from any well-written essay, especially if the apparatus is systematic in design. For each selection in this text there is a brief introduction. After each essay, there are questions organized in a common format created to reinforce essential reading, writing, and oral communication skills. Arranged in three categories—Comprehension, Rhetoric, and Writing—these questions reflect current compositional theory as they move students from audience analysis to various modes and processes of composition. All specialized terms used in the questions are defined for students in an extensive Glossary of Terms at the end of the text. The integrated design of these questions makes each essay—simple or complex, short or long, old or new—accessible to college students who possess mixed reading and writing abilities.

Supplementing *The McGraw-Hill Reader* is a comprehensive instructor's manual. Unlike many manuals, this one is a complete teacher's guide. *A Guide to the McGraw-Hill Reader* offers sample syllabi, well-considered strategies for teaching individual essays, sample rhetorical analyses, answers to questions, additional thought-provoking questions, comparative essay discussion formats, and tips for prewriting and guided writing activities. There is also a bibliography of criticism and research on the teaching of composition.

As teachers and students today, we might very well be inclinded to agree with Dr. Johnson's definition of the essay as "loose sally of the mind; an irregular, undigested piece; not a regular and orderly performance." There is, of course, an ideal essay lurking behind Johnson's whimsical definition. In this better sense of the essay, *The McGraw-Hill Reader* offers orderly performances. Here, there are regular prose models commensurate with our need and desire to read, write, and think well.

ACKNOWLEDGMENTS

It is a pleasure to acknowledge the support, assistance, and guidance of numerous individuals who helped to create *The McGraw-Hill Reader*. Foremost among these people are the many McGraw-Hill sales representatives who obtained teacher responses to questionnaires when the text was in its formative stages. I also want to thank the excellent McGraw-Hill family of assistants, editors, and executives who participated enthusiastically in the project from the outset and who encouraged me at every step.

The final design and content of *The McGraw-Hill Reader* reflects the expertise and advice offered by college teachers across the country who gave generously of their time when asked to respond to questionnaires submitted to them by McGraw-Hill sales representatives. These include: Howard Eitland, Boston College; Jack Williams, California State College, Stanislaus; John Gordon, Connecticut College; A. Harris Fairbanks, University of Connecticut; Scott Elledge, Cornell University; Bernard Beranek, G. F. Provost, Duquesne University; J. A. LaBashak, Edinboro State College; Robert Hogenson, Ferris State College; John McGrail, Fitchburg State College; James Fetler, Foothill College; Lynn Garrett, Louisiana State University; Gloria Conforti, Loyola University of Chicago; Florence Frank, University of Massachusetts; Robert L. Brown, University of Minnesota; Lee Nicholson, Modesto Junior College; Mary McHenry, Mount Holyoke College; Mary Wagoner, University of New Orleans; Linda Barlow, Walter Beale, and Erika Lindemann, University of North Carolina; June Verbillion, Northeastern Illinois University; Penny Hirsch, Northwestern University; David Fite, University of Santa Clara; Tony Tyler, State University College, Potsdam; and Peter DeBlois, Syracuse University.

Warm appreciation is also extended to those college and university English professors who carefully read the manuscript in part or in its entirety and who made many constructive suggestions for improvement of the first and second editions. I am most grateful to David Bartl, New Mexico Military Institute; Kathleen Bell, University of Miami; Robert L. Brown, University of Minnesota; Irene Clark, University of Southern California; David Fite, University of Santa Clara; Dennis R. Gabriel, Cuyahoga Community College; Alan Golding, University of California, Los Angeles; Lillian Gottesman, Bronx Community College; Eugene Hammond, University of Maryland; John Hanes, Duquesne University; Pamela Howell, Midland College; James Mauch, Foothill College; Mary McFarland, Fresno Community College; Susan Miller, University of Wisconsin; Albert Nicolai, Middlesex Community College; Patricia Owen, Nassau Community College; Robert J. Pelinski, University of Illinois; Linda H. Peterson, Yale University; Rosentine Purnell, California State University, Northridge; Carl Quesnell, Iowa State University; Grayce F. Salerno, Seton Hall University; Maragaret A. Strom, George Washington University; Beverly Thorsen, Central State University; Randall Wells, University of South Carolina; Jack Wilson, Old Dominion University; Mary Ann Wilson, Georgia State University; and Carl Wooton, University of Southwestern Louisiana.

Special recognition must also be given to those specialists in various liberal arts fields who provided advice: Jane S. Zembaty, Department of Philosophy, University of Dayton; Linda Davidoff, Department of Psychology, Essex Community College; Curtis Williams, Department of Biology, The State University of New York; and Diane Papalia-Finlay, Department of Psychology, University of Wisconsin.

For the fourth edition, I thank the following reviewers for their supportive and most helpful evaluations: Susan Aylworth, California State University; Lynette Black, Memphis State University; Mary Edge Blevetty, Cardinal Stritch College; Nadia Creamer, Columbia-Greene Community College; Paula Friedman, Cardinal Stritch College; James Fuller, Midland College; LaVerne Gonzalez, San Jose State University; Peter Hardon, Bradley University; Elyce Rae Helford, University of Iowa; Glenda Linsey Hicks, Midland College; Katherine Kernberger, Linfield College; Diane Koenig, Columbia-Greene Community College; Mary Kay Mahoney, Merrimack College; Ross Primm, Mount Senario College; Audrey Schmidt, Cardinal Stritch College; Patrick Shaw, Texas Tech University; Kathy Sheldon, Iowa University; Emma Johanne Thomas, Prairie View A&M University; Jeanne Westcott, Miami Dade Community College; Clifford Wood, University of Wisconsin; and Robert J. Wurster, Western Kentucky University.

Finally, I am pleased to acknowledge support from the Mellon Foundation, the Graduate Center of The City University of New York, and the United States Office of Education (Title III) that enabled me to concentrate on the development of this text.

Gilbert H. Muller

The
McGraw-Hill
Reader

Personal Narrative

LANGSTON HUGHES

Salvation

James Langston Hughes (1902–1967), poet, playwright, fiction writer, biographer, and essayist, was for more than fifty years one of the most productive and significant modern American authors. In The Weary Blues *(1926),* Simple Speaks His Mind *(1950),* The Ways of White Folks *(1940),* Selected Poems *(1959), and dozens of other books, he strove, in his own words, "to explain the Negro condition in America." This essay, from his 1940 autobiography* The Big Sea, *reflects the sharp, humorous, often bittersweet insights contained in Hughes's examination of human behavior.*

 was saved from sin when I was going on thirteen. But not really saved. It happened like this. There was a big revival at my Auntie Reed's church. Every night for weeks there had been much preaching, singing, praying, and shouting, and some very hardened sinners had been brought to Christ, and the membership of the church had grown by leaps and bounds. Then just before the revival ended, they held a special meeting for children, "to bring the young lambs to the fold." My aunt spoke of it for days ahead. That night I was escorted to the front row

1

and placed on the mourners' bench with all the other young sinners, who had not yet been brought to Jesus.

My aunt told me that when you were saved you saw a light, 2 and something happened to you inside! And Jesus came into your life! And God was with you from then on! She said you could see and hear and feel Jesus in your soul. I believed her. I had heard a great many old people say the same thing and it seemed to me they ought to know. So I sat there calmly in the hot, crowded church, waiting for Jesus to come to me.

The preacher preached a wonderful rhythmical sermon, all 3 moans and shouts and lonely cries and dire pictures of hell, and then he sang a song about the ninety and nine safe in the fold, but one little lamb was left out in the cold. Then he said: "Won't you come? Won't you come to Jesus? Young lambs, won't you come?" And he held out his arms to all us young sinners there on the mourners' bench. And the little girls cried. And some of them jumped up and went to Jesus right away. But most of us just sat there.

A great many old people came and knelt around us and 4 prayed, old women with jet-black faces and braided hair, old men with work-gnarled hands. And the church sang a song about the lower lights are burning, some poor sinners to be saved. And the whole building rocked with prayer and song.

Still I kept waiting to *see* Jesus. 5

Finally all the young people had gone to the altar and were 6 saved, but one boy and me. He was a rounder's son named Westley. Westley and I were surrounded by sisters and deacons praying. It was very hot in the church, and getting late now. Finally Westley said to me in a whisper: "God damn! I'm tired o' sitting here. Let's get up and be saved." So he got up and was saved.

Then I was left all alone on the mourners' bench. My aunt 7 came and knelt at my knees and cried, while prayers and song swirled all around me in the little church. The whole congregation prayed for me alone, in a mighty wail of moans and voices. And I kept waiting serenely for Jesus, waiting, waiting—but he didn't come. I wanted to see him, but nothing happened to me. Nothing! I wanted something to happen to me, but nothing happened.

I heard the songs and the minister saying: "Why don't you 8 come? My dear child, why don't you come to Jesus? Jesus is waiting for you. He wants you. Why don't you come? Sister Reed, what is this child's name?"

"Langston," my aunt sobbed. 9

"Langston, why don't you come? Why don't you come and 10 be saved? Oh, Lamb of God! Why don't you come?"

Now it was really getting late. I began to be ashamed of my- 11 self, holding everything up so long. I began to wonder what God thought about Westley, who certainly hadn't seen Jesus either, but who was now sitting proudly on the platform, swinging his knicker-bockered legs and grinning down at me, surrounded by deacons and old women on their knees praying. God had not struck Westley dead for taking his name in vain or for lying in the temple. So I decided that maybe to save further trouble, I'd better lie, too, and say that Jesus had come, and get up and be saved.

So I got up. 12

Suddenly the whole room broke into a sea of shouting, as they 13 saw me rise. Waves of rejoicing swept the place. Women leaped in the air. My aunt threw her arms around me. The minister took me by the hand and led me to the platform.

When things quieted down, in a hushed silence, punctuated 14 by a few ecstatic "Amens," all the new young lambs were blessed in the name of God. Then joyous singing filled the room.

That night, for the last time in my life but one—for I was a 15 big boy twelve years old—I cried. I cried, in bed alone, and couldn't stop. I buried my head under the quilts, but my aunt heard me. She woke up and told my uncle I was crying because the Holy Ghost had come into my life, and because I had seen Jesus. But I was really crying because I couldn't bear to tell her that I had lied, that I had deceived everybody in the church, that I hadn't seen Jesus, and that now I didn't believe there was a Jesus any more, since he didn't come to help me.

COMPREHENSION

1. What does the title tell you about the subject of this essay? How would you state, in your own words, the thesis that emerges from the title and the essay?

2. How does Hughes recount the revival meeting he attended? What is the dominant impression?

3. Explain Hughes's shifting attitude toward salvation in this essay. Why is he disappointed in the religious answers provided by his church? What does he say about salvation in the last paragraph?

RHETORIC

1. Key words and phrases in this essay relate to the religious experience. Locate five of these words and expressions, and explain their connotations.

2. Identify the level of language in the essay. How does Hughes employ language effectively?

3. Where is the thesis statement in the essay? Consider the following: the use of dialogue; the use of phrases familiar to you (idioms); and the sentence structure. Cite examples of these elements.

4. How much time elapses, and why is this important to the effect? How does the author achieve narrative coherence?

5. Locate details and examples in the essay that are especially vivid and interesting. Compare your list with what others have listed. What are the similarities? The differences?

6. What is the tone of the essay? What is the relationship between tone and point of view?

WRITING

1. Describe a time in your life when you suppressed your feelings before adults because you thought they would misunderstand.

2. Recount an event in your life during which you surrendered to group pressures.

3. Write a narrative account of the most intense religious experience in your life.

4. Narrate an episode in which you played a trick on people simply to win their approval or satisfy their expectations.

EUDORA WELTY

One Writer's Beginnings

Eudora Welty (1909–   ) was born and raised in Mississippi. She attended the University of Wisconsin, from which she received a B.A. in 1929, and Columbia University, where she studied advertising. Rejecting a career in advertising, Welty turned to writing, publishing her first short story in 1936. After a decade of writing short fiction, she published her first novel, Delta Wedding, *in 1946. Welty is considered one of our most important regional writers and one of the few contemporary masters of both the short story and the novel. Among her major works are* The Optimist's Daughter *(1972), which won a Pulitzer Prize, and* One Writer's Beginnings *(1984). She is a recipient of the National Medal for literature (1980) and the Presidential Medal of Freedom (1980). In this vivid reminiscence, Welty explores the relationship between reality and the imagination as she attempts to trace her origins as a writer.*

EUDORA WELTY

had the window seat. Beside me, my father checked the progress of our train by moving his finger down the timetable and springing open his pocket watch. He explained to me what the position of the arms of the semaphore meant; before we were to pass through a switch we would watch the signal lights change. Along our track, the mileposts could be read; he read them. Right on time by Daddy's watch, the next town sprang into view, and just as quickly was gone.

Side by side and separately, we each lost ourselves in the experience of not missing anything, of seeing everything, of knowing each time what the blows of the whistle meant. But of course it was not the same experience: what was new to me, not older than ten, was a landmark to him. My father knew our way mile by mile; by day or by night, he knew where we were. Everything that changed under our eyes, in the flying countryside, was the known world to him, the imagination to me. Each in our own way, we hungered for all of this: my father and I were in no other respect or situation so congenial.

In Daddy's leather grip was his traveler's drinking cup, collapsible; a lid to fit over it had a ring to carry it by; it traveled in a round leather box. This treasure would be brought out at my request, for me to bear to the water cooler at the end of the Pullman car, fill to the brim, and bear back to my seat, to drink water over its smooth lip. The taste of silver could almost be relied on to shock your teeth.

After dinner in the sparkling dining car, my father and I walked back to the open-air observation platform at the end of the train and sat on the folding chairs placed at the railing. We watched the sparks we made fly behind us into the night. Fast as our speed was, it gave us time enough to see the rose-red cinders turn to ash, each one, and disappear from sight. Sometimes a house far back in the empty hills showed a light no bigger than a star. The sleeping countryside seemed itself to open a way through for our passage, then close again behind us.

The swaying porter would be making ready our berths for the night, pulling the shade down just so, drawing the green fishnet hammock across the window so the clothes you took off could ride along beside you, turning down the tight-made bed, standing up the two snowy pillows as high as they were wide, switching on the eye of the reading lamp, starting the tiny electric fan—you suddenly saw its blades turn into gauze and heard its insect murmur; and drawing across it all the pair of thick green theaterlike curtains—billowing, smelling of cigar smoke—between which you would crawl or dive headfirst to button them together with yourself inside, to be seen no more that night.

When you lay enclosed and enwrapped, your head on a pillow parallel to the track, the rhythm of the rail clicks pressed closer to your body as if it might be your heart beating, but the sound of the engine seemed to come from farther away than when it carried you in daylight. The whistle was almost too far away to be heard, its sound wavering back from the engine over the roofs of the cars. What you listened for was the different sound that ran under you when your own car crossed on a trestle, then another sound on an iron bridge; a low or a high bridge—each had its pitch, or drumbeat, for your car.

Riding in the sleeper rhythmically lulled me and waked me. 7 From time to time, waked suddenly, I raised my window shade and looked out at my own strip of the night. Sometimes there was unexpected moonlight out there. Sometimes the perfect shadow of our train, with our car, with me invisibly included, ran deep below, crossing a river with us by the light of the moon. Sometimes the encroaching walls of mountains woke me by clapping at my ears. The tunnels made the train's passage resound like the "loud" pedal of a piano, a roar that seemed to last as long as a giant's temper tantrum.

But my father put it all into the frame of regularity, predict- 8 ability, that was his fatherly gift in the course of our journey. I saw it going by, the outside world, in a flash. I dreamed over what I could see as it passed, as well as over what I couldn't. Part of the dream was what lay beyond, where the path wandered off through the pasture, the red clay road climbed and went over the hill or made a turn and was hidden in trees, or toward a river whose bridge I could see but whose name I'd never know. A house back at its distance at night showing a light from an open doorway, the morning faces of the children who stopped still in what they were doing, perhaps picking blackberries or wild plums, and watched us go by—I never saw with the thought of their continuing to be there just the same after we were out of sight. For now, and for a long while to come, I was proceeding in fantasy.

COMPREHENSION

1. At the end of the second paragraph, the narrator says, "Each in our own way, we hungered for all of this." Do father and child hunger for the same thing? Describe what each one is enjoying. In what way do they crave the same thing?

2. According to the author, what constitutes a writer's "beginnings"?

3. What does the narrator mean when she says that regularity and predictability were the gifts her father gave her "in the course of our journey"?

RHETORIC

1. The author makes vivid use of sensory language. Give instances where she employs her senses of touch, sound, taste, and smell.

EUDORA WELTY

2. Why is the "flying countryside" an important image? What other images of movement and acceleration can you find?

3. Is the time frame of this story one day or several? Why is the author compressing experience? What effect does this achieve?

4. Is the narrator writing this from the point of view of a child or an adult? Is there any place where the narrator judges something in retrospect? How is Welty's handling of point of view similar to that of Langston Hughes in "Salvation"?

5. What is the purpose of this narrative? Is the thesis overstated? Explain your answer.

6. In what sense is this trip a metaphor for the relationship between father and child?

WRITING

1. Discuss what qualities life had for you as a child. In what ways have your perceptions of the world changed over time?

2. In a narrative essay, describe an experience you had that served as a metaphor for your relationship to the world.

3. Select a particularly memorable childhood trip that you took with your family or a member of your family. As Welty does, try to recapture the event by using vivid sensory language.

4. Compare and contrast what we learn about Welty and Hughes from their respective essays about childhood events.

MARK TWAIN

The Mesmerizer

Mark Twain (1835–1910) was the pseudonym of Samuel Langhorne Clemens. In The Adventures of Tom Sawyer *(1876),* Life on the Mississippi *(1883), and* The Adventures of Huckleberry Finn *(1885), Twain celebrated the challenge of the frontier experience and the promise of a new world. Adventurous, democratic, individualistic, hardheaded, and sentimental, he projected the image of the essential American, a role that did not always correspond to the bitter and tragic aspects of his later life. This selection, from Twain's autobiography, captures the young Clemens as a humorous crowd pleaser and perpetrator of hoaxes—characteristics that became central to his adult life and career.*

THE MESMERIZER

An exciting event in our village was the arrival of the mesmerizer. I think the year was 1850. As to that I am not sure but I know the month—it was May; that detail has survived the wear of fifty years. A pair of connected little incidents of that month have served to keep the memory of it green for me all this time; incidents of no consequence and not worth embalming, yet my memory has preserved them carefully and flung away things of real value to give them space and make them comfortable. The truth is, a person's memory has no more sense than his conscience and no appreciation whatever of values and proportions. However, never mind those trifling incidents; my subject is the mesmerizer now.

He advertised his show and promised marvels. Admission as usual: 25 cents, children and negroes half price. The village had heard of mesmerism in a general way but had not encountered it yet. Not many people attended the first night but next day they had so many wonders to tell that everybody's curiosity was fired and after that for a fortnight the magician had prosperous times. I was fourteen or fifteen years old, the age at which a boy is willing to endure all things, suffer all things short of death by fire, if thereby he may be conspicuous and show off before the public; and so, when I saw the "subjects" perform their foolish antics on the platform and make the people laugh and shout and admire I had a burning desire to be a subject myself.

Every night for three nights I sat in the row of candidates on the platform and held the magic disk in the palm of my hand and gazed at it and tried to get sleepy, but it was a failure; I remained wide awake and had to retire defeated, like the majority. Also, I had to sit there and be gnawed with envy of Hicks, our journeyman; I had to sit there and see him scamper and jump when Simmons the enchanter exclaimed, "See the snake! See the snake!" and hear him say, "My, how beautiful!" in response to the suggestion that he was observing a splendid sunset; and so on—the whole insane business. I couldn't laugh, I couldn't applaud; it filled me with bitterness to have others do it and to have people make a hero of Hicks and crowd around him when the show was over and ask him for more and more particulars of the wonders he had seen in his visions and manifest in many ways that they were proud to be acquainted with him. Hicks—the idea! I couldn't stand it; I was getting boiled to death in my own bile.

On the fourth night temptation came and I was not strong enough to resist. When I had gazed at the disk a while I pretended to be sleepy and began to nod. Straightway came the professor and made passes over my head and down my body and legs and arms, finishing each pass with a snap of his fingers in the air to discharge

MARK TWAIN

the surplus electricity; then he began to "draw" me with the disk, holding it in his fingers and telling me I could not take my eyes off it, try as I might; so I rose slowly, bent and gazing, and following that disk all over the place, just as I had seen the others do. Then I was put through the other paces. Upon suggestion I fled from snakes, passed buckets at a fire, became excited over hot steamboat-races, made love to imaginary girls and kissed them, fished from the platform and landed mud cats that outweighed me—and so on, all the customary marvels. But not in the customary way. I was cautious at first and watchful, being afraid the professor would discover that I was an imposter and drive me from the platform in disgrace; but as soon as I realized that I was not in danger, I set myself the task of terminating Hick's usefulness as a subject and of usurping his place.

It was a sufficiently easy task. Hicks was born honest, I without that incumbrance—so some people said. Hicks saw what he saw and reported accordingly, I saw more than was visible and added to it such details as could help. Hicks had no imagination; I had a double supply. He was born calm, I was born excited. No vision could start a rapture in him and he was constipated as to language, anyway; but if I saw a vision I emptied the dictionary onto it and lost the remnant of my mind into the bargain.

At the end of my first half-hour Hicks was a thing of the past, a fallen hero, a broken idol, and I knew it and was glad and said in my heart, "Success to crime!" Hicks could never have been mesmerized to the point where he could kiss an imaginary girl in public or a real one either, but I was competent. Whatever Hicks had failed in, I made it a point to succeed in, let the cost be what it might, physically or morally. He had shown several bad defects and I had made a note of them. For instance, if the magician asked, "What do you see?" and left him to invent a vision for himself, Hicks was dumb and blind, he couldn't see a thing nor say a word, whereas the magician soon found out that when it came to seeing visions of a stunning and marketable sort I could get along better without his help than with it.

Then there was another thing: Hicks wasn't worth a tallow dip on mute mental suggestion. Whenever Simmons stood behind him and gazed at the back of his skull and tried to drive a mental suggestion into it, Hicks sat with vacant face and never suspected. If he had been noticing he could have seen by the rapt faces of the audience that something was going on behind his back that required a response. Inasmuch as I was an imposter I dreaded to have this test put upon me, for I knew the professor would be "willing" me to do something, and as I couldn't know what it was, I should be exposed and denounced. However, when my time came, I took my chance. I perceived by the tense and expectant faces of the people that Simmons was behind me willing me with all his might. I tried my best to imagine what he wanted but nothing suggested itself. I felt ashamed and miserable then. I believed that the hour of my disgrace was come and that in another moment I should go out of that place disgraced. I ought to be ashamed to confess it but my next thought was not how I could win the compassion of kindly hearts by going out humbly and in sorrow for my misdoings, but how I could go out most sensationally and spectacularly.

There was a rusty and empty old revolver lying on the table among the "properties" employed in the performances. On May Day two or three weeks before there had been a celebration by the schools and I had had a quarrel with a big boy who was the school bully and I had not come out of it with credit. That boy was now seated in the middle of the house, halfway down the main aisle. I crept stealthily and impressively toward the table, with a dark and murderous scowl on my face, copied from a popular romance, seized the revolver suddenly, flourished it, shouted the bully's name, jumped off the platform and made a rush for him and chased him out of the house before the paralyzed people could interfere to save him. There was a storm of applause, and the magician, addressing the house, said, most impressively—

"That you may know how really remarkable this is and how wonderfully developed a subject we have in this boy, I assure you that without a single spoken word to guide him he has carried out what I mentally commanded him to do, to the minutest detail. I could have stopped him at a moment in his vengeful career by a mere exertion of my will, therefore the poor fellow who has escaped was at no time in danger."

So I was not in disgrace. I returned to the platform a hero and happier than I have ever been in this world since. As regards mental suggestion, my fears of it were gone. I judged that in case I failed to guess what the professor might be willing me to do, I could count on putting up something that would answer just as well. I was right, and exhibitions of unspoken suggestion became a favorite with the public. Whenever I perceived that I was being willed to do something I got up and did something—anything that occurred to me—and the magician, not being a fool, always ratified it. When people asked me, "How *can* you tell what he is willing you to do?" I said, "It's just as easy," and they always said admiringly, "Well, it beats *me* how you can do it."

Hicks was weak in another detail. When the professor made passes over him and said "his whole body is without sensation now—come forward and test him, ladies and gentlemen," the ladies and gentlemen always complied eagerly and stuck pins into Hicks, and if they went deep Hicks was sure to wince, then that poor professor

8

9

10

11

MARK TWAIN

would have to explain that Hicks "wasn't sufficiently under the influence." But I didn't wince; I only suffered and shed tears on the inside. The miseries that a conceited boy will ensure to keep up his "reputation"! And so will a conceited man; I know it in my own person and have seen it in a hundred thousand others. That professor ought to have protected me and I often hoped he would, when the tests were unusually severe, but he didn't. It may be that he was deceived as well as the others, though I did not believe it nor think it possible. Those were dear good people but they must have carried simplicity and credulity to the limit. They would stick a pin in my arm and bear on it until they drove it a third of its length in, and then be lost in wonder that by a mere exercise of will power the professor could turn my arm to iron and make it insensible to pain. Whereas it was not insensible at all; I was suffering agonies of pain.

After that fourth night, that proud night, that triumphant 12 night, I was the only subject. Simmons invited no more candidates to the platform. I performed alone every night the rest of the fortnight. Up to that time a dozen wise old heads, the intellectual aristocracy of the town, had held out as implacable unbelievers. I was as hurt by this as if I were engaged in some honest occupation. There is nothing surprising about this. Human beings feel dishonor the most, sometimes, when they most deserve it. That handful of overwise old gentlemen kept on shaking their heads all the first week and saying they had seen no marvels there that could not have been produced by collusion; and they were pretty vain of their unbelief too and liked to show it and air it and be superior to the ignorant and the gullible. Particularly old Dr. Peake, who was the ringleader of the irreconcilables and very formidable; for he was an F.F.V., he was learned, white-haired and venerable, nobly and richly clad in the fashions of an earlier and a courtlier day, he was large and stately, and he not only seemed wise but was what he seemed in that regard. He had great influence and his opinion upon any matter was worth much more than that of any other person in the community. When I conquered him at last, I knew I was undisputed master of the field; and now after more than fifty years I acknowledge with a few dry old tears that I rejoiced without shame.

COMPREHENSION

1. Where in his essay does Twain reveal his purpose? How does the author justify his trick?

2. What reasons does Twain give for his triumph over Hicks?

3. Explain the persona or image that Twain creates for himself in the course of the narrative.

THE MESMERIZER

RHETORIC

1. Twain uses abstract language in the first paragraph. Does this conflict with the informality of his style? Why, or why not?

2. Use these words in sentences: *embalming* (paragraph 1); *bile* (paragraph 3); *terminating* (paragraph 4); *incumbrance* (paragraph 5); *stealthily* (paragraph 8).

3. What method of introduction does Twain employ? What is the effect? In what way does the paragraph establish the tone of the essay?

4. What is the point of view in the essay? What advantage does Twain gain from his selection of point of view?

5. Cite three instances of comic techniques and effects in the essay, and explain their significance.

6. What is the function of Twain's editorializing in the account?

WRITING

1. Speaking of memory, Twain declares that "a person's memory has no more sense than his conscience and no appreciation whatever of values and proportions." Do you agree or disagree with this opinion? Justify your answer in an argumentative essay.

2. Recall a memorable event that occurred in your neighborhood when you were a child and that created excitement and controversy. Write a narrative essay about your role in it.

3. Compare and contrast this essay and "Salvation," by Langston Hughes, in regard to the theme of deception.

MAXINE HONG KINGSTON

The Woman Warrior

Maxine Hong Kingston (1940–   ) has written three books on the Chinese-American experience that have established her as a major contemporary prose stylist. The Woman Warrior *(1976) and* China Men *(1980) are brilliant explorations of personal and ethnic consciousness. Her newest work, a novel, is entitled* Trip-master Monkey *(1989). This selection from her first book is filled with the mysteries, family tales, and legends that she uses to create the tapestry of her complex cultural identity.*

MAXINE HONG KINGSTON

My American life has been such a disappointment. 1

"I got straight A's, Mama." 2

"Let me tell you a true story about a girl who saved her 3
village."

I could not figure out what was my village. And it was im- 4
portant that I do something big and fine, or else my parents would
sell me when we made our way back to China. In China there were
solutions for what to do with little girls who ate up food and threw
tantrums. You can't eat straight A's.

When one of my parents or the emigrant villagers said, "Feed- 5
ing girls is feeding cowbirds," I would thrash on the floor and scream
so hard I couldn't talk. I couldn't stop.

"What's the matter with her?" 6

"I don't know. Bad, I guess. You know how girls are. 'There's 7
no profit in raising girls. Better to raise geese than girls.'"

"I would hit her if she were mine. But then there's no use 8
wasting all that discipline on a girl. 'When you raise girls, you're
raising children for strangers.'"

"Stop that crying!" my mother would yell. "I'm going to hit 9
you if you don't stop. Bad girl! Stop!" I'm going to remember never
to hit or to scold my children for crying, I thought, because then they
will only cry more.

"I'm not a bad girl," I would scream. "I'm not a bad girl. I'm 10
not a bad girl." I might as well have said, "I'm not a girl."

"When you were little, all you had to say was 'I'm not a bad 11
girl,' and you could make yourself cry," my mother says, talking-story
about my childhood.

I minded that the emigrant villagers shook their heads at my 12
sister and me. "One girl—and another girl," they said, and made our
parents ashamed to take us out together. The good part about my
brothers being born was that people stopped saying, "All girls," but
I learned new grievances. "Did you roll an egg on *my* face like that
when *I* was born?" "Did you have a full-month party for *me*?" "Did
you turn on all the lights?" "Did you send *my* picture to Grandmother?" "Why not? Because I'm a girl? Is that why not?" "Why
didn't you teach me English?" "You like having me beaten up at
school, don't you?"

"She is very mean, isn't she?" the emigrant villagers would say. 13

"Come, children. Hurry. Hurry. Who wants to go out with 14
Great-Uncle?" On Saturday mornings, my great-uncle, the ex-river
pirate, did the shopping. "Get your coats, whoever's coming."

"I'm coming. I'm coming. Wait for me." 15

When he heard girls' voices, he turned on us and roared, "No 16
girls!" and left my sisters and me hanging our coats back up, not
looking at one another. The boys came back with candy and new toys.

When they walked through Chinatown, the people must have said, "A boy—and another boy—and another boy!" At my great-uncle's funeral I secretly tested out feeling glad that he was dead—the six-foot bearish masculinity of him.

I went away to college—Berkeley in the sixties—and I studied, 17 and I marched to change the world, but I did not turn into a boy. I would have liked to bring myself back as a boy for my parents to welcome with chickens and pigs. That was for my brother, who returned alive from Vietnam.

If I went to Vietnam, I would not come back; females desert 18 families. It was said, "There is an outward tendency in females," which meant that I was getting straight A's for the good of my future husband's family, not my own. I did not plan ever to have a husband. I would show my mother and father and the nosey emigrant villagers that girls have no outward tendency. I stopped getting straight A's.

And all the time I was having to turn myself American- 19 feminine, or no dates.

There is a Chinese word for the female I—which is "slave." 20 Break the women with their own tongues!

I refused to cook. When I had to wash dishes, I would crack 21 one or two. "Bad girl," my mother yelled, and sometimes that made me gloat rather than cry. Isn't a bad girl almost a boy?

"What do you want to be when you grow up, little girl?" 22

"A lumberjack in Oregon." 23

Even now, unless I'm happy, I burn the food when I cook. I 24 do not feed people. I let the dirty dishes rot. I eat at other people's tables but won't invite them to mine, where the dishes are rotting.

If I could not-eat, perhaps I could make myself a warrior like 25 the swordswoman who drives me. I will—I must—rise and plow the fields as soon as the baby comes out.

Once I get outside the house, what bird might call me; on 26 what horse could I ride away? Marriage and childbirth strengthen the swordswoman, who is not a maid like Joan of Arc. Do the women's work; then do more work, which will become ours too. No husband of mine will say, "I could have been a drummer, but I had to think about the wife and kids. You know how it is." Nobody supports me at the expense of his own adventure. Then I get bitter: no one supports me; I am not loved enough to be supported. That I am not a burden has to compensate for the sad envy when I look at women loved enough to be supported. Even now China wraps double binds around my feet.

When urban renewal tore down my parents' laundry and 27 paved over our slum for a parking lot, I only made up gun and knife fantasies and did nothing useful.

From the fairy tales, I've learned exactly who the enemy are. 28

I easily recognize them—business-suited in their modern American executive guise, each boss two feet taller than I am and impossible to meet eye to eye.

I once worked at an art supply house that sold paints to art- 29
ists. "Order more of that nigger yellow, willya?" the boss told me. "Bright, isn't it? Nigger yellow."

"I don't like that word," I had to say in my bad, smallperson's 30
voice that makes no impact. The boss never deigned to answer.

I also worked at a land developer's association. The building 31
industry was planning a banquet for contractors, real estate dealers, and real estate editors. "Did you know the restaurant you chose for the banquet is being picketed by CORE and the NAACP?" I squeaked.

"Of course I know." The boss laughed. "That's why I chose 32
it."

"I refuse to type these invitations," I whispered, voice unre- 33
liable.

He learned back in his leather chair, his bossy stomach opu- 34
lent. He picked up his calendar and slowly circled a date. "You will be paid up to here," he said. "We'll mail you the check."

If I took the sword, which my hate must surely have forged 35
out of the air, and gutted him, I would put color and wrinkles into his shirt.

It's not just the stupid racists that I have to do something 36
about, but the tyrants who for whatever reason can deny my family food and work. My job is my own only land.

To avenge my family, I'd have to storm across China to take 37
back our farm from the Communists; I'd have to rage across the United States to take back the laundry in New York and the one in California. Nobody in history has conquered and united both North America and Asia. A descendant of eighty pole fighters, I ought to be able to set out confidently, march straight down our street, get going right now. There's work to do, ground to cover. Surely, the eighty pole fighters, though unseen would follow me and lead me and pro- tect me, as is the wont of ancestors.

Or it may well be that they're resting happily in China, their 38
spirits dispersed among the real Chinese, and not nudging me at all with their poles. I mustn't feel bad that I haven't done as well as the swordswoman did; after all, no bird called me, no wise old people tutored me. I have no magic beads, or water gourd sight, no rabbit that will jump in the fire when I'm hungry. I dislike armies.

I've looked for the bird. I've seen clouds make pointed angel 39
wings that stream past the sunset, but they shred into clouds. Once at a beach after a long hike I saw a seagull, tiny as an insect. But when I jumped up to tell what miracle I saw, before I could get the words out I understood that the bird was insect-size because it was far away.

My brain had momentarily lost its depth perception. I was that eager to find an unusual bird.

The news from China has been confusing. It also had some- 40 thing to do with birds. I was nine years old when the letters made my parents, who are rocks, cry. My father screamed in his sleep. My mother wept and crumpled up the letters. She set fire to them page by page in the ashtray, but new letters came almost every day. The only letters they opened without fear were the ones with red borders, the holiday letters that mustn't carry bad news. The other letters said that my uncles were made to kneel on broken glass during their trials and had confessed to being land-owners. They were all executed, and the aunt whose thumbs were twisted off drowned herself. Other aunts, mothers-in-law, and cousins disappeared; some suddenly began writing to us again from communes or from Hong Kong. They kept asking for money. The ones in communes got four ounces of fat and one cup of oil a week, they said, and had to work from 4 A.M. to 9 P.M. They had to learn to do dances waving red kerchiefs; they had to sing nonsense syllables. The communists gave axes to the old ladies and said, "Go and kill yourself. You're useless." If we overseas Chinese would just send money to the Communist bank, our relatives said, they might get a percentage of it for themselves. The aunts in Hong Kong said to send money quickly; their children were begging on the sidewalks and mean people put dirt in their bowls.

When I dream that I am wire without flesh, there is a letter 41 on blue airmail paper that floats above the night ocean between here and China. It must arrive safely or else my grandmother and I will lose each other.

My parents felt bad whether or not they sent money. Some- 42 times they got angry at their brothers and sisters for asking. And they would not simply ask but have to talk-story too. The revolutionaries had taken Fourth Aunt and Uncle's store, house, and lands. They attacked the house and killed the grandfather and oldest daughter. The grandmother escaped with the loose cash and did not return to help. Fourth Aunt picked up her sons, one under each arm, and hid in the pig house, where they slept that night in cotton clothes. The next day she found her husband, who had also miraculously escaped. The two of them collected twigs and yams to sell while their children begged. Each morning they tied the faggots on each other's back. Nobody bought from them. They ate the yams and some of the children's rice. Finally Fourth Aunt saw what was wrong. "We have to shout 'Fuel for sale' and 'Yams for sale,'" she said, "We can't just walk unobtrusively up and down the street." "You're right," said my uncle, but he was shy and walked in back of her. "Shout," my aunt ordered, but he could not. "They think we're carrying these sticks home for our own fire," she said. "Shout." They walked about miserably, silently, until sundown, neither of them able to advertise themselves. Fourth Aunt, an orphan since the age of ten, mean as my mother, threw her bundle down at his feet and scolded Fourth Uncle, "Starving to death, his wife and children starving to death, and he's too damned shy to raise his voice." She left him standing by himself and afraid to return empty-handed to her. He sat under a tree to think, when he spotted a pair of nesting doves. Dumping his bag of yams, he climbed up and caught the birds. That was when the Communists trapped him, in the tree. They criticized him for selfishly taking food for his own family and killed him, leaving his body in the tree as an example. They took the birds to a commune kitchen to be shared.

It is confusing that my family was not the poor to be cham-   43
pioned. They were executed like the barons in the stories, when they were not barons. It is confusing that birds tricked us.

What fighting and killing I have seen have not been glorious   44
but slum grubby. I fought the most during junior high school and always cried. Fights are confusing as to who has won. The corpses I've seen had been rolled and dumped, sad little dirty bodies covered with a police khaki blanket. My mother locked her children in the house so we couldn't look at dead slum people. But at news of a body, I would find a way to get out; I had to learn about dying if I wanted to become a swordswoman. Once there was an Asian man stabbed next door, word on cloth pinned to his corpse. When the police came around asking questions, my father said, "No read Japanese. Japanese words. Me Chinese."

I've also looked for old people who could be my gurus. A   45
medium with red hair told me that a girl who died in a far country follows me wherever I go. This spirit can help me if I acknowledge her, she said. Between the head line and heart line in my right palm, she said, I have the mystic cross. I could become a medium myself. I don't want to be a medium. I don't want to be a crank taking "offer-ings" in a wicker plate from the frightened audience, who, one after another, asked the spirits how to raise rent money, how to cure their coughs and skin diseases, how to find a job. And martial arts are for unsure little boys kicking away under fluorescent lights.

I live now where there are Chinese and Japanese, but no emi-   46
grants from my own village looking at me as if I had failed them. Living among one's own emigrant villagers can give a good Chinese far from China glory and a place. "That old busboy is really a swords-man," we whisper when he goes by, "He's a swordsman who's killed fifty. He has a tong ax in his closet." But I am useless, one more girl who couldn't be sold. When I visit the family now, I wrap my Amer-ican successes around me like a private shawl; I *am* worthy of eating the food. From afar I can believe my family loves me fundamentally. They only say, "When fishing for treasures in the flood, be careful not

to pull in girls," because that is what one says about daughters. But I watched such words come out of my own mother's and father's mouths; I looked at their ink drawing of poor people snagging their neighbor's flotage with long flood hooks and pushing the girl babies on down the river. And I had to get out of hating range. I read in an anthropology book that Chinese say, "Girls are necessary too"; I have never heard the Chinese I know make this concession. Perhaps it was a saying in another village. I refuse to shy my way anymore through our Chinatown, which tasks me with the old sayings and the stories.

The swordswoman and I are not so dissimilar. May my people   47
understand the resemblance soon so that I can return to them. What we have in common are the words at our backs. The ideographs for *revenge* are "report at crime" and "report to five families." The reporting is the vengeance—not the beheading, not the gutting, but the words. And I have so many words—"chink" words and "gook" words too—that they do not fit on my skin.

COMPREHENSION

1. What is the historical context of this personal narrative? What assumptions does the author make about her audience?

2. Summarize the "autobiography" that Kingston presents of herself in this selection. What are her family and its individual members like?

3. Explain the author's American life. How does she relate to Chinese culture *and* to American culture? What is her major problem? How would she overcome it?

RHETORIC

1. What connotations does Kingston explore for the words *girls* and *females*? What connotations does she bring to the word *swordswoman*?

2. Locate five Chinese expressions or sayings in this selection. What is their effect on the tone of the essay?

3. The author's introductory paragraph consists of a single sentence. How effective is this strategy, and why?

4. Analyze the author's presentation of chronology. List the scenes into which the action is divided. Where are there stories within stories? Why does Kingston present such a complex tapestry of chronology and events? How, finally, does the author use narration to advance expository or explanatory ends?

5. Why is characterization important to the development of Kingston's thesis? How does the author *create* vivid characters? Cite specific examples and techniques. Compare her technique of characterization to that of Twain in "The Mesmerizer."

MAXINE HONG KINGSTON

6. Which paragraphs comprise the conclusion? How do these paragraphs reflect some of the major motifs of the essay?

WRITING

1. In *China Men*, Kingston speaks of "trying to unravel the mysteries" of her family. What mysteries does she explore here? Look up the word *mystery* in your dictionary. What "mysteries" concerning your family or your origins would you like to explore? Write an essay exploring this topic.

2. Write an autobiographical or narrative essay tracing a particular problem that you had to face while growing up in your family.

3. Narrate an event that happened to one of your relatives or ancestors in the "old country," the nation of your family's origin.

An American Childhood

Annie Dillard (1945–   ) often writes about nature, finding dramatic and important meanings in everyday natural events. Her writing is extremely meticulous, and she describes things with an exacting eye. She brings an intensity of spirit to all her subjects, which may range from water bugs to airplane accidents. Her most well-known work includes Pilgrim at Tinker Creek *(1974),* Holy the Firm *(1977), and* An American Childhood *(1987). In this selection, Dillard presents a vivid picture of a trip downriver with her father, while, at the same time, she depicts the relationship between them.*

Years before this, on long-ago summer Sundays, before   1
Father went down the Ohio and ended up selling his boat, he used to take me out with him on the water. It was a long drive to the Allegheny River; it was a long wait, collecting insects in the grass among the pebbles on shore, till Father got the old twenty-four-foot cabin cruiser ready to go. But the Allegheny River, once we got out on it, was grand. Its distant shores were mostly wooded on both sides; coal barges, sand barges, and shallow-draft oil tankers floated tied up at a scattering of docks. Father wore tennis shoes on his long feet, and a sun-bleached cotton captain-style hat. He always squinted outside, hat or no hat, because his eyes

were such a pale blue; the sun got in them. He was so tall he had to lean under the housetop to man the wheel.

We stopped at islands and swam. There were wooded islands 2
in the river—like Smoky Island at Pittsburgh's point, where Indians had tortured their English and Scotch-Irish captives by night. The Indians had tied the soldiers and settlers to trees, heaped hot coals on their feet, and let their small boys practice archery on them. Indian women heated rifle barrels and ramrods over fires till they glowed, then drove them through prisoners' nostrils or ears. The screams of the tortured settlers on Smoky Island reached French soldiers at Fort Duquesne, who had handed them over to the Indians reluctantly, they said. "Humanity groans at being forced to use such monsters."

Father and I tied up at Nine-Mile Island, upstream from 3
Smoky Island, and I jumped from a high rope-swing into the water, after poor Father told me all about those boaters' children who'd been killed or maimed dropping from this very swing. He could not bear to watch; he shut his eyes. From the tree branch at the top of the ladder I jumped onto the swing; when I let go over the water, momentum shot me forward like a slung stone. I swam up to find the water's surface again, and called to Father on shore, "It's okay now."

Our boat carved through the glossy water. Pittsburgh's sum- 4
mer skies are pale, as they are in many river valleys. The blinding haze spread overhead and glittered up from the river. It was the biggest sky in town.

We rode up in the locks and down in the locks. The locks 5
scared me, for the huge doors that locked out the river leaked, and loud tons of water squirted in, and we sat helpless below the river with nothing to do but wait for the doors to give way. Enormous whirlpools dragged at the boat; we held on to the lock walls, clawed, with a single hand line and a boat hook. Once I dropped the boat hook, a new one with a teak handle, and the whirlpools sucked it down. To where? Where did the whirlpools put the water they took, and where would they put you, all ground up, if you fell in?

Oh, the river was grand. Outside the lock and back on the go, 6
I sang wild songs at the top of my voice out over the roaring boat's stern. We raced under old steel bridges set on stone pilings in the river. How do people build bridges? How did anyone set those pilings, pile those stones, under the water?

Whenever I was on the river, I seemed to be visiting a fasci- 7
nating place I had forgotten all about, where physical causes had physical effects, and great things got done, slowly, heavily, because people understood materials and forces.

Father on these boat outings answered my questions at length. 8
He explained that people built coffer dams to set bridge pilings in a river. They lowered a kind of big pipe, or tight set of walls, to the

ANNIE DILLARD

bottom, and pumped all the water out of it; then the men could work there. I imagined the men piling and mortaring stones, with the unhurried ease of stone masons; they stood on gasping catfish and stinky silt. They were working under the river, at the bottom of a well of air. Just a few inches away, outside their coffer dam, a complete river of water was sliding downhill from western New York to the Gulf of Mexico. Above the workers' heads, boats and barges went by, their engines probably buzzing the coffer-dam walls. What a life. Father said that some drowned in accidents, or got crushed; it was dangerous work. He said, answering my question, that these workers made less money than the men I knew, men I privately considered wholly unskilled. The bridge pilings obsessed me; I thought and thought about the brave men who built them in the rivers. I tried to imagine their families, their lunches, their boots. I tried to imagine what it would feel like to accomplish something so useful as building a bridge. What a queer world was the river, where I admired everything and knew nothing.

Father explained how to make glass from sand. He explained, over and over, because I was usually too frightened to hear right, how the river locks worked; they ran our boat up or down beside the terrible dams. The concrete navigation dams made slick spillways like waterfalls across the river. From upstream it was hard to see the drop's smooth line. Drunks forgot about the dams from time to time, and drove their boats straight over, killing themselves and everyone else on board. How did the drunks feel, while they were up loose in the air at the wheels of their boats for a split second, when they remembered all of a sudden the dam? "Oh yes, the dam." It seemed like a familiar feeling.   9

On the back of a chart—a real nautical chart, with shoals and soundings, just as in *Life on the Mississippi*—Father drew a diagram of a water system. The diagram made clear something I'd always wondered about: how water got up to the top floors of houses. The water tower was higher than the highest sinks, that was all; through all those labyrinthine pipes, the water sought its own level, seeming to climb up, but really still trickling down. He explained how steam engines worked, and suspension bridges, and pumps.   10

Father explained so much technology to me that for a long time I confused it with American culture. If pressed, I would have claimed that an American invented the irrigation ditch. Certainly the coffer dam was American, I thought, and the water tower, the highway tunnel—these engineering feats—and everything motorized, and everything electrical, and in short, everything I saw about me newer than fishnets, sailboats, and spoons.   11

Technology depended on waterworks. The land of the forty-eight states was an extended and mighty system of controlled slopes,   12

a combination Grand Coulee Dam and Niagara Falls. The water fell and the turbines spun and the lights came on, so steel mills could run all night. Then the steel made cars, millions of cars, and workers bought the cars, because Henry Ford in 1910 had come up with the idea of paying them enough to buy things. So the water rolled down the continent—just plain fell—and everyone got rich.

Now, years later, Father had picked Amy and me up after church. When we got out of the car in the garage, we could hear Dixieland, all rambling brasses and drums, coming from the house. We hightailed it inside through the snow on the back walk and kicked off our icy dress shoes. I was in stockings. I could eat something, and go to my room. I had my own room now, and when I was home I stayed there and read or sulked. 13

While we were making sandwiches, though, Father started explaining the world to us once again. I stuck around. There in the kitchen, Father embarked upon on explanation of American economics. I don't know what prompted it. His voice took on urgency; he paced. Money worked like water, he said. 14

We were all listening, even little Molly. Molly, at four, had an open expression, smooth and quick, and fine blond hair; she was eating on the hoof, like the rest of us, and looking up, a pale face at thigh level, following the conversation. Mother futzed around the kitchen in camel-colored wool slacks; she rarely ate. 15

Did we know how water got up to our attic bathroom? Money worked the same way, he said, worked the way locks on the river worked, worked the way water flowed down from high water towers into our attic bathroom, the way the Allegheny and the Monongahela flowed into the Ohio, and the Ohio flowed into the Mississippi and out into the Gulf of Mexico at New Orleans. The money, once you got enough of it high enough, would flow by gravitation, all over everybody. 16

"It doesn't work that way," our mother said. She offered Molly tidbits: a drumstick, a beet slice, cheese. "Remember those shacks we see in Georgia? Those barefoot little children who have to quit school to work in the fields, their poor mothers not able to feed them enough"—we could all hear in her voice that she was beginning to cry—"not even able to keep them dressed?" Molly was looking at her, wide-eyed; she was bent over looking at Molly, wide-eyed. 17

"They shouldn't have so many kids," Father said. "They must be crazy." 18

The trouble was, I no longer believed him. It was beginning to strike me that Father, who knew the real world so well, got some of it wrong. Not much; just some. 19

ANNIE DILLARD

COMPREHENSION

1. What is Dillard's main purpose in this selection? Does a thesis emerge? Explain your answer.

2. What is the significance of the title? What distinguishes Dillard's childhood as an American one? How does her "American" childhood contrast with that of Maxine Hong Kingston?

3. What type of man is Dillard's father? What do his observations and perceptions reveal about his view of the world?

RHETORIC

1. How does Dillard's choice of images in describing her father reveal the perspective of a child? How is their relationship similar to that of Eudora Welty and *her* father in "One Writer's Beginnings"?

2. In paragraph 2, Dillard describes how Indians tortured settlers. What other images does Dillard use that evoke fear in her? How do they contribute to the mood of the essay?

3. Neither section opening reveals when the events of the essay took place or Dillard's age at the time. What is her purpose in presenting time so circumspectly?

4. How is Dillard's view of her father transformed in the second section? In the concluding paragraph? How does this three-part structure determine the organization of the essay?

5. Dillard alternates between description of what she observes and fantasies based on her observations. How does this strategy make the essay more interesting than a straightforward description?

6. Dillard's mother is not introduced until the end of the essay. How do the mother's observations help transform Dillard's view of the world? How do they contribute toward the essay's sense of closure?

WRITING

1. Is Dillard's attitude and response toward the technology she sees around her typical of a child's viewpoint? How might an adult's perception of the same technology differ? Explain these differing perceptions in an essay of causal analysis.

2. Describe a technology from the viewpoint of a child—for example, an elevator, a computer, or an amusement park ride. What would be your attitude, associations, or fantasies concerning the thing observed?

3. Write a two- or three-part portrait of someone you have known for a long time, and demonstrate through your description how your perception of that person transformed through time.

Travels in Georgia

John McPhee (1931–   ) began his career writing for television and was an associate editor of Time *magazine and a staff writer for* The New Yorker. *He received an A.B. from Princeton and did graduate work at Cambridge University in England. He is known for his off-beat subjects—often agriculture and geography—and detailed, lucid prose. McPhee often focuses on little-known aspects of his subject matter, which results in making the commonplace interesting. Among the best known of his over twenty nonfiction books are* Oranges *(which describes the history and growth cycle of the fruit and the manufacture of its by-products), published in 1967;* The Survival of the Bark Canoe *(1975); and* Coming into the Country *(1977). His awards include four Litt.D.'s from various universities and the Woodrow Wilson Award from Princeton. In this selection from* Pieces of the Frame *(1975), a seemingly insignificant incident reveals a lot about character, place, and attitude.*

asked for the gorp. Carol passed it to me. Breakfast had been heavy with cathead biscuits, sausage, boiled eggs, Familia, and chicory coffee, but that was an hour ago and I was again hungry. Sam said, "The little Yankee bastard wants the gorp, Carol. Shall we give him some?" Sam's voice was as soft as sphagnum, with inflections of piedmont Georgia.   1

"The little Yankee bastard can have all he wants this morning," Carol said. "It's such a beautiful day."   2

Although Sam was working for the state, he was driving his own Chevrolet. He was doing seventy. In a reverberation of rubber, he crossed Hunger and Hardship Creek and headed into the sun on the Swainsboro Road. I took a ration of gorp—soybeans, sunflower seeds, oats, pretzels, Wheat Chex, raisins, and kelp—and poured another ration into Carol's hand. At just about that moment, a snapping turtle was hit on the road a couple of miles ahead of us, who knows by what sort of vehicle, a car, a pickup; run over like a manhole cover, probably with much the same sound, and not crushed, but gravely wounded. It remained still. It appeared to be dead on the road.   3

Sam, as we approached, was the first to see it. "D.O.R.," he said. "Man, that is a big snapper." Carol and I both sat forward. Sam pressed hard on the brakes. Even so, he was going fifty when he passed the turtle.   4

Carol said, "He's not dead. He didn't look dead."   5

Sam reversed. He drove backward rapidly, fast as the car   6 would go. He stopped on the shoulder, and we all got out. There was a pond beyond the turtle. The big, broad head was shining with blood, but there was, as yet, very little blood on the road. The big jaws struck as we came near, opened and closed bloodily—not the kind of strike that, minutes ago, could have cut off a finger, but still a strike with power. The turtle was about fourteen inches long and a shining horn-brown. The bright spots on its marginal scutes were like light bulbs around a mirror. The neck lunged out. Carol urged the turtle, with her foot, toward the side of the road. "I know, big man," she said to it. "I know it's bad. We're not tormenting you. Honest we're not." Sam asked her if she thought it had a chance to live and she said she was sure it had no chance at all. A car, coming west, braked down and stopped. The driver got out, with some effort and a big paunch. He looked at the turtle and said, "Fifty years old if he's a day." That was the whole of what the man had to say. He got into his car and drove on. Carol nudged the snapper, but it was too hurt to move. It could only strike the air. Now, in a screech of brakes, another car came onto the scene. It went by us, then spun around with squealing tires and pulled up on the far shoulder. It was a two-tone, high-speed, dome-lighted Ford, and in it was the sheriff of Laurens County. He got out and walked toward us, all Technicolor in his uniform, legs striped like a pine-barrens tree frog's, plastic plate on his chest, name of Wade.

"Good morning," Sam said to him.   7

"How y'all?" said Sheriff Wade.   8

Carol said, "Would you mind shooting this turtle for us,   9
please?"

"Surely, Ma'am," said the sheriff, and he drew his .38. He   10
extended his arm and took aim.

"Uh, Sheriff," I said. "If you don't mind . . ." And I asked him   11
if he would kindly shoot the turtle over soil and not over concrete. The sheriff paused and looked slowly, with new interest, from one of us to another: a woman in her twenties, good-looking, with long tawny hair, no accent (that he could hear), barefoot, and wearing a gray sweatshirt and brown dungarees with a hunting knife in the belt; a man (Sam) around forty, in weathered khaki, also without an accent, and with a full black beard divided by a short white patch at the chin—an authentic, natural split beard; and then this incongruous lit-tle Yankee bastard telling him not to shoot the road. Carol picked up the turtle by its long, serrated tail and carried it, underside toward her leg, beyond the shoulder of the highway, where she set it down on a patch of grass. The sheriff followed with his .38. He again took aim. He steadied the muzzle of the pistol twelve inches from the tur-tle. He fired, and missed. The gun made an absurdly light sound, like a screen door shutting. He fired again. The third shot killed the turtle.

The pistol smoked. The sheriff blew the smoke away, and smiled, apparently at himself. He shook his head a little. "He should be good," he said, with a nod at the turtle. The sheriff crossed the road and got into his car. "Y'all be careful," he said. With a great screech of tires, he wheeled around and headed on west.

Carol guessed that the turtle was about ten years old. By the tail, she carried it down to the edge of the pond, like a heavy suitcase with a broken strap. Sam fetched plastic bags from the car. I found a long two-by-ten plank and carried it to the edge of the water. Carol placed the snapper upside down on the plank. Kneeling, she un-sheathed her hunting knife and began, in a practiced and professional way, to slice around the crescents in the plastron, until the flesh of the legs—in thick steaks of red meat—came free. Her knife was very sharp. She put the steaks into a plastic bag. All the while, she talked to the dead turtle, soothingly, reassuringly, nurse to patient, doctor to child, and when she reached in under the plastron and found an ovary, she shifted genders with a grunt of surprise. She pulled out some globate yellow fat and tossed it into the pond. Hundreds of mosquito fish came darting through the water, sank their teeth, shook their heads, worried the fat. Carol began to remove eggs from the turtle's body. The eggs were like ping-pong balls in size, shape, and color, and how they all fitted into the turtle was more than I could comprehend, for there were fifty-six of them in there, fully finished, and a number that had not quite taken their ultimate form. "Look at those eggs. Aren't they beautiful?" Carol said. "Oh, that's sad. You were just about to do your thing, weren't you, girl?" That was why the snapper had gone out of the pond and up onto the road. She was going to bury her eggs in some place she knew, perhaps drawn by an atavistic attachment to the place where she herself had hatched out and where many generations of her forebears had been born when there was no road at all. The turtle twitched. Its neck moved. Its nerves were still working, though its life was gone. The nails on the ends of the claws were each an inch long. The turtle draped one of these talons over one of Carol's fingers. Carol withdrew more fat and threw a huge hunk into the pond. "Wouldn't it be fun to analyze *that* for pesticides?" she said. "You're fat as a pig, Mama. You sure lived high off the hog." Finishing the job—it took forty minutes—Carol found frog bones in the turtle. She put more red meat into plastic sacks and divided the eggs. She kept half for us to eat. With her knife she carefully buried the remaining eggs, twenty-eight or so, in a sand-bank, much as the mother turtle might have been doing at just that time. Carol picked away some leeches from between her fingers. The leeches had come off the turtle's shell. She tied the sacks and said, "All right. That's all we can say grace over. Let's send her back whence she came." Picking up the inedible parts—plastron, carapace,

JOHN McPHEE

neck, claws—she heaved them into the pond. They hit with a slap and sank without bubbles.

COMPREHENSION

1. What is the narrator's role during the sequence of events that occur in the essay?

2. Why is the turtle so important to Carol and Sam? At what point do you understand its significance to them?

3. What was your emotional response to this essay? Why did the essay affect you as it did?

RHETORIC

1. McPhee explains, in detail, his breakfast, the composition of gorp, and the innards of the turtle. What function does this straightforward reporting serve? How does the diction mirror the attitudes and behaviors of the characters?

2. In addition to reportage, McPhee uses a considerable amount of figurative language in his descriptions. Locate examples of this language in the essay. How do they enrich the effect of the writing?

3. How effective is the opening sentence of the essay in attracting your attention? Why is it effective?

4. How does the dialogue between the sheriff and Carol contribute to the overall tone and mood of the essay? How does it strengthen the portrait of the locale and its people?

5. Why does McPhee devote so much attention to describing the turtle in paragraph 12? What do Carol's behavior and comments reveal about her personality and profession?

6. How do Carol and Sam's initial comments about the narrator set up his role in the story? How is this role maintained throughout the action?

WRITING

1. Had the story been told through the point of view of Carol or Sam, how would it have differed from McPhee's version? How does McPhee's perspective determine which elements are focused on? Write a brief analysis of this rhetorical issue.

2. Have you ever visited a place where you were an "outsider"? Write an essay about this visit, and explain how others responded to you and how you responded to them. Title your essay, "Travels in _____ ."

3. Narrate an event in which you witnessed the killing or death of an animal. Capture your emotional response to the event as well as the response of any others who might have witnessed it.

Why the Geese Shrieked

Isaac Bashevis Singer (1904–   ) was born in Radzymin, Poland, and came to the United States in 1935. He became an American citizen in 1943. Singer, who writes in Yiddish, is the author of several superlative short story collections, including Gimpel the Fool *(1957),* The Seance *(1968), and* The Spinoza of Market Street *(1961). He also has written novels, books for children, and memoirs, notably* A Day of Pleasure *(1969) and* Lost in America *(1981). Singer received the Nobel Prize for Literature in 1975. A former rabbinical student, Singer injects elements of religion into his work, often in a comic way. "Why the Geese Shrieked" is typical of Singer's seriocomic approach to the conflicts and tribulations of this world.*

n our home there was always talk about spirits of the 1
dead that possess the bodies of the living, souls reincarnated as animals, houses inhabited by hobgoblins, cellars haunted by demons. My father spoke of these things, first of all because he was interested in them, and second because in a big city children so easily go astray. They go everywhere, see everything, read nonreligious books. It is necessary to remind them from time to time that there are still mysterious forces at work in the world.

One day, when I was about eight, he told us a story found in 2
one of the holy books. If I am not mistaken, the author of that book is Rabbi Eliyahu Graidiker, or one of the other Graidiker sages. The story was about a girl possessed by four demons. It was said that they could actually be seen crawling around in her intestines, blowing up her belly, wandering from one part of her body to another, slithering into her legs. The Rabbi of Graidik had exorcised the evil spirits with the blowing of the ram's horn, with incantations, and the incense of magic herbs.

When my brother Joshua questioned these things, my father 3
became very excited. He argued: "Was then the great Rabbi of Graidik, God forbid, a liar? Are all the rabbis, saints, and sages deceivers, while only atheists speak the truth? Woe is us! How can one be so blind?"

Suddenly the door opened, and a woman entered. She was 4
carrying a basket with two geese in it. The woman looked frightened. Her matron's wig was tilted to one side. She smiled nervously.

Father never looked at strange women, because it is forbidden 5
by Jewish law, but Mother and we children saw immediately that something had greatly upset our unexpected visitor.

"What is it?" Father asked, at the same time turning his back 6 so as not to look upon her.

"Rabbi, I have a very unusual problem." 7

"What is it?" 8

"It's about these geese." 9

"What's the matter with them?" 10

"Dear Rabbi, the geese were slaughtered properly. Then I cut 11 off their heads. I took out the intestines, the livers, all the other organs, but the geese keep shrieking in such a sorrowful voice . . ."

Upon hearing these words, my father turned pale. A dreadful 12 fear befell me, too. But my mother came from a family of rationalists and was by nature a skeptic.

"Slaughtered geese don't shriek," she said. 13

"You will hear for yourself," replied the woman. 14

She took one of the geese and placed it on the table. Then she 15 took out the second goose. The geese were headless, disemboweled— in short, ordinary dead geese.

A smile appeared on my mother's lips. "And *these geese* 16 shriek?"

"You will soon hear." 17

The woman took one goose and hurled it against the other. 18 At once a shriek was heard. It is not easy to describe that sound. It was like the cackling of a goose, but in such a high, eerie pitch, with such groaning and quaking, that my limbs grew cold. I could actually feel the hairs on my earlocks pricking me. I wanted to run from the room. But where would I run? My throat constricted with fear. Then I, too, shrieked and clung to my mother's skirt, like a child of three.

Father forgot that one must avert one's eyes from a woman. 19 He ran to the table. He was no less frightened than I was. His red beard trembled. In his blue eyes could be seen a mixture of fear and vindication. For my father this was a sign that not only to the Rabbi of Graidik, but to him too, omens were sent from heaven. But perhaps this was a sign from the Evil One, from Satan himself?

"What do you say now?" asked the woman. 20

My mother was no longer smiling. In her eyes there was 21 something like sadness, and also anger.

"I cannot understand what is going on here," she said, with 22 a certain resentment.

"Do you want to hear it again?" 23

Again the woman threw one goose against the other. And 24 again the dead geese gave forth an uncanny shriek—the shriek of dumb creatures slain by the slaughterer's knife who yet retain a living force; who still have a reckoning to make with the living, an injustice to avenge. A chill crept over me. I felt as though someone had struck me with all his might.

My father's voice became hoarse. It was broken as though by 25 sobs. "Well, can anyone still doubt that there *is* a Creator?" he asked.

"Rabbi, what shall I do and where shall I go?" The woman 26 began to croon in a mournful singsong. "What has befallen me? Woe is me! What shall I do with them? Perhaps I should run to one of the Wonder Rabbis? Perhaps they were not slaughtered properly? I am afraid to take them home. I wanted to prepare them for the Sabbath meal, and now, such a calamity! Holy Rabbi, what shall I do? Must I throw them out? Someone said they must be wrapped in shrouds and buried in a grave. I am a poor woman. Two geese! They cost me a fortune!"

Father did not know what to answer. He glanced at his book- 27 case. If there was an answer anywhere, it must be there.

Suddenly he looked angrily at my mother. "And what do you 28 say now, eh?"

Mother's face was growing sullen, smaller, sharper. In her 29 eyes could be seen indignation and also something like shame.

"I want to hear it again." Her words were half-pleading, half 30 commanding.

The woman hurled the geese against each other for the third 31 time, and for the third time the shrieks were heard. It occurred to me that such must have been the voice of the sacrificial heifer.

"Woe, woe, and still they blaspheme . . . It is written that the 32 wicked do not repent even at the very gates of hell." Father had again begun to speak. "They behold the truth with their own eyes, and they continue to deny their Maker. They are dragged into the bottomless pit and they maintain that all is nature, or accident . . ."

He looked at Mother as if to say: You take after *them*. 33

For a long time there was silence. Then the woman asked, 34 "Well, did I just imagine it?"

Suddenly my mother laughed. There was something in her 35 laughter that made us all tremble. I knew, by some sixth sense, that Mother was preparing to end the mighty drama being enacted before our eyes.

"Did you remove the windpipes?" my mother asked. 36

"The windpipes? No . . ." 37

"Take them out," said my mother, "and the geese will stop 38 shrieking."

My father became angry. "What are you babbling? What has 39 this got to do with windpipes?"

Mother took hold of one of the geese, pushed her slender 40 finger inside the body, and with all her might pulled out the thin tube that led from the neck to the lungs. Then she took the other goose and removed its windpipe also. I stood trembling, aghast at my mother's courage. Her hands had become bloodied. On her face could be seen the wrath of the rationalist whom someone has tried to frighten in broad daylight.

Father's face turned white, calm, a little disappointed. He 41 knew what had happened here: logic, cold logic, was again tearing down faith, mocking it, holding it up to ridicule and scorn.

"Now, if you please, take one goose and hurl it against the 42 other!" commanded my mother.

Everything hung in the balance. If the geese shrieked, Mother 43 would have lost all: her rationalist's daring, her skepticism, which she had inherited from her intellectual father. And I? Although I was afraid, I prayed inwardly that the geese *would* shriek, shriek so loud that people in the street would hear and come running.

But, alas, the geese were silent, silent as only two dead geese 44 without windpipes can be.

"Bring me a towel!" Mother turned to me. 45

I ran to get the towel. There were tears in my eyes. Mother 46 wiped her hands on the towel like a surgeon after a difficult operation.

"That's all it was!" she announced victoriously. 47

"Rabbi, what do you say?" asked the woman. 48

Father began to cough, to mumble. He fanned himself with 49 his skullcap.

"I have never before heard of such a thing," he said at last. 50

"Nor have I," echoed the woman. 51

"Nor have I," said my mother. "But there is always an expla- 52 nation. Dead geese don't shriek."

"Can I go home now and cook them?" asked the woman. 53

"Go home and cook them for the Sabbath." Mother pro- 54 nounced the decision. "Don't be afraid. They won't make a sound in your pot."

"What do you say, Rabbi?" 55

"Hmm ... they are kosher," murmured Father. "They can be 56 eaten." He was not really convinced, but now he could not pronounce the geese unclean.

Mother went back to the kitchen. I remained with my father. 57 Suddenly he began to speak to me as though I were an adult. "Your mother takes after your grandfather, the Rabbi of Bilgoray. He is a great scholar, but a cold-blooded rationalist. People warned me before our betrothal ..."

And then Father threw up his hands, as if to say: It is too late 58 now to call off the wedding.

COMPREHENSION

1. Explain the conflict between the author's mother and father.

2. Where does Singer, as a child, stand in relation to the conflict? What do you think that he learns from this episode?

3. Does this essay have a thesis? Justify your answer.

RHETORIC

1. This essay contains strong *visual* and *auditory* imagery. Cite examples, and explain how such imagery contributes to the effect of the narrative.

2. Locate and analyze examples of parallel sentence structure in paragraphs 1 and 2. What effects are achieved?

3. What is the function of the first three paragraphs? How are they connected to the body of the essay?

4. Trace Singer's development of conflict, terror, and suspense in the story he narrates. How does he handle these elements successfully?

5. What is the tone of the essay? How does Singer achieve it?

6. What do the last two paragraphs contribute to the essay?

WRITING

1. Do you accept Singer's implied premise that children often get caught between the conflicting value systems of their parents? Why, or why not? Can you think of an example from your personal experience? Narrate a personal experience that grew out of a conflict of opinions or beliefs between parents, relatives, or friends.

2. Examine the conflicts in values and family beliefs in the essays by Hughes, Kingston, and Singer.

3. Are you a "rationalist" or a believer in "mysterious forces"? Describe an episode in your life that supports your response to this question.

CARSON McCULLERS

Home for Christmas

Carson McCullers (1917–1967) was the author of a small but impressive body of fiction, including The Heart Is a Lonely Hunter *(1940),* Reflections in a Golden Eye *(1941),* A Member of

the Wedding (1946), and The Ballad of the Sad Cafe (1951). Al-
though she was preoccupied in her fiction with the theme of
loneliness, this selection from her autobiography reveals instead
the love, joy, and sense of community permeating one episode
from her Georgia childhood.

ometimes in August, weary of the vacant, broiling after- 1
noon, my younger brother and sister and I would gather
in the dense shade under the oak tree in the back yard
and talk of Christmas and sing carols. Once after such
a conclave, when the tunes of the carols still lingered in the heat-
shimmered air, I remember climbing up into the tree-house and
sitting there alone for a long time.

Brother called up: "What are you doing?" 2

"Thinking," I answered. 3

"What are you thinking about?" 4

"I don't know." 5

"Well, how can you be thinking when you don't know what 6
you are thinking about?"

I did not want to talk with my brother. I was experiencing the 7
first wonder about the mystery of Time. Here I was, on this August
afternoon, in the tree-house, in the burnt, jaded yard, sick and tired
of all our summer ways. (I had read *Little Women* for the second time,
Hans Brinker and the Silver Skates, Little Men, and *Twenty Thousand
Leagues under the Sea.* I had read movie magazines and even tried to
read love stories in the *Woman's Home Companion*—I was so sick of
everything.) How could it be that I was I and now was now when in
four months it would be Christmas, wintertime, cold weather, twilight
and the glory of the Christmas tree? I puzzled about the *now* and *later*
and rubbed the inside of my elbow until there was a little roll of dirt
between my forefinger and thumb. Would the *now* I of the tree-house
and the August afternoon be the same *I* of winter, firelight and the
Christmas tree? I wondered.

My brother repeated: "You say you are thinking but you don't 8
know what you are thinking about. What are you really doing up
there? Have you got some secret candy?"

September came, and my mother opened the cedar chest and 9
we tried on winter coats and last year's sweaters to see if they would
do again. She took the three of us downtown and bought us new shoes
and school clothes.

Christmas was nearer on the September Sunday that Daddy 10
rounded us up in the car and drove us out on dusty country roads to
pick elderberry blooms. Daddy made wine from elderberry blos-
soms—it was a yellow-white wine, the color of weak winter sun. The
wine was dry to the wry side—indeed, some years it turned to vine-

gar. The wine was served at Christmastime with slices of fruitcake when company came. On November Sundays we went to the woods with a big basket of fried chicken dinner, thermos jug and coffee-pot. We hunted partridge berries in the pine woods near our town. These scarlet berries grew hidden underneath the glossy brown pine needles that lay in a slick carpet beneath the tall wind-singing trees. The bright berries were a Christmas decoration, lasting in water through the whole season.

In December the windows downtown were filled with toys, 11 and my brother and sister and I were given two dollars apiece to buy our Christmas presents. We patronized the ten-cent stores, choosing between jackstones, pencil boxes, water colors and satin handkerchief holders. We would each buy a nickel's worth of lump milk chocolate at the candy counter to mouth as we trudged from counter to counter, choice to choice. It was exacting and final—taking several afternoons—for the dime stores would not take back or exchange.

Mother made fruitcakes, and for weeks ahead the family 12 picked out the nut meats of pecans and walnuts, careful of the bitter layer of the pecans that lined your mouth with nasty fur. At the last I was allowed to blanch the almonds, pinching the scalded nuts so that they sometimes hit the ceiling or bounced across the room. Mother cut slices of citron and crystallized pineapple, figs and dates, and candied cherries were added whole. We cut rounds of brown paper to line the pans. Usually the cakes were mixed and put into the oven when we were in school. Late in the afternoon the cakes would be finished, wrapped in white napkins on the breakfast-room table. Later they would be soaked in brandy. These fruitcakes were famous in our town, and Mother gave them often as Christmas gifts. When company came thin slices of fruitcake, wine and coffee were always served. When you held a slice of fruitcake to the window or the firelight the slice was translucent, pale citron green and yellow and red, with the glow and richness of our church windows.

Daddy was a jeweler, and his store was kept open until mid- 13 night all Christmas week. I, as the eldest child, was allowed to stay up late with Mother until Daddy came home. Mother was always nervous without a "man in the house." (On those rare occasions when Daddy had to stay overnight on business in Atlanta, the children were armed with a hammer, saw and a monkey wrench. When pressed about her anxieties Mother claimed she was afraid of "escaped convicts or crazy people." I never saw an escaped convict, but once a "crazy" person did come to see us. She was an old, old lady dressed in elegant black taffeta, my mother's second cousin once removed, and came on a tranquil Sunday morning and announced that she had always liked our house and she intended to stay with us until she died. Her sons and daughters and grandchildren gathered around to plead with her as she sat rocking in our front porch rocking chair and she left not unwillingly when they promised a car ride and ice cream.) Nothing ever happened on those evenings in Christmas week, but I felt grown, aged suddenly by trust and dignity. Mother confided in secrecy what the younger children were getting from Santa Claus. I knew where the Santa Claus things were hidden, and was appointed to see that my brother and sister did not go into the back-room closet or the wardrobe in our parents' room.

Christmas Eve was the longest day, but it was lined with the glory of tomorrow. The sitting-room smelled of floor wax and the clean, cold odor of the spruce tree. The Christmas tree stood in a corner of the front room, tall as the ceiling, majestic, undecorated. It was our family custom that the tree was not decorated until after we children were in bed on Christmas Eve night. We went to bed very early, as soon as it was winter dark. I lay in bed beside my sister and tried to keep her awake. 14

"You want to guess again about your Santa Claus?" 15

"We've already done that so much," she said. 16

My sister slept. And there again was another puzzle. How could it be that when she opened her eyes it would be Christmas while I lay awake in the dark for hours and hours? The time was the same for both of us, and yet not at all the same. What was it? How? I thought of Bethlehem and cherry candy, Jesus and skyrockets. It was dark when I awoke. We were allowed to get up on Christmas at five o'clock. Later I found out that Daddy juggled the clock Christmas Eve so that five o'clock was actually six. Anyway it was always still dark when we rushed in to dress by the kitchen stove. The rule was that we dress and eat breakfast before we could go in to the Christmas tree. On Christmas morning we always had fish roe, bacon and grits for breakfast. I grudged every mouthful—for who wanted to fill up on breakfast when there in the sitting-room was candy, at least three whole boxes? After breakfast we lined up, and carols were started. Our voices rose naked and mysterious as we filed through the door to the sitting-room. The carol, unfinished, ended in raw yells of joy. 17

The Christmas tree glittered in the glorious, candlelit room. There were bicycles and bundles wrapped in tissue paper. Our stockings hanging from the mantlepiece bulged with oranges, nuts and smaller presents. The next hours were paradise. The blue dawn at the window brightened, and the candles were blown out. By nine o'clock we had ridden the wheel presents and dressed in the clothes gifts. We visited the neighborhood children and were visited in turn. Our cousins came and grown relatives from distant neighborhoods. All through the morning we ate chocolates. At two or three o'clock the Christmas dinner was served. The dining-room table had been let out with extra leaves and the very best linen was laid—satin damask with 18 a rose design. Daddy asked the blessing, then stood up to carve the turkey. Dressing, rice and giblet gravy were served. There were cut-glass dishes of sparkling jellies and stateliness of festal wine. For dessert there was always sillabub or charlotte and fruitcake. The afternoon was almost over when dinner was done.

At twilight I sat on the front steps, jaded by too much pleasure, sick at the stomach and worn out. The boy next door skated down the street in his new Indian suit. A girl spun around on a crackling son-of-a-gun. My brother waved sparklers. Christmas was over. I thought of the monotony of Time ahead, unsolaced by the distant glow of paler festivals, the year that stretched before another Christmas—eternity. 19

COMPREHENSION

1. What, according to the author, is the essence of Christmas?

2. Trace chronologically the preparations for Christmas by the McCullers family.

3. What is the author's attitude toward time? Paraphrase the last sentence of the essay.

RHETORIC

1. This essay is rich in sensory language. Cite five words or phrases that are especially vivid, and analyze their effect. To which senses does the writing appeal?

2. Define these words: *conclave* (paragraph 1); *patronized* (paragraph 11); *blanch* (paragraph 12); *tranquil* (paragraph 13); and *festal* (paragraph 19). Use them in sentences of your own.

3. McCullers writes in paragraph 7 that she "was experiencing the first wonder about the mystery of Time." How does this theme serve as the organizing principle for the essay? How does the author convey the mystery of time? What is her dual attitude toward time, and how does this serve as a structuring device in the essay? How does the author's treatment of time resemble that of Welty in "One Writer's Beginnings"?

4. What principles of emphasis do you find in McCullers's treatment of chronology?

5. How and why does the author connect the many and varied details in the essay? How effective are her details in conveying a sense of her childhood and evolving personality? How is this reflected in point of view?

6. How does the conclusion relate to the rest of the essay? Do you find the conclusion effective? Why, or why not?

1.   Do you still look forward to special holidays or celebrations, or does the type of anticipation of which McCullers speaks exist only for children? Why do children have different perceptions of time than adults? Evaluate this matter in an essay.

2.   Write a narrative account of a vivid holiday event in your childhood.

3.   Analyze McCullers's use of sensory language to create a dominant impression in "Home for Christmas."

DYLAN THOMAS

A Visit to Grandpa's

Dylan Thomas (1914–1953), Welsh poet and prose writer, had one of the most lyric voices in contemporary literature. Both his poetry and prose are filled with an animated primitivism, forceful sounds and rhythms, and complex patterns of symbolism and imagery. His poetry collections include Eighteen Poems *(1934),* Twenty-five Poems *(1936), and* In Country Sleep *(1952). The following autobiographical sketch from* Portrait of the Artist as a Young Dog *(1952) contains many of his most expressive techniques.*

n the middle of the night I woke from a dream full of whips and lariats as long as serpents, and runaway coaches on mountain passes, and wide, windy gallops over cactus fields, and I heard the old man in the next room crying, "Gee-up!" and "Whoa!" and trotting his tongue on the roof of his mouth. 1

It was the first time I had stayed in grandpa's house. The floorboards had squeaked like mice as I climbed into bed, and the mice between the walls had creaked like wood as though another visitor was walking on them. It was a mild summer night, but curtains had flapped and branches beaten against the window. I had pulled the sheets over my head, and soon was roaring and riding in a book. 2

"Whoa there, my beauties!" cried grandpa. His voice sounded very young and loud, and his tongue had powerful hooves, and he made his bedroom into a great meadow. I thought I would see if he was ill, or had set his bed-clothes on fire, for my mother had said that he lit his pipe under the blankets, and had warned me to run to his 3 help if I smelt smoke in the night. I went on tiptoe through the darkness to his bedroom door, brushing against the furniture and upsetting a candlestick with a thump. When I saw there was a light in the room I felt frightened, and as I opened the door I heard grandpa shout, "Gee-up!" as loudly as a bull with a megaphone.

He was sitting straight up in bed and rocking from side to side as though the bed were on a rough road; the knotted edges of the counterpane were his reins; his invisible horses stood in a shadow beyond the bedside candle. Over a white flannel nightshirt he was wearing a red waistcoat with walnut-sized brass buttons. The over-filled bowl of his pipe smouldered among his whiskers like a little, burning hayrick on a stock. At the sight of me, his hands dropped from the reins and lay blue and quiet, the bed stopped still on a level road, he muffled his tongue into silence, and the horses drew softly up.

"Is there anything the matter, grandpa?" I asked, though the clothes were not on fire. His face in the candlelight looked like a ragged quilt pinned upright on the black air and patched all over with goat-beards.

He stared at me mildly. Then he blew down his pipe, scattering the sparks and making a high, wet dog-whistle of the stem, and shouted: "Ask no questions."

After a pause, he said shyly: "Do you ever have nightmares, boy?"

I said: "No."

"Oh, yes, you do," he said.

I said I was woken by a voice that was shouting to horses.

"What did I tell you?" he said. "You eat too much. Who ever heard of horses in a bedroom?"

He fumbled under his pillow, brought out a small, tinkling bag, and carefully untied its strings. He put a sovereign in my hand, and said "Buy a cake." I thanked him and wished him good night.

As I closed my bedroom door, I heard his voice crying loudly and gaily, "Gee-up! gee-up!" and the rocking of the travelling bed.

In the morning I woke from a dream of fiery horses on a plain that was littered with furniture, and of large, cloudy men who rode six horses at a time and whipped them with burning bed-clothes. Grandpa was at breakfast, dressed in deep black. After breakfast he said, "There was a terrible loud wind last night," and sat in his arm-chair by the hearth to make clay balls for the fire. Later in the morning he took me for a walk, through Johnstown village and into the fields on the Llanstephan road.

A man with a whippet said, "There's a nice morning, Mr. Thomas," and when he had gone, leanly as his dog, into the short-treed green wood he should not have entered because of the notices, grandpa said: "There, do you hear what he called you? Mister!"

We passed by small cottages, and all the men who leant on 16 the gates congratulated grandpa on the fine morning. We passed through the wood full of pigeons, and their wings broke the branches as they rushed to the tops of the trees. Among the soft, contented voices and the loud, timid flying, grandpa said, like a man calling across a field: "If you heard those old birds in the night, you'd wake me up and say there were horses in the trees."

We walked back slowly, for he was tired, and the lean man 17 stalked out of the forbidden wood with a rabbit held as gently over his arm as a girl's arm in a warm sleeve.

On the last day but one of my visit I was taken to Llanstephan 18 in a governess cart pulled by a short, weak pony. Grandpa might have been driving a bison, so tightly he held the reins, so ferociously cracked the long whip, so blasphemously shouted warning to boys who played in the road, so stoutly stood with his gaitered legs apart and cursed the demon strength and wilfulness of his tottering pony.

"Look out, boy!" he cried when we came to each corner, and 19 pulled and tugged and jerked and sweated and waved his whip like a rubber sword. And when the pony had crept miserably round each corner, grandpa turned to me with a sighing smile: "We weathered that one, boy."

When we came to Llanstephan village at the top of the hill, 20 he left the cart by the "Edwinsford Arms" and patted the pony's muzzle and gave it sugar, saying: "You're a weak little pony, Jim, to pull big men like us."

He had strong beer and I had lemonade, and he paid Mrs 21 Edwinsford with a sovereign out of the tinkling bag; she inquired after his health, and he said that Llangadock was better for the tubes. We went to look at the churchyard and the sea, and sat in the wood called the Sticks, and stood on the concert platform in the middle of the wood where visitors sang on mid-summer nights and, year by year, the innocent of the village was elected mayor. Grandpa paused at the churchyard and pointed over the iron gate at the angelic headstones and the poor wooden crosses. "There's no sense in lying there," he said.

We journeyed back furiously: Jim was a bison again. 22

I woke late on my last morning, out of dreams where the 23 Llanstephan sea carried bright sailing-boats as long as liners; and heavenly choirs in the Sticks, dressed in bards' robes and brass-buttoned waistcoats, sang in a strange Welsh to the departing sailors. Grandpa was not at breakfast; he rose early. I walked in the fields with a new sling, and shot at the Towy gulls and the rooks in the parsonage trees. A warm wind blew from the summer points of the weather; a morning mist climbed from the ground and floated among the trees and hid the noisy birds; in the mist and the wind my pebbles flew lightly up like hailstones in a world on its head. The morning passed without a bird falling.

I broke my sling and returned for the midday meal through the parson's orchard. Once, grandpa told me, the parson had bought three ducks at Carmarthen Fair and made a pond for them in the centre of the garden; but they waddled to the gutter under the crumbling doorsteps of the house, and swam and quacked there. When I reached the end of the orchard path, I looked through a hole in the hedge and saw that the parson had made a tunnel through the rockery that was between the gutter and the pond and had set up a notice in plain writing: "This way to the pond."

The ducks were still swimming under the steps.

Grandpa was not in the cottage. I went into the garden, but grandpa was not staring at the fruit-trees. I called across to a man who leant on a spade in the fields beyond the garden hedge: "Have you seen my grandpa this morning?"

He did not stop digging, and answered over his shoulder: "I seen him in his fancy waistcoat."

Griff, the barber, lived in the next cottage. I called to him through the open door: "Mr Griff, have you seen my grandpa?"

The barber came out in his shirtsleeves.

I said: "He's wearing his best waistcoat." I did not know if it was important, but grandpa wore his waistcoat only in the night.

"Has grandpa been to Llanstephan?" asked Mr Griff anxiously.

"We went there yesterday in a little trap," I said.

He hurried indoors and I heard him talking in Welsh, and he came out again with his white coat on, and he carried a striped and coloured walking-stick. He strode down the village street and I ran by his side.

When we stopped at the tailor's shop, he cried out, "Dan!" and Dan Tailor stepped from his window where he sat like an Indian priest but wearing a derby hat. "Dai Thomas has got his waistcoat on," said Mr Griff, "and he's been to Llanstephan."

As Dan Tailor searched for his overcoat, Mr Griff was striding on. "Will Evans," he called outside the carpenter's shop, "Dai Thomas has been to Llanstephan, and he's got his waistcoat on."

"I'll tell Morgan now," said the carpenter's wife out of the hammering, sawing darkness of the shop.

We called at the butcher's shop and Mr Price's house, and Mr Griff repeated his message like a town crier.

We gathered together in Johnstown square. Dan Tailor had

DYLAN THOMAS

his bicycle, Mr Price his pony-trap. Mr Griff, the butcher, Morgan Carpenter, and I climbed into the shaking trap, and we trotted off towards Carmarthen town. The tailor led the way, ringing his bell as though there were a fire or a robbery, and an old woman by the gate of a cottage at the end of the street ran inside like a pelted hen. Another woman waved a bright handkerchief.

"Where are we going?" I asked. 39

Grandpa's neighbours were as solemn as old men with black 40 hats and jackets on the outskirts of a fair. Mr Griff shook his head and mourned: "I didn't expect this again from Dai Thomas."

"Not after last time," said Mr Price sadly. 41

We trotted on, we crept up Constitution Hill, we rattled down 42 into Lammas Street, and the tailor still rang his bell and a dog ran, squealing, in front of his wheels. As we clop-clopped over the cobbles that led down to the Towy bridge, I remembered grandpa's nightly noisy journeys that rocked the bed and shook the walls, and I saw his gay waistcoat in a vision and his patchwork head tufted and smiling in the candlelight. The tailor before us turned round on his saddle, his bicycle wobbled and skidded. "I see Dai Thomas!" he cried.

The trap rattled on to the bridge, and I saw grandpa there; 43 the buttons of his waistcoat shone in the sun, he wore his tight, black Sunday trousers and a tall, dusty hat I had seen in a cupboard in the attic, and he carried an ancient bag. He bowed to us. "Good morning, Mr Price," he said, "and Mr Griff and Mr Morgan and Mr Evans." To me, he said, "Good morning, boy."

Mr Griff pointed his coloured stick at him. 44

"And what do you think you are doing on Carmarthen bridge 45 in the middle of the afternoon," he said sternly, "with your best waistcoat and your old hat?"

Grandpa did not answer, but inclined his face to the river 46 wind, so that his beard was set dancing and wagging as though he talked, and watched the coracle men move, like turtles, on the shore.

Mr Griff raised his stunted barber's pole. "And where do you 47 think you are going," he said, "with your old black bag?"

Grandpa said: "I am going to Llangadock to be buried." And 48 he watched the coracle shells slip into the water lightly, and the gulls complain over the fish-filled water as bitterly as Mr Price complained:

"But you aren't dead yet, Dai Thomas." 49

For a moment grandpa reflected, then: "There's no sense in 50 lying dead in Llanstephan," he said. "The ground is comfy in Llangadock; you can twitch your legs without putting them in the sea."

His neighbours moved close to him. They said: "You aren't 51 dead, Mr. Thomas."

"How can you be buried, then?" 52

"Nobody's going to bury you in Llanstephan." 53

"Come on home, Mr Thomas."   54
"There's strong beer for tea."   55
"And cake."   56
But grandpa stood firmly on the bridge, and clutched his bag 57
to his side, and stared at the flowing river and the sky, like a prophet
who has no doubt.

COMPREHENSION

1. Do you find any implied purpose in this essay? Does Thomas merely want
to recount a childhood memory, or might he have a different purpose?

2. What do we learn about Thomas's childhood, his views of himself, his attitude toward his grandfather, and his perceptions of the world?

3. Characterize the personality of Thomas's grandfather. Can we infer whether
or not the grandfather will continue his journey at the end of the story? Why, or
why not?

RHETORIC

1. The prose style in this narrative might be termed "poetic." How does Thomas's poetic style influence mood and tone in the essay? What are the components
of his style? Isolate five instances of poetic style in the essay, and explain their
effects. Locate instances of poetic style in two other essays in this chapter.

2. A major motif in the essay involves nature imagery. Trace this motif, citing
examples. Why is this motif important?

3. How does Thomas use dreams to structure and to inform the essay? In what
ways are the dreams symbolic?

4. The author uses an episodic technique in the essay, yet he achieves unity
and coherence in the presentation of episodes. How? How does he handle proportion?

5. Discuss point of view with regard to the author's relationship to the action
and time of the story.

6. Assess Thomas's conclusion. Evaluate its effectiveness.

WRITING

1. Thomas presents a microcosm of Welsh society in this essay. What are its
contours and cultural points of reference? How do people relate to each other
within these social contexts?

2. Relate an episode or series of episodes about a memorable visit to one of
your relatives or friends.

3. Analyze the pleasures and pains of childhood as presented by at least three
of the writers in this chapter.

GEORGE ORWELL

Shooting an Elephant

George Orwell (1903–1950) was the pseudonym of Eric Blair, an English novelist, essayist, and journalist. Orwell served with the Indian Imperial Police from 1922 to 1927 in Burma, fought in the Spanish Civil War, and acquired from his experiences a disdain of totalitarian and imperialistic systems. This attitude is reflected in the satiric fable Animal Farm *(1945) and in his bleak, futuristic novel,* 1984 *(1949). In this essay, Orwell invokes personal experience to expose the contradictions inherent in British imperialism.*

n Moulmein, in Lower Burma, I was hated by large numbers of people—the only time in my life that I have been important enough for this to happen to me. I was subdivisional police officer of the town, and in an aimless, petty kind of way anti-European feeling was very bitter. No one had the guts to raise a riot, but if a European woman went through the bazaars alone somebody would probably spit betel juice over her dress. As a police officer I was an obvious target and was baited whenever it seemed safe to do so. When a nimble Burman tripped me up on the football field and the referee (another Burman) looked the other way, the crowd yelled with hideous laughter. This happened more than once. In the end the sneering yellow faces of young men that met me everywhere, the insults hooted after me when I was at a safe distance, got badly on my nerves. The young Buddhist priests were the worst of all. There were several thousands of them in the town and none of them seemed to have anything to do except stand on street corners and jeer at Europeans.

All this was perplexing and upsetting. For at that time I had already made up my mind that imperialism was an evil thing and the sooner I chucked up my job and got out of it the better. Theoretically—and secretly, of course—I was all for the Burmese and all against their oppressors, the British. As for the job I was doing, I hated it more bitterly than I can perhaps make clear. In a job like that you see the dirty work of Empire at close quarters. The wretched prisoners huddling in the stinking cages of the lock-ups, the grey, cowed faces of the long-term convicts, the scarred buttocks of the men who had been flogged with bamboos—all these oppressed me with an intolerable sense of guilt. But I could get nothing into perspective. I was young and ill-educated and I had had to think out my problems in the utter silence that is imposed on every Englishman in the East. I did not even know that the British Empire is dying, still less did I

1

2

know that it is a great deal better than the younger empires that are going to supplant it. All I knew was that I was stuck between my hatred of the empire I served and my rage against the evil-spirited little beasts who tried to make my job impossible. With one part of my mind I thought of the British Raj as an unbreakable tyranny, as something clamped down, *in saecula saeculorum,* upon the will of prostrate peoples; with another part I thought that the greatest joy in the world would be to drive a bayonet into a Buddhist priest's guts. Feelings like these are the normal by-products of imperialism; ask any Anglo-Indian official, if you can catch him off duty.

One day something happened which in a roundabout way   3
was enlightening. It was a tiny incident in itself, but it gave me a better glimpse than I had had before of the real nature of imperialism—the real motives for which despotic governments act. Early one morning the sub-inspector at a police station the other end of the town rang me up on the phone and said that an elephant was ravaging the bazaar. Would I please come and do something about it? I did not know what I could do, but I wanted to see what was happening and I got on to a pony and started out. I took my rifle, an old .44 Winchester and much too small to kill an elephant, but I thought the noise might be useful *in terrorem.* Various Burmans stopped me on the way and told me about the elephant's doings. It was not, of course, a wild elephant, but a tame one which had gone "must." It had been chained up as tame elephants always are when their attack of "must" is due, but on the previous night it had broken its chain and escaped. Its mahout, the only person who could manage it when it was in that state, had set out in pursuit, but he had taken the wrong direction and was now twelve hours' journey away, and in the morning the elephant had suddenly reappeared in the town. The Burmese population had no weapons and were quite helpless against it. It had already destroyed somebody's bamboo hut, killed a cow and raided some fruit-stalls and devoured the stock; also it had met the municipal rubbish van, and, when the driver jumped out and took to his heels, had turned the van over and inflicted violence upon it.

The Burmese sub-inspector and some Indian constables were   4
waiting for me in the quarter where the elephant had been seen. It was a very poor quarter, a labyrinth of squalid bamboo huts, thatched with palm-leaf, winding all over a steep hillside. I remember that it was a cloudy stuffy morning at the beginning of the rains. We began questioning the people as to where the elephant had gone, and, as usual, failed to get any definite information. That is invariably the case in the East; a story always sounds clear enough at a distance, but the nearer you get to the scene of events the vaguer it becomes. Some of the people said that the elephant had gone in one direction, some

said that he had gone in another, some professed not even to have heard of any elephant. I had almost made up my mind that the whole story was a pack of lies, when we heard yells a little distance away. There was a loud, scandalized cry of "Go away, child! Go away this instant!" and an old woman with a switch in her hand came round the corner of a hut, violently shooing away a crowd of naked children. Some more women followed, clicking their tongues and exclaiming; evidently there was something there that the children ought not to have seen. I rounded the hut and saw a man's dead body sprawling in the mud. He was an Indian, a black Dravidian coolie, almost naked, and he could not have been dead many minutes. The people said that the elephant had come suddenly upon him round the corner of the hut, caught him with its trunk, put its foot on his back and ground him into the earth. This was the rainy season and the ground was soft, and his face had scored a trench a foot deep and a couple of yards long. He was lying on his belly with arms crucified and head sharply twisted to one side. His face was coated with mud, the eyes wide open, the teeth bared and grinning with an expression of unendurable agony. (Never tell me, by the way, that the dead look peaceful. Most of the corpses I have seen looked devilish.) The friction of the great beast's foot had stripped the skin from his back as neatly as one skins a rabbit. As soon as I saw the dead man I sent an orderly to a friend's house nearby to borrow an elephant rifle. I had already sent back the pony, not wanting it to go mad with fright and throw me if it smelled the elephant.

The orderly came back in a few minutes with a rifle and five 5 cartridges, and meanwhile some Burmans had arrived and told us that the elephant was in the paddy fields below, only a few hundred yards away. As I started forward practically the whole population of the quarter flocked out of their houses and followed me. They had seen the rifle and were all shouting excitedly that I was going to shoot the elephant. They had not shown much interest in the elephant when he was merely ravaging their homes, but it was different now that he was going to be shot. It was a bit of fun to them, as it would be to an English crowd; besides, they wanted the meat. It made me vaguely uneasy. I had no intention of shooting the elephant—I had merely sent for the rifle to defend myself if necessary—and it is always un-nerving to have a crowd following you. I marched down the hill, looking, and feeling a fool, with the rifle over my shoulder and an ever-growing army of people jostling at my heels. At the bottom, when you got away from the huts, there was a metalled road and beyond that a miry waste of paddy fields a thousand yards across, not yet ploughed but soggy from the first rains and dotted with coarse grass. The elephant was standing eighty yards from the road, his left

 SHOOTING AN ELEPHANT

side towards us. He took not the slightest notice of the crowd's approach. He was tearing up bunches of grass, beating them against his knees to clean them and stuffing them into his month.

I had halted on the road. As soon as I saw the elephant I knew 6 with perfect certainty that I ought not to shoot him. It is a serious matter to shoot a working elephant—it is comparable to destroying a huge and costly piece of machinery—and obviously one ought not to do it if it can possibly be avoided. And at a distance, peacefully eating, the elephant looked no more dangerous than a cow. I thought then and I think now that his attack of "must" was already passing off; in which case he would merely wander harmlessly about until the mahout came back and caught him. Moreover, I did not in the least want to shoot him. I decided that I would watch him for a little while to make sure that he did not turn savage again, and then go home.

But at that moment I glanced round at the crowd that had 7 followed me. It was an immense crowd, two thousand at the least and growing every minute. It blocked the road for a long distance on either side. I looked at the sea of yellow faces above the garish clothes—faces all happy and excited over this bit of fun, all certain that the elephant was going to be shot. They were watching me as they would watch a conjuror about to perform a trick. They did not like me, but with the magical rifle in my hands I was momentarily worth watching. And suddenly I realised that I should have to shoot the elephant after all. The people expected it of me and I had got to do it; I could feel their two thousand wills pressing me forward, irresistibly. And it was at this moment, as I stood there with the rifle in my hands, that I first grasped the hollowness, the futility of the white man's dominion in the East. Here was I, the white man with his gun, standing in front of the unarmed native crowd—seemingly the leading actor of the piece, but in reality I was only an absurd puppet pushed to and fro by the will of those yellow faces behind. I perceived in this moment that when the white man turns tyrant it is his own freedom that he destroys. He becomes a sort of hollow, posing dummy, the conventionalised figure of a sahib. For it is the condition of his rule that he shall spend his life in trying to impress the "natives" and so in every crisis he has got to do what the "natives" expect of him. He wears a mask, and his face grows to fit it. I had got to shoot the elephant. I had committed myself to doing it when I sent for the rifle. A sahib has got to act like a sahib; he has got to appear resolute, to know his own mind and do definite things. To come all that way, rifle in hand, with two thousand people marching at my heels, and then to trail feebly away, having done nothing—no, that was impossible. The crowd would laugh at me. And my whole life, every white man's life in the East, was one long struggle not to be laughed at.

GEORGE ORWELL

But I did not want to shoot the elephant. I watched him beat- 8
ing his bunch of grass against his knees, with that preoccupied grand-
motherly air that elephants have. It seemed to me that it would be
murder to shoot him. At that age I was not squeamish about killing
animals, but I had never shot an elephant and never wanted to. (Somehow it always seems worse to kill a *large* animal.) Besides, there was
the beast's owner to be considered. Alive, the elephant was worth at
least a hundred pounds; dead, he would only be worth the value of
his tusks—five pounds, possibly. But I had got to act quickly. I turned
to some experienced-looking Burmans who had been there when we
arrived, and asked them how the elephant had been behaving. They
all said the same thing: he took no notice of you if you left him alone,
but he might charge if you went too close to him.

It was perfectly clear to me what I ought to do. I ought to 9
walk up to within, say, twenty-five yards of the elephant and test his
behaviour. If he charged I could shoot, if he took no notice of me it
would be safe to leave him until the mahout came back. But also I
knew that I was going to do no such thing. I was a poor shot with a
rifle and the ground was soft mud into which one would sink at every
step. If the elephant charged and I missed him, I should have about
as much chance as a toad under a steam-roller. But even then I was
not thinking particularly of my own skin, only the watchful yellow
faces behind. For at that moment, with the crowd watching me, I was
not afraid in the ordinary sense, as I would have been if I had been
alone. A white man mustn't be frightened in front of "natives"; and
so, in general, he isn't frightened. The sole thought in my mind was
that if anything went wrong those two thousand Burmans would see
me pursued, caught, trampled on and reduced to a grinning corpse
like that Indian up the hill. And if that happened it was quite probable
that some of them would laugh. That would never do. There was only
one alternative. I shoved the cartridges into the magazine and lay
down on the road to get a better aim.

The crowd grew very still, and a deep, low, happy sigh, as of 10
people who see the theatre curtain go up at last, breathed from innumerable throats. They were going to have their bit of fun after all.
The rifle was a beautiful German thing with cross-hair sights. I did
not then know that in shooting an elephant one should shoot to cut
an imaginary bar running from ear-hole to ear-hole. I ought therefore,
as the elephant was sideways on, to have aimed straight at his ear-
hole; actually I aimed several inches in front of this, thinking the brain
would be further forward.

When I pulled the trigger I did not hear the bang or feel the 11
kick—one never does when a shot goes home—but I heard the devilish roar of glee that went up from the crowd. In that instant, in too
short a time, one would have thought, even for the bullet to get there,

a mysterious, terrible change had come over the elephant. He neither stirred nor fell, but every line of his body had altered. He looked suddenly stricken, shrunken, immensely old, as though the frightful impact of the bullet had paralysed him without knocking him down. At last, after what seemed a long time—it might have been five seconds, I dare say—he sagged flabbily to his knees. His mouth slobbered. An enormous senility seemed to have settled upon him. One could have imagined him thousands of years old. I fired again into the same spot. At the second shot he did not collapse but climbed with desperate slowness to his feet and stood weakly upright, with legs sagging and head drooping. I fired a third time. That was the shot that did for him. You could see the agony of it jolt his whole body and knock the last remnant of strength from his legs. But in falling he seemed for a moment to rise, for as his hind legs collapsed beneath him he seemed to tower upwards like a huge rock toppling, his trunk reaching skyward like a tree. He trumpeted, for the first and only time. And then down he came, his belly towards me, with a crash that seemed to shake the ground even where I lay.

I got up. The Burmans were already racing past me across the mud. It was obvious that the elephant would never rise again, but he was not dead. He was breathing very rhythmically with long rattling gasps, his great mound of a side painfully rising and falling. His mouth was wide open—I could see far down into caverns of pale pink throat. I waited a long time for him to die, but his breathing did not weaken. Finally I fired my two remaining shots into the spot where I thought his heart must be. The thick blood welled out of him like red velvet, but still he did not die. His body did not even jerk when the shots hit him, the tortured breathing continued without a pause. He was dying, very slowly and in great agony, but in some world remote from me where not even a bullet could damage him further. I felt that I had got to put an end to that dreadful noise. It seemed dreadful to see the great beast lying there, powerless to move and yet powerless to die, and not even to be able to finish him. I sent back for my small rifle and poured shot after shot into his heart and down his throat. They seemed to make no impression. The tortured gasps continued as steadily as the ticking of a clock.

In the end I could not stand it any longer and went away. I heard later that it took him half an hour to die. Burmans were arriving with dahs and baskets even before I left, and I was told they had stripped his body almost to the bones by the afternoon.

Afterwards, of course, there were endless discussions about the shooting of the elephant. The owner was furious, but he was only an Indian and could do nothing. Besides, legally I had done the right thing, for a mad elephant has to be killed, like a mad dog, if its owner fails to control it. Among the Europeans opinion was divided. The older men said I was right, the younger men said it was a damn shame to shoot an elephant for killing a coolie, because an elephant was worth more than any damn Coringhee coolie. And afterwards I was very glad that the coolie had been killed; it put me legally in the right and it gave me a sufficient pretext for shooting the elephant. I often wondered whether any of the others grasped that I had done it solely to avoid looking a fool.

COMPREHENSION

1. State in your own words the thesis of this essay.

2. How does the shooting of the elephant give Orwell a better understanding of "the real nature of imperialism—the real motives for which despotic governments act" (paragraph 3)? Why does Orwell kill the elephant? What is his attitude toward the Burmese people?

3. Why does Orwell concentrate on the prolonged death of the elephant? What effect does it have?

RHETORIC

1. How would you describe the level of language in the essay? Point to specific words, sentences, and phrases to support your answer.

2. Define *supplant* (paragraph 2); *labyrinth* (paragraph 4); *jostling* (paragraph 5); *conjuror* (paragraph 7); and *senility* (paragraph 11).

3. What is the function of the first two paragraphs? Where is the thesis stated in the essay?

4. Analyze Orwell's use of dramatic techniques to develop the narrative. Examine consecutive paragraphs in the essay to determine the author's presentation of action from different perspectives. What other essays in this chapter strike you as dramatic, and why?

5. Select and analyze some of the details in the essay that are designed to impress the reader's senses and emotions. Why does Orwell rely so heavily on the presentation and accumulation of detail in the essay?

6. How is the entire essay structured by irony of situation and paradox? How do these devices relate to the ethical issues raised by Orwell?

WRITING

1. In this essay, written in 1936, Orwell declares: "I did not even know that the British Empire is dying, still less did I know that it is a great deal better than the younger empires that are going to supplant it" (paragraph 2). In what ways is Orwell's statement prophetic?

2.   Write a narrative essay about an episode in your life when you came into conflict with social or political forces.

3.   In a comparative essay, examine the ways in which Orwell and McPhee use the death of an animal to reflect on the human condition.

4.   For a research project, consult library sources, and then write a report, employing proper documentation, on one of the authors in this chapter.

The Sense of Place

HARRY CREWS

Why I Live Where I Live

Harry Crews (1935–) is a Southern writer who is a master of the art of the grotesque. His novels include Karate Is a Thing of the Spirit *(1971),* The Gypsy's Curse *(1974), and* A Feast of Snakes *(1976). His more recent work includes* All We Know of Hell *(1987) and* The Knockout Artist *(1988). He contributes regularly to* Playboy, The Sewanee Review, Esquire, *and other publications. In this personal essay, Crews examines the relationship between the writer's surroundings and the creative process.*

can leave the place where I live a couple of hours before daylight and be on a deserted little strip of sand called Crescent Beach in time to throw a piece of meat on a fire and then, in a few minutes, lie back sucking on a vodka bottle and chewing on a hunk of bloody beef while the sun lifts out of the Atlantic Ocean (somewhat unnerving but also mystically beautiful to a man who never saw a body of water bigger than a pond until he was grown) and while the sun rises lie on a blanket, brain singing from vodka and a bellyful of beef, while the beautiful bikinied children from the University of Florida drift down the beach, their

1

51

smooth bodies sweating baby oil and the purest kind of innocent lust (which of course is the rankest sort) into the bright air. If all that starts to pall—and what *doesn't* start to pall?—I can leave the beach and be out on the end of a dock, sitting in the Captain's Table eating hearts-of-palm salad and hot boiled shrimp and sipping on a tall, icy glass of beer while the sun I saw lift out of the Atlantic that morning sinks into the warm, waveless Gulf of Mexico. It makes for a hell of a day. But that isn't really why I live in the north-central Florida town of Gainesville.

2   Nor do I live in Gainesville because seven blocks from my house there are two enormous libraries filled with the most courteous, helpful people you can imagine, people who, after explaining some of the more intricate mysteries of how the place works, including the purposes of numerous indices, will go ahead and cheerfully find what I cannot: for example, the car capacity of drive-in theaters in Bakers-field, California, in 1950. A man never knows when he may need a bit of information like that, but it isn't enough to keep him living in a little town in Florida as opposed to, say, Ann Arbor, Michigan.

3   I love the size of Gainesville. I can walk anywhere I want to go, and consequently I have very little to do with that abomination before the Lord, the car. It's a twenty-minute stroll to my two favorite bars, Lillian's Music Store and the Winnjammer; ten minutes to a lovely square of grass and trees called the Plaza of the Americas; less than ten minutes to the house of a young lady who has been hyp-notizing me for six years. Some people get analyzed; I get hypnotized. It leaves me with the most astonishing and pleasurable memories. But there must be ten thousand towns like Gainesville in this country, and surely several hundred of them would have good places to drink and talk and at least one house where a young lady lived who would consent to hypnotize me into astonishing and pleasurable memories. So I cannot lean too heavily on walking and memories to justify being where I am.

4   The reason I live where I do is more complicated than the sorts of things I've been talking about thus far—more complicated and, I expect, ultimately inexplicable. Or, said another way: anyone other than I may find that the explanation does not satisfy. To start, I live right in the middle of town on three acres of land, land thick with pines a hundred feet tall, oak, wild plum trees, and all manner of tangled, unidentifiable underbrush. The only cleared space is the very narrow road leading down to the house. No lawn. (There are many things I absolutely refuse to do on this world, but the three things leading the list are: wash my car, shine my shoes, and mow a lawn). The back wall of the room I work in at the rear of the house is glass, and when I raise my eyes from the typewriter I look past an enormous bull bay tree through a thin stand of reeds into a tiny creek,

the banks of which are thick with the greenest fern God ever made. In my imagination I can follow that little creek upstream to the place where, after a long, circuitous passage, it joins the Suwannee River, and then follow the dark waters of the Suwannee upriver to the place where it rises in the nearly impenetrable fastness of the Okefenokee Swamp. Okefenokee: Creek Indian word for Land of the Trembling Earth, because most of the islands in the swamp—some of them holding hundreds of huge trees growing so thick that their roots are matted and woven as closely as a blanket—actually float on the water, and when a black bear crashes across one of them, the whole thing trembles.

I saw the Okefenokee Swamp long before I saw the Suwannee 5 River, and the Suwannee River long before I saw the little creek I'm looking at as I write this. When I was a boy, I was in the swamp a lot, on the edges of it practically all the time that I was not in the fields working. I went deep into the Okefenokee with T. J., the husband of one of my first cousins. His left leg was cut off at the knee and he wore a peg, but he got along fine with it because we were usually in a flat skiff casting nets for crawfish, which he sold for fish bait at a penny apiece. I did not know enough then and do not know enough now to go into the deep middle swamp, but T. J. did; he knew the twisting maze of sloughs like his back yard, could read every sign of every living thing in the swamp, and made a good living with the crawfish nets and his string of traps and his gun. He sold alligator, wore alligator, and ate alligator. This was long before the federal government made the place a national wildlife refuge.

T. J. made his living out of the swamp, and I make mine now 6 out of how the swamp shaped me, how the rhythms and patterns of speech in that time and place are still alive in my mouth today and, more important, alive in my ear. I feed off now and hope always to feed off the stories I heard told in the early dark around fires where coffee boiled while our clothes, still wet from stringing traps all day, slowly dried to our bodies. Even when I write stories not set in Georgia and not at all about anything in the South, that writing is of necessity still informed by my notions of the world and of what it is to be caught in it. Those notions obviously come out of South Georgia and out of everything that happened to me there, or so I believe.

Living here in North Florida, I am a little more than a 7 hundred miles from where I was born and raised to manhood. I am just far enough away from the only place that was ever mine to still see it, close enough to the only people to whom I was ever kin in ways deeper than blood to still hear them. I know that what I have just written will sound precious and pretentious to many people. So be it. Let them do their work as they will, and I'll do mine.

I've tried to work—that is, to write—in Georgia, but I could 8 not. Even under the best of circumstances, at my mama's farm, for instance, it was all too much for me. I was too deep in it, too close to it to use it, to make anything out of it. My memory doesn't even seem to work when I'm writing in Georgia. I can't seem to hold a story in my head. I write a page, and five pages later what I wrote earlier has begun to slide out of focus. If this is all symptomatic of some more profound malaise, I don't want to know about it and I certainly don't want to understand it.

Living here in Gainesville seems to give me a kind of geographic and emotional distance I need to write. I can't write if I get too far away. I tried to work on a novel in Tennessee once and after a ruined two months gave it up in despair. I once spent four months near Lake Placid in a beautiful house lent to me by a friend—perfect place to write—and I didn't do a damn thing but eat my guts and look out the window at the mountains. 9

And that, all of it, precious, pretentious, or whatever, is why I live where I live. And unless something happens that I cannot control, I plan to die here. 10

COMPREHENSION

1. What purpose other than to explain why he lives in northern Florida do you find in Crews's essay?

2. The author gives uncomplicated reasons to explain why he lives where he does. What are these reasons? Why does he raise them?

3. How does Crews's sense of place relate to his conception of himself as a writer?

RHETORIC

1. What are the key words in the first, long sentence of the essay that create a persona for the author? To what extent is the language in this sentence sustained or modified throughout the essay?

2. Locate words and phrases in paragraphs 4 and 5 that convey connotations of mystery and the unknown. What do these words indicate about the theme of the essay?

3. Study Crews's introductory paragraph. What is the effect of the first sentence? Of the parenthetical asides? Of the last two sentences? How does the introduction function in relation to the next two paragraphs?

4. How does description function in relation to the causal patterns that Crews develops?

5. Notice the shift in tone between the first half of the essay (paragraphs 1 to 5) and the second half (paragraphs 6 to 10). Why does the author do this? What does he achieve by "breaking" tonal consistency?

6. Describe the method of development in the concluding paragraph. What new element is introduced? Justify its placement and effectiveness.

WRITING

1. Crews speaks of "a kind of geographic and emotional distance" that he needs to work or to create. Why can being too close to a place or neighborhood be harmful? Conversely, how can such closeness be a strength? Examine these questions in an essay.

2. Write a paper about the ideal place for you to live if you had the opportunity.

3. Compose your own essay entitled "Why I Live Where I Live."

HENRY DAVID THOREAU

Economy

Henry David Thoreau (1817–1862), author of the masterpiece Walden *(1854), is one of the most important figures in American thought and literature. A social and political activist, he opposed the Mexican War, protested slavery, and refused to pay his poll taxes. As a naturalist, he believed in the preeminence of individualism and nature over technology, materialism, and nationalism. In 1845, Thoreau went to live at Walden Pond, "living deep and sucking the marrow out of life." Walden, describing his life at the pond, is one of the most challenging, exuberant, and innovative works of American literature. This account from Thoreau's masterpiece, tracing the construction of his dwelling, reflects his preoccupation with economy, natural process, and self-reliance.*

Near the end of March, 1845, I borrowed an axe and went 1 down to the woods by Walden Pond, nearest to where I intended to build my house, and began to cut down some tall arrowy white pines, still in their youth, for timber. It is difficult to begin without borrowing, but perhaps it is the most generous course thus to permit your fellow-men to have an interest in your enterprise. The owner of the axe, as he released his hold on it, said that it was the apple of his eye; but I returned it sharper than I received it. It was a pleasant hillside where I worked, covered with pine woods, through which I looked out on the pond, and a small open field in the woods where pines and hickories were springing up. The ice in the pond was not yet dissolved, though there were some open spaces, and it was all dark colored and saturated with water. There were some slight flurries of snow during the days that I worked there; but for the most part when I came out onto the railroad, on my way home, its yellow sand heap stretched away gleaming in the hazy atmosphere, and the rails shone in the spring sun, and I heard the lark and pewee and other birds already come to commence another year with us. They were pleasant spring days, in which the winter of man's discontent was thawing as well as the earth, and the life that had lain torpid began to stretch itself. One day, when my axe had come off and I had cut a green hickory for a wedge, driving it with a stone, and had placed the whole to soak in a pond hole in order to swell the wood, I saw a striped snake run into the water, and he lay on the bottom, apparently without inconvenience, as long as I stayed there, or more than a quarter of an hour; perhaps because he had not yet fairly come out of the torpid state. It appeared to me that for a like reason men remain in their present low and primitive condition; but if they should feel the influence of the spring of springs arousing them, they would of necessity rise to a higher and more ethereal life. I had previously seen the snakes in frosty mornings in my path with portions of their bodies still numb and inflexible, waiting for the sun to thaw them. On the 1st of April it rained and melted the ice, and in the early part of the day, which was very foggy, I heard a stray goose groping about over the pond and cackling as if lost, or like the spirit of the fog.

So I went on for some days cutting and hewing timber, and also studs and rafters, all with my narrow axe, not having many communicable or scholar-like thoughts, singing to myself. 2

> Men say they know many things;
> But lo! they have taken wings—
> The arts and sciences,
> And a thousand appliances;
> The wind that blows
> Is all that anybody knows.

I hewed the main timber six inches square, most of the studs on two sides only, and the rafters and floor timbers on one side, leaving the rest of the bark on, so that they were just as straight and much stronger than sawed ones. Each stick was carefully mortised or tenoned by its stump, for I had borrowed other tools by this time. My days in the woods were not very long ones; yet I usually carried my dinner of bread and butter, and read the newspaper in which it was wrapped, at noon, sitting amid the green pine boughs which I had cut off, and to my bread was imparted some of their fragrance, for my hands were covered with a thick coat of pitch. Before I had done I was more the friend than the foe of the pine tree, though I had cut down some of them, having become better acquainted with it. Sometimes a rambler in the wood was attracted by the sound of my axe, and we chatted pleasantly over the chips which I had made.

By the middle of April, for I made no haste in my work, but rather made the most of it, my house was framed and ready for the raising. I had already bought the shanty of James Collins, an Irishman who worked on the Fitchburg Railroad, for boards. James Collins' shanty was considered an uncommonly fine one. When I called to see it he was not at home. I walked about the outside, at first unobserved from within, the window was so deep and high. It was of small dimensions, with a peaked cottage roof, and not much else to be seen, the dirt being raised five feet all around as if it were a compost heap. The roof was the soundest part, though a good deal warped and made brittle by the sun. Doorsill there was none, but a perennial passage for the hens under the door board. Mrs. C. came to the door and asked me to view it from the inside. The hens were driven in by my approach. It was dark, and had a dirt floor for the most part, dank, clammy, and aguish, only here a board and there a board which would not bear removal. She lighted a lamp to show me the inside of the roof and the walls, and also that the board floor extended under the bed, warning me not to step into the cellar, a sort of dust hole two feet deep. In her own words, they were "good boards overhead, good boards all around, and a good window"—of two whole squares originally, only the cat had passed out that way lately. There was a stove, a bed, and a place to sit, an infant in the house where it was born, a silk parasol, gilt-framed looking-glass, and a patent new coffee-mill nailed to an oak sapling, all told. The bargain was soon concluded, for James had in the meanwhile returned. I to pay four dollars and twenty-five cents tonight, he to vacate at five tomorrow morning, selling to nobody else meanwhile: I to take possession at six. It were well, he said, to be there early, and anticipate certain indistinct but wholly unjust claims on the score of ground rent and fuel. This he assured me was the only encumbrance. At six I passed him and his family on the road. One large bundle held their all—bed, coffee-mill, looking-glass, hens—all but the cat; she took to the woods and became a wild cat and, as I learned afterward, trod in a trap set for woodchucks, and so became a dead cat at last.

I took down this dwelling the same morning, drawing the nails, and removed it to the pond side by small cartloads, spreading the boards on the grass there to bleach and warp back again in the sun. One early thrush gave me a note or two as I drove along the woodland path. I was informed treacherously by a young Patrick that neighbor Seeley, an Irishman, in the intervals of the carting, transferred the still tolerable, straight, and drivable nails, staples, and spikes to his pocket, and then stood when I came back to pass the time of day, and look freshly up, unconcerned, with spring thoughts, at the devastation; there being a dearth of work, as he said. He was there to represent spectatordom, and help make this seemingly insignificant event one with the removal of the gods of Troy.

I dug my cellar in the side of a hill sloping to the south, where 5
a woodchuck had formerly dug his burrow, down through sumach and blackberry roots, and the lowest stain of vegetation, six feet square by seven deep, to a fine sand where potatoes would not freeze in any winter. The sides were left shelving, and not stoned; but the sun having never shone on them, the sand still keeps its place. It was but two hours' work. I took particular pleasure in this breaking of ground, for in almost all latitudes men dig into the earth for an equable temperature. Under the most splendid house in the city is still to be found the cellar where they store their roots as of old, and long after the superstructure had disappeared posterity remark its dent in the earth. The house is still but a sort of porch at the entrance of a burrow.

At length, in the beginning of May, with the help of some of 6
my acquaintances, rather to improve so good an occasion for neighborliness than from any necessity, I set up the frame of my house. No man was ever more honored in the character of his raisers than I. They are destined, I trust, to assist at the raising of loftier structures one day. I began to occupy my house on the 4th of July, as soon as it was boarded and roofed, for the boards were carefully feather-edged and lapped, so that it was perfectly impervious to rain, but before boarding I laid the foundation of a chimney at one end, bringing two cartloads of stones up the hill from the pond in my arms. I built the chimney after my hoeing in the fall, before a fire became necessary for warmth, doing my cooking in the meanwhile out of doors on the ground, early in the morning: which mode I still think is in some respects more convenient and agreeable than the usual one. When it stormed before my bread was baked, I fixed a few boards over the fire, and sat under them to watch my loaf, and passed some pleasant hours in that way. In those days, when my hands were much employed, I read but little, but the least scraps of paper which lay on the ground, my holder, or tablecloth, afforded me as much entertainment, in fact answered the same purpose as the Iliad.

COMPREHENSION

1. Explain the process by which Thoreau builds his house. What are the main steps in this process?

2. What is Thoreau's attitude toward economy in this selection? Which of the details Thoreau has included most successfully reveal this attitude?

3.   Compare Thoreau's evocation of place in this essay with Crews's presentation of place in "Why I Live Where I Live." Are the two authors addressing readers the same way? Justify your response.

RHETORIC

1.   In paragraph 1, what connotation does the author develop for the word *borrowing*? How do words related to economics serve as a motif in the essay?

2.   What is the analogy in paragraph 1?

3.   How does Thoreau use process analysis? Why is this rhetorical technique reinforced by the natural processes depicted in the essay?

4.   How does Thoreau particularize the generalizations he makes in the essay?

5.   What is the tone of the essay? Does an implied thesis for the essay emerge? Justify your answer.

6.   What is the relationship of the last two sentences in paragraph 6 to the rest of the selection?

WRITING

1.   Analyze Thoreau's poem in paragraph 2. Identify the poem's theme. Then write a brief essay explaining its relevance to "Economy."

2.   Using Thoreau's method, write an essay in which you trace the process of building or creating something that was important to you.

3.   Write a letter to the editor of your college newspaper arguing the need to economize in some aspect of personal or public life. Refer to Thoreau in this letter.

PABLO NERUDA

The Odors of Homecoming

Pablo Neruda (1904–1973), one of the greatest modern poets writing in Spanish, was born in Parral, Chile, the son of a railwayworker. He studied in Santiago from 1923 to 1926, publishing five volumes of poetry. Later he served as Chilean counsel in Burma, Ceylon, Java, Spain, and Mexico. Neruda, a communist, was elected to the Chilean senate in 1945 but was driven into hiding and eventual exile in 1948. He returned to Chile in 1952 and remained active as a poet-politician up to his untimely death, twelve days after the coup that overthrew Allende. Neruda's major volumes of poetry include Residence on Earth *(1925–1945),* Elementary Odes *(1954–1957),* Estravagaria *(1958), and* A Hundred Love Sonnets *(1960). The following essay, in a translation by Margaret Sayers Peden, comes from* Passions and Impressions *(1983). It reflects the broad range of images, figurative language, and heightened meanings that also endow Neruda's poetry with such power.*

M y house nestles among many trees. After a long absence, 1 I like to lose myself in hidden nooks to savor my homecoming. Mysterious, fragrant thickets have appeared that are new to me. The poplar I planted in the back of the garden, so slim it could barely be seen, is now an adult tree. Its bark is patterned with wrinkles of wisdom that rise toward the sky to express themselves in a constant tremor of new leaves in the treetop.

The chestnut trees were the last to recognize me. When I ar- 2 rived, their naked, dry branches, towering and unseeing, seemed imperious and hostile, though the prevading spring of Chile was germinating amid their trunks. Every day I went to call on them, for I understood that they demanded my homage, and in the cold of morning stood motionless beneath the leafless branches, until one day a timid green bud, high overhead, came out to look at me, and others followed. So my reappearance was communicated to the wary, hidden leaves of the tallest chestnut tree, which now greets me with condescension, tolerating my return.

In the trees the birds renew their age-old trills, as if nothing 3 ever happened beneath the leaves.

A pervasive odor of winter and years lingers in the library. 4 Of all places, this was the most suffused with absence.

There is something of mortality about the smell of musty 5 books; it assaults the nostrils and strikes the rugged terrain of the soul, because it is the odor of oblivion, of buried memory.

Standing beside the weathered window, staring at the blue 6 and white Andean sky, I sense that behind my back the aroma of spring is pitting its strength against the books. They resist being rooted out of their long neglect, and still exude signs of oblivion. Spring enters every room, clad in a new dress and the odor of honeysuckle.

The books have been unruly in my absence. None is missing, 7 but none is in its place. Beside an austere volume of Bacon, a rare seventeenth-century edition, I find Salgari's *The Captain of Yucatan,* and in spite of everything, they've got along rather well together. On the other hand, as I pick up a solitary Byron, its cover drops off like the dark wing of an albatross. Laboriously, I stitch spine and cover, but not before a puff of cold Romanticism clouds my eyes.

The shells are the most silent occupants of my house. They   8
endured the years of the ocean, solidifying their silence. Now, to those years have been added time and dust. Their cold, glinting mother-of-pearl, their concentric Gothic ellipses, their open valves, remind me of distant coasts, long-ago events. This incomparable lance of rosy light is the *Rostellaria*, which the Cuban malacologist Carlos de la Torre, a magus of the deep, once conferred upon me like an underseas decoration. And here, slightly more faded and dusty, is the black "olive" of the California seas, and, of the same provenance, the oyster of red spines and the oyster of black pearls. We almost drowned in that treasure-laden sea.

There are new occupants, books and objects liberated from   9
boxes long sealed. The pine boxes come from France. The boards smell of sunny noon in the Midi, and as I pry them open, they creak and sing, and the golden light falls on the red bindings of Victor Hugo. *Les Misérables*, in an early edition, arrives to crowd the walls of my house with its multitude of heartrending lives.

Then, from a large box resembling a coffin, comes the sweet   10
face of a woman, firm wooden breasts that once cleaved the wind, hands saturated with music and brine. It is the figure of a woman, a figurehead. I baptize her María Celeste, because she has all the mystery of a lost ship. I discovered her radiant beauty in a Paris *bric-á-brac*, buried beneath used hardware, disfigured by neglect, hidden beneath the sepulchral rags and tatters of the slums. Now, aloft, she sails again, alive and new. Every morning her checks will be covered by mysterious dew or saltwater tears.

All at once the roses are in bloom. Once I was an enemy of   11
the rose, of its interminable literary associations, of its arrogance. But as I watched them grow, having endured the winter with nothing to wear and nothing to cover their heads, and then as snowy breasts or glowing fires peered from among hard and thorny stems, little by little I was filled with tenderness, with admiration for their ox-like health, for the daring, secret wave of perfume and light they implacably extract from the black earth at just the right moment, as if duty were a miracle, as if they thrived on precise maneuvers in harsh weather. And now roses grow everywhere, with a moving solemnity I share— remote, both they and I, from pomp and frivolity, each absorbed in creating its individual flash of lightning.

Now every wave of air bears a soft, trembling movement, a   12
flowery palpitation that pierces the heart. Forgotten names, forgotten springs, hands that touched briefly, haughty eyes of yellow stone,

THE ODORS OF HOMECOMING   **61**

tresses lost in time: youth, insistently throbbing with memories and ecstatic aromas.

It is the perfume of the honeysuckle, the first kisses of spring. 13

COMPREHENSION

1. What is the season? What are some of the "odors of homecoming" that Neruda detects? What do the odors and sights remind him of?

2. List the various objects that Neruda describes. What is his attitude toward them? Is it the same attitude as the one expressed by Thoreau in "Economy"? Justify your answer.

3. What responses by Neruda to the odors of homecoming contribute to your understanding of the author?

RHETORIC

1. Analyze the sensory language in this essay. What senses does Neruda evoke? Cite examples. Describe the mood or atmosphere that the imagery creates.

2. Locate similes and metaphors in the essay. What do they contribute to the dominant impression?

3. What sentence in the introductory paragraph establishes the purpose of Neruda's description of his home? Is this the thesis statement? Why, or why not?

4. How does Neruda arrange descriptive details in paragraphs 1 to 3, 4 to 6, 7 to 10, and 11 to 13?

5. Neruda employs a considerable amount of personification in this essay. Cite and explain examples of this method. What cumulative impression is created?

6. What effect is achieved by the relatively short paragraphs 3, 4, and 5 and by the one-sentence conclusion?

WRITING

1. Is Neruda excessively impressionistic, romantic, or sentimental in this essay? Justify your response in a brief essay.

2. Describe a particularly vivid homecoming of your own. Incorporate sensory details and other poetic devices.

3. Write a descriptive paragraph that captures the dominant impression of a specific month or season.

4. Develop a comparative essay on the use of figurative language in "The Odors of Homecoming" and "Why I Live Where I Live," by Crews.

GRETEL EHRLICH

Wyoming: The Solace of Open Spaces

Gretel Ehrlich (1949–   ) was born in California and educated at Bennington College, UCLA, and The New School for Social Research. She currently lives on a ranch in Shell, Wyoming. She has worked as a professional documentary filmmaker. Her essays have appeared in The New York Times, The Atlantic, Harper's, *and the* New Age Journal. *She has also published two books of poetry and a story collection,* City Tales, Wyoming Stories. *Ehrlich has received awards from the National Endowment for the Arts and the Wyoming Council for the Arts. In the following selection, with the eyes and ears of an anthropologist and the knowledge of a historian, Ehrlich provides us with a comprehensive view of a life most Americans are no longer familiar with.*

t's May, and I've just awakened from a nap, curled against sagebrush the way my dog taught me to sleep— sheltered from wind. A weather front is pulling the huge sky over me, and from the dark a hailstone has hit me on the head.   1

I'm trailing a band of 2000 sheep across a stretch of Wyoming badland, a 50-mile trip that takes five days because sheep shade up in the hot sun and won't budge until it cools. Bunched together now, and excited into a run by the storm, they drift across dry land, tumbling into draws like water and surging out again onto the rugged, choppy plateaus that are the building blocks of this state.   2

The name "Wyoming" comes from an Indian word meaning "at the great plains," but the plains are really valleys, great arid valleys, 1600 square miles' worth of them, with the horizon bending up on all sides into mountain ranges. This gives the vastness a sheltering look.   3

Winter lasts six months here. Prevailing winds spill snowdrifts to the east, and new storms from the northwest replenish them. This white bulk is sometimes dizzying, even nauseating, to look at. At 20, 30, 40 degrees below zero, it is not only your car that doesn't work but also your mind and body.   4

The landscape hardens into a dungeon of space. During the winter, while I was riding to find a new calf, my legs half froze to the saddle, and in the silence that such cold creates, I felt like the first person on earth, or the last.   5

Today the sun is out—only a few clouds billowing. In the east, where the sheep have started off without me, the benchland tilts up   6

in a series of red-earthed, eroded mesas, planed flat on top by a million years of water. Behind them, a bold line of muscular scraps rears up 10,000 feet to become the Big Horn Mountains. A tidal pattern is engraved into the ground, as if left by the sea that once covered this state. Canyons curve down like galaxies to meet the oncoming rush of flat land.

To live and work in this kind of open country, with its 100-mile views, is to lose the distinction between background and foreground. When I asked an older ranch hand to describe Wyoming's openness, he said, "It's all a bunch of nothing—wind and rattlesnakes—and so much of it you can't tell where you're going or where you've been and it don't make much difference." 7

John, a sheepman I know, is tall and handsome and has an explosive temperament. He has a perfect intuition about people and sheep. They call him "Highpockets" because he's so long-legged; his graceful stride matches the distances he has to cover. 8

"Open space hasn't affected me at all. It's all the people moving in on it," he said. The huge ranch he was born on takes up much of one county and spreads into another state. For him to put 100,000 miles on his pickup in three years and never leave home is not unusual. 9

Most of Wyoming has a "lean-to" look. Instead of big, roomy barns and Victorian houses, there are dugouts, low sheds, log cabins, sheep camps and fence lines that look like driftwood blown haphazardly into place. People in Wyoming still feel pride because they live in such a harsh place, part of the glamorous cowboy past, and they are determined not to be the victims of a mining-dominated future. 10

Most characteristic of the state's landscape is what a developer euphemistically describes as "indigenous growth right up to your front door"—a reference to waterless stands of salt sage, snakes, jackrabbits, deerflies, red dust, a brief respite of wildflowers, dry washes and no trees. 11

Sagebrush covers 58,000 square miles of Wyoming. The biggest city has a population of 50,000, and there are only five settlements that could be called cities in the whole state. The rest are towns, scattered across the expanse with as much as 60 miles between them, their populations 2000, 50 or 10. They are fugitive-looking, perched on a barren, windblown bench, or tagged onto a river or a railroad, or laid out straight in a farming valley with implement stores and a block-long Mormon church. 12

In the eastern part of the state, which slides down into the Great Plains, the new mining settlements are boomtowns, trailer cities, metal knots on flat land. 13

Despite the desolate look, there's a coziness to living in this state. 14

There are so few people (only 470,000) that ranchers who buy 15 and sell cattle know each other statewide. The kids who choose to go to college usually go to the state's one university, in Laramie. Hired hands work their way around Wyoming in a lifetime of hirings and firings. And, despite the physical separation, people stay in touch, often driving two or three hours to another ranch for dinner.

Seventy-five years ago, when travel was by buckboard or horseback, cowboys who were temporarily out of work rode the grub line—drifting from ranch to ranch, mending fences or milking cows, and receiving in exchange a bed and meals. Gossip and messages traveled this slow circuit with them, creating an intimacy among ranchers who were three and four weeks' ride apart. 16

One old-time couple I know, whose turn-of-the-century home- stead was used by an outlaw gang as a relay station for stolen horses, recall that if you were traveling, desperado or not, any lighted ranch house was a welcome sign. 17

Even now, for someone who lives in a remote spot, arriving at a ranch or coming to town for supplies is cause for celebration. To emerge from isolation can be disorienting. Everything looks bright, new, vivid. After I had been herding sheep for only three days, the sound of the camp-tender's pickup flustered me. Longing for human company, I felt a foolish grin take over my face, yet I had to resist an urgent temptation to run and hide. 18

Things happen suddenly in Wyoming: the change of seasons and weather; for people, the violent swings into and out of isolation. But goodnaturedness goes hand in hand with severity. Friendliness is a tradition. Strangers passing on the road wave hello. 19

A common sight is two pickups stopped side by side far out on a range, on a dirt track winding through the sage. The drivers will share a cigarette, uncap their Thermos bottles, and pass a battered cup, steaming with coffee, between windows. These meetings sum- mon up the details of several generations, because in Wyoming pri- vate histories are largely public knowledge. 20

In most parts of Wyoming, the human population is visibly outnumbered by the animal. Not far from my town of 50, I rode into a narrow valley and startled a herd of 200 elk. Eagles look like small people as they eat car-killed deer by the road. Antelope, moving in small, graceful bands, travel at 60 m.p.h., their mouths open as if drinking in the space. 21

The solitude in which Westerners live makes them quiet. They telegraph thoughts and feelings by the way they tilt their heads and listen; pulling their Stetsons into a steep dive over their eyes or pigeon-toeing one boot over the other, they lean against a fence and take the whole scene in. These detached looks of quiet amusement are sometimes cynical, but they can also come from a dry-eyed humility as lucid as the air is clear. 22

 WYOMING: THE SOLACE OF OPEN SPACES

Conversation goes on in what sounds like a private code. A few phrases imply a complex of meanings. Asking directions you get a curious list of details. While trailing sheep, I was told to "ride up to that kinda upturned rock, follow the pin wash, turn left at the dump, and then you'll see the waterhole." 23

I've spent hours riding to sheep camp at dawn in a pickup when nothing was said and eaten meals in the cookhouse when the only words spoken were a mumbled "Thank you, ma'am" at the end of dinner. The silence is profound. Instead of talking, we seem to share one eye. The landscape is engorged with detail, every movement on it chillingly sharp. The air between people is charged. 24

Spring weather is capricious and mean. It snows, then blisters with heat. There have been tornadoes. They lay their elephant trunks out in the sage until they find houses, then slurp everything up and leave. I've noticed that melting snowbanks hiss and rot, viperous, then drip into calm pools where ducklings hatch and livestock, being trailed to summer range, drink. 25

With the ice cover gone, rivers churn a milkshake brown, taking culverts and small bridges with them. Water in such an arid place (the average annual rainfall where I live is less than eight inches) is like blood. It festoons drab land with green veins: a line of cottonwoods following a stream; a strip of alfalfa, and on ditchbanks, wild asparagus growing. 26

I try to imagine a world of uncharted land, in which one could look over an uncompleted map and ride a horse past where all the lines have stopped. There is no real wilderness left; wilderness, yes, but true wilderness has been gone on this continent since the time of Lewis and Clark's overland journey. 27

Two hundred years ago, the Crow, Shoshone, Arapaho, Cheyenne, and Sioux roamed the intermountain West, orchestrating their movements according to hunger, season, and warfare. Once they acquired horses, they traversed the spines of all the big Wyoming ranges—the Absarokas, the Wind Rivers, the Tetons, the Big Horns—and wintered on the unprotected plains that fan out from them. Space was life. The word was their home. 28

What was life-giving to native Americans was often nightmarish to sod-busters who arrived encumbered with families and ethnic pasts to be transplanted in nearly uninhabitable land. The great distances, the shortage of water and trees, and the loneliness created unexpected hardships for them. 29

In her book *O Pioneers!* Willa Cather gives a settler's version of the black landscape: "The little town behind them had vanished as if it had never been, had fallen behind the swell of the prairie, and the stern frozen country received them into its bosom. The homesteads 30 were few and far apart; here and there a windmill gaunt against the sky, a sod house crouching in a hollow."

The emptiness of the West was for others a geography of possibility. Men and women who amassed great chunks of land and struggled to preserve unfenced empires were, despite their self-serving motives, unwitting geographers. They understood the lay of the land. 31

But by the 1850s, the Oregon and Mormon trails sported bumper-to-bumper traffic. Wealthy landowners, many of them aristocratic absentee landlords, known as remittance men because they were paid to come West and get out of their families' hair, overstocked the range with more than a million head of cattle. By 1885, the feed and water were desperately short, and the winter of 1886 laid out the gaunt bodies of dead animals so closely together that when the thaw came, one rancher from Kaycee claimed to have walked on cowhide all the way to Crazy Woman Creek, 20 miles away. 32

Territorial Wyoming was a boy's world. The land was generous with everything but water. At first there was room enough and food enough for everyone. And, as with all beginnings, an expansive mood set in. The young cowboys, drifters, shopkeepers, and schoolteachers were heroic, lawless, generous, rowdy, and tenacious. The individualism and optimism generated during those times have endured. 33

Cattle barons tried to control all the public grazing land by restricting membership in the Wyoming Stock Growers Association, as if it were a country club. They ostracized from roundups and brandings cowboys and ranchers who were not members, then denounced them as rustlers. 34

One cold-blooded murder of a small-time stockman kicked off the Johnson County cattle war, which was no simple good guy–bad guy shootout but a complicated class struggle between landed gentry and less affluent settlers—a shocking reminder that the West was not an egalitarian sanctuary after all. 35

Fencing ultimately enforced boundaries, but barbed wire abolished space. It was stretched across the beautiful valleys, into mountains, over desert badlands, through buffalo grass. 36

The "anything is possible" fever—the lure of any place—was constricted. The integrity of the land as a geographical body, and the freedom to ride anywhere on it, was lost. 37

I punched cows with a young man named Martin, who is the great-grandson of John Tisdale. His inheritance is not the open land that Tisdale knew and prematurely lost but a rage against restraint. 38

In all this open space, values crystallize quickly. People are strong on scruples but tenderhearted about quirky behavior. A friend 39 and I found one ranch hand, who's "not right in the head," sitting in front of the badly decayed carcass of a cow, shaking his finger and saying, "Now, I don't want you to do this ever again!"

When I asked what was wrong with him, I was told, "He's goofier than hell, just like the rest of us." 40

Perhaps because the West is historically new, conventional morality is still felt to be less important than rock-bottom truths. Though there's always a lot of teasing and sparring around, people are blunt with each other, sometimes even cruel, believing honesty is stronger medicine than sympathy, which may console but often conceals. 41

The formality that goes hand in hand with the rowdiness is known as "the Western Code." It's a list of practical do's and don'ts, faithfully observed. A friend, Cliff, who runs a trapline in the winter, cut off half his foot while axing a hole in the ice. Alone, he dragged himself to his pickup and headed for town, stopping to open the ranch gate as he left, and getting out to close it again, thus losing, in his observance of rules, precious time and blood. 42

Later, he commented, "How would it look, them having to come to the hospital to tell me their cows had gotten out?" 43

The roominess of the state has affected political attitudes. Ranchers keep up with world politics and the convulsions of the economy but are basically isolationists. Used to running their own small empires of land and livestock, they're suspicious of big government. 44

It's a "don't fence me in" holdover from a century ago. They still want the elbow room their grandfathers had, so they're strongly conservative, but with a populist twist. 45

Summer is the season when we get our "cowboy tans"—on the lower parts of our faces and on three fourths of our arms. Excessive heat, in the 90s and higher, sends us outside with the mosquitoes. 46

After the brief lushness of summer, the sun moves south. The range grass is brown. Livestock has been trailed back down from the mountains. Waterholes begin to frost over at night. Last fall Martin asked me to accompany him on a pack trip. With five horses, we followed a river into the mountains behind the tiny Wyoming town of Meeteetse. Groves of aspen, red and orange, gave off a light that made us look toasted. 47

One of our evening entertainments was to watch the night sky. My dog, who also came on the trip, a dingo bred to herd sheep, is so used to the silence and empty skies that when an airplane flies over he always looks up and eyes the distant intruder quizzically. 48

The sky, lately, seems to be much more crowded than it used to be. Satellites make their silent passes in the dark with great regularity. We counted 18 in one hour's viewing. How odd to think that while they circumnavigated the planet, Martin and I had moved only 49

GRETEL EHRLICH

six miles into our local wilderness, and had seen no other human for the two weeks we stayed there.

At night, by moonlight, the land is whittled to slivers—a 50 ridge, a river, a strip of grassland stretching to the mountains, then the huge sky. One morning a full moon was setting in the west just as the sun was rising. I felt precariously balanced between the two as I loped across a meadow. For a moment, I could believe that the stars, which were still visible, work like cooper's bands, holding everything above Wyoming together.

Space has a spiritual equivalent, and can heal what is divided 51 and burdensome in us. My grandchildren will probably use space shuttles for a honeymoon trip or to recover from heart attacks, but closer to home we might also learn how to carry space inside ourselves in the effortless way we carry our skins. Space represents sanity, not a life purified, dull, or "spaced out" but one that might accommodate intelligently any idea or situation.

COMPREHENSION

1. What is Wyoming's predominant appeal to the author? Why has she chosen to live in its rather inhospitable climate?

2. Explain the ways in which Wyoming, for Ehrlich, symbolizes the American West.

3. In the concluding paragraph, Ehrlich says, "Space has a spiritual equivalent." What does she mean by this? How do the Wyoming natives display this spirituality? How has it affected the author?

RHETORIC

1. How do the following descriptions help create the nature of Wyoming space: "This gives the vastness a sheltering look" (paragraph 3); "The landscape hardens into a dungeon of space" (paragraph 5); and "Canyons curve down like galaxies" (paragraph 6)?

2. None of the direct speech in this essay is in the form of a dialogue. How is this indicative of the Westerner's attitude toward speech? How does it support the idea that "A few phrases imply a complex of meanings" (paragraph 23)?

3. How does Ehrlich's introductory comment that "my dog taught me to sleep" (paragraph 1) set the general tone for the bond between humans and nature in Wyoming? What other evidence is there in the essay of this special relationship?

4. Paragraphs 28 through 37 describe Wyoming's history. What function does this serve in the essay? How does it explain life in present-day Wyoming?

5. In the conclusion, Ehrlich suggests that the relationship of humans to space as it exists in Wyoming may be dying out. What references are there in the essay that seem to move toward this conclusion?

6. Compare the use of direct speech in this essay to that in McPhee's "Travels in Georgia." In what way does the dialogue suggest that the residents depicted in the two essays are similar in their outlook and attitudes?

WRITING

1. How can one's environment affect the nature of one's relationship with others? How can it affect one's "communicative style"? For example, do city dwellers speak differently from rural ones? Do people from one region—for example, the South—relate differently toward one another than people from another region? Explore these issues in an essay focusing on a locale you are familiar with. Your topics don't have to be limited to speech but may include body language, dress, jewelry, and so forth.

2. Compare and contrast the sense of space in this essay with that in Orwell's "Shooting an Elephant."

3. Think about some quality that is important to you—for example, solitude or brightness—and then write an essay about a place or environment that captures this quality.

N. SCOTT MOMADAY

The Way to Rainy Mountain

Navarre Scott Momaday (1934–   ), Pulitzer Prize–winning poet, critic, and academician, is the author of House Made of Dawn *(1968),* The Way to Rainy Mountain *(1969),* The Names *(1976), and other works. "I am an American Indian (Kiowa), and am vitally interested in American Indian art, history and culture," Momaday has written. In this essay, he elevates personal experience to the realm of poetry and tribal myth.*

 single knoll rises out of the plain in Oklahoma, north   1
and west of the Wichita Range. For my people, the
Kiowas, it is an old landmark, and they gave it the name
Rainy Mountain. The hardest weather in the world is
there. Winter brings blizzards, hot tornadic winds arise in the spring,
and in summer the prairie is an anvil's edge. The grass turns brittle
and brown, and it cracks beneath your feet. There are green belts
along the rivers and creeks, linear groves of hickory and pecan, willow
and witch hazel. At a distance in July or August the steaming foliage
seems almost to writhe in fire. Great green and yellow grasshoppers

are everywhere in the tall grass, popping up like corn to sting the flesh, and tortoises crawl about on the red earth, going nowhere in the plenty of time. Loneliness is an aspect of the land. All things in the plain are isolate; there is no confusion of objects in the eye, but *one* hill or *one* tree or *one* man. To look upon that landscape in the early morning, with the sun at your back, is to lose the sense of proportion. Your imagination comes to life, and this, you think, is where Creation was begun.

I returned to Rainy Mountain in July. My grandmother had died in the spring, and I wanted to be at her grave. She had lived to be very old and at last infirm. Her only living daughter was with her when she died, and I was told that in death her face was that of a child.   2

I like to think of her as a child. When she was born, the Kiowas were living the last great moment of their history. For more than a hundred years they had controlled the open range from the Smoky Hill River to the Red, from the headwaters of the Canadian to the fork of the Arkansas and Cimarron. In alliance with the Comanches, they had ruled the whole of the southern Plains. War was their sacred business, and they were among the finest horsemen the world has ever known. But warfare for the Kiowas was preeminently a matter of disposition rather than of survival, and they never understood the grim, unrelenting advance of the U.S. Cavalry. When at last, divided and ill-provisioned, they were driven onto the Staked Plains in the cold rains of autumn, they fell into panic. In Palo Duro Canyon they abandoned their crucial stores to pillage and had nothing then but their lives. In order to save themselves, they surrendered to the soldiers at Fort Sill and were imprisoned in the old stone corral that now stands as a military museum. My grandmother was spared the humiliation of those high gray walls by eight or ten years, but she must have known from birth the affliction of defeat, the dark brooding of old warriors.   3

Her name was Aho, and she belonged to the last culture to evolve in North America. Her forebears came down from the high country in western Montana nearly three centuries ago. They were a mountain people, a mysterious tribe of hunters whose language has never been positively classified in any major group. In the late seventeenth century they began a long migration to the south and east. It was a journey toward the dawn, and it led to a golden age. Along the way the Kiowas were befriended by the Crows, who gave them the culture and religion of the Plains. They acquired horses, and their ancient nomadic spirit was suddenly free of the ground. They acquired Tai-me, the sacred Sun Dance doll, from that moment the object and symbol of their worship, and so shared in the divinity of the sun. Not least, they acquired the sense of destiny, therefore courage and   4 pride. When they entered upon the southern Plains they had been transformed. No longer were they slaves to the simple necessity of survival; they were a lordly and dangerous society of fighters and thieves, hunters and priests of the sun. According to their origin myth, they entered the world through a hollow log. From one point of view, their migration was the fruit of an old prophecy, for indeed they emerged from a sunless world.

Although my grandmother lived out her long life in the 5 shadow of Rainy Mountain, the immense landscape of the continental interior lay like memory in her blood. She could tell of the Crows, whom she had never seen, and of the Black Hills, where she had never been. I wanted to see in reality what she had seen more perfectly in the mind's eye, and traveled fifteen hundred miles to begin my pilgrimage.

Yellowstone, it seemed to me, was the top of the world, a 6 region of deep lakes and dark timber, canyons and waterfalls. But, beautiful as it is, one might have the sense of confinement there. The skyline in all directions is close at hand, the high wall of the woods and deep cleavages of shade. There is a perfect freedom in the mountains, but it belongs to the eagle and the elk, the badger and the bear. The Kiowas reckoned their stature by the distance they could see, and they were bent and blind in the wilderness.

Descending eastward, the highland meadows are a stairway 7 to the plain. In July the inland slope of the Rockies is luxuriant with flax and buckwheat, stonecrop and larkspur. The earth unfolds and the limit of the land recedes. Clusters of trees, and animals grazing far in the distance, cause the vision to reach away and wonder to build upon the mind. The sun follows a longer course in the day, and the sky is immense beyond all comparison. The great billowing clouds that sail upon it are shadows that move upon the grain like water, dividing light. Farther down, in the land of the Crows and Blackfeet, the plain is yellow. Sweet clover takes hold of the hills and bends upon itself to cover and seal the soil. There the Kiowas paused on their way; they had come to the place where they must change their lives. The sun is at home on the plains. Precisely there does it have the certain character of a god. When the Kiowas came to the land of the Crows, they could see the dark lees of the hills at dawn across the Bighorn River, the profusion of light on the grain shelves, the oldest deity ranging after the solstices. Not yet would they veer southward to the caldron of the land that lay below; they must wean their blood from the northern winter and hold the mountains a while longer in their view. They bore Tai-me in procession to the east.

A dark mist lay over the Black Hills, and the land was like 8 iron. At the top of a ridge I caught sight of Devil's Tower upthrust against the gray sky as if in the birth of time the core of the earth had broken through its crust and the motion of the world was begun. There are things in nature that engender an awful quiet in the heart of man; Devil's Tower is one of them. Two centuries ago, because they could not do otherwise, the Kiowas made a legend at the base of the rock. My grandmother said:

> Eight children were there at play, seven sisters and their brother. Suddenly the boy was struck dumb; he trembled and began to run upon his hands and feet. His fingers became claws, and his body was covered with fur. Directly there was a bear where the boy had been. The sisters were terrified; they ran, and the bear after them. They came to the stump of a great tree, and the tree spoke to them. It bade them climb upon it, and as they did so it began to rise into the air. The bear came to kill them, but they were just beyond its reach. It reared against the tree and scored the bark all around with its claws. The seven sisters were borne into the sky, and they became the stars of the Big Dipper.

From that moment, and so long as the legend lives, the Kiowas have kinsmen in the night sky. Whatever they were in the mountains, they could be no more. However tenuous their well-being, however much they had suffered and would suffer again, they had found a way out of the wilderness.

My grandmother had a reverence for the sun, a holy regard 9 that now is all but gone out of mankind. There was a wariness in her, and an ancient awe. She was a Christian in her later years, but she had come a long way about, and she never forgot her birthright. As a child she had been to the Sun Dances; she had taken part in those annual rites, and by them she had learned the restoration of her people in the presence of Tai-me. She was about seven when the last Kiowa Sun Dance was held in 1887 on the Washita River above Rainy Mountain Creek. The buffalo were gone. In order to consummate the ancient sacrifice—to impale the head of a buffalo bull upon the medicine tree—a delegation of old men journeyed into Texas, there to beg and barter for an animal from the Goodnight herd. She was ten when the Kiowas came together for the last time as a living Sun Dance culture. They could find no buffalo; they had to hang an old hide from the sacred tree. Before the dance could begin, a company of soldiers rode out from Fort Sill under orders to disperse the tribe. Forbidden without cause the essential act of their faith, having seen the wild herds slaughtered and left to rot upon the ground, the Kiowas backed away forever from the medicine tree. That was July 20, 1890, at the great bend of the Washita. My grandmother was there.

 THE WAY TO RAINY MOUNTAIN

Without bitterness, and for as long as she lived, she bore a vision of deicide.

Now that I can have her only in memory, I see my grand- 10
mother in the several postures that were peculiar to her: standing at the wood stove on a winter morning and turning meat in a great iron skillet; sitting at the south window, bent above her beadwork, and afterwards, when her vision failed, looking down for a long time into the fold of her hands; going out upon a cane, very slowly as she did when the weight of age came upon her; praying. I remember her most often at prayer. She made long, rambling prayers out of suffering and hope, having seen many things. I was never sure that I had the right to hear, so exclusive were they of all mere custom and company. The last time I saw her she prayed standing by the side of her bed at night, naked to the waist, the light of a kerosene lamp moving upon her dark skin. Her long, black hair, always drawn and braided in the day, lay upon her shoulders and against her breasts like a shawl. I do not speak Kiowa, and I never understood her prayers, but there was something inherently sad in the sound, some merest hesitation upon the syllables of sorrow. She began in a high and descending pitch, exhausting her breath to silence; then again and again—and always the same intensity of effort, of something that is, and is not, like urgency in the human voice. Transported so in the dancing light among the shadows of her room, she seemed beyond the reach of time. But that was illusion; I think I knew then that I should not see her again.

Houses are like sentinels in the plain, old keepers of the 11
weather watch. There, in a very little while, wood takes on the appearance of great age. All colors wear soon away in the wind and rain, and then the wood is burned gray and the grain appears and the nails turn red with rust. The windowpanes are black and opaque; you imagine there is nothing within, and indeed there are many ghosts, bones given up to the land. They stand here and there against the sky, and you approach them for a longer time than you expect. They belong in the distance; it is their domain.

Once there was a lot of sound in my grandmother's house, a 12
lot of coming and going, feasting and talk. The summers there were full of excitement and reunion. The Kiowas are a summer people; they abide the cold and keep to themselves, but when the season turns and the land becomes warm and vital they cannot hold still; an old love of going returns upon them. The aged visitors who came to my grandmother's house when I was a child were made of lean and leather, and they bore themselves upright. They wore great black hats and bright ample shirts that shook in the wind. They rubbed fat upon their hair and wound their braids with strips of colored cloth. Some of them painted their faces and carried the scars of old and cherished enmities. They were an old council of warlords, come to remind and be re-

minded of who they were. Their wives and daughters served them well. The women might indulge themselves; gossip was at once the mark and compensation of their servitude. They made loud and elaborate talk among themselves, full of jest and gesture, fright and false alarm. They went abroad in fringed and flowered shawls, bright beadwork and German silver. They were at home in the kitchen, and they prepared meals that were banquets.

There were frequent prayer meetings, and great nocturnal feasts. When I was a child I played with my cousins outside, where the lamplight fell upon the ground and the singing of the old people rose up around us and carried away into the darkness. There were a lot of good things to eat, a lot of laughter and surprise. And afterwards, when the quiet returned, I lay down with my grandmother and could hear the frogs away by the river and feel the motion of the air. **13**

Now there is funeral silence in the rooms, the endless wake of some final word. The walls have closed in upon my grandmother's house. When I returned to it in mourning, I saw for the first time in my life how small it was. It was late at night, and there was a white moon, nearly full. I sat for a long time on the stone steps by the kitchen door. From there I could see out across the land; I could see the long row of trees by the creek, the low light upon the rolling plains, and the stars of the Big Dipper. Once I looked at the moon and caught sight of a strange thing. A cricket had perched upon the handrail, only a few inches away from me. My line of vision was such that the creature filled the moon like a fossil. It had gone there, I thought, to live and die, for there, of all places, was its small definition made whole and eternal. A warm wind rose up and purled like the longing within me. **14**

The next morning I awoke at dawn and went out on the dirt road to Rainy Mountain. It was already hot, and the grasshoppers began to fill the air. Still, it was early in the morning, and the birds sang out of the shadows. The long yellow grass on the mountain shone in the bright light, and a scissortail hied above the land. There, where it ought to be, at the end of a long and legendary way, was my grandmother's grave. Here and there on the dark stones were ancestral names. Looking back once, I saw the mountain and came away. **15**

COMPREHENSION

1. What is the significance of Momaday's title? How does the title help to explain the author's purpose?

2. Why does Momaday return to his grandmother's house and journey to her grave?

3. List the various myths and legends the author mentions in the essay. What subjects do they treat? How are these subjects interrelated?

RHETORIC

1. Locate and explain instances of sensory, metaphorical, and symbolic language in the essay. Why are these modes of language consistent with the subject and theme elaborated by Momaday?

2. How does Momaday's use of abstract language affect the concrete vocabulary in the essay?

3. What is the method of development in the first paragraph? How does the introduction serve as a vehicle for the central meanings in the essay?

4. Consider the relationship of narration to description in the organization of the essay. What forms of narrative serve to unify the selection? Are the narrative patterns strictly linear, or do they shift for other purposes? Explain. In what sense is Momaday's descriptive technique cinematic?

5. How do the land, the Kiowas, and Momaday's grandmother serve as reinforcing frames of the essay?

6. Describe in detail the creation of mood in this essay. Explain specifically the mood at the conclusion.

WRITING

1. Momaday implies that myth is central to his life and the life of the Kiowas. What *is* myth? Do you think that myth is as strong in general American culture as it is in Kiowa culture? In what ways does it operate? How can myth sustain the individual, community, and nation? Write an analytical essay on this subject.

2. Write about a person and place that, taken together, inspire a special reverence in you.

3. In an essay, explore the ways in which environment molds personality in "The Way to Rainy Mountain," by Momaday, and "Wyoming: The Solace of Open Spaces," by Ehrlich.

BARRY LOPEZ

Perimeter

Barry Lopez (1945–   ) is a distinguished American writer on natural history, the environment, and our community obligations to the planet. He was born in Port Chester, New York; raised in rural California and New York City; and educated at the Univer-

sity of Notre Dame and the University of Oregon. Since the early 1970s, he has lived on the McKenzie River in western Oregon. His award-winning books include Of Wolves and Men *(1978),* Winter Count *(1981), and* Arctic Dreams *(1986). A frequent contributor to periodicals, Lopez has collected some of his best essays and short fiction in* Crossing Open Ground *(1988). Lopez is a keen, poetic observer of landscape, by which he means "the complete lay of the land." In the following selection from* Desert Notes *(1976), Lopez invites us to see a particular landscape and understand our relationship to its various elements.*

I.

n the west, in the blue mountains, there are creeks of grey water. They angle out of the canyons, come across the brown scratched earth to the edge of the desert and run into nothing. When these creeks are running they make a terrific noise.

No one to my knowledge has ever counted the number, but I think there are more than twenty; it is difficult to be precise. For example, some of the creeks have been given names that, over the years, have had to be given up because a creek has run three or four times and then the channel has been abandoned.

You can easily find the old beds, where the dust has been washed out to reveal a level of rock rubble—cinnabar laced with mercury, fool's gold, clear quartz powder, and fire opal; but it is another thing to find one of the creeks, even when they are full. I have had some success by going at night and listening for the noise.

There is some vegetation in this area; it does not seem to depend on water. The rattlesnakes live here along with the rabbits. When there is any thunder it is coming from this direction. During the day the wind is here. The smells include the hellebore, vallo weed and punchen; each plant puts out its own smell and together they make a sort of pillow that floats a few feet off the ground where they are not as likely to be torn up by the wind.

II.

To the north the blue mountains go white and the creeks become more dependable though there are fewer of them. There is a sort of swamp here at the edge of the desert where the creeks pool and where grasses and sedges grow and the water takes a considerable time to evaporate and seep into the earth. There are some ducks here, but I do not know where they come from or where they go when the swamp dries up in the summer. I have never seen them flying. They are always hiding, slipping away; you will see their tail feathers disappearing in the screens of wire grass. They never quack.

 PERIMETER

There are four cottonwood trees here and two black locusts.   6
The cottonwoods smell of balsam, send out seeds airborne in a mesh of exceedingly fine white hair, and produce a glue which the bees use to cement their honeycombs. Only one of the cottonwoods, the oldest one, is a female. The leaf stem meets the leaf at right angles and this allows the leaves to twitter and flash in the slightest breeze. The underside of the leaf is a silver green. I enjoy watching this windflash of leaves in strong moonlight.

The black locusts are smaller, younger trees and grow off by   7 themselves a little. They were planted by immigrants and bear sweet smelling pea-like flowers with short, rose-like thorns at the leaf nodes. There are a few chokecherry bushes and also a juniper tree. You can get out of the sun here at noon and sleep. The wind runs down the sides of the cottonwoods like water and cools you.

An old tawny long-haired dog lives here. Sometimes you will   8 see him, walking along and always leaning to one side. There is also part of a cabin made with finished lumber lying on its back; the dark brown boards are dotted with red and yellow lichen and dry as sun-baked, long forgotten shoes.

III.

To the east the white mountains drop off and there is a flat place on   9 the horizon and then the red mountains start. There is almost nothing growing in these mountains, just a little sagebrush. At the base, where they come to the desert, there are dunes, white like gypsum.

Inside the mountains are old creeks that run in circles over   10 the floors of low-ceilinged caves. The fish in these waters are white and translucent; you can see a pink haze of organs beneath the skin. Where there should be eyes there are grey bulges that do not move. On the walls are white spiders like tight buttons of surgical cotton suspended on long hairy legs. There are white beetles, too, scurrying through the hills of black bat dung.

I have always been suspicious of these caves because the walls   11 crumble easily under your fingertips; there is no moisture in the air and it smells like balloons. The water smells like oranges but has no taste. Nothing you do here makes any sound.

You have to squeeze through these red mountains to get   12 around them; you can't walk over them. You have to wedge yourself in somewhere at the base and go in. There is always a moment of panic before you slip in when you are stuck. Your eyes are pinched shut and the heels of your shoes wedge and make you feel foolish.

At night the wind lies in a trough at the base of the red moun-   13 tains, sprawled asleep over the white sand dunes like a caterpillar. The edge of the desert is most indistinct in this place where the white

       BARRY LOPEZ

sand and the alkaline dust blow back and forth in eddies of the wind's breath while it sleeps.

IV.
In the south the red mountains fall away and yellow mountains rise   14
up, full of silver and turquoise rock. There are plenty of rabbits here, a little rain in the middle of the summer, fine clouds tethered on the highest peaks. If you are out in the middle of the desert, this is the way you always end up facing.

    In the south twelve buckskin horses are living along the edge   15
of the yellow mountains. The creeks here are weak; the horses have to go off somewhere for water but they always come back. There is a little grass but the horses do not seem to eat it. They seem to be waiting, or finished. Ten miles away you can hear the clack of their hooves against the rocks. In the afternoon they are motionless, with their heads staring down at the ground, at the little stones.

    At night they go into the canyons to sleep standing up.   16

    From the middle of the desert even on a dark night you can   17
look out at the mountains and perceive the differences in direction. From the middle of the desert you can see everything well, even in the black dark of a new moon. You know where everything is coming from.

COMPREHENSION

1. Explain what happens and what is described in each of the essay's four sections.

2. What is the author trying to communicate about the desert and its ecology? What assumptions does he make about his audience?

3. What does the author mean when he says in paragraph 17 that in the desert "you know where everything is coming from"?

RHETORIC

1. Does the author use pure description in this essay, or does he draw upon other rhetorical methods? Be specific in your answer.

2. Where does the author use personification?

3. Identify the tone of this selection. How does the tone contribute to the meaning of the piece?

4. What contribution do the concrete details make to this selection? Is it necessary to know the smell of vallo weed or balsam or to be able to distinguish cinnabar from fire opal to enjoy the author's use of detail? Why, or why not?

Conversely, why does Lopez name the mountains blue, white, red, and yellow rather than telling us their actual names? How does this support his purpose?

5. Why does Lopez organize this selection into four parts?

6. How do you imagine Lopez would describe his relationship to the desert? Do you think he believes he belongs there? Which paragraphs support your answer?

WRITING

1. What do we learn when we gain deep knowledge about a place? How do you suppose Lopez's understanding of the desert has altered his perceptions about himself?

2. Write a description of a place you know very well, a place where you feel at home. What has this place taught you about yourself and your relationship to the world?

3. Ehrlich, Momaday, and Lopez offer us visions of the American West. Write your own definition of the American West, basing your observations on material in these three essays.

E. B. WHITE

Once More to the Lake

Elwyn Brooks White (1899–1985), perhaps the finest contemporary American essayist, is at his most distinctive in his treatments of people and nature. A recipient of the National Medal for Literature, and associated for years with The New Yorker, *White is the author of* One Man's Meat *(1942),* Here is New York *(1949), and* The Second Tree from the Corner *(1954), among numerous other works. He is also one of the most talented writers of literature for children, the author of* Stuart Little *(1945),* Charlotte's Web *(1952), and* The Trumpet of the Swan *(1970). In this essay, White combines narration and description to render a poignant and vivid statement about past and present, youth and age, life and death.*

ne summer, along about 1904, my father rented a camp on a lake in Maine and took us all there for the month of August. We all got ringworm from some kittens and had to rub Pond's Extract on our arms and legs night and morning, and my father rolled over in a canoe with all his clothes on; but outside of that the vacation was a success and from then on   1 none of us ever thought there was any place in the world like that lake in Maine. We returned summer after summer—always on August 1st for one month. I have since become a salt-water man, but sometimes in summer there are days when the restlessness of the tides and the fearful cold of the sea water and the incessant wind which blows across the afternoon and into the evening make me wish for the placidity of a lake in the woods. A few weeks ago this feeling got so strong I bought myself a couple of bass hooks and a spinner and returned to the lake where we used to go, for a week's fishing and to revisit old haunts.

2   I took along my son, who had never had any fresh water up his nose and who had seen lily pads only from train windows. On the journey over to the lake I began to wonder what it would be like. I wondered how time would have marred this unique, this holy spot—the coves and streams, the hills that the sun set behind, the camps and the paths behind the camps. I was sure the tarred road would have found it out and I wondered in what other ways it would be desolated. It is strange how much you can remember about places like that once you allow your mind to return into the grooves which lead back. You remember one thing, and that suddenly reminds you of another thing. I guess I remembered clearest of all the early mornings, when the lake was cool and motionless, remembered how the bedroom smelled of the lumber it was made of and of the wet woods whose scent entered through the screen. The partitions in the camp were thin and did not extend clear to the top of the rooms, and as I was always the first up I would dress softly so as not to wake the others, and sneak out into the sweet outdoors and start out in the canoe, keeping close along the shore in the long shadows of the pines. I remembered being very careful never to rub my paddle against the gunwale for fear of disturbing the stillness of the cathedral.

3   The lake had never been what you would call a wild lake. There were cottages sprinkled around the shores, and it was in farming country although the shores of the lake were quite heavily wooded. Some of the cottages were owned by nearby farmers, and you would live at the shore and eat your meals at the farmhouse. That's what our family did. But although it wasn't wild, it was a fairly large and undisturbed lake and there were places in it which, to a child at least, seemed infinitely remote and primeval.

4   I was right about the tar: it led to within half a mile of the shore. But when I got back there, with my boy, and we settled into a camp near a farmhouse and into the kind of summertime I had known, I could tell that it was going to be pretty much the same as it had been before—I knew it, lying in bed the first morning, smelling the bedroom, and hearing the boy sneak quietly out and go off along the shore in a boat. I began to sustain the illusion that he was I, and

ONCE MORE TO THE LAKE

81

therefore, by simple transposition, that I was my father. This sensation persisted, kept cropping up all the time we were there. It was not an entirely new feeling, but in this setting it grew much stronger. I seemed to be living a dual existence. I would be in the middle of some simple act, I would be picking up a bait box or laying down a table fork, or I would be saying something, and suddenly it would be not I but my father who was saying the words or making the gesture. It gave me a creepy sensation.

We went fishing the first morning. I felt the same damp moss 5 covering the worms in the bait can, and saw the dragonfly alight on the tip of my rod as it hovered a few inches from the surface of the water. It was the arrival of this fly that convinced me beyond any doubt that everything was as it always had been, that the years were a mirage and there had been no years. The small waves were the same, chucking the rowboat under the chin as we fished at anchor, and the boat was the same boat, the same color green and the ribs broken in the same place, and under the floor-boards the same fresh-water leavings and débris—the dead hellgrammite, the wisps of moss, the rusty discarded fishhook, the dried blood from yesterday's catch. We stared silently at the tips of our rods, at the dragonflies that came and went. I lowered the tip of mine into the water, tentatively, pensively dislodging the fly, which darted two feet away, poised, darted two feet back, and came to rest again a little farther up the rod. There had been no years between the ducking of this dragonfly and the other one— the one that was part of memory. I looked at the boy, who was silently watching his fly, and it was my hands that held his rod, my eyes watching. I felt dizzy and didn't know which rod I was at the end of.

We caught two bass, hauling them in briskly as though they 6 were mackerel, pulling them over the side of the boat in a businesslike manner without any landing net, and stunning them with a blow on the back of the head. When we got back for a swim before lunch, the lake was exactly where we had left it, the same number of inches from the dock, and there was only the merest suggestion of a breeze. This seemed an utterly enchanted sea, this lake you could leave to its own devices for a few hours and come back to, and find that it had not stirred, this constant and trustworthy body of water. In the shallows, the dark, water-soaked sticks and twigs, smooth and old, were undulating in clusters on the bottom against the clean ribbed sand, and the track of the mussel was plain. A school of minnows swam by, each minnow with its small individual shadow, doubling the attendance, so clear and sharp in the sunlight. Some of the other campers were in swimming, along the shore, one of them with a cake of soap, and the water felt thin and clear and unsubstantial. Over the years there had been this person with the cake of soap, this cultist, and here he was. There had been no years.

E. B. WHITE

Up to the farmhouse to dinner through the teeming, dusty 7 field, the road under our sneakers was only a two-track road. The middle track was missing, the one with the marks of the hooves and the splotches of dried, flaky manure. There had always been three tracks to choose from in choosing which track to walk in; now the choice was narrowed down to two. For a moment I missed terribly the middle alternative. But the way led past the tennis court, and something about the way it lay there in the sun reassured me; the tape had loosened along the backline, the alleys were green with plaintains and other weeds, and the net (installed in June and removed in September) sagged in the dry noon, and the whole place steamed with midday heat and hunger and emptiness. There was a choice of pie for dessert, and one was blueberry and one was apple, and the waitresses were the same country girls, there having been no passage of time, only the illusion of it as in a dropped curtain—the waitresses were still fifteen; their hair had been washed, that was the only difference— they had been to the movies and seen the pretty girls with the clean hair.

Summertime, oh summertime, pattern of life indelible, the 8 fade-proof lake, the woods unshatterable, the pasture with the sweet-fern and the juniper forever and ever, summer without end; this was the background, and the life along the shore was the design, the cottagers with their innocent and tranquil design, their tiny docks with the flagpole and the American flag floating against the white clouds in the blue sky, the little paths over the roots of the trees leading from camp to camp and the paths leading back to the outhouses and the can of lime for sprinkling, and at the souvenir counters at the store the miniature birch-bark canoes and the post cards that showed things looking a little better than they looked. This was the American family at play, escaping the city heat, wondering whether the newcomers in the camp at the head of the cove were "common" or "nice," wondering whether it was true that the people who drove up for Sunday dinner at the farmhouse were turned away because there wasn't enough chicken.

It seemed to me, as I kept remembering all this, that those 9 times and those summers had been infinitely precious and worth saving. There had been jollity and peace and goodness. The arriving (at the beginning of August) had been so big a business in itself, at the railway station the farm wagon drawn up, the first smell of the pine-laden air, the first glimpse of the smiling farmer, and the great importance of the trunks and your father's enormous authority in such matters, and the feel of the wagon under you for the long ten-mile haul, and at the top of the last long hill catching the first view of the lake after eleven months of not seeing this cherished body of water. The shouts and cries of the other campers when they saw you, and the trunks to be unpacked, to give up their rich burden. (Arriving was less exciting nowadays, when you sneaked up in your car and parked it under a tree near the camp and took out the bags and in five minutes it was all over, no fuss, no loud wonderful fuss about trunks.)

Peace and goodness and jollity. The only thing that was wrong now, really, was the sound of the place, an unfamiliar nervous sound of the outboard motors. This was the note that jarred, the one thing that would sometimes break the illusion and set the years moving. In those other summertimes all motors were inboard; and when they were at a little distance, the noise they made was a sedative, an ingredient of summer sleep. They were one-cylinder and two-cylinder engines, and some were make-and-break and some were jump-spark, but they all made a sleepy sound across the lake. The one-lungers throbbed and fluttered, and the twin-cylinder ones purred and purred, and that was a quiet sound too. But now the campers all had outboards. In the daytime, in the hot mornings, these motors made a petulant, irritable sound; at night, in the still evening when the afterglow lit the water, they whined about one's ears like mosquitoes. My boy loved our rented outboard, and his great desire was to achieve singlehanded mastery over it, and authority, and he soon learned the trick of choking it a little (but not too much), and the adjustment of the needle valve. Watching him I would remember the things you could do with the old one-cylinder engine with the heavy flywheel, how you could have it eating out of your hand if you got really close to it spiritually. Motor boats in those days didn't have clutches, and you would make a landing by shutting off the motor at the proper time and coasting in with a dead rudder. But there was a way of reversing them, if you learned the trick, by cutting the switch and putting it on again exactly on the final dying revolution of the flywheel, so that it would kick back against compression and begin reversing. Approaching a dock in a strong following breeze, it was difficult to slow up sufficiently by the ordinary coasting method, and if a boy felt he had complete mastery over his motor, he was tempted to keep it running beyond its time and then reverse it a few feet from the dock. It took a cool nerve, because if you threw the switch a twentieth of a second too soon you would catch the flywheel when it still had speed enough to go up past center, and the boat would leap ahead, charging bull-fashion at the dock.

We had a good week at the camp. The bass were biting well and the sun shone endlessly, day after day. We would be tired at night and lie down in the accumulated heat of the little bedrooms after the long hot day and the breeze would stir almost imperceptibly outside and the smell of the swamp drift in through the rusty screens. Sleep would come easily and in the morning the red squirrel would be on

E. B. WHITE

the roof, tapping out his gay routine. I kept remembering everything, lying in bed in the mornings—the small steamboat that had a long rounded stern like the lip of a Ubangi, and how quietly she ran on the moonlight sails, when the older boys played their mandolins and the girls sang and we ate doughnuts dipped in sugar, and how sweet the music was on the water in the shining night, and what it had felt like to think about girls then. After breakfast we would go up to the store and the things were in the same place—the minnows in a bottle, the plugs and spinners disarranged and pawed over by the youngsters from the boys' camp, the fig newtons and the Beeman's gum. Outside, the road was tarred and cars stood in front of the store. Inside, all was just as it had always been, except there was more Coca-Cola and not so much Moxie and root beer and birch beer and sarsaparilla. We would walk out with a bottle of pop apiece and sometimes the pop would backfire up our noses and hurt. We explored the streams, quietly, where the turtles slid off the sunny logs and dug their way into the soft bottom; and we lay on the town wharf and fed worms to the tame bass. Everywhere we went I had trouble making out which was I, the one walking at my side, the one walking in my pants.

One afternoon while we were there at that lake a thunderstorm came up. It was like the revival of an old melodrama that I had seen long ago with childish awe. The second-act climax of the drama of the electrical disturbance over a lake in America had not changed in any important respect. This was the big scene, still the big scene. The whole thing was so familiar, the first feeling of oppression and heat and a general air around camp of not wanting to go very far away. In midafternoon (it was all the same) a curious darkening of the sky, and a lull in everything that had made life tick; and then the way the boats suddenly swung the other way at their moorings with the coming of a breeze out of the new quarter, and the premonitory rumble. Then the kettle drum, then the snare, then the bass drum and cymbals, then crackling light against the dark, and the gods grinning and licking their chops in the hills. Afterward the calm, the rain steadily rustling in the calm lake, the return of light and hope and spirits, and the campers running out in joy and relief to go swimming in the rain, their bright cries perpetuating the deathless joke about how they were getting simply drenched, and the children screaming with delight at the new sensation of bathing in the rain, and the joke about getting drenched linking the generations in a strong indestructible chain. And the comedian who waded in carrying an umbrella.

When the others went swimming my son said he was going in too. He pulled his dripping trunks from the line where they had hung all through the shower, and wrung them out. Languidly, and with no thought of going in, I watched him, his hard little body,

12

13

skinny and bare, saw him wince slightly as he pulled up around his vitals the small, soggy, icy garment. As he buckled the swollen belt suddenly my groin felt the chill of death.

COMPREHENSION

1. At what point in the essay do you begin to sense White's main purpose? What *is* his purpose? What type of reader might his purpose appeal to?

2. What motivates White to return to the lake in Maine? Explain the "simple transposition" that he mentions in paragraph 4. List the illustrations that he gives of this phenomenon. What change does he detect in the lake?

3. Explain the significance of White's last sentence. Where are there foreshadowings of this statement?

RHETORIC

1. Describe the author's use of figurative language in paragraphs 2, 10, and 12.

2. Identify those words and phrases that White invokes to establish the sense of mystery about the lake. Why are these words and their connotations important to the nature of the illusion that he describes?

3. Explain the organization of the essay in terms of the following paragraph units: 1 to 4; 5 to 7; 8 to 10; and 11 to 13. Explain the function of paragraphs 8 and 12.

4. There are many vivid and unusual descriptive details in this essay—for example, the dragonfly in paragraph 2 and the two-track road in paragraph 7. How does White create symbolic overtones for these descriptive details and others? Why is the lake itself a complex symbol? Explain with reference to paragraph 6.

5. Describe the persona that White creates for himself in the essay. How does this persona function?

6. What is the relation between the introductory and concluding paragraphs, specifically in terms of irony of statement?

WRITING

1. Explore in an essay the theme of nostalgia in "Once More to the Lake." What are the beauties and the dangers of nostalgia? Can the past ever be recaptured or relived? Justify your answer.

2. Write a descriptive account of a return to a favorite location and of your reaction to the experience. Explore the interrelationship of past and present.

3. Explain, in a short essay, the appeal of this classic essay by White.

4. One of White's favorite authors is Thoreau. Reread Thoreau's "Economy," and in a brief essay, identify the influence that you see at work in "Once More to the Lake."

E. B. WHITE

GEORGE ORWELL

Marrakech

George Orwell (1903–1950) was the pseudonym of Eric Blair, an English novelist, essayist, and journalist. Orwell served with the Indian Imperial Police from 1922 to 1927 in Burma, fought in the Spanish Civil War, and acquired from his experiences a disdain of totalitarian and imperialistic systems. This attitude is reflected in the satiric fable Animal Farm *(1945) and in his bleak, futuristic novel,* 1984 *(1949). In the following essay, Orwell depicts vividly third world poverty and criticizes colonial responses to it.*

A s the corpse went past the flies left the restaurant table 1
in a cloud and rushed after it, but they came back a few minutes later.

The little crowd of mourners—all men and boys, 2
no women—threaded their way across the market-place between the piles of pomegranates and the taxis and the camels, wailing a short chant over and over again. What really appeals to the flies is that the corpses here are never put into coffins, they are merely wrapped in a piece of rag and carried on a rough wooden bier on the shoulders of four friends. When the friends get to the burying-ground they hack an oblong hole a foot or two deep, dump the body in it and fling over it a little of the dried-up, lumpy earth, which is like broken brick. No gravestone, no name, no identifying mark of any kind. The burying-ground is merely a huge waste of hummocky earth, like a derelict building-lot. After a month or two no one can even be certain where his own relatives are buried.

When you walk through a town like this—two hundred thou- 3
sand inhabitants, of whom at least twenty thousand own literally nothing except the rags they stand up in—when you see how people live, and still more how easily they die, it is always difficult to believe that you are walking among human beings. All colonial empires are in reality founded upon that fact. The people have brown faces—besides, there are so many of them! Are they really the same flesh as yourself? Do they even have names? Or are they merely a kind of undifferentiated brown stuff, about as individual as bees or coral insects? They rise out of the earth, they sweat and starve for a few years, and then they sink back into the nameless mounds of the graveyard and nobody notices that they are gone. And even the graves themselves soon fade back into the soil. Sometimes, out for a walk, as you break your way through the prickly pear, you notice that it is rather bumpy underfoot, and only a certain regularity in the bumps tells you that you are walking over skeletons.

I was feeding one of the gazelles in the public gardens. 4

Gazelles are almost the only animals that look good to eat 5
when they are still alive, in fact, one can hardly look at their hind-
quarters without thinking of mint sauce. The gazelle I was feeding
seemed to know that this thought was in my mind, for though it took
the piece of bread I was holding out it obviously did not like me. It
nibbled rapidly at the bread, then lowered its head and tried to butt
me, then took another nibble and then butted again. Probably its idea
was that if it could drive me away the bread would somehow remain
hanging in mid-air.

An Arab navvy working on the path nearby lowered his 6
heavy hoe and sidled towards us. He looked from the gazelle to the
bread and from the bread to the gazelle, with a sort of quiet amazement, as though he had never seen anything quite like this before.
Finally he said shyly in French:

"I could eat some of that bread." 7

I tore off a piece and he stowed it gratefully in some secret 8
place under his rags. This man is an employee of the Municipality.

When you go through the Jewish quarters you gather some 9
idea of what the medieval ghettoes were probably like. Under their
Moorish rulers the Jews were only allowed to own land in certain
restricted areas, and after centuries of this kind of treatment they have
ceased to bother about overcrowding. Many of the streets are a good
deal less than six feet wide, the houses are completely windowless,
and sore-eyed children cluster everywhere in unbelievable numbers,
like clouds of flies. Down the centre of the street there is generally
running a little river of urine.

In the bazaar huge families of Jews, all dressed in the long 10
black robe and little black skull-cap, are working in dark fly-infested
booths that look like caves. A carpenter sits cross-legged at a prehistoric lathe, turning chair-legs at lightning speed. He works the lathe
with a bow in his right hand and guides the chisel with his left foot,
and thanks to a lifetime of sitting in this position his left leg is warped
out of shape. At his side his grandson, aged six, is already starting on
the simpler parts of the job.

I was just passing the coppersmiths' booths when somebody 11
noticed that I was lighting a cigarette. Instantly, from the dark holes
all round, there was a frenzied rush of Jews, many of them old grandfathers with flowing grey beards, all clamouring for a cigarette. Even
a blind man somewhere at the back of one of the booths heard a
rumour of cigarettes and came crawling out, groping in the air with
his hand. In about a minute I had used up the whole packet. None of
these people, I suppose, works less than twelve hours a day, and every
one of them looks on a cigarette as a more or less impossible luxury.

As the Jews live in self-contained communities they follow the 12 same trades as the Arabs, except for agriculture. Fruit-sellers, potters, silversmiths, blacksmiths, butchers, leather-workers, tailors, water-carriers, beggars, porters—whichever way you look you see nothing but Jews. As a matter of fact there are thirteen thousand of them, all living in the space of a few acres. A good job Hitler isn't here. Perhaps he is on his way, however. You hear the usual dark rumours about the Jews, not only from the Arabs but from the poorer Europeans.

"Yes, *mon vieux*, they took my job away from me and gave it 13 to a Jew. The Jews! They're the real rulers of this country, you know. They've got all the money. They control the banks, finance—everything."

"But," I said, "isn't it a fact that the average Jew is a labourer 14 working for about a penny an hour?"

"Ah, that's only for show! They're all moneylenders really. 15 They're cunning, the Jews."

In just the same way, a couple of hundred years ago, poor old 16 women used to be burned for witchcraft when they could not even work enough magic to get themselves a square meal.

All people who work with their hands are partly invisible, 17 and the more important the work they do, the less visible they are. Still, a white skin is always fairly conspicuous. In northern Europe, when you see a labourer ploughing a field, you probably give him a second glance. In a hot country, anywhere south of Gibraltar or east of Suez, the chances are that you don't even see him. I have noticed this again and again. In a tropical landscape one's eye takes in everything except the human beings. It takes in the dried-up soil, the prickly pear, the palm-tree and the distant mountain, but it always misses the peasant hoeing at his patch. He is the same colour as the earth, and a great deal less interesting to look at.

It is only because of this that the starved countries of Asia and 18 Africa are accepted as tourist resorts. No one would think of running cheap trips to the Distressed Areas. But where the human beings have brown skins their poverty is simply not noticed. What does Morocco mean to a Frenchman? An orange-grove or a job in government service. Or to an Englishman? Camels, castles, palm-trees, Foreign Legionnaires, brass trays and bandits. One could probably live here for years without noticing that for nine-tenths of the people the reality of life is an endless, back-breaking struggle to wring a little food out of an eroded soil.

Most of Morocco is so desolate that no wild animal bigger 19 than a hare can live on it. Huge areas which were once covered with forest have turned into a treeless waste where the soil is exactly like broken-up brick. Nevertheless a good deal of it is cultivated, with frightful labour. Everything is done by hand. Long lines of women, bent double like inverted capital Ls, work their way slowly across the fields, tearing up the prickly weeds with their hands, and the peasant gathering lucerne for fodder pulls it up stalk by stalk instead of reaping it, thus saving an inch or two on each stalk. The plough is a wretched wooden thing, so frail that one can easily carry it on one's shoulder, and fitted underneath with a rough iron spike which stirs the soil to a depth of about four inches. This is as much as the strength of the animals is equal to. It is usual to plough with a cow and a donkey yoked together. Two donkeys would not be quite strong enough, but on the other hand two cows would cost a little more to feed. The peasants possess no harrows, they merely plough the soil several times over in different directions, finally leaving it in rough furrows, after which the whole field has to be shaped with hoes into small oblong patches, to conserve water. Except for a day or two after the rare rainstorms there is never enough water. Along the edges of the fields channels are hacked out to a depth of thirty or forty feet to get at the tiny trickles which run through the subsoil.

Every afternoon a file of very old women passes down the 20 road outside my house, each carrying a load of firewood. All of them are mummified with age and the sun, and all of them are tiny. It seems to be generally the case in primitive communities that the women, when they get beyond a certain age, shrink to the size of children. One day a poor old creature who could not have been more than four feet tall crept past me under a vast load of wood. I stopped her and put a five-sou piece (a little more than a farthing) into her hand. She answered with a shrill wail, almost a scream, which was partly gratitude but mainly surprise. I suppose that from her point of view, by taking any notice of her, I seemed almost to be violating a law of nature. She accepted her status as an old woman, that is to say as a beast of burden. When a family is travelling it is quite usual to see a father and a grown-up son riding ahead on donkeys, and an old woman following on foot, carrying the baggage.

But what is strange about these people is their invisibility. For 21 several weeks, always at about the same time of day, the file of old women had hobbled past the house with their firewood, and though they had registered themselves on my eyeballs I cannot truly say that I had seen them. Firewood was passing—that was how I saw it. It was only that one day I happened to be walking behind them, and the curious up-and-down motion of a load of wood drew my attention to the human being underneath it. Then for the first time I noticed the poor old earth-coloured bodies, bodies reduced to bones and leathery skin, bent double under the crushing weight. Yet I suppose I had not been five minutes on Moroccan soil before I noticed the overloading of the donkeys and was infuriated by it. There is no question that the donkeys are damnably treated. The Moroccan donkey is hardly bigger than a St. Bernard dog, it carries a load which in the British army would be considered too much for a fifteen-hands mule, and very often its pack-saddle is not taken off its back for weeks together. But what is peculiarly pitiful is that it is the most willing creature on earth, it follows its master like a dog and does not need either bridle or halter. After a dozen years of devoted work it suddenly drops dead, whereupon its master tips it into the ditch and the village dogs have torn its guts out before it is cold.

This kind of thing makes one's blood boil, whereas—on the 22 whole—the plight of the human beings does not. I am not commenting, merely pointing to a fact. People with brown skins are next door to invisible. Anyone can be sorry for the donkey with its galled back, but it is generally owing to some kind of accident if one even notices the old woman under her load of sticks.

As the storks flew northward the Negroes were marching 23 southward—a long, dusty column, infantry, screw-gun batteries and then more infantry, four or five thousand men in all, winding up the road with a clumping of boots and a clatter of iron wheels.

They were Senegalese, the blackest Negroes in Africa, so black 24 that sometimes it is difficult to see whereabouts on their necks the hair begins. Their splendid bodies were hidden in reach-me-down khaki uniforms, their feet squashed into boots that looked like blocks of wood, and every tin hat seemed to be a couple of sizes too small. It was very hot and the men had marched a long way. They slumped under the weight of their packs and the curiously sensitive black faces were glistening with sweat.

As they went past a tall, very young Negro turned and caught 25 my eye. But the look he gave me was not in the least the kind of look you might expect. Not hostile, not contemptuous, not sullen, not even inquisitive. It was the shy, wide-eyed Negro look, which actually is a look of profound respect. I saw how it was. This wretched boy, who is a French citizen and has therefore been dragged from the forest to scrub floors and catch syphilis in garrison towns, actually has feelings of reverence before a white skin. He has been taught that the white race are his masters, and he still believes it.

But there is one thought which every white man (and in this 26 connection it doesn't matter twopence if he calls himself a Socialist) thinks when he sees a black army marching past. "How much longer can we go on kidding these people? How long before they turn their guns in the other direction?"

It was curious, really. Every white man there has this thought 27 stowed somewhere or other in his mind. I had it, so had the other onlookers, so had the officers on their sweating chargers and the white NCOs marching in the ranks. It was a kind of secret which we all knew and were too clever to tell; only the Negroes didn't know it. And really it was almost like watching a flock of cattle to see the long column, a mile or two miles of armed men, flowing peacefully up the road, while the great white birds drifted over them in the opposite direction, glittering like scraps of paper.

COMPREHENSION

1. Orwell's title is decidedly simple. What is the reason for this simplicity?

2. Describe the major scenes that Orwell develops to render his impression of Marrakech. What relationships do you perceive among the scenes? What dominant impression emerges from the presentation of scenes?

3. What is Orwell's attitude toward the misery he describes? What does he say about certain foreign responses to misery and poverty?

RHETORIC

1. Orwell uses both subjective and objective language in this essay. Cite examples of both. Why does he combine these two modes? What effect is created?

2. Locate and evaluate Orwell's use of similes, juxtaposed imagery, personification, and onomatopoeia in the essay. Compare his use of figurative language with his procedure in "A Hanging."

3. How does Orwell's short initial paragraph set the stage for the entire essay?

4. Analyze Orwell's technique of juxtaposition in the presentation of major paragraph units in the essay. What is the effect of his decision not to provide normal transitions between major segments? How are the segments related in terms of theme, tone, and mood? Is there final essay coherence? Why, or why not?

5. How does Orwell's persistent use of contrasting elements relate to his treatment of characterization? How does characterization relate to animal life?

6. Account for paragraphs 3, 8, 16, 22, and 27 in terms of their antecedents.

WRITING

1. Orwell states that it is easy to ignore glaring poverty and to pretend that the poor and exploited do not exist. What explains this behavior? Offer your own examples to confirm or refute Orwell's thesis.

2. Write a descriptive essay illuminating your personal encounter with poverty, as you have either observed or experienced it.

3. Evaluate Orwell's social and political thinking, using "Marrakech" and "A Hanging" as evidence.

ALFRED KAZIN

The Kitchen

Alfred Kazin (1915–   ) was born in Brooklyn and holds degrees from City College of New York and Columbia University. A literary critic and professor of literature, he has taught at New York University, the State University of New York, and the City University of New York, among other institutions. Kazin has written literary criticism, and he specializes in nineteenth and twentieth century literature of the United States. He has been an editor of the works of Herman Melville, Ralph Waldo Emerson, and Nathaniel Hawthorne. His books of criticism include On Native Ground *(1942) and* Contemporaries *(1962). He also has written three autobiographies,* Starting Out in the Thirties *(1965),* New York Jew *(1978), and* A Walker in the City *(1951). The following passage is from* A Walker in the City. *It provides a picture filled with careful detail of tenement life in the 1920s and concludes with an intimate glimpse into the emotional life of the author's mother.*

I n Brownsville tenements the kitchen is always the largest room and the center of the household. As a child I felt that we lived in a kitchen to which four other rooms were annexed. My mother, a "home" dressmaker, had her workshop in the kitchen. She told me once that she had begun dressmaking in Poland at thirteen; as far back as I can remember, she was always making dresses for the local women. She had an innate sense of design, a quick eye for all the subtleties in the latest fashions, even when she despised them, and great boldness. For three or four dollars she would study the fashion magazines with a customer, go with the customer to the remnants store on Belmont Avenue to pick out the material, argue the owner down—all remnants stores, for some reason, were supposed to be shady, as if the owners dealt in stolen goods—and then for days would patiently fit and baste and sew and fit again. Our apartment was always full of women in their housedresses sitting around the kitchen table waiting for a fitting. My little bedroom next to the kitchen was the fitting room. The sewing machine, an old nut-brown Singer with golden scrolls painted along the black arm and engraved along the two tiers of little drawers massed with needles and thread on each side of the treadle, stood next to the window and the great coalblack stove which up to my last year in college was our main source of heat. By December the two outer bedrooms were closed off, and used to chill bottles of milk and cream, cold borscht and jellied calves' feet.

1

THE KITCHEN

93

The kitchen held our lives together. My mother worked in it 2
all day long, we ate in it almost all meals except the Passover *seder*, I
did my homework and first writing at the kitchen table, and in winter
I often had a bed made up for me on three kitchen chairs near the
stove. On the wall just over the table hung a long horizontal mirror
that sloped to a ship's prow at each end and was lined in cherry wood.
It took up the whole wall, and drew every object in the kitchen
to itself. The walls were a fiercely stippled whitewash, so often
rewhitened by my father in slack seasons that the paint looked as if
it had been squeezed and cracked into the walls. A large electric bulb
hung down the center of the kitchen at the end of a chain that had
been hooked into the ceiling; the old gas ring and key still jutted out
of the wall like antlers. In the corner next to the toilet was the sink at
which we washed, and the square tub in which my mother did our
clothes. Above it, tacked to the shelf on which were pleasantly ranged
square, blue-bordered white sugar and spice jars, hung calendars from
the Public National Bank on Pitkin Avenue and the Minsker Progressive Branch of the Workman's Circle; receipts for the payment of insurance premiums, and household bills on a spindle; two little boxes
engraved with Hebrew letters. One of these was for the poor, the other
to buy back the Land of Israel. Each spring a bearded little man would
suddenly appear in our kitchen, salute us with a hurried Hebrew
blessing, empty the boxes (sometimes with a sidelong look of disdain
if they were not full), hurriedly bless us again for remembering our
less fortunate Jewish brothers and sisters, and so take his departure
until the next spring, after vainly trying to persuade my mother to
take still another box. We did occasionally remember to drop coins in
the boxes, but this was usually only on the dreaded morning of "mid-
terms" and final examinations, because my mother thought it would
bring me luck. She was extremely superstitious, but embarrassed
about it, and always laughed at herself whenever, on the morning of
an examination, she counseled me to leave the house on my right foot.
"I know it's silly," her smile seemed to say, "but what harm can it
do? It may calm God down."

The kitchen gave a special character to our lives; my mother's 3
character. All my memories of that kitchen are dominated by the nearness of my mother sitting all day long at her sewing machine, by the
clacking of the treadle against the linoleum floor, by the patient twist
of her right shoulder as she automatically pushed at the wheel with
one hand or lifted the foot to free the needle where it had got stuck
in a thick piece of material. The kitchen was her life. Year by year, as
I began to take in her fantastic capacity for labor and her anxious zeal,
I realized it was ourselves she kept stitched together. I can never remember a time when she was not working. She worked because the

law of her life was work, work and anxiety; she worked because she would have found life meaningless without work. She read almost no English; she could read the Yiddish paper, but never felt she had time to. We were always talking of a time when I would teach her how to read, but somehow there was never time. When I awoke in the morning she was already at her machine, or in the great morning crowd of housewives at the grocery getting fresh rolls for breakfast. When I returned from school she was at her machine, or conferring over *McCall's* with some neighborhood woman who had come in pointing hopefully to an illustration—"Mrs. Kazin! Mrs. Kazin! Make me a dress like it shows here in the picture!" When my father came home from work she had somehow mysteriously interrupted herself to make supper for us, and the dishes cleared and washed, was back at her machine. When I went to bed at night, often she was still there, pounding away at the treadle, hunched over the wheel, her hands steering a piece of gauze under the needle with a finesse that always contrasted sharply with her swollen hands and broken nails. Her left hand had been pierced through when as a girl she had worked in the infamous Triangle Shirtwaist Factory on the East Side. A needle had gone straight through the palm, severing a large vein. They had sewn it up for her so clumsily that a tuft of flesh always lay folded over the palm.

The kitchen was the great machine that set our lives running; 4 it whirred down a little only on Saturdays and holy days. From my mother's kitchen I gained my first picture of life as a white, overheated, starkly lit workshop redolent with Jewish cooking, crowded with women in housedresses, strewn with fashion magazines, patterns, dress material, spools of thread—and at whose center, so lashed to her machine that bolts of energy seemed to dance out of her hands and feet as she worked, my mother stamped the treadle hard against the floor, hard, hard, and silently, grimly at war, beat out the first rhythm of the world for me.

Every sound from the street roared and trembled at our win- 5 dows—a mother feeding her child on the doorstep, the screech of the trolley cars on Rockaway Avenue, the eternal smash of a handball against the wall of our house, the clatter of *"der Italyéner"*'s cart packed with watermelons, the sing-song of the old-clothes men walking Chester Street, the cries *"Árbes! Árbes! Kinder! Kinder! Heyse gute árbes!"* All day long people streamed into our apartment as a matter of course—"customers," upstairs neighbors, downstairs neighbors, women who would stop in for a half-hour's talk, salesmen, relatives, insurance agents. Usually they came in without ringing the bell— everyone knew my mother was always at home. I would hear the front door opening, the wind whistling through our front hall, and then some familiar face would appear in our kitchen with the same bland, matter-of-fact inquiring look: no need to stand on ceremony: my mother and her kitchen were available to everyone all day long.

At night the kitchen contracted around the blaze of light on the cloth, the patterns, the ironing board where the iron had burned a black border around the tear in the muslin cover; the finished dresses looked so frilly as they jostled on their wire hangers after all the work my mother had put into them. And then I would get that strangely ominous smell of tension from the dress fabrics and the burn in the cover of the ironing board—as if each piece of cloth and paper crushed with light under the naked bulb might suddenly go up in flames. Whenever I pass some small tailoring shop still lit up at night and see the owner hunched over his steam press; whenever in some poorer neighborhood of the city I see through a window some small crowded kitchen naked under the harsh light glittering in the ceiling, I still smell that fiery breath, that warning of imminent fire. I was always holding my breath. What I must have felt most about ourselves, I see now, was that we ourselves were like kindling—that all the hard-pressed pieces of ourselves and all the hard-used objects in that kitchen were like so many slivers of wood that might go up in flames if we came too near the white-blazing filaments in that naked bulb. Our tension itself was fire, we ourselves were forever burning—to live, to get down the foreboding in our souls, to make good. 6

Twice a year, on the anniversaries of her parents' deaths, my mother placed on top of the ice-box an ordinary kitchen glass packed with wax, the *yortsayt,* and lit the candle in it. Sitting at the kitchen table over my homework, I would look across the threshold to that mourning-glass, and sense that for my mother the distance from our kitchen to *der heym,* from life to death, was only a flame's length away. Poor as we were, it was not poverty that drove my mother so hard; it was loneliness—some endless bitter brooding over all those left behind, dead or dying or soon to die; a loneliness locked up in her kitchen that dwelt every day on the hazardousness of life and the nearness of death, but still kept struggling in the lock, trying to get us through by endless labor. 7

With us, life started up again only on the last shore. There seemed to be no middle ground between despair and the fury of our ambition. Whenever my mother spoke of her hopes for us, it was with such unbelievingness that the likes of us would ever come to anything, such abashed hope and readiness for pain, that I finally came to see in the flame burning on top of the ice-box death itself burning away the bones of poor Jews, burning out in us everything but courage, the blind resolution to live. In the light of that mourning-candle, there were ranged around me how many dead and dying—how many eras 8

ALFRED KAZIN

of pain, of exile, of dispersion, of cringing before the powers of this world!

It was always at dusk that my mother's loneliness came home most to me. Painfully alert to every shift in the light at her window, she would suddenly confess her fatigue by removing her pince-nez, and then wearily pushing aside the great mound of fabrics on her machine, would stare at the street as if to warm herself in the last of the sun. "How sad it is!" I once heard her say. "It grips me! It grips me!" Twilight was the bottommost part of the day, the chillest and loneliest time for her. Always so near to her moods, I knew she was fighting some deep inner dread, struggling against the returning tide of darkness along the streets that invariably assailed her heart with the same foreboding—Where? Where now? Where is the day taking us now? 9

Yet one good look at the street would revive her. I see her now, perched against the windowsill, with her face against the glass, her eyes almost asleep in enjoyment, just as she starts up with the guilty cry—"What foolishness is this in me!"—and goes to the stove to prepare supper for us: a moment, only a moment, watching the evening crowd of women gathering at the grocery for fresh bread and milk. But between my mother's pent-up face at the window and the winter sun dying in the fabrics—"Alfred, see how beautiful!"—she has drawn for me one single line of sentience. 10

COMPREHENSION

1. Kazin says, "The kitchen held our lives together" (paragraph 2). How did it do this?

2. What references "date" the essay? What decade of the twentieth century is Kazin describing? What does he say about this period?

3. Why does Kazin concentrate on his mother? What is she like? Cite specific paragraphs to support your answer.

RHETORIC

1. Images of light abound in the essay. Review these references to light. What impact do they have on the mood of Kazin's home? On the mood of the essay? What significance does Kazin find in his mother's relationship to the various lights?

2. In paragraph 4, Kazin says, "The kitchen was the great machine that set our lives running." Where and how does Kazin describe the kitchen like a machine?

3. As in "Wyoming: The Solace of Open Spaces," there is a notable lack of dialogue in the essay. What factors about Kazin's homelife could account for

this silence? How does this absence affect the tone of the essay? How do these factors compare to the reasons for silence in the former essay, by Ehrlich?

4. Why does Kazin introduce the essay with a sentence that makes a general observation about his neighborhood?

5. The title of the essay is "The Kitchen." Would a more appropriate title have been "The Mother"? Explain your view.

6. There is a marked change in mood beginning with paragraph 6. What specific images does Kazin employ that contribute to this change? What impact does this change have on the overall thesis of the essay?

WRITING

1. In paragraph 6, Kazin states that "we ourselves were like kindling." What other explicit or implicit metaphors and similes can you find in the essay? Are there any central metaphors that are suggestive of the essay's theme? Analyze this figurative language in a short essay.

2. Can a room have a "personality" of its own? Select a room that has special significance to you. Describe it with a central metaphor, for example, "my room is a haven." Then proceed to explain your metaphor, using specific examples.

3. Interview someone alive at the time that Kazin is writing about. Write a descriptive essay based on the information he or she gives you about the life of the period.

4. In part, Kazin's mother works hard so that her son can succeed in life. In the United States today, do you think that people still can escape poverty by hard work? What evidence can you cite to support your position? Investigate this issue in an essay.

ALFRED KAZIN

Manners and Morals

MARYA MANNES

Wasteland

Marya Mannes (1904–   ) has written several novels and some light verse, but she is best known for her essays, which have appeared in Vogue, McCall's, Harper's, *and* The New Republic. *She has collected her essays in* More In Anger *(1958) and in* The New York I Know *(1961). Mannes has also written on such subjects as suicide and euthanasia in* Last Rights *(1974) and television in* Who Owns the Air? *(1960). Throughout her career, she has always been concerned with and critical of the quality of American life. In "Wasteland," Mannes describes the modern American landscape.*

ans. Beer cans. Glinting on the verges of a million miles   1
of roadways, lying in scrub, grass, dirt, leaves, sand,
mud, but never hidden. Piels, Rheingold, Ballantine,
Schaefer, Schlitz, shining in the sun or picked by moon
or the beams of headlights at night; washed by rain or flattened by

wheels, but never dulled, never buried, never destroyed. Here is the mark of savages, the testament of wasters, the stain of prosperity.

Who are these men who defile the grassy borders of our roads 2 and lanes, who pollute our ponds, who spoil the purity of our ocean beaches with the empty vessels of their thirst? Who are the men who make these vessels in millions and then say, "Drink—and discard"? What society is this that can afford to cast away a million tons of metal and to make of wild and fruitful land a garbage heap?

What manner of men and women need thirty feet of steel and 3 two hundred horsepower to take them, singly, to their small destinations? Who demand that what they eat is wrapped so that forests are cut down to make the paper that is thrown away, and what they smoke and chew is sealed so that the sealers can be tossed in gutters and caught in twigs and grass?

What kind of men can afford to make the streets of their 4 towns and cities hideous with neon at night, and their roadways hideous with signs by day, wasting beauty; who leave the carcasses of cars to rot in heaps; who spill their trash into ravines and make smoking mountains of refuse for the town's rats? What manner of men choke off the life in rivers, streams and lakes with the waste of their produce, making poison of water?

Who is as rich as that? Slowly the wasters and despoilers are 5 impoverishing our land, our nature, and our beauty, so that there will not be one beach, one hill, one lane, one meadow, one forest free from the debris of man and the stigma of his improvidence.

Who is so rich that he can squander forever the wealth of 6 earth and water for the trivial needs of vanity or the compulsive demands of greed; or so prosperous in land that he can sacrifice nature for unnatural desires? The earth we abuse and the living things we kill will, in the end, take their revenge; for in exploiting their presence we are diminishing our future.

And what will we leave behind us when we are long dead? 7 Temples? Amphora? Sunken treasure?

Or mountains of twisted, rusted steel, canyons of plastic containers, and a million miles of shores garlanded, not with the lovely 8 wrack of the sea, but with the cans and bottles and light-bulbs and boxes of a people who conserved their convenience at the expense of their heritage, and whose ephemeral prosperity was built on waste.

COMPREHENSION

1. What is Mannes's main purpose in "Wasteland"?

2. What evidence of wastefulness does Mannes give in the essay?

3. How does Mannes relate prosperity to waste?

RHETORIC

1. What are the multiple meanings of the title "Wasteland"? How are they represented in the essay?

2. Why does Mannes use fragments in the first paragraph and in paragraphs 7 and 8? What is the significance of the term "ephemeral prosperity" in the last paragraph?

3. What is the effect of the author's use of rhetorical questions to structure her essay? Explain the use of irony in Mannes's answers to her questions.

4. Identify the concrete objects listed in the essay. How does Mannes's selection of objects support her thesis?

5. How does Mannes describe such things as cars, cigarette wrappers, street-lights, and road signs? Why is her technique, called *periphrasis*, successful?

6. Paragraph 6 is made up of a question and a declarative sentence. Although the declarative sentence does not directly answer the question, the two are related. How?

WRITING

1. Describe several objects that, taken as a whole, make a positive or negative statement about pollution, elections, education, or sports.

2. Write an editorial for your college newspaper in which you attack some aspect of a local pollution problem.

3. Write a comparative essay on Thoreau's "Economy" and Mannes's "Wasteland."

IMAMU AMIRI BARAKA

Soul Food

Imamu Amiri Baraka (1934–   ) is a playwright, novelist, editor, poet, essayist, and community leader. Baraka's most famous work, the play Dutchman *(1964), is about the often destructive relations between black and white Americans. During his career, Baraka has, through the powerful use of the black idiom, introduced the public to the richness of black culture.*

Recently, a young Negro novelist writing in *Esquire* about   1
the beauties of America mentioned that one of the things
wrong with Negroes was that, unlike the Chinese, boots
have neither a language of their own nor a characteristic
cuisine. And this to me is the deepest stroke, the unkindest cut, of
oppression, especially as it has distorted Black Americans. America,
where the suppliant, far from rebelling or even disagreeing with the
forces that have caused him to suffer, readily backs them up and finally tries to become an honorary oppressor himself.

No language? No characteristic food? Oh, man, come on.   2

Maws are things ofays seldom get to peck, nor are you likely   3
ever to hear about Charlie eating a chitterling. Sweet potatoe pies, a
good friend of mine asked recently, "Do they taste anything like
pumpkin?" Negative. They taste more like memory, if you're not uptown.

All those different kinds of greens (now quick frozen for any-   4
one) once were all Sam got to eat. (Plus the potlikker, into which one
slipped some throwed away meat.) Collards and turnips and kale and
mustards were not fit for anybody but the woogies. So they found a
way to make them taste like something somebody would want to
freeze and sell to a Negro going to Harvard as exotic European spin-
ach.

The watermelon, friend, was imported from Africa (by   5
whom?) where it had been growing many centuries before it was necessary for some people to deny that they had ever tasted one.

Did you ever hear of a black-eyed pea? (Whitey used it for   6
forage, but some folks couldn't.) And all those weird parts of the hog?
(After the pig was stripped of its choicest parts, the feet, snout, tail,
intestines, stomach, etc., were all left for the "members," who treated
them mercilessly.) Is it mere myth that shades are death on chickens?
(Deep fat frying, the Dutch found out in 17th century New Amster-
dam, was an African speciality: and if you can get hold of a fried
chicken leg, or a fried porgie, you can find out what happened to that
tradition.)

I had to go to Rutgers before I found people who thought   7
grits were meant to be eaten with milk and sugar, instead of gravy
and pork sausage . . . and that's one of the reasons I left.

Away from home, you must make the trip uptown to get   8
really straight as far as a good grease is concerned. People kill chickens all over the world, but chasing them through the dark on somebody else's property would probably insure, once they went in the
big bag, that you'd find some really beautiful way to eat them. I mean,
after all the risk involved. The fruit of that tradition unfolds everywhere above 100th Street. There are probably more restaurants in Harlem whose staple is fried chicken, or chicken in the basket, than any

other place in the world. Ditto, barbecued ribs—also straight out of the South with the West Indians, *i.e.*, Africans from farther south in the West, having developed the best sauce for roasting whole oxen and hogs, spicy and extremely hot.

Hoppin' John (black-eyed peas and rice), hushpuppies (crusty cornmeal bread cooked in fish grease and best with fried fish, especially fried salt fish, which ought to soak overnight unless you're over fifty and can take all that salt), hoecake (pan bread), buttermilk biscuits and pancakes, fatback, *i.e.*, streak'alean-streak'afat, dumplings, neck bones, knuckles (both good for seasoning limas or string beans), okra (another African importation, other name gumbo), pork chops—some more staples of the Harlem cuisine. Most of the food came North when the people did. 9

There are hundreds of tiny restaurants, food shops, rib joints, shrimp shacks, chicken shacks, "rotisseries" throughout Harlem that serve "soul food"—say, a breakfast of grits, eggs and sausage, pancakes and Alaga syrup—and even tiny booths where it's at least possible to get a good piece of barbecue, hot enough to make you whistle, or a chicken wing on a piece of greasy bread. You can *always* find a fish sandwich: a fish sandwich is something you walk with, or "Two of those small sweet potato pies to go." The Muslim temple serves bean pies which are really separate. It is never necessary to go to some big expensive place to get a good filling grease. You *can* go to the Red Rooster, or Wells, or Joch's, and get a good meal, but Jennylin's, a little place on 135th near Lenox, is more filling, or some place like the A&A food shop in a basement up in the 140's, and you can really get away. I guess a square is somebody who's in Harlem and eats at Nedicks. 10

COMPREHENSION

1. Who is Baraka's primary audience for this essay? What is the author's attitude toward this audience? Cite evidence to support your answer.

2. According to Baraka, what foods and cooking styles originated in African or Afro-American culture?

3. The theme of white oppression and the black response to it recurs frequently in the essay. Identify some of the different ways in which the theme is put forth. Why does the author state and restate the theme?

RHETORIC

1. List the various words that come from the black language and define them. There are also serveral references to "uptown" in the essay, which can be considered examples of metonymy. Explain.

2. Why is slang so effective in this essay?

3. What are the two opinions Baraka sets out to disprove? He uses two different methods of refuting these opinions. What are they?

4. How does the essay use inductive reasoning?

5. Why does Baraka present historical information in parentheses?

6. Analyze the way that Baraka develops his concluding paragraph.

WRITING

1. Write an essay that develops your own definition of soul food, ethnic food, or junk food.

2. Write an argumentative essay on the value of a "separate" language used by some ethnic, social, or professional group.

3. Develop an appreciative essay on your favorite national cuisine.

RUSSELL BAKER

Making It

Russell Baker (1925–   ), Pulitzer Prize-winning humorist and journalist, has written a syndicated column called "The Observer" since 1962. His humor runs from allegorical satires on American politics and taste to witty criticisms of current jargon and slang. Baker's columns have been collected in such books as An American in Washington *(1961),* No Cause for Panic *(1964), and* Poor Russell's Almanac *(1972). He has also written a fine autobiography,* Growing Up *(1982). In this essay, the author satirizes our assumptions about commonly held values.*

When I go back to my hometown with my world-weary   1
New York eyes and my expensive New York teeth the
folks always look at me in that sly superior country way.
That's partly because they're country people and my
hometown—Morrisonville, Va.—is a country town, nestled as it is
three miles south of metropolitan Lovettsville and two miles north of
Wheatland, which is not a town at all but just a sign on the side of
the road.

Partly though, it's also because of Frank Sinatra, whose voice   2
reaches everywhere, even to Morrisonville, with his musical paean to

RUSSELL BAKER

New York City, a song that says if a person can "make it there" he can "make it anywhere."

I've noticed that dyed-in-the-wool New Yorkers—maybe I 3 should call them spray-painted-in-the-subway New Yorkers—always look as if they're having a hard time keeping from patting themselves on the back when Frank sings this song. It seems to make them feel like heroic achievers, especially the way Frank phrases it with those big notes on the "make it" lines.

Morrisonville people don't seem to respond the same way. 4 Truth is, if they weren't such sweet people, I'd say their response is an inner sneer. I first detected this a few weeks ago when Lester, with the big house down by the creek, asked if I was "making it up there in New York."

Since my idea of "making it" in New York is not getting run 5 down by a bicyclist or a car running a red light, I said, "Guess so, Lester."

"Just what is it you're making?" he asked. 6

"Well, you know, day by day—getting by—I'm making it 7 O.K."

"Sure, but making what?" 8

Was Lester pulling my beautifully tailored New York leg? 9

"I heard the man sing that if you can make it in New York 10 you can make it anywhere," he said. "And Morrisonville is just about as close to anywhere as you can get. Whatever it is you're making in New York, I'd sort of like you to make some right here."

"It's just a song, Lester. You know songs are silly." 11

He went off to make hay, after pointing out that though he 12 could make hay right there in Morrisonville nobody ever claimed that if you could make hay there you could make it anywhere, for the simple reason that though hay was very easy to make in much of the country, even those who made it best wouldn't be able to make it in downtown Los Angeles, if there was such a place.

In this I detected a gentle rustic contempt for my suave New 13 York worldliness. True, I couldn't make hay in Morrisonville because I didn't know the recipe, but on the other hand Lester probably couldn't navigate the Union Square subway station without getting lost. I let it pass.

On the next visit, however, I encountered the ghost of my 14 Uncle Bruce outside the ruins of my grandmother's house in the very spot where he used to hide his moonshine behind the lime barrel and he, too, had been listening to Frank Sinatra.

Uncle Bruce, who had lived and died in Morrisonville, was 15 in an uncharacteristically melancholy mood. "Guess you're making it up there in New York, boy," he said.

"Getting along. Day by day. Paying the rent. Keeping the 16
spray paint off my Sunday suit," I said.

"I did that much right here in Morrisonville," he said, "and 17
it was hard toil. Of course, I wouldn't say I was making it. Then, on
the other hand, it wasn't easy to make it in Morrisonville. That's what
grinds me every time I hear Sinatra sing that song."

"How does a ghost hear, Uncle Bruce?" 18

"What that song should say, if the writer knew anything," he 19
said, ignoring my question, "is that making it in New York is a lark
beside trying to make it in Morrisonville."

"I always thought it ought to be about Baltimore," I said. 20
"Compared to Baltimore, New York is a piece of cake. If you can make
it in Baltimore, you can make it anywhere."

"Lord o' mercy, boy, I used to think that just getting to Bal- 21
timore would be making it. But Mama always told me, 'Bruce, you
stay right here in Morrisonville and test yourself, because if you can
make it in Morrisonville, you can make it anywhere.' "

"Why are you talking to yourself?" asked my cousin Ruth 22
Lee, who had wandered around from across the road. "Is that the
way you make it?"

"Don't make fun of us New Yorkers, Ruth Lee," I said. "I 23
understand how you feel, what with it being so hard for you to make
it here in Morrisonville."

"Goodness gracious," she said. "Morrisonville is a picnic 24
compared to Wheatland. If you can make it in Wheatland you can
make it anywhere."

COMPREHENSION

1. At what or at whom is Baker's humor directed in this essay?

2. What implicit comment is Baker making about the term "making it"?

3. How do New Yorkers and Morrisonville residents contrast?

4. What offends Morrisonville residents about the term "making it"?

RHETORIC

1. How does the first paragraph provide clues that the essay is humorous?

2. In paragraph 13, Baker refers to his "suave New York worldliness." Why is
this description ironic? Where else does Baker use irony in the essay?

3. In paragraph 14, Baker encounters his uncle's ghost. What is there about
his being a ghost that makes his comments about "making it" particularly poignant?

4. How does Ruth Lee's final comment (paragraph 24) conclude the essay so
effectively?

5. The direct speech of the local residents has a particular tone. What is the nature of this tone? How does it contribute to revealing their attitudes about the term "making it"? Why is this more interesting than Baker merely explaining their attitudes?

6. What makes this essay typical of the narrative form? What makes it atypical?

WRITING

1. Prepare a paper analyzing the elements in the essay that contribute to its humor.

2. Select an everyday expression that suggests success and satirize it. In your satire, try to reveal what makes the expression silly or meaningless. Some suggestions: "top of his/her profession"; "living on easy street"; "making the grade."

3. Select a popular expression from an advertisement that suggests achievement, and satirize it.

ANN GRACE MOJTABAI

Polygamy

Ann Grace Mojtabai (1938–   ) spent several years living in Iran. She has written several novels, including Mundome *(1974),* The Four Hundred Eels of Sigmund Freud *(1976), and* A Stopping Place *(1979). In the following essay, Mojtabai tries to look clearly at a particularly disturbing—from our perspective—aspect of Iranian culture.*

eheran, 1960. A warm evening. The courtyard in which we were sitting was not very beautiful. There was a narrow strip of ground that ran along the edge of the wall, spotted with shrubbery and some insignificant roses; the rest was flagstone surrounding the customary small pool for ablutions, set like a turquoise in the center.

I had come to Iran expecting nightingales and roses, but had not yet heard a nightingale above the sounds of streets hawkers and traffic, and the famed rose gardens of Persia were nowhere in evidence; they remained out of sight, if they ever existed, sealed off by high proprietary walls.

But my interest of the moment was not in the garden; my eyes were fixed on my father-in-law. He was a large, imposing man in his mid-90's, with high color, still-black eyebrows and the scrub of a heavy beard. He might have passed for a much younger man and, in fact, claimed to be in his young, vigorous 70's.

"What do you think of this?" he asked, pointing to his wives, 4 one large, one small, on either side of him. His wives smiled in my direction, then at each other. My father-in-law continued to stare at me and to wait; he really wanted to know what I thought.

For the few separate moments it took to translate his question 5 and my reply (with what distortion I shall never know), we gazed coolly at each other, each an anthropologist confronting opacity—the mind of a stranger. I thought I could hear him taking notes. I, for my part, was certainly jotting things down—but only impressions. I would see; I wasn't going to judge prematurely. My judgment, when it came, wouldn't be narrow, biased or culture-bound. "Customs differ," I said.

Long before meeting my father-in-law, I had been prepared 6 for this—or, rather, I had been briefed, and imagined that I was prepared. It had been a briefing full of history (polygamy as a practical solution to the decimation of the male population in warfare and the resulting disproportionate preponderance of females over males); it had been a briefing on principle as well (the Koranic requirement that the husband distribute his affection equally among the co-wives).

But, of course, I was not ready to confront the live instance— 7 three individuals who would bear an intimate family relation to me. Mother, father and what—aunt? mother-surrogate? I decided that the other party would simply be my Other Mother-in-Law. At that moment, the language barrier turned out to be an opportune cover for, really, I did not know what I thought.

The happy threesome sat cross-legged on a takhte, a low 8 wooden platform, covered with a rug. My particular mother-in-law, the tiny one, was the junior wife, chosen, I later learned, by the older woman as someone agreeable to herself, someone she thought the old man would like, too. The senior wife's passion was for talking, and her husband's silence had long been wearing her down. She wanted someone in the house willing to hear her out and, she hoped, to respond from time to time.

I was left to imagine the precise formalities, but it seemed to 9 me to be a marriage welcome to all the parties concerned. It was an arrangement not without its share of bickerings and quarrels, for however well-disposed the women were to each other, their respective children were rivals, and the wives were partisan for their children.

Still, as marriages go, theirs seemed to be a reasonably happy 10 one.

When it grew chilly, we moved indoors. The sitting room was 11 also my father-in-law's bedroom. He sat on a fine, ancient rug, with

ANN GRACE MOJTABAI

bolsters at his back, a bay of windows on his left and, in front of him, an array of small vials: vitamins, elixirs, purges. He didn't believe in modern medicine, but was taking no chances.

Stiff, wooden chairs of mismatching shapes were lined against the walls of the room. I eyed them, but, noticing that they were mantled in dust, furred with a thin, unbroken velvet, decided they were not really for use, and sat on the floor instead. In fact, the chairs were chiefly ceremonial, a reluctant concession to the times, to the imposition of Westernization around the world. Not like the television set, which was an ecstatic testimony to the march of *universal* human progress, and which held, along with the samovar, pride of place among the old man's possessions. 12

The wives stepped out to bring refreshments. With a sinking sense, I noticed my husband getting up to speak to his mother in private. I was utterly adrift, alone with my father-in-law, a total stranger. The old man turned to me and said what I later learned was: "When hearts speak, no language is necessary." I recognized none of the words, but I guessed from his face and tone that whatever it was he had said was meant to be comforting and, trusting in a language of gesture and sign, I ventured a smile by way of reply. 13

Even today, I do not know what I think about polygamy. Or, perhaps, I know what I think—it's only that my feelings are mixed. Abstractly, I oppose the custom. These bonds ought to be reciprocal, one-to-one. Sexual favors *may* be distributed equally as required (a night with A, a night with B), but I doubt whether affection can be distributed so neatly. And, of course, the custom speaks of the poverty of opportunities for women. 14

On the other hand, the custom of mut'a, or temporary marriage, practiced by Shiites, though not by Sunnites, seems to me to be possessed of some merits and, on the whole, somewhat more enlightened than prostitution, or the vaguely polygamous custom of balancing wife (with legal rights) with mistress (having no rights), which is so widely prevalent in the West. 15

In the mut'a marriage, a term is stipulated—a night, a year, a decade, an hour, whatever. A set term, a mehr—a wedding endowment for the woman—mutual consent and a contract specifying all this are required. The children of such unions are legitimate and entitled to a share of the father's inheritance, although the sigheh, the temporary wife, has no claim to maintenance beyond the initial marriage endowment. 16

But polygamy is meant to be more than a mere alternative to such clearly deficient institutions as prostitution. And my feelings for polygamy as a true and viable form of marriage remain contrary, held in suspension. My opposition in theory is muffled by my observation of one palpable contrary fact. I saw a polygamous marriage work, and 17 work well. That my mothers-in-law were deeply attached to each other, I have no doubt. I tend to question rather more their devotion to the husband who brought them together.

As for two mothers-in-law in one household, an old proverb 18 would seem to apply: "Better two tigers in one cage than two mistresses in one household." But, in point of fact, the laws of addition don't always apply. After all, one shark and one codfish equal one shark; one raindrop and one raindrop equal one raindrop. The two women worked off their intensities on each other, with less energy left for me. So, actually, I had one mother-in-law, which, as all the proverbs of all nations attest, was quite sufficient.

COMPREHENSION

1. How do paragraphs 1 to 5 serve the author's purpose?

2. What effects of Westernization appear in the essay? Of which ones do the Iranians approve? Of which ones do they disapprove?

3. What academic-sounding reasons for polygamy has Mojtabai been given? Do they help her to confront the reality of it? Why, or why not? What is her final attitude toward polygamy?

RHETORIC

1. Identify Iranian words in the essay, and explain what they mean.

2. What does Mojtabai mean when she describes her first meeting with her father-in-law as "each an anthropologist confronting opacity" (paragraph 5)? What level of language does that suggest Mojtabai uses in the essay? Can these words be used by Westerners to describe aspects of Western culture?

3. What is the function of the opening narrative? Why is it effective?

4. In this essay, the narrator is both actor and observer. How does this affect the tone of the essay? Where else in the anthology have we seen this strategy?

5. Why does Mojtabai spend considerable time describing *mut'a*? What elements of contrast does she utilize here? For what purpose?

6. One paragraph is considerably shorter than the others. How does this contribute to the structure and meaning of the essay?

WRITING

1. Discuss a custom you have confronted that was alien to your own values. Compare your response to Mojtabai's response.

2. Write your own evaluation of polygamy.

3. Does the United States have a more enlightened perspective on woman and marriage than the Iran depicted by Mojtabai? Discusss this question in an essay.

ANN GRACE MOJTABAI

Erotica and Pornography

Gloria Steinem (1934–   ) was born and raised in Toledo, Ohio; she attended Smith College, receiving a B.A. in government in 1956. A noted feminist and political activist, Steinem in 1968 helped to found New York *magazine; in 1971 she co-founded* Ms. *magazine and has served as its editor since then. Whether campaigning for Robert Kennedy and George McGovern or helping to defend and raise money for Angela Davis and the United Farmworkers, Steinem has been on the cutting edge of American politics for more than two decades. Her most recent book, a collection of essays, is* Outrageous Acts and Everyday Rebellions *(1983). The essay that follows reflects Steinem's keen ability to relate ideas and issues to the lives of women today.*

uman beings are the only animals that experience the   1
same sex drive at times when we can—and cannot—conceive.

Just as we developed uniquely human capacities   2
for language, planning, memory, and invention along our evolutionary path, we also developed sexuality as a form of expression; a way of communicating that is separable from our need for sex as a way of perpetuating ourselves. For humans alone, sexuality can be and often is primarily a way of bonding, of giving and receiving pleasure, bridging differentness, discovering sameness, and communicating emotion.

We developed this and other human gifts through our ability   3
to change our environment, adapt physically, and in the long run, to affect our own evolution. But as an emotional result of this spiraling path away from other animals, we seem to alternate between periods of exploring our unique abilities to change new boundaries, and feelings of loneliness in the unknown that we ourselves have created; a fear that sometimes sends us back to the comfort of the animal world by encouraging us to exaggerate our sameness.

The separation of "play" from "work," for instance, is a prob-   4
lem only in the human world. So is the difference between art and nature, or an intellectual accomplishment and a physical one. As a result, we celebrate play, art, and invention as leaps into the unknown; but any imbalance can send us back to nostalgia for our primate past and the conviction that the basics of work, nature, and physical labor are somehow more worthwhile or even moral.

In the same way, we have explored our sexuality as separable   5
from conception: a pleasurable, emphathetic bridge to strangers of the

same species. We have even invented contraception—a skill that has probably existed in some form since our ancestors figured out the process of birth—in order to extend this uniquely human difference. Yet we also have times of atavistic suspicion that sex is not complete— or even legal or intended-by-god—if it cannot end in conception.

No wonder the concepts of "erotica" and "pornography" can 6 be so crucially different, and yet so confused. Both assume that sexuality can be separated from conception, and therefore can be used to carry a personal message. That's a major reason why, even in our current culture, both may be called equally "shocking" or legally "obscene," a word whose Latin derivative means "dirty, containing filth." This gross condemnation of all sexuality that isn't harnessed to childbirth and marriage has been increased by the current backlash against women's progress. Out of fear that the whole patriarchal structure might be upset if women really had the autonomous power to decide our reproductive futures (that is, if we controlled the most basic means of production), right-wing groups are not only denouncing prochoice abortion literature as "pornographic," but are trying to stop the sending of all contraceptive information through the mails by invoking obscenity laws. In fact, Phyllis Schlafly recently denounced the entire Women's Movement as "obscene."

Not surprisingly, this religious, visceral backlash has a secu- 7 lar, intellectual counterpart that relies heavily on applying the "natural" behavior of the animal world to humans. That is questionable in itself, but these Lionel Tiger-ish studies make their political purpose even more clear in the particular animals they select and the habits they choose to emphasize. The message is that females should accept their "destiny" of being sexually dependent and devote themselves to bearing and rearing their young.

Defending against such reaction in turn leads to another 8 temptation: to merely reverse the terms, and declare that *all* nonprocreative sex is good. In fact, however, this human activity can be as constructive as destructive, moral or immoral, as any other. Sex as communication can send messages as different as life and death; even the origins of "erotica" and "pornography" reflect that fact. After all, "erotica" is rooted in *eros* or passionate love, and thus in the idea of positive choice, free will, the yearning for a particular person. (Interestingly, the definition of erotica leaves open the question of gender.) "Pornography" begins with a root meaning "prostitution" or "female captives," thus letting us know that the subject is not mutual love, or love at all, but domination and violence against women. (Though, of course, homosexual pornography may imitate this violence by putting a man in the "feminine" role of victim.) It ends with a root meaning "writing about" or "description of" which puts still more distance

GLORIA STEINEM

between subject and object, and replaces a spontaneous yearning for closeness with objectification and a voyeur.

The difference is clear in the words. It becomes even more so 9 by example.

Look at any photo or film of people making love; really making love. The images may be diverse, but there is usually a sensuality and touch and warmth, an acceptance of bodies and nerve endings. There is always a spontaneous sense of people who are there because they *want* to be, out of shared pleasure. 10

Now look at any depiction of sex in which there is clear force, 11 or an unequal power that spells coercion. It may be very blatant, with weapons or torture or bondage, wounds and bruises, some clear humiliation, or an adult's sexual power being used over a child. It may be much more subtle: a physical attitude of conqueror and victim, the use of race or class difference to imply the same thing, perhaps a very unequal nudity, with one person exposed and vulnerable while the other is clothed. In either case, there is no sense of equal choice or equal power.

The first is erotic: a mutually pleasurable, sexual expression 12 between people who have enough power to be there by positive choice. It may or may not strike a sense-memory in the viewer, or be creative enough to make the unknown seem real; but it doesn't require us to identify with a conquerer or a victim. It is truly sensuous, and may give us a contagion of pleasure.

The second is pornographic: its message is violence, domi- 13 nance, and conquest. It is sex being used to reinforce some inequality, or to create one, or to tell us the lie that pain and humiliation (ours or someone else's) are really the same as pleasure. If we are to feel anything, we must identify with conqueror or victim. That means we can only experience pleasure through the adoption of some degree of sadism or masochism. It also means that we may feel diminished by the role of conqueror, or enraged, humiliated, and vengeful by sharing identity with the victim.

Perhaps one could simply say that erotica is about sexuality, 14 but pornography is about power and sex-as-weapon—in the same way we have come to understand that rape is about violence, and not really about sexuality at all.

Yes, it's true that there are women who have been forced by 15 violent families and dominating men to confuse love with pain; so much so that they have become masochists. (A fact that in no way excuses those who administer such pain.) But the truth is that, for most women—and for men with enough humanity to imagine themselves into the predicament of women—true pornography could serve as aversion therapy for sex.

 EROTICA AND PORNOGRAPHY

Of course, there will always be personal differences about   16
what is and is not erotic, and there may be cultural differences for a
long time to come. Many women feel that sex makes them vulnerable
and therefore may continue to need more sense of personal connection
and safety before allowing any erotic feelings. We now find competence and expertise erotic in men, but that may pass as we develop
those qualities in ourselves. Men, on the other hand, may continue to
feel less vulnerable, and therefore more open to such potential danger
as sex with strangers. As some men replace the need for submission
from childlike women with the pleasure of cooperation from equals,
they may find a partner's competence to be erotic, too.

Such group changes plus individual differences will continue   17
to be reflected in sexual love between people of the same gender, as
well as between women and men. The point is not to dictate sameness,
but to discover ourselves and each other through sexuality that is an
exploring, pleasurable, empathetic part of our lives; a human sexuality
that is unchained both from unwanted pregnancies and from violence.

But that is a hope, not a reality. At the moment, fear of change   18
is increasing both the indiscriminate repression of all nonprocreative
sex in the religious and "conservative" male world, and the pornographic vengeance against women's sexuality in the secular world of
"liberal" and "radical" men. It's almost futuristic to debate what is
and is not truly erotic, when many women are again being forced into
compulsory motherhood, and the number of pornographic murders,
tortures, and woman-hating images are on the increase in both popular culture and real life.

It's a familiar division: wife or whore, "good" woman who is   19
constantly vulnerable to pregnancy or "bad" woman who is unprotected from violence. *Both* roles would be upset if we were to control
our own sexuality. And that's exactly what we must do.

In spite of all our atavistic suspicions and training for the   20
"natural" role of motherhood, we took up the complicated battle for
reproductive freedom. Our bodies had borne the health burden of
endless births and poor abortions, and we had a greater motive for
separating sexuality and conception.

Now we have to take up the equally complex burden of ex-   21
plaining that all nonprocreative sex is *not* alike. We have a motive:
our right to a uniquely human sexuality, and sometimes even to survival. As it is, our bodies have too rarely been enough our own to
develop erotica in our own lives, much less in art and literature. And
our bodies have too often been the objects of pornography and the
woman-hating, violent practice that it preaches. Consider also our
spirits that break a little each time we see ourselves in chains or full
labial display for the conquering male viewer, bruised or on our
knees, screaming a real or pretended pain to delight the sadist, pre-

tending to enjoy what we don't enjoy, to be blind to the images of our sisters that really haunt us—humiliated often enough ourselves by the truly obscene idea that sex and the domination of women must be combined.

Sexuality *is* human, free, separate—and so are we.   22

But until we untangle the lethal confusion of sex with vio-   23
lence, there will be more pornography and less erotica. There will be little murders in our beds—and very little love.

COMPREHENSION

1. What thesis does the author develop in this essay?

2. How does Steinem define the terms *erotica* and *pornography*? What is the essential distinction that the author draws between these two words?

3. In what ways do the concepts of erotica and pornography affect women's lives?

RHETORIC

1. Look up the words *erotica* and *pornography* in the *Oxford English Dictionary (OED)* or any large dictionary. Trace the etymology of these two words and any shifts in meaning.

2. Use the dictionary as necessary to understand the following biological, psychological, and sociological terms: *evolutionary* (paragraph 2), *environment* (paragraph 3), *primate* (paragraph 5), *atavistic* (paragraph 5), *patriarchal* (paragraph 6), *voyeur* (paragraph 8), *sadism* and *masochism* (paragraph 12), and *aversion therapy* (paragraph 14).

3. Why does the author delay the introduction of her key topic until paragraph 6? What is the relevance of the first five paragraphs? How are these paragraphs developed?

4. What is the relevance of the definition to the essay's development?

5. Explain Steinem's use of comparison and contrast to structure parts of this essay.

6. Examine the author's use of illustration in these representative paragraphs.

WRITING

1. Do you accept the author's distinction between erotica and pornography? Answer this question in an argumentative essay.

2. Describe and evaluate an erotic scene that you have viewed in a film or read in a book.

3. Should pornography be banned? Answer this question in an essay.

A Bachelor's Complaint

Charles Lamb (1775–1834) was a famous essayist in England in the early nineteenth century. His writings ranged from children's tales to plays, but his forte was the personal essay. In The Essays of Elia *(London Magazine, 1820–1825), Lamb described his friends, himself, and his society in a light, satiric style. In* Specimens of English Dramatic Poets *(1808), he inspired renewed interest in Elizabethan drama. Lamb describes the failures of matrimony under the persona of Elia, an eccentric bachelor, in the following selection, "A Bachelor's Complaint of the Behavior of Married People."*

s a single man, I have spent a good deal of my time in noting down the infirmities of Married People, to console myself for those superior pleasures, which they tell me I have lost by remaining as I am. 1

I cannot say that the quarrels of men and their wives ever made any great impression upon me, or had much tendency to strengthen me in those anti-social resolutions, which I took up long ago upon more substantial considerations. What oftenest offends me at the houses of married persons where I visit, is an error of quite a different description; it is that they are too loving. 2

Not too loving neither: that does not explain my meaning. Besides, why should that offend me? The very act of separating themselves from the rest of the world, to have the fuller enjoyment of each other's society, implies that they prefer one another to all the world. 3

But what I complain of is, that they carry this preference so undisguisedly, they perk it up in the faces of us single people so shamelessly, you cannot be in their company a moment without being made to feel, by some indirect hint or open avowal, that *you* are not the object of this preference. Now there are some things which give no offence, while implied or taken for granted merely; but expressed, there is much offence in them. If a man were to accost the first homely-featured or plain-dressed young woman of his acquaintance, and tell her bluntly, that she was not handsome or rich enough for him, and he could not marry her, he would deserve to be kicked for his ill manners; yet no less is implied in the fact, that having access and opportunity of putting the question to her, he has never yet thought fit to do it. The young woman understands this as clearly as if it were put into words; but no reasonable young woman would think of making this the ground of a quarrel. Just as little right have a married couple to tell me by speeches, and looks that are scarce less plain than 4 speeches, that I am not the happy man—the lady's choice. It is enough that I know that I am not: I do not want this perpetual reminding.

The display of superior knowledge or riches may be made 5 sufficiently mortifying; but these admit of a palliative. The knowledge which is brought out to insult me, may accidentally improve me; and in the rich man's houses and pictures, his parks and gardens, I have a temporary usufruct at least. But the display of married happiness has none of these palliatives; it is throughout pure, unrecompensed, unqualified insult.

Marriage by its best title is a monopoly, and not of the least 6 invidious sort. It is the cunning of most possessors of any exclusive privilege to keep their advantage as much out of sight as possible, that their less favored neighbors, seeing little of the benefit, may be less disposed to question the right. But these married monopolists thrust the most obnoxious part of their patent into our faces.

Nothing is to me more distasteful than that entire compla- 7 cency and satisfaction which beam in the countenances of a new-married couple—in that of the lady particularly; it tells you, that her lot is disposed of in this world: that *you* can have no hopes of her. It is true, I have none; nor wishes either, perhaps; but this is one of those truths which ought, as I said before, to be taken for granted, not expressed.

The excessive airs which those people give themselves, 8 founded on the ignorance of us unmarried people, would be more offensive if they were less irrational. We will allow them to understand the mysteries belonging to their own craft better than we, who have not had the happiness to be made free of the company: but their arrogance is not content within these limits. If a single person presume to offer his opinion in their presence, though upon the most indifferent subject, he is immediately silenced as an incompetent person. Nay, a young married lady of my acquaintance, who, the best of the jest was, had not changed her condition above a fortnight before, in a question on which I had the misfortune to differ from her, respecting the properest mode of breeding oysters for the London market, had the assurance to ask with a sneer, how such an old Bachelor as I could pretend to know anything about such matters!

But what I have spoken of hitherto is nothing to the airs which 9 these creatures give themselves when they come, as they generally do, to have children. When I consider how little of a rarity children are—that every street and blind alley swarms with them—that the poorest people commonly have them in most abundance—that there are few marriages that are not blest with at least one of these bargains—how often they turn out ill, and defeat the fond hope of their parents, taking to vicious courses, which end in poverty, disgrace, the gallows, &c., I cannot for my life tell what cause for pride there can possibly

 A BACHELOR'S COMPLAINT

be in having them. If they were young phoenixes, indeed, that were born but one in a year, there might be a pretext. But when they are so common—

I do not advert to the insolent merit which they assume with their husbands on these occasions. Let *them* look to that. But why *we*, who are not their natural-born subjects, should be expected to bring our spices, myrrh, and incense—our tribute and homage of admiration—I do not see.

"Like as the arrows in the hand of the giant, even so are the young children": so says the excellent office in our Prayer-book appointed for the churching of women. "Happy is the man that hath his quiver full of them": So say I; but then don't let him discharge his quiver upon us that are weaponless; let them be arrows, but not to gall and stick us. I have generally observed that these arrows are double-headed: they have two forks, to be sure to hit with one or the other. As for instance, where you come into a house which is full of children, if you happen to take no notice of them (you are thinking of something else, perhaps, and turn a deaf ear to their innocent caresses), you are set down as untractable, morose, a hater of children. On the other hand, if you find them more than usually engaging—if you are taken with their pretty manners, and set about in earnest to romp and play with them, some pretext or other is sure to be found for sending them out of the room; they are too noisy or boisterous, or Mr.——does not like children. With one or other of these forks the arrow is sure to hit you.

I could forgive their jealousy, and dispense with toying with their brats, if it gives them any pain; but I think it unreasonable to be called upon to *love* them, where I see no occasion—to love a whole family, perhaps eight, nine, or ten indiscriminately—to love all the pretty dears, because children are so engaging!

I know there is a proverb, "Love me, love my dog": that is not always so very practicable, particularly if the dog be set upon you to tease you or snap at you in sport. But a dog, or a lesser thing—any inanimate substance, as a keepsake, a watch or a ring, a tree, or the place where we last parted when my friend went away upon a long absence, I can make shift to love, because I love him, and anything that reminds me of him, provided it be in its nature indifferent, and apt to receive whatever hue fancy can give it. But children have a real character, and an essential being of themselves: they are amiable or unamiable *per se*; I must love or hate them, as I see cause for either in their qualities. A child's nature is too serious a thing to admit of its being regarded as a mere appendage to another being, and to be loved or hated accordingly: they stand with me upon their own stock, as much as men and women do. Oh! but you will say, sure it is an attractive age—there is something in the tender years of infancy that

CHARLES LAMB

of itself charms us? That is the very reason why I am more nice about them. I know that a sweet child is the sweetest thing in nature, not even excepting the delicate creatures which bear them; but the prettier the kind of a thing is, the more desirable it is that it should be pretty of its kind. One daisy differs not much from another in glory; but a violet should look and smell the daintiest. I was always rather squeamish in my women and children.

But this is not the worst: one must be admitted into their   14 familiarity at least, before they can complain of inattention. It implies visits, and some kind of intercourse. But if the husband be a man with whom you have lived on a friendly footing before marriage—if you did not come in on the wife's side—if you did not sneak into the house in her train, but were an old friend in fast habits of intimacy before their courtship was so much as thought on,—look about you—your tenure is precarious—before a twelve-month shall roll over your head, you shall find your old friend gradually grow cool and altered towards you, and at last seek opportunities of breaking with you. I have scarce a married friend of my acquaintance, upon whose firm faith I can rely, whose friendship did not commence *after the period of his marriage*. With some limitations, they can endure that; but that the good man should have dared to enter into a solemn league of friendship in which they were not consulted, though it happened before they knew him,—before they that are now man and wife ever met,— this is intolerable to them. Every long friendship, every old authentic intimacy, must be brought into their office to be new stamped with their currency, as a sovereign prince calls in the good old money that was coined in some reign before he was born or thought of, to be new marked and minted with the stamp of his authority, before he will let it pass current in the world. You may guess what luck generally befalls such a rusty piece of metal as I am in these *new mintings*.

Innumerable are the ways which they take to insult and worm   15 you out of their husbands' confidence. Laughing at all you say with a kind of wonder, as if you were a queer kind of fellow that said good things, *but an oddity*, is one of the ways;—they have a particular kind of stare for the purpose;—till at last the husband, who used to defer to your judgment, and would pass over some excrescenses of understanding and manner for the sake of a general vein of observation (not quite vulgar) which he perceived in you, begins to suspect whether you are not altogether a humorist—a fellow well enough to have consorted with in his bachelor days, but not quite so proper to be introduced to ladies. This may be called the staring way; and is that which has oftenest been put in practice against me.

Then there is the exaggerating way, or the way of irony; that   16 is, where they find you an object of especial regard with their husband, who is not so easily to be shaken from the lasting attachment

    A BACHELOR'S COMPLAINT   119

founded on esteem which he has conceived towards you, by never qualified exaggerations to cry up all that you say or do, till the good man, who understands well enough that it is all done in compliment to him, grows weary of the debt of gratitude which is due to so much candor, and by relaxing a little on his part, and taking down a peg or two in his enthusiasm, sinks at length to the kindly level of moderate esteem—that "decent affection and complacent kindness" towards you, where she herself can join in sympathy with him without much stress and violence to her sincerity.

Another way (for the ways they have to accomplish so desir- 17 able a purpose are infinite) is, with a kind of innocent simplicity, continually to mistake what it was which first made their husband fond of you. If an esteem for something excellent in your moral character was that which riveted the chain which she is to break, upon any imaginary discovery of a want of poignancy in your conversation, she will cry, "I thought, my dear, you described your friend, Mr.———, as a great wit?" If, on the other hand, it was for some supposed charm in your conversation that he first grew to like you, and was content for this to overlook some trifling irregularities in your moral deportment, upon the first notice of any of these she as readily exclaims, "This, my dear, is your good Mr.———!" One good lady whom I took the liberty of expostulating with for not showing me quite so much respect as I thought due to her husband's old friend, had the candor to confess to me that she had often heard Mr.———speak of me before marriage, and that she had conceived a great desire to be acquainted with me, but that the sight of me had very much disappointed her expectations; for from her husband's representations of me, she had formed a notion that she was to see a fine, tall officer-like-looking man (I use her very words), the very reverse of which proved to be the truth. This was candid; and I had the civility not to ask her in return, how she came to pitch upon a standard of personal accomplishments for her husband's friends which differed so much from his own; for my friend's dimensions as near as possible approximate to mine; he standing five feet five in his shoes, in which I have the advantage of him by about half an inch; and he no more than myself exhibiting any indications of a martial character in his air or countenance.

These are some of the mortifications which I have encountered 18 in the absurd attempt to visit at their houses. To enumerate them all would be a vain endeavor; I shall therefore just glance at the very common impropriety of which married ladies are guilty,—of treating us as if we were their husbands, and *vice versa*. I mean, when they use us with familiarity, and their husbands with ceremony. *Testacea*, for instance, kept me the other night two or three hours beyond my usual time of supping, while she was fretting because Mr.———did not come home, till the oysters were all spoiled, rather than she would be guilty of the impoliteness of touching one in his absence. This was reversing the point of good manners; for ceremony is an invention to take off the uneasy feeling which we derive from knowing ourselves to be less the object of love and esteem with a fellow-creature than some other person is. It endeavors to make up, by superior attentions in little points, for that invidious preference which it is forced to deny in the greater. Had *Testacea* kept the oysters back for me, and withstood her husband's importunities to go to supper, she would have acted according to the strict rules of propriety. I know no ceremony that ladies are bound to observe to their husbands, beyond the point of a modest behavior and decorum: therefore I must protest against the vicarious gluttony of *Cerasia*, who at her own table sent away a dish of Morellas, which I was applying to with great good-will, to her husband at the other end of the table, and recommended a plate of less extraordinary gooseberries to my unwedded palate in their stead. Neither can I excuse the wanton affront of———

But I am weary of stringing up all my married acquaintance   19
by Roman denominations. Let them amend and change their manners, or I promise to record the full-length English of their names, to the terror of all such desperate offenders in future.

COMPREHENSION

1. Is Lamb being serious or humorous in this essay? Cite examples to support your answer.

2. Lamb labels several ways that women alienate their husbands from their friends. What are the labels, and what are the ways?

3. What are the author's complaints about children?

RHETORIC

1. What is the effect of using such words as *usufruct, monopoly,* and *patent?* From what field are they derived?

2. Give examples of connotative words used to describe women and children. How do these words reveal the author's attitudes?

3. What is the thesis of the essay? Why is it so surprising?

4. Show where Lamb uses conventional essay techniques such as classification, definition, and exemplification.

5. This essay is part of the series *Essays of Elia;* thus, Lamb does not speak in his own voice. What effect does this have upon your sense of the tone of the essay?

6. What techniques does Lamb use to criticize conventional attitudes toward marriage?

 A BACHELOR'S COMPLAINT

WRITING

1. Do you think that marriage is overrated? Justify your answer in an essay.

2. Write a satiric essay on the supposed "evils" of friendship, motherhood, patriotism, or another, similar, convention.

3. Set forth a case in favor of marriage, family, and children, contrary to Lamb's purported argument.

VLADIMIR NABOKOV

Philistines and Philistinism

Vladimir Nabokov (1899–1977) was born into an aristocratic family in czarist Russia. Following the Russian Revolution, he went into exile in England in 1919. In 1922, he graduated with honors from Cambridge University. Subsequently he lived in Germany and France, writing in Russian, giving tennis lessons, and collecting butterflies—all recounted in his poignant autobiography, Speak Memory *(1966). He came to the United States in 1940. Nabokov taught at Wellesley College from 1944 to 1948 and at Cornell University from 1948 to 1958. Nabokov, who once termed himself the greatest Russian novelist writing in English, gained enormous success with* Lolita *(1956). His later novels include* Pale Fire *(1962) and* Ada *(1969). He died in Montreux, Switzerland. With stylistic grace and satiric precision, Nabokov in the following essay defines both a state of mind and a social condition of our times.*

A philistine is a full-grown person whose interests are of a material and commonplace nature, and whose mentality is formed of the stock ideas and conventional ideals of his or her group and time. I have said "full-grown person" because the child or the adolescent who may look like a small philistine is only a small parrot mimicking the ways of confirmed vulgarians, and it is easier to be a parrot than to be a white heron. "Vulgarian" is more or less synonymous with "philistine": the stress in a vulgarian is not so much on the conventionalism of a philistine as on the vulgarity of some of his conventional notions. I may also use the terms *genteel* and *bourgeois*. *Genteel* implies the lace-curtain refined vulgarity which is worse than simple coarseness. To burp in company may be rude, but to say "excuse me" after a burp is genteel and thus worse than vulgar. The term *bourgeois* I use following Flaubert, not Marx. *Bourgeois* in Flaubert's sense is a state of mind, not a state of pocket. A bourgeois is a smug philistine, a dignified vulgarian.

A philistine is not likely to exist in a very primitive society   2
although no doubt rudiments of philistinism may be found even there. We may imagine, for instance, a cannibal who would prefer the human head he eats to be artistically colored, just as the American philistine prefers his oranges to be painted orange, his salmon pink, and his whisky yellow. But generally speaking philistinism presupposes a certain advanced state of civilization where throughout the ages certain traditions have accumulated in a heap and have started to stink.

Philistinism is international. It is found in all nations and in   3
all classes. An English duke can be as much of a philistine as an American Shriner or a French bureaucrat or a Soviet citizen. The mentality of a Lenin or a Stalin or a Hitler in regard to the arts and the sciences was utterly bourgeois. A laborer or a coal miner can be just as bourgeois as a banker or a housewife or a Hollywood star.

Philistinism implies not only a collection of stock ideas but   4
also the use of set phrases, clichés, banalities expressed in faded words. A true philistine has nothing but these trivial ideas of which he entirely consists. But it should be admitted that all of us have our cliché side; all of us in everyday life often use words not as words but as signs, as coins, as formulas. This does not mean that we are all philistines, but it does mean that we should be careful not to indulge too much in the automatic process of exchanging platitudes. On a hot day every other person will ask you, "Is it warm enough for you?" but that does not necessarily mean that the speaker is a philistine. He may be merely a parrot or a bright foreigner. When a person asks you "Hullo, how *are* you?" it is perhaps a sorry cliché to reply, "Fine"; but if you made to him a detailed report of your condition you might pass for a pedant and a bore. It also happens that platitudes are used by people as a kind of disguise or as the shortest cut for avoiding conversation with fools. I have known great scholars and poets and scientists who in the cafeteria sank to the level of the most commonplace give and take.

The character I have in view when I say "smug vulgarian" is,   5
thus, not the part-time philistine, but the total type, the genteel bourgeois, the complete universal product of triteness and mediocrity. He is the conformist, the man who conforms to his group, and he also is typified by something else: he is a pseudo-idealist, he is pseudo-compassionate, he is pseudo-wise. The fraud is the closest ally of the true philistine. All such great words as "Beauty," "Love," "Nature," "Truth," and so on become masks and dupes when the smug vulgarian employs them. In *Dead Souls* you have heard Chichikov. In *Bleak House* you have heard Skimpole. You have heard Homais in *Madame*

Bovary. The philistine likes to impress and he likes to be impressed, in consequence of which a world of deception, of mutual cheating, is formed by him and around him.

The philistine in his passionate urge to conform, to belong, to join, is torn between two longings: to act as everybody does, to admire, to use this or that thing because millions of people do; or else he craves to belong to an exclusive set, to an organization, to a club, to a hotel patronage or an ocean liner community (with the captain in white and wonderful food), and to delight in the knowledge that there is the head of a corporation or a European count sitting next to him. The philistine is often a snob. He is thrilled by riches and rank— "Darling, I've actually talked to a duchess!" 6

A philistine neither knows nor cares anything about art, including literature—his essential nature is anti-artistic—but he wants information and he is trained to read magazines. He is a faithful reader of the *Saturday Evening Post*, and when he reads he identifies himself with the characters. If he is a male philistine he will identify himself with the fascinating executive or any other big shot—aloof, single, but a boy and a golfer at heart; or if the reader is a female philistine—a philistinette—she will identify herself with the fascinating strawberry-blond secretary, a slip of a girl but a mother at heart, who eventually marries the boyish boss. The philistine does not distinguish one writer from another; indeed, he reads little and only what may be useful to him, but he may belong to a book club and choose beautiful, *beautiful* books, a jumble of Simone de Beauvoir, Dostoevski, Marquand, Somerset Maugham, *Dr. Zhivago*, and Masters of the Renaissance. He does not much care for pictures, but for the sake of prestige he may hang in his parlor reproductions of Van Gogh's or Whistler's respective mothers, although secretly preferring Norman Rockwell. 7

In his love for the useful, for the material goods of life, he becomes an easy victim of the advertisement business. Ads may be very good ads—some of them are very artistic—that is not the point. The point is that they tend to appeal to the philistine's pride in possessing things whether silverware or underwear. I mean the following kind of ad: just come to the family is a radio set or a television set (or a car, or a refrigerator, or table silver—anything will do). It has just come to the family: mother clasps her hands in dazed delight, the children crowd around all agog: junior and the dog strain up to the edge of the table where the Idol is enthroned; even Grandma of the beaming wrinkles peeps out somewhere in the background; and somewhat apart, his thumbs gleefully inserted in the armpits of his waistcoat, stands triumphant Dad or Pop, the Proud Donor. Small boys and girls in ads are invariably freckled, and the smaller fry have front teeth missing. I have nothing against freckles (in fact I find them 8

VLADIMIR NABOKOV

very becoming in live creatures) and quite possibly a special survey might reveal that the majority of small American-born Americans *are* freckled, or else perhaps another survey might reveal that all successful executives and handsome housewives had been freckled in their childhood. I repeat, I have really nothing against freckles as such. But I do think there is considerable philistinism involved in the use made of them by advertisers and other agencies. I am told that when an unfreckled, or only slightly freckled, little boy actor has to appear on the screen in television, an artificial set of freckles is applied to the middle of his face. Twenty-two freckles is the minimum: eight over each cheekbone and six on the saddle of the pert nose. In the comics, freckles look like a case of bad rash. In one series of comics they appear as tiny circles. But although the good cute little boys of the ads are blond or redhaired, with freckles, the handsome young men of the ads are generally dark haired and always have thick dark eyebrows. The evolution is from Scotch to Celtic.

The rich philistinism emanating from advertisements is due   9
not to their exaggerating (or inventing) the glory of this or that serviceable article but to suggesting that the acme of human happiness is purchasable and that its purchase somehow ennobles the purchaser. Of course, the world they create is pretty harmless in itself because everybody knows that it is made up by the seller with the understanding that the buyer will join in the make-believe. The amusing part is not that it is a world where nothing spiritual remains except the ecstatic smiles of people serving or eating celestial cereals, or a world where the game of the senses is played according to bourgeois rules, but that it is a kind of satellite shadow world in the actual existence of which neither sellers nor buyers really believe in their heart of hearts—especially in this wise quiet country.

Russians have, or had, a special name for smug philistinism—   10
poshlust. Poshlism is not only the obviously trashy but mainly the falsely important, the falsely beautiful, the falsely clever, the falsely attractive. To apply the deadly label of *poshlism* to something is not only an esthetic judgment but also a moral indictment. The genuine, the guileless, the good is never *poshlust*. It is possible to maintain that a simple, uncivilized man is seldom if ever a *poshlust* since *poshlism* presupposes the veneer of civilization. A peasant has to become a townsman in order to become vulgar. A painted necktie has to hide the honest Adam's apple in order to produce *poshlism*.

It is possible that the term itself has been so nicely devised by   11
Russians because of the cult of simplicity and good taste in old Russia. The Russia of today, a country of moral imbeciles, of smiling slaves and poker-faced bullies, has stopped noticing *poshlism* because Soviet Russia is so full of its special brand, a blend of despotism and pseudoculture; but in the old days a Gogol, a Tolstoy, a Chekhov in quest of

the simplicity of truth easily distinguished the vulgar side of things as well as the trashy systems of pseudo-thought. But *poshlists* are found everywhere, in every country, in this country as well as in Europe—in fact *poshlism* is more common in Europe than here, despite our American ads.

COMPREHENSION

1. What does Nabokov reveal of his own background, beliefs, and behavior in this essay?

2. What, according to the author, is a philistine? Explain the representative characteristics of a philistine.

3. What does philistinism tell us about the state of society? Why is philistinism international? What does Nabokov say about the degree of philistinism in Europe and America?

RHETORIC

1. Nabokov employs several synonyms for *philistine* and *philistinism*. List them, and explain their shades of meaning.

2. Identify and explain the effectiveness of the various literary allusions in the essay.

3. Identify the topic sentence in each paragraph. Why are they so consistently placed? Relate their placement to the movement from general or abstract to specific and concrete in three representative paragraphs.

4. Does the author use actual examples or hypothetical examples in the essay? Explain.

5. How does Nabokov use definition? For what purpose does he employ it? What instances of comparison and contrast and causal analysis do you find?

6. What is the tone of the essay? What effect does that tone have on the way that Nabokov describes the philistine?

WRITING

1. What is your opinion of Nabokov's assertion that philistinism is rampant in the modern world? Respond to this question in an argumentative essay.

2. Write an extended definition of philistinism, using examples drawn from personal experience, reading, and the media.

3. Write an essay that uses definition to make a comic or satiric point about manners or social behavior.

VLADIMIR NABOKOV

Falling for Apples

Noel Perrin (1927–   ) was born in New York City. He graduated from Williams College in Massachusetts and earned an M.A. at Duke University. His first writing assignment was as associate editor for the journal Medical Economics. *Since 1959, he has been a professor in the Department of English at Dartmouth College in New Hampshire. He has twice been a Guggenheim Fellow, and he received a Fulbright Fellowship to teach for one year at the University of Warsaw. He has published articles, essays, novels, and a historical work on Japan. His most recent book is a collection of essays entitled* A Reader's Delight *(1988). In the following essay, from* Second Person Rural *(1980), Perrin shares with us his enthusiasm for making apple cider. At the same time he provides us with an excellent "how-to" that departs quite drastically from the typical instruction manual format.*

The number of children who eagerly help around a farm is rather small. Willing helpers do exist, but many more of them are five years old than fifteen. In fact, there seems to be a general law that says as long as a kid is too little to help effectively, he or she is dying to. Then, just as they reach the age when they really could drive a fence post or empty a sap bucket without spilling half of it, they lose interest. Now it's cars they want to drive, or else they want to stay in the house and listen for four straight hours to The Who. That sort of thing. 1

There is one exception to this rule. Almost no kid that I have ever met outgrows an interest in cidering. In consequence, cider making remains a family time on our farm, even though it's been years since any daughter trudged along a fencerow with me, dragging a new post too heavy for her to carry, or begged for lessons in chain-sawing. 2

It's not too hard to figure out why. In the first place, cidering gives the child instant gratification. There's no immediate reward for weeding a garden (unles the parents break down and offer cash), still less for loading a couple of hundred hay bales in the barn. But the minute you've ground and pressed the first bushel of apples, you can break out the glasses and start drinking. Good stuff, too. Cider has a wonderful fresh sweetness as it runs from the press. 3

In the second place, making cider on a small scale is simple enough so that even fairly young children—say, a pair of nine-year-olds—can do the whole operation by themselves. Yet it's also pictur- 4 esque enough to tempt people of any age. When my old college room-mate was up last fall—and we've been out of college a long time—he and his wife did four pressings in the course of the weekend. They only quit then because I ran out of apples.

Finally, cider making appeals to a deep human instinct. It's the same one that makes a housewife feel so good when she takes a bunch of leftovers and produces a memorable casserole. At no cost, and using what would otherwise be wasted, she has created some-thing. In fact, she has just about reversed entropy.

Cidering is like that. You take apples that have been lying on the ground for a week, apples with blotches and cankers and bad spots, apples that would make a supermarket manager turn pale if you merely brought them in the store, and out of this unpromising material you produce not one but two delicious drinks. Sweet cider now. Hard cider later.

The first step is to have a press. At the turn of the century, almost every farm family did. They ordered them from the Sears or Montgomery Ward catalogue as routinely as one might now order a toaster. Then about 1930 little presses ceased to be made. Pasteurized apple juice had joined the list of American food-processing triumphs. It had no particular flavor (still hasn't), but it would keep almost in-definitely. Even more appealing, it was totally sterile. That was the era when the proudest boast that, let's say, a bakery could make was that its bread was untouched by human hands. Was touched only by stainless-steel beaters and stainless-steel wrapping machines.

Eras end, though, and the human hand came back into favor. One result: in the 1970s home cider presses returned to the market. They have not yet returned to the Sears catalogue, but they are readily available. I know of two companies in Vermont that make them, an-other in East Aurora, New York, and one out in Washington state. If there isn't someone making them in Michigan or Wisconsin, there soon will be. Prices range from about 175 to 250 dollars.

Then you get a couple of bushels of apples. There *may* be people in the country who buy cider apples, but I don't know any of them. Old apple trees are too common. I get mine by the simple process of picking up windfalls in a derelict orchard that came with our place. I am not choosy. Anything that doesn't actually squish goes in the basket.

With two kids to help, collecting takes maybe twenty minutes. Kids tend to be less interested in gathering the apples than in running the press, but a quiet threat of no-pickee, no-pressee works wonders. Kids also worry about worms sometimes, as they scoop apples from the ground—apples that may be wet with dew, spiked with stubble, surrounded by hungry wasps. Occasionally I have countered with a short lecture on how much safer our unsprayed apples are than the

NOEL PERRIN

shiny, wormless, but heavily sprayed apples one finds in stores. But usually I just say that I have yet to see a worm in our cider press. That's true, too. Whether it's because there has never been one, or whether it's because in the excitement and bustle of grinding you just wouldn't notice one little worm, I don't dare to say.

As soon as you get back with the apples, it's time to make 11 cider. Presses come in two sizes: one-bushel and a-third-of-a-bushel. We have tried both. If I lived in a suburb and had to buy apples, I would use the very efficient third-of-a-bushel press and make just under a gallon at a time. Living where I do, I use the bigger press and make two gallons per pressing, occasionally a little more.

The process has two parts. First you set your pressing tub 12 under the grinder, line it with a pressing cloth, and start grinding. Or, better, your children do. One feeds apples into the hopper, the other turns the crank. If there are three children present, the third can hold the wooden hopper plate, and thus keep the apples from bouncing around. If there are four, the fourth can spell off on cranking. Five or more is too many, and any surplus over four is best made into a separate crew for the second pressing. I once had two three-child crews present, plus a seventh child whom my wife appointed the official timer. We did two pressings and had 4¼ gallons of cider in 43 minutes and 12 seconds. (Who won? The second crew, by more than a minute. Each crew had one of our practiced daughters on it, but the second also had the advantage of watching the first.)

As soon as the apples are ground, you put the big pressing 13 plate on and start to turn the press down. If it's a child crew, and adult meddling is nevertheless tolerated, it's desirable to have the kids turn the press in order of their age, starting with the youngest: at the end it takes a fair amount of strength (though it's not beyond two nine-year-olds working together), and a little kid coming after a big one may fail to produce a single drop.

The pressing is where all the thrills come. As the plate begins 14 to move down and compact the ground apples, you hear a kind of sighing, bubbling noise. Then a trickle of cider begins to run out. Within five or ten seconds the trickle turns into a stream, and the stream into a ciderfall. Even kids who've done it a dozen times look down in awe at what their labor has wrought.

A couple of minutes later the press is down as far as it will 15 go, and the container you remembered to put below the spout is full of rich, brown cider. Someone has broken out the glasses, and everybody is having a drink.

This pleasure goes on and on. In an average year we start 16 making cider the second week of September, and we continue until early November. We make all we can drink ourselves, and quite a lot to give away. We have supplied whole church suppers. One year the

FALLING FOR APPLES

girls sold about ten gallons to the village store, which made them some pocket money they were prouder of than any they ever earned by baby-sitting. Best of all, there are two months each year when all of us are running the farm together, just like a pioneer family.

COMPREHENSION

1. What does Perrin see as the advantages of cidering?

2. How does the title of the essay establish its tone? What pun does the author intend the reader to understand?

3. What is the purpose of the essay? To inform? To entertain? To instruct? Who is the implicit audience for the essay?

RHETORIC

1. Perrin uses words and terms such as *kids, good stuff, squish,* and *no pickee, no-pressee.* How is the diction of the essay appropriate to its topic?

2. How does Perrin describe the pressing process in paragraph 12 so that it is obvious he is an expert "presser"?

3. Paragraph 1 makes no specific references to cidering. How effective is it as an introduction? How does the first sentence of paragraph 2 provide a strong transition to the main topic?

4. Paragraphs 2 through 6 constitute a subsection of the essay. How does Perrin achieve unity among these paragraphs? How does he use transitions to strengthen their coherence?

5. Paragraphs 7 and 8 digress from explaining the cidering process. What is the function of these two paragraphs? Do they strengthen or weaken the structure of the essay as a whole?

6. Does the essay prepare you for its concluding sentence? In what way does this sentence modify the thesis of the essay?

WRITING

1. How do you as a reader endow a writer with authority? What in this essay makes you confident that Perrin is an expert on the subject? Examine this issue in a brief essay.

2. Describe a little-known but enjoyable activity to an audience unfamiliar with it. Explain the steps of the process and why it is enjoyable.

3. Defend, in an essay, some cultural ritual, acknowledging and refuting any potential detractors.

Gifts

Ralph Waldo Emerson (1803–1882) is among the most important writers and thinkers in American history. The son of a Unitarian minister, Emerson himself was briefly the pastor of the Old North Church in Boston. Leaving the ministry after a dispute with his congregation, he traveled in Europe, where he became friends with many of the leading writers and intellectuals of his day, including Wordsworth and Coleridge. This European sojourn profoundly influenced his ideas, especially his belief in transcendentalism. Emerson's work is notable for encouraging the development of American art and literature, and his influence on his contemporaries, notably Thoreau and Hawthorne, was profound. Among his major works are Nature *(1836),* "The American Scholar" *(1837), and* Essays *(1841 and 1844). In this selection, Emerson distinguishes between common and special gifts, explores the relationship of gifts to the receiver, and explores the implications of gift giving for human nature and society.*

Gifts of one who loved me,—
'Twas high time they came;
When he ceased to love me,
Time they stopped for shame.

t is said that the world is in a state of bankruptcy, that   1
the world owes the world more than the world can pay, and ought to go into chancery, and be sold. I do not think this general insolvency, which involves in some sort all the population, to be the reason of the difficulty experienced at Christmas and New Year, and other times, in bestowing gifts; since it is always so pleasant to be generous, though very vexatious to pay debts. But the impediment lies in the choosing. If, at any time, it comes into my head that a present is due from me to somebody, I am puzzled what to give until the opportunity is gone. Flowers and fruits are always fit presents; flowers, because they are a proud assertion that a ray of beauty out values all the utilities of the world. These gay natures contrast with the somewhat stern countenance of ordinary nature; they are like music heard out of a workhouse. Nature does not cocker us: we are children, not pets: she is not fond: everything is dealt to us without fear or favor, after severe universal laws. Yet these delicate flowers look like the frolic and interference of love and beauty. Men used to tell us that we love flattery, even though we are

not deceived by it, because it shows that we are of importance enough to be courted. Something like that pleasure, the flowers give us: what am I to whom these sweet hints are addressed? Fruits are acceptable gifts, because they are the flower of commodities, and admit of fantastic values being attached to them. If a man should send to me to come a hundred miles to visit him, and should set before me a basket of fine summer-fruit, I should think there was some proportion between the labour and the reward.

For common gifts, necessity makes pertinences and beauty 2
every day, and one is glad when an imperative leaves him no option, since if the man at the door has no shoes you have not to consider whether you could procure him a paint-box. And as it is always pleasing to see a man eat bread, or drink water, in the house or out of doors, so it is always a great satisfaction to supply these first wants. Necessity does everything well. In our condition of universal dependence, it seems heroic to let the petitioner be the judge of his necessity, and to give all that is asked, though at great inconvenience. If it be a fantastic desire, it is better to leave to others the office of punishing him. I can think of many parts I should prefer playing to that of the Furies. Next to things of necessity, the rule for a gift, which one of my friends prescribed, is, that we might convey to some person that which properly belonged to his character, and was easily associated with him in thought. But our tokens of compliment and love are for the most part barbarous. Rings and other jewels are not gifts, but apologies for gifts. The only gift is a portion of thyself. Thou must bleed for me. Therefore the poet brings his poem; the shepherd, his lamb; the farmer, corn; the miner, a gem; the sailor, coral and shells; the painter, his picture; the girl, a handkerchief of her own sewing. This is right and pleasing, for it restores society in so far to its primary basis, when a man's biography is conveyed in his gift, and every man's wealth is an index of his merit. But it is a cold, lifeless business when you go to the shops to buy me something, which does not represent your life and talent, but a goldsmith's. This is fit for kings, and rich men who represent kings, and a false state of property, to make presents of gold and silver stuffs, as a kind of symbolical sin-offering, or payment of blackmail.

The law of benefits is a difficult channel, which requires care- 3
ful sailing, or rude boats. It is not the office of a man to receive gifts. How dare you give them? We wish to be self-sustained. We do not quite forgive a giver. The hand that feeds us is in some danger of being bitten. We can receive anything from love, for that is a way of receiving it from ourselves; but not from anyone who assumes to bestow. We sometimes hate the meat which we eat, because there seems something of degrading dependence in living by it.

"Brother, if Jove to thee a present make,
Take heed that from his hands thou nothing take."

We ask the whole. Nothing less will content us. We arraign society if it does not give us besides earth, and fire, and water, opportunity, love, reverence, and objects of veneration.

He is a good man who can receive a gift well. We are either   4
glad or sorry at a gift, and both emotions are unbecoming. Some violence, I think, is done, some degradation borne, when I rejoice or grieve at a gift. I am sorry when my independence is invaded, or when a gift comes from such as do not know my spirit, and so the act is not supported; and if the gift pleases me overmuch, then I should be ashamed that the donor should read my heart, and see that I love his commodity, and not him. The gift, to be true, must be the flowing of the giver unto me, correspondent to my flowing unto him. When the waters are at a level, then my goods pass to him, and his to me. All his are mine, all mine his. I say to him, "How can you give me this pot of oil, or this flagon of wine, when all your oil and wine is mine?" which belief of mine this gift seems to deny. Hence the fitness of beautiful, not useful things for gifts. This giving is flat usurpation, and therefore when the beneficiary is ungrateful, as all beneficiaries hate all Timons, not at all considering the value of the gift, but looking back to the greater store it was taken from, I rather sympathize with the beneficiary than with the anger of my lord Timon. For, the expectation of gratitude is mean, and is continually punished by the total insensibility of the obliged person. It is a great happiness to get off without injury and heart-burning from one who has had the ill luck to be served by you. It is a very onerous business, this of being served, and the debtor naturally wishes to give you a slap. A golden text for these gentlemen is that which I so admire in the Buddhist, who never thanks, and who says, "Do not flatter your benefactors."

The reason of these discords I conceive to be, that there is no   5
commensurability between a man and any gift. You cannot give anything to a magnanimous person. After you have served him, he at once puts you in debt by his magnanimity. The service a man renders his friend is trivial and selfish, compared with the service he knows his friend stood in readiness to yield him, alike before he had begun to serve his friend, and now also. Compared with that goodwill I bear my friend, the benefit it is in my power to render him seems small. Besides, our action on each other, good as well as evil, is so incidental and at random, that we can seldom hear the acknowledgements of any person who would thank us for a benefit without some shame and humiliation. We can rarely strike a direct stroke, but must be content with an oblique one; we seldom have the satisfaction of yield-

ing a direct benefit which is directly received. But rectitude scatters favors on every side without knowing it, and receives with wonder the thanks of all people.

I fear to breathe any treason against the majesty of love, which is the genius and god of gifts and to whom we must not affect to prescribe. Let him give kingdoms or flower leaves indifferently. There are persons from whom we always expect fairy tokens; let us not cease to expect them. This is prerogative, and not to be limited by our municipal rules. For the rest, I like to see that we cannot be bought and sold. The best of hospitality and of generosity is also not in the will, but in fate. I find that I am not much to you; you do not need me; you do not feel me; then am I thrust out of doors, though you proffer me house and lands. No services are of any value, but only likeness. When I have attempted to join myself to others by services, it proved an intellectual trick—no more. They eat your service like apples, and leave you out. But love them, and they feel you and delight in you all the time.

6

COMPREHENSION

1. On what assumptions about his audience does Emerson base his advice? Provide examples to support your answer.

2. What is the main idea of this selection? What does Emerson wish to convey about gifts and giving?

3. Why does Emerson say, in paragraph 2, that "our tokens of compliment and love are for the most part barbarous"?

RHETORIC

1. Use a classical dictionary or an encyclopedia to look up the following references: the Furies, Jove, Timon.

2. Stylistically, what about this piece identifies it as belonging to an era aesthetically different from our own?

3. What is the tone of this piece? How would you characterize Emerson's role in the essay?

4. Comment on the structure of this essay. How does Emerson proceed from his introduction to the conclusion?

5. Does Emerson support his thesis with specific examples, or does he use more general, abstract support? What are the advantages or disadvantages of his approach?

6. Is Emerson's shifting use of the pronouns *I*, *we*, and *you* deliberate? Explain. Give an example of each, and discuss the effect.

RALPH WALDO EMERSON

WRITING

1. Mark Twain observed that the only difference between a starving dog and a man is that if you feed the dog, he will not bite you. In this essay, Emerson articulates a slightly less cynical version of the same thought in paragraph 3: "The hand that feeds us is in some danger of being bitten." What responsibility do we have toward our fellow men and women? What would Emerson say about our modern Christmas celebrations, the welfare state, and our concerts for farmers or Africa? Answer these questions in an essay.

2. In an argumentative essay, discuss the following: Human nature has/has not changed fundamentally since 1844, when Emerson wrote "Gifts." People reflect/do not reflect the same bankruptcy that Emerson derided in his essay.

3. Present the case for giving gifts. Cite Emerson in your essay.

4 Education

ELLEN GOODMAN

Bamama Goes to College

Ellen Holtz Goodman (1941–   ) is an award-winning journalist who writes a syndicated column for The Boston Globe. *She is the author of* Close to Home *(1979) and other essay collections and has been a commentator on television and radio. Goodman is an adept practitioner of the personal essay. In "Bamama Goes to College," she takes a bemused look at higher education.*

oston—My friend received another degree this month. 1
She became a B.A., M.A., M.A., or as we fondly call her, a Bamama.

This latest degree raised her academic tempera- 2
ture and the quality of her resume. In fact, my friend Bamama officially became qualified to be unemployed in yet a better class of jobs.

Let me explain. When she got a B.A. in philosophy four years 3
ago at the cost of $12,000 (them was the bargain basement days), Bamama had the choice between becoming an overeducated waitress or an overeducated office worker. So she became an overeducated day-camp counselor and went back to school.

The next year, for $4,000, she got a degree in library science. 4

Now, qualified as a librarian, she won a job as an overeducated part-time library assistant. In her off-hours, she became an overqualified clerk at a cheese counter. Rumors that she arranged the cheddar according to the Dewey Decimal system were greatly exaggerated.

In any case, her course was clear. Before she entirely coated 5 her brain as well as her arteries with brie, she went back to school. Now, $5,000 later, she is qualified not only as a librarian, but as a school librarian, teacher, administrator, etc., for a school system in need of an efficient, caring, well-educated Bamama. No such luck or, rather, no such system.

So, Bamama has done the only logical thing: applied for and 6 been accepted for a Ph.D. program. With that degree, Bamamaphd, three years older and deeper in debt, would be qualified as a college professor and might therefore be able to find a job as an overqualified school librarian.

She had, you see, followed the life pattern of Woody Allen, 7 who says that success has meant that he is now turned down for dates by a better class of women. Bamama may be particularly adroit at choosing a career track on which 90 percent of the stations have been closed. But the problem is not uniquely hers.

There are more than one million Americans getting bachelor's 8 degrees this year, more than 300,000 getting master's degrees and more than 32,000 getting doctorates.

They and/or their parents are up to their ears in debt. The 9 economy is up to its ears in the overeducated underemployed.

Eighty percent of the recent college graduates, we are told, 10 are doing work which was once done quite capably by people without college degrees. The point is that you don't need the degree to do the job. But nowadays you do need the degree to get the job.

College graduates may be getting the jobs once filled by non- 11 graduates, but they are not automatically filling the spots once guaranteed by a degree. There is more educational competition at every level. In fact, by 1985, 2.5 college graduates will be competing for every "college" job.

This is the name of the 1980s war game called Defensive Ed- 12 ucation. As economist Lester Thurow put it: "As the supply of more highly educated labor increases, individuals find that they must improve their own education qualification simply to defend their current income position. If they do not go to college, others will and they will not find their current job open to them."

This is described as the "tiptoe syndrome" in Michael Har- 13 rington's book, "Decade of Decision." At any parade, the people in the second row stand on tiptoe to see over the heads of those in the front row. Then everyone else behind them stands on tiptoe, just to stay in the same position.

As more and more people go to college, a degree no longer 14
guarantees who will get ahead. But the lack of a degree still can determine who will fall behind. We keep raising the education threshold
to the job market.

This is the sort of new truth that makes us feel trapped and 15
cynical and furious. Trapped into paying a fortune, not for advance
but for defense. Cynical about the real motivation for "Higher Education."

Meanwhile, even as we play the game, the gap between our 16
educational level and job level grows and is filled with the discontent
of the "underemployed."

Remember the movie "Goodbye Columbus"? There was a 17
moment when the father who owns a trucking business shakes his
head watching his son work. Finally he sighs, "Four years of college,
and he can't load a truck."

Just a few years ago, that was funny. But at the current rate 18
of the education escalation war, the kid won't even be able to get a
tryout without a Ph.D.

COMPREHENSION

1. How important is the issue that Goodman discusses? Why does she treat the issue humorously?

2. According to Goodman, how much does it cost to become a Bamama?

3. What does Goodman mean by "Defensive Education"?

RHETORIC

1. What is the effect of using the acronym Bamama in the title and in identifying Goodman's friend?

2. Goodman uses two terms to describe modern higher education. Define "tip-toe syndrome" and "education escalation war."

3. What is the effect of repetititon in the essay?

4. What different rhetorical strategies are used in paragraph groups 1 to 7, 8 to 11, 12 to 16, and 17 to 18?

5. How does Goodman use humor to forward her argument?

6. In this argumentative essay, what kinds of evidence are given? Why?

WRITING

1. A second kind of education is alluded to in the essay: practical education. How valuable do you believe education through experience is to your career goals? Write an essay answering this question.

2. Statistics are crucial to this essay. Write an argumentative essay that com-

ELLEN GOODMAN

bines anecdote and statistical information, addressing the proposition, "College is a waste of time and money."

3. Invent your own "Bamama," a holder of multiple degrees, and create your own comic scenario for this individual.

E. B. WHITE

Education

Elwyn Brooks White (1899–1985), perhaps the finest contemporary American essayist, is at his most distinctive in his treatments of people, nature, and social conventions. A recipient of the National Medal for literature, and associated for years with The New Yorker, *White is the author of* One Man's Meat *(1942),* Here Is New York *(1949), and* The Second Tree from the Corner *(1954), among numerous other works. He is also one of the most talented writers of literature for children, the author of* Stuart Little *(1945),* Charlotte's Web *(1952), and* The Trumpet of the Swan *(1970). Most writers and lovers of language have read and reread his witty, cogent explanation of English grammar in* The Elements of Style *(1959). In the following essay, White reveals his abiding love for the country experience as he muses on the comparative values of urban and rural, private and public education.*

 have an increasing admiration for the teacher in the country school where we have a third-grade scholar in attendance. She not only undertakes to instruct her charges in all the subjects of the first three grades, but she manages to function quietly and effectively as a guardian of their health, their clothes, their habits, their mothers, and their snowball engagements. She has been doing this sort of Augean task for twenty years, and is both kind and wise. She cooks for the children on the stove that heats the room, and she can cool their passions or warm their soup with equal competence. She conceives their costumes, cleans up their messes, and shares their confidences. My boy already regards his teacher as his great friend, and I think tells her a great deal more than he tells us.

The shift from city school to country school was something we worried about quietly all last summer. I have always rather favored public school over private school, if only because in public school you meet a greater variety of children. This bias of mine, I

1

2

suspect, is partly an attempt to justify my own past (I never knew anything but public schools) and partly an involuntary defense against getting kicked in the shins by a young ceramist on his way to the kiln. My wife was unacquainted with public schools, never having been exposed (in her early life) to anything more public than the washroom of Miss Winsor's. Regardless of our backgrounds, we both knew that change in schools was something that concerned not us but the scholar himself. We hoped it would work out all right. In New York our son went to a medium-priced private institution with semi-progressive ideas of education, and modern plumbing. He learned fast, kept well, and we were satisfied. It was an electric, colorful, regimented existence with moments of pleasurable pause and giddy incident. The day the Christmas angel fainted and had to be carried out by one of the Wise Men was educational in the highest sense of the term. Our scholar gave imitations of it around the house for weeks afterward, and I doubt if it ever goes completely out of his mind.

His days were rich in formal experience. Wearing overalls and 3 an old sweater (the accepted uniform of the private seminary), he sallied forth at morn accompanied by a nurse or a parent and walked (or was pulled) two blocks to a corner where the school bus made a flag stop. This flashy vehicle was as punctual as death: seeing us waiting at the cold curb, it would sweep to a halt, open its mouth, suck the boy in, and spring away with an angry growl. It was a good deal like a train picking up a bag of mail. At school the scholar was worked on for six or seven hours by half a dozen teachers and a nurse, and was revived on orange juice in mid-morning. In a cinder court he played games supervised by an athletic instructor, and in a cafeteria he ate lunch worked out by a dietitian. He soon learned to read with gratifying facility and discernment and to make Indian weapons of a semi-deadly nature. Whenever one of his classmates fell low of a fever the news was put on the wires and there were breathless phone calls to physicians, discussing periods of incubation and allied magic.

In the country all one can say is that the situation is different, 4 and somehow more casual. Dressed in corduroys, sweatshirt, and short rubber boots, and carrying a tin dinner-pail, our scholar departs at crack of dawn for the village school, two and a half miles down the road, next to the cemetery. When the road is open and the car will start, he makes the journey by motor, courtesy of his old man. When the snow is deep or the motor is dead or both, he makes it on the hoof. In the afternoons he walks or hitches all or part of the way home in fair weather, gets transported in foul. The schoolhouse is a two-room frame building, bungalow type, shingles stained a burnt brown with weather-resistant stain. It has a chemical toilet in the basement and two teachers above stairs. One takes the first three grades, the other the fourth, fifth, and sixth. They have little or no time for indi-

E. B. WHITE

vidual instruction, and no time at all for the esoteric. They teach what they know themselves, just as fast and as hard as they can manage. The pupils sit still at their desks in class, and do their milling around outdoors during recess.

There is no supervised play. They play cops and robbers (only 5 they call it "Jail") and throw things at one another—snowballs in winter, rose hips in fall. It seems to satisfy them. They also construct darts, pinwheels, and "pick-up sticks" (jackstraws), and the school itself does a brisk trade in penny candy, which is for sale right in the classroom and which contains "surprises." The most highly prized surprise is a fake cigarette, made of cardboard, fiendishly lifelike.

The memory of how apprehensive we were at the beginning 6 is still strong. The boy was nervous about the change too. The tension, on that first fair morning in September when we drove him to school, almost blew the windows out of the sedan. And when later we picked him up on the road, wandering along with his little blue lunch-pail, and got his laconic report "All right" in answer to our inquiry about how the day had gone, our relief was vast. Now, after almost a year of it, the only difference we can discover in the two school experiences is that in the country he sleeps better at night—and *that* probably is more the air than the education. When grilled on the subject of school-in-country vs. school-in-city, he replied that the chief difference is that the day seems to go so much quicker in the country. "Just like lightning," he reported.

COMPREHENSION

1. How does White define his subject in this essay? Does he present a limited or comprehensive view of his subject? Justify your answer.

2. Why were the Whites "quietly" worried about the shift from private to public school? What were the two schools like? Which school does the author prefer? How do you know?

3. Explain the connections between the city and private schools and the country and public schools.

RHETORIC

1. White refers to his son as the "scholar" several times in this essay. What are the purpose and effect of this strategy? How does "scholar" resemble Goodman's use of the word "Bamama"?

2. What is the significance of the word "Education" as used in the title? Is this significance a matter of connotation or denotation? Explain.

3. What is White's thesis? Is it ever explicitly stated? Why, or why not?

4. What standard means of exposition does the author employ in the introduction? Why is the introductory paragraph especially effective?

EDUCATION

5. How does the author develop his pattern of comparison and contrast in this essay? What major and minor points in the contrast does he develop?

6. How are the rhetorical strategies of narration, description, and argumentation reflected in this essay?

WRITING

1. Debate this proposition: Rural schools cannot provide the educational advantages of urban private schools.

2. Write a comparative essay on the type of school that you prefer—public or private.

3. Compare and contrast the relative advantages and disadvantages of urban and rural (or, if you wish, suburban) education.

4. In a comparative essay, examine the father-son relationship in this essay and in White's "Once More to the Lake."

MAYA ANGELOU

Graduation

Maya Angelou (1928–   ) is an American poet, playwright, television screen writer, actress, and singer. Her autobiographical books, notably I Know Why the Caged Bird Sings *(1970), from which the following selection is taken, provide one of the fullest accounts of the black female experience in contemporary literature. Fluent in six languages and active in artistic, educational, and political affairs, Angelou often presents autobiographical material against the backdrop of larger cultural concerns. In this vivid reminiscence of her 1940 graduation from grade school in Stamps, Arkansas, she provides insights into a community of young scholars who gain inspiration and wisdom from their experience during commencement ceremonies.*

he children in Stamps trembled visibly with anticipation.   1
Some adults were excited too, but to be certain the whole
young population had come down with graduation epidemic. Large classes were graduating from both the grammar school and the high school. Even those who were years removed from their own day of glorious release were anxious to help with preparations as a kind of dry run. The junior students who were

142   MAYA ANGELOU

moving into the vacating classes' chairs were tradition-bound to show their talents for leadership and management. They strutted through the school and around the campus exerting pressure on the lower grades. Their authority was so new that occasionally if they pressed a little too hard it had to be overlooked. After all, next term was coming, and it never hurt a sixth grader to have a play sister in the eighth grade, or a tenth-year student to be able to call a twelfth grader Bubba. So all was endured in a spirit of shared understanding. But the graduating classes themselves were the nobility. Like travelers with exotic destinations on their minds, the graduates were remarkably forgetful. They came to school without their books, or tablets or even pencils. Volunteers fell over themselves to secure replacements for the missing equipment. When accepted, the willing workers might or might not be thanked, and it was of no importance to the pre-graduation rites. Even teachers were respectful of the now quiet and aging seniors, and tended to speak to them, if not as equals, as beings only slightly lower than themselves. After tests were returned and grades given, the student body, which acted like an extended family, knew who did well, who excelled, and what piteous ones had failed.

Unlike the white high school, Lafayette County Training 2
School distinguished itself by having neither lawn, nor hedges, nor tennis court, nor climbing ivy. Its two buildings (main classrooms, the grade school and home economics) were set on a dirt hill with no fence to limit either its boundaries or those of bordering farms. There was a large expanse to the left of the school which was used alternately as a baseball diamond or a basketball court. Rusty hoops on the swaying poles represented the permanent recreational equipment, although bats and balls could be borrowed from the P.E. teacher if the borrower was qualified and if the diamond wasn't occupied.

Over this rocky area relieved by a few shady tall persimmon 3
trees the graduating class walked. The girls often held hands and no longer bothered to speak to the lower students. There was a sadness about them, as if this old world was not their home and they were bound for higher ground. The boys, on the other hand, had become more friendly, more outgoing. A decided change from the closed attitude they projected while studying for finals. Now they seemed not ready to give up the old school, the familiar paths and classrooms. Only a small percentage would be continuing on to college—one of the South's A & M (agricultural and mechanical) schools, which trained Negro youths to be carpenters, farmers, handymen, masons, maids, cooks and baby nurses. Their future rode heavily on their shoulders, and blinded them to the collective joy that had pervaded the lives of the boys and girls in the grammar school graduating class.

Parents who could afford it had ordered new shoes and 4
ready-made clothes for themselves from Sears and Roebuck or Mont-

gomery Ward. They also engaged the best seamstresses to make the floating graduating dresses and to cut down secondhand pants which would be pressed to a military slickness for the important event.

Oh, it was important, all right. Whitefolks would attend the ceremony, and two or three would speak of God and home, and the Southern way of life, and Mrs. Parsons, the principal's wife, would play the graduation march while the lower-grade graduates paraded down the aisles and took their seats below the platform. The high school seniors would wait in empty classrooms to make their dramatic entrance.

In the Store I was the person of the moment. The birthday girl. The center. Bailey had graduated the year before, although to do so he had had to forfeit all pleasures to make up for his time lost in Baton Rouge.

My class was wearing butter-yellow piqué dresses, and Momma launched out on mine. She smocked the yoke into tiny criss-crossing puckers, then shirred the rest of the bodice. Her dark fingers ducked in and out of the lemony cloth as she embroidered raised daisies around the hem. Before she considered herself finished she had added a crocheted cuff on the puff sleeves, and a pointy crocheted collar.

I was going to be lovely. A walking model of all the various styles of fine hand sewing and it didn't worry me that I was only twelve years old and merely graduating from the eighth grade. Besides, many teachers in Arkansas Negro schools had only that diploma and were licensed to impart wisdom.

The days had become longer and more noticeable. The faded beige of former times had been replaced with strong and sure colors. I began to see my classmate's clothes, their skin tones, and the dust that waved off pussy willows. Clouds that lazed across the sky were objects of great concern to me. Their shiftier shapes might have held a message that in my new happiness and with a little bit of time I'd soon decipher. During that period I looked at the arch of heaven so religiously my neck kept a steady ache. I had taken to smiling more often, and my jaws hurt from the unaccustomed activity. Between the two physical sore spots, I suppose I could have been uncomfortable, but that was not the case. As a member of the winning team (the graduating class of 1940) I had outdistanced unpleasant sensations by miles. I was headed for the freedom of open fields.

Youth and social approval allied themselves with me and we trammeled memories of slights and insults. The wind of our swift passage remodeled my features. Lost tears were pounded to mud and then to dust. Years of withdrawal were brushed aside and left behind, as hanging ropes of parasitic moss.

My work alone had awarded me a top place and I was going

to be one of the first called in the graduating ceremonies. On the classroom blackboard, as well as on the bulletin board in the auditorium, there were blue stars and white stars and red stars. No absences, no tardiness, and my academic work was among the best of the year. I could say the preamble to the Constitution even faster than Bailey. We timed ourselves often: "WethepeopleoftheUnitedStatesinordertoformamoreperfectunion ..." I had memorized the Presidents of the United States from Washington to Roosevelt in chronological as well as alphabetical order.

My hair pleased me too. Gradually the black mass had lengthened and thickened, so that it kept at last to its braided pattern, and I didn't have to yank my scalp off when I tried to comb it. 12

Louise and I had rehearsed the exercises until we tired out ourselves. Henry Reed was class valedictorian. He was a small, very black boy with hooded eyes, a long, broad nose and an oddly shaped head. I had admired him for years because each term he and I vied for the best grades in our class. Most often he bested me, but instead of being disappointed, I was pleased that we shared top places between us. Like many Southern black children, he lived with his grandmother, who was as strict as Momma and as kind as she knew how to be. He was courteous, respectful and softspoken to elders, but on the playground he chose to play the roughest games. I admired him. Anyone, I reckoned, sufficiently afraid or sufficiently dull could be polite. But to be able to operate at a top level with both adults and children was admirable. 13

His valedictory speech was entitled "To Be or Not to Be." The rigid tenth-grade teacher had helped him write it. He'd been working on the dramatic stresses for months. 14

The weeks until graduation were filled with heady activities. A group of small children were to be presented in a play about buttercups and daisies and bunny rabbits. They could be heard throughout the building practicing their hops and their little songs that sounded like silver bells. The older girls (non-graduates, of course) were assigned the task of making refreshments for the night's festivities. A tangy scent of ginger, cinnamon, nutmeg and chocolate wafted around the home economics building as the budding cooks made samples for themselves and their teachers. 15

In every corner of the workshop, axes and saws split fresh timber as the woodshop boys made sets and stage scenery. Only the graduates were left out of the general bustle. We were free to sit in the library at the back of the building or look in quite detachedly, naturally, on the measures being taken for our event. 16

Even the minister preached on graduation the Sunday before. His subject was, "Let your light so shine that men will see your good works and praise your Father, Who is in Heaven." Although the ser- 17

 GRADUATION

mon was purported to be addressed to us, he used the occasion to speak to backsliders, gamblers and general ne'er-do-wells. But since he had called our names at the beginning of the service we were mollified.

Among Negroes the tradition was to give presents to children 18 going only from one grade to another. How much more important this was when the person was graduating at the top of the class. Uncle Willie and Momma had sent away for a Mickey Mouse watch like Bailey's. Louise gave me four embroidered handkerchiefs. (I gave her three crocheted doilies.) Mrs. Sneed, the minister's wife, made me an underskirt to wear for graduation, and nearly every customer gave me a nickel or maybe even a dime with the instruction "Keep on moving to higher ground," or some such encouragement.

Amazingly the great day finally dawned and I was out of bed 19 before I knew it. I threw open the back door to see it more clearly, but Momma said, "Sister, come away from that door and put your robe on."

I hoped the memory of that morning would never leave me. 20 Sunlight was itself still young, and the day had none of the insistence maturity would bring it in a few hours. In my robe and barefoot in the backyard, under cover of going to see about my new beans, I gave myself up to the gentle warmth and thanked God that no matter what evil I had done in my life He had allowed me to live to see this day. Somewhere in my fatalism I had expected to die, accidentally, and never have the chance to walk up the stairs in the auditorium and gracefully receive my hard-earned diploma. Out of God's merciful bosom I had won reprieve.

Bailey came out in his robe and gave me a box wrapped in 21 Christmas paper. He said he had saved his money for months to pay for it. It felt like a box of chocolates, but I knew Bailey wouldn't save money to buy candy when we had all we could want under our noses.

He was as proud of the gift as I. It was a soft-leather-bound 22 copy of a collection of poems by Edgar Allan Poe, or, as Bailey and I called him, "Eap." I turned to "Annabel Lee" and we walked up and down the garden rows, the cool dirt between our toes, reciting the beautifully sad lines.

Momma made a Sunday breakfast although it was only Fri- 23 day. After we finished the blessing, I opened my eyes to find the watch on my plate. It was a dream of a day. Everything went smoothly and to my credit. I didn't have to be reminded or scolded for anything. Near evening I was too jittery to attend to chores, so Bailey volunteered to do all before his bath.

Days before, we had made a sign for the Store, and as we 24 turned out the lights Momma hung the cardboard over the doorknob. It read clearly: CLOSED. GRADUATION.

My dress fitted perfectly and everyone said that I looked like 25
a sunbeam in it. On the hill, going toward the school, Bailey walked
behind with Uncle Willie, who muttered, "Go on, Ju." He wanted him
to walk ahead with us because it embarrassed him to have to walk so
slowly. Bailey said he'd let the ladies walk together, and the men
would bring up the rear. We all laughed, nicely.

Little children dashed by out of the dark like fireflies. Their 26
crepe-paper dresses and butterfly wings were not made for running
and we heard more than one rip, dryly, and the regretful "uh uh"
that followed.

The school blazed without gaiety. The windows seemed cold 27
and unfriendly from the lower hill. A sense of ill-fated timing crept
over me, and if Momma hadn't reached for my hand I would have
drifted back to Bailey and Uncle Willie, and possibly beyond. She
made a few slow jokes about my feet getting cold, and tugged me
along to the now-strange building.

Around the front steps, assurance came back. There were my 28
fellow "greats," the graduating class. Hair brushed back, legs oiled,
new dresses and pressed pleats, fresh pocket handkerchiefs and little
handbags, all homesewn. Oh, we were up to snuff, all right. I joined
my comrades and didn't even see my family go in to find seats in the
crowded auditorium.

The school band struck up a march and all classes filed in as 29
had been rehearsed. We stood in front of our seats, as assigned, and
on a signal from the choir director, we sat. No sooner had this been
accomplished than the band started to play the national anthem. We
rose again and sang the song, after which we recited the pledge of
allegiance. We remained standing for a brief minute before the choir
director and the principal signaled to us, rather desperately I thought,
to take our seats. The command was so unusual that our carefully
rehearsed and smooth-running machine was thrown off. For a full
minute we fumbled for our chairs and bumped into each other awk-
wardly. Habits change or solidify under pressure, so in our state of
nervous tension we had been ready to follow our usual assembly pattern: the American national anthem, then the pledge of allegiance,
then the song every Black person I knew called the Negro National
Anthem. All done in the same key, with the same passion and most
often standing on the same foot.

Finding my seat at last, I was overcome with a presentiment 30
of worse things to come. Something unrehearsed, unplanned, was
going to happen, and we were going to be made to look bad. I distinctly remember being explicit in the choice of pronoun. It was "we,"
the graduating class, the unit, that concerned me then.

The principal welcomed "parents and friends" and asked the 31
Baptist minister to lead us in prayer. His invocation was brief and

punchy, and for a second I thought we were getting back on the high road to right action. When the principal came back to the dais, however, his voice had changed. Sounds always affected me profoundly and the principal's voice was one of my favorites. During assembly it melted and lowed weakly into the audience. It had not been in my plan to listen to him, but my curiosity was piqued and I straightened up to give him my attention.

He was talking about Booker T. Washington, our "late great 32 leader," who said we can be as close as the fingers on the hand, etc. . . . Then he said a few vague things about friendship and the friendship of kindly people to those less fortunate than themselves. With that his voice nearly faded, thin, away. Like a river diminishing to a stream and then to a trickle. But he cleared his throat and said, "Our speaker tonight, who is also our friend, came from Texarkana to deliver the commencement address, but due to the irregularity of the train schedule, he's going to, as they say, 'speak and run.' " He said that we understood and wanted the man to know that we were most grateful for the time he was able to give us and then something about how we were willing always to adjust to another's program, and without more ado—"I give you Mr. Edward Donleavy."

Not one but two white men came through the door offstage. 33 The shorter one walked to the speaker's platform, and the tall one moved over to the center seat and sat down. But that was our principal's seat, and already occupied. The dislodged gentleman bounced around for a long breath or two before the Baptist minister gave him his chair, then with more dignity than the situation deserved, the minister walked off the stage.

Donleavy looked at the audience once (on reflection, I'm sure 34 that he wanted only to reassure himself that we were really there), adjusted his glasses and began to read from a sheaf of papers.

He was glad "to be here and to see the work going on just as 35 it was in the other schools."

At the first "Amen" from the audience I willed the offender 36 to immediate death by choking on the word. But Amens and Yes, sir's began to fall around the room like rain through a ragged umbrella.

He told us of the wonderful changes we children in Stamps 37 had in store. The Central School (naturally, the white school was Central) had already been granted improvements that would be in use in the fall. A well-known artist was coming from Little Rock to teach art to them. They were going to have the newest microscopes and chemistry equipment for their laboratory. Mr. Donleavy didn't leave us long in the dark over who made these improvements available to Central High. Nor were we to be ignored in the general betterment scheme he had in mind.

He said that he had pointed out to people at a very high level 38

MAYA ANGELOU

that one of the first-line football tacklers at Arkansas Agricultural and Mechanical College had graduated from good old Lafayette County Training School. Here fewer Amens were heard. Those few that did break through lay dully in the air with the heaviness of habit.

He went on to praise us. He went on to say how he had 39 bragged that "one of the best basketball players at Fisk sank his first ball right here at Lafayette County Training School."

The white kids were going to have a chance to become Gali- 40 leos and Madame Curies and Edisons and Gauguins, and our boys (the girls weren't even in on it) would try to be Jesse Owenses and Joe Louises.

Owens and the Brown Bomber were great heroes in our 41 world, but what school official in the white-goddom of Little Rock had the right to decide that those two men must be our only heroes? Who decided that for Henry Reed to become a scientist he had to work like George Washington Carver, as a bootblack, to buy a lousy microscope? Bailey was obviously always going to be too small to be an athlete, so which concrete angel glued to what country seat had decided that if my brother wanted to become a lawyer he had to first pay penance for his skin by picking cotton and hoeing corn and studying correspondence books at night for twenty years?

The man's dead words fell like bricks around the auditorium 42 and too many settled in my belly. Constrained by hard-learned manners I couldn't look behind me, but to my left and right the proud graduating class of 1940 had dropped their heads. Every girl in my row had found something new to do with her handkerchief. Some folded the tiny squares into love knots, some into triangles, but most were wadding them, then pressing them flat on their yellow laps.

On the dais, the ancient tragedy was being replayed. Professor 43 Parsons sat, a sculptor's reject, rigid. His large, heavy body seemed devoid of will or willingness, and his eyes said he was no longer with us. The other teachers examined the flag (which was draped stage right) or their notes, or the windows which opened on our now-famous playing diamond.

Graduation, the hush-hush magic time of frills and gifts and 44 congratulations and diplomas, was finished for me before my name was called. The accomplishment was nothing. The meticulous maps, drawn in three colors of ink, learning, and spelling decasyllabic words, memorizing the whole of *The Rape of Lucrece*—it was for nothing. Donleavy had exposed us.

We were maids and farmers, handymen and washerwomen, 45 and anything higher that we aspired to was farcical and presumptuous.

Then I wished that Gabriel Prosser and Nat Turner had killed 46 all whitefolks in their beds and that Abraham Lincoln had been assassinated before the signing of the Emancipation Proclamation, and that Harriet Tubman had been killed by that blow on her head and Christopher Columbus had drowned in the *Santa Maria*.

It was awful to be Negro and have no control over my life. It was brutal to be young and already trained to sit quietly and listen to charges brought against my color with no chance of defense. We should all be dead. I thought I should like to see us all dead, one on top of the other. A pyramid of flesh with the whitefolks on the bottom, as the broad base, then the Indians with their silly tomahawks and tepees and wigwams and treaties, the Negroes with their mops and recipes and cotton sacks and spirituals sticking out of their mouths. The Dutch children should all stumble in their wooden shoes and break their necks. The French should choke to death on the Louisiana Purchase (1803) while silkworms ate all the Chinese with their stupid pigtails. As a species, we were an abomination. All of us. 47

Donleavy was running for election, and assured our parents that if he won we could count on having the only colored paved playing field in that part of Arkansas. Also—he never looked up to acknowledge the grunts of acceptance—also, we were bound to get some new equipment for the home economics building and the workshop. 48

He finished, and since there was no need to give any more than the most perfunctory thank-you's, he nodded to the men on the stage, and the tall white man who was never introduced joined him at the door. They left with the attitude that now they were off to something really important. (The graduation ceremonies at Lafayette County Training School had been a mere preliminary.) 49

The ugliness they left was palpable. An uninvited guest who wouldn't leave. The choir was summoned and sang a modern arrangement of "Onward, Christian Soldiers," with new words pertaining to graduates seeking their place in the world. But it didn't work. Elouise, the daughter of the Baptist minister, recited "Invictus," and I could have cried at the impertinence of "I am the master of my fate, I am the captain of my soul." 50

My name had lost its ring of familiarity and I had to be nudged to go and receive my diploma. All my preparations had fled. I neither marched up to the stage like a conquering Amazon, nor did I look in the audience for Bailey's nod of approval. Marguerite Johnson, I heard the name again, my honors were read, there were noises in the audience of appreciation, and I took my place on the stage as rehearsed. 51

I thought about colors I hated: ecru, puce, lavender, beige and black. 52

There was shuffling and rustling around me, then Henry Reed was giving his valedictory address, "To Be or Not to Be." Hadn't he 53 heard the whitefolks? We couldn't *be* so the question was a waste of time. Henry's voice came clear and strong. I feared to look at him. Hadn't he got the message? There was no "nobler in the mind" for Negroes because the world didn't think we had minds, and they let us know it. "Outrageous fortune"? Now, that was a joke. When the ceremony was over I had to tell Henry Reed some things. That is, if I still cared. Not "rub," Henry, "erase." "Ah, there's the erase." Us.

Henry had been a good student in elocution. His voice rose   54 on tides of promise and fell on waves of warnings. The English teacher had helped him to create a sermon winging through Hamlet's soliloquy. To be a man, a doer, a builder, a leader, or to be a tool, an unfunny joke, a crusher of funky toadstools, I marveled that Henry could go through the speech as if we had a choice.

I had been listening and silently rebutting each sentence with   55 my eyes closed; then there was a hush, which in an audience warns that something unplanned is happening. I looked up and saw Henry Reed, the conservative, the proper, the A student, turn his back to the audience and turn to us (the proud graduating class of 1940) and sing, nearly speaking,

> "Lift ev'ry voice and sing
> Till earth and heaven ring
> Ring with the harmonies of Liberty . . ."

It was the poem written by James Weldon Johnson. It was the music composed by J. Rosamond Johnson. It was the Negro national anthem. Out of habit we were singing it.

Our mothers and fathers stood in the dark hall and joined the   56 hymn of encouragement. A kindergarten teacher led the small children onto the stage and the buttercups and daisies and bunny rabbits marked time and tried to follow:

> "Stony the road we trod
> Bitter the chastening rod
> Felt in the days when hope, unborn, had died.
> Yet with a steady beat
> Have not our weary feet
> Come to the place for which our father sighed?"

Every child I knew had learned that song with his ABC's and   57 along with "Jesus Loves Me This I Know." But I personally had never heard it before. Never heard the words, despite the thousands of times I had sung them. Never thought they had anything to do with me.

On the other hand, the words of Patrick Henry had made such   58 an impression on me that I had been able to stretch myself tall and trembling and say, "I know not what course others may take, but as for me, give me liberty or give me death."

And now I heard, really for the first time:

59

"We have come over a way that with tears has been watered,
We have come, treading our path through the blood of the slaughtered."

While echoes of the song shivered in the air, Henry Reed bowed his head, said "Thank you," and returned to his place in the line. The tears that slipped down many faces were not wiped away in shame.

60

We were on top again. As always, again. We survived. The depths had been icy and dark, but now a bright sun spoke to our souls. I was no longer simply a member of the proud graduating class of 1940; I was a proud member of the wonderful beautiful Negro race.

61

COMPREHENSION

1. Is Angelou a neutral observer or subjective participant in the events of this narrative? How can you tell?

2. How is the author's "presentiment of worse things to come" actually borne out? What is the "ancient tragedy" alluded to? How, specifically, does education relate to this allusion?

3. What do you learn about Marguerite—the young Maya Angelou—from this essay? What are her moods, emotions, thoughts, and attitudes? In what way is she "bound for higher ground"?

RHETORIC

1. Angelou is a highly impressionistic stylist in this essay. Provide examples of details that create vivid descriptive impressions. How do these details control the shifting moods of the selection?

2. Explain Angelou's allusions to *The Rape of Lucrece,* Gabriel Prosser and Nat Turner, Harriet Tubman, and "Invictus." How are these allusions and others related to the thesis? State that thesis in your own words.

3. What is the purpose of the relatively long five-paragraph introduction? What contrasts and latent ironies do you detect?

4. Cite examples of the author's ability to blend description, narration, and exposition. At what points is the expository mode the strongest? What is Angelou's purpose?

5. Why are the descriptions of Henry Reed and Donleavy juxtaposed?

6. Which paragraphs constitute the conclusion? How does Angelou achieve the transition from the body to the end?

WRITING

1. To what extent does American education still try to "track" students? What are the implications of such tracking? Discuss this issue in an essay; be certain to provide appropriate evidence.

2. Reconstruct your own graduation from grade school or high school.

3. Analyze and evaluate the many strategies that Angelou employs to honor and celebrate black culture and black wisdom in this essay.

RICHARD WRIGHT

The Library Card

Richard Wright (1908–1960), an American author, spoke eloquently about the racial experience in America in his novels and essays. Wright was born on a Mississippi plantation. As a young man he moved to Chicago, where he joined a Federal Writers Project in the 1930s. His experiences in Mississippi and Chicago appear in his early fiction: Uncle Tom's Children *(1938), about racial oppression in the South, and* Native Son *(1940), about discrimination and exploitation in Chicago during the Depression. Wright became an expatriate after World War II. From Paris, he wrote an autobiography,* Black Boy *(1945), and two novels,* The Outsider *(1953) and* The Long Dream *(1958), among other works. This story, an excerpt from* Black Boy, *describes a turning point in Wright's intellectual development.*

 ne morning I arrived early at work and went into the bank lobby where the Negro porter was mopping. I stood at a counter and picked up the Memphis *Commercial Appeal* and began my free reading of the press. I came finally to the editorial page and saw an article dealing with one H. L. Mencken. I knew by hearsay that he was the editor of the *American Mercury*, but aside from that I knew nothing about him. The article was a furious denunciation of Mencken, concluding with one hot, short sentence: Mencken is a fool.

I wondered what on earth this Mencken had done to call down upon him the scorn of the South. The only people I had ever heard denounced in the South were Negroes, and this man was not a Negro. Then what ideas did Mencken hold that made a newspaper like the *Commercial Appeal* castigate him publicly? Undoubtedly he must be advocating ideas that the South did not like. Were there, then, people other than Negroes who criticized the South? I knew that during the Civil War the South had hated northern whites, but I had not encountered such hate during my life. Knowing no more of Mencken than I did at that moment, I felt a vague sympathy for him. Had not the South, which had assigned me the role of a non-man, cast at him its hardest words?

Now, how could I find out about this Mencken? There was a   3
huge library near the riverfront, but I knew that Negroes were not allowed to patronize its shelves any more than they were the parks and playgrounds of the city. I had gone into the library several times to get books for the white men on the job. Which of them would now help me to get books? And how could I read them without causing concern to the white men with whom I worked? I had so far been successful in hiding my thoughts and feelings from them, but I knew that I would create hostility if I went about this business of reading in a clumsy way.

I weighed the personalities of the men on the job. There was   4
Don, a Jew; but I distrusted him. His position was not much better than mine and I knew that he was uneasy and insecure; he had always treated me in an offhand, bantering way that barely concealed his contempt. I was afraid to ask him to help me to get books; his frantic desire to demonstrate a racial solidarity with the whites against Negroes might make him betray me.

Then how about the boss? No, he was a Baptist and I had the   5
suspicion that he would not be quite able to comprehend why a black boy would want to read Mencken. There were other white men on the job whose attitudes showed clearly that they were Kluxers or sympathizers, and they were out of the question.

There remained only one man whose attitude did not fit into   6
an anti-Negro category, for I had heard the white men refer to him as a "Pope lover." He was an Irish Catholic and was hated by the white Southerners. I knew that he read books, because I had got him volumes from the library several times. Since he, too, was an object of hatred, I felt that he might refuse me but would hardly betray me. I hesitated, weighing and balancing the imponderable realities.

One morning I paused before the Catholic fellow's desk.   7
"I want to ask you a favor," I whispered to him.   8
"What is it?"   9
"I want to read. I can't get books from the library. I wonder   10
if you'd let me use your card?"
He looked at me suspiciously.   11

       RICHARD WRIGHT

"My card is full most of the time," he said. 12

"I see," I said and waited, posing my question silently. 13

"You're not trying to get me into trouble, are you, boy?" he 14
asked, staring at me.

"Oh, no, sir." 15

"What book do you want?" 16

"A book by H. L. Mencken." 17

"Which one?" 18

"I don't know. Has he written more than one?" 19

"He has written several." 20

"I didn't know that." 21

"What makes you want to read Mencken?" 22

"Oh, I just saw his name in the newspaper," I said. 23

"It's good of you to want to read," he said. "But you ought 24
to read the right things."

I said nothing. Would he want to supervise my reading? 25

"Let me think," he said. "I'll figure out something." 26

I turned from him and he called me back. He stared at me 27
quizzically.

"Richard, don't mention this to the other white men," he said. 28

"I understand," I said. "I won't say a word." 29

A few days later he called me to him. 30

"I've got a card in my wife's name," he said. "Here's mine." 31

"Thank you, sir." 32

"Do you think you can manage it?" 33

"I'll manage fine," I said. 34

"If they suspect you, you'll get in trouble," he said. 35

"I'll write the same kind of notes to the library that you wrote 36
when you sent me for books," I told him. "I'll sign your name."

He laughed. 37

"Go ahead. Let me see what you get," he said. 38

That afternoon I addressed myself to forging a note. Now, 39
what were the names of books written by H. L. Mencken? I did not
know any of them. I finally wrote what I thought would be a foolproof
note: *Dear Madam: Will you please let this nigger boy*—I used the word
"nigger" to make the librarian feel that I could not possibly be the
author of the note—*have some books by H. L. Mencken?* I forged the
white man's name.

I entered the library as I had always done when on errands 40
for whites, but I felt that I would somehow slip up and betray myself.
I doffed my hat, stood a respectful distance from the desk, looked as
unbookish as possible, and waited for the white patrons to be taken
care of. When the desk was clear of people, I still waited. The white
librarian looked at me.

"What do you want, boy?" 41

As though I did not possess the power of speech, I stepped 42
forward and simply handed her the forged note, not parting my lips.

"What books by Mencken does he want?" she asked. 43

"I don't know, ma'am," I said, avoiding her eyes. 44

"Who gave you this card?" 45

"Mr. Falk," I said. 46

"Where is he?" 47

"He's at work, at the M—Optical Company," I said. "I've 48
been in here for him before."

"I remember," the woman said. "But he never wrote notes 49
like this."

Oh, God, she's suspicious. Perhaps she would not let me have 50
the books? If she had turned her back at that moment, I would have
ducked out the door and never gone back. Then I thought of a bold
idea.

"You can call him up, ma'am," I said, my heart pounding. 51

"You're not using these books, are you?" she asked pointedly. 52

"Oh, no, ma'am. I can't read." 53

"I don't know what he wants by Mencken," she said under 54
her breath.

I knew now that I had won; she was thinking of other things 55
and the race question had gone out of her mind. She went to the
shelves. Once or twice she looked over her shoulder at me, as though
she was still doubtful. Finally she came forward with two books in
her hand.

"I'm sending him two books," she said. "But tell Mr. Falk to 56
come in next time, or send me the names of the books he wants. I
don't know what he wants to read."

I said nothing. She stamped the card and handed me the 57
books. Not daring to glance at them, I went out of the library, fearing
that the woman would call me back for further questioning. A block
away from the library I opened one of the books and read a title: *A
Book of Prefaces*. I was nearing my nineteenth birthday and I did not
know how to pronounce the word "preface." I thumbed the pages
and saw strange words and strange names. I shook my head, disappointed. I looked at the other book; it was called *Prejudices*. I knew
what that word meant; I had heard it all my life. And right off I was
on guard against Mencken's books. Why would a man want to call a
book *Prejudices*? The word was so stained with all my memories of
racial hate that I could not conceive of anybody using it for a title.
Perhaps I had made a mistake about Mencken? A man who had prejudices must be wrong.

When I showed the books to Mr. Falk, he looked at me and 58
frowned.

"That librarian might telephone you," I warned him. 59

"That's all right," he said. "But when you're through reading 60
those books, I want you to tell me what you get out of them."

That night in my rented room, while letting the hot water run 61
over my can of pork and beans in the sink, I opened *A Book of Prefaces*
and began to read. I was jarred and shocked by the style, the clear,
clean, sweeping sentences. Why did he write like that? And how did
one write like that? I pictured the man as a raging demon, slashing
with his pen, consumed with hate, denouncing everything American,
extolling everything European or German, laughing at the weaknesses
of people, mocking God, authority. What was this? I stood up, trying
to realize what reality lay behind the meaning of the words . . . Yes,
this man was fighting, fighting with words. He was using words as a
weapon, using them as one would use a club. Could words be weapons? Well, yes, for here they were. Then, maybe, perhaps, I could use
them as a weapon? No. It frightened me. I read on and what amazed
me was not what he said, but how on earth anybody had the courage
to say it.

Occasionally I glanced up to reassure myself that I was alone 62
in the room. Who were these men about whom Mencken was talking
so passionately? Who was Anatole France? Joseph Conrad? Sinclair
Lewis, Sherwood Anderson, Dostoevski, George Moore, Gustave
Flaubert, Maupassant, Tolstoy, Frank Harris, Mark Twain, Thomas
Hardy, Arnold Bennett, Stephen Crane, Zola, Norris, Gorky, Bergson,
Ibsen, Balzac, Bernard Shaw, Dumas, Poe, Thomas Mann, O. Henry,
Dreiser, H. G. Wells, Gogol, T. S. Eliot, Gide, Baudelaire, Edgar Lee
Masters, Stendhal, Turgenev, Hunekar, Nietzsche, and scores of oth-
ers? Were these men real? Did they exist or had they existed? And
how did one pronounce their names?

I ran across many words whose meanings I did not know, 63
and I either looked them up in a dictionary or, before I had a chance
to do that, encountered the word in a context that made its meaning
clear. But what strange world was this? I concluded the book with the
conviction that I had somehow overlooked something terribly important in life. I had once tried to write, had once reveled in feeling, had
let my crude imagination roam, but the impulse to dream had been
slowly beaten out of me by experience. Now it surged up again and
I hungered for books, new ways of looking and seeing. It was not a
matter of believing or disbelieving what I read, but of feeling something new, of being affected by something that made the look of the
world different.

As dawn broke I ate my pork and beans, feeling dopey, 64
sleepy. I went to work, but the mood of the book would not die; it
lingered, coloring everything I saw, heard, did. I now felt that I knew
what the white men were feeling. Merely because I had read a book
that had spoken of how they lived and thought, I identified myself

with that book. I felt vaguely guilty. Would I, filled with bookish notions, act in a manner that would make the whites dislike me?

I forged more notes and my trips to the library became fre- 65 quent. Reading grew into a passion. My first serious novel was Sinclair Lewis's *Main Street*. It made me see my boss, Mr. Gerald, and identify him as an American type. I would smile when I saw him lugging his golf bags into the office. I had always felt a vast distance separating me from the boss, and now I felt closer to him, though still distant. I felt now that I knew him, that I could feel the very limits of his narrow life. And this had happened because I had read a novel about a mythical man called George F. Babbitt.

The plots and stories in the novels did not interest me so much 66 as the point of view revealed. I gave myself over to each novel without reserve, without trying to criticize it; it was enough for me to see and feel something different. And for me, everything was something different. Reading was like a drug, a dope. The novels created moods in which I lived for days. But I could not conquer my sense of guilt, my feeling that the white men around me knew that I was changing, that I had begun to regard them differently.

Whenever I brought a book to the job, I wrapped it in news- 67 paper—a habit that was to persist for years in other cities and under other circumstances. But some of the white men pried into my packages when I was absent and they questioned me.

"Boy, what are you reading those books for?" 68

"Oh, I don't know, sir." 69

"That's deep stuff you're reading, boy." 70

"I'm just killing time, sir." 71

"You'll addle your brains if you don't watch out." 72

I read Dreiser's *Jennie Gerhardt* and *Sister Carrie* and they re- 73 vived in me a vivid sense of my mother's suffering; I was overwhelmed. I grew silent, wondering about the life around me. It would have been impossible for me to have told anyone what I derived from these novels, for it was nothing less than a sense of life itself. All my life had shaped me for the realism, the naturalism of the modern novel, and I could not read enough of them.

Steeped in new moods and ideas, I bought a ream of paper 74 and tried to write; but nothing would come, or what did come was flat beyond telling. I discovered that more than desire and feeling were necessary to write and I dropped the idea. Yet I still wondered how it was possible to know people sufficiently to write about them? Could I ever learn about life and people? To me, with my vast ignorance, my Jim Crow station in life, it seemed a task impossible of achievement. I now knew what being a Negro meant. I could endure the hunger. I had learned to live with hate. But to feel that there were feelings denied me, that the very breath of life itself was beyond my

RICHARD WRIGHT

reach, that more than anything else hurt, wounded me. I had a new hunger.

In buoying me up, reading also cast me down, made me see 75 what was possible, what I had missed. My tension returned, new, terrible, bitter, surging, almost too great to be contained. I no longer *felt* that the world about me was hostile, killing; I *knew* it. A million times I asked myself what I could do to save myself, and there were no answers. I seemed forever condemned, ringed by walls.

I did not discuss my reading with Mr. Falk, who had lent me 76 his library card; it would have meant talking about myself and that would have been too painful. I smiled each day, fighting desperately to maintain my old behavior, to keep my disposition seemingly sunny. But some of the white men discerned that I had begun to brood.

"Wake up there, boy!" Mr. Olin said one day. 77

"Sir!" I answered for the lack of a better word. 78

"You act like you've stolen something," he said. 79

I laughed in the way I knew he expected me to laugh, but I 80 resolved to be more conscious of myself, to watch my every act, to guard and hide the new knowledge that was dawning within me.

If I went north, would it be possible for me to build a new 81 life then? But how could a man build a life upon vague, unformed yearnings? I wanted to write and I did not even know the English language. I bought English grammars and found them dull. I felt that I was getting a better sense of the language from novels than from grammars. I read hard, discarding a writer as soon as I felt that I had grasped his point of view. At night the printed page stood before my eyes in sleep.

Mrs. Moss, my landlady, asked me one Sunday morning: 82 "Son, what is this you keep on reading?"

"Oh, nothing. Just novels." 83

"What you get out of 'em?" 84

"I'm just killing time," I said. 85

"I hope you know your own mind," she said in a tone which 86 implied that she doubted if I had a mind.

I knew of no Negroes who read the books I liked and I won- 87 dered if any Negroes ever thought of them. I knew that there were Negro doctors, lawyers, newspapermen, but I never saw any of them. When I read a Negro newspaper I never caught the faintest echo of my preoccupation in its pages. I felt trapped and occasionally, for a few days, I would stop reading. But a vague hunger would come over me for books, books that opened up new avenues of feeling and seeing, and again I would forge another note to the white librarian. Again I would read and wonder as only the naïve and unlettered can read and wonder, feeling that I carried a secret, criminal burden about with me each day.

That winter my mother and brother came and we set up   88
housekeeping, buying furniture on the installment plan, being cheated
and yet knowing no way to avoid it. I began to eat warm food and
to my surprise found that regular meals enabled me to read faster. I
may have lived through many illnesses and survived them, never suspecting that I was ill. My brother obtained a job and we began to save
toward the trip north, plotting our time, setting tentative dates for
departure. I told none of the white men on the job that I was planning
to go north; I knew that the moment they felt I was thinking of the
North they would change toward me. It would have made them feel
that I did not like the life I was living, and because my life was completely conditioned by what they said or did, it would have been
tantamount to challenging them.

I could calculate my chances for life in the South as a Negro   89
fairly clearly now.

I could fight the southern whites by organizing with other   90
Negroes, as my grandfather had done. But I knew that I could never
win that way; there were many whites and there were but few blacks.
They were strong and we were weak. Outright black rebellion could
never win. If I fought openly I would die and I did not want to die.
News of lynchings were frequent.

I could submit and live the life of a genial slave, but that was   91
impossible. All of my life had shaped me to live by my own feelings
and thoughts. I could make up to Bess and marry her and inherit the
house. But that, too, would be the life of a slave; if I did that, I would
crush to death something within me, and I would hate myself as much
as I knew the whites already hated those who had submitted. Neither
could I ever willingly present myself to be kicked, as Shorty had done.
I would rather have died than do that.

I could drain off my restlessness by fighting with Shorty and   92
Harrison. I had seen many Negroes solve the problem of being black
by transferring their hatred of themselves to others with a black skin
and fighting them. I would have to be cold to do that, and I was not
cold and I could never be.

I could, of course, forget what I had read, thrust the whites   93
out of my mind, forget them; and find release from anxiety and longing in sex and alcohol. But the memory of how my father had conducted himself made that course repugnant. If I did not want others
to violate my life, how could I voluntarily violate it myself?

I had no hope whatever of being a professional man. Not only   94
had I been so conditioned that I did not desire it, but the fulfillment
of such an ambition was beyond my capabilities. Well-to-do Negroes
lived in a world that was almost as alien to me as the world inhabited
by whites.

What, then, was there? I held my life in my mind, in my   95

RICHARD WRIGHT

consciousness each day, feeling at times that I would stumble and drop it, spill it forever. My reading had created a vast sense of distance between me and the world in which I lived and tried to make a living, and that sense of distance was increasing each day. My days and nights were one long, quiet, continuously contained dream of terror, tension, and anxiety. I wondered how long I could bear it.

COMPREHENSION

1. Point out the main episodes in this narrative. What is Wright's purpose in offering readers these episodes?

2. How do books function as the catalyst for the narrator's transformation in this selection? Characterize this transformation. How does the transformation resemble Angelou's in "Graduation"?

3. When does the narrator begin to "hunger for books"? What is "the new hunger" (paragraph 74) that replaces it?

RHETORIC

1. Use an encyclopedia to look up the term "Jim Crow." What does it mean? How does the spirit of Jim Crow infuse the tone of this selection?

2. Define the following words: *castigate* (paragraph 2); *solidarity* (paragraph 4); *doffed* (paragraph 40); and *tantamount* (paragraph 88). Overall, how would you characterize the level of language in this piece?

3. How is the style of paragraphs 1 to 54 different from that of paragraphs 55 to 95? What change in the narrator does this change in style reflect?

4. What impact does the extensive use of dialogue have on the reader?

5. How does Wright break this selection up into specific events? What events are described? What patterns emerge?

6. To what extent is Wright being polemical in this selection? Cite examples to support your response.

WRITING

1. In light of the changes that occur in the main character, was his decision to read entirely positive? In what ways is he worse off? What new burden has he taken on? In an essay, examine the positive and negative results of Wright's experience.

2. Write an essay on the importance of books in a person's education and life.

3. Write an essay in which you compare and contrast the educations of Richard Wright and Maya Angelou.

THE LIBRARY CARD

A Liberal Education

Thomas Henry Huxley (1825–1895) was one of the nineteenth century's most brilliant adventurers, educators, polemicists, and scientists. He defended Charles Darwin's theory of evolution to an often hostile English scientific community. He reformed the organization of the English elementary school. He labored incessantly to explain science to Britain's middle and working classes. Most of Huxley's works were republished in his Collected Essays *(nine volumes, 1894–1908). In this essay, Huxley employs striking allusions, metaphors, and analogies to explain the essence of a liberal education.*

1 Suppose it were perfectly certain that the life and fortune of every one of us would, one day or other, depend upon his winning or losing a game of chess. Don't you think that we should all consider it to be a primary duty to learn at least the names and the moves of the pieces; to have a notion of a gambit, and a keen eye for all the means of giving and getting out of check? Do you not think that we should look with a disapprobation amounting to scorn, upon the father who allowed his son, or the state which allowed its members, to grow up without knowing a pawn from a knight?

2 Yet it is a very plain and elementary truth, that the life, the fortune, and the happiness of every one of us, and, more or less, of those who are connected with us, do depend upon our knowing something of the rules of a game infinitely more difficult and complicated than chess. It is a game which has been played for untold ages, every man and woman of us being one of the two players in a game of his or her own. The chessboard is the world, the pieces are the phenomena of the universe, the rules of the game are what we call the laws of Nature. The player on the other side is hidden from us. We know that his play is always fair, just, and patient. But also we know, to our cost, that he never overlooks a mistake, or makes the smallest allowance for ignorance. To the man who plays well, the highest stakes are paid, with that sort of overflowing generosity with which the strong shows delight in strength. And one who plays ill is check-mated—without haste, but without remorse.

3 My metaphor will remind some of you of the famous picture in which Retzsch has depicted Satan playing at chess with man for his soul. Substitute for the mocking fiend in that picture, a calm, strong angel who is playing for love, as we say, and would rather lose than win—and I should accept it as an image of human life.

Well, what I mean by Education is learning the rules of this mighty game. In other words, education is the instruction of the intellect in the laws of Nature, under which name I include not merely things and their forces, but men and their ways; and the fashioning of the affections and of the will into an earnest and loving desire to move in harmony with those laws. For me education means neither more nor less than this. Anything which professes to call itself education must be tried by this standard, and if it fails to stand the test, I will not call it education, whatever may be the force of authority, or of numbers, upon the other side.

It is important to remember that, in strictness, there is no such thing as an uneducated man. Take an extreme case. Suppose that an adult man, in the full vigor of his faculties, could be suddenly placed in the world, as Adam is said to have been, and then left to do as he best might. How long would he be left uneducated? Not five minutes. Nature would begin to teach him, through the eye, the ear, the touch, the properties of objects. Pain and pleasure would be at his elbow telling him to do this and avoid that; and by slow degrees the man would receive an education, which, if narrow, would be thorough, real, and adequate to his circumstances, though there would be no extras and very few accomplishments.

And if to this solitary man entered a second Adam, or better still, an Eve, a new and greater world, that of social and moral phenomena, would be revealed. Joys and woes, compared with which all others might seem but faint shadows, would spring from the new relations. Happiness and sorrow would take the place of the coarser monitors, pleasure and pain; but conduct would still be shaped by the observation of the natural consequences of actions; or, in other words, by the laws of the nature of man.

To every one of us the world was once as fresh and new as to Adam. And then, long before we were susceptible of any other mode of instruction, Nature took us in hand, and every minute of waking life brought its educational influence, shaping our actions into rough accordance with Nature's laws, so that we might not be ended untimely by too gross disobedience. Nor should I speak of this process of education as past for any one, be he as old as he may. For every man the world is as fresh as it was at the first day, and as full of untold novelties for him who has the eyes to see them. And Nature is still continuing her patient education of us in that great university, the universe, of which we are all members—Nature having no Test Acts.

Those who take honors in Nature's university, who learn the laws which govern men and things and obey them, are the really great and successful men in this world. The great mass of mankind are the "Poll," who pick up just enough to get through without much discredit. Those who won't learn at all are plucked; and then you can't come up again. Nature's pluck means extermination.

Thus the question of compulsory education is settled so far as 9 Nature is concerned. Her bill on that question was framed and passed long ago. But, like all compulsory legislation, that of Nature is harsh and wasteful in its operation. Ignorance is visited as sharply as willful disobedience—incapacity meets with the same punishment as crime. Nature's discipline is not even a word and a blow, and the blow first; but the blow without the word. It is left to you to find out why your ears are boxed.

The object of what we commonly call education—that edu- 10 cation in which man intervenes and which I shall distinguish as artificial education—is to make good these defects in Nature's methods; to prepare the child to receive Nature's education, neither incapably nor ignorantly, nor with willful disobedience; and to understand the preliminary symptoms of her displeasure, without waiting for the box on the ear. In short, all artificial education ought to be an anticipation of natural education. And a liberal education is an artificial education, which has not only prepared a man to escape the great evils of disobedience to natural laws, but has trained him to appreciate and to seize upon the rewards, which Nature scatters with as free a hand as her penalties.

That man, I think, has had a liberal education, who has been 11 so trained in youth that his body is the ready servant of his will, and does with ease and pleasure all the work that, as a mechanism, it is capable of; whose intellect is a clear, cold, logic engine, with all its parts of equal strength, and in smooth working order; ready, like a steam engine, to be turned to any kind of work, and spin the gossamers as well as forge the anchors of the mind; whose mind is stored with a knowledge of the great and fundamental truths of Nature and of the laws of her operations; one who, no stunted ascetic, is full of life and fire, but whose passions are trained to come to heel by a vigorous will, the servant of a tender conscience; who has learned to love all beauty, whether of Nature or of art, to hate all vileness, and to respect others as himself.

Such a one and no other, I conceive, has had a liberal edu- 12 cation; for he is, as completely as a man can be, in harmony with Nature. He will make the best of her, and she of him. They will get on together rarely; she as his ever beneficent mother; he as her mouthpiece, her conscious self, her minister and interpreter.

COMPREHENSION

1. In which paragraphs do you find these purposes: illustration, explanation, exhortation? What is the main idea that Huxley wants to convey to his audience?

T. H. HUXLEY

2. What is the main analogy in this essay? What concept does it explain? Define that concept in your own words.

3. According to the author, what is the relationship of mature people to Adam and Eve?

RHETORIC
1. Does the author's use of analogy make his language more concrete or abstract? Explain.

2. In addition to analogy, what figurative language does Huxley employ, and for what purpose?

3. Exactly how does the author use analogy to structure this essay? Does he use a single analogy or multiple ones? Explain.

4. In what way is the author's essay a definition of "liberal education"?

5. How does the author use examples in the essay?

6. Of what value is Huxley's use of the pronouns *I, we,* and *us* in this essay?

WRITING
1. Huxley speaks of taking "honors in Nature's university." What does Nature have to do with a liberal education? Why, do you think, would Huxley have based his definitions of a liberal education on the laws of nature? Write an analytical essay on this topic.

2. Write your own definition of a liberal education.

3. Use an analogy to explain what Nature can teach us. Try to avoid sentimentality in handling this topic.

4. Explain how either Maya Angelou in "Graduation" or Richard Wright in "The Library Card" obtained a liberal education.

SANTHA RAMA RAU

By Any Other Name

Santha Rama Rau (1923–   ) is an Indian novelist and essayist who throughout her career has interpreted the Eastern experience for Western audiences. She is a gifted travel writer and memorist. Her principal works include Home to India *(1944),* Remember the House *(1955), and* Gifts of Passage *(1961). This narrative essay sensitively portrays the conflict in cultures perceived by the author in her early childhood.*

t the Anglo-Indian day school in Zorinabad to which my sister and I were sent when she was eight and I was five and a half, they changed our names. On the first day of school, a hot, windless morning of a north Indian September, we stood in the headmistress's study and she said, "Now you're the *new* girls. What are your names?"

My sister answered for us. "I am Premila, and she"—nodding in my direction—"is Santha."

The headmistress had been in India, I suppose, fifteen years or so, but she still smiled her helpless inability to cope with Indian names. Her rimless half-glasses glittered, and the precarious bun on top of her head trembled as she shook her head. "Oh, my dears, those are much too hard for me. Suppose we give you pretty English names. Wouldn't that be more jolly? Let's see, now—Pamela for you, I think." She shrugged in a baffled way at my sister. "That's as close as I can get. And for *you*," she said to me, "how about Cynthia? Isn't that nice?"

My sister was always less easily intimidated than I was, and while she kept a stubborn silence, I said, "Thank you," in a very tiny voice.

We had been sent to that school because my father, among his responsibilities as an officer of the civil service, had a tour of duty to perform in the villages around that steamy little provincial town, where he had his headquarters at that time. He used to make his shorter inspection tours on horseback, and a week before, in the stale heat of a typically postmonsoon day, we had waved good-by to him and a little procession—an assistant, a secretary, two bearers, and the man to look after the bedding rolls and luggage. They rode away through our large garden, still bright green from the rains, and we turned back into the twilight of the house and the sound of fans whispering in every room.

Up to then, my mother had refused to send Premila to school in the British-run establishments of that time, because, she used to say, "you can bury a dog's tail for seven years and it still comes out curly, and you can take a Britisher away from his home for a lifetime, and he still remains insular." The examinations and degrees from entirely Indian schools were not, in those days, considered valid. In my case, the question had never come up, and probably never would have come up if Mother's extraordinary good health had not broken down. For the first time in my life, she was not able to continue the lessons she had been giving us every morning. So our Hindi books were put away, the stories of the Lord Krishna as a little boy were left in mid-air, and we were sent to the Anglo-Indian school.

That first day at school is still, when I think of it, a remarkable one. At that age, if one's name is changed, one develops a curious form of dual personality. I remember having a certain detached and disbelieving concern in the actions of "Cynthia," but certainly no responsibility. Accordingly, I followed the thin, erect back of the headmistress down the veranda to my classroom feeling, at most, a passing interest in what was going to happen to me in this strange, new atmosphere of School.

The building was Indian in design, with wide verandas opening onto a central courtyard, but Indian verandas are usually whitewashed, with stone floors. These, in the tradition of British schools, were painted dark brown and had matting on the floors. It gave a feeling of extra intensity to the heat. 8

I suppose there were about a dozen Indian children in the school—which contained perhaps forty children in all—and four of them were in my class. They were all sitting at the back of the room, and I went to join them. I sat next to a small, solemn girl who didn't smile at me. She had long, glossy-black braids and wore a cotton dress, but she still kept on her Indian jewelry—a gold chain around her neck, thin gold bracelets, and tiny ruby studs in her ears. Like most Indian children, she had a rim of black kohl around her eyes. The cotton dress should have looked strange, but all I could think of was that I should ask my mother if I couldn't wear a dress to school, too, instead of my Indian clothes. 9

I can't remember too much about the proceedings in class that day, except for the beginning. The teacher pointed to me and asked me to stand up. "Now, dear, tell the class your name." 10

I said nothing. 11

"Come along," she said frowning slightly. "What's your name, dear?" 12

"I don't know," I said, finally. 13

The English children in the front of the class—there were about eight or ten of them—giggled and twisted around in their chairs to look at me. I sat down quickly and opened my eyes very wide, hoping in that way to dry them off. The little girl with the braids put out her hand and very lightly touched my arm. She still didn't smile. 14

Most of that morning I was rather bored. I looked briefly at the children's drawings pinned to the wall, and then concentrated on a lizard clinging to the ledge of the high, barred window behind the teacher's head. Occasionally it would shoot out its long yellow tongue for a fly, and then it would rest, with its eyes closed and its belly palpitating, as though it were swallowing several times quickly. The lessons were mostly concerned with reading and writing and simple numbers—things that my mother had already taught me—and I paid very little attention. The teacher wrote on the easel blackboard words like "bat" and "cat," which seemed babyish to me; only "apple" was new and incomprehensible. 15

When it was time for the lunch recess, I followed the girl with braids out onto the veranda. There the children from the other classes were assembled. I saw Premila at once and ran over to her, as she had charge of our lunchbox. The children were all opening packages and sitting down to eat sandwiches. Premila and I were the only ones who had Indian food—thin wheat chapatties, some vegetable curry, and a bottle of buttermilk. Premila thrust half of it into my hand and whispered fiercely that I should go and sit with my class, because that was what the others seemed to be doing.

The enormous black eyes of the little Indian girl from my class looked at my food longingly, so I offered her some. But she only shook her head and plowed her way solemnly through her sandwiches.

I was very sleepy after lunch, because at home we always took a siesta. It was usually a pleasant time of day, with the bedroom darkened against the harsh afternoon sun, the drifting off into sleep with the sound of Mother's voice reading a story in one's mind, and, finally, the shrill, fussy voice of the ayah waking one for tea.

At school, we rested for a short time on low, folding cots on the veranda, and then we were expected to play games. During the hot part of the afternoon we played indoors, and after the shadows had begun to lengthen and the slight breeze of the evening had come up we moved outside to the wide courtyard.

I had never really grasped the system of competitive games. At home, whenever we played tag or guessing games, I was always allowed to "win"—"because," Mother used to tell Premila, "she is the youngest, and we have to allow for that." I had often heard her say it, and it seemed quite reasonable to me, but the result was that I had no clear idea of what "winning" meant.

When we played twos-and-threes that afternoon at school, in accordance with my training, I let one of the small English boys catch me, but was naturally rather puzzled when the other children did not return the courtesy. I ran about for what seemed like hours without ever catching anyone, until it was time for school to close. Much later I learned that my attitude was called "not being a good sport," and I stopped allowing myself to be caught, but it was not for years that I really learned the spirit of the thing.

When I saw our car come up to the school gate, I broke away from my classmates and rushed toward it yelling, "Ayah! Ayah!" It seemed like an eternity since I had seen her that morning—a wizened, affectionate figure in her white cotton sari, giving me dozens of urgent and useless instructions on how to be a good girl at school. Premila followed more sedately, and she told me on the way home never to do that again in front of the other children.

When we got home we went straight to Mother's high, white room to have tea with her, and I immediately climbed onto the bed

SANTHA RAMA RAU

and bounced gently up and down on the springs. Mother asked how we had liked our first day in school. I was so pleased to be home and to have left that peculiar Cynthia behind that I had nothing whatever to say about school, except to ask what "apple" meant. But Premila told Mother about the classes, and added that in her class they had weekly tests to see if they learned their lessons well.

I asked, "What's a test?" 24

Premila said, "You're too small to have them. You won't have 25
them in your class for donkey's years." She had learned the expression that day and was using it for the first time. We all laughed enormously at her wit. She also told Mother, in an aside, that we should take sandwiches to school the next day. Not, she said, that *she* minded. But they would be simpler for me to handle.

That whole lovely evening I didn't think about school at all. 26
I sprinted barefoot across the lawns with my favorite playmate, the cook's son, to the stream at the end of the garden. We quarreled in our usual way, waded in the tepid water under the lime trees, and waited for the night to bring out the smell of the jasmine. I listened with fascination to his stories of ghosts and demons, until I was too frightened to cross the garden alone in the semidarkness. The ayah found me, shouted at the cook's son, scolded me, hurried me into supper—it was an entirely usual, wonderful evening.

It was a week later, the day of Premila's first test, that our 27
lives changed rather abruptly. I was sitting at the back of my class, in my usual inattentive way, only half listening to the teacher. I had started a rather guarded friendship with the girl with the braids, whose name turned out to be Nalini (Nancy, in school). The three other Indian children were already fast friends. Even at that age it was apparent to all of us that friendship with the English or Anglo-Indian children was out of the question. Occasionally, during the class, my new friend and I would draw pictures and show them to each other secretly.

The door opened sharply and Premila marched in. At first, 28
the teacher smiled at her in a kindly and encouraging way and said, "Now, you're little Cynthia's sister?"

Premila didn't even look at her. She stood with her feet 29
planted firmly apart and her shoulders rigid, and addressed herself directly to me. "Get up," she said. "We're going home."

I didn't know what had happened, but I was aware that it 30
was a crisis of some sort. I rose obediently and started to walk toward my sister.

"Bring your pencils and your notebook," she said. 31

I went back for them, and together we left the room. The 32
teacher started to say something just as Premila closed the door, but we didn't wait to hear what it was.

4 BY ANY OTHER NAME   169

In complete silence we left the school grounds and started to walk home. Then I asked Premila what the matter was. All she would say was "We're going home for good." 33

It was a very tiring walk for a child of five and a half, and I dragged along behind Premila with my pencils growing sticky in my hand. I can still remember looking at the dusty hedges, and the tangles of thorns in the ditches by the side of the road, smelling the faint fragrance from the eucalyptus trees and wondering whether we would ever reach home. Occasionally a horse-drawn tonga passed us, and the women, in their pink or green silks, stared at Premila and me trudging along on the side of the road. A few coolies and a line of women carrying baskets of vegetables on their heads smiled at us. But it was nearing the hottest time of day, and the road was almost deserted. I walked more and more slowly, and shouted to Premila, from time to time, "Wait for me!" with increasing peevishness. She spoke to me only once, and that was to tell me to carry my notebook on my head, because of the sun. 34

When we got to our house the ayah was just taking a tray of lunch into Mother's room. She immediately started a long, worried questioning about what are you children doing back here at this hour of the day. 35

Mother looked very startled and very concerned, and asked Premila what had happened. 36

Premila said, "We had our test today, and she made me and the other Indians sit at the back of the room, with a desk between each one." 37

Mother said, "Why was that, darling?" 38

"She said it was because Indians cheat," Premila added. "So I don't think we should go back to that school." 39

Mother looked very distant, and was silent a long time. At last she said, "Of course not, darling." She sounded displeased. 40

We all shared the curry she was having for lunch, and afterward I was sent off to the beautifully familiar bedroom for my siesta. I could hear Mother and Premila talking through the open door. 41

Mother said, "Do you suppose she understood all that?" 42

Premila said, "I shouldn't think so. She's a baby." 43

Mother said, "Well, I hope it won't bother her." 44

Of course, they were both wrong. I understood it perfectly, and I remember it all very clearly. But I put it happily away, because it had all happened to a girl called Cynthia, and I never was really particularly interested in her. 45

COMPREHENSION

1. What does the title of this essay mean? State the thesis that emerges from it.

2. Cite five examples the author gives to demonstrate that her attendance at

the Anglo-Indian day school was an alien experience for her. How is the author's experience similar to Angelou's in "Graduation"?

3. According to the author's inferences, what was the effect of British rule on Indian society? How does the headmistress embody this impact? Compare and contrast Rau's perception of colonialism and that of Orwell in "A Hanging."

RHETORIC

1. Define these Indian words, preferably from the contexts in which they are used: *kohl* (paragraph 9), *chapatties* (paragraph 17), *ayah* (paragraph 18), *sari* (paragraph 22), and *tonga* (paragraph 34).

2. Explain the author's use of sensory language in paragraphs 1, 3, 5, 8, 9, 15, 26, and 34.

3. What is the theme of this narrative essay? How does the author state it?

4. Identify the tone and mood of the essay.

5. What is the utility and value of the author's use of dialogue in the essay?

6. How do various causal patterns inform the narrative?

WRITING

1. Although dealing specifically with a colonial situation, the author also illuminates the universal experience of being made to feel different, strange, or alien. Why is this ironic for the author? Why does it remain so vivid in her memory? Do we become more or less conscious of this phenomenon at a later age? Write a narrative essay centering on a time when you were made to feel strange or foreign in an educational situation.

2. Tell of a time when you felt that someone or some group was trying to change your identity or sense of self.

3. Write a comparative essay on this selection and Angelou's "Graduation."

FRANCES FITZGERALD

America Revised:
HISTORY SCHOOLBOOKS
IN THE TWENTIETH CENTURY

Frances Fitzgerald (1940–   ), winner of the Pulitzer Prize for Fire in the Lake: The Vietnamese and Americans in Vietnam *(1972), is an American journalist who has contributed to the At-*

lantic, *the* New Yorker, *the* New York Times Book Review, *and other magazines. Fitzgerald's interest in contemporary affairs and in the history of modern education resulted in the controversial study* America Revised: History Schoolbooks in the Twentieth Century *(1979), from which this selection is taken.*

t is a commonplace to say that the texts of the fifties were superpatriotic—dominated, almost to the exclusion of all else, by the concerns of the Cold War. But it is now hard to remember exactly what this meant, or how it happened. It is interesting, therefore, to watch the ideological drift as it crossed over the subsequent junior-high-school texts of the mid-century. First published in 1931, Casner and Gabriel's *Exploring American History* has had a life span of almost fifty years and was for much of the time a best-selling American history for seventh and eighth graders. Initially, at least, it was the product of a collaboration between a Yale history professor, Ralph Henry Gabriel, and a West Haven, Connecticut, schoolteacher, Mabel B. Casner. According to its first editor, at Harcourt Brace, it did well in the market because of its thematic approach to American history and its "ingenious" teaching strategies.

The first edition is clearly the work of liberals, and it has more than a touch of John Dewey about it. The foreword states that history should be "socially helpful" and should lead to "an understanding of how the life about us has evolved out of the life of the past." The text begins by drawing a parallel between a child's exploration of his own world and the wanderings of an imaginary knight over medieval Europe—the point of which is to explain "why did Europeans wait 500 years to discover America again?" It goes on to draw a picture of pre-Colonial North American Indian life in a manner so stylized that it might have been taken from the backdrop of a case in the American Museum of Natural History. The forest is deep, birds are flitting, squirrels are chattering, and so forth. The Indians, so the book says, were "deeply religious," the proof being that they worshipped so many different spirits; their tragedy was that they had no domestic animals, and therefore "could not progress toward a higher way of life." There are a certain number of poor people in the book—Jacob Riis is mentioned and there is a drawing of the immigrant boats—and very little chauvinism. The War of 1812 is said to have been won by no one, and the Mexican War to have occurred because President James Polk wanted to buy some empty land from the Mexicans and the Mexicans, though poor, were too proud to sell it. Such attempts at balance run through the narrative. The book reports that the United States was "drawn into" world affairs before the First World War, and in the title of the last foreign-policy chapter it asks, "What Steps

FRANCES FITZGERALD

Has the United States Taken Recently to Promote International Peace?" (a question that provides a perfect logical parallel to "When did you stop beating your wife?").

The 1938 edition of Casner and Gabriel has a new title, *The Rise of American Democracy*, and is said to be a complete reworking of the original volume. It has a new rationale. In their foreword, the authors say that democracy is now being challenged by other forms of government, including "swift-striking dictatorships," and that we therefore have to ask, "What does the word, *democracy*, mean?" The book never quite gets around to answering this question, but its focus is more political than that of the first edition, and its tone more urgent. The story of the knight in the first chapter has been condensed, and the American scenery of birds, squirrels, and leafy boughs has largely disappeared. The Indians are now said to have practiced democracy, not religion; they are no longer "deeply religious." Jacob Riis is still around, but the United States government has become a much more positive actor in social reform. Whereas a mid-thirties edition seems to judge some of President Franklin Roosevelt's legislation to have been unconstitutional, this one simply credits him with having helped the country out of the Depression. In foreign policy, too, the government has taken a positive role: it "helps" the Allies in the First World War and "promotes" world peace thereafter, within the limits of its isolationist position. In the last part of the book, "American Democracy Faces a Confused World," the text maintains that Americans now have new ideals, including a balanced economy, Social Security, and well-being for all citizens. But it ends, rather ominously, "The struggle still goes on. It was never more intense than in our day. The outcome will depend upon the intelligence and alertness of this generation and of future generations."

The 1942 edition, now called *The Story of American Democracy*, has an update on the Second World War and a new preface that refers to the "perilous times" we are living in. Apparently because of this emergency, the Indian sections have been condensed. (They drop out completely in subsequent editions.) In the central part of the book, the titles have changed, and these give a rather different tone to the book. Where once there were "problems" to "challenge democracy," there is now only progress: "American Life Becomes Better for the Common Man," and so on. The Constitutional period is headed "Free Americans Organize a Strong Democratic Nation," and the words "freedom" and "strength" crop up a lot elsewhere. In the last chapter—a completely new one, entitled "The United States Fights for Its Life and for a Free, Democratic World"—there is a photograph caption that reads, "This picture shows citizens enjoying the democratic privilege of free discussion. ... The leader is helping them to carry on their business in an orderly way." The photograph shows several men on a dais facing a seated audience; it is clearly a meeting of some sort. In contrast to the final worryings of the 1938 edition, this book ends on a note of optimism concerning air travel.

Over the next eight years, the authors—or whoever did the revising of the text—must have felt justified in their optimism, for the 1950 text is a victorious book. The United States now "leads the struggle for democracy"; it has "faced problems," "met challenges"; it has risen "to a position of world leadership" and become "a bastion of the free nations." All of this is, of course, in the twentieth century, but retrospectively the nation has made other gains as well—notably in its nineteenth-century wars. It has not exactly won the War of 1812, but the war is now said to have helped "build the nation." (In earlier editions, the war, less grandly, "develops national feeling.") The Mexican War, which in the first two editions brought the country only empty land, now has brought it vast territories rich in oil and precious metals. In addition, the country has become more prosperous: there are no more poor people or bad social conditions. Pages have been added explaining the superiority of the American democratic system to the Russian police state.

In accordance with the authors' new belief that "perhaps the most important event of the first half of the twentieth century was the rise of the United States to a position of world leadership," the last quarter of the book deals mainly with foreign affairs. These sections portray the United States as playing an essentially benevolent and pacific role in the world. The nation is always attempting to improve communications with the Soviet Union and to "gain peace by mutual understanding"—this in spite of continual rebuffs. In an echo of the liberal internationalism of the first edition, the book talks about the need for international control of atomic energy and the effort to remove the causes of war through the United Nations. The last section, "Democracy Enriches the Lives of Americans," confidently describes recent "advances" in art, education, and science, and points up the American belief in the importance of the individual, of whatever race or creed.

Five years later, this confidence has evaporated; the book is a bundle of anxieties. In the first place, the authors no longer appear to believe that the United States exerts "world leadership." In their foreword, they say that the United States leads "those people in the world who believe in freedom" (a worrying kind of group), and that it is "locked in a struggle" with "another powerful world leader . . . the Soviet Union." Faced with the need to prepare "young people" for the "struggle" in a "complicated and often dangerous world," the authors propose to compare the Russian and American ways of life— American history apparently being of no use anymore. Later on in the book, the authors fulfill their promise by giving an account of Soviet institutions. In this section, one is told that "Russia" is a police state, where "the leader of the Communist party has absolute power over ... every person." (The book cautiously does not name this leader; Stalin had died two years before publication.) Russia, one learns, is a "fake democracy" and a "fake republic"; worse yet, its industry is geared not to the production of television sets but to war production. In addition, one learns that Russia is tremendously powerful—perhaps even more powerful than the United States, because, in spite of all the American aid to free nations, Russia has managed to block progress and block the growth of prosperity. It is now threatening the free world. (In this section, there is a map of the world color-coded to show which nations are "Communist," which are "free," and which are "neutral." This map classifies all of Indo-China and all of sub-Sahara Africa as "free" and classifies Saudi Arabia, Iran, and most of Latin America, including Mexico, as "neutral." This assessment is mysterious, since the book appeared a year after Dien Bien Phu, several years before the decolonization of most of Africa, and some time after the C.I.A. had brought the Shah of Iran to power and had overturned the Arbenz government in Guatemala.) Internationally, nothing is safe from the Communists, and the home front is not very secure, either. The United States may be a free country, with "wonderful machines" and a free-enterprise system (over which the government now presides in the much reduced capacity of referee), but the Russians are in the process of undermining it. They have already stolen American state secrets through Alger Hiss and the Rosenbergs. They lie a lot, and the Communist Party in the United States espouses violent, undemocratic means. The book therefore approves of the Internal Security Act, the Loyalty Board, and the firm hand of J. Edgar Hoover in the F.B.I.

The most surprising thing about this 1955 edition is the attitude that its authors take toward children. In the thirties editions, they had tried to engage their young readers with adventure stories and romance; here they do nothing but lecture—as if the children might turn out to be small subversives. The last page, subheaded "A Citizen's Rights and Duties," is terribly stern. A citizen's duties, they warn, include military service, jury duty, and paying taxes without cheating. The last few pages—usually given over to science and technology—now include a warning against "false news" and "dangerous propaganda." What the authors are referring to here can only be conjectured, since they are no more explicit than they were when they warned in an earlier section against the questionable practices of "some investigating committees of Congress"—surely the House Un-American Activities Committee and Senator Joseph R. McCarthy's subcommittee. But these two things are probably connected, because the authors offer this explicit piece of advice:

> The FBI urges Americans to report directly to its offices any suspicions they may have about Communist activity on the part of their fellow Americans. The FBI is expertly trained to sift out the truth of such reports under the laws of our free nation. When Americans handle their suspicions in this way, rather than by gossip and publicity, they are acting in line with American traditions.

What this paragraph literally says is that an American tradition is that of the police informer. The authors, however, appear to have thought of the F.B.I. as the liberal alternative to the McCarthy subcommittee.

This edition of Casner and Gabriel was not untypical of the texts of the period—certainly in its emphasis on the Communist threat. Virtually all the texts of the mid-fifties made the same estimates of Soviet power and Soviet aggressiveness in foreign policy. Virtually all of them expressed similar doubts about the survival of democracy in this country. The texts of the early forties had not portrayed the Nazis as half so aggressive, or the Second World War as half such a threat to the country. Now the danger was everywhere, invisible. According to Bragdon and McCutchen, one of the most respectable of the high-school texts of the period:

> Unquestioning party members are found everywhere. Everywhere they are willing to engage in spying, sabotage, and the promotion of unrest on orders from Moscow.

And

> Agents of the worldwide Communist conspiracy have been active inside the United States. Some of them have been trusted officials of the State Department, regularly furnishing information to Russia. Others have passed on atomic secrets; still others have even represented the United States in the UN.

Bragdon and McCutchen were quoting Senator McCarthy and representing his charges as true.

The subversion anxieties of the texts peaked in the mid-fifties, subsiding gradually after that. The early-sixties texts did not repudiate McCarthy except by saying, "Some Americans said there was too much fuss being made about the Communists since there were so relatively few in the United States," or "The struggle divided us when we should have been united." Only now do some texts actually denounce McCarthy's "scare tactics" and take issue with the general assessment of the Soviet Union in the fifties. The aspect of fifties texts that persisted most strongly into the sixties was a certain tone of grimness toward children, and particularly toward young children. It was the junior-high-school books, rather than the high-school ones, that gave such warnings as "Some forces in the world today want to abolish freedom. [But] your heritage as an American provides you with the ideals and faith to give you strength to preserve the rights that are yours as a free American. It is your duty to preserve these rights." And so on. Since these books never defined what they meant by "freedom," the burden they laid on children was truly awesome.

COMPREHENSION

1. What sort of audience would be interested in this essay? Does it appeal to a general audience? Explain.

2. Trace the changes in the "ideological drift" of the Casner and Gabriel textbook from 1931 to the mid-1950s.

3. What assumptions and inferences does Fitzgerald make about the teaching of American history in the junior high school classroom?

RHETORIC

1. Although this is an analytical essay, the diction tends to be informal. Point to examples of this informal style. What is the effect of the diction on the analysis itself?

2. Explain the allusions to John Dewey and Jacob Riis in paragraph 2. Identify the allusion in paragraph 8.

3. How does the term *ideological drift* serve to structure the entire essay? What type of process analysis is involved in the development? Identify the steps in the process.

4. Comment on the effectiveness of the author's topic sentences. How do they reinforce the implied thesis in the essay?

5. Explain how Fitzgerald uses causal analysis. Analyze one paragraph in detail to illuminate this procedure.

6. What is the author's tone in her analysis of the Casner and Gabriel text? Cite examples to support your position.

WRITING

1. Analyze the presentation of American history in a textbook with which you are familiar. What connections can you make among the text, the author, and the era in which it was written?

2. Write an analysis of a textbook, dealing with its assumptions, its content, its intended audience, and its purpose.

 AMERICA REVISED

3. Should various interest groups put pressure on publishers to present topics in textbooks—for example, creationism vs. evolutionary theory—in a certain way? Deal with this question in an argumentative essay.

Credo

Richard Rodriguez (1944–   ) was born in San Francisco and received degrees from Stanford University and Columbia University. He also did graduate study at the University of California, Berkeley and the Warburg Institute, London. Rodriguez became a nationally known writer with the publication of his autobiography, Hunger of Memory: The Education of Richard Rodriguez *(1982). In it, he describes the struggles of growing up biculturally—feeling alienated from his Spanish-speaking parents yet not wholly comfortable in the dominant culture of the United States. He opposes bilingualism and affirmative action as they are now practiced in the United States, and his stance has caused much controversy in educational and intellectual circles. Rodriguez continues to write about social issues such as acculturation, education, and language. The following essay continues Rodriguez's personal interrogation into his own experience of growing up in a bicultural environment, this time focusing on the different roles Mexican and "gringo" Catholicism played in his childhood.*

 remember my early Catholic schooling and recall an experience of religion very different from anything I have known since. Never since have I felt so much at home in the Church, so easy at mass. My grammar school years especially were the years when the great Church doors opened to enclose me, filling my day as I was certain the Church filled all time. Living in a community of shared faith, I enjoyed much more than mere social reenforcement of religious belief. Experienced continuously in public and private, Catholicism shaped my whole day. It framed my experience of eating and sleeping and washing; it named the season and the hour.

The sky was full then and the coming of spring was a religious event. I would awaken to the sound of garage doors creaking open and know without thinking that it was Friday and that my father was on his way to six-thirty mass. I saw, without bothering to notice, statues at home and at school of the Virgin and of Christ. I would write

1

2

RICHARD RODRIGUEZ

at the top of my arithmetic or history homework the initials *Jesus, Mary,* and *Joseph.* (All my homework was thus dedicated.) I felt the air was different, somehow still and more silent on Sundays and high feastdays. I felt lightened, transparent as sky, after confessing my sins to a priest. Schooldays were routinely divided by prayers said with classmates. I would not have forgotten to say grace before eating. And I would not have turned off the light next to my bed or fallen asleep without praying to God.

The institution of the Church stood an extraordinarily physi-   3
cal presence in my world. One block from the house was Sacred Heart Church. In the opposite direction, another block away, was Sacred Heart Grammar School, run by the Sisters of Mercy. And from our backyard, I could see Mercy Hospital, Sacramento's only Catholic hospital. All day I would hear the sirens of death. Well before I was a student myself, I would watch the Catholic school kids walk by the front of the house, dressed in gray and red uniforms. From the front lawn I could see people on the steps of the church, coming out, dressed in black after funerals, or standing, the ladies in bright-colored dresses in front of the church after a wedding. When I first went to stores on errands for my mother, I could be seen by the golden-red statue of Christ, where it hovered over the main door of the church.

I was *un católico* before I was a Catholic. That is, I acquired   4
my earliest sense of the Church—and my membership in it—through my parents' Mexican Catholicism. It was in Spanish that I first learned to pray. I recited family prayers—not from any book. And in those years when we felt alienated from *los gringos,* my family went across town every week to the wooden church of Our Lady of Guadalupe, which was decorated with yellow Christmas tree lights all year long.

Very early, however, the *gringo* church in our neighborhood   5
began to superimpose itself on our family life. The first English-speaking dinner guest at our house was a priest from Sacred Heart Church. I was about four years old at the time, so I retain only random details with which to remember the evening. But the visit was too important an event for me to forget. I remember how my mother dressed her four children in outfits it had taken her weeks to sew. I wore a white shirt and blue woolen shorts. (It was the first time I had been dressed up for a stranger.) I remember hearing the priest's English laughter. (It was the first time I had heard such sounds in the house.) I remember that my mother served a *gringo* meat loaf and that I was too nervous or shy to look up more than two or three times to study the priest's jiggling layers of face. (Smoothly, he made believe that there was conversation.) After dinner we all went to the front room where the priest took a small book from his jacket to recite some prayers, consecrating our house and our family. He left a large picture of a sad-eyed Christ, exposing his punctured heart. (A caption below

records the date of his visit and the imprimatur of Francis Cardinal Spellman.) That picture survives. Hanging prominently over the radio or, later, the television set in the front room, it has retained a position of prominence in all the houses my parents have lived in since. It has been one of the few permanent fixtures in the environment of my life. Visitors to our house doubtlessly noticed it when they entered the door—saw it immediately as the sign we were Catholics. But I saw the picture too often to pay it much heed.

I saw a picture of the Sacred Heart in the grammar school 6 classroom I entered two years after the priest's visit. The picture drew an important continuity between home and the classroom. When all else was different for me (as a scholarship boy) between the two worlds of my life, the Church provided an essential link. During my first months in school, I remember being struck by the fact that— although they worshipped in English—the nuns and my classmates shared my family's religion. The *gringos* were, in some way, like me, *católicos*. Gradually, however, with my assimilation in the schoolroom, I began to think of myself and my family as Catholics. The distinction blurred. At home and in class I heard about sin and Christ and Satan and the consoling presence of Mary the Virgin. It became one Catholic faith for me.

Only now do I trouble to notice what intricate differences 7 separated home Catholicism from classroom Catholicism. In school, religious instruction stressed that man was a sinner. Influenced, I suspect, by a bleak melancholic strain in Irish Catholicism, the nuns portrayed God as a judge. I was carefully taught the demands He placed upon me. In the third grade I could distinguish between venial and mortal sin. I knew—and was terrified to know—that there was one unforgivable sin (against the Holy Ghost): the sin of despair. I knew the crucial distinction between perfect and imperfect contrition. I could distinguish sins of commission from sins of omission. And I learned how important it was to be in a state of grace at the moment of death.

Death. (How much nearer it seemed to the boy than it seems 8 to me now.) Again and again the nuns would pull out the old stories of deathbed conversions; of Roman martyrdoms; of murdered African missionaries; of pious children dying of cancer to become tiny saints; of souls going immediately to heaven. We were taught how to baptize in case of emergency. I knew why some souls went to Limbo after the death of the body, and others went for a time to Purgatory, and why others went to heaven or hell—"forever and ever."

Among the assortment of possible sins to commit, sexual 9 sins—the cherries—were certainly mentioned. With the first years of puberty, the last years of grammar school, we began hearing about "sins of the flesh." There were those special mornings when the priest

RICHARD RODRIGUEZ

would come over from church to take the boys to the cafeteria, while the nun remained with the girls—"the young ladies"—in the classroom. For fifty minutes the priest would talk about the dangers of masturbation or petting, and some friend of mine would turn carefully in his chair to smirk in my direction or somebody else would jab me in the back with a pencil.

Unlike others who have described their Catholic schooling, I 10 do not remember the nuns or the priests to have been obsessed with sexual sins. Perhaps that says more about me or my Mexican Catholicism than it says about what actually went on in the classroom. I remember, in any case, that I would sometimes hear with irony warnings about sins of the flesh. When we were in eighth grade the priest told us how dangerous it was to look at our naked bodies, even while taking a bath—and I noticed that he made the remark directly under a near-naked figure of Christ on the cross.

The Church, in fact, excited more sexual wonderment than it 11 repressed. I regarded with awe the "wedding ring" on a nun's finger, her black "wedding veil"—symbols of marriage to God. I would study pictures of martyrs—white-robed virgins fallen in death and the young, almost smiling, St. Sebastian, transfigured in pain. At Easter high mass I was dizzied by the mucous perfume of white flowers at the celebration of rebirth. At such moments, the Church touched alive some very private sexual excitement; it pronounced my sexuality important.

Sin remained, nevertheless. Confession was a regular part of 12 my grammar school years. (One sought forgiveness through the ritual plea: "Bless me, father, for I have sinned. . . .") Sin—the distance separating man from God—sin that burdened a sorrowful Christ; sin remained. ("I have disobeyed my parents fourteen times . . . I have lied eight times . . . I am heartily sorry for having offended Thee. . . .") God the Father judged. But Christ the Son had interceded. I was forgiven each time I sought forgiveness. The priest murmured Latin words of forgiveness in the confessional box. And I would leave the dark.

In contrast to the Catholicism of school, the Mexican Catholicism of home was less concerned with man the sinner than with man the supplicant. God the Father was not so much a stern judge as One with the power to change our lives. My family turned to God not in guilt so much as in need. We prayed for favors and at desperate times. I prayed for help in finding a quarter I had lost on my way home. I prayed with my family at times of illness and when my father was temporarily out of a job. And when there was death in the family, we prayed.

I remember my family's religion, and I hear the whispering 14 voices of women. For although men in my family went to church,

 CREDO

women prayed most audibly. Whether by man or woman, however, God the Father was rarely addressed directly. There were intermediaries to carry one's petition to Him. My mother had her group of Mexican and South American saints and near-saints (persons moving toward canonization). She favored a black Brazilian priest who, she claimed, was especially efficacious. Above all mediators there was Mary, *Santa María*, the Mother. Whereas at school the primary mediator was Christ, at home that role was assumed by the Mexican Virgin, *Nuestra Señora de Guadalupe*, the focus of devotion and pride for Mexican Catholics. The Mexican Mary "honored our people," my mother would say. "She could have appeared to anyone in the whole world, but she appeared to a Mexican." Someone like us. And she appeared, I could see from her picture, as a young Indian maiden—dark just like me.

On her feastday in early December my family would go to the Mexican church for a predawn high mass. The celebration would begin in the cold dark with a blare of trumpets imitating the cries of a cock. The Virgin's wavering statue on the shoulders of men would lead a procession into the warm yellow church. Often an usher would roughly separate me from my parents and pull me into a line of young children. (My mother nodded calmly when I looked back.) Sometimes alone, sometimes with my brother and sisters, I would find myself near the altar amid two or three hundred children, many of them dressed like Mexican cowboys and cowgirls. Sitting on the floor it was easier to see the congregation than the altar. So, as the mass progressed, my eye would wander through the crowd. Invariably, my attention settled on old women—mysterious supplicants in black—bent deep, their hands clasped tight to hold steady the attention of the Mexican Virgin, who was pictured high over the altar, astride a black moon. 15

The *gringo* Catholic church, a block from our house, was a very different place. In the *gringo* church Mary's statue was relegated to a side altar, imaged there as a serene white lady who matter-of-factly squashed the Genesis serpent with her bare feet. (Very early I knew that I was supposed to believe that the shy Mexican Mary was the same as this European Mary triumphant.) In the *gringo* church the floors were made not of squeaky wood but of marble. And there was not the devotional clutter of so many pictures and statues and candle racks. "It doesn't feel like a church," my mother complained. But as it became our regular church, I grew to love its elegant simplicity: the formal march of its eight black pillars toward the altar; the Easter-egg-shaped sanctuary that arched high over the tabernacle; and the dim pink light suffused throughout on summer afternoons when I came in not to pray but to marvel at the cool calm. 16

The holy darkness of church never frightened me. It was 17

RICHARD RODRIGUEZ

never nighttime darkness. Religion at school and at church was never nighttime religion like religion at home. Catholicism at home was shaped by the sounds of the "family rosary": tired voices repeating the syllables of the Hail Mary; our fingers inching forward on beads toward the point of beginning; my knees aching; the coming of sleep.

Religion at home was a religion of bedtime. Prayers before 18 sleeping spoke of death coming during the night. It was then a religion of shadows. The last thing I'd see before closing my eyes would be the cheap statue of Mary aglow next to my bed.

But the dark at the foot of my bed billowed with malevolent 19 shapes. Those nights when I'd shudder awake from a nightmare, I'd remember my grandmother's instruction to make a sign of the cross in the direction of my window. (That way Satan would find his way barred.) Sitting up in bed, I'd aim the sign of the cross against the dim rectangle of light. Quickly, then, I'd say the Prayer to My Guardian Angel, which would enable me to fall back to sleep.

In time dawn came. 20

A child whose parents could not introduce him to books like 21 *Grimm's Fairy Tales*, I was introduced to the spheres of enchantment by the nighttime Catholicism of demons and angels. The superstitious Catholicism of home provided a kind of proletarian fairy-tale world.

Satan was mentioned in the classroom. And depicted on the 22 nuns' cartoon placards as bringing all his evil to bear on the temptation of nicely dressed boys and girls. In the morning's bright light and in the safe company of classmates, Satan never aroused very much terror. Around the time I was in fourth grade, moreover, religion classes became increasingly academic. I was introduced to that text familiar to generations of Catholic students, *The Baltimore Catechism*. It is a text organized by questions about the Catholic faith. (Who is God? What is Penance? What is Hope?)

Today's Catholic elementary schools attempt a less mechani- 23 cal approach to religious instruction. Students are taught—what I never had to be taught—that religion is not simply a matter of dogmas or theological truths; that religion involves a person's whole way of life. To make the point, emphasis has shifted from the theological to the ethical. Students are encouraged to consider social problems and responses to "practical" dilemmas in a modern world through which angels and devils no longer dance.

My schooling belonged to another time. *The Baltimore Cate-* 24 *chism* taught me to trust the authority of the Church. That was the central lesson conveyed through the experience of memorizing hundreds of questions and answers. I learned an answer like, God made us to know, love, and serve Him in this life, and to be happy with Him in the next. The answer was memorized *along with* the question (it belonged with the question), Why did God make us? I learned, in other words, question and answer together. Beyond what the answer literally stated, two things were thus communicated. First, the existence of a question implies the existence of an answer. (There are no stray questions.) And second, that my questions about religion had answers. (The Church knows.)

Not only in religion class was memory exercised. During those years when I was memorizing the questions and answers of *The Baltimore Catechism,* I was also impressing on my memory the spelling of hundreds of words, grammar rules, division and multiplication tables. The nuns deeply trusted the role of memorization in learning. Not coincidentally, they were excellent teachers of basics. They would stand in front of the room for hours, drilling us over and over (5 times 5 . . . 5 times 9; *i* before *e* except after *c*; God made us to know, love, and serve Him in this world . . .). Stressing memorization, my teachers implied that education is largely a matter of acquiring knowledge already discovered. And they were right. For contrary to more progressive notions of learning, much that is learned in a classroom must be the already known; and much that is already known must be learned before a student can achieve truly independent thought. 25

Stressing memorization, the nuns assumed an important Catholic bias. Stated positively, they believed that learning is a social activity; learning is a rite of passage into the group. (Remembrance is itself an activity that establishes a student's dependence upon and union with others.) Less defensibly, the nuns distrusted intellectual challenges to authority. In religion class especially, they would grow impatient with the relentlessly questioning student. When one nun told my parents that their youngest daughter had a 'mind of her own,' she meant the remark to be a negative criticism. And even though I was urged to read all that I could, several teachers were dismayed to learn that I had read the novels of Victor Hugo and Flaubert. ('Those writers are on the Index, Richard.') With classmates I would hear the nuns' warning about non-Catholic colleges, stories of Faustian Catholics falling victim to the foolish sin of intellectual pride. 26

Trust the Church. It was the institution established by the instruction of Christ to his disciple: 'Thou art Peter and upon this rock I will build. . . .' (How could Protestants not hear?) The nun drew her pointer to the chart in front of the classroom where the line of popes connected the name of St. Peter to that of Pope Pius XII. Trust the Church, the nun said. It was through the Church that God was best known. I came to believe: 'I am a Catholic.' (My faith in the Christian God was enclosed by my faith in the Church.) 27

I never read the Bible alone. In fifth grade, when I told a teacher that I intended to read the New Testament over the summer, I did not get the praise I expected. Instead, the nun looked worried and said I should delay my plan for a while. ('Wait until we read it 28

RICHARD RODRIGUEZ

in class.') In the seventh and eighth grades, my class finally did read portions of the Bible. We read together. And our readings were guided by the teachings of Tradition—the continuous interpretation of the Word passing through generations of Catholics. Thus, as a reader I never forgot the ancient Catholic faith—that the Church serves to help solitary man comprehend God's Word.

COMPREHENSION

1. What two contrasting definitions of the word *credo* are implied in Rodriguez's title? How does each distinct meaning influence the author's perceptions and behaviors as a child?

2. What is the author's attitude toward his early experience? Positive? Negative? A combination of the two? Support your view.

3. State, in your own words, the thesis of this essay.

RHETORIC

1. In paragraph 3, Rodriguez comments that the church was an "extraordinarily physical presence." What descriptions in paragraphs 2 and 3 support this impression?

2. Rodriguez uses many special terms in the context of the Catholic religion, for example, *consecrate* (paragraph 5), *imprimatur* (paragraph 5), and *venial* (paragraph 7). How do these contribute to the tone of the essay?

3. Does the introduction provide a clue as to the purpose of the essay? Why, or why not? Where in the essay does Rodriguez make his purpose clear?

4. Paragraph 20 is composed of only four words. What purpose does it serve in the overall organization of the essay? What double meaning is implied in the word *dawn*?

5. Why does Rodriguez digress to a description of contemporary religion in paragraph 23? Does this strengthen or weaken the essay's unity?

6. How does Rodriguez use the concluding paragraph to provide an example of the philosophy behind Catholic instruction he describes in paragraph 26? How does the repetition of the phrase "trust the Church" in the final paragraph create a strong ending to the essay?

WRITING

1. Rodriguez compares and contrasts the two churches that held sway over him as a child. How else can the experience of growing up in two cultures expose a child to alternative traditions, viewpoints, and behavior? Answer this question in a comparative essay.

2. Write a comparison/contrast essay describing one tradition as it is practiced by two different cultural groups.

3. Write a brief essay summarizing the main differences that Rodriguez found between Mexican Catholicism and school Catholicism.

4. Rodriguez claims that the church was a "physical presence" (paragraph 3). Select something in your own life that is not usually thought of in physical terms, and write an essay describing your experience of its "physicality."

BERTRAND RUSSELL

Knowledge and Wisdom

Bertrand Arthur William Russell (1872–1970), who was born in Monmouthshire, England, was one of the great philosophers, mathematicians, liberal political theorists, and authors of the twentieth century. His works, comprising more than sixty volumes, range from abstract explanations of mathematical theory to fascinating memoirs that record British culture in the early years of the twentieth century. From the early Principles of Mathematics *(1903) through* An Inquiry into Meaning and Truth *(1940) to his three-volume* Autobiography *(1967–1969), Russell demonstrated his multivarious talents as a writer, socialist thinker, and activist. He was awarded the Nobel Prize in Literature in 1950. In 1955 he received the Silver Pears Trophy for work on behalf of world peace. In this essay from* Portraits from Memory *(1956), Russell argues that as we advance in knowledge, wisdom becomes an increasingly necessary quality in peoples and cultures.*

Most people would agree that, although our age far surpasses all previous ages in knowledge, there has been no correlative increase in wisdom. But agreement ceases as soon as we attempt to define "wisdom" and consider means of promoting it. I want to ask first what wisdom is, and then what can be done to teach it.

There are several factors that contribute to wisdom. Of these I should put first *a sense of proportion*: the capacity to take account of all the important factors in a problem and to attach to each its due weight. This has become more difficult than it used to be owing to the extent and complexity of the specialised knowledge required of various kinds of technicians. Suppose, for example, that you are engaged in research in scientific medicine. The work is difficult and is likely to absorb the whole of your intellectual energy. You have not time to consider the effect which your discoveries or inventions may have outside the field of medicine. You succeed (let us say), as modern medicine has succeeded, in enormously lowering the infant death-rate, not only in Europe and America, but also in Asia and Africa. This has the entirely unintended result of making the food supply inadequate and lowering the standard of life in the most populous parts of the world. To take an even more spectacular example, which is in everybody's mind at the present time: you study the composition of the atom from a disinterested desire for knowledge, and incidentally place in the hands of powerful lunatics the means of destroying the human race. In such ways the pursuit of knowledge may become harmful unless it is combined with wisdom; and wisdom in the sense of comprehensive vision is not necessarily present in specialists in the pursuit of knowledge.

Comprehensiveness alone, however, is not enough to constitute wisdom. There must be, also, a certain awareness of the ends of human life. This may be illustrated by the study of history. Many eminent historians have done more harm than good because they viewed facts through the distorting medium of their own passions: Hegel had a philosophy of history which did not suffer from any lack of comprehensiveness, since it started from the earliest times and continued into an indefinite future. But the chief lesson of history which he sought to inculcate was that from the year A.D. 400 down to his own time, Germany had been the most important nation and the standard-bearer of progress in the world. Perhaps one could stretch the comprehensiveness that constitutes wisdom to include not only intellect but also feeling. It is by no means uncommon to find men whose knowledge is wide but whose feelings are narrow. Such men lack what I am calling wisdom. 3

It is not only in public ways, but in private life equally, that wisdom is needed. It is needed in the choice of ends to be pursued and in emancipation from personal prejudice. Even an end which it would be noble to pursue if it were attainable may be pursued unwisely if it is inherently impossible of achievement. Many men in past ages devoted their lives to a search for the Philosopher's Stone and the Elixir of Life. No doubt, if they could have found them, they would have conferred great benefits upon mankind, but as it was their lives were wasted. To descend to less heroic matters, consider the case of two men, Mr. A and Mr. B, who hate each other and, through mutual hatred, bring each other to destruction. Suppose you go to Mr. A and say, "Why do you hate Mr. B?" He will no doubt give you an appalling list of Mr. B's vices, partly true, partly false. And now suppose you go to Mr. B. He will give you an exactly similar list of Mr. A's vices with an equal admixture of truth and falsehood. Suppose you now come back to Mr. A and say, "You will be surprised to learn 4 that Mr. B says the same things about you as you say about him," and you go to Mr. B and make a similar speech. The first effect, no doubt, will be to increase their mutual hatred, since each will be so horrified by the other's injustice. But, perhaps, if you have sufficient patience and sufficient persuasiveness, you may succeed in convincing each that the other has only the normal share of human wickedness, and their enmity is harmful to both. If you do this, you will have instilled some fragment of wisdom.

The essence of wisdom is emancipation, as far as possible, 5 from the tyranny of the here and the now. We cannot help the egoism of our senses. Sight and sound and touch are bound up with our own bodies and cannot be made impersonal. Our emotions start similarly from ourselves. An infant feels hunger and discomfort, and is unaffected except by his own physical condition. Gradually, with the years, his horizon widens, and, in proportion as his thoughts and feelings become less personal and less concerned with his own physical states, he achieves growing wisdom. This is, of course, a matter of degree. No one can view the world with complete impartiality; and if anyone could, he would hardly be able to remain alive. But it is possible to make a continual approach towards impartiality: on the one hand, by knowing things somewhat remote in time or space; and, on the other hand, by giving to such things their due weight in our feelings. It is this approach towards impartiality that constitutes growth in wisdom.

Can wisdom in this sense be taught? And, if it can, should 6 the teaching of it be one of the aims of education? I should answer both these questions in the affirmative. We are told on Sundays that we should love our neighbor as ourselves. On the other six days of the week, we are exhorted to hate him. You may say that this is nonsense, since it is not our neighbor whom we are exhorted to hate. But you will remember that the precept was exemplified by saying that the Samaritan was our neighbour. We no longer have any wish to hate Samaritans and so we are apt to miss the point of the parable. If you want to get its point, you should substitute "communist" or "anticommunist," as the case may be, for "Samaritan." It might be objected that it is right to hate those who do harm. I do not think so. If you hate them, it is only too likely that you will become equally harmful; and it is very unlikely you will induce them to abandon their evil ways. Hatred of evil is itself a kind of bondage to evil. The way out is through understanding, not through hate. I am not advocating non-resistance. But I am saying that resistance, if it is to be effective in preventing the spread of evil, should be combined with the greatest degree of understanding and the smallest degree of force that is compatible with the survival of the good things that we wish to preserve.

It is commonly urged that a point of view such as I have been 7 advocating is incompatible with vigour in action. I do not think history bears out this view. Queen Elizabeth I in England and Henry IV in France lived in a world where almost everybody was fanatical, either on the Protestant or on the Catholic side. Both remained free from the errors of their time and both, by remaining free, were beneficent and certainly not ineffective. Abraham Lincoln conducted a great war without ever departing from what I have been calling wisdom.

I have said that in some degree wisdom can be taught. I think that this teaching should have a larger intellectual element than has been customary in what has been thought of as moral instruction. The disastrous results of hatred and narrow-mindedness to those who feel them can be pointed out incidentally in the course of giving knowledge. I do not think that knowledge and morals ought to be too much separated. It is true that the kind of specialised knowledge which is required for various kinds of skill has little to do with wisdom. But it should be supplemented in education by wider surveys calculated to put it in its place in the total of human activities. Even the best technicians should also be good citizens; and when I say "citizens," I mean citizens of the world and not of this or that sect or nation. With every increase of knowledge and skill, wisdom becomes more necessary, for every such increase augments our capacity for realising our purposes, and therefore augments our capacity for evil, if our purposes are unwise. The world needs wisdom as it has never needed it before; and if knowledge continues to increase, the world will need wisdom in the future even more than it does now.

8

COMPREHENSION

1. Does Russell's essay give evidence of any purpose other than to inform? Cite examples to support your response.

2. According to Russell, what is the difference between knowledge and wisdom? What constitutes true wisdom? What is the essence of wisdom?

3. How does Russell answer this question, "can wisdom . . . be taught"?

RHETORIC

1. Explain how the author shades his connotations of the words *knowledge* and *wisdom* so that the audience understands that Russell thinks the latter more important.

2. Define these words: *correlative* (paragraph 1), *eminent* (paragraph 3), *enmity* (paragraph 4), *exhorted* (paragraph 6), and *advocating* (paragraph 7).

3. What sort of introductory paragraph does the author develop?

4. How does Russell employ a pattern of comparison and contrast to structure his essay?

5. Explain the way that Russell integrates a pattern of exemplification into his comparative essay. How does this strategy help him achieve the definition of wisdom?

6. What elements of argumentation and persuasion do you encounter in this essay? Is Russell arguing the same point as Huxley in "A Liberal Education"? Explain.

WRITING

1. How successful have your teachers been in imparting wisdom to you? Do you think that a teacher *should* impart wisdom, or is knowledge sufficient?

2. Write your own essay on knowledge and wisdom, using personal examples to highlight differences in the two concepts.

3. Using examples drawn from this chapter and earlier sections, evaluate the ways in which, individuals, through a variety of educational processes, can achieve "wisdom."

Human Development and Behavior

VIRGINIA WOOLF

The Death of the Moth

Virginia Woolf (1882–1941), English novelist and essayist, was the daughter of Leslie Stephen, a famous critic and writer on economics. An experimental novelist, Woolf attempted to portray consciousness through a poetic, symbolic, and concrete style. Her novels include Jacob's Room *(1922),* Mrs. Dalloway *(1925),* To the Lighthouse *(1927), and* The Waves *(1931). She was also a perceptive reader and critic, and her criticism appears in* The Common Reader *(1925) and* The Second Common Reader *(1933). The following essay, which demonstrates Woolf's capacity to convey profound meaning even in commonplace events, appeared in* The Death of a Moth and Other Essays *(1948).*

 oths that fly by day are not properly to be called moths; they do not excite that pleasant sense of dark autumn nights and ivy-blossom which the commonest yellow-underwing asleep in the shadow of the curtain never fails to rouse in us. They are hybrid creatures, neither gay like butterflies nor sombre like their own species. Nevertheless the present specimen, with his narrow hay-coloured wings, fringed with a tassel

1

of the same colour, seemed to be content with life. It was a pleasant morning, mid-September, mild, benignant, yet with a keener breath than that of the summer months. The plough was already scoring the field opposite the window, and where the share had been, the earth was pressed flat and gleamed with moisture. Such vigour came rolling in from the fields and the down beyond that it was difficult to keep the eyes strictly turned upon the book. The rooks too were keeping one of their annual festivities; soaring round the tree tops until it looked as if a vast net with thousands of black knots in it had been cast up into the air; which, after a few moments sank slowly down upon the trees until every twig seemed to have a knot at the end of it. Then, suddenly, the net would be thrown into the air again in a wider circle this time, with the utmost clamour and vociferation, as though to be thrown into the air and settle down upon the tree tops were a tremendously exciting experience.

The same energy which inspired the rooks, the ploughmen, 2 the horses, and even, it seemed, the lean bare-backed downs, sent the moth fluttering from side to side of his square of the windowpane. One could not help watching him. One, was, indeed, conscious of a queer feeling of pity for him. The possibilities of pleasure seemed that morning so enormous and so various that to have only a moth's part in life, and a day moth's at that, appeared a hard fate, and his zest in enjoying his meagre opportunities to the full, pathetic. He flew vigorously to one corner of his compartment, and, after waiting there a second, flew across to the other. What remained for him but to fly to a third corner and then to a fourth? That was all he could do, in spite of the size of the downs, the width of the sky, the far-off smoke of houses, and the romantic voice, now and then, of a steamer out at sea. What he could do he did. Watching him, it seemed as if a fibre, very thin but pure, of the enormous energy of the world had been thrust into his frail and diminutive body. As often as he crossed the pane, I could fancy that a thread of vital light became visible. He was little or nothing but life.

Yet, because he was so small, and so simple a form of the 3 energy that was rolling in at the open window and driving its way through so many narrow and intricate corridors in my own brain and in those of other human beings, there was something marvellous as well as pathetic about him. It was as if someone had taken a tiny bead of pure life and decking it as lightly as possible with down and feathers, had set it dancing and zigzagging to show us the true nature of life. Thus displayed one could not get over the strangeness of it. One is apt to forget all about life, seeing it humped and bossed and garnished and cumbered so that it has to move with the greatest circumspection and dignity. Again, the thought of all that life might have

VIRGINIA WOOLF

been had he been born in any other shape caused one to view his simple activities with a kind of pity.

After a time, tired by his dancing apparently, he settled on the window ledge in the sun, and, the queer spectacle being at an end, I forgot about him. Then, looking up, my eye was caught by him. He was trying to resume his dancing, but seemed either so stiff or so awkward that he could only flutter to the bottom of the window-pane; and when he tried to fly across it he failed. Being intent on other matters I watched these futile attempts for a time without thinking, unconsciously waiting for him to resume his flight, as one waits for a machine, that has stopped momentarily, to start again without considering the reason of its failure. After perhaps a seventh attempt he slipped from the wooden ledge and fell, fluttering his wings, on to his back on the window sill. The helplessness of his attitude roused me. It flashed upon me that he was in difficulties; he could no longer raise himself; his legs struggled vainly. But, as I stretched out a pencil, meaning to help him to right himself, it came over me that the failure and awkwardness were the approach of death. I laid the pencil down again.

The legs agitated themselves once more. I looked as if for the enemy against which he struggled. I looked out of doors. What had happened there? Presumably it was midday, and work in the fields had stopped. Stillness and quiet had replaced the previous animation. The birds had taken themselves off to feed in the brooks. The horses stood still. Yet the power was there all the same, massed outside, indifferent, impersonal, not attending to anything in particular. Somehow it was opposed to the little hay-coloured moth. It was useless to try to do anything. One could only watch the extraordinary efforts made by those tiny legs against an oncoming doom which could, had it chosen, have submerged an entire city, not merely a city, but masses of human beings; nothing, I knew had any chance against death. Nevertheless after a pause of exhaustion the legs fluttered again. It was superb this last protest, and so frantic that he succeeded at last in righting himself. One's sympathies, of course, were all on the side of life. Also, when there was nobody to care or to know, this gigantic effort on the part of an insignificant little moth, against a power of such magnitude, to retain what no one else valued or desired to keep, moved one strangely. Again, somehow, one saw life, a pure bead. I lifted the pencil again, useless though I knew it to be. But even as I did so, the unmistakable tokens of death showed themselves. The body relaxed, and instantly grew stiff. The struggle was over. The insignificant little creature now knew death. As I looked at the dead moth, this minute wayside triumph of so great a force over so mean an antagonist filled me with wonder. Just as life had been strange a

4

5

few minutes before, so death was now as strange. The moth having righted himself now lay most decently and uncomplainingly composed. O yes, he seemed to say, death is stronger than I am.

COMPREHENSION

1. Why is Woolf so moved by the moth's death? Why does she call the moth's protest (paragraph 5) "superb"?

2. What, according to Woolf, is the "true nature of life"?

3. What paradox is inherent in the death of the moth?

RHETORIC

1. Examine Woolf's use of similes in paragraph 1. Where else does she use similes? Are any of them similar to the similes used in paragraph 1?

2. Why does the author personify the moth?

3. What sentences constitute the introduction of this essay? What rhetorical device do they use?

4. Divide the essay into two parts. Why did you divide the essay where you did? How are the two parts different? How are they similar?

5. Explain the importance of description in this essay. Where, particularly, does Woolf describe the setting of her scene? How does that description contribute to the development of her essay? How does she describe the moth, and how does this description affect tone?

6. How is narration used to structure the essay?

WRITING

1. Woolf implicitly connects insect and human life. What else can we learn about human development by looking at other forms of life? Analyze this connection in an essay.

2. Write a detailed description of a small animal. Try to invest it with the importance that Woolf gives his moth.

3. Analyze Woolf's use of figurative language in "The Death of the Moth."

ELIZABETH KÜBLER-ROSS

The Emotional Quadrant

Elizabeth Kübler-Ross (1926–   ) was born in Zurich, Switzerland, but became a naturalized American citizen in 1961. She received her M.D. from Zurich University in 1957 and, since then, has divided her time among medicine, teaching, and writing. Voted Woman of the Decade in 1979 by Ladies' Home Journal, *Kübler-Ross is one of the world's greatest authorities on the subject of death and dying. Among her works are* On Death and Dying *(1969),* Questions and Answers on Death and Dying *(1974), and* Remember the Secret *(1981). This essay is an examination of the often hidden but enduring hurt the death of a parent may give a child.*

Very young children have no fear of death, although they have the two innate fears of sudden loud noises and of falling from high places. Later on children are naturally afraid of separation, since the fear of abandonment and the absence of a loving caretaker is very basic and meaningful. Children are aware of their dependency, and those who have been exposed to early traumas in life are scarred. They will need to relive the trauma and learn to let go of the panic, pain, anxiety and rage of the abandonment. 1

These violent feelings arise often, not solely when a member of the family dies. Abandonments of all sorts happen thousands of times over in our society, and if the loss is not associated with the death of a loved one, few people will recognize this. The emergency support systems or shoulders to lean on will not be called into action, and there will be no sympathy visits by neighbors. So the child who feels abandoned in some manner is left vulnerable; his future mindset could include a general mistrust, a fear of ever allowing a close relationship, an alienation from the person who is blamed for the separation, and a deep grief over the absence of love. 2

Rene was such a child, and he needed thirty years to heal. He was only five years old when his father told him to get into the car, because they were going somewhere together. Rene was very excited. His father had been drinking for many years; his mom had been in and out of mental hospitals, and there had been very little laughter and happiness in his life. And now his dad was going to take him somewhere. He did not dare to ask him where they were going. To the zoo? To the park? To a football game? He could not understand why Dad had come home in the middle of the week, but he knew that his mom was very sick again, because she had slept all day and never came down even to fix him a sandwich. 3

In the car, Rene and his father approached a huge building and parked. His father silently opened the car door and let Rene out. The father was very quiet; he did not even smile once. Rene wondered if his father was mad at him. He remembered he had fixed his own breakfast. He had even put the dishes in the sink. He was never noisy when his mom and dad had their fights, and he stayed in the den and 4

THE EMOTIONAL QUADRANT

out of the way. He had not heard them fighting today, and therefore Rene had hoped it would be a good day.

His dad took him by the hand and led him into a strange room with a funny smell. A Catholic sister came and talked to his father, but no one talked to him. Then his father left the room, and a short time later the sister left also. Rene sat very quietly and waited, but no one came. Maybe his dad had to go to the bathroom. Finally he got up, and out the window he saw his dad walking out of the house toward the car. He ran as fast as he could: "Dad, Dad, don't leave me!" But the car door shut, and he saw the old familiar car turn the corner—out of sight.

Rene never saw his mother again. She returned to the mental hospital, where two years later she killed herself. He didn't see his father again for many years. It was much later that a strange woman came to visit him one day; she told him that his dad had married her and that they had planned to take him out of the home of the sisters to see if it could "work out."

Rene tried to please his dad in every way he could. He painted the new house and worked every free moment he had to get a nod of approval from him. But his dad remained as silent as he had always been. This silence always brought back to Rene the memory of that nightmarish day when he had been taken away from home without so much as an explanation, much less a good-bye or last hug from his mom.

His father never said "thank you" or "I am pleased with you," just as he never brought up the reasons for Rene's placement in the home and the lack of warning. So Rene grew up trying to please, not knowing that the fear of rejection and abandonment was still with him in adulthood. But Rene was afraid of alcoholism, afraid of mental illness, afraid of getting close to anyone. His whole life consisted of work and more work to please his father. He never allowed himself to get angry, to speak up, to express displeasure. The only time his face lit up was at the sight of a parent playing with a child in the park or swinging on a swing in a schoolyard. He spent his free time in those places, vicariously enjoying the laughter of these children, unaware of why he could not experience love and laughter in his own life.

As a mature adult he took an opportunity to look at his pain, anguish, despair, and incomprehension of this totally unexpected abandonment in early childhood, and he emerged a free man. It took him only one week, touched by others who shared their agonies in a safe place where it was regarded as a blessing to get rid of old tears and anger. During that week, Rene felt loved unconditionally. This man has just resolved his conflicts and has begun to understand his inability to trust and relate.

ELIZABETH KÜBLER-ROSS

If someone—preferably his parents—had talked with this little boy and made an effort to understand his play, his drawings, his sullen withdrawal and isolation, much pain and unresolved conflict, carried within for decades, could have easily been avoided. You think those things happened in the last century? No, they still happen every day in our society.

Many, many adults suffer from never having resolved the hurts of their childhood. So children need to be allowed to grieve without being labeled crybaby or sissy, or hearing the ridiculous statement "Big boys don't cry." If children of both sexes are not allowed to express their natural emotions in childhood, they will have problems later on in the form of self-pity and many psychosomatic symptoms. Grief and fear, when allowed to be expressed and shared in childhood, can prevent much future heartache.

COMPREHENSION

1. Explain in your own words Rene's relationship to his parents.

2. What is the thesis of this selection? Where is it stated?

3. What is the "emotional quadrant" mentioned in the title? In what sense is Kübler-Ross using the word *quadrant*?

RHETORIC

1. Look up the word *vicariously* (paragraph 8). How is it being used in this context? What other meaning does it have? How does the word illuminate the author's purpose and also Woolf's purpose in "The Death of the Moth"?

2. Describe the author's style. Is it abstract or concrete? How does the style contribute to the purpose of the selection?

3. What kind of transition words does Kübler-Ross use? How does this contribute to the organization of her essay?

4. Where does Kübler-Ross argue by example? What purpose does this serve?

5. Where does the author introduce unsupported hypotheses as facts? Why doesn't she support them?

6. Is the example of Rene typical? Explain your response. How does the example affect the author's argument?

WRITING

1. Name some of the nonpsychological attitudes that Kübler-Ross says shape our response to our emotions. Have these attitudes changed? Should they? Evaluate this matter in an essay.

2. Filmmaker François Truffaut once observed that people who remember their

childhoods as happy do not have good memories. Write an essay analyzing how your childhood has shaped the adult you have become.

3.   Develop your own case study of an individual—preferably a child—whom you know. Develop a case study of this individual, offering an analysis of his or her personality.

MARY LEAKEY

Footprints in the Ashes of Time

Mary Douglas Leakey (1913–   ) is the director of the Olduvai Gorge Excavations, one of the most important paleontological sites in the world. Among her publications are Olduvai Gorge *(1971);* Africa's Vanishing Art *(1983); and* Disclosing the Past *(1984), an autobiography. In addition, Mrs. Leakey has contributed numerous papers to* Nature *and other scientific journals. In this essay, a preliminary report on a remarkable find, Leakey provides insight into the challenging field of paleontology.*

It happened some 3,600,000 years ago, at the onset of a rainy season. The East African landscape stretched then, much as it does now, in a series of savannas punctuated by wind-sculptured acacia trees. To the east the volcano now called Sadiman heaved restlessly, spewing ash over the flat expanse known as Laetoli. 1

The creatures that inhabited the region, and they were plentiful, showed no panic. They continued to drift on their random errands. Several times Sadiman blanketed the plain with a thin layer of ash. Tentative showers, precursors of the heavy seasonal rains, moistened the ash. Each layer hardened, preserving in remarkable detail the footprints left by the ancient fauna. The Laetolil Beds, as geologists designate the oldest deposits at Laetoli, captured a frozen moment of time from the remote past—a pageant unique in prehistory. 2

Our serious survey of the beds, which lie in northern Tanzania 30 miles by road south of Olduvai Gorge, began in 1975 and gained intensity last summer after the discovery of some startling footprints. This article must stand as a preliminary report; further findings will almost certainly modify early interpretations. 3

Still, what we have discovered to date at Laetoli will cause yet another upheaval in the study of human origins. For in the gray, petrified ash of the beds—among the spoor of the extinct predecessors 4 of today's elephants, hyenas, hares—we have found hominid foot-prints that are remarkably similar to those of modern man. Prints that, in my opinion, could only have been left by an ancestor of man. Prints that were laid down an incredible 3,600,000 years ago . . . !

In 1976 Peter Jones, my assistant and a specialist in stone tools, and my youngest son, Philip, noticed what they believed to be a trail of hominid footprints. After considerable analysis I agreed and an-nounced the discovery the following year. Of the five prints, three were obscured by overlying sediment impossible to remove. The two clear examples, broad and rather curiously shaped, offered few clues to the primate that had trudged across the plain so long ago.

Nonetheless, the implications of this find were enormous. Dr. Garniss Curtis of the University of California at Berkeley undertook to date the footprint strata. These deposits possess relatively large crystals of biotite, or black mica. Biotite from ash overlying the prints, when subjected to potassium-argon testing, showed an age of about 3.6 million years; that from below tested at about 3.8 million years. The footprints had been preserved sometime within this span. Dr. Richard L. Hay, also of Berkeley, showed that the ash forming the layers fell within a month's time.

The hominid footprints attested, in my considered opinion, to the existence of a direct ancestor of man half a million years before the earliest previous evidence—fossils unearthed by Dr. Donald C. Johanson and his party in the Afar triangle of Ethiopia beginning in 1973.

Faced with this, we largely abandoned our hunt for fossils and focused our three-month campaign of 1978 on the footprints—plotting and photographing them, making plaster and latex casts, and even removing certain specimens. While Dr. Paul Abell of the Uni-versity of Rhode Island was attempting—delicately and successfully—to quarry out a block of rhinoceros tracks, he noticed a barely exposed, hominidlike heel print.

When we removed the surrounding overburden, we found a trail some 23 meters long; only the end of the excavation season in September prevented our following it still farther. Two individuals, one larger, one smaller, had passed this way 3,600,000 years ago.

The footsteps come from the south, progress northward in a fairly straight line, and end abruptly where seasonal streams have eroded a small, chaotic canyon through the beds. The nature of the terrain leads us to believe that the footprints, though now covered, remain largely intact to the south. And that is where we will continue our effort.

The closeness of the two sets of prints indicates that their own-ers were not walking abreast. Other clues suggest that the hominids may have passed at different times. For example, the imprints of the smaller individual stand out clearly. The crispness of definition and sharp outlines convince me that they were left on a damp surface that retained the form of the foot.

On the other hand, the prints of the larger are blurred, as if   12
he had shuffled or dragged his feet. In fact, I think that the surface when he passed was loose and dusty, hence the collapsed appearance of his prints. Nonetheless, luck favored us again; the bigger hominid left one absolutely clear print, probably on a patch of once damp ash.

What do these footprints tell us? First, they demonstate once   13
and for all that at least 3,600,000 years ago, in Pliocene times, what I believe to be man's direct ancestor walked fully upright with a bipe-dal, free-striding gait. Second, that the form of his foot was exactly the same as ours.

One cannot overemphasize the role of bipedalism in hominid   14
development. It stands as perhaps the salient point that differentiated the forebears of man from other primates. This unique ability freed the hands for myriad possibilities—carrying, tool-making, intricate manipulation. From this single development, in fact, stems all modern technology.

Somewhat oversimplified, the formula holds that this new   15
freedom of forelimbs posed a challenge. The brain expanded to meet it. And mankind was formed.

Even today, millions of years beyond that unchronicled Ru-   16
bicon, *Homo sapiens* is the only primate to walk upright as a matter of course. And, for better or for worse, *Homo sapiens* dominates the world.

But what of those two hominids who crossed the Laetolil Beds   17
so long ago? We have measured their footprints and the length of their stride. Was the larger one a male, the smaller a female? Or was one mature, the other young? It is unlikely that we will ever know with certainty. For convenience, let us postulate a case of sexual di-morphism and consider the smaller one a female.

Incidentally, following her path produces, at least for me, a   18
kind of poignant time wrench. At one point, and you need not be an expert tracker to discern this, she stops, pauses, turns to the left to glance at some possible threat or irregularity, and then continues to the north. This motion, so intensely human, transcends time. Three million six hundred thousand years ago, a remote ancestor—just as you or I—experienced a moment of doubt.

The French have a proverb: *Plus ça change, plus c'est la même*   19
chose—"The more it changes, the more it is the same." In short, noth-ing really alters. Least of all, the human condition.

Measurements show the length of the smaller prints to be 18.5   20
centimeters (slightly more than 7 inches) and 21.5 centimeters for the larger. Stride length averages 38.7 centimeters for the smaller hominid,

MARY LEAKEY

47.2 centimeters for the larger. Clearly we are dealing with two small creatures.

An anthropological rule of thumb holds that the length of the 21
foot represents about 15 percent of an individual's height. On this basis—and it is far from exact—we can estimate the height of the male as perhaps four feet eight inches (1.4 meters); the female would have stood about four feet.

Leg structure must have been very similar to our own. It 22
seems clear to me that the Laetoli hominid, although much older, relates very closely to the remains found by Dr. Johanson in Ethiopia. Dr. Owen Lovejoy of Kent State University in Ohio studied a knee joint from Ethiopia—the bottom of the femur and the top of the tibia— and concluded that the Afar hominid had walked upright, with a free, bipedal gait.

Our footprints confirm this. Furthermore, Dr. Louise Robbins 23
of the University of North Carolina, Greensboro, an anthropologist who specializes in the analysis of footprints, visited Laetoli and con- cluded: "The movement pattern of the individual is a bipedal walking gait, actually a stride—and quite long relative to the creature's small size. Weight-bearing pressure patterns in the prints resemble human ones. . . ."

I can only assume that the prints were left by the hominids 24
whose fossils we also found in the beds. In addition to part of a child's skeleton, we uncovered adult remains—two lower jaws, a section of upper jaw, and a number of teeth.

Where can we place the Laetoli hominids and their Afar cou- 25
sins in the incomplete mosaic of the rise of man? This question, quite honestly, is a subject of some contention among paleontologists. One school, including Dr. Johanson, classifies them as australopithecines.

But the two forms of *Australopithecus*, gracile and robust, rep- 26
resent, in my opinion, evolutionary dead ends. These man apes flour- ished for their season, and perished—unsuccessful twigs on the branch that produced mankind. Of course, the Laetoli hominid resem- bles the gracile *Australopithecus*, but I believe that, so far back in time, all the hominids shared certain characteristics. However, the simple evidence of the footprints, so very much like our own, indicates to me that the Laetoil hominid stands in the direct line of man's ancestry.

We have encountered one anomaly. Despite three years of 27
painstaking search by Peter Jones, no stone tools have been found in the Laetolil Beds. With their hands free, one would have expected this species to have developed tools or weapons of some kind. But, except for the ejecta of erupting volcanoes, we haven't found a single stone introduced into the beds. So we can only conclude, at least for the moment, that the hominids we discovered had not yet attained the toolmaking stage.

But in the end one cannot escape the supreme importance of 28
the presence of hominids at Laetoli. Sometimes, during the excavating
season, I go out and watch the dusk settle over the gray tuff with its
eerie record of time long past. The slanting light of evening throws
the hominid prints into sharp relief, so sharp that they could have
been left this morning.

I cannot help but think about the distant creatures who made 29
them. Where did they come from? Where were they going? We simply
do not know. It has been suggested that they were merely crossing
this scorched plain toward the greener ridges to the north. Perhaps
so.

In any case, those footprints out of the deep past, left by the 30
oldest known hominids, haunt the imagination. Across the gulf of
time I can only wish them well on that prehistoric trek. It was, I believe, part of a greater and more perilous journey, one that—through
millions of years of evolutionary trial and error, fortune and misfortune—culminated in the emergence of modern man.

COMPREHENSION

1. What is the author's main purpose in this essay? Cite evidence to support
your answer.

2. In which paragraph do you discover that Leakey is describing human footprints? What effect is she trying to achieve by delaying this revelation? Does
Leakey do an effective job of proving that the footprints "could only have been
left by an ancestor of man"? What other interpretation is there? What facts support another interpretation?

3. What is the author's relationship to Donald C. Johanson? How often and
where do his theories appear?

RHETORIC

1. Define the following words: hominid (paragraph 4); Bliocene (paragraph 13);
and dimorphism (paragraph 17). Is the language in this section specialized? Explain.

2. Use a dictionary or encyclopedia to define Rubicon (paragraph 16). In what
sense is "that unchronicled Rubicon" a turning point? How does the allusion
strengthen the idea?

3. How does the author create her introduction in this essay?

4. What sort of reasoning process does Leakey apply to the development of
her essay? Trace this process as carefully as you can.

5. Many of Leakey's paragraphs are relatively short. Cite representative examples, and explain why the overall strategy is successful.

MARY LEAKEY

6. Is this report meant to be read by scientists or by lay people? What clues tell you this?

WRITING

1. If Leakey is right, what implications are there to the discovery that humankind is far older than we once believed? In what ways are we like our hominid ancestors? Write an essay explaining the connection between humans and hominids.

2. There is a school of thought that entirely rejects the findings of Leakey and others on the subject of evolution and fossil remains. This school, called "creationism," argues that the biblical account in the book of Genesis is incompatible with scientific evidence and that where the two disagree, the revealed word of God is a better indicator than is a fossil record. Write an essay explaining which side of this debate you find more compelling. Offer reasons and evidence to support your position.

3. Leakey asserts, ". . . nothing really alters. Least of all the human condition." From your reading of this essay and your perspective, is she right or wrong? Answer this question in an argumentative essay.

FRANZ BOAS

The Diffusion of Cultural Traits

Franz Boas (1858–1942) was a highly influential anthropologist who was known for his rigorous use of scientific method. His most famous works are The Mind of Primitive Man *(1911),* Primitive Art *(1927),* Anthropology and Modern Life *(1928), and two volumes of collected essays,* Race, Language, and Culture *(1940) and* Race and Democratic Society *(1945). "The Diffusion of Cultural Traits" shows Boas's wide-ranging cultural expertise and, perhaps more important, his humanism.*

he study of the types of cultures found the world over   1
gives the impression of an enormous diversity of forms. The differences are so great that we may be inclined to think that every one of these cultures developed quite independently and that the peculiar genius of the people has found expression in the forms under which they live. This impression is strengthened by the fact that the people themselves differ in appearance. The African Negro, the Australian, the Siberian native, the peo-

ple of the Pacific Islands, each have their own peculiar bodily build and their own peculiar culture.

Added to this is the observation that the people constituting 2 every one of these societies consider themselves as independent units, specifically distinct from all their neighbors. This finds its strongest expression in the fact that many primitive people designate themselves as human beings, while all their neighbors are designated by specific names in the same way as animals are designated by names. Thus the Eskimos call themselves human beings, the Indians whom they know in some regions only by hearsay are considered as doglike animals, and the white people with whom they came into contact in later times are considered as descended from dogs. The specific differences are keenly felt, while the similarities are neglected.

The objective study of cultures and of types of man shows 3 that notwithstanding all these apparently fundamental differences cultural strains have passed from one people to the other, that no culture can be assumed to be self-developed and no type to be pure, unmixed with foreign strains.

This can be most easily shown by a study of the distribution 4 of languages. The migrations of primitive people in early times covered whole continents. A few examples will suffice. A certain American language is spoken in the vast area extending from the Yukon to Hudson Bay; south of this area live people speaking entirely different languages, but dialects of the same language which is spoken in the north reappear locally in Oregon and California and in the vast territory north and south of the Rio Grande. This can be understood only on the assumption that at one time these people migrated over this immense area. In southern Brazil the Carib language is spoken. It reappears locally north of the Amazon River and on the West Indian Islands. The Bantu languages spoken in Africa cover the whole district from south of the Sahara, southward almost to the extreme southern end of Africa. The language of the Malay, which is spoken in southeastern Asia, found its way eastward to all the islands of the Pacific Ocean and is also spoken by the inhabitants of part of Madagascar.

These inferences based on similarities of languages can also 5 be proved by historical migrations. The great Arab migration, which started in Arabia and at the time of its greatest extent covered the whole of north Africa and part of Spain, and which also influenced all the languages of the Near East, occurred after Mohammed's time. We know that the so-called Aryans invaded India at a very early time. The Greeks migrated from the north into what later became Greece. The Celts of western Europe migrated eastward as far as Asia Minor. The Teutonic migrations destroyed the Roman Empire, and later on the great Turkish migrations swept over a large part of eastern Europe as well as over a large part of Siberia. Thus we actually see mankind

FRANZ BOAS

on the move since the very earliest times. The whole settlement of America occurred within a comparatively short period. Evidently the American aborigines lived on the continent not earlier than the beginning of the last warm period before the last ice age, coming presumably over the land bridge which is now Bering Sea, and spreading from there as far as the extreme southern part of South America.

It is not only language that was carried by migrations all over the world; it is also easy to show that inventions and ideas were carried from one area to another, partly by migration, partly by cultural contact. One of the most striking examples is found in the distribution of folk tales. The European folk tale of the couple that escaped a pursuing monster by throwing backwards a number of objects which were transformed into obstacles is well known all over Europe. A comb thrown down becomes an impenetrable thicket, a whetstone an insurmountable mountain, a small amount of oil becomes an extensive lake, all of which detain the pursuer. This complicated story containing all the elements mentioned is found not only all over Europe but all over the Asiatic continent and also in northwestern America reaching as far as California, and eastward even in Greenland and Nova Scotia. In more recent times we find that the most isolated tribes of South America tell tales which were carried by Negro slaves to the coast of Brazil. 6

Equally striking are certain similarities in political organization characteristic of the Old World but entirely absent in America and other outlying regions. The whole political organization of Africa shows a high development of administration through kings and their ministers in charge of war, judicial procedure and so on—analogous to the ancient organization of European states. Judicial procedure by means of courts taking evidence, administering the oath and finally ascertaining the truth by ordeal is found in a vast part of the Old World, while it is entirely foreign to people that had never been in contact with the Old World. 7

Perhaps still more convincing is the distribution of agriculture. Wheat and barley are two characteristic plants on which early agriculture is based all over the temperate zone of the Old World, while rice is characteristic of another extended area. The home of the wild plants from which wheat and barley are derived must be looked for somewhere in western Asia, from where they spread from tribe to tribe. In the same way early American agriculture is based on the use of Indian corn which was developed from a native plant of the western highlands of Mexico, from where it spread southward as far as the Argentine republic and northward to the Great Lakes. 8

Thus a detailed study of cultural traits proves beyond cavil that there is not a single people in the primitive world that has developed its culture independently. 9

 THE DIFFUSION OF CULTURAL TRAITS   205

Much of the diffusion must have been accompanied by actual   10
intermingling of tribes. The people speaking the language of the Yukon River, to whom we referred before and who live now on the Rio Grande, differ in type from the people of the north but are similar in appearance to their neighbors who speak an unrelated language. This would not have happened if they had not intermingled with them at the same time that they adopted many important traits of their culture. In South Africa the intermingling of types is perhaps not equally clear but another striking feature of mutual influence may be seen in a linguistic change. The Bushmen of southern Africa have a peculiarity of speech which does not occur in any other part of the world. They produce sounds not by breathing out but by sucking in. This habit, which is considered an ancient African trait, is found in weak traits on the Gold Coast in equatorial West Africa, but only one of the Bantu tribes, who are neighbors of the Bushmen, have adopted the habit of producing strong sounds by sucking in, as the Bushmen do.

It we want to understand the way in which these fundamental   11
modifications of cultures occur we have to remember that the conditions of contact among primitive tribes are very different from what has occurred in more modern times. Most primitive tribes are small; sometimes the whole number of individuals may not be more than a few hundred. Wars between neighboring groups are common and almost everywhere it is customary for the men to be killed, while the women are taken along as captives. These become the mothers of the following generation, so that it may happen that a large number of children grow up bilinguals, with the cultural habits of the mother having a far-reaching influence upon the behavior of the children.

The study of distribution of cultural traits brings out one very   12
characteristic feature: the details of the culture may be similar among different tribes but the general structure will retain fundamental differences. To give an example, one of the most important ceremonials of our North American Indians is the Sun Dance, an elaborate ceremonial the details of which are widespread over our western plains. The meaning of the ceremonial is quite different in the different areas and it is fitted into the fundamental religious ideas of each tribe. We can perhaps best understand these differences when we consider our own culture. All over Europe, and wherever the white race has gone, the fundamental traits are the same; inventions, religion, fundamental traits of state organization are alike. And nevertheless there are decided national patterns which allow us to differentiate between the cultural life of different areas as well as of different times.

It is interesting to follow the processes of acculturation. Evidently in many cases it is due to war. We have already mentioned the   13
importance of the introduction of foreign women. In many cases conquest leads to the establishment of stratified societies of a class of

masters to whom the native population becomes subject. This has been the case in the history of Europe as well as in the history of Africa. In Africa we see that pastoral people conquered agricultural communities and became the nobility to whom the natives became subjects. Such conquests led to economic adjustments, and in many traits the conquerors adopted the customs of the old population while these in turn adopted the traits of the invaders. It must not be assumed that every stratified society originated in this manner, because sometimes internal conditions, family privileges and so on have led to similar results. In other cases economic and social advantages favored the adoption of foreign customs. This was obviously the case in the spread of agriculture both in the Old World and in America. In a similar way new religious ideas which strengthen the emotional energy of the people and awaken them from indifferent attitudes have had a powerful influence in modifying cultural life.

One of the many remarkable changes of culture due to an 14 introduction of foreign invention is the change all over North America which occurred with the introduction of the horse. After the introduction of the horse the pursuit of the buffalo became easier and some of the tribes which had been hunting the buffalo on foot were now able to roam over a wider area and gave up agriculture almost entirely, becoming more or less nomadic hunters. Notwithstanding the readiness with which foreign cultural traits are adopted we may also observe in many cases a strong resistance to changes of life. This occurs particularly when new ideas cannot be fitted into the general cultural habits of the people. As an instance may be mentioned the difficulty of adjusting native tribes to the fundamental idea of capitalism. Very rarely do we find among primitive people that wealth can be used to produce more wealth by utilizing the power it may give over other members of the community. Wealth is of value only insofar as it enables the owner to improve his social standing by liberality, or by making a show with his property. In this lies one of the reasons which make it so difficult to assimilate the American Indians, to whom the idea of capital as producing wealth is entirely foreign.

In modern society the conditions favorable to cultural contact 15 are ever so much greater than those existing in primitive society. First of all, the numbers of individuals constituting each unit are infinitely larger than those occurring in primitive society, and within each group diffusion occurs with the greatest rapidity. Our schools, the commercial exploitation of inventions, are of such a character that new ideas and new objects are distributed with incredible rapidity. Most of these extend beyond national boundaries because international trade and international communication make it impossible for any idea to be confined to a single nation. On the other hand general, structural attitudes find much greater resistance than in the small tribes because the inertia of the enormous masses of the population is much greater than that of a small tribal group. It is less difficult to introduce a new idea into the well established structure of a small group than to break down the habits of thought of millions.

We are too much inclined to consider the development of civ- 16 ilization in Europe as an achievement of Europe alone, and to assume that Europe has always been the giver, not the recipient of new ideas. We are likely to forget that in antiquity the exchange of inventions and ideas extended from China all over the continent to Europe, and that the indirect contact between the Far East and Europe contributed much to the development of European civilization. We are likely to forget the immense service that Arab scientists did to Europe in re-establishing contact with Greek thought. Later on, when contact with the Far East was interrupted by the Turkish invasion of eastern Europe and the development of the Mongolian empire, the need for contact with the East led to maritime discoveries, and the discovery of America brought inventions to Europe which modified life in many parts of the Old World. I need only mention the introduction of Indian corn, which in an incredibly short time found its way to all parts of the Old World that were adapted to its cultivation, or the use of tobacco, which has reached all parts of the inhabitable world.

Peculiar types of cultural assimilation developed with colo- 17 nization. Greek colonies sprang up on all the shores of the Mediterranean and hand in hand with them went a strong influence of Greek culture upon the surrounding people. Still more effective was Roman colonization, which not only carried the habits of Roman life into outlying provinces but led to Latin becoming the language of these countries, so that the languages of what is now Spain, of France, of what is now Romania disappeared and provincial Latin took their place. During the Middle Ages a similar process occurred in central Europe when German colonists reoccupied the former habitat of German tribes which had been filled by Slavic groups. The process that occurred there may still be observed in Mexico, where Spaniards are still colonizing in Indian territory and where we see the Indian languages gradually giving way to Spanish. There is little doubt that the process of assimilation which occurred in Greek and Roman colonization and later on in Germany was of the same type. In Mexico we see the Spaniards settling in small towns. A hybrid population develops with fair rapidity and the town as a trade center attracts the Indians. Intercourse is first by means of poorly developed Spanish, which is gradually adopted by a large part of the native population. Gradually the influence of the town increases in importance, with the final result that the native language disappears and the natives and the Spaniards form a single community. According to the character of the migrating population there would of course be differences in the resultant social structure. When the colonists are poor and uneducated the native population and colonists may merge into a single community. When the colonists are supported by a central power they may become the masters of the territory and a stratified society results.

It is interesting to compare with this the conditions of immigration into countries which are already more or less settled. We may observe this in our own country as well as in South America, Australia, or South Africa. The immigrants who arrive are drawn from many different countries and form always a minority in a larger and economically stronger group, so that their only hope of success in the new country is based on a gradual assimilation. It is not only economic stress, however, which brings about the assimilation of the new colonists to the new environment but also the strong social influence of the majority among whom they live. An interesting example of this kind was observed about thirty years ago in a New York school in a part of the city which had been inhabited by an Irish population then being replaced by Italians. The school had been for some time Irish, with a sprinkling of Italian children. The Italian children had learned an Irish pronunciation of English, and even when they increased to about ninety per cent of all the children they all spoke English with an Irish accent. By the pressure of the majority all immigrants become assimilated, no matter what nationality they belong to, and their own influence is comparatively slight. 18

It is of considerable practical interest for us to understand what happens in the process of assimilation, how far old habits are stable and how far they are influenced by their new environment. A number of studies made on American immigrants throw light on this question. It has repeatedly been shown that the physical development of children of immigrants differs from that of their parents. During the last century the stature of Americans and also of Europeans has increased noticeably, but the immigrants who came here during the last seventy years have always belonged to the same economic level and their stature has remained quite stable. Their children, however, follow the general increase which is found in the American population. Furthermore, the form of the body of immigrants' children undergoes certain changes, and though the cause is still obscure the result is that in bodily form they differ from their parents. This does not mean that they tend to approach a general American type, but merely that the new environment and new mode of life influence the bodily build. 19

The changes in their behavior are much more noticeable. It is not only that they adopt American tastes and language, a process which results from contact between children of many nationalities in school, but their motor habits also change from foreign types to what we might call an American type. The Italians and the Jews accompany 20 speech with characteristic gestures. The Italian describes what he has to say with a wide sweep of motions, while the Jew follows his line of thought with short, rather jerky movements. The assimilated Italians and Jews substitute for these movements the descriptive and emphatic motions which are characteristic of American habits, or when they belong to more sophisticated classes tend to suppress all gestures. Statistics also show that the immigrant becomes adjusted very quickly to American social habits. This becomes particularly striking in criminal statistics. On the whole, crimes against property among the immigrants from Europe are comparatively rare, while they are exceedingly common in our American city population. But the distribution of crime in the second generation, that is, among the descendants of immigrants, is quite similar to that found in the American population of native parentage. All this is merely an expression of the fact that when an individual is exposed to a new environment his descent is almost irrelevant when compared to the stress to which he is exposed in his new mode of life.

A review of all the data which have been summarized here   21
altogether too briefly shows that the assumption that any culture is autonomous, uninfluenced from outside sources, or that each type of man produces a culture which is an expression of the biological make-up of the race to which he belongs, is quite untenable. We see everywhere types of culture which develop historically under the impact of multifarious influences that come from neighboring people or those living far away.

COMPREHENSION

1. Identify the "types" of culture that Boas refers to in this essay. What is his purpose?

2. Does Boas believe that there is such a thing as a purely autonomous culture? What evidence does he give to prove or disprove this thesis?

3. What ways of acculturation does Boas present? What kinds of things are exchanged by cultures?

RHETORIC

1. As an early anthropologist, Boas might be expected to write in a scientific style. Is there any reflection in word choice or point of view of a scientific method? Is the style of Boas or Leakey more technical? Explain.

2. Explain Boas's use of the word *invention*. How does it differ from the way we use it? How does the difference reflect his anthropological viewpoint?

3. If you were to divide this essay into three parts, where would you divide it? Why did you divide it where you did?

4. How does Boas use process and analysis to support his thesis?

5. What kinds of evidence does he offer to support his thesis?

6. How does Boas use contrast and comparison? Are they his primary rhetorical methods? If so, why do you think he chose them? If not, why not?

WRITING

1. All Americans either are immigrants or have forebearers who were. How thoroughly have you been assimilated into the mainstream of American life? Do you believe that assimilation is valuable? Explain in an essay.

2. Many of us have had to acclimate ourselves to new cultural settings. When we do that, we are in a small way repeating the acts of nations that Boas describes. Describe objectively the process of assimilation you underwent when you did one of the following things: (a) went out for your first sports team; (b) moved to a new school, for instance, college; (c) moved into a new neighborhood.

3. Write an essay in which you predict how the diffusion of cultural traits will develop in the twenty-first century.

ANAÏS NIN

Notes on Feminism

Anaïs Nin (1903–1977), diarist, novelist, essayist, and feminist, was an American born in Paris. A student of psychology under Otto Rank, Nin always retained her interest in the inner self and specifically in the consciousness of women. In her words, she wished "to unmask the deeper self that lies hidden behind the self that we present to the world." Her diaries, started as letters to her father in 1931, were published in seven volumes between 1966 and 1980. These diaries, an imposing collection termed by Gunther Stuhlmann "one of the unique literary documents of our century," have been compared in method to the work of Marcel Proust. In this essay, Nin writes about the need for women to develop their inner selves.

he nature of my contribution to the Women's Liberation Movement is not political but psychological. I get thousands of letters from women who have been liberated by the reading of my diaries, which are a long study of the psychological obstacles that have prevented woman from her fullest evolution and flowering. I studied the negative influence of religion, of racial and cultural patterns, which action alone and no political slogans can dissolve. I describe in the diaries the many restrictions confining woman. The diary itself was an escape from judgment, a place in which to analyze the truth of woman's situation. I believe that is where the sense of freedom has to begin. I say begin, not remain. A reformation of woman's emotional attitudes and beliefs will enable her to act more effectively. I am not speaking of the practical, economic, sociological problems, as I believe many of them are solvable with clear thinking and intelligence. I am merely placing the emphasis on a confrontation of ourselves because it is a source of strength. Do not confuse my shifting of responsibility with blame. I am not blaming woman. I say that if we take the responsibility for our situation, we can feel less helpless than when we put the blame on society or man. We waste precious energy in negative rebellions. Awareness can give us a sense of captainship over our fate, and to take destiny into our own hands is more inspiring than to expect others to direct our destiny for us. No matter what ideas, psychology, history, or art I learned from man, I learned to convert it into the affirmation of my own identity and my own beliefs, to serve my own growth. At the same time, I loved woman and was fully aware of her problems, and I watched her struggles for development. I believe the lasting revolution comes from deep changes in ourselves which influence our collective life.

Many of the chores women accepted were ritualistic; they 2 were means of expressing love and care and protection. We have to find other ways of expressing these devotions. We cannot solve the problem of freeing ourselves of all chores without first understanding why we accomplished them and felt guilty when we did not. We have to persuade those we love that there are other ways of enriching their lives. Part of these occupations were compensatory. The home was our only kingdom, and it returned many pleasures. We were repaid with love and beauty and a sense of accomplishment. If we want our energy and strength to go into other channels, we have to work at a transitional solution which may deprive us of a personal world altogether. But I also think we have to cope with our deep-seated, deeply instilled sense of responsibility. That means finding a more creative way of love and collaboration, of educating our children, or caring for a house, and we have to convince those we love that there are other ways of accomplishing these things. The restrictions of women's lives, confined to the personal, also created in us qualities men lost to a degree in a competitive world. I think woman retains a more human relationship to human beings and is not corrupted by the impersonality of powerful interests. I have watched woman in law, in politics, and in education. Because of her gift for personal relationships she deals more effectively with injustice, war, prejudice. I have a dream about woman pouring into all professions a new quality. I want a different world, not the same world born of man's need of power which is the origin of war and injustice. We have to create a new woman.

What of ghettos and poverty? A new kind of human being 3 would not allow them to be born in the first place. It is the quality of human beings I want to see improved, because we already know that drugs, crime, war, and injustice are not curable by a change of system. It is humanism which is lacking in our leaders. I do not want to see women follow in the same pattern. To assert individual qualities and thought was tabooed by puritanism and is now being equally tabooed by militant fanatics. But practical problems are often solved by psychological liberation. The imagination, the skills, the intelligence, are freed to discover solutions. I see so many women in the movement thinking in obsessional circles about problems which are solvable when one is emotionally free to think and act clearly. Undirected, blind anger and hostility are not effective weapons. They have to be converted into lucid action. Each woman has to consider her own problems before she can act effectively within her radius; otherwise she is merely adding the burden of her problems to the collective overburdened majority. Her individual solution, courage, become in turn like cellular growth, organic growth. It is added to the general synthesis. Slogans do not give strength because generalizations are untrue. Many intelligent women, many potentially collaborative men, are alienated by generalizations. To recruit all women for a work for which some are unfit is not effective. The group does not always give strength, because it moves only according to the lowest denominator of understanding. The group weakens the individual will and annihilates the individual contribution. To object to individual growth of awareness in women is to work against the benefit of the collective whose quality is raised by individual research and learning. Each woman has to know herself, her problems, her obstacles. I ask woman to realize she can be master of her own destiny. This is an inspiring thought. To blame others means one feels helpless. What I liked best about psychology is the concept that destiny is interior, in our own hands. While we wait for others to free us, we will not develop the strength to do it ourselves. When a woman has not solved her personal, intimate defeats, her private hostilities, her failures, she brings the dregs of this to the group and only increases its negative reactions. This is placing liberation on too narrow a basis. Liberation means the power to transcend obstacles. The obstacles are educational, religious, racial, and cultural patterns. These have to be confronted, and there is no political solution which serves them all. The real tyrants are guilt, taboos, educational inheritance—these are our enemies. And we can grapple with them. The real enemy is what we were taught, not always by man, but often by our mothers and grandmothers.

The trouble with anger is that it makes us overstate our case 4 and prevents us from reaching awareness. We often damage our case by anger. It is like resorting to war.

Poverty and injustice and prejudice are not solved by any 5 man-made system. I want them to be solved by a higher quality of human being who, by his own law of valuation upon human life, will not permit such inequalities. In that sense whatever we do for the development of this higher quality will eventually permeate all society. The belief that all of us, untrained, unprepared and unskilled, can be conscripted for mass action is what has prevented woman from developing, because it is the same old-fashioned assertion that the only good we can do is outside of ourselves, salvaging others. When we do this we ignore the fact that the evil comes from individual flaws, undeveloped human beings. We need models. We need heroes and leaders. Out of the many lawyers who came from Harvard, we were given only one Nader. But one Nader has incalculable influence. If we continue in the name of politics to denigrate those who have developed their skills to the maximum pitch as elite, privileged, or exceptional people, we will never be able to help others achieve their potential. We need blueprints for the creation of human beings as well as for architecture.

The attack against individual development belongs to the 6 dark ages of socialism. If I am able to inspire or help women today, it is because I persisted in my development. I was often derailed by other duties, but I never gave up this relentless disciplined creation of my awareness because I realized that at the bottom of every failed system to improve the lot of man lies an imperfect, corruptible human being.

It is inspiring to read of the women who defied the codes and 7 taboos of their period: Ninon de Lenclos in the seventeenth century, Lou Andreas-Salomé in the time of Freud, Nietzsche, and Rilke, and in our time Han Suyin. Or the four heroines of Lesley Blanch's *Wilder Shores of Love*.

I see a great deal of negativity in the Women's Liberation 8 Movement. It is less important to attack male writers than to discover and read women writers, to attack male-dominated films than to make films by women. If the passivity of woman is going to erupt like a volcano or an earthquake, it will not accomplish anything but disaster. This passivity can be converted to creative will. If it expresses itself in war, then it is an imitation of man's methods. It would be good to study the writings of women who were more concerned with personal relationships than with the power struggles of history. I have a dream

214

ANAÏS NIN

of a more human lawyer, a more human educator, a more human politician. To become man, or like man, is no solution. There is far too much imitation of man in the women's movement. That is merely a displacement of power. Woman's definition of power should be different. It should be based on relationships to others. The women who truly identify with their oppressors, as the cliché phrase goes, are the women who are acting like men, masculinizing themselves, not those who seek to convert or transform man. There is no liberation of one group at the expense of another. Liberation can only come totally and in unison.

Group thinking does not give strength. It weakens the will. 9 Majority thinking is oppressive because it inhibits individual growth and seeks a formula for all. Individual growth makes communal living of higher quality. A developed woman will know how to take care of all her social duties and how to act effectively.

COMPREHENSION

1. Why do people write to Nin? Who is her audience for this essay?

2. What arguments does Nin give against group action? What arguments does she offer for individual growth? Does she support feminism? Explain.

3. According to Nin, what are the main differences between man and woman? Why does this difference make women so important to the development of social justice?

RHETORIC

1. Give examples of Nin's hortatory style. Examine particularly her point of view and verb forms.

2. Give examples of Nin's use of psychological vocabulary in this essay. How does the vocabulary reflect the theme? Cite other examples of jargon from the essays in this chapter.

3. Where in this essay does Nin describe her personal experience? How is this placement important for the development of the essay?

4. Does Nin use such conventional forms of organization as comparison and contrast or classification? If not, what kinds of organizational devices does she use? If she does, detail how.

5. The most explicit criticism of the woman's liberation movement occurs in paragraph 8. Why does Nin defer this criticism until so late in her essay?

6. Nin's conclusion clearly recapitulates most of the points of her essay. Why does she write such a conventional conclusion?

WRITING

1. Do you agree that personal growth must precede social growth? Explain in an argumentative essay.

2. Write an essay describing your idea of the new woman or new man.

3. For one week, keep a diary in which you focus on the restrictions you have sensed in your personal life. These restrictions might be sexual, racial, academic, economic, religious, or cultural.

ADRIENNE RICH

The Anger of a Child

Adrienne Rich (1929–   ) was born in Baltimore and graduated from Radcliffe College. She has taught at many universities, including the City University of New York, Columbia University, and Brandeis University. Presently she is a professor of English and feminist studies at Stanford. Author of over twenty books of poetry and five books of prose, Rich is considered one of America's most important feminist poets, her latter poems often dealing with women's struggle for identity and power. Her book Diving Into the Wreck: Poems, 1971–1972 was awarded a National Book Award. She has also received a Guggenheim Fellowship, a Bollingen Foundation translation grant, and a grant from the National Endowment for the Arts. In "The Anger of a Child," Rich describes how deeply the dynamics of her family affected her own attitudes toward herself as a woman and a mother, and even her very concept of personhood itself.

It is hard to write about my mother. Whatever I do write,   1
it is my story I am telling, my version of the past. If she were to tell her own story other landscapes would be revealed. But in my landscape or hers, there would be old, smoldering patches of deep-burning anger. Before her marriage, she had trained seriously for years both as a concert pianist and a composer. Born in a southern town, mothered by a strong, frustrated woman, she had won a scholarship to study with the director at the Peabody Conservatory in Baltimore, and by teaching at girls' schools had earned her way to further study in New York, Paris, and Vienna. From the age of sixteen, she had been a young belle, who could have married at any time, but she also possessed unusual talent, determination, and independence for her time and place. She read—and reads—widely and wrote—as her journals from my childhood and her letters of today reveal—with grace and pungency.

She married my father after a ten years' engagement during   2 which he finished his medical training and began to establish himself in academic medicine. Once married, she gave up the possibility of a concert career, though for some years she went on composing, and she is still a skilled and dedicated pianist. My father, brilliant, ambitious, possessed by his own drive, assumed that she would give her life over to the enhancement of his. She would manage his household with the formality and grace becoming to a medical professor's wife, though on a limited budget; she would "keep up" her music, though there was no question of letting her composing and practice conflict with her duties as a wife and mother. She was supposed to bear him two children, a boy and a girl. She had to keep her household books to the last penny—I still can see the big blue-gray ledgers, inscribed in her clear, strong hand; she marketed by streetcar, and later, when they could afford a car, she drove my father to and from his laboratory or lectures, often awaiting him for hours. She raised two children, and taught us all our lessons, including music. (Neither of us was sent to school until the fourth grade.) I am sure that she was made to feel responsible for all our imperfections.

My father, like the transcendentalist Bronson Alcott, believed   3
that he (or rather, his wife) could raise children according to his unique moral and intellectual plan, thus proving to the world the values of enlightened, unorthodox child-rearing. I believe that my mother, like Abigail Alcott, at first genuinely and enthusiastically embraced the experiment, and only later found that in carrying out my father's intense, perfectionist program, she was in conflict with her deep instincts as a mother. Like Abigail Alcott, too, she must have found that while ideas might be unfolded by her husband, their daily, hourly practice was going to be up to her. (" 'Mr. A. aids me in general principles, but nobody can aid me in the detail,' she mourned. ... Moreover her husband's views kept her constantly wondering if she were doing a good job. 'Am I doing what is right? Am I doing enough? Am I doing too much?' " The appearance of "temper" and "will" in Louisa, the second Alcott daughter, was blamed by her father on her inheritance from her mother.) Under the institution of motherhood, the mother is the first to blame if theory proves unworkable in practice, or if anything whatsoever goes wrong. But even earlier, my mother had failed at one part of the plan: she had not produced a son.

For years, I felt my mother had chosen my father over me,   4
had sacrificed me to his needs and theories. When my first child was born, I was barely in communication with my parents. I had been fighting my father for my right to an emotional life and a selfhood beyond his needs and theories. We were all at a draw. Emerging from the fear, exhaustion, and alienation of my first childbirth, I could not admit even to myself that I wanted my mother, let alone tell her how

much I wanted her. When she visited me in the hospital neither of us could uncoil the obscure lashings of feeling that darkened the room, the tangled thread running backward to where she had labored for three days to give birth to me, and I was not a son. Now, twenty-six years later, I lay in a contagious hospital with my allergy, my skin covered with a mysterious rash, my lips and eyelids swollen, my body bruised and sutured, and, in a cot beside my bed, slept the perfect, golden, male child I had brought forth. How could I have interpreted her feelings when I could not begin to decipher my own? My body had spoken all too eloquently, but it was, medically, just my body. I wanted her to mother me again, to hold my baby in her arms as she had once held me; but that baby was also a gauntlet flung down: *my son*. Part of me longed to offer him for her blessing; part of me wanted to hold him up as a badge of victory in our tragic, unnecessary rivalry as women.

But I was only at the beginning. I know now as I could not possibly know then, that among the tangle of feelings between us, in that crucial yet unreal meeting, was her guilt. Soon I would begin to understand the full weight and burden of maternal guilt, that daily, nightly, hourly, *Am I doing what is right? Am I doing enough? Am I doing too much?* The institution of motherhood finds all mothers more or less guilty of having failed their children; and my mother, in particular, had been expected to help create, according to my father's plan, a perfect daughter. This "perfect" daughter, though gratifyingly precocious, had early been given to tics and tantrums, had become permanently lame from arthritis at twenty-two; she had finally resisted her father's Victorian paternalism, his seductive charm and controlling cruelty, had married a divorced graduate student, had begun to write "modern," "obscure," "pessimistic" poetry, lacking the fluent sweetness of Tennyson, had had the final temerity to get pregnant and bring a living baby into the world. She had ceased to be the demure and precocious child or the poetic, seducible adolescent. Something, in my father's view, had gone terribly wrong. I can imagine that whatever else my mother felt (and I know that part of her *was* mutely on my side) she also was made to feel blame. Beneath the "numbness" that she has since told me she experienced at that time, I can imagine the guilt of Everymother, because I have known it myself.

But I did not know it yet. And it is difficult for me to write of my mother now, because I have known it too well. I struggle to describe what it felt like to be her daughter, but I find myself divided, slipping under her skin; a part of me identified too much with her. I know deep reservoirs of anger toward her still exist: the anger of a four-year-old locked in the closet (my father's orders, but my mother carried them out) for childish misbehavior; the anger of a six-year-old

ADRIENNE RICH

kept too long at piano practice (again, at his insistence, but it was she who gave the lessons) till I developed a series of facial tics. (As a mother I know what a child's facial tic is—a lancet of guilt and pain running through one's own body.) And I still feel the anger of a daughter, pregnant, wanting my mother desperately and feeling she had gone over to the enemy.

And I know there must be deep reservoirs of anger in her; every mother has known overwhelming, unacceptable anger at her children. When I think of the conditions under which my mother became a mother, the impossible expectations, my father's distaste for pregnant women, his hatred of all that he could not control, my anger at her dissolves into grief and anger *for* her, and then dissolves back again into anger at her: the ancient, unpurged anger of the child. 7

My mother lives today as an independent woman, which she was always meant to be. She is a much-loved, much-admired grandmother, an explorer in new realms; she lives in the present and future, not the past. I no longer have fantasies—they are the unhealed child's fantasies, I think—of some infinitely healing conversation with her, in which we could show all our wounds, transcend the pain we have shared as mother and daughter, say everything at last. But in writing these pages, I am admitting, at least, how important her existence is and has been for me. 8

COMPREHENSION

1. Who is Rich's audience in this essay? Might there be more than one audience? Why, or why not?

2. What is the basis of Rich's anger toward her father? Toward her mother? Does she resolve this anger? Explain.

3. Compare the attitude toward women that existed in Rich's family to that of Kingston's family in "The Woman Warrior."

RHETORIC

1. How do the following examples of figurative language contribute to the tone of the essay: "smoldering patches of deep-burning anger" (paragraph 1); "obscure lashings of feeling" (paragraph 4); "deep reservoirs of anger" (paragraph 6)?

2. Note the length and structure of the following sentence. Why has the author compressed so much information into it? How would the effect on the reader differ if it were broken down into shorter sentences? "This 'perfect' daughter, though gratifyingly precocious, had early been given to tics and tantrums, had become permanently lame from arthritis at twenty-two; she had finally resisted her father's Victorian paternalism, his seductive charm and controlling cruelty, had married a divorced graduate student, had begun to write 'modern,' 'obscure,' 'pessimistic' poetry, lacking the fluent sweetness of Tennyson, had had

THE ANGER OF A CHILD   219 the final temerity to get pregnant and bring a living baby into the world" (paragraph 5).

3. Why has Rich chosen to include information about Bronson Alcott? Would the essay have been just as effective without it?

4. Why are the questions in paragraph 5 italicized?

5. In paragraph 6, Rich makes extensive use of parentheses. How does this punctuation complement the content of the paragraph?

6. Rich concludes the essay by stating her purpose. Why has she saved it for last?

WRITING

1. Who bears the greatest responsibility for Rich's anger? Her father? Her mother? The society that condoned oppression of women? Rich herself? Analyze these issues in an essay.

2. Write an essay explaining how your father or mother influenced your lifestyle, goals, attitudes, or behavior.

3. The father's view concerning the role of women no longer exists in our society. Agree or disagree with this statement in a brief essay.

4. Compare and contrast the essays by Nin and Rich.

SIGMUND FREUD

Libidinal Types

Sigmund Freud (1956–1939), founder of psychoanalysis, was an excellent writer. His theories concerning the pleasure principle, repression, and infantile sexuality are still controversial; nevertheless, they have had a profound impact upon culture, education, and art. Some of Freud's psychological works include The Interpretation of Dreams *(1900),* The Psychopathology of Everyday Life *(1904), and* The Ego and the Id *(1923). He also analyzed the relation of culture and psychology in* Totem and Taboo *(1913) and* Moses and Monotheism *(1939). In the following essay, Freud discusses several character types derived from his theory of the libido.*

bservation teaches us that in individual human beings the general features of humanity are embodied in almost infinite variety. If we follow the promptings of a legitimate desire to distinguish particular types in this multiplicity, we must begin by selecting the characteristics to look for and the points of view to bear in mind in making our differentiation. For this purpose physical qualities will be no less useful than mental; it will be most valuable of all if we can make our classification on the basis of a regularly occurring combination of physical and mental characteristics.

It is doubtful whether we are as yet able to discover types of this order, although we shall certainly be able to do so something on a basis of which we are still ignorant. If we confine our efforts to defining certain purely psychological types, the libidinal situation will have the first claim to serve as the basis of our classification. It may fairly be demanded that this classification should not merely be deduced from our knowledge or our conjectures about the libido, but that it should be easily verified in actual experience and should help to clarify the mass of our observations and enable us to grasp their meaning. Let it be admitted at once that there is no need to suppose that, even in the psychical sphere, these libidinal types are the only possible ones; if we take other characteristics as our basis of classification we might be able to distinguish a whole series of other psychological types. But there is one rule which must apply to all such types: they must not coincide with specific clinical pictures. On the contrary, they should embrace all the variations which according to our practical standards fall within the category of the normal. In their extreme developments, however, they may well approximate to clinical pictures and so help to bridge the gulf which is assumed to exist between the normal and the pathological.

Now we can distinguish three main libidinal types, according as the subject's libido is mainly allocated to one or another region of the mental apparatus. To name these types is not very easy; following the lines of our depth-psychology, I should be inclined to call them the *erotic*, the *narcissistic* and the *obsessional* type.

The *erotic* type is easily characterized. Erotics are persons whose main interest—the relatively largest amount of their libido—is focused on love. Loving, but above all being loved, is for them the most important thing in life. They are governed by the dread of loss of love, and this makes them peculiarly dependent on those who may withhold their love from them. Even in its pure form this type is a very common one. Variations occur according as it is blended with another type and as the element of aggression in it is strong or weak. From the social and cultural standpoint this type represents the elementary instinctual claims of the id, to which the other psychical agencies have become docile.

The second type is that which I have termed the *obsessional*— a name which may at first seem rather strange; its distinctive characteristic is the supremacy exercised by the super-ego, which is segregated from the ego with great accompanying tension. Persons of this type are governed by anxiety of conscience instead of by the dread of losing love; they exhibit, we might say, an inner instead of an outer dependence; they develop a high degree of self-reliance, from the social standpoint they are the true upholders of civilization, for the most part in a conservative spirit.

The characteristics of the third type, justly called the *narcissistic*, are in the main negatively described. There is no tension between ego and super-ego—indeed, starting from this type one would hardly have arrived at the notion of a super-ego; there is no preponderance of erotic needs; the main interest is focused on self-preservation; the type is independent and not easily overawed. The ego has a considerably amount of aggression available, one manifestation of this being a proneness to activity; where love is in question, loving is preferred to being loved. People of this type impress others as being "personalities"; it is on them that their follow-men are specially likely to lean; they readily assume the role of leader, give a fresh stimulus to cultural development or break down existing conditions.

These pure types will hardly escape the suspicion of being deduced from the theory of the libido. But we feel that we are on the firm ground of experience when we turn to the mixed types which are to be found so much more frequently than the unmixed. These new types: the *erotic-obsessional*, the *erotic-narcissistic* and the *narcissistic-obsessional* do really seem to provide a good grouping of the individual psychical structures revealed in analysis. If we study these mixed types we find in them pictures of characters with which we have long been familiar. In the *erotic-obsessional* type the preponderance of the instincts is restricted by the influence of the super-ego: dependence on persons who are *contemporary* objects and, at the same time, on the residues of *former* objects—parents, educators and ideal figures—is carried by this type to the furthest point. The *erotic-narcissistic* type is perhaps the most common of all. It combines contrasting characteristics which are thus able to moderate one another; studying this type in comparison with the other two erotic types, we can see how aggressiveness and activity go with a predominance of narcissism. Finally, the *narcissistic-obsessional* type represents the variation most valuable from the cultural standpoint, for it combines independence of external factors and regard for the requirements of conscience with the capacity for energetic action, and it reinforces the ego against the super-ego.

It might be asked in jest why no mention has been made of 8
another mixed type which is theoretically possible: the *erotic-obses-
sional-narcissistic*. But the answer to this jest is serious: such a type
would no longer be a type at all, but the absolute norm, the ideal
harmony. We thereupon realize that the phenomenon of different
types arises just in so far as one or two of the three main modes of
expending the libido in the mental economy have been favoured at
the cost of the others.

Another question that may be asked is what is the relation of 9
these libidinal types to pathology, whether some of them have a special disposition to pass over into neurosis and, if so, which types lead
to which forms of neurosis. The answer is that the hypothesis of these
libidinal types throws no fresh light on the genesis of the neuroses.
Experience testifies that persons of all these types can live free from
neurosis. The pure types marked by the undisputed predominance of
a single psychical agency seem to have a better prospect of manifesting themselves as pure character-formations, while we might expect
that the mixed types would provide a more fruitful soil for the con-
ditioning factors of neurosis. But I do not think that we should make
up our mind on these points until they have been carefully submitted
to appropriate tests.

It seems easy to infer that when persons of the erotic type fall 10
ill they will develop hysteria, just as those of the obsessional type will
develop obsessional neurosis; but even this conclusion partakes of the
uncertainty to which I have just alluded. People of the narcissistic
type, who, being otherwise independent, are exposed to frustration
from the external world, are peculiarly disposed to psychosis; and
their mental composition also contains some of the essential condi-
tioning factors which make for criminality.

We know that we have not as yet exact certainty about the 11
aetiological conditions of neurosis. The precipitating occasions are
frustrations and inner conflicts: conflicts between the three great
psychical agencies, conflicts arising in the libidinal economy by reason
of our bisexual disposition, conflicts between the erotic and the aggressive instinctual components. It is the endeavor of the psychology
of the neurosis to discover what imparts a pathogenic character to
these processes, which are a part of the normal course of mental life.

COMPREHENSION

1. State, in your own words, Freud's thesis in this selection.

2. According to Freud, what types of individuals uphold society? What are their
psychological characteristics?

3. What relationship does Freud see between mental illness and these character
types?

RHETORIC

1. Freud assumes that the reader is familiar with several psychological terms. Make sure you understand the following: *depth-psychology* (paragraph 3); *id* (paragraph 4); *ego* (paragraph 5); *neuroses* (paragraph 9); *psychosis* (paragraph 10); and *aetiological* (paragraph 11).

2. Does Freud use general or specific language in this essay? How does his choice of language relate to the conclusions he draws in paragraphs 9 to 11?

3. Freud's primary rhetorical technique is classification. Identify his categories, and list the distinguishing characteristics of each class.

4. Explain the relations of paragraphs 1 and 2 to the body of the essay.

5. Freud uses definition frequently in this essay. What kinds of definitions does he use? How do they contribute to the structuring of the essay?

6. Explain the importance of paragraph 7 to the essay's structure. What effect does it have on the classification the author has established?

WRITING

1. Judging from your own observations, how valid is Freud's classification of libidinal types? Write an essay defending or attacking Freud's system.

2. There are innumerable ways to classify people. In a classification essay, devise your own method for analyzing a particular group of people.

3. Take one of Freud's terms—for example, *neurosis*—and write an extended definition of it.

RICHARD WRIGHT

The Psychological Reactions of Oppressed People

Richard Wright (1908–1960), American author, spoke eloquently about the black experience in America in his novels and essays. Wright was born on a Mississippi plantation. As a young man he moved to Chicago, where he joined a Federal Writers' Project in the 1930s. His experiences in Mississippi and Chicago appear in his early fiction: Uncle Tom's Children *(1938) is about racial oppression in the South, and* Native Son *(1940) is about discrimination and exploitation in Chicago during the Depression. Wright became an expatriate after World War II. From Paris, he wrote an autobiography,* Black Boy *(1945), and two novels,* The Outsider *(1953) and* The Long Dream *(1958). Wright visited the African Gold Coast, where, as the following essay demonstrates, he observed the oppression of blacks once more.*

Buttressed by their belief that their God had entrusted the earth into their keeping, drunk with power and possibility, waxing rich through trade in commodities, human and non-human, with awesome naval and merchant marines at their disposal, their countries filled with human debris anxious for any adventures, psychologically armed with new facts, white Western Christian civilization during the fourteenth, fifteenth, sixteenth, and seventeenth centuries, with a long, slow, and bloody explosion, hurled itself upon the sprawling masses of colored humanity in Asia and Africa. 1

I say to you white men of the West: Don't be too proud of how easily you conquered and plundered those Asians and Africans. You had unwitting allies in your campaigns; you had Fifth Columns in the form of indigenous cultures to facilitate your military, missionary, and mercenary efforts. Your collaborators in those regions consisted of the mental habits of the people, habits for which they were in no way responsible, no more than you were responsible for yours. Those habits constituted corps of saboteurs, of spies, if you will, that worked in the interests of European aggression. You must realize that it was not your courage or racial superiority that made you win, nor was it the racial inferiority or cowardice of the Asians and Africans that made them lose. This is an important point that you must grasp, or your concern with this problem will be forever wide of the facts. How, then, did the West, numerically the minority, achieve, during the last four centuries, so many dazzling victories over the body of colored mankind? Frankly, it took you centuries to do a job that could have been done in fifty years! You had the motive, the fire power, the will, the religious spur, the superior organization, but you dallied. Why? You were not aware exactly of what you were doing. You didn't suspect your impersonal strength, or the impersonal weakness on the other side. You were as unconscious, at bottom, as were your victims about what was really taking place. 2

Your world of culture clashed with the culture-worlds of colored mankind, and the ensuing destruction of traditional beliefs among a billion and a half of black, brown, and yellow men has set off a tide of social, cultural, political, and economic revolution that grips the world today. That revolution is assuming many forms, absolutistic, communistic, fascistic, theocratistic etc.—all marked by unrest, violence, and an astounding emotional thrashing about as men seek new objects about which they can center their loyalties. 3

It is of the reactions, tortured and turbulent, of those Asians   4
and Africans, in the New and Old World, that I wish to speak to you.
Naturally I cannot speak for those Asians and Africans who are still
locked in their mystical or ancestor-worshiping traditions. They are
the voiceless ones, the silent ones. Indeed, I think that they are the
doomed ones, men in a tragic trap. Any attempt on their part to wage
a battle to protect their outmoded traditions and religions is a battle
that is lost before it starts. And I say frankly that I suspect any white
man who loves to dote upon those "naked nobles," who wants to
leave them as they are, who finds them "primitive and pure," for such
mystical hankering is, in my opinion, the last refuge of reactionary
racists and psychological cripples tired of their own civilization. My
remarks will, of necessity, be confined to those Asians and Africans
who, having been partly Westernized, have a quarrel with the West.
They are the ones who feel that they are oppressed. In a sense, this is
a fight of the West with *itself*, a fight that the West blunderingly began,
and the West does not to this day realize that it is the sole responsible
agent, the sole instigator. For the West to disclaim responsibility for
what it so clearly did is to make every white man alive on earth today
a criminal. In history as in law, men must be held strictly responsible
for the consequences of their historic actions, whether they intended
those consequences or not. For the West to accept its responsibility is
to create the means by which white men can liberate themselves from
their fears, panic, and terror while they confront the world's colored
majority of men who are also striving for liberation from the irrational
ties which the West prompted them to disown—ties of which the West
has partially robbed them.

Let's imagine a mammoth flying saucer from Mars landing,   5
say, in a peasant Swiss village and debouching swarms of fierce-
looking men whose skins are blue and whose red eyes flash lightning
bolts that deal instant death. The inhabitants are all the more terrified
because the arrival of these men had been predicted. The religious
myths of the Western world—the Second Coming of Christ, the Last
Judgment, etc., have conditioned Europeans for just such an improbable event. Hence, those Swiss natives will feel that resistance is useless for a while. As long as the blue strangers are casually kind, they
are obeyed and served. They become the Fathers of the people. Is this
a fragment of paperback science fiction? No. It's more prosaic than
that. The image I've sketched above is the manner, by and large, in
which white Europe overran Asia and Africa. (Remember the Cortés-
Montezuma drama!)

But why did Europe do this? Did it only want gold, power,   6
women, raw materials? It was more complicated than that.

The fifteenth-, sixteenth-, and seventeenth-century neurotic   7
European, sick of his thwarted instincts, restless, filled with self-

disgust, was looking for not only spices and gold and slaves when he set out; he was looking for an Arcadia, a Land's End, a Shangri-la, a world peopled by shadow men, a world that would permit free play for his repressed instincts. Stripped of tradition, these misfits, adventurers, indentured servants, convicts and freebooters were the most advanced individualists of their time. Rendered socially superfluous by the stifling weight of the Church and nobility, buttressed by the influence of the ideas of Hume and Descartes, they had been brutally molded toward attitudes of emotional independence and could doff the cloying ties of custom, tradition, and family. The Asian-African native, anchored in family-dependence systems of life, could not imagine why or how these men had left their homelands, could not conceive of the cold, arid emotions sustaining them. . . . Emotional independence was a state of mind not only utterly inconceivable, but an attitude toward life downright evil to the Asian-African native— something to be avoided at all costs. Bound by a charged array of humble objects that made up an emotionally satisfying and exciting world, they, trapped by their limited mental horizon, could not help thinking that the white men invading their lands had been driven forcibly from their homes!

Living in a waking dream, generations of emotionally impoverished colonial European whites wallowed in the quick gratification of greed, reveled in the cheap superiority of racial domination, slaked their sensual thirst in illicit sexuality, draining off the dammed-up libido that European morality had condemned, amassing through trade a vast reservoir of economic fat, thereby establishing vast accumulations of capital which spurred the industrialization of the West. Asia and Africa thus became a neurotic habit that Europeans could forgo only at the cost of a powerful psychic wound, for this emotionally crippled Europe had, through the centuries, grown used to leaning upon this black crutch. 8

But what of the impact of those white faces upon the personalities of the native? Steeped in dependence systems of family life and anchored in ancestor-worshiping religions, the native was prone to identify those powerful white faces falling athwart his existence with the potency of his dead father who had sustained him in the past. Temporarily accepting the invasion, he transferred his loyalties to those white faces, but, because of the psychological, racial, and economic luxury which those faces derived from their domination, the native was kept at bay. 9

Today, as the tide of white domination of the land mass of Asia and Africa recedes, there lies exposed to view a procession of shattered cultures, disintegrated societies, and a writhing sweep of more aggressive, irrational religion than the world has known for centuries. And, as scientific research, partially freed from the blight of 10 colonial control, advances, we are witnessing the rise of a new genre of academic literature dealing with colonial and post-colonial facts from a wider angle of vision than ever possible before. The personality distortions of hundreds of millions of black, brown, and yellow people that are being revealed by this literature are confounding and will necessitate drastic alteration of our past evaluations of colonial rule. In this new literature one enters a universe of menacing shadows where disparate images coalesce—white turning into black, the dead coming to life, the top becoming the bottom—until you think you are seeing Biblical beasts with seven heads and ten horns rising out of the sea. Imperialism turns out to have been much more morally foul a piece of business than even Marx and Lenin imagined!

An agony was induced into the native heart, rotting and pul- 11
verizing it as it tried to live under a white domination with which it could not identify in any real sense, a white domination that mocked it. The more Westernized that native heart became, the more anti-Western it had to be, for the heart was now weighing itself in terms of white Western values that made it feel degraded. Vainly attempting to embrace the world of white faces that rejected it, it recoiled and sought refuge in the ruins of moldering tradition. But it was too late; it was trapped; it found haven in neither. This is the psychological stance of the elite of the populations, free or still in a state of subjection, of present-day Asia and Africa; this is the profound revolution that the white man cast into the world; this is the revolution (a large part of which has been successfully captured by the Communists) that the white man confronts today with fear and paralysis.

COMPREHENSION

1.   Who is Wright's audience? How do you know? What attitude does he take toward this audience?

2.   Whom does Wright blame for the state of oppressed nations? What reasons does he give for blaming them?

3.   According to Wright, what are the cultural traits of Western people in the fifteenth, sixteenth, seventeenth, and eighteenth centuries? What is his purpose in presenting these traits?

RHETORIC

1.   Explain what Wright means by "advanced individualists" (paragraph 7). What other words does he use to describe Westerners? What connotations do these words tend to have?

2.   Give examples of Wright's hortatory style. What other styles of writing appear in this essay?

RICHARD WRIGHT

3. How does Wright develop his history? Is his chronological structure linear? Does he repeat events? How does his choice here reflect the goals of the essay?

4. Explain how contrast is used as a structural device in this essay.

5. What words introduce the hypothetical example in paragraph 5? How does this example contribute to the theme of the essay?

6. Identify an instance of syllogistic reasoning in Wright's argument. Is the essay strictly logical? Explain.

WRITING

1. In an age of diminishing resources and burgeoning populations, can Americans afford to be concerned with the plight of oppressed peoples? How do you think Wright would answer this question? How do you? Answer these questions in a brief essay.

2. Write an essay on the new psychology of third world nations.

3. People often engage in actions whose consequences are damaging. Show how this insight is true in your experience.

4. Write a comparative essay on the ways that Freud and Wright employ the word *neurosis.*

Social 6 Processes and Institutions

E. M. FORSTER

My Wood

Edward Morgan Forster (1879–1970), English essayist, novelist, biographer, and literary critic, wrote several notable works of fiction dealing with the constricting effects of social and national conventions upon human relationships. These novels include A Room with a View *(1908),* Howards End *(1910), and* A Passage to India *(1924). In addition, his lectures on fiction, collected as* Aspects of the Novel *(1927), remain graceful elucidations of the genre. In "My Wood," taken from his essay collection* Abinger Harvest *(1936), Forster writes with wit and wisdom about the effect of property upon human behavior—notably his own.*

 few years ago I wrote a book which dealt in part with the difficulties of the English in India. Feeling that they would have had no difficulties in India themselves, the Americans read the book freely. The more they read it the better it made them feel, and a cheque to the author was the result. I bought a wood with the cheque. It is not a large wood—it contains scarcely any trees, and it is intersected, blast it, by a public footpath. Still, it is the first property that I have owned, so it is right that other people should participate in my shame, and should ask themselves, in accents that will vary in horror, this very important question: What is the effect of property upon the character? Don't let's touch economics; the effect of private ownership upon the community as a whole is another question—a more important question, perhaps, but another one. Let's keep to psychology. If you own things, what's their effect on you? What's the effect on me of my wood?

In the first place, it makes me feel heavy. Property does have 2 this effect. Property produces men of weight, and it was a man of weight who failed to get into the Kingdom of Heaven. He was not wicked, that unfortunate millionaire in the parable, he was only stout; he stuck out in front, not to mention behind, and as he wedged himself this way and that in the crystalline entrance and bruised his well-fed flanks, he saw beneath him a comparatively slim camel passing through the eye of a needle and being woven into the robe of God. The Gospels all through couple stoutness and slowness. They point out what is perfectly obvious, yet seldom realized: that if you have a lot of things you cannot move about a lot, that furniture requires dusting, dusters require servants, servants require insurance stamps, and the whole tangle of them makes you think twice before you accept an invitation to dinner or go for a bathe in the Jordan. Sometimes the Gospels proceed further and say with Tolstoy that property is sinful; they approach the difficult ground of asceticism here, where I cannot follow them. But as to the immediate effects of property on people, they just show straightforward logic. It produces men of weight. Men of weight cannot, by definition, move like the lightning from the East unto the West, and the ascent of a fourteen-stone bishop into a pulpit is thus the exact antithesis of the coming of the Son of Man. My wood makes me feel heavy.

In the second place, it makes me feel it ought to be larger. 3

The other day I heard a twig snap in it. I was annoyed at first, 4 for I thought that someone was blackberrying, and depreciating the value of the undergrowth. On coming nearer, I saw it was not a man who had trodden on the twig and snapped it, but a bird, and I felt pleased. My bird. The bird was not equally pleased. Ignoring the relation between us, it took fright as soon as it saw the shape of my face, and flew straight over the boundary hedge into a field, the property of Mrs. Henessy, where it sat down with a loud squawk. It had become Mrs. Henessy's bird. Something seemed grossly amiss here, something that would not have occurred had the wood been larger. I could not afford to buy Mrs. Henessy out, I dared not murder her, and limitations of this sort beset me on every side. Ahab did not want that vineyard—he only needed it to round off his property, preparatory to plotting a new curve—and all the land around my wood has become necessary to me in order to round off the wood. A boundary protects. But—poor little thing—the boundary ought in its turn to be protected. Noises on the edge of it. Children throw stones. A little more, and then a little more, until we reach the sea. Happy Canute! Happier Alexander! And after all, why should even the world be the limit of possession? A rocket containing a Union Jack, will, it is hoped, be shortly fired at the moon. Mars. Sirius. Beyond which . . . But these immensities ended by saddening me. I could not suppose that my wood was the destined nucleus of universal dominion—it is so very small and contains no mineral wealth beyond the blackberries. Nor was I comforted when Mrs. Henessy's bird took alarm for the second time and flew clean away from us all, under the belief that it belonged to itself.

   In the third place, property makes its owner feel that he ought   5
to do something to it. Yet he isn't sure what. A restlessness comes over him, a vague sense that he has a personality to express—the same sense which, without any vagueness, leads the artist to an act of creation. Sometimes I think I will cut down such trees as remain in the wood, at other times I want to fill up the gaps between them with new trees. Both impulses are pretentious and empty. They are not honest movements towards money-making or beauty. They spring from a foolish desire to express myself and from an inability to enjoy what I have got. Creation, property, enjoyment form a sinister trinity in the human mind. Creation and enjoyment are both very, very good, yet they are often unattainable without a material basis, and at such moments property pushes itself in as a substitute, saying, "Accept me instead—I'm good enough for all three." It is not enough. It is, as Shakespeare said of lust, "The expense of spirit in a waste of shame": it is "Before, a joy proposed; behind, a dream." Yet we don't know how to shun it. It is forced on us by our economic system as the alternative to starvation. It is also forced on us by an internal defect in the soul, by the feeling that in property may lie the germs of self-development and of exquisite or heroic deeds. Our life on earth is, and ought to be, material and carnal. But we have not yet learned to manage our materialism and carnality properly; they are still entangled with the desire for ownership, where (in the words of Dante) "Possession is one with loss."

   And this brings us to our fourth and final point: the black-   6
berries.

   Blackberries are not plentiful in this meagre grove, but they   7
are easily seen from the public footpath which traverses it, and all too easily gathered. Foxgloves, too—people will pull up the foxgloves, and ladies of an educational tendency even grub for toadstools to show them on the Monday in class. Other ladies, less educated, roll down the bracken in the arms of their gentlemen friends. There is paper, there are tins. Pray, does my wood belong to me or doesn't it?

E. M. FORSTER

And, if it does, should I not own it best by allowing no one else to walk there? There is a wood near Lyme Regis, also cursed by a public footpath, where the owner has not hesitated on this point. He had built high stone walls each side of the path, and has spanned it by bridges, so that the public circulate like termites while he gorges on the blackberries unseen. He really does own his wood, this able chap. Dives in Hell did pretty well, but the gulf dividing him from Lazarus could be traversed by vision, and nothing traverses it here. And perhaps I shall come to this in time. I shall wall in and fence out until I really taste the sweets of property. Enormously stout, endlessly avaricious, pseudo-creative, intensely selfish, I shall weave upon my forehead the quadruple crown of possession until those nasty Bolshies come and take it off again and thrust me aside into the outer darkness.

COMPREHENSION

1. What sort of essay is Forster writing for his audience? What is his purpose? How do you know?

2. List the four effects that property ownership has upon the author. How serious is he in describing these effects? Explain.

3. Describe the persona that emerges from the essay. What is the relationship of the last sentence to this persona?

RHETORIC

1. What words and phrases does the author use to create a conversational style in the essay?

2. Analyze biblical, historical, and literary allusions in the essay. What is their function?

3. What is the purpose of Forster's reference to Americans at the outset of the essay?

4. How is the thesis reinforced in the first paragraph? How are essay clarity and proper sequence achieved through placement of topic sentences?

5. Analyze the manner in which Forster integrates the analysis of effects with a personal definition of property.

6. Explain the shift in tone, and the movement from concrete to abstract, in paragraph 5.

WRITING

1. Do you agree with Forster that property ownership is as difficult as he declares it to be? Give the basis of your response, and elucidate in an essay.

2. Write an essay of definition in which you explain an abstract term in personal, concrete, and carefully organized terms.

3. Write a comparative essay on the theme of property and nature developed by Forster in "My Wood" and Thoreau in "Economy."

RUTH BENEDICT

Are Families Passé?

Ruth Benedict (1887–1948), an anthropologist and educator, began her career as a poet. Later, she studied anthropology under Franz Boas and succeeded him as chairman of the department of anthropology at Columbia University (1936–1939). In 1934, she wrote Patterns of Culture, *and in 1940* Race: Science and Politics. *In her work, Benedict attempted to study anthropology through sociology, psychology, and philosophy. The following essay illustrates her ability to work in an interdisciplinary manner in order to illuminate a core American institution.*

A great many people today speak as if the family were in some special sort of danger in our times. We hear a great deal about "saving the family" and about "preserving the home." Authors and lecturers describe how the family is threatened by divorce, or by mothers who work outside of the home, or by unemployment, or by lack of religious training of children. Each of them, depending on his experience in his own home and on his observations in the families he knows, selects something which he thinks should be changed—or should be preserved—and says that, if this or that were done, the family would be "saved."

To an anthropologist such phrasings are dangerously misleading. He has studied the family among naked savages and in contemporary civilizations and he knows that it has survived in all human societies known in the record of mankind. Just as surely he knows that the family takes all kinds of different forms. It is not merely that unlettered primitive nomads have family arrangements different from Western industrial nations; even in Western nations around the Atlantic shores the family differs profoundly. The ethics of marriage, the specific close emotional ties which the family fosters, the disciplines and freedoms for the child, the nature of the dependency of the children upon the parents, even the personnel which makes up the family—all these differ in Western civilized nations. The anthropologist knows that the changes taking place in the home in any decade in any country do not mean that the family is now about to disintegrate under our eyes unless we do something about it. The problem as he states it is quite different: how do legal and customary arrangements in the family tally with the arrangements and premises of the whole way of life which is valued in any tribe or nation? If, for instance, the father has a heavy, authoritarian hand upon his children, the anthropologist asks: Is this in keeping with authoritarianism in the state and in industry? Or is it at odds with a society which values non-authoritarianism and the pursuit of happiness? He asks the same kind of question about a nation's laws of inheritance from father to son, about the divorce laws, about the architectural layout of the house, about the reasons that are given to children when they are told to be good.

Customs enshrined in the family in any tribe or nation are likely to be sensitively adjusted to the values and customs of each particular people. This is no mystic correspondence; the persons who make up the family are the same people who are the citizens of that nation—the business men, the farmers, the churchgoers or nonchurch-goers, the readers of newspapers, and the listeners to the radio. In all their roles they are molded more or less surely into a people with certain habits, certain hopes, and a certain *espirit de corps*. Americans come to share certain slogans, behavior, and judgments which differ from those of Frenchmen or Czechs. This is inevitable. And in the process the role of the family also becomes different. By the same token, just as economic and political changes occur over a period of time in the United States or in France or in Czechoslovakia, the family also changes. 3

An anthropologist, therefore, when he reads about the failure of the family, finds in such criticism a somewhat special meaning. He remembers how often the family is made a convenient whipping boy among many peoples who disapprove of the way their world is going. He has seen it in Amazon jungles and on the islands of the Pacific. The author remembers an American Indian tribe which used to talk about the family in a most uncomplimentary fashion. They were a people who, not long before, had roamed over the great plains hunting buffalo and proving their courage by war exploits. Now they lived on a reservation, and tending crops was no adequate substitute for their old way of life. Their old economic arrangements of boastful gift giving, their political life, and their religious practices had either been destroyed by circumstances or had lost their old meaningfulness. Life had become pointless to them. These men talked with gusto about the failure of the family. They said that in the family the children no longer learned manners, or religion, or generosity, or whatever it was the individual Indian favored as a cure-all. The family, too, weighed a man down, they said; it was a burden to him. 4

To the anthropologist studying this tribe, however, the family 5 was precisely the best arranged, most trustworthy institution in their whole culture. It was hard beset and it had not escaped the tragic effects of the general disintegration of tribal life, but it was what provided the warm, human ties and the dependable security which were left in that Indian tribe. The children were loved and cared for, the husbands and wives often had comfortable relations with each other, and family hospitality had a graciousness that was absent in more public life. At birth and marriage and death the family still functioned as an effective institution. And there seemed to be no man or woman of childbearing age who was not married or would not have preferred to be.

The writer thinks of this Indian tribe when she hears Americans talk about the decay of the family. Instead of viewing the family with such alarm, suppose we look at it as it exists in this decade in this country and see how it is arranged to fulfill its functions in American schemes of life. Let us leave aside for the moment the questions of whether conditions are provided that would keep it from preventable overstrain and of whether as human beings we are able to get all the satisfaction we might out of this institution; let us consider only the arrangements of the family as we know it and how these fit in with our values and with the way we should like to plan our lives. 6

Suppose we take marriage first. Marriage sets up the new family, and it seems to make a great deal of difference whether a society dictates that the new home shall be begun in tears and heartache or with rejoicing. Many human societies would not recognize a marriage without a wailing bride and a sullen groom. Often the bride has to be surrounded by her mourning women, who lament her coming lifelong separation from her parents and her brothers and sisters, as well as her future misery as she goes to work for her mother-in-law. Often they cut her long hair and remove her jewelry as a sign that she is now a worker and no longer alluring. The groom's role, too, may be that of an unwilling victim. Often marriages are arranged by the parents without giving the two young people any chance to know each other. 7

All these circumstances are absent in marriage in the United States. The young people are hardly hampered in their choice of a mate; if occasionally parents deplore their choice, public opinion allows the young couple to outface them and expects the parents to accept the inevitable with as much decency as they can muster. We expect that the bride and groom will be in love or will have chosen each other for reasons known to themselves. Whether they marry for love or for money or to show they can win a sought-after mate from a rival, in any case they are making a personal choice and are not acting on command. Because in every field of life American culture puts such a high value on this kind of freedom and so bitterly resents 8 its curtailment in peace time, the fact that young people do make their own choice of a mate is an important and auspicious arrangement. The arranged marriage which is traditional in France or the careful class restrictions which have been observed in Holland would be difficult to manage in the United States. The wide range of choice of a mate and the fact that the young people make their own selection are conditions which could hardly be made more satisfactory for Americans with their particular habits and demands.

9 After marriage, too, the new family has a wide range of choices about where to live, how the wife shall occupy herself, when to start a family, and a host of other important matters. Such freedom is extremely unusual in the world. Sometimes the couple must live with the husband's family, sometimes with the wife's. Often in other countries, until one or two children are born, the young man continues to work for his father and has no say about the farm or the flock and no money which he can control. But in the United States a young couple plans the family budget before the wedding and what they earn is theirs to spend.

10 The way the new family in this country sets up its own separate home makes possible a rare and delightful circumstance: the two of them can have an incomparable privacy. No matter how hard it has been to arrange for privacy before marriage, as soon as the wedding is over everybody expects them to have their own latch key and their own possessions around them. If they cannot manage this, they feel cheated and other people think something is wrong. It is the same if they have to give a home to a parent. In most civilized countries this is a duty to which as a good son and good daughter they are bound, but if it is necessary in the United States their friends and neighbors will regard them as exceptionally burdened. Even the scarcity and high wages of domestic servants give the young family a greater privacy. Considering that they have chosen each other to their own liking, this privacy in the home is made to order to gratify them; the only problem is whether they can use it to their own happiness.

11 When they cannot, and when they find that their choice of a mate was not fool-proof just because they made it on their own, there is in the United States great freedom to get a divorce. Our growing divorce rate is the subject of much viewing-with-alarm; yet in a culture built as ours is on ever expanding personal choice, an important goal of which is the pursuit of happiness, the right to terminate an unhappy marriage is the other side of the coin of which the fair side is the right to choose one's spouse. Weak and stunted individuals will of course abuse both privileges, yet it is difficult to see how divorce could consistently be denied in a culture like ours. Certainly if we accepted it more honestly as a necessary phase of our way of life, however sorrowful, and put honest effort and sympathy into not pen-

ARE FAMILIES PASSÉ?

alizing the divorced, we should be acting more appropriately and in our own best interests. At any rate, the high divorce rate in the United States is no attack on marriage, for it is precisely the divorced—those who have failed in one or two attempts—who have the highest rate of marriage. Between the ages of twenty-five and thirty-five not even the unmarried or the widowed marry at so great a rate as the divorced.

Besides free choice and privacy, the American family has unusual potential leisure because of the labor-saving devices, prepared foods, and ready-made clothes available under modern conditions. The basic labor-saver is running water in the sink, and Americans have little idea how many millions of homes in civilized countries do not have it. Thus we are saved an endless round of drudgery that ties down women—and men also—in countries where homes have no running water, no gas and electricity, no farm tools but those which are driven into the earth by human hands or are swung in human arms, and no use of ready-made soaps and foods and clothes. Americans put high value on lessened drudgery, but they deprecate having free spaces of truly leisure time; the more time they save the more they fill up their days and nights with a round of engagements and complications. They are unwilling to admit that they have leisure, but the schedules of their lives prove clearly how much they have. 12

Universal schooling in the United States also frees the family of many duties when children have come. It is hard for Americans to imagine the difference which regular school hours make in a mother's role. For a great part of the working day, American children are in the responsibility of the teacher and not of the mother. As nursery schools spread over the country, younger and younger children get trained care outside the home and the mother's labors are correspondingly relieved. As the children grow older the mother's leisure increases until finally she reaches that idle middle age with its round of card parties and clubs and window shopping and movies which engross and waste the energy of so many millions of American women. Her husband is earning more money now than when he was younger, and her children have flown; she has a plethora of privileges and freedom and leisure. In one sense she has everything. 13

It is obviously unfair to talk about the incomparable freedom from drudgery which the American home offers without emphasizing that interval of a few years when there is no leisure for the mother in the home—the years when the babies are little. In our great cities where each family is strange to all the others, a mother is likely to have to be baby tender every hour of the day, with no one to relieve her. Along with these duties she must do all her cooking and washing and cleaning. And, as all our magazines and women's pages reiterate, she must make efforts to keep her husband. She must keep herself 14

RUTH BENEDICT

looking attractive, must keep up social contacts, and be a companion to him. To European wives this program looks formidable. "I was always told that American women were so free," a Polish woman said to me, "but when I came here and saw how they had to manage with the babies and the house without any older women of the family to help, and then how they had to play around with their husbands in the evening to keep them happy, I decided I wouldn't change places with them for anything. In Poland a woman doesn't have to 'keep' her husband; it's all settled when they're married."

The striking fact about the nursery years in the United States 15 is that in comparison with those in other countries they are so short and that nevertheless we do not really treat them as an interim. Mothers who are going through this period give remarkably little thought to the leisure that will come soon. They are often vocal enough about the turmoil of their present lives, and sometimes bitter, but the fact that the nursery years last so short a time in the United States and could be treated as an interim—like a professor's going into the government during war time—is all too seldom part of their thinking. No doubt this is due in part to a lag in our culture, since even with our grandparents conditions were different; but in part it is a result of the sentiment which selects this period, no matter how short, as the fulfillment of a woman's chief duty in life. A social engineer looking at the family, however, would certainly put his major effort into better arrangements for the overburdened mother during these years and into thinking about effecting some transition from this period into that next one during which, in the United States, millions of women become idle parasites upon society—and dull and unhappy into the bargain.

Another notable feature of the American family is its pecul- 16 iarly non-authoritarian character. The old rules that a child should be seen and not heard and the adage, "Spare the rod and spoil the child," are anachronistic in the United States; they are dispensed with even in immigrant groups which honored them in their native country. The rule of the father over the family is still a reality in some European nations, but in the United States the mother is the chief responsible agent in bringing up her children; here the father's opinions are something the children are more likely to play off against the mother's, to their own advantage, rather than a court of last authority from which there is no appeal. Children take the noisy center of the stage at the breakfast table and in the living room in a way that is quite impossible in European countries. The fact that they are expected to know right from wrong in their tenderest years and to act upon it on their own is often commented on by European mothers who have lived here. A Dutch mother once spoke to the author about how hard we are on our children because we expect this of them; she said "I don't expect it of my children before they are seven; until then, I am there to see that they act correctly." But an American mother expects a child of three or four to be a responsible moral agent, and she gives him great latitude in which to prove that he can manage his little affairs by himself.

All this lack of strong authoritarianism in American families   17
accords well with the values that are chiefly sought after in this country. No strong father image is compatible with our politics or our economics. We seek the opportunity to prove that we are as good as the next person, and we do not find comfort in following an authoritarian voice—in the state or in the home, from the landowner or the priest—which will issue a command from on high. We learn as children to measure ourselves against Johnny next door, or against Mildred whose mother our mother knows in church, and this prepares us for living in a society with strongly egalitarian ideals. We do not learn the necessity of submitting to unquestioned commands as the children of many countries do. The family in the United States has become democratic.

These free-choice and non-authoritarian aspects of the family,   18
along with its privacy and potential leisure, evidence only a few of the many ways in which it has become consistent with major emphases in our national life. They seem, when one compares them with arrangements of other civilized nations, to be quite well fitted to the role the family must play in a culture like the United States. This does not mean, however, that Americans capitalize to their own advantage upon all these consistently contrived arrangements which are institutionalized in the family as we know it. At the beginning of this essay two subjects were left for later discussion—how well our society protects the family from dangerous overstrain, and how well as human beings with special insights and blind spots we are able to get all the satisfactions we might out of our version of the home. These two subjects cannot be omitted.

In spite of all our American sentiment about the home and   19
the family, we do not show great concern about buttressing it against catastrophe. Any well-considered national program must have regard for the children; if they are housed and fed below a certain minimum, if their health is not attended to, the nation suffers in the next generation. The lack of a tolerable economic floor under the family is especially crucial in a society like that of the United States, where competition is so thoroughly relied upon as an incentive and where so few families have anything but the weekly pay envelope to use for food and doctors' bills. When factories close, when inflation comes, the family gets little consideration in the United States. Especially in economic crises it gets the little end of the horn. Today the necessity of providing tens of thousands of new homes is of the greatest im-

RUTH BENEDICT

portance for healthy family life in the United States, but adequate housing programs are notoriously unsupported. Sickness insurance, too, which would provide preventive care as well as relieve the family budget of all expenses in a crisis, needs high priority in a national program. When one reads about families in trouble, it is clear that many of the reefs which are threatening shipwreck are avoidable by intelligent local, state, or national programs. Such programs have worked satisfactorily in non-communist countries—as, for instance, in the Scandinavian nations. But they cost money, and Americans have not been willing to be taxed for the sake of taking the excessive strain off the family and providing better circumstances for growing children. It could be done, and if it were done the incidental disadvantages of our highly competitive and unregulated economic system would be largely removed; it should be the surest way to ensure the successful continuance of what is known as the democratic way of life.

Besides this American political attitude toward the family, there is also a very different difficulty which threatens it. We have seen how as an institution it is particularly tailored to American ways of living. But the very best suit of clothes may be badly worn by a careless and irresponsible person. So, too, people may abuse a home well designed to suit them. It is no less true of marriage and the family. These exist as institutions remarkably well adjusted to American life. But many Americans are miserably unable to achieve happiness within them.

It is of course easy to say that a culture like that of the United States, which allows individuals so much free choice among alternatives, is asking a great deal of human beings. In social life, as in literature, some of the finest human achievements have been within restrictions as rigid as those of the sonnet form. Our American culture is more like a sprawling novel where every page may deal with a new encounter and with a special choice. We ask a great deal of individuals when we give them such wide latitude and so little respected authority. But the United States is built on the premise that this is possible, and if ever we as a people decide otherwise our nation will change beyond recognition. We shall have lost the very thing we have been trying to build in this country.

It must not be imagined that this craving for individual freedom is what prevents Americans from enjoying the family as much as it might be enjoyed. In so far as the family is an overheavy economic burden on some wage earners, a more careful welfare program could take care of this complaint. Certainly women and children have a freedom in the American family which is hard to match elsewhere in the world, and from all portents this will probably increase rather than diminish.

ARE FAMILIES PASSÉ?

The crucial difficulty in American happiness in marriage is, 23
rather, a certain blind spot which is especially fostered in our privileged United States. An extreme instance of this was mentioned in
connection with the millions of idle, middle-aged wives in this country. These are women who as a group are well set up and favored
beyond any such great numbers of women in any other part of the
world. But privilege to them is separate from responsibility. Comparatively few of them feel that it is compatible with their status to do
responsible work in which they have had experience in their own
households and which must now be done outside their homes, and
few take the initiative in getting the training they would need in jobs
which they can see need to be done—except in war time. In periods
of peace they have a blind spot about what it takes to live happily.
For that the motto is *Noblesse oblige*, or "Privilege obligates one to do
something in return."

It is not only the middle-aged woman who accepts privilege 24
without a sense of obligation. In marriage, the right of both men and
women to choose their mates freely is a privilege which carries with
it, if they are to live happily, an accompanying conviction that when
things go wrong it is doubly their obligation—to themselves as well
as to their spouse—to deal tolerantly. Perhaps a young man realizes
that his wife is more petulant than he knew; exactly because he chose
her, however, she is "a poor thing; but his own." Privileged as he was
to choose her, he has a corresponding responsibility.

It is the same with children. In the United States the reason 25
for having children is not, as it is in most of the world, the perpetua-
tion of the family line down many generations. In most countries people have children because there must be someone to till the piece of
land in the village where the family has lived for centuries, there must
be an heir to inherit the *Hof*, or there must be a son to perform the
ancestral rites. In our atomistic American families these motivations
seldom arise. We have children, not because our parents are sitting in
judgment, not because of the necessity of having an heir, but because
we personally want them—whether as company in the home or to
show our friends we can have them. It is a privileged phase of par-
enthood, and if it is to bring us happiness it implies an acceptance of
responsibility. Nothing is all pleasure in this life, and bringing up two
or three noisy children in our small urban apartments is no exception
to the rule. But with us it is based on choice—far more than it is
elsewhere in the world—and we can only make the most of a choice
if we follow it through wholeheartedly in all its implications.

It is partly because of this blind spot in the American family, 26
this walling off of privilege from responsibility and tolerance, that we
so often ask of life an average happiness—as if it could be presented
to us on a platter. Full normal happiness only comes to men and

RUTH BENEDICT

women who give as well as take—who, in this instance, give themselves warmly to their family life, and do not merely arrogate to themselves the rights they are so freely allowed in our society. In the United States, if happiness proves impossible they can get a divorce, but, until they have made this decision, they can capitalize on their privileges only if they bind around their arms the motto "Privilege has its obligations."

The family in the United States is an institution remarkably   27
adapted to our treasured way of life. The changes that are occurring in it do not mean that it is decaying and needs to be saved. It offers a long array of privileges. It needs more consideration in political tax-supported programs, by means of which many difficulties that beset it could be eradicated. Finally, Americans, in order to get the maximum happiness out of such a free institution as the family in the United States, need to parallel their privileges with an awakening responsibility. It is hard to live up to being so privileged as we are in the United States, but it is not impossible.

COMPREHENSION

1.   Does Benedict write as an anthropologist to a specialized audience? Why, or why not?

2.   Why is the anthropological perspective established by Benedict at the outset of the essay important to our understanding of the selection?

3.   List the "notable features" about the American family that the author analyzes. According to the author, how does the American family differ from families in other cultures?

RHETORIC

1.   How does the writer achieve an informal yet reflective style in presenting her materials?

2.   Define the following foreign words used by the author: *esprit de corps* (paragraph 3); *noblesse oblige* (paragraph 23); and *Hof* (paragraph 25). Do they conflict with the intent of a popular essay?

3.   What rhetorical strategies does Benedict employ in the introductory section, paragraphs 1 to 5? What is the function of paragraph 6? What other paragraph in the essay has a smiliar function?

4.   How does the author's use of comparison and contrast throughout paragraphs 7 to 18 advance her thesis? What are the main comparative topics?

5.   Analyze Benedict's presentation of illustration to develop the thesis. What is the unifying principle behind these illustrations? How are they ordered?

6.   Explain the techniques in the development of the concluding paragraph.

 ARE FAMILIES PASSÉ?

WRITING

1. Benedict wrote this essay in 1948. Do any of her observations require reconsideration today? What assumptions does the author make about "our treasured way of life"? Do you agree or disagree with her assumptions? Why? Develop an essay on these issues.

2. Write an analysis of the relative strength or weakness of the American family today.

3. Test Benedict's assumptions about the American family against examples of family life provided by such writers as Hughes, Kingston, McCullers, White, and Angelou.

4. Compare and contrast the nuclear family and the extended family.

THOMAS JEFFERSON

The Declaration of Independence
In CONGRESS, JULY 4, 1776

The Unanimous Declaration
of the thirteen united States of America

Thomas Jefferson (1743–1826) was governor of Virginia during the American Revolution, America's first Secretary of State, and the third President of the United States. He had a varied and monumental career as politician, public servant, scientist, architect, educator (he founded the University of Virginia), and man of letters. Jefferson attended the Continental Congress in 1775, where he wrote the rough draft of the Declaration of Independence and revised it; other hands made contributions to the document that was signed on July 4, 1776, but the wording, style, structure, and spirit of the final version are distinctly Jefferson's. Like Thomas Paine, Benjamin Franklin, James Madison, and other major figures of the Revolutionary era, Jefferson was notable for his use of prose as an instrument for social and political change. In the Declaration of Independence, we see the direct, precise, logical, and persuasive statement of revolutionary principles that makes the document one of the best known and best written texts in world history. Jefferson died in his home at Monticello on July 4, fifty years to the day of the signing of the Declaration of Independence.

THOMAS JEFFERSON

hen in the Course of human events it becomes necessary 1 for one people to dissolve the political bands which have connected them with another, and to assume among the powers of the earth, the separate and equal station to which the Laws of Nature and of Nature's God entitle them, a decent respect to the opinions of mankind requires that they should declare the causes which impel them to the separation.

We hold these truths to be self-evident, that all men are cre- 2 ated equal, that they are endowed by their Creator with certain un- alienable Rights, that among these are Life, Liberty and the pursuit of Happiness.

That to secure these rights, Governments are instituted among 3 Men, deriving their just powers from the consent of the governed.

That whenever any Form of Government becomes destructive 4 of these ends, it is the Right of the People to alter or to abolish it, and to institute new Government, laying its foundation on such principles and organizing its powers in such form, as to them shall seem most likely to effect their Safety and Happiness. Prudence, indeed, will dic- tate that Governments long established should not be changed for light and transient causes; and accordingly all experience hath shewn that mankind are more disposed to suffer, while evils are sufferable, than to right themselves by abolishing the forms to which they are accustomed. But when a long train of abuses and usurpations, pur- suing invariably the same Object evinces a design to reduce them under absolute Despotism, it is their right, it is their duty, to throw off such Government, and to provide new Guards for their future security.

Such has been the patient sufferance of these Colonies; and 5 such is now the necessity which constrains them to alter their former Systems of Government. The history of the present King of Great Brit- ain is a history of repeated injuries and usurpations, all having in direct object the establishment of an absolute Tyranny over these States. To prove this, let Facts be submitted to a candid world.

He has refused his Assent to Laws, the most wholesome and 6 necessary for the public good.

He has forbidden his Governors to pass Laws of immediate 7 and pressing importance, unless suspended in their operation till his Assent should be obtained; and when so suspended, he has utterly neglected to attend to them.

He has refused to pass other Laws for the accommodation of 8 large districts of people, unless those people would relinquish the right of Representation in the Legislature, a right inestimable to them and formidable to tyrants only.

He has called together legislative bodies at places unusual, 9 uncomfortable, and distant from the depository of their public

Records, for the sole purpose of fatiguing them into compliance with his measures.

He has dissolved Representative Houses repeatedly, for opposing with manly firmness his invasions on the rights of the people. 10

He has refused for a long time, after such dissolutions, to cause others to be elected; whereby the Legislative powers, incapable of Annihilation, have returned to the People at large for their exercise; the State remaining in the mean time exposed to all the dangers of invasion from without, and convulsions within. 11

He has endeavoured to prevent the population of these States; for that purpose obstructing the Laws for Naturalization of Foreigners; refusing to pass others to encourage their migrations hither, and raising the conditions of new Appropriations of Lands. 12

He has obstructed the Administration of Justice, by refusing his Assent to Laws for establishing Judiciary powers. 13

He was made Judges dependent on his Will alone, for the tenure of their offices, and the amount and payment of their salaries. 14

He has erected a multitude of New Offices, and sent hither swarms of Officers to harass our people, and eat out their substance. 15

He has kept among us, in times of peace, Standing Armies without the Consent of our legislatures. 16

He has affected to render the Military independent of and superior to the Civil power. 17

He has combined with others to subject us to a jurisdiction foreign to our constitution, and unacknowledged by our laws; giving his Assent to their Acts of pretended Legislation: 18

For quartering large bodies of armed troops among us:

For protecting them, by a mock Trial, from punishment of any Murders which they should commit on the Inhabitants of these States:

For cutting off our Trade with all parts of the world:

For imposing Taxes on us without our Consent:

For depriving us in many cases, of the benefits of Trial by Jury:

For transporting us beyond Seas to be tried for pretended offences:

For abolishing the free System of English Laws in a neighboring Province, establishing therein an Arbitrary government, and enlarging its Boundaries so as to render it at once an example and fit instrument for introducing the same absolute rule into these Colonies:

For taking away our Charters, abolishing our most valuable Laws and altering fundamentally the Forms of our Governments:

For suspending our own Legislatures, and declaring themselves invested with power to legislate for us in all cases whatsoever.

He has abdicated Government here, by declaring us out of his Protection and waging War against us. 19

THOMAS JEFFERSON

He has plundered our seas, ravaged our Coasts, burnt our towns, and destroyed the Lives of our people. 20

He is at this time transporting large Armies of foreign Mercenaries to compleat the works of death, desolation and tyranny, already begun with circumstances of Cruelty & perfidy scarcely paralleled in the most barbarous ages, and totally unworthy the Head of a civilized nation. 21

He has constrained our fellow Citizens taken Captive on the high Seas to bear Arms against their Country, to become the executioners of their friends and Brethren, or to fall themselves by their Hands. 22

He has excited domestic insurrections amongst us, and has endeavoured to bring on the inhabitants of our frontiers, the merciless Indian Savages, whose known rule of warfare, is an undistinguished destruction of all ages, sexes and conditions. 23

In every stage of these Oppressions We have Petitioned for Redress in the most humble terms: Our repeated Petitions have been answered only by repeated injury. A Prince, whose character is thus marked by every act which may define a Tyrant, is unfit to be the ruler of a free people. Nor have We been wanting in attentions to our British brethren. We have warned them from time to time of attempts by their legislature to extend an unwarrantable jurisdiction over us. We have reminded them of the circumstances of our emigration and settlement here. We have appealed to their native justice and magnanimity, and we have conjured them by the ties of our common kindred to disavow these usurpations, which would inevitably interrupt our connections and correspondence. They too have been deaf to the voice of justice and of consanguinity. We must, therefore, acquiesce in the necessity, which denounces our Separation, and hold them, as we hold the rest of mankind, Enemies in War, in Peace Friends. 24

We, therefore, the Representatives of the united States of America, in General Congress, Assembled, appealing to the Supreme Judge of the world for the rectitude of our intentions, do, in the Name, and by Authority of the good People of these Colonies, solemnly publish and declare, That these United Colonies are, and of Right ought to be, Free and Independent States; that they are Absolved from all Allegiance to the British Crown, and that all political connection between them and the State of Great Britain, is and ought to be totally dissolved; and that as Free and Independent States, they have full Power to levy War, conclude Peace, contract Alliances, establish Commerce, and to do all other Acts and Things which Independent States may of right do. 25

And for the support of this Declaration, with a firm reliance on the protection of divine Providence, we mutually pledge to each other our Lives, our Fortunes and our sacred Honor. 26

COMPREHENSION

1. Explain Jefferson's main and subordinate purposes in this document.

2. What is Jefferson's key assertion or argument? Mention several reasons that he gives to support his argument.

3. Summarize Jefferson's definition of human nature and of government. Reconsider Forster's "My Wood," and how Forster might respond to Jefferson's definition.

RHETORIC

1. There are many striking words and phrases in the Declaration of Independence, notably in the beginning. Locate three such examples, and explain their connotative power and effectiveness.

2. Jefferson and his colleagues had to draft a document designed for several audiences. What audiences did they have in mind? How do language and style reflect an awareness of multiple audiences?

3. The Declaration of Independence is a classic model of syllogistic reasoning and deductive argument (see the Glossary). What is the major premise, and where is it stated? The minor premise? The conclusion?

4. What sort of inductive evidence does Jefferson offer?

5. Why is the middle portion, or body, of the Declaration of Independence considerably longer than the introduction or conclusion? What holds the body together?

6. Explain the function and effect of parallel structure in this document.

WRITING

1. Do you believe that "all men are created equal"? Justify your answer.

2. Discuss the relevance of the Declaration of Independence to politics today.

3. Explain why the Declaration of Independence is a model of effective prose.

4. Write your own declaration of independence—from family, employer, required courses, or the like. Develop this declaration as an "op-ed" piece for a newspaper.

THOMAS JEFFERSON

J. B. PRIESTLEY

Wrong Ism

John Boynton Priestley (1894–1984), best-selling English novelist and popular dramatist, was also a prolific writer of essays, many of them involving social and political criticism. His work includes The English Novel *(1927),* The Good Companions *(1929),* Time and the Conways *(1937),* An Inspector Calls *(1946), and* The English *(1973). This selection from* Essays of Five Decades *(1968) offers an astute analysis of contemporary political habits.*

here are three isms that we ought to consider very carefully—regionalism, nationalism, internationalism. Of these three the one there is most fuss about, the one that starts men shouting and marching and shooting, the one that seems to have all the depth and thrust and fire, is of course nationalism. Nine people out of ten, I fancy, would say that of this trio it is the one that really counts, the big boss. Regionalism and internationalism, they would add, are comparatively small, shadowy, rather cranky. And I believe all this to be quite wrong. Like many another big boss, nationalism is largely bogus. It is like a bunch of flowers made of plastics.

The real flowers belong to regionalism. The mass of people everywhere may never have used the term. They are probably regionalists without knowing it. Because they have been brought up in a certain part of the world, they have formed perhaps quite unconsciously a deep attachment to its landscape and speech, its traditional customs, its food and drink, its songs and jokes. (There are of course always the rebels, often intellectuals and writers, but they are not the mass of people.) They are rooted in their region. Indeed, without this attachment a man can have no roots.

So much of people's lives, from earliest childhood onwards, is deeply intertwined with the common life of the region, they cannot help feeling strongly about it. A threat to it is a knife pointing at the heart. How can life ever be the same if bullying strangers come to change everything? The form and colour, the very taste and smell of dear familiar things will be different, alien, life-destroying. It would be better to die fighting. And it is precisely this, the nourishing life of the region, for which common men have so often fought and died.

This attachment to the region exists on a level far deeper than that of any political hocus-pocus. When a man says "my country" with real feeling, he is thinking about his region, all that has made up his life, and not about that political entity, the nation. There can be some confusion here simply because some countries are so small—

and ours is one of them—and so old, again like ours, that much of what is national is also regional. Down the centuries, the nation, itself, so comparatively small, has been able to attach to itself the feeling really created by the region. (Even so there is something left over, as most people in Yorkshire or Devon, for example, would tell you.) This probably explains the fervent patriotism developed early in small countries. The English were announcing that they were English in the Middle Ages, before nationalism had arrived elsewhere.

If we deduct from nationalism all that it has borrowed or stolen from regionalism, what remains is mostly rubbish. The nation, as distinct from the region, is largely the creation of power-men and political manipulators. Almost all nationalist movements are led by ambitious frustrated men determined to hold office. I am not blaming them. I would do the same if I were in their place and wanted power so badly. But nearly always they make use of the rich warm regional feeling, the emotional dynamo of the movement, while being almost untouched by it themselves. This is because they are not as a rule deeply loyal to any region themselves. Ambition and a love of power can eat like acid into the tissues of regional loyalty. It is hard, if not impossible, to retain a natural piety and yet be for ever playing both ends against the middle.

Being itself a power structure, devised by men of power, the nation tends to think and act in terms of power. What would benefit the real life of the region, where men, women and children actually live, is soon sacrificed for the power and prestige of the nation. (And the personal vanity of presidents and ministers themselves, which historians too often disregard.) Among the new nations of our time innumerable peasants and labourers must have found themselves being cut down from five square meals a week to three in order to provide unnecessary airlines, military forces that can only be used against them and nobody else, great conference halls and official yachts and the rest. The last traces of imperialism and colonialism may have to be removed from Asia and Africa, where men can no longer endure being condemned to a permanent inferiority by the colour of their skins; but even so, the modern world, the real world of our time, does not want and would be far better without more and more nations, busy creating for themselves the very paraphernalia that western Europe is now trying to abolish. You are compelled to answer more questions when trying to spend half a day in Cambodia than you are now travelling from the Hook of Holland to Syracuse.

This brings me to internationalism. I dislike this term, which I used only to complete the isms. It suggests financiers and dubious promoters living nowhere but in luxury hotels; a shallow world of entrepreneurs and impresarios. (Was it Sacha Guitry who said that impresarios were men who spoke many languages but all with a foreign accent?) The internationalism I have in mind here is best described as world civilisation. It is life considered on a global scale. Most of our communications and transport already exist on this high wide level. So do many other things from medicine to meteorology. Our astronomers and physicists (except where they have allowed themselves to be hush-hushed) work here. The UN special agencies, about which we hear far too little, have contributed more and more to this world civilisation. All the arts, when they are arts and not chunks of nationalist propaganda, naturally take their place in it. And it grows, widens, deepens, in spite of the fact that for every dollar, ruble, pound or franc spent in explaining and praising it, a thousand are spent by the nations explaining and praising themselves.

This world civilisation and regionalism can get along together, 8 especially if we keep ourselves sharply aware of their quite different but equally important values and rewards. A man can make his contribution to world civilisation and yet remain strongly regional in feeling: I know several men of this sort. There is of course the danger—it is with us now—of the global style flattening out the regional, taking local form, colour, flavour, away for ever, disinheriting future generations, threatening them with sensuous poverty and a huge boredom. But to understand and appreciate regionalism is to be on guard against this danger. And we must therefore make a clear distinction between regionalism and nationalism.

It is nationalism that tries to check the growth of world civ- 9 ilisation. And nationalism, when taken on a global scale, is more aggressive and demanding now than it has ever been before. This in the giant powers is largely disguised by the endless fuss in public about rival ideologies, now a largely unreal quarrel. What is intensely real is the glaring nationalism. Even the desire to police the world is nationalistic in origin. (Only the world can police the world.) Moreover, the nation-states of today are for the most part far narrower in their outlook, far more inclined to allow prejudice against the foreigner to impoverish their own style of living, than the old imperial states were. It should be part of world civilisation that men with particular skills, perhaps the product of the very regionalism they are rebelling against, should be able to move easily from country to country, to exercise those skills, in anything from teaching the violin to running a new type of factory to managing an old hotel. But nationalism, especially of the newer sort, would rather see everything done badly than allow a few non-nationals to get to work. And people face a barrage of passports, visas, immigration controls, labour permits; and in this respect are worse off than they were in 1900. But even so, in spite of all that nationalism can do—so long as it keeps its nuclear bombs to itself—the internationalism I have in mind, slowly creating a world civilisation, cannot be checked.

WRONG ISM   251

Nevertheless, we are still backing the wrong ism. Almost all 10
our money goes on the middle one, nationalism, the rotten meat between the two healthy slices of bread. We need regionalism to give
us roots and that very depth of feeling which nationalism unjustly
and greedily claims for itself. We need internationalism to save the
world and to broaden and heighten our civilisation. While regional
man enriches the lives that international man is already working to
keep secure and healthy, national man, drunk with power, demands
our loyalty, money and applause, and poisons the very air with his
dangerous nonsense.

COMPREHENSION

1. What thesis does Priestley present? State the thesis in your own words.

2. Define *regionalism, nationalism,* and *internationalism* as Priestley presents
these terms.

3. Explain Priestley's objections to nationalism. Where does he state these objections in the essay? What alternative does he propose?

RHETORIC

1. What striking metaphor does the author develop to capture the essence of
nationalism? What is its sensory impact? Analyze another example of metaphorical language in the essay.

2. How does the suffix "-ism" function stylistically in the essay?

3. What is Priestley's principle of classification in this essay? How does he
maintain proportion in the presentation of categories?

4. Analyze the relationship between definition and classification in the essay.

5. Examine Priestley's use of comparison and contrast.

6. Explain the connection between the introductory and concluding paragraphs.

WRITING

1. Priestley makes many assumptions about regionalism, nationalism, and
internationalism. Which assumptions do you accept? Which assumptions do you
reject? Explain in an essay.

2. Write a classification essay on at least three related "-isms": capitalism,
socialism, and communism; Protestantism, Catholicism, and Judaism; regionalism, nationalism, and internationalism.

3. Reread Wright's "The Psychological Reactions of Oppressed People," and
in an essay explain how Priestley's article illuminates the issues raised by Wright.

J. B. PRIESTLEY

Of the Meaning of Progress

William Edward Burghardt Du Bois (1868–1963) was born in Massachusetts, the descendant of French Huguenots and slaves. He studied at Harvard and Berlin, and was a professor of economics and history at Atlanta University from 1896 to 1910. Emerging as a leader of the militant wing of the black movement in America, Du Bois wrote The Souls of Black Folk *(1903) and other sociological studies. His increasing militancy moved him toward socialism and communism, culminating in renunciation of American citizenship and residence in Ghana, where he died. In this chapter from* The Souls of Black Folk, *Du Bois presents a highly personalized sociological account of black education in the South.*

nce upon a time I taught school in the hills of Tennessee, where the broad dark vale of the Mississippi begins to roll and crumple to greet the Alleghenies. I was a Fisk student then, and all Fisk men thought that Tennessee—beyond the Veil—was theirs alone, and in vacation time they sallied forth in lusty bands to meet the county school-commissioners. Young and happy, I too went, and I shall not soon forget that summer, seventeen years ago. 1

First, there was a Teachers' Institute at the countyseat; and there distinguished guests of the superintendent taught the teachers fractions and spelling and other mysteries,—white teachers in the morning, Negroes at night. A picnic now and then, and a supper, and the rough world was softened by laughter and song. I remember how—But I wander. 2

There came a day when all the teachers left the Institute and began the hunt for schools. I learn from hearsay (for my mother was mortally afraid of firearms) that the hunting of ducks and bears and men is wonderfully interesting, but I am sure that the man who has never hunted a country school has something to learn of the pleasures of the chase. I see now the white, hot roads lazily rise and fall and wind before me under the burning July sun; I feel the deep weariness of heart and limb as ten, eight, six miles stretch relentlessly ahead; I feel my heart sink heavily as I hear again and again, "Got a teacher? Yes." So I walked on and on—horses were too expensive—until I had wandered beyond railways, beyond stage lines, to a land of "varmints" and rattlesnakes, where the coming of a stranger was an event, and men lived and died in the shadow of one blue hill. 3

Sprinkled over hill and dale lay cabins and farmhouses, shut 4 out from the world by the forests and the rolling hills toward the east. There I found at last a little school. Josie told me of it; she was a thin, homely girl of twenty, with a dark-brown face and thick, hard hair. I had crossed the stream at Watertown, and rested under the great willows; then I had gone to the little cabin in the lot where Josie was resting on her way to town. The gaunt farmer made me welcome, and Josie, hearing my errand, told me anxiously that they wanted a school over the hill; that but once since the war had a teacher been there; that she herself longed to learn—and thus she ran on, talking fast and loud, with much earnestness and energy.

Next morning I crossed the tall round hill, lingered to look at 5
the blue and yellow mountains stretching toward the Carolinas, then plunged into the wood, and came out at Josie's home. It was a dull frame cottage with four rooms, perched just below the brow of the hill, amid peach-trees. The father was a quiet, simple soul, calmly ignorant, with no touch of vulgarity. The mother was different,— strong, bustling, and energetic, with a quick, restless tongue, and an ambition to live "like folks." There was a crowd of children. Two boys had gone away. There remained two growing girls; a shy midget of eight; John, tall awkward, and eighteen; Jim, younger, quicker, and better looking; and two babies of indefinite age. Then there was Josie herself. She seemed to be the centre of the family: always busy at service, or at home, or berrypicking, a little nervous and inclined to scold, like her mother, yet faithful, too, like her father. She had about her a certain fineness, the shadow of an unconscious moral heroism that would willingly give all of life to make life broader, deeper, and fuller for her and hers. I saw much of this family afterwards, and grew to love them for their honest efforts to be decent and comfortable, and for their knowledge of their own ignorance. There was with them no affectation. The mother would scold the father for being so "easy"; Josie would roundly berate the boys for carelessness; and all knew that it was a hard thing to dig a living out of a rocky side-hill.

I secured the school. I remember the day I rode horseback out 6
to the commissioner's house with a pleasant young white fellow who wanted the white school. The road ran down the bed of a stream; the sun laughed and the water jingled, and we rode on. "Come in," said the commissioner,—come in. Have a seat. Yes, that certificate will do. Stay to dinner. What do you want a month?" "Oh," thought I, "this is lucky"; but even then fell the awful shadow of the Veil, for they ate first, then I—alone.

The schoolhouse was a log hut, where Colonel Wheeler used 7
to shelter his corn. It sat in a lot behind a rail fence and thorn bushes, near the sweetest of springs. There was an entrance where a door once was, and within a massive rickety fireplace; great chinks between the logs served as windows. Furniture was scarce. A pale blackboard

W. E. B. DU BOIS

crouched in the corner. My desk was made of three boards, reinforced at critical points, and my chair, borrowed from the landlady, had to be returned every night. Seats for the children—these puzzled me much. I was haunted by a New England vision of neat little desks and chairs, but, alas! the reality was rough plank benches without backs, and at times without legs. They had the one virtue of making naps dangerous,—possibly fatal, for the floor was not to be trusted.

It was a hot morning late in July when the school opened. I trembled when I heard the patter of little feet down the dusty road, and saw the growing row of dark solemn faces and bright eager eyes facing me. First came Josie and her brothers and sisters. The longing to know, to be a student in the great school at Nashville, hovered like a star above this child-woman amid her work and worry, and she studied doggedly. There were the Dowells from their farm over toward Alexandria,—Fanny, with her smooth black face and wondering eyes; Martha, brown and dull; the pretty girl-wife of a brother, and the younger brood. ⁸

There were the Burkes,—two brown and yellow lads, and a tiny haughty-eyed girl. Fat Reuben's little chubby girl came, with golden face and old-gold hair, faithful and solemn. Thenie was on hand early,—a jolly, ugly, goodhearted girl, who slyly dipped snuff and looked after her little bow-legged brother. When her mother could spare her, Tildy came,—a midnight beauty, with starry eyes and tapering limbs; and her brother, correspondingly homely. And then the big boys,—the hulking Lawrences; and lazy Neills, unfathered sons of mother and daughter; Hickman, with a stoop in his shoulders; and the rest. ⁹

There they sat, nearly thirty of them, on the rough benches, their faces shading from a pale cream to a deep brown, the little feet bare and swinging, the eyes full of expectation, with here and there a twinkle of mischief, and the hands grasping Webster's blue-back spelling-book. I loved my school, and the fine faith the children had in the wisdom of their teacher was truly marvellous. We read and spelled together, wrote a little, picked flowers, sang, and listened to stories of the world beyond the hill. At times the school would dwindle away, and I would start out. I would visit Mun Eddings, who lived in two very dirty rooms, and ask why little Lugene, whose flaming face seemed ever ablaze with the dark-red hair uncombed, was absent all last week, or why I missed so often the inimitable rags of Mack and Ed. Then the father, who worked Colonel Wheeler's farm on shares, would tell me how the crops needed the boys; and the thin, slovenly mother, whose face was pretty when washed, assured me that Lugene must mind the baby. "But we'll start them again next week." When the Lawrences stopped, I knew that the doubts of the old folks about book-learning had conquered again, and so, toiling up the hill, and ¹⁰

getting as far into the cabin as possible, I put Cicero "pro Archia Poeta" into the simplest English with local applications, and usually convinced them—for a week or so.

On Friday nights I often went home with some of the chil- 11 dren,—sometimes to Doc Burke's farm. He was a great, loud, thin Black, ever working, and trying to buy the seventy-five acres of hill and dale where he lived; but people said that he would surely fail, and the "white folks would get it all." His wife was a magnificent Amazon, with saffron face and shining hair, uncorseted and bare-footed, and the children were strong and beautiful. They lived in a one-and-a-half room cabin in the hollow of the farm, near the spring. The front room was full of great fat white beds, scrupulously neat; and there were bad chromos on the walls, and a tired centre-table. In the tiny back kitchen I was often invited to "take out and help" myself to fried chicken and wheat biscuit, "meat" and corn pone, string-beans and berries. At first I used to be a little alarmed at the approach of bedtime in the one lone bedroom, but embarrassment was very deftly avoided. First, all the children nodded and slept, and were stowed away in one great pile of goose feathers; next, the mother and the father discreetly slipped away to the kitchen while I went to bed; then, blowing out the dim light, they retired in the dark. In the morning all were up and away before I thought of awaking. Across the road, where fat Reuben lived, they all went outdoors while the teacher re-tired, because they did not boast the luxury of a kitchen.

I liked to stay with the Dowells, for they had four rooms and 12 plenty of good country fare. Uncle Bird had a small, rough farm, all woods and hills, miles from the big road; but he was full of tales,— he preached now and then,—and with his children, berries, horses, and wheat he was happy and prosperous. Often, to keep the peace, I must go where life was less lovely; for instance, Tildy's mother was incorrigibly dirty, Reuben's larder was limited seriously, and herds of untamed insects wandered over the Eddingses' beds. Best of all I loved to go to Josie's, and sit on the porch, eating peaches, while the mother bustled and talked: how Josie had bought the sewing-machine; how Josie worked at service in winter, but that four dollars a month was "mighty little" wages; how Josie longed to go away to school, but that it "looked like" they never could get far enough ahead to let her; how the crops failed and the well was yet unfinished; and, finally, how "mean" some of the white folks were.

For two summers I lived in this little world; it was dull and 13 humdrum. The girls looked at the hill in wistful longing, and the boys fretted and haunted Alexandria. Alexandria was "town,"—a strag-gling, lazy village of houses, churches, and shops, and an aristocracy of Toms, Dicks, and Captains. Cuddled on the hill to the north was the village of the colored folks who lived in three- or four-room un-

W. E. B. DU BOIS

painted cottages, some neat and homelike, and some dirty. The dwellings were scattered rather aimlessly, but they centered about the twin temples of the hamlet, the Methodist, and the Hard-Shell Baptist churches. These, in turn, leaned gingerly on a sad-colored schoolhouse. Hither my little world wended its crooked way on Sunday to meet other worlds, and gossip, and wonder, and make the weekly sacrifice with frenzied priest at the altar of the "old-time religion." Then the soft melody and mighty cadences of Negro song fluttered and thundered.

I have called my tiny community a world, and so its isolation 14 made it; and yet there was among us but a half-awakened common consciousness, sprung from common joy and grief, at burial, birth, or wedding; from a common hardship in poverty, poor land, and low wages; and, above all, from the sight of the Veil that hung between us and Opportunity. All this caused us to think some thoughts together; but these, when ripe for speech, were spoken in various languages. Those whose eyes twenty-five and more years before had seen "the glory of the coming of the Lord," saw in every present hindrance or help a dark fatalism bound to bring all things right in His own good time. The mass of those to whom slavery was a dim recollection of childhood found the world a puzzling thing: it asked little of them, and they answered with little, and yet it ridiculed their offering. Such a paradox they could not understand, and therefore sank into listless indifference, or shiftlessness, or reckless bravado. There were, however, some—such as Josie, Jim, and Ben—to whom War, Hell, and Slavery were but childhood tales, whose young appetites had been whetted to an edge by school and story and half-awakened thought. Ill could they be content, born without and beyond the World. And their weak wings beat against their barriers,—barriers of caste, of youth, of life; at last, in dangerous moments, against everything that opposed even a whim.

The ten years that follow youth, the years when first the real- 15 ization comes that life is leading somewhere,—these were the years that passed after I left my little school. When they were past, I came by chance once more to the walls of Fisk University, to the halls of the chapel of melody. As I lingered there in the joy and pain of meeting old school-friends, there swept over me a sudden longing to pass again beyond the blue hill, and to see the homes and the school of other days, and to learn how life had gone with my schoolchildren; and I went.

Josie was dead, and the gray-haired mother said simply, 16 "We've had a heap of trouble since you've been away." I had feared for Jim. With a cultured parentage and a social caste to uphold him, he might have made a venturesome merchant or a West Point cadet.

But here he was, angry with life and reckless; and when Farmer Durham charged him with stealing wheat, the old man had to ride fast to escape the stones which the furious fool hurled after him. They told Jim to run away; but he would not run, and the constable came that afternoon. It grieved Josie, and great awkward John walked nine miles every day to see his little brother through the bars of Lebanon jail. At last the two came back together in the dark night. The mother cooked supper, and Josie emptied her purse, and the boys stole away. Josie grew thin and silent, yet worked the more. The hill became steep for the quiet old father, and with the boys away there was little to do in the valley. Josie helped them to sell the old farm, and they moved nearer town. Brother Dennis, the carpenter, built a new house with six rooms; Josie toiled a year in Nashville, and brought back ninety dollars to furnish the house and change it to a home.

When the spring came, and the birds twittered, and the stream 17 ran proud and full, little sister Lizzie, bold and thoughtless, flushed with the passion of youth, bestowed herself on the tempter, and brought home a nameless child. Josie shivered and worked on, with the vision of schooldays all fled, with a face wan and tired,—worked until, on a summer's day, some one married another; then Josie crept to her mother like a hurt child, and slept—and sleeps.

I paused to scent the breeze as I entered the valley. The Law- 18 rences have gone,—the father and son forever,—and the other son lazily digs in the earth to live. A new young widow rents out their cabin to fat Reuben. Reuben is a Baptist preacher now, but I fear as lazy as ever, though his cabin has three rooms; and little Ella has grown into a bouncing woman, and is ploughing corn on the hot hillside. There are babies a-plenty, and one half-witted girl. Across the valley is a house I did not know before, and there I found, rocking one baby and expecting another one of my schoolgirls, a daughter of Uncle Bird Dowell. She looked somewhat worried with her new duties, but soon bristled into pride over her neat cabin and the tale of her thrifty husband, and the horse and cow, and the farm they were planning to buy.

My log schoolhouse was gone. In its place stood Progress; and 19 Progress, I understand, is necessarily ugly. The crazy foundation stones still marked the former site of my poor little cabin, and not far away, on six weary boulders, perched a jaunty board house, perhaps twenty by thirty feet, with three windows and a door that locked. Some of the window-glass was broken, and part of an old iron stove lay mournfully under the house. I peeped through the window half reverently, and found things that were more familiar. The blackboard had grown by about two feet, and the seats were still without backs. The county owns the lot now, I hear, and every year there is a session

W. E. B. DU BOIS

of school. As I sat by the spring and looked on the Old and the New I felt glad, very glad, and yet—

After two long drinks I started on. There was the great double log-house on the corner. I remembered the broken, blighted family that used to live there. The strong, hard face of the mother, with its wilderness of hair, rose before me. She had driven her husband away, and while I taught school a strange man lived there, big and jovial, and people talked. I felt sure that Ben and Tildy would come to naught from such a home. But this is an odd world; for Ben is a busy farmer in Smith County, "doing well, too," they say, and he had cared for little Tildy until last spring, when a lover married her. A hard life the lad had led, toiling for meat, and laughed at because he was homely and crooked. There was a Sam Carlon, an impudent old skin-flint, who had definite notions about "niggers," and hired Ben a summer and would not pay him. Then the hungry boy gathered his sacks together, and in broad daylight went to Carlon's corn; and when the hard-fisted farmer set upon him the angry boy flew at him like a beast. Doc Burke saved a murder and a lynching that day. [20]

The story reminded me again of the Burkes, and an impatience seized me to know who won in the battle, Doc or the seventy-five acres. For it is a hard thing to make a farm out of nothing, even in fifteen years. So I hurried on, thinking of the Burkes. They used to have a certain magnificent barbarism about them that I liked. They were never vulgar, never immoral, but rather rough and primitive, with an unconventionality that spent itself in loud guffaws, slaps on the back, and naps in the corner. I hurried by the cottage of the mis-born Neill boys. It was empty, and they were grown into fat, lazy farm-hands. I saw the home of the Hickmans, but Albert, with his stooping shoulders, had passed from the world. Then I came to the Burkes' gate and peered through; the inclosure looked rough and un-trimmed, and yet there were the same fences around the old farm save to the left, where lay twenty-five other acres. And Lo! the cabin in the hollow had climbed the hill and swollen to a half-finished six-room cottage. [21]

The Burkes held a hundred acres, but they were still in debt. Indeed, the gaunt father who toiled night and day would scarcely be happy out of debt, being so used to it. Some day he must stop, for his massive frame is showing decline. The mother wore shoes, but the lion-like physique of other days was broken. The children had grown up. Rob, the image of his father, was loud and rough with laughter. Birdie, my school baby of six, had grown to a picture of maiden beauty, tall and tawny. "Edgar is gone," said the mother, with head half bowed—"gone to work in Nashville; he and his father couldn't agree." [22]

OF THE MEANING OF PROGRESS

259

Little Doc, the boy born since the time of my school, took me 23
horseback down the creek next morning toward Farmer Dowell's. The
road and the stream were battling for mastery, and the stream had
the better of it. We splashed and waded, and the merry boy, perched
behind me, chattered and laughed. He showed me where Simon
Thompson had bought a bit of ground and a home; but his daughter
Lana, a plump, brown, slow girl, was not there. She had married a
man and a farm twenty miles away. We wound on down the stream
till we came to a gate that I did not recognize, but the boy insisted
that it was "Uncle Bird's." The farm was fat with the growing crop.
In that little valley was a strange stillness as I rode up; for death and
marriage had stolen youth and left age and childhood there. We sat
and talked that night after the chores were done. Uncle Bird was
grayer, and his eyes did not see so well, but he was still jovial. We
talked of the acres bought,—one hundred and twenty-five,—of the
new guest-chamber added, of Martha's marrying. Then we talked of
death: Fanny and Fred were gone; a shadow hung over the other
daughter and when it lifted she was to go to Nashville to school. At
last we spoke of the neighbors, and as night fell, Uncle Bird told me
how, on a night like that, 'Thenie came wandering back to her home
over yonder, to escape the blows of her husband. And next morning
she died in the home that her little bow-legged brother, working and
saving, had bought for their widowed mother.

My journey was done, and behind me lay hill and dale, and 24
Life and Death. How shall man measure Progress there where the
dark-faced Josie lies? How many heartfuls of sorrow shall balance a
bushel of wheat? How hard a thing is life to the lowly, and yet how
human and real! And all this life and love and strife and failure,—is
it the twilight of nightfall or the flush of some faint-dawning day?

Thus sadly musing, I rode to Nashville in the Jim Crow car. 25

COMPREHENSION

1. According to the author, what did he learn from his "journey"?

2. In general, what is the author's basic attitude toward progress? Where does
he state this attitude most clearly?

3. Put into your own words the feelings Du Bois projects in his description of
the people he taught in the hills of Tennessee.

RHETORIC

1. Would you label the language in the essay subjective or objective? Justify
your answer by citing passages from the text.

2. How does the symbolism of "the Veil," first introduced in paragraph 1,
influence the tone of the essay? How does the author control mood through
shifting patterns of imagery? Cite examples.

　　　　　　　　　　　　　　　W. E. B. DU BOIS

3. What are the primary rhetorical patterns employed by the author to develop his definition of progress?

4. The essay divides into two main narrative segments. What are they? Analyze the relationship between these segments. How does Du Bois maintain unity? How does the time element affect the mood and tone that are generated?

5. Analyze the spatial transitions that the author uses in the essay.

6. Assess the effectiveness of the short concluding paragraph.

WRITING

1. Discuss the value of personal experience and observation as a sociological method. Why do you think that Du Bois mistrusted scientific objectivity in sociological analysis? Compare and contrast the methods of Du Bois, Benedict, and Forster in this chapter.

2. Write a definition of *progress* based on personal experience and observation.

3. A national magazine has asked you to write a short article on racial progress and pluralism at your college. Prepare this article, which should run between 1,000 and 1,250 words.

BRUCE CATTON

Grant and Lee: A Study in Contrasts

Bruce Catton (1899–1978) was born in Petosky, Michigan. After serving in the Navy during World War I, he attended Oberlin College but left in his junior year to pursue a career in journalism. From 1942 to 1952, Catton served in the government, first on the War Production Board and later in the Departments of Commerce and the Interior. He left government to devote himself to literary work as a columnist for the Nation *and a historian of the Civil War. His many works include* A Stillness at Appomattox, *which won the 1954 Pulitzer Prize;* Mr. Lincoln's Army; The Centennial History of the Civil War; *and* Prefaces to History. *In this selection, Catton presents vivid portraits of two well-known but little-understood figures from American history.*

When Ulysses S. Grant and Robert E. Lee met in the parlor 1
of a modest house at Appomattox Court House, Virginia, on April 9, 1865, to work out the terms for the surrender of Lee's Army of Northern Virginia, a great chapter in American life came to a close, and a great new chapter began.

These men were bringing the Civil War to its virtual finish. 2
To be sure, other armies had yet to surrender, and for a few days the fugitive Confederate government would struggle desperately and vainly, trying to find some way to go on living now that its chief support was gone. But in effect it was all over when Grant and Lee signed the papers. And the little room where they wrote out the terms was the scene of one of the poignant, dramatic contrasts in American History.

They were two strong men, these oddly different generals, 3
and they represented the strengths of two conflicting currents that, through them, had come into final collision.

Back of Robert E. Lee was the notion that the old aristocratic 4
concept might somehow survive and be dominant in American life.

Lee was tidewater Virginia, and in his background were family, culture, and tradition . . . the age of chivalry transplanted to a New 5
World which was making its own legends and its own myths. He embodied a way of life that had come down through the age of knighthood and the English country squire. America was a land that was beginning all over again, dedicated to nothing much more complicated than the rather hazy belief that all men had equal rights and should have an equal chance in the world. In such a land Lee stood for the feeling that it was somehow of advantage to human society to have a pronounced inequality in the social structure. There should be a leisure class, backed by ownership of land; in turn, society itself should be keyed to the land as the chief source of wealth and influence. It would bring forth (according to this ideal) a class of men with a strong sense of obligation to the community; men who lived not to gain advantage for themselves, but to meet the solemn obligations which had been laid on them by the very fact that they were privileged. From them the country would get its leadership; to them it could look for the higher values—of thought, of conduct, of personal deportment—to give it strength and virtue.

Lee embodied the noblest elements of this aristocratic ideal. 6
Through him, the landed nobility justified itself. For four years, the Southern states had fought a desperate war to uphold the ideals for which Lee stood. In the end, it almost seemed as if the Confederacy fought for Lee; as if he himself was the Confederacy . . . the best thing that the way of life for which the Confederacy stood could ever have to offer. He had passed into legend before Appomattox. Thousands

of tired, underfed, poorly clothed Confederate soldiers, long since past the simple enthusiasm of the early days of the struggle, somehow considered Lee the symbol of everything for which they had been willing to die. But they could not quite put this feeling into words. If the Lost Cause, sanctified by so much heroism and so many deaths, had a living justification, its justification was General Lee.

Grant, the son of a tanner on the Western frontier, was every- 7 thing Lee was not. He had come up the hard way and embodied nothing in particular except the eternal toughness and sinewy fiber of the men who grew up beyond the mountains. He was one of a body of men who owed reverence and obeisance to no one, who were self-reliant to a fault, who cared hardly anything for the past but who had a sharp eye for the future.

These frontier men were the precise opposites of the tidewater 8 aristocrats. Back of them, in the great surge that had taken people over the Alleghenies and into the opening Western country, there was a deep, implicit dissatisfaction with a past that had settled into grooves. They stood for democracy, not from any reasoned conclusion about the proper ordering of human society, but simply because they had grown up in the middle of democracy and knew how it worked. Their society might have privileges, but they would be privileges each man had won for himself. Forms and patterns meant nothing. No man was born to anything, except perhaps to a chance to show how far he could rise. Life was competition.

Yet along with this feeling had come a deep sense of belong- 9 ing to a national community. The Westerner who developed a farm, opened a shop, or set up in business as a trader, could hope to prosper only as his own community prospered—and his community ran from the Atlantic to the Pacific and from Canada down to Mexico. If the land was settled, with towns and highways and accessible markets, he could better himself. He saw his fate in terms of the nation's own destiny. As its horizons expanded, so did his. He had, in other words, an acute dollars-and-cents stake in the continued growth and development of his country.

And that, perhaps, is where the contrast between Grant and Lee 10 becomes most striking. The Virginia aristocrat, inevitably, saw himself in relation to his own region. He lived in a static society which could endure almost anything except change. Instinctively, his first loyalty would go to the locality in which that society existed. He would fight to the limit of endurance to defend it, because in defending it he was defending everything that gave his own life its deepest meaning.

The Westerner, on the other hand, would fight with an equal 11 tenacity for the broader concept of society. He fought so because everything he lived by was tied to growth, expansion, and a constantly widening horizon. What he lived by would survive or fall with the nation itself. He could not possibly stand by unmoved in the face of an attempt to destroy the Union. He would combat it with everything he had, because he could only see it as an effort to cut the ground out from under his feet.

So Grant and Lee were in complete contrast, representing two   12
diametrically opposed elements in American life. Grant was the modern man emerging; beyond him, ready to come on the stage, was the great age of steel and machinery, of crowded cities and a restless burgeoning vitality. Lee might have ridden down from the old age of chivalry, lance in hand, silken banner fluttering over his head. Each man was the perfect champion of his cause, drawing both his strengths and his weaknesses from the people he led.

Yet it was not all contrast, after all. Different as they were—   13
in background, in personality, in underlying aspiration—these two great soldiers had much in common. Under everything else, they were marvelous fighters. Furthermore, their fighting qualities were really very much alike.

Each man had, to begin with, the great virtue of utter tenacity   14
and fidelity. Grant fought his way down the Mississippi Valley in spite of acute personal discouragement and profound military handicaps. Lee hung on in the trenches at Petersburg after hope itself had died. In each man there was an indomitable quality . . . the born fighter's refusal to give up as long as he can still remain on his feet and lift his two fists.

Daring and resourcefulness they had, too; the ability to think   15
faster and move faster than the enemy. These were the qualities which gave Lee the dazzling campaigns of Second Manassas and Chancellorsville and won Vicksburg for Grant.

Lastly, and perhaps greatest of all, there was the ability, at   16
the end, to turn quickly from war to peace once the fighting was over. Out of the way these two men behaved at Appomattox came the possibility of a peace of reconciliation. It was a possibility not wholly realized, in the years to come, but which did, in the end, help the two sections to become one nation again . . . after a war whose bitterness might have seemed to make such a reunion wholly impossible. No part of either man's life became him more than the part he played in their brief meeting in the McLean house at Appomattox. Their behavior there put all succeeding generations of Americans in their debt. Two great Americans, Grant and Lee—very different, yet under everything very much alike. Their encounter at Appomattox was one of the great moments of American history.

COMPREHENSION

1. What is the central purpose of Catton's study? Cite evidence to support your view. Who is his audience?

BRUCE CATTON

2. What is the primary appeal to readers of describing history through the study of individuals rather than through the recording of events? How does Catton's essay reflect this appeal?

3. According to Catton, what special qualities did Grant and Lee share, and what qualities set them apart?

RHETORIC

1. What role does the opening paragraph have in setting the tone for the essay? Is the tone typical of what you would expect of an essay describing military generals? Explain your view. How does the conclusion echo the introductory paragraph?

2. Note that the sentence, "Two great Americans, Grant and Lee—very different, yet under everything very much alike" (paragraph 16), has no verb. What does this indicate about Catton's style? What other sentences contain atypical syntax? What is *their* contribution to the unique quality of the writing?

3. While this essay is about an historical era, there is a notable lack of specific facts—for example, dates, statistics, and events. What has Catton focused on instead?

4. What is the function of the one-sentence paragraph 3?

5. Paragraphs 9, 10, 12, and 13 begin with coordinating conjunctions. How do these transitional words give the paragraphs their special coherence? How would more typical introductory expressions, such as "in addition," "furthermore," or "moreover," have altered this coherence?

6. What strategy does Catton use in comparing and contrasting the two generals? Study paragraphs 5 through 16. Which are devoted to describing each man separately, and which include aspects of each man? What is the overall development of the comparisons?

WRITING

1. Does Lee's vision of society exist in the United States today? If not, why not? If so, where do you find this vision? Write a brief essay on this topic.

2. Select two well-known individuals in the same profession—for example, politics, entertainment, or sports. Make a list for each, enumerating the different aspects of their character, behavior, beliefs, and background. Using this list as an outline, devise an essay wherein you compare and contrast the two.

3. Apply, in a comparative essay, Catton's observation about "two diametrically opposed elements in American life" to the current national scene.

I Have a Dream

Martin Luther King Jr. (1929–1968) was born in Atlanta, Georgia, and earned degrees from Morehouse College, Crozer Theological Seminary, Boston University, and Chicago Theological Seminary. As Baptist clergyman, civil rights leader, founder and president of the Southern Christian Leadership Council, and, in 1964, Nobel Peace Prize winner, King was a celebrated advocate of nonviolent resistance to achieve equality and racial integration in the world. King was a gifted orator and a highly persuasive writer. His books include Stride toward Freedom *(1958);* Letter from Birmingham City Jail *(1963);* Strength to Love *(1963);* Why We Can't Wait *(1964); and* Where Do We Go from Here: Chaos or Community? *(1967), a book published shortly before Reverend King was assassinated on April 4, 1968, in Memphis, Tennessee. This selection, a milestone of American oratory, was the keynote address at the March on Washington, August 28, 1963.*

1   I am happy to join with you today in what will go down in history as the greatest demonstration for freedom in the history of our nation.

2   Fivescore years ago, a great American, in whose symbolic shadow we stand today, signed the Emancipation Proclamation. This momentous decree came as a great beacon light of hope to millions of Negro slaves who had been seared in the flames of withering injustice. It came as a joyous daybreak to end the long night of their captivity.

3   But one hundred years later, the Negro still is not free; one hundred years later, the life of the Negro is still sadly crippled by the manacles of segregation and the chains of discrimination; one hundred years later, the Negro lives on a lonely island of poverty in the midst of a vast ocean of material prosperity; one hundred years later, the Negro is still languishing in the corners of American society and finds himself in exile in his own land.

4   So we've come here today to dramatize a shameful condition. In a sense we've come to our nation's capital to cash a check. When the architects of our republic wrote the magnificent words of the Constitution and the Declaration of Independence, they were signing a promissory note to which every American was to fall heir. This note was the promise that all men, yes, black men as well as white men, would be guaranteed the unalienable rights of life, liberty, and the pursuit of happiness.

5   It is obvious today that America has defaulted on this prom-

issory note in so far as her citizens of color are concerned. Instead of honoring this sacred obligation, America has given the Negro people a bad check; a check which has come back marked "insufficient funds." We refuse to believe that there are insufficient funds in the great vaults of opportunity of this nation. And so we've come to cash this check, a check that will give us upon demand the riches of freedom and the security of justice.

We have also come to this hallowed spot to remind America 6 of the fierce urgency of now. This is no time to engage in the luxury of cooling off or to take the tranquilizing drug of gradualism. Now is the time to make real the promises of democracy; now is the time to rise from the dark and desolate valley of segregation to the sunlit path of racial justice; now is the time to lift our nation from the quicksands of racial injustice to the solid rock of brotherhood; now is the time to make justice a reality for all God's children. It would be fatal for the nation to overlook the urgency of the moment. This sweltering summer of the Negro's legitimate discontent will not pass until there is an invigorating autumn of freedom and equality.

Nineteen sixty-three is not an end, but a beginning. And those 7 who hope that the Negro needed to blow off steam and will now be content, will have a rude awakening if the nation returns to business as usual.

There will be neither rest nor tranquility in America until the 8 Negro is granted his citizenship rights. The whirlwinds of revolt will continue to shake the foundations of our nation until the bright day of justice emerges.

But there is something that I must say to my people who stand 9 on the warm threshold which leads into the palace of justice. In the process of gaining our rightful place we must not be guilty of wrongful deeds.

Let us not seek to satisfy our thirst for freedom by drinking 10 from the cup of bitterness and hatred. We must forever conduct our struggle on the high plane of dignity and discipline. We must not allow our creative protest to degenerate into physical violence. Again and again we must rise to the majestic heights of meeting physical force with soul force.

The marvelous new militancy which has engulfed the Negro 11 community must not lead us to a distrust of all white people, for many of our white brothers, as evidenced by their presence here today, have come to realize that their destiny is tied up with our destiny and they have come to realize that their freedom is inextricably bound to our freedom. This offense we share mounted to storm the battlements of injustice must be carried forth by a biracial army. We cannot walk alone.

And as we walk, we must make the pledge that we shall al- 12 ways march ahead. We cannot turn back. There are those who are asking the devotees of civil rights, "When will you be satisfied?" We can never be satisfied as long as the Negro is the victim of the unspeakable horrors of police brutality.

We can never be satisfied as long as our bodies, heavy with 13 fatigue of travel, cannot gain lodging in the motels of the highways and the hotels of the cities. We cannot be satisfied as long as the Negro's basic mobility is from a smaller ghetto to a larger one.

We can never be satisfied as long as our children are stripped 14 of their selfhood and robbed of their dignity by signs stating "for whites only." We cannot be satisfied as long as a Negro in Mississippi cannot vote and a Negro in New York believes he has nothing for which to vote. No, we are not satisfied, and we will not be satisfied until justice rolls down like waters and righteousness like a mighty stream.

I am not unmindful that some of you have come here out of 15 excessive trials and tribulation. Some of you have come fresh from narrow jail cells. Some of you have come from areas where your quest for freedom left you battered by the storms of persecution and staggered by the winds of police brutality. You have been the veterans of creative suffering. Continue to work with the faith that unearned suffering is redemptive.

Go back to Mississippi; go back to Alabama; go back to South 16 Carolina; go back to Georgia; go back to Louisiana; go back to the slums and ghettos of the northern cities, knowing that somehow this situation can, and will be changed. Let us not wallow in the valley of despair.

So I say to you, my friends, that even though we must face 17 the difficulties of today and tomorrow, I still have a dream. It is a dream deeply rooted in the American dream that one day this nation will rise up and live out the true meaning of its creed—we hold these truths to be self-evident, that all men are created equal.

I have a dream that one day on the red hills of Georgia, sons 18 of former slaves and sons of former slave-owners will be able to sit down together at the table of brotherhood.

I have a dream that one day, even the state of Mississippi, a 19 state sweltering with the heat of injustice, sweltering with the heat of oppression, will be transformed into an oasis of freedom and justice.

I have a dream my four little children will one day live in a 20 nation where they will not be judged by the color of their skin but by content of their character. I have a dream today!

I have a dream that one day, down in Alabama, with its vicious racists, with its governor having his lips dripping with the words of interposition and nullification, that one day, right there in Alabama, little black boys and black girls will be able to join hands with little white boys and white girls as sisters and brothers. I have a dream today!

I have a dream that one day every valley shall be exalted, 22 every hill and mountain shall be made low, the rough places shall be made plain, and the crooked places shall be made straight and the glory of the Lord will be revealed and all flesh shall see it together.

This is our hope. This is the faith that I go back to the South 23 with.

With this faith we will be able to hear out of the mountain of 24 despair a stone of hope. With this faith we will be able to transform the jangling discords of our nation into a beautiful symphony of brotherhood.

With this faith we will be able to work together, to pray to- 25 gether, to struggle together, to go to jail together, to stand up for freedom together, knowing that we will be free one day. This will be the day when all of God's children will be able to sing with new meaning—"my country 'tis of thee; sweet land of liberty; of thee I sing; land where my fathers died, land of the pilgrim's pride; from every mountain side, let freedom ring"—and if America is to be a great nation, this must become true.

So let freedom ring from the prodigious hilltops of New 26 Hampshire.

Let freedom ring from the mighty mountains of New York. 27

Let freedom ring from the heightening Alleghenies of Penn- 28 sylvania.

Let freedom ring from the snow-capped Rockies of Colorado. 29

Let freedom ring from the curvaceous slopes of California. 30

But not only that. 31

Let freedom ring from Stone Mountain of Georgia. 32

Let freedom ring from Lookout Mountain of Tennessee. 33

Let freedom ring from every hill and molehill of Mississippi, 34 from every mountainside, let freedom ring.

And when we allow freedom to ring, when we let it ring from 35 every village and hamlet, from every state and city, we will be able to speed up that day when all of God's children—black men and white men, Jews and Gentiles, Catholics and Protestants—will be able to join hands and to sing in the words of the old Negro spiritual, "Free at last, free at last; thank God Almighty, we are free at last."

COMPREHENSION

1. What is the main purpose behind this speech? Where does King state this purpose most clearly?

2. Why does King make use of "fivescore years ago" (paragraph 2)? How is this more appropriate than simply saying, "a hundred years ago"?

3. Who is King's audience? Where does he acknowledge the special historic circumstances influencing his speech?

RHETORIC

1. Where else does King adapt phrases from other sources to give his work allusive richness?

2. What do the terms *interposition* and *nullification* (paragraph 21) mean? What is their historical significance?

3. Why does King make use of repetition? Does this technique work well in print? Explain.

4. What is the purpose of the extended metaphor in paragraphs 4 and 5? Which point in paragraph 3 does it refer to?

5. In which paragraphs does King address the problems of African Americans?

6. Why is this selection entitled "I Have a Dream"? How do dreams serve as a motif for this speech?

WRITING

1. "I Have a Dream" is considered by many people to be among the greatest speeches delivered by an American. Do you think that it deserves to be? Explain in an essay.

2. Write a comparative essay analyzing King's assessment of black Americans' condition in 1963 and their condition today. What do you think King would say if he knew of contemporary conditions?

3. Write your own "I Have a Dream" essay, basing it on your vision of America or of a special people.

4. Prepare a newspaper editorial advocating a solution to one aspect of racial, ethnic, or sexual injustice.

VACLAV HAVEL

The Revolution Has Just Begun

Vaclav Havel (1936–   ) is an internationally acclaimed Czech dramatist, dissident, and human rights activist. He began writing drama in the 1950s, and his plays are influenced strongly by the absurdist literature of Kafka, Beckett, and Ionesco. Jailed fre-

quently for his activism, Havel was instrumental in the success of the 1989 reform movement in Czechoslovakia, and in 1990 he was elected to his nation's presidency. His major work includes his plays The Garden Party *(1963) and* The Memorandum *(1965), along with a dazzling collection of prison correspondence to his wife,* Letters to Olga *(1984). In the following selection, delivered in 1990 to a joint meeting of the United States Congress, Havel offers his vision of the changing global political structure.*

 wice in this century the world has been threatened by a catastrophe. 1

Twice this catastrophe was born in Europe, and twice you Americans, along with others, were called upon to save Europe, the whole world and yourselves. 2

In the meantime, the U.S. became the most powerful nation on earth, and it understood the responsibility that flowed from this. But something else was happening as well. The Soviet Union appeared, grew and transformed the enormous sacrifices of its people suffering under totalitarian rule into a strength that, after World War II, made it the second most powerful nation in the world. 3

CREATING THE FAMILY OF MEN

All of this taught us to see the world in bipolar terms as two enormous forces—one a defender of freedom, the other a source of nightmares. Europe became the point of friction between these two powers, and thus it turned into a single enormous arsenal divided into two parts. In this process, one half of the arsenal became part of that nightmarish power, while the other, the free part, bordering on the ocean and having no wish to be driven into it, was compelled, together with you, to build a complicated security system to which we probably owe the fact that we still exist. 4

The totalitarian system in the Soviet Union and in most of its satellites is breaking down, and our nations are looking for a way to democracy and independence. 5

This, I am convinced, is a historically irreversible process and, as a result, Europe will begin again to seek its own identity without being compelled to be a divided armory any longer. Perhaps this will create the hope that sooner or later, your boys will no longer have to stand on guard for freedom in Europe or come to our rescue, because Europe will at last be able to stand guard over itself. 6

But that is still not the most important thing. The main thing is, it seems to me, that these revolutionary changes will enable us to escape from the rather antiquated straitjacket of this bipolar view of the world and to enter at last into an era of multipolarity in which all 7 of us, large and small, former slaves and former masters, will be able to create what your great President Lincoln called "the family of men."

THE PATH OF PLURALISM
How can the U.S. help us today? My reply is as paradoxical as the whole of my life has been. You can help us most of all if you help the Soviet Union on its irreversible but immensely complicated road to democracy. It is far more complicated than the road open to its former European satellites. You yourselves know best how to support as rapidly as possible the nonviolent evolution of this enormous multinational body politic toward democracy and autonomy for all its people. Therefore, it is not fitting for me to offer you any advice. 8

I can only say that the sooner, the more quickly and the more peacefully the Soviet Union begins to move along the road toward genuine political pluralism, respect for the rights of the nations to their own integrity and to a working—that is, a market—economy, the better it will be not just for Czechs and Slovaks but for the whole world. 9

And the sooner you yourselves will be able to reduce the burden of the military budget borne by the American people. To put it metaphorically, the millions you give to the East today will soon return to you in the form of billions in savings. American soldiers shouldn't have to be separated from their mothers just because Europe is incapable of being a guarantor of world peace, which it ought to be in order to make some amends, at least, for having given the world two world wars. 10

THE LEGACY OF OPPRESSION
As long as people are people, democracy, in the full sense of the word, will always be no more than an ideal. In this sense, you too are merely approaching democracy. But you have one great advantage: you have been approaching democracy uninterruptedly for more than 200 years, and your journey toward the horizon has never been disrupted by a totalitarian system. 11

The communist type of totalitarian system has left both our nations, Czechs and Slovaks, as it has all the nations of the Soviet Union and the other countries the Soviet Union subjugated in its time, a legacy of countless dead, an infinite spectrum of human suffering, profound economic decline and, above all, enormous human humiliation. It has brought us horrors that fortunately you have not known. 12

It has given us something positive, a special capacity to look from time to time somewhat further than someone who has not undergone this bitter experience. A person who cannot move and lead a somewhat normal life because he is pinned under a boulder has more 13

VACLAV HAVEL

time to think about his hopes than someone who is not trapped that way.

What I'm trying to say is this: we must all learn many things   14
from you, from how to educate our offspring, how to elect our representatives, all the way to how to organize our economic life so that
it will lead to prosperity and not to poverty. But it doesn't have to be
merely assistance from the well educated, powerful and wealthy to
someone who has nothing and therefore has nothing to offer in return.

We too can offer something to you: our experience and the   15
knowledge that has come from it. The specific experience I'm talking
about has given me one certainty: consciousness precedes being, and
not the other way around, as the Marxists claim. For this reason, the
salvation of this human world lies nowhere else than in the human
heart, in the human power to reflect, in human meekness and in human responsibility.

A NEW WAY OF THINKING

Without a global revolution in the sphere of human consciousness,   16
nothing will change for the better in the sphere of our being as humans, and the catastrophe toward which this world is headed—be it
ecological, social, demographic or a general breakdown of civilization—will be unavoidable. If we are no longer threatened by world
war or by the danger that the absurd mountains of accumulated nuclear weapons might blow up the world, this does not mean that we
have definitely won. We are still incapable of understanding that the
only genuine backbone of all our actions, if they are to be moral, is
responsibility. Responsibility to something higher than my family, my
country, my company, my success—responsibility to the order of
being where all our actions are indelibly recorded and where and only
where they will be properly judged.

I think that you Americans should understand this way of   17
thinking. When Thomas Jefferson wrote that "governments are instituted among men, deriving their just powers from the consent of the
governed," it was a simple and important act of the human spirit.
What gave meaning to that act, however, was the fact that the author
backed it up with his life. It was not just his words, it was his deeds
as well.

COMPREHENSION

1.   Havel was directing this speech to a joint meeting of the United States Congress. How does he tailor his remarks to his primary audience? Are there other
audiences that he seems to be conscious of? Explain.

2.   Summarize the main concepts that Havel discusses in this selection. How
does he define such ideas as *freedom*, *bipolarity*, *totalitarianism*, *political pluralism*, and *revolution*? What thesis holds these concepts together?

3. What does Havel mean when he writes, "consciousness precedes being" (paragraph 15)?

RHETORIC

1. What is Havel's purpose in quoting from Lincoln in paragraph 7 and Jefferson in paragraph 17? What is the author's stylistic debt to Jefferson? (Reread "The Declaration of Independence" in this section.)

2. How does Havel manipulate the pronouns *you, us,* and *we* to frame his remarks and convey his thesis?

3. Havel sets up several points of comparison and contrast. What are they, and how do these comparative elements help to unify the selection?

4. Does Havel argue from general or specific evidence, or from both? Explain your answer by referring to examples in this selection.

5. How does the author utilize the rhetorical modes of definition and causal analysis to advance his thesis?

6. Analyze the first two paragraphs and the last two paragraphs in this selection. What are the similarities and differences? How do they focus the selection and permit it to cohere?

WRITING

1. Write a brief essay explaining the power or force of Havel's speech. (The members of Congress, after hearing this speech, gave Havel a standing ovation.) What elements give the speech its intellectual and emotional impact?

2. Explain the influence of "The Declaration of Independence" on Havel's remarks. Compare and contrast the social and political visions deriving from these two documents.

3. Both Havel and Martin Luther King, Jr., in their speeches have a "dream." In a comparative essay, analyze the nature of their respective dreams.

4. Write your own essay on contemporary world events entitled, "The Revolution Has Just Begun."

BARBARA TUCHMAN

An Inquiry into the Persistence of Unwisdom in Government

Barbara Tuchman (1912–1989), an eminent American historian, twice winner of the Pulitzer Prize, began her career as a research assistant for the Institute of Pacific Relations in 1933. She was a

BARBARA TUCHMAN

staff writer and correspondent for the Nation, *covering the Spanish Civil War from 1935 to 1937. Tuchman gained her first significant literary recognition for* The Zimmerman Telegram *(1958); she followed this initial success with* The Guns of August *(1962),* The Proud Tower *(1966), and* Stilwell and the American Experience in China, 1911–45 *(1971). This article offers a wide-ranging historical assessment of the causes of failure, mediocrity, and unwisdom in political life.*

A problem that strikes one in the study of history, regard- 1
less of period, is why man makes a poorer performance of government than of almost any other human activity. In this sphere, wisdom—meaning judgment acting on experience, common sense, available knowledge, and a decent appreciation of probability—is less operative and more frustrated than it should be. Why do men in high office so often act contrary to the way that reason points and enlightened self-interest suggests? Why does intelligent mental process so often seem to be paralyzed?

Why, to begin at the beginning, did the Trojan authorities 2
drag that suspicious-looking wooden horse inside their gates? Why did successive ministries of George III—that "bundle of imbecility," as Dr. Johnson called them collectively—insist on coercing rather than conciliating the Colonies though strongly advised otherwise by many counselors? Why did Napoleon and Hitler invade Russia? Why did the kaiser's government resume unrestricted submarine warfare in 1917 although explicitly warned that this would bring in the United States and that American belligerency would mean Germany's defeat? Why did Chiang Kai-shek refuse to heed any voice of reform or alarm until he woke up to find that his country had slid from under him? Why did Lyndon Johnson, seconded by the best and the brightest, progressively involve this nation in a war both ruinous and halfhearted and from which nothing but bad for our side resulted? Why does the present Administration continue to avoid introducing effective measures to reduce the wasteful consumption of oil while members of OPEC follow a price policy that must bankrupt their customers? How is it possible that the Central Intelligence Agency, whose function it is to provide, at taxpayers' expense, the information necessary to conduct a realistic foreign policy, could remain unaware that discontent in a country crucial to our interests was boiling up to the point of insurrection and overthrow of the ruler upon whom our policy rested? It has been reported that the CIA was ordered *not* to investigate the opposition to the shah of Iran in order to spare him any indication that we took it seriously, but since this sounds more like the theater of the absurd than like responsible government, I cannot bring myself to believe it.

There was a king of Spain once, Philip III, who is said to have died of a fever he contracted from sitting too long near a hot brazier, helplessly overheating himself because the functionary whose duty it was to remove the brazier when summoned could not be found. In the late twentieth century, it begins to appear as if mankind may be approaching a similar stage of suicidal incompetence. The Italians have been sitting in Philip III's hot seat for some time. The British trade unions, in a lunatic spectacle, seem periodically bent on dragging their country toward paralysis, apparently under the impression that they are separate from the whole. Taiwan was thrown into a state of shock by the United States' recognition of the People's Republic of China because, according to one report, in the seven years since the Shanghai Communiqué, the Kuomintang rulers of Taiwan had "refused to accept the new trend as a reality."

Wooden-headedness is a factor that plays a remarkably large role in government. Wooden-headedness consists of assessing a situation in terms of preconceived, fixed notions while ignoring or rejecting any contrary signs. It is acting according to wish while not allowing oneself to be confused by the facts.

A classic case was the French war plan of 1914, which concentrated everything on a French offensive to the Rhine, leaving the French left flank from Belgium to the Channel virtually unguarded. This strategy was based on the belief that the Germans would not use reserves in the front line and, without them, could not deploy enough manpower to extend their invasion through the French left. Reports by intelligence agents in 1913 to the effect that the Germans were indeed preparing their reserves for the front line in case of war were resolutely ignored because the governing spirits in France, dreaming only of their own offensive, did not want to believe in any signals that would require them to strengthen their left at the expense of their march to the Rhine. In the event, the Germans could and did extend themselves around the French left with results that determined a long war and its fearful consequences for our country.

Wooden-headedness is also the refusal to learn from experience, a form in which fourteenth-century rulers were supreme. No matter how often and obviously devaluation of the currency disrupted the economy and angered the people, French monarchs continued to resort to it whenever they were desperate for cash until they provoked insurrection among the bourgeoisie. No matter how often a campaign that depended on living off a hostile country ran into want and even starvation, campaigns for which this fate was inevitable were regularly undertaken.

Still another form is identification of self with the state, as currently exhibited by the ayatollah Khomeini. No wooden-headedness is so impenetrable as that of a religious zealot. Because he is

BARBARA TUCHMAN

connected with a private wire to the Almighty, no idea coming in on a lesser channel can reach him, which leaves him ill equipped to guide his country in its own best interests.

Philosophers of government ever since Plato have devoted their thinking to the major issues of ethics, sovereignty, the social contract, the rights of man, the corruption of power, the balance between freedom and order. Few—except Machiavelli, who was concerned with government as it is, not as it should be—bothered with mere folly, although this has been a chronic and pervasive problem. "Know, my son," said a dying Swedish statesman in the seventeenth century, "with how little wisdom the world is governed." More recently, Woodrow Wilson warned, "In public affairs, stupidity is more dangerous than knavery." 8

Stupidity is not related to type of regime; monarchy, oligarchy, and democracy produce it equally. Nor is it peculiar to nation or class. The working class as represented by the Communist governments functions no more rationally or effectively in power than the aristocracy or the bourgeoisie, as has notably been demonstrated in recent history. Mao Tse-tung may be admired for many things, but the Great Leap Forward, with a steel plant in every backyard, and the Cultural Revolution were exercises in unwisdom that greatly damaged China's progress and stability, not to mention the chairman's reputation. The record of the Russian proletariat in power can hardly be called enlightened, although after sixty years of control it must be accorded a kind of brutal success. If the majority of Russians are better off now than before, the cost in cruelty and tyranny has been no less and probably greater than under the czars. 9

After the French Revolution, the new order was rescued only by Bonaparte's military campaigns, which brought the spoils of foreign wars to fill the treasury, and subsequently by his competence as an executive. He chose officials not on the basis of origin or ideology but on the principle of "la carrière ouverte aux talents"—the said talents being intelligence, energy, industry, and obedience. That worked until the day of his own fatal mistake. 10

I do not wish to give the impression that men in office are incapable of governing wisely and well. Occasionally, the exception appears, rising in heroic size above the rest, a tower visible down the centuries. Greece had her Pericles, who ruled with authority, moderation, sound judgment, and a certain nobility that imposes natural dominion over others. Rome had Caesar, a man of remarkable governing talents, although it must be said that a ruler who arouses opponents to resort to assassination is probably not as smart as he ought to be. Later, under Marcus Aurelius and the other Antonines, Roman citizens enjoyed good government, prosperity, and respect for about a century. Charlemagne was able to impose order upon a mass of 11 contending elements, to foster the arts of civilization no less than those of war, and to earn a prestige supreme in the Middle Ages—probably not equaled in the eyes of contemporaries until the appearance of George Washington.

Possessor of an inner strength and perseverance that enabled him to prevail over a sea of obstacles, Washington was one of those critical figures but for whom history might well have taken a different course. He made possible the physical victory of American independence, while around him, in extraordinary fertility, political talent bloomed as if touched by some tropical sun. For all their flaws and quarrels, the Founding Fathers, who established our form of government, were, in the words of Arthur Schlesinger Sr., "the most remarkable generation of public men in the history of the United States or perhaps of any other nation." It is worth noting the qualities Schlesinger ascribes to them: They were fearless, high-principled, deeply versed in ancient and modern political thought, astute and pragmatic, unafraid of experiment, and—this is significant—"convinced of man's power to improve his condition through the use of intelligence." That was the mark of the Age of Reason that formed them, and though the eighteenth century had a tendency to regard men as more rational than they in fact were, it evoked the best in government from these men.   12

For our purposes, it would be invaluable if we could know what produced this burst of talent from a base of only two million inhabitants. Schlesinger suggests some contributing factors: wide diffusion of education, challenging economic opportunities, social mobility, training in self-government—all these encouraged citizens to cultivate their political aptitudes to the utmost. Also, he adds, with the Church declining in prestige and with business, science, and art not yet offering competing fields of endeavor, statecraft remained almost the only outlet for men of energy and purpose. Perhaps the need of the moment—the opportunity to create a new political system—is what brought out the best.   13

Not before or since, I believe, has so much careful and reasonable thinking been invested in the creation of a new political system. In the French, Russian, and Chinese revolutions, too much class hatred and bloodshed were involved to allow for fair results or permanent constitutions. The American experience was unique, and the system so far has always managed to right itself under pressure. In spite of accelerating incompetence, it still works better than most. We haven't had to discard the system and try another after every crisis, as have Italy and Germany, Spain and France. The founders of the United States are a phenomenon to keep in mind to encourage our estimate of human possibilities, but their example, as a political sci-   14 entist has pointed out, is "too infrequent to be taken as a basis for normal expectations."

The English are considered to have enjoyed reasonably benign 15 government during the eighteenth and nineteenth centuries, except for their Irish subjects, debtors, child laborers, and other unfortunates in various pockets of oppression. The folly that lost the American colonies reappeared now and then, notably in the treatment of the Irish and the Boers, but a social system can survive a good deal of folly when circumstances are historically favorable or when it is cushioned by large resources, as in the heyday of the British Empire, or absorbed by sheer size, as in this country during our period of expansion. Today there are no more cushions, which makes folly less affordable.

Elsewhere than in government, man has accomplished mar- 16 vels: invented the means in our time to leave the world and voyage to the moon; in the past, harnessed wind and electricity, raised earthbound stone into soaring cathedrals, woven silk brocades out of the spinnings of a worm, composed the music of Mozart and the dramas of Shakespeare, classified the forms of nature, penetrated the mysteries of genetics. Why is he so much less accomplished in government? What frustrates, in that sphere, the operation of the intellect? Isaac Bashevis Singer, discoursing as a Nobel laureate on mankind, offers the opinion that God had been frugal in bestowing intellect but lavish with passions and emotions. "He gave us," Singer says, "so many emotions and such strong ones that every human being, even if he is an idiot, is a millionaire in emotions."

I think Singer has made a point that applies to our inquiry. 17 What frustrates the workings of intellect is the passions and the emotions: ambition, greed, fear, facesaving, the instinct to dominate, the needs of the ego, the whole bundle of personal vanities and anxieties.

Reason is crushed by these forces. If the Athenians out of 18 pride and overconfidence had not set out to crush Sparta for good but had been content with moderate victory, their ultimate fall might have been averted. If fourteenth-century knights had not been obsessed by the idea of glory and personal prowess, they might have defeated the Turks at Nicopolis with incalculable consequence for all of Eastern Europe. If the English, 200 years ago, had heeded Chatham's knocking on the door of what he called "this sleeping and confounded Ministry" and his urgent advice to repeal the Coercive Acts and withdraw the troops before the "inexpiable drop of blood is shed in an impious war with a people contending in the great cause of publick liberty," or, given a last chance, if they had heeded Edmund Burke's celebrated plea for conciliation and his warning that it would prove impossible to coerce a "fierce people" of their own pedigree, we might still be a united people bridging the Atlantic, with incalculable consequence for the history of the West. It did not happen that way, because king and Parliament felt it imperative to affirm sovereignty over arrogant colonials. The alternative choice, as in Athens and medieval Europe, was close to psychologically impossible.

In the case we know best—the American engagement in Vietnam—fixed notions, preconceptions, wooden-headed thinking, and emotions accumulated into a monumental mistake and classic humiliation. The original idea was that the lesson of the failure to halt fascist aggression during the appeasement era dictated the necessity of halting the so-called aggression by North Vietnam, conceived to be the spearhead of international communism. This was applying the wrong model to the wrong facts, which would have been obvious if our policy makers had taken into consideration the history of the people on the spot instead of charging forward wearing the blinders of the cold war. 19

The reality of Vietnamese nationalism, of which Ho Chi Minh had been the standard-bearer since long before the war, was certainly no secret. Indeed, Franklin Roosevelt had insisted that the French should not be allowed to return after the war, a policy that we instantly abandoned the moment the Japanese were out: Ignoring the Vietnamese demand for self-government, we first assisted the return of the French, and then, when incredibly, they had been put to rout by the native forces, we took their place, as if Dien Bien Phu had no significance whatever. Policy founded upon error multiplies, never retreats. The pretense that North versus South Vietnam represented foreign aggression was intensified. If Asian specialists with knowledge of the situation suggested a reassessment, they were not persuasive. As a Communist aggressor, Hanoi was presumed to be a threat to the United States, yet the vital national interest at stake, which alone may have justified belligerency, was never clear enough to sustain a declaration of war. 20

A further, more fundamental, error confounded our policy. This was the nature of the client. In war, as any military treatise or any soldier who has seen active service will tell you, it is essential to know the nature—that is, the capabilities *and* intentions—of the enemy and no less so of an ally who is the primary belligerent. We fatally underestimated the one and foolishly overestimated the other. Placing reliance on, or hope in, South Vietnam was an advanced case of wooden-headedness. Improving on the Bourbons, who forgot nothing and learned nothing, our policy makers forgot everything and learned nothing. The oldest lesson in history is the futility and, often, fatality of foreign interference to maintain in power a government unwanted or hated at home. As far back as 500 B.C., Confucius stated, "Without the confidence of the people, no government can stand," and political philosophers have echoed him down through the ages. What else was 21

BARBARA TUCHMAN

the lesson of our vain support of Chiang Kai-shek, within such recent experience? A corrupt or oppressive government may be maintained by despotic means but not for long, as the English occupiers of France learned in the fifteenth century. The human spirit protests and generates a Joan of Arc, for people will not passively endure a government that is in fact unendurable.

The deeper we became involved in Vietnam during the Johnson era, the greater grew the self-deception, the lies, the false body counts, the cheating on Tonkin Gulf, the military mess, domestic dissent, and all those defensive emotions in which, as a result, our leaders became fixed. Their concern for personal ego, public image, and government status determined policy. Johnson was not going to be the first President to preside over defeat; generals could not admit failure nor civilian advisers risk their jobs by giving unpalatable advice. 22

Males, who so far in history have managed government are obsessed with potency, which is the reason, I suspect, why it is difficult for them to admit error. I have rarely known a man who, with a smile and a shrug, could easily acknowledge being wrong. Why not? *I* can, without any damage to self-respect. I can only suppose the difference is that deep in their psyches, men somehow equate being wrong with being impotent. For a Chief of State, it is almost out of the question, and especially so for Johnson and Nixon, who both seem to me to have had shaky self-images. Johnson's showed in his deliberate coarseness and compulsion to humiliate others in crude physical ways. No self-confident man would have needed to do that. Nixon was a bundle of inferiorities and sense of persecution. I do not pretend to be a psychohistorian, but in pursuit of this inquiry, the psychological factors must be taken into account. Having no special knowledge of Johnson and Nixon, I will not pursue the question other than to say that it was our misfortune during the Vietnam period to have had two Presidents who lacked the self-confidence for a change of course, much less for a grand withdrawal. "Magnanimity in politics," said Edmund Burke, "is not seldom the truest wisdom, and a great Empire and little minds go ill together." 23

An essential component of that "truest wisdom" is the self-confidence to reassess. Congressman Morris Udall made this point in the first few days after the nuclear accident at Three Mile Island. Cautioning against a hasty decision on the future of nuclear power, he said, "We have to go back and reassess. There is nothing wrong about being optimistic or making a mistake. The thing that is wrong, as in Vietnam, is *persisting* in a mistake when you see you are going down the wrong road and are caught in a bad situation." 24

The test comes in recognizing when persistence has become a fatal error. A prince, says Machiavelli, ought always to be a great asker and a patient hearer of truth about those things of which he has 25 inquired, and he should be angry if he finds that anyone has scruples about telling him the truth. Johnson and Nixon, as far as an outsider can tell, were not great askers; they did not want to hear the truth or to face it. Chiang Kai-shek knew virtually nothing of real conditions in his domain because he lived a headquarters life amid an entourage all of whom were afraid to be messengers of ill report. When, in World War I, a general of the headquarters staff visited for the first time the ghastly landscape of the Somme, he broke into tears, saying, "If I had known we sent men to fight in that, I could not have done it." Evidently he was no great asker either.

Neither, we now know, was the shah of Iran. Like Chiang   26
Kai-shek, he was isolated from actual conditions. He was educated abroad, took his vacations abroad, and toured his country, if at all, by helicopter.

Why is it that the major clients of the United States, a country   27
founded on the principle that government derives its just powers from the consent of the governed, tend to be unpopular autocrats? A certain schizophrenia between our philosophy and our practice afflicts American policy, and this split will always make the policy based on it fall apart. On the day the shah left Iran, an article summarizing his reign said that "except for the generals, he has few friends or allies at home." How useful to us is a ruler without friends or allies at home? He is a kind of luftmensch, no matter how rich or how golden a customer for American business. To attach American foreign policy to a ruler who does not have the acceptance of his countrymen is hardly intelligent. By now, it seems to me, we might have learned that. We must understand conditions—and by conditions, I mean people and history—on the spot. Wise policy can only be made on the basis of *informed*, not automatic, judgments.

When it has become evident to those associated with it that a   28
course of policy is pointed toward disaster, why does no one resign in protest or at least for the peace of his own soul? They never do. In 1917, the German chancellor Bethmann Hollweg pleaded desperately against the proposed resumption of unrestricted submarine warfare, since, by bringing in the United States, it would revive the Allies' resources, their confidence in victory, and their will to endure. When he was overruled by the military, he told a friend who found him sunk in despair that the decision meant "finis Germaniae." When the friend said simply, "You should resign," Bethmann said he could not, for that would sow dissension at home and let the world know he believed Germany would fail.

This is always the refuge. The officeholder tells himself he can   29
do more from within and that he must not reveal division at the top to the public. In fact if there is to be any hope of change in a democratic society, that is exactly what he must do. No one of major influ-

ence in Johnson's circle resigned over our Vietnam policy although several, hoping to play it both ways, hinted their disagreement. Humphrey, waiting for the nod, never challenged the President's policy, although he campaigned afterward as an opponent of the war. Since then, I've always thought the adulation given to him misplaced.

Basically, what keeps officeholders attached to a policy they believe to be wrong is nothing more nor less, I believe, than the lure of office, or Potomac fever. It is the same whether the locus is the Thames or the Rhine or, no doubt, the Nile. When Herbert Lehman ran for a second term as senator from New York after previously serving four terms as governor, his brother asked him why on earth he wanted it. "Arthur," replied the senator, "after you have once ridden behind a motorcycle escort, you are never the same again." 30

Here is a clue to the question of why our performance in government is worse than in other activities: because government offers power, excites that lust for power, which is subject to emotional drives—to narcissism, fantasies of omnipotence, and other sources of folly. The lust for power, according to Tacitus, "is the most flagrant of all the passions" and cannot really be satisfied except by power over others. Business offers a kind of power but only to the very successful at the very top, and even they, in our day, have to play it down. Fords and Du Ponts, Hearsts and Pulitzers, nowadays are subdued, and the Rockefeller who most conspicuously wanted power sought it in government. Other activities—in sports, science, the professions, and the creative and performing arts—offer various satisfactions but not the opportunity for power. They may appeal to status seeking and, in the form of celebrity, offer crowd worship and limousines and recognition by headwaiters, but these are the trappings of power, not the essence. Of course, mistakes and stupidities occur in nongovernmental activities too, but since these affect fewer people, they are less noticeable than they are in public affairs. Government remains the paramount field of unwisdom because it is there that men seek power over others—and lose it over themselves. 31

There are, of course, other factors that lower competence in public affairs, among them the pressure of overwork and overscheduling; bureaucracy, especially big bureaucracy; the contest for votes that gives exaggerated influence to special interests and an absurd tyranny to public opinion polls. Any hope of intelligent government would require that the persons entrusted with high office should formulate and execute policy according to their best judgment and the best knowledge available, not according to every breeze of public opinion. But reelection is on their minds, and that becomes the criterion. Moreover, given schedules broken down into fifteen-minute appointments and staffs numbering in the hundreds and briefing memos of never less than thirty pages, policy makers never have time to think. 32

This leaves a rather important vacuum. Meanwhile, bureaucracy rolls on, impervious to any individual or cry for change, like some vast computer that when once penetrated by error goes on pumping it out forever.

Under the circumstances, what are the chances of improving 33 the conduct of government? The idea of a class of professionals trained for the task has been around ever since Plato's Republic. Something of the sort animates, I imagine, the new Kennedy School of Government at Harvard. According to Plato, the ruling class in a just society should be men apprenticed to the art of ruling, drawn from the rational and the wise. Since he acknowledged that in natural distribution these are few, he believed they would have to be eugenically bred and nurtured. Government, he said, was a special art in which competence, as in any other profession, could be acquired only by study of the discipline and could not be acquired otherwise.

Without reference to Plato, the Mandarins of China were 34 trained, if not bred, for the governing function. They had to pass through years of study and apprenticeship and weeding out by successive examinations, but they do not seem to have developed a form of government much superior to any other, and in the end, they petered out in decadence and incompetence.

In seventeenth-century Europe, after the devastation of the 35 Thirty Years' War, the electors of Brandenburg, soon to be combined with Prussia, determined to create a strong state by means of a disciplined army and a trained civil service. Applicants for the civil positions, drawn from commoners in order to offset the nobles' control of the military, had to complete a course of study covering political theory, law and legal philosophy, economics, history, penology, and statutes. Only after passing through various stages of examination and probationary terms of office did they receive definitive appointments and tenure and opportunity for advancement. The higher civil service was a separate branch, not open to promotion from the middle and lower levels.

The Prussian system proved so effective that the state was 36 able to survive both military defeat by Napoleon in 1807 and the revolutionary surge of 1848. By then it had begun to congeal, losing many of its most progressive citizens in emigration to America; nevertheless, Prussian energies succeeded in 1871 in uniting the German states in an empire under Prussian hegemony. Its very success contained the seed of ruin, for it nourished the arrogance and power hunger that from 1914 through 1918 was to bring it down.

In England, instead of responding in reactionary panic to the 37 thunders from the Continent in 1848, as might have been expected, the authorities, with commendable enterprise, ordered an investigation of their own government practices, which were then the virtually private preserve of the propertied class. The result was a report on the need for a permanent civil service to be based on training and specialized skills and designed to provide continuity and maintenance of the long view as against transient issues and political passions. Though heavily resisted, the system was adopted in 1870. It has produced distinguished civil servants but also Burgess, Maclean, Philby, and the fourth man. The history of British government in the last 100 years suggests that factors other than the quality of its civil service determine a country's fate.

In the United States, civil service was established chiefly as a barrier to patronage and the pork barrel rather than in search of excellence. By 1937, a presidential commission, finding the system inadequate, urged the development of a "real career service . . . requiring personnel of the highest order, competent, highly trained, loyal, skilled in their duties by reason of long experience, and assured of continuity." After much effort and some progress, that goal is still not reached, but even if it were, it would not take care of elected officials and high appointments—that is, of government at the top. 38

I do not know if the prognosis is hopeful or, given the underlying emotional drives, whether professionalism is the cure. In the Age of Enlightenment, John Locke thought the emotions should be controlled by intellectual judgment and that it was the distinction and glory of man to be able to control them. As witnesses of the twentieth century's record, comparable to the worst in history, we have less confidence in our species. Although professionalism can help, I tend to think that fitness of character is what government chiefly requires. How that can be discovered, encouraged, and brought into office is the problem that besets us. 39

No society has yet managed to implement Plato's design. Now, with money and image-making manipulating our elective process, the chances are reduced. We are asked to choose by the packaging, yet the candidate seen in a studio-filmed spot, sincerely voicing lines from the Tele-PrompTer, is not the person who will have to meet the unrelenting problems and crucial decisions of the Oval Office. It might be a good idea if, without violating the First Amendment, we could ban all paid political commercials and require candidates (who accept federal subsidy for their campaigns) to be televised live only. 40

That is only a start. More profound change must come if we are to bring into office the kind of person our form of government needs if it is to survive the challenges of this era. Perhaps rather than educating officials according to Plato's design, we should concentrate on educating the electorate—that is, ourselves—to look for, recognize, and reward character in our representatives and to reject the ersatz. 41

COMPREHENSION

1. Why does Tuchman term her essay an "inquiry"? How does the term govern audience response?

2. According to Tuchman, what are the causes of the persistence of unwisdom in government?

3. What is the author's attitude toward the French, Russian, Chinese, and Iranian revolutions, respectively? Cite evidence to support your response.

RHETORIC

1. How do such phrases as the following contribute to the author's purpose and tone: "theatre of the absurd" (paragraph 2); "lunatic spectacle" (paragraph 3); "the whole bundle of personal vanities and anxieties" (paragraph 17); "charging forward wearing the blinkers of the Cold War" (paragraph 19); and "schizophrenia between our philosophy and our practice" (paragraph 27)?

2. Analyze the connotations that develop around Tuchman's use of the word *unwisdom.*

3. How does the author's use of rhetorical questions, notably in the introduction, contribute to the thesis? To the causal analysis?

4. How selective are the author's illustrations? What types of illustration does she use in the essay?

5. Analyze the author's transitions for paragraphs 7 to 8, 14 to 15, 23 to 24, 30 to 31, and 39 to 40.

6. What particulars develop Tuchman's generalizations about the emotional and psychological drives of politicians?

WRITING

1. A significant part of Tuchman's critique of unwisdom in government deals specifically with the problems of men as rulers. What is your response to her emotional and psychological profile of men as political leaders? Would women be less susceptible to these emotional and psychological problems? Analyze the issue in an essay.

2. Write your own inquiry into the persistence of unwisdom in government, using a series of relevant examples to support your generalizations.

3. Compare and contrast the principles enunciated in "The Declaration of Independence" and the realities dealt with by Tuchman.

The Circle of Governments

Niccolò Machiavelli (1469–1527), Italian patriot, statesman, and writer, is one of the seminal figures in the history of Western political thought. His inquiries into the nature of the state, the amoral quality of political life, and the primacy of power are distinctly modernist in outlook. He began his studies of political and historical issues after being forced to retire from Florentine politics in 1512. Exiled outside the city, Machiavelli wrote The Prince *(1513),* The Discourses (1519), The Art of War *(1519–1520), and* The Florentine History *(1525). The following selection from* The Discourses *(conceived as commentaries by the author on the first ten books of Livy's* History of Rome*) analyzes the varieties of government and their political implications in history.*

H aving proposed to myself to treat of the kind of government established at Rome, and of the events that led to its perfection, I must at the beginning observe that some of the writers on politics distinguished three kinds of government, vis. the monarchical, the aristocratic, and the democratic; and maintain that the legislators of a people must choose from these three the one that seems to them most suitable. Other authors, wiser according to the opinion of many, count six kinds of governments, three of which are very bad, and three good in themselves, but so liable to be corrupted that they become absolutely bad. The three good ones are those which we have just named; the three bad ones result from the degradation of the other three, and each of them resembles its corresponding original, so that the transition from the one to the other is very easy. Thus monarchy becomes tyranny; aristocracy degenerates into oligarchy; and the popular government lapses readily into licentiousness. So that a legislator who gives to a state which he founds either of these three forms of government, constitutes it but for a brief time; for no precautions can prevent either one of the three that are reputed good from degenerating into its opposite kind; so great are in these the attractions and resemblances between the good and the evil. 1

Chance has given birth to these different kinds of governments amongst men; for at the beginning of the world the inhabitants were few in number and lived for a time dispersed, like beasts. As the human race increased, the necessity for uniting themselves for defence made itself felt; the better to attain this object they chose the strongest and most courageous from amongst themselves and placed him at their head promising to obey him. Thence they began to know 2 the good and the honest, and to distinguish them from the bad and vicious; for seeing a man insure his benefactor aroused at once two sentiments in every heart, hatred against the ingrate and love for the benefactor. They blamed the first, and on the contrary honoured those the more who showed themselves grateful, for each felt that he in turn might be subject to a like wrong; and to prevent similar evils, they set to work to make laws, and to institute punishments for those who contravened them. Such was the origin of justice. This caused them, when they had afterwards to choose a prince, neither to look to the strongest nor bravest, but to the wisest and most just. But when they began to make sovereignty hereditary and non-elective, the children quickly degenerated from their fathers; and, so far from trying to equal their virtues, they considered that a prince had nothing else to do than to excel all the rest in luxury, indulgence, and every other variety of pleasure. The prince consequently soon drew upon himself the general hatred. An object of hatred, he naturally felt fear; fear in turn dictated to him precautions and wrongs, and thus tyranny quickly developed itself. Such were the beginning and causes of disorders, conspiracies, and plots against the sovereigns, set on foot, not by the feeble and timid, but by those citizens who, surpassing the others in grandeur of soul, in wealth, and in courage, could not submit to the outrages and excesses of their princes.

Under such powerful leaders the masses armed themselves 3 against the tyrant, and after having rid themselves of him, submitted to these chiefs as their liberators. These, abhorring the very name of prince, constituted themselves a new government; and at first bearing in mind the past tyranny, they governed in strict accordance with the laws which they had established themselves; preferring public interests to their own, and to administer and protect with greatest care both public and private affairs. The children succeeded their fathers, and ignorant of the changes of fortune, having never experienced its reverses, and indisposed to remain content with this civil equality, they in turn gave themselves up to cupidity, ambition, libertinage, and violence, and soon caused the aristocratic government to degenerate into an oligarchic tyranny, regardless of all civil rights. They soon, however, experienced the same fate as the first tyrant; the people, disgusted with their government, placed themselves at the command of whoever was willing to attack them, and this disposition soon produced an avenger, who was sufficiently well seconded to destroy them. The memory of the prince and the wrongs committed by him being still fresh in their minds, and having overthrown the oligarchy, the people were not willing to return to the government of a prince. A popular government was therefore resolved upon, and it was so organized that the authority would not again fall into the hands of a prince or a small number of nobles. And as all governments are at

NICCOLÒ MACHIAVELLI

first looked up to with some degree of reverence, the popular state also maintained itself for a time, but which was never of long duration, and lasted generally only about as long as the generation that had established it; for it soon ran into that kind of licence which inflicts injury upon public as well as private interests. Each individual only consulted his own passions, and a thousand acts of injustice were daily committed, so that, constrained by necessity, or directed by the counsels of some good man, or for the purpose of escaping from this anarchy, they returned anew to the government of a prince, and from this they generally lapsed again into anarchy, step-by-step, in the same manner and from the same causes as we have indicated.

Such is the circle which all republics are destined to run 4 through. Seldom, however, do they come back to the original form of government, which results from the fact that their duration is not sufficiently long to be able to undergo these repeated changes and preserve their existence. But it may well happen that a republic lacking strength and good counsel in its difficulties becomes subject after a while to some neighbouring state, that is better organized than itself; and if such is not the case, then they will be apt to revolve indefinitely in the circle of revolutions. I say, then, that all kinds of government are defective; those three which we have qualified as good because they are too short-lived, and the three bad ones because of their inherent viciousness. Thus sagacious legislators, knowing the vices of each of these systems of government by themselves, have chosen one that should partake of all of them, judging that to be the most stable and solid. In fact, when there is combined under the same constitution a prince, a nobility, and the power of the people, then these three powers will watch and keep each other reciprocally in check.

COMPREHENSION

1. Explain Machiavelli's view of human nature in this selection.

2. Explain the relation between the author's three forms of government and six forms of government.

3. Describe the "circle which all republics are destined to run through" (paragraph 4).

RHETORIC

1. Analyze the definitions Machiavelli provides in context for the key political terms *monarchy, tyranny, aristocracy, oligarchy, democracy,* and *anarchy.*

2. What does the term *justice* mean to the author?

3. The author uses classification as a method of essay development. Analyze the way in which the key categories are introduced and developed.

4. Explain the relationship of the "circle" as a metaphor to the development of the essay. Is the application purely figurative or based on logic? Explain.

5. Explain the use of comparison and contrast as a strategy in the essay.

6. Where does the author present his thesis? How is it reinforced by other materials in the essay?

WRITING

1. What is your opinion concerning Machiavelli's definition of good or viable government? Are Machiavelli's types of government obsolete, or are they universal? Explain in an essay.

2. Write a classification essay on the types of government in the modern world or on the branches or levels of government in the United States.

3. Write a comparative essay on Machiavelli's and Tuchman's visions of human nature.

JONATHAN SWIFT

A Modest Proposal
FOR PREVENTING THE CHILDREN OF POOR PEOPLE IN IRELAND FROM BEING A BURDEN TO THEIR PARENTS OR COUNTRY, AND FOR MAKING THEM BENEFICIAL TO THE PUBLIC

Jonathan Swift (1667–1745) is best known as the author of three satires: A Tale of a Tub *(1704),* Gulliver's Travels *(1726), and* A Modest Proposal *(1729). In these satires, Swift pricks the balloon of many of his contemporaries' and our own most cherished prejudices, pomposities, and delusions. He was also a famous churchman, an eloquent spokesman for Irish rights, and a political journalist. The following selection, perhaps the most famous satiric essay in the English language, offers modest advice to a nation suffering from poverty, overpopulation, and political injustice.*

 t is a melancholy object to those who walk through this great town or travel in the country, when they see the streets, the roads, and cabin doors, crowded with beggars of the female-sex, followed by three, four, or six children, all in rags and importuning every passenger for an alms. These mothers, instead of being able to work for their honest liveli-

1

hood, are forced to employ all their time in strolling to beg sustenance for their helpless infants, who, as they grow up, either turn thieves for want of work, or leave their dear native country to fight for the Pretender in Spain, or sell themselves to the Barbadoes.

I think it is agreed by all parties that this prodigious number 2 of children in the arms, or on the backs, or at the heels of their mothers, and frequently of their fathers, is in the present deplorable state of the kingdom a very great additional grievance; and therefore whoever could find out a fair, cheap, and easy method of making these children sound, useful members of the commonwealth would deserve so well of the public as to have his statue set up for a preserver of the nation.

But my intention is very far from being confined to provide 3 only for the children of professed beggars; it is of a much greater extent, and shall take in the whole number of infants at a certain age who are born of parents in effect as little able to support them as those who demand our charity in the streets.

As to my own part, having turned my thoughts for many 4 years upon this important subject, and maturely weighed the several schemes of other projectors, I have always found them grossly mistaken in their computation. It is true, a child just dropped from its dam may be supported by her milk for a solar year, with little other nourishment; at most not above the value of two shillings, which the mother may certainly get, or the value in scraps, by her lawful occupation of begging; and it is exactly at one year old that I propose to provide for them in such a manner as instead of being a charge upon their parents or the parish, or wanting food and raiment for the rest of their lives, they shall on the contrary contribute to the feeding, and partly to the clothing, of many thousands.

There is likewise another great advantage in my scheme, that 5 it will prevent those voluntary abortions, and that horrid practice of women murdering their bastard children, alas, too frequent among us, sacrificing the poor innocent babes, I doubt, more to avoid the expense than the shame, which would move tears and pity in the most savage and inhuman breast.

The number of souls in this kingdom being usually reckoned 6 one million and a half, of these I calculate there may be about two hundred thousand couples whose wives are breeders; from which number I subtract thirty thousand couples who are able to maintain their own children, although I apprehend there cannot be so many under the present distresses of the kingdom; but this being granted, there will remain an hundred and seventy thousand breeders. I again subtract fifty thousand for those women who miscarry, or whose children die by accident or disease within the year. There only remain an hundred and twenty thousand children of poor parents annually born.

The question therefore is, how this number shall be reared and provided for, which, as I have already said, under the present situation of affairs, is utterly impossible by all the methods hitherto proposed. For we can neither employ them in handicraft or agriculture; we neither build houses (I mean in the country) nor cultivate land. They can very seldom pick up a livelihood by stealing till they arrive at six years old, except where they are of towardly parts; although I confess they learn the rudiments much earlier, during which time they can however be looked upon only as probationers, as I have been informed by a principal gentlemen in the county of Cavan, who protested to me that he never knew above one or two instances under the age of six, even in a part of the kingdom so renowned for the quickest proficiency in that art.

    I am assured by our merchants that a boy or girl before twelve 7
years old is no salable commodity; and even when they come to this age they will not yield above three pounds, or three pounds and half a crown at most on the Exchange; which cannot turn to account either to the parents or the kingdom, the charge of nutriment and rags having been at least four times that value.

    I shall now therefore humbly propose my own thoughts, 8
which I hope will not be liable to the least objection.

    I have been assured by a very knowing American of my ac- 9
quaintance in London, that a young healthy child well nursed is at a year old a most delicious, nourishing, and wholesome food, whether stewed, roasted, baked or boiled; and I make no doubt that it will equally serve in a fricassee or a ragout.

    I do therefore humbly offer it to public consideration that of 10
the hundred and twenty thousand children, already computed, twenty thousand may be reserved for breed, whereof only one fourth part to be males, which is more than we allow to sheep, black cattle, or swine; and my reason is that these children are seldom the fruits of marriage, a circumstance not much regarded by our savages, therefore one male will be sufficient to serve four females. That the remaining hundred thousand may at a year old be offered in sale to the persons of quality and fortune through the kingdom, always advising the mother to let them suck plentifully in the last month, so as to render them plump and fat for a good table. A child will make two dishes at an entertainment for friends; and when the family dines alone, the fore or hind quarter will make a reasonable dish, and seasoned with a little pepper or salt will be very good boiled on the fourth day, especially in winter.

    I have reckoned upon a medium that a child just born will 11
weigh twelve pounds, and in a solar year if tolerably nursed increaseth to twenty-eight pounds.

    I grant this food will be somewhat dear, and therefore very 12

          JONATHAN SWIFT

proper for landlords, who, as they have already devoured most of the parents, seem to have the best title to the children.

Infant's flesh will be in season throughout the year, but more 13 plentiful in March, and a little before and after. For we are told by a grave author, an eminent French physician, that fish being a prolific diet, there are more children born in Roman Catholic countries about nine months after Lent than at any other season: therefore, reckoning a year after Lent, the markets will be more glutted than usual, because the number of popish infants is at least three to one in this kingdom; and therefore it will have one other collateral advantage, by lessening the number of Papists among us.

I have already computed the charge of nursing a beggar's 14 child (in which list I reckon all cottagers, laborers, and four fifths of the farmers) to be about two shillings per annum, rags included: and I believe no gentleman would repine to give ten shillings for the carcass of a good fat child, which, as I have said, will make four dishes of excellent nutritive meat, when he hath only some particular friend or his own family to dine with him. Thus the squire will learn to be a good landlord, and grow popular among the tenants; the mother will have eight shillings net profit, and be fit for work till she produces another child.

Those who are more thrifty (as I must confess the times 15 require) may flay the carcass; the skin of which artificially dressed will make admirable gloves for ladies, and summer boots for fine gentlemen.

As to our city of Dublin, shambles may be appointed for this 16 purpose in the most convenient parts of it, and butchers we may be assured will not be wanting; although I rather recommend buying the children alive, and dressing them hot from the knife as we do roasting pigs.

A very worthy person, a true lover of his country, and whose 17 virtues I highly esteem, was lately pleased in discoursing on this matter to offer a refinement upon my scheme. He said that many gentlemen of this kingdom, having of late destroyed their deer, he conceived that the want of venison might be well supplied by the bodies of young lads and maidens, not exceeding fourteen years of age nor under twelve, so great a number of both sexes in every county being now ready to starve for want of work and service; and these to be disposed of by their parents, if alive, or otherwise by their nearest relations. But with due deference to so excellent a friend and so deserving a patriot, I cannot be altogether in his sentiments; for as to the males, my American acquaintance assured me from frequent experience that their flesh was generally tough and lean, like that of our schoolboys, by continual exercise, and their taste disagreeable; and to fatten them would not answer the charge. Then as to the females, it would, I think with humble submission, be a loss to the public, because they soon would become breeders themselves: and besides, it is not improbable that some scrupulous people might be apt to censure such a practice (although indeed very unjustly) as a little bordering upon cruelty; which, I confess, hath always been with me the strongest objection against any project, how well soever intended.

But in order to justify my friend, he confessed that this expedient was put into his head by the famous Psalmanazar, a native of the island Formosa, who came from thence to London above twenty years ago, and in conversation told my friend that in his country when any young person happened to be put to death, the executioner sold the carcass to persons of quality as a prime dainty; and that in his time the body of a plump girl of fifteen, who was crucified for an attempt to poison the emperor, was sold to his Imperial Majesty's prime minister of state, and other great mandarins of the court, in joints from the gibbet, at four hundred crowns. Neither indeed can I deny that if the same use were made of several plump young girls in this town, who without one single groat to their fortunes cannot stir abroad without a chair, and appear at the playhouse and assemblies in foreign fineries which they never will pay for, the kingdom would not be the worse. 18

Some persons of a desponding spirit are in great concern about that vast number of poor people who are aged, diseased, or maimed, and I have been desired to employ my thoughts what course may be taken to ease the nation of so grievous an encumbrance. But I am not in the least pain upon that matter, because it is very well known that they are every day dying and rotting by cold and famine, and filth and vermin, as fast as can be reasonably expected. And as to the younger laborers, they are now in almost as hopeful a condition. They cannot get work, and consequently pine away for want of nourishment to a degree that if at any time they are accidentally hired to common labor, they have not strength to perform it; and thus the country and themselves are happily delivered from the evils to come. 19

I have too long digressed, and therefore shall return to my subject. I think the advantages by the proposal which I have made are obvious and many, as well as of the highest importance. 20

For first, as I have already observed, it would greatly lessen the number of Papists, with whom we are yearly overrun, being the principal breeders of the nation as well as our most dangerous enemies; and who stay at home on purpose to deliver the kingdom to the Pretender, hoping to take their advantage by the absence of so many good Protestants, who have chosen rather to leave their country than to stay at home and pay tithes against their conscience to an Episcopal curate. 21

Secondly, the poorer tenants will have something valuable of 22

JONATHAN SWIFT

their own, which by law may be made liable to distress, and help to pay their landlord's rent, their corn and cattle being already seized and money a thing unknown.

Thirdly, whereas the maintenance of an hundred thousand 23
children, from two years old and upwards, cannot be computed at less than ten shillings a piece per annum, the nation's stock will be thereby increased fifty thousand pounds per annum, besides the profit of a new dish introduced to the tables of all gentlemen of fortune in the kingdom who have any refinement in taste. And the money will circulate among ourselves, the goods being entirely of our own growth and manufacture.

Fourthly, the constant breeders, besides the gain of eight shill- 24
ings sterling per annum by the sale of their children, will be rid of the charge of maintaining them after the first year.

Fifthly, this food would likewise bring great custom to tav- 25
erns, where the vintners will certainly be so prudent as to procure the best receipts for dressing it to perfection, and consequently have their houses frequented by all the fine gentlemen, who justly value themselves upon their knowledge in good eating; and a skillful cook, who understands how to oblige his guests, will contrive to make it as expensive as they please.

Sixthly, this would be a great inducement to marriage, which 26
all wise nations have either encouraged by rewards or enforced by laws and penalties. It would increase the care and tenderness of mothers toward their children, when they were sure of a settlement for life to the poor babes, provided in some sort by the public, to their annual profit instead of expense. We should see an honest emulation among the married women, which of them could bring the fattest child to the market. Men would become as fond of their wives during the time of their pregnancy as they are now of their mares in foal, their cows in calf, or sows when they are ready to farrow; nor offer to beat or kick them (as is too frequent a practice) for fear of a miscarriage.

Many other advantages might be enumerated. For instance, 27
the addition of some thousand carcasses in our exportation of barreled beef, the propagation of swine's flesh, and improvement in the art of making good bacon, so much wanted among us by the great destruction of pigs, too frequent at our tables, which are no way comparable in taste or magnificence to a well-grown, fat yearling child, which roasted whole will make a considerable figure at a lord mayor's feast or any other public entertainment. But this and many others I omit, being studious of brevity.

Supposing that one thousand families in this city would be 28
constant customers for infants' flesh, besides others who might have it at merry meetings, particularly weddings and christenings, I compute that Dublin would take off annually about twenty thousand car-

casses, and the rest of the kingdom (where probably they will be sold somewhat cheaper) the remaining eighty thousand.

I can think of no one objection that will possibly be raised 29 against this proposal, unless it should be urged that the number of people will be thereby much lessened in the kingdom. This I freely own, and it was indeed one principal design in offering it to the world. I desire the reader will observe, that I calculate my remedy for this one individual kingdom of Ireland and for no other that ever was, is, or I think ever can be upon earth. Therefore let no man talk to me of other expedients: of taxing our absentees at five shillings a pound: of using neither clothes nor household furniture except what is of our own growth and manufacture: of utterly rejecting the materials and instruments that promote foreign luxury: of curing the expensiveness of pride, vanity, idleness, and gaming in our women: of introducing a vein of parsimony, prudence, and temperance: of learning to love our country, in the want of which we differ even from Laplanders and the inhabitants of Topinamboo: of quitting our animosities and factions, nor acting any longer like the Jews, who were murdering one another at the very moment their city was taken: of being a little cautious not to sell our country and conscience for nothing: of teaching landlords to have at least one degree of mercy toward their tenants: lastly, of putting a spirit of honesty, industry, and skill into our shopkeepers; who, if a resolution could be now taken to buy only our native goods, would immediately unite to cheat and exact upon us in the price, the measure and the goodness, nor could ever yet be brought to make one fair proposal of just dealing, though often and earnestly invited to it.

Therefore I repeat, let no man talk to me of these and the like 30 expedients, till he hath at least some glimpse of hope that there will ever be some hearty and sincere attempt to put them in practice.

But as to myself, having been wearied out for many years 31 with offering vain, idle, visonary thoughts, and at length utterly despairing of success, I fortunately fell upon this proposal, which, as it is wholly new, so it hath something solid and real, of no expense and little trouble, full in our own power, and whereby we can incur no danger in disobliging England. For this kind of commodity will not bear exportation, the flesh being of too tender a consistence to admit a long continuance in salt, although perhaps I could name a country which would be glad to eat up our whole nation without it.

After all, I am not so violently bent upon my own opinion as 32 to reject any offer proposed by wise men, which shall be found equally innocent, cheap, easy, and effectual. But before something of that kind shall be advanced in contradiction to my scheme, and offering a better, I desire the author or authors will be pleased maturely to consider two points. First, as things now stand, how they will be able to find

JONATHAN SWIFT

food and raiment for an hundred thousand useless mouths and backs. And secondly, there being a round million of creatures in human figure throughout this kingdom, whose sole subsistence put into a common stock would leave them in debt two millions of pounds sterling, adding those who are beggars by profession to the bulk of farmers, cottagers, and laborers, with their wives and children who are beggars in effect; I desire those politicians who dislike my overture, and may perhaps be so bold to attempt an answer, that they will first ask the parents of these mortals whether they would not at this day think it a great happiness to have been sold for food at a year old in the manner I prescribe, and thereby have avoided such a perpetual scene of misfortunes as they have since gone through by the oppression of landlords, the impossibility of paying rent without money or trade, the want of common sustenance, with neither house nor clothes to cover them from the inclemencies of the weather, and the most inevitable prospect of entailing the like or greater miseries upon their breed forever.

      I profess, in the sincerity of my heart, that I have not the least   33 personal interest in endeavoring to promote this necessary work, having no other motive than the public good of my country, by advancing our trade, providing for infants, relieving the poor, and giving some pleasure to the rich. I have no children by which I can propose to get a single penny; the youngest being nine years old, and my wife past childbearing.

COMPREHENSION

1. Who is Swift's audience for this essay? Defend your answer.

2. Describe the persona in this essay. How is the unusual narrative personality (as distinguished from Swift's personality) revealed by the author in degrees? How can we tell that the speaker's opinions are not shared by Swift?

3. What are the major propositions behind Swift's modest proposal? What are the minor propositions?

RHETORIC

1. Explain the importance of the word *modest* in the title. What stylistic devices does this "modesty" contrast with?

2. What is the effect of Swift's persistent reference to people as "breeders," "dams," "carcass," and the like? Why does he define children in economic terms? Find other words that contribute to this motif.

3. Analyze the purpose of the relatively long introduction consisting of paragraphs 1 to 7. How does Swift establish his ironic-satiric tone in this initial section?

A MODEST PROPOSAL   **297**

4. What contrasts and discrepancies are at the heart of Swift's ironic statement in paragraphs 9 and 10? Explain both the subtlety and savagery of the satire in paragraph 12.

5. Paragraphs 13 to 20 develop six advantages of Swift's proposal, while paragraphs 24 to 26 list them in enumerative manner. Analyze the progression of these propositions. What is the effect of the listing? Why is Swift parodying argumentative techniques?

6. How does the author both sustain and suspend the irony in paragraph 29? How is the strategy repeated in paragraph 32? How does the concluding paragraph cap his satiric commentary on human nature?

WRITING

1. Write a modest proposal—on, for example, how to end the drug problem—advancing an absurd proposition through various argumentative techniques.

2. Discuss Swift's social, political, religious, and economic views as they are revealed in the essay.

3. Review the essays in this chapter, and then write a comprehensive summary and critique of America's social and political institutions today.

7 Business and Economics

ADAM SMITH

"You Keep Bringing Up Exogenous Variables"

Adam Smith (1930–   ) is the pseudonym of George J. W. Goodman, who in 1966 started a witty and irreverent column on business and economics in New York *magazine. Born in St. Louis and educated at Harvard and Oxford universities, he has successfully combined careers as a corporate director, financial analyst, editor, essayist, and novelist. His books include* The Money Game, Supermoney, *and* Paper Money. *In this selection from* Paper Money *(1981), the modern-day "Adam Smith" talks about his eighteenth-century predecessor and other figures as he shrewdly pokes fun at certain types of economic inquiry.*

 have a friend called Arthur, who has a pleasant smile, a   1
wife, two children, two sets of skis, and who has, in
economics, what is called an ideal quantitative background. Practically from second grade, Arthur loved
math. It was a mystery to him why some people had to chew their
pencils in math exams; to him, math was as easy as watching tele-

vision was to some of his contemporaries. And although excellent marks came showering upon him all through school, he was never a serious, innovative mathematician. Great mathematicians, like competitive swimmers, mature early. At sixteen they have solved Fermat's Last Theorem, and at twenty-six they had better be teaching somewhere, because they are burned out. Arthur knew, at eighteen, that he was not that kind of scholar-mathematician, so he looked around at college and found a congenial home in economics. Arthur's hardest course came in his freshman year; it was English, and he had to write a paper on two Joseph Conrad stories, *Heart of Darkness* and *The Secret Agent*. He had a ghastly time with it. When he finished the Conrad paper, he says, he was very glad that he would never again have to do anything like that.

The graduate students who taught sections of the economics   2 courses were very strong in econometrics, which is a mathematical and statistical form of economics, and Arthur was marvelously adept at that. After he got his Ph.D., Arthur thought about teaching. But one of his professors was a consultant to a commercial firm I will call Economics, Inc., which had built a computer model of the whole economy and which sold this service to various businesses. Economics, Inc., offered Arthur such a high starting salary that he went right to work there and has been very happy ever since.

At various times I visited Arthur, and we would sit at his   3 computer console. His cuffs would shoot out of his sport jacket, and his fingers would be poised over the computer keyboard like those of E. Power Biggs at the organ. The computer keyboard was like a typewriter keyboard, *q-w-e-r-t-y-u-i-o-p*, except that it had a lot of extra keys you had to press before you could ask it questions. Once, I had just come back from the Middle East and I was worried that the price of oil might go to $15 a barrel, or even $20 a barrel.

"Ask it what the inflation rate will be if oil goes to fifteen   4 dollars a barrel," I would say, and Arthur would go tapety-tapety-tap on the keyboard. The answer—when the computer did not ask us for more information, or tell us to start over—would appear on the CRT screen. "Wow," said Arthur. "Inflation of nine percent, all other things being equal."

"Ask it what the mortgage rate will be with oil at fifteen dol-   5 lars a barrel," I said. Tapety-tapety-tap. "Ten percent?" Arthur said. "That's awfully high. It can't be right. Maybe we have to have an assumption about housing starts, too." Tapety-tapety-tapety-tapety-*tap*.

I have called Arthur, periodically, over the years, but I have   6 never had to act specifically on his information. In 1973, for example, Economics, Inc., missed the inflation rate by a wide margin. "Well, we did better than the Council of Economic Advisers," Arthur said, referring to the group appointed by the President, which sits in Washington. "They predicted inflation would be down to two and a half percent." Indeed they had, and Economics, Inc., had done better.

In order to have something as neat and symmetrical as an equation, you have to have assumptions, even if the assumption is very basic—let x equal the unknown, let Σ mean "the sum of." There is an old joke, used by economists at departmental dinners, in which three men are stranded on a desert island and all they have is one huge can of tuna, but the tuna is inside the can and they are starving. The first man, a physicist, suggests a way to make a fire hot enough to melt the can. The second is an engineer, who is thinking up a complicated slingshot that will hurl the can against a rock with enough force to puncture it. The third is an economist. He has the answer. He says, "Assume a can opener." Then he proceeds with a theory. 7

Economics, Inc., had all kinds of assumptions and all kinds of assessments. 8

None of this, by the way, hurt Economics, Inc. Businessmen and institutions quested for certainty, and the computer at Economics, Inc., was very certain, even if it was not always right. The CRT screen would say ERROR if the processing was inconsistent, but not if the conclusions didn't match the brawling world outside. 9

As I said, I was worried about the Middle East. If the price of oil went high enough fast enough, we would have a depression because all that money for imports would get taken out of our economy, unless the oil countries reinvested the money productively, unless the Federal Reserve loosened the money to make up for the oil, unless the new price of oil brought up more oil . . . you see the process. So I was talking to Arthur about Saudi Arabia, and the health of King Khalid, and the Shiites of the eastern province who worked in the oil fields, and I could tell it all sounded to Arthur like Conrad's Congo in *Heart of Darkness*—unfathomable. Revolutionary Iran had thrown out the Shah, the price of oil was doubling, gold was going to new highs, and I had been saying how far off the great Economics, Inc., model was; it wasn't telling me what I so urgently needed to know. Arthur lost his temper. 10

"You keep bringing up exogenous variables!" he shouted. 11

Like *economist, exogenous* is another Greek-rooted word, from *exo*, "outside, coming from outside."

"Who the hell knew there was an ayatollah?" Arthur said. "Who knew the Russian wheat crop was going to bomb? Who cares about whoever it is in the eastern province?" 12

"But *life* is exogenous variables," I said. All I wanted was the answers. I was worried that if *one* ayatollah could, in a short time, cause oil to go up, the truckers then to go on strike, the airlines to 13 flirt with bankruptcy, the defense budget to gather momentum, the Japanese to replace us as the buyers of Iranian oil—what if there was *another* fanatic Islamic cleric somewhere dictating into cassettes? What if there was a sorehead colonel in an oil country deciding that Allah wished the prime minister to meet with a nine-millimeter bullet?

But Arthur had hung up. And suddenly I knew one of the problems with economics. Arthur was brilliant. He had never sold a can of shoe polish, or bought a carload of lumber, or hired anybody, or fired anybody, or even worried about his checking account; in fact, he had never done anything but economics. In his own shop he could make lemmas dance around stochastic equilibria, he could rip off multiple regressions, he could make equations whistle "Dixie." The trouble came from that joke, "Assume a can opener." For deep, deep in the Economics, Inc., computer was a very tiny person upon whom the assumptions were based. Would the tiny person spend? Would the tiny person save? If you tapped the tiny person on the knee, his leg would jerk; if you tickled him, he would laugh. But the tiny, tiny person, upon whom all the vast panoply of computer modeling had been done, *was an economist.* If you asked him something, he would take a tiny sheet of yellow paper and ask, "What are the costs, and what are the benefits?" With a column for each, very coolly and rationally. He never threw an ashtray at his tiny wife, breaking a window and raising the gross national product by the price of the new window. Fear and greed and panic and emotion and nationalism and religious fervor, ayatollahs and Shiites and sinister Middle Eastern colonels were not part of his world.

This is *not* meant to be a trivial complaint about the limits of models. That is of interest to the people who use them, who naturally want to do the best possible job, and the subject has been well debated by such respected figures as Harvard's Hendrik Houthakker, an expert on econometric models and the varying relationships known as elasticities. I have another friend, Princeton's Geoffrey Watson, who, many years ago, with James Durbin, derived an equation that made them both famous in the field. The Durbin-Watson equation is one test for the mathematical work upon which the complex computer models are based. "Mathematics has so much prestige," Geoffrey says, "that people sometimes back away from their own intuitive judgments. What used to be called 'political economy' at Oxford and Cambridge has been overshadowed. I had a distinguished economics professor at Cambridge, Richard Stern, whose background was in classics."

There were once two kinds of economists, one might argue: the Smiths and the Ricardos. The Smith is the 1723 Adam Smith, and the Ricardo is David Ricardo, his immediate successor. Both the Smiths and the Ricardos were concerned with human activity and with the institutions that produce, preserve, and distribute wealth. The Smiths observed; the Ricardos sought the universal and logical principles, using algebra and its succeeding languages. The Smiths looked for what is to be explained, the Ricardos for the principles that did the explaining. Until comparatively recently, economists could write in both languages; that is, they could describe human activity in some detail, using the detail in written analysis, and they could reason mathematically and abstractly about the governing principles.

Today the Ricardos are fashionable and the Smiths are not. 17 Economists who write well in English—there may be eight of them— run the risk of being labeled with the pejorative term "literary." The Ricardos admire the elegance of perfect equations; the highest terms of their praise are "rigorous" and "scientific."

When the problem was contained enough, when the numbers 18 were discrete enough, the mathematical descriptions of the Ricardos worked. Government economists who favored deregulation of the airline industry found that scenario unfolding much as they had planned. But too often the real world did not match the movements of that tiny economist inside the computer. All through the 1970s, the economists missed the impact of OPEC because, when they described it mathematically, they treated it as if it were a rational, profit-maximizing convention of economists. They did not know about *asibaya*, the Arab sense of community, nor could they quantify Third World indignation at past histories, or Middle East rivalries, or Western myopia, all of which became more important than the more easily quantified data. Some years ago the sociologist and pollster Daniel Yankelovich described a process he called the McNamara fallacy, after the Secretary of Defense who had so carefully quantified the Vietnam War.

"The first step," he said, "is to measure what can easily be 19 measured. The second is to disregard what can't be measured, or give it an arbitrary quantitative value. This is artificial and misleading. The third step is to presume that what can't be measured easily isn't very important. This is blindness. The fourth step is to say that what can't be easily measured really doesn't exist." The philosopher A. N. Whitehead called this tendency, in another form, "the fallacy of misplaced concreteness."

The Hopi language, an American Indian language, contains 20 no words, grammatical forms, constructions, or expressions that refer to what we call "time," or to past, present, future. The whole structure we base on "time"—wages, rent, credit, interest, depreciation, insurance—cannot be expressed in Hopi and is not part of that world view. The main Eskimo language has twenty-seven different words for snow, each connoting another nuance of texture, utility, and consistency, so the Eskimo's ability to communicate about snow is far greater than ours. The picture of the universe, of "reality," shifts from language to language. The economists whose counsel we seek—as do presidents and prime ministers—speak from a world within the world, just as the Hopi spoke from a world without time, credit, wages, and rent. That cold, neat, elegant world of mathematics views a different reality than blunt, ambiguous English.

Poets know they must use the slippery sibilances and jagged 21 edges of language, as well as the meanings of the words, to communicate. Poets know that life throws up exogenous variables. I made a note that at the next meeting of the Advisory Council of the university Department of Economics on which I serve I would propose that we recruit some poets. I am sure the council will treat the suggestion as merely amusing, and I'm not totally sure it's a great idea; but I know it's aimed in the right direction. I sent Arthur the classic *Language, Thought, and Reality* by Benjamin Whorf, from which I took the example of the Hopi, but I haven't heard back. Maybe it reminds him of *Heart of Darkness*, and maybe he's just too busy.

COMPREHENSION

1. From what perspective does Smith make his comments about contemporary economics? What is your response to the content as the author presents it? How does the essay's title affect reader response?

2. Who uses the phrase "exogenous variables"? What does it mean? How does it serve to characterize contemporary economists?

3. Explain the distinction between the Smiths and the Ricardos. According to the author, which group or school of economists is more powerful today, and why? What are the consequences?

RHETORIC

1. Explain what the language of paragraph 1 gains from the author's use of hyperbolic style.

2. Analyze the various levels of diction in this essay. What impression emerges?

3. Cite and explain the author's use of anecdotes in this essay. What is the effect? How do the anecdotes compare with those Goodman uses in "Bamama Goes to College"?

4. What use does the author make of the personal "I" in this essay? What dominant impression of the speaker emerges?

5. How important is proportion in this essay? In other words, how does the author arrange the major parts of his analysis?

6. What is the relationship of logical reasoning to the ironic pattern of development in this essay?

WRITING

1. Assess the value of humor in exposing the foibles and problems of economic operations. Use this essay as an extended example.

2. Create an imaginary economics expert, and write a comic account of this person.

3. Is economics a science or discipline that is as precise as mathematics? Answer this question in an argumentative essay.

4. Analyze the ways in which economists use specialized language to confuse lay readers, deceive the public, or cover up the obvious.

ELLEN GOODMAN

Being a Secretary Can Be Hazardous to Your Health

Ellen Holtz Goodman (1941–   ) is an award-winning journalist who writes a syndicated column for The Boston Globe. *She is the author of* Close to Home *(1979) and* At Large *(1981) and has been a commentator on television and radio. Goodman is an adept practitioner of the personal essay. In the following selection, her celebrated penchant for irony and satire finds a perfect focus in the working lives of women.*

 hey used to say it with flowers or celebrate it with a somewhat liquid lunch. National Secretaries Week was always good for at least a token of appreciation. But the way the figures add up now, the best thing a boss can do for a secretary this week is cough up for her cardiogram.

"Stress and the Secretary" has become the hottest new syndrome on the heart circuit.

It seems that it isn't those Daring Young Women in their Dress-for-Success Suits who are following men down the cardiovascular trail to ruin. Nor is it the female professionals who are winning their equal place in intensive care units.

It is powerlessness and not power that corrupts women's hearts. And clerical workers are the number one victims.

In the prestigious Framingham study, Dr. Suzanne Haynes, an epidemiologist with the National Heart, Lung and Blood Institute, found that working women as a whole have no higher rate of heart

disease than housewives. But women employed in clerical and sales occupations do. Their coronary disease rates are twice that of other women.

"This is not something to ignore," says Dr. Haynes, "since such a high percent of women work at clerical jobs." In fact, 35 percent of all working women, or 18 million of us, hold these jobs. 6

When Dr. Haynes looked into their private lives, she found the women at greatest risk—with a one in five chance of heart disease—were clerical workers with blue-collar husbands, and three or more children. When she then looked at their work lives, she discovered that the ones who actually developed heart disease were those with nonsupportive bosses who hadn't changed jobs very often and who had trouble letting their anger out. 7

In short, being frustrated, dead-ended, without a feeling of control over your life is bad for your health. 8

The irony in all the various and sundry heart statistics is that we now have a weird portrait of the Cardiovascular Fun Couple of the Office: The Type A Boss and his secretary. The male heart disease stereotype is, after all, the Type A aggressive man who always needs to be in control, who lives with a great sense of time urgency . . . and is likely to be a white-collar boss. 9

"The Type A man is trying to be in control. But given the way most businesses are organized there are, in fact, few ways for them to be in control of their jobs," says Dr. Haynes. The only thing the Type A boss can be in control of is his secretary who in turn feels . . . well you get the picture. He's not only getting heart disease, he's giving it. 10

As if all this weren't enough to send you out for the annual three martini lunch, clerical workers are increasingly working for a new Type A boss: the computer. 11

These days fewer women are sitting in front of bosses with notepads and more are sitting in front of Visual Display Terminals. Word processors, data processors, microprocessors . . . these are the demanding, time-conscious, new automatons of automation. 12

There is nothing intrinsically evil about computers. I am writing this on a VDT and if you try to take it away from me, I will break your arm. But as Working Women, the national association of office workers, puts it in their release this week, automation is increasingly producing clerical jobs that are de-skilled, down-graded, dead-ended and dissatisfying. 13

As Karen Nussbaum of the Cleveland office described it, the office of the future may well be the factory of the past. Work on computers is often reduced to simple, repetitive, monotonous tasks. Workers are often expected to produce more for no more pay, and there are also reports of a disturbing trend to processing speed-ups and 14

ELLEN GOODMAN

piece-rate pay, and a feeling among clerical workers that their jobs are computer controlled.

"It's not the machine, but the way it's used by employers," 15 says Working Women's research director, Judith Gregory. Too often, automation's most important product is stress.

Groups, like Working Women, are trying to get clerical work- 16 ers to organize in what they call "a race against time" so that computers will become their tools instead of their supervisors.

But in the meantime, if you are 1) a female clerical worker, 2) 17 with a blue-collar husband, 3) with three or more children, 4) in a dead-end job, 5) without any way to express anger, 6) with a Type A boss, 7) or a Type A computer controlling your work day . . . *You better start jogging.*

COMPREHENSION

1. What slogan does the author's title play upon? How does it prepare us for Goodman's thesis? What is her thesis?

2. What major problem does Goodman discuss in this essay? What are the causes of the problem?

3. How does the author describe the Type A boss and the Type A female employee?

RHETORIC

1. How does Goodman use colloquial language to help establish the tone of the essay?

2. List examples of comic language. What is Goodman's purpose? Comment on the relationship of Goodman's use of comic language to Smith's in "You Keep Bringing Up Exogenous Variables."

3. What technique does Goodman use to establish the topic of her essay?

4. What types of examples does Goodman use to reinforce her generalizations? Do any of the examples qualify as expert testimony? Explain.

5. Where does Goodman state her thesis? How does her conclusion reinforce this thesis?

6. What patterns of comparison and contrast do you find? Why does the author employ this technique?

WRITING

1. Does Goodman's range of humor work for or against the seriousness of her topic? Explain your response in an evaluative essay.

2. Analyze the varieties of stress that you have felt while employed at a particular job.

3. Argue for or against the proposition that working women do not experience any more stress than working men.

4. Describe the Type A worker or professional, and propose solutions to his or her problem.

ROSABETH MOSS KANTER

The "Roast Pig" Problem

Rosabeth Moss Kanter is active as an educator, business adviser, and author. Currently professor of sociology and of organization and management at Yale University, Kanter is also chairman of the board of directors of Goodmeasure Inc., a company of which she was a founder. She is the author of many books, among them Men and Women of the Corporation, *the winner of the 1977 C. Wright Mills Award for the year's best book on social issues. Professor Kanter lives in Cambridge, Massachusetts. In this selection from* The Change Masters, *she explores the problems of innovation for corporations.*

Pervading the time of institutionalizing innovations, when leaders want to ensure that their benefits can be derived repeatedly, is the nagging question of defining accurately the practice or method or cluster of attributes that is desired. Out of all the events and elements making up an innovation, what is the core that needs to be preserved? What *is* the essence of the innovation? This is a problem of theory, an intellectual problem of understanding exactly *why* something works.   1

I call this the "Roast Pig" problem after Charles Lamb's classic 1822 essay "A Dissertation on Roast Pig," a satirical account of how the art of roasting was discovered in a Chinese village that did not cook its food. A mischievous child accidentally set fire to a house with a pig inside, and the villagers poking around in the embers discovered a new delicacy. This eventually led to a rash of house fires. The moral of the story is: when you do not understand how the pig gets cooked, you have to burn a whole house down every time you want a roast-pork dinner.   2

The "Roast Pig" problem can plague any kind of organization that lacks a solid understanding of itself. One striking example comes from a high-technology firm I'll call "Precision Scientific Corporation." Precision grew steadily and rapidly from its founding to a po-   3 sition of industry preeminence. To the founders, many of whom still manage it, this success is due to a strongly entrepreneurial environment and an equally strong aversion to formal bureaucratic structures. But recently, growth has slackened, margins are down, competition is up, and Precision is even beginning to contemplate cutting back the work force. Increasingly Precision's leaders have the feeling that something needs to be done, but cannot agree on what it should be.

One obvious issue at Precision is waste and duplication. For example, there are a dozen nearly identical model shops on the same small site, neighboring operating units have their own systems for labeling and categorizing parts, and purchases tend to be haphazard and uncoordinated. But although this is well known, and although a number of middle-level "entrepreneurs" surface from time to time with systems innovations to solve the problems, the leaders express considerable reluctance to change anything. So each wave of good ideas for operational improvements that washes up from the middle goes out again with the tide.

The reason is simple: Roast Pig. Precision senior executives have been part of a very successful history, but they do not seem to fully understand that history. They have no theory to guide them. They do not act as though they knew exactly which aspects of the culture and structure they have built are critical, and which could profitably and safely be modified. They are afraid that changing *anything* would begin to unravel *everything*, like a loosely knit sweater. In the absence of a strong theory, they feel compelled to keep burning down the houses, even though house costs are rising and other villages are reputed to have learned new and less expensive cooking methods.

In many companies, management practices are much more vulnerable to the Roast Pig problem than products, because the depth of understanding of technology and markets sometimes far exceeds the understanding of organizational behavior and organizational systems. So among a dozen failures to diffuse successful work innovations were a number that did not spread because of uncertainty or confusion about what the "it" was that was to be used elsewhere. Or I see "superstitious behavior," the mindless repetition of unessential pieces of a new practice in the false belief that it will not work without them—e.g., in the case of quality circles which companies often burden with excessive and unnecessary formulas for their operation from which people become afraid to depart.

Beliefs may indeed help something work, but beliefs can also be modified by information and theory. The consequences of failing to perform this intellectual task are twofold: first, as one innovation gets locked rigidly into place, further experimentation may be discouraged—house burning may become so ritualistic that the search for other cooking methods is stifled; and perhaps more important, the company may waste an awful lot of houses.

The other extreme also poses problems, of course: reductionism, or the stripping down to apparent "essentials," thus missing some critical piece out of the cluster of elements that makes the innovation work. This fallacy of understanding also needs to be corrected by theory and analysis. As usual, the issue is balance between inclusion of unnecessary rituals and the elimination of key supports. 8

Thus, the task of conceptualization is as important at the "end" of a change sequence, when the time comes to institutionalize an innovation, as it was at the beginning. Behind every institutionalized practice is a theory about why things work as they do; the success and efficiency of the organization's use of the practice depend on the strength of that theory. 9

COMPREHENSION

1. In your own words, state Kanter's thesis.

2. What is the "roast pig" problem? Why is it an appropriate analogy?

3. What does Kanter suggest is the relationship between theory and practice in business? Why are theories necessary?

RHETORIC

1. What is the level of language in this piece? Is Kanter writing for professionals or for lay readers? How do you know?

2. How does the label "superstitious behavior" function stylistically in this essay? What other labels does Kanter use?

3. Why doesn't the author use concrete examples to support her thesis? Is this a defect, or not? Explain.

4. What visual metaphors does Kanter use to describe the problem of modifying practices? How do these metaphors help to structure the essay?

5. What kind of example is "Precision Scientific Corporation"? What is the purpose of this example?

6. Where does the author begin her conclusion? Does the conclusion raise a new point in the essay? Explain.

WRITING

1. How useful are theories of behavior or operation to everyday life? How much of your practice as students or workers has a theoretical basis? Do your theories need revision? Evaluate these issues in an essay.

2. Take some activity—like studying for a test, going on a successful date, or

ROSABETH MOSS KANTER

running a business—and write an essay describing the theory behind it. Where did your theory originate? Has it been successful? Does it require modification?

3. Report on your own "roast pig" problem, where you had to burn or destroy everything in order to achieve a goal.

4. For a research paper, look into a company that has been especially successful at innovation. Explain the reasons for the company's success.

JOHN KENNETH GALBRAITH

The Higher Economic Purpose of Women

John Kenneth Galbraith (1908–   ), America's best known economist and commentator on our economic system, was born on a farm in Ontario, Canada. He received his doctorate from the University of California at Berkeley and has taught at Princeton and Harvard Universities. Galbraith also has held posts in government since 1940; from 1961 to 1963, he served as U.S. ambassador to India. Among Galbraith's numerous books are American Capitalism, The Concept of Countervailing Power *(1952),* The Affluent Society *(1958), and* The New Industrial State *(1967). In this essay from* Annals of an Abiding Liberal *(1979), Galbraith relates economic theory to "convenient social virtue."*

n the nineteen-fifties, for reasons that were never revealed to me, for my relations with academic administrators have often been somewhat painful, I was made a trustee of Radcliffe College. It was not a highly demanding position. Then, as now, the college had no faculty of its own, no curriculum of its own and, apart from the dormitories, a gymnasium and a library, no academic plant of its own. We were a committee for raising money for scholarships and a new graduate center. The meetings or nonmeetings of the trustees did, however, encourage a certain amount of reflection on the higher education of women, there being no appreciable distraction. This reflection was encouraged by the mood of the time at Harvard. As conversation and numerous formal and informal surveys reliably revealed, all but a small minority of the women students felt that they were a failure unless they were firmly set for marriage by the time they got their degree. I soon learned that my fellow trustees of both sexes thought this highly meritorious. Often at our meetings there was impressively solemn mention of our responsibility, which was to help women prepare themselves for their life's work. Their life's work, it was held, was care of home, husband and children. In inspired moments one or another of my colleagues would ask, "Is there anything else so important?"

Once, and rather mildly, for it was more to relieve tedium 2 than to express conviction, I asked if the education we provided wasn't rather expensive and possibly also ill-adapted for these tasks, even assuming that they were combined with ultimate service to the New Rochelle Library and the League of Women Voters. The response was so chilly that I subsided. I've never minded being in a minority, but I dislike being thought eccentric.

It was, indeed, mentioned that a woman should be prepared 3 for what was called a *second* career. After her children were raised and educated, she should be able to essay a re-entry into intellectual life— become a teacher, writer, researcher or some such. All agreed that this was a worthy, even imaginative design which did not conflict with *basic* responsibilities. I remember contemplating but censoring the suggestion that this fitted in well with the common desire of husbands at about this stage in life to take on new, younger and sexually more inspiring wives.

In those years I was working on the book that eventually be- 4 came *The Affluent Society*. The task was a constant reminder that much information solemnly advanced as social wisdom is, in fact, in the service of economic convenience—the convenience of some influential economic interest. I concluded that this was so of the education of women and resolved that I would one day explore the matter more fully. This I have been doing in these last few years, and I've decided that while the rhetorical commitment of women to home and husband as a career has been weakened in the interim, the economic ideas by which they are kept persuaded to serve economic interests are still almost completely intact. Indeed, these ideas are so generally assumed that they are very little discussed.

Women are kept in the service of economic interests by ideas 5 that they do not examine and that even women who are professionally involved as economists continue to propagate, often with some professional pride. The husband, home and family that were celebrated in those ghastly Radcliffe meetings are no longer part of the litany. But the effect of our economic education is still the same.

Understanding of this begins with a look at the decisive but 6 little-perceived role of women in modern economic development and at the economic instruction by which this perception is further dulled.

The decisive economic contribution of women in the devel- 7

JOHN KENNETH GALBRAITH

oped industrial society is rather simple—or at least it so becomes once the disguising myth is dissolved. It is, overwhelmingly, to make possible a continuing and more or less unlimited increase in the sale and use of consumer goods.

The test of success in modern economic society, as all know, is the annual rate of increase in Gross National Product. At least until recent times this test was unquestioned; a successful society was one with a large annual increase in output, and the most successful society was the one with the largest increase. Even when the social validity of this measure is challenged, as on occasion it now is, those who do so are only thought to be raising an interesting question. They are not imagined to be practical. 8

Increasing production, in turn, strongly reflects the needs of the dominant economic interest, which in modern economic society, as few will doubt, is the large corporation. The large corporation seeks relentlessly to get larger. The power, prestige, pay, promotions and perquisites of those who command or who participate in the leadership of the great corporation are all strongly served by its expansion. That expansion, if it is to be general, requires an expanding or growing economy. As the corporation became a polar influence in modern economic life, economic growth became the accepted test of social performance. This was not an accident. It was the predictable acceptance of the dominant economic value system. 9

Economic growth requires manpower, capital and materials for increased production. It also, no less obviously, requires increased consumption, and if population is relatively stable, as in our case, this must be increased per-capita consumption. But there is a further and equally unimpeachable truth which, in economics at least, has been celebrated scarcely at all: just as the production of goods and services requires management or administration, so does their consumption. The one is no less essential than the other. Management is required for providing automobiles, houses, clothing, food, alcohol and recreation. And management is no less required for their possession and use. 10

The higher the standard of living, that is to say the greater the consumption, the more demanding is this management. The larger the house, the more numerous the automobiles, the more elaborate the attire, the more competitive and costly the social rites involving food and intoxicants, the more complex the resulting administration. 11

In earlier times this administration was the function of a menial servant class. To its great credit, industrialization everywhere liquidates this class. People never remain in appreciable numbers in personal service if they have alternative employment. Industry supplies this employment, so the servant class, the erstwhile managers of con- 12 sumption, disappears. If consumption is to continue and expand, it is an absolute imperative that a substitute administrative force be found. This, in modern industrial societies, is the function that wives perform. The higher the family income and the greater the complexity of the consumption, the more nearly indispensable this role. Within broad limits the richer the family, the more indispensably menial must be the role of the wife.

It is, to repeat, a vital function for economic success as it is 13 now measured. Were women not available for managing consumption, an upper limit would be set thereon by the administrative task involved. At some point it would become too time-consuming, too burdensome. We accept, without thought, that a bachelor of either sex will lead a comparatively simple existence. (We refer to it as the bachelor life.) That is because the administrative burden of a higher level of consumption, since it must be assumed by the individual who consumes, is a limiting factor. When a husband's income passes a certain level, it is expected that his wife will be needed "to look after the house" or simply "to manage things." So, if she has been employed, she quits her job. The consumption of the couple has reached the point where it requires full-time attention.

Although without women appropriately conditioned to the 14 task there would be an effective ceiling on consumption and thus on production and economic expansion, this would not apply uniformly. The ceiling would be especially serious for high-value products for the most affluent consumers. The latter, reflecting their larger share of total income—the upper 20 percent of income recipients received just under 42 percent of all income in 1977—account for a disproportionate share of total purchases of goods. So women are particularly important for lifting the ceiling on this kind of consumption. And, by a curious quirk, their doing so opens the way for a whole new range of consumer products—washing machines, dryers, dishwashers, vacuum cleaners, automatic furnaces, sophisticated detergents, cleaning compounds, tranquilizers, pain-relievers—designed to ease the previously created task of managing a high level of consumption.

Popular sociology and much associated fiction depict the ex- 15 tent and complexity of the administrative tasks of the modern diversely responsible, high-bracket, suburban woman. But it seems likely that her managerial effectiveness, derived from her superior education, her accumulating experience as well as her expanding array of facilitating gadgetry and services, keeps her more or less abreast of her increasingly large and complex task. Thus the danger of a ceiling on consumption, and therefore on economic expansion, caused by the exhaustion of her administrative capacities does not seem imminent. One sees here, more than incidentally, the economic rationale, even if

JOHN KENNETH GALBRAITH

it was unsuspected for a long time by those involved, of the need for a superior education for the upper-bracket housewife. Radcliffe prepared wives for the higher-income family. The instinct that this required superior intelligence and training was economically sound.

The family of higher income, in turn, sets the consumption patterns to which others aspire. That such families be supplied with intelligent, well-educated women of exceptional managerial competence is thus of further importance. It allows not only for the continued high-level consumption of these families, but it is important for its demonstration effect for families of lesser income. 16

That many women are coming to sense that they are instruments of the economic system is not in doubt. But their feeling finds no support in economic writing and teaching. On the contrary, it is concealed, and on the whole with great success, by modern neoclassical economics—the everyday economics of the textbook and classroom. This concealment is neither conspiratorial nor deliberate. It reflects the natural and very strong instinct of economics for what is convenient to influential economic interest—for what I have called the convenient social virtue. It is sufficiently successful that it allows many hundreds of thousands of women to study economics each year without their developing any serious suspicion as to how they will be used. 17

The general design for concealment has four major elements: 18

First, there is the orthodox identification of an increasing consumption of goods and services with increasing happiness. The greater the consumption, the greater the happiness. This proposition is not defended; it is again assumed that only the philosophically minded will cavil. They are allowed their dissent, but, it is held, no one should take it seriously. 19

Second, the tasks associated with the consumption of goods are, for all practical purposes, ignored. Consumption being a source of happiness, one cannot get involved with the problems in managing happiness. The consumer must exercise choice; happiness is maximized when the enjoyment from an increment of expenditure for one object of consumption equals that from the same expenditure for any other object or service. As all who have ever been exposed, however inadequately, to economic instruction must remember, satisfactions are maximized when they are equalized at the margin. 20

Such calculation does require some knowledge of the quality and technical performance of goods as well as thought in general. From it comes the subdivision of economics called consumer economics; this is a moderately reputable field that, not surprisingly, is thought especially appropriate for women. But this decision-making is not a burdensome matter. And once the decision between objects 21 of expenditure is made, the interest of economics is at an end. No attention whatever is given to the effort involved in the care and management of the resulting goods.[1]

The third requisite for the concealment of women's economic role is the avoidance of any accounting for the value of household work. This greatly helps it to avoid notice. To include in the Gross National Product the labor of housewives in managing consumption, where it would be a very large item which would increase as consumption increases, would be to invite thought on the nature of the service so measured. And some women would wonder if the service was one they wished to render. To keep these matters out of the realm of statistics is also to help keep them innocuously within the sacred domain of the family and the soul. It helps sustain the pretense that, since they are associated with consumption, the toil involved is one of its joys.

The fourth and final element in the concealment is more complex and concerns the concept of the household. The intellectual obscurantism that is here involved is accepted by all economists, mostly without thought. It would, however, be defended by very few.

The avowed focus of economics is the individual. It is the individual who distributes her or his expenditures so as to maximize satisfactions. From this distribution comes the instruction to the market and ultimately to the producing firm that makes the individual the paramount power in economic society. (There are grave difficulties with this design, including the way in which it reduces General Motors to the role of a mere puppet of market forces, but these anomalies are not part of the present story.)

Were this preoccupation with the individual pursued to the limit, namely to the individual, there would be grave danger that the role of women would attract attention. There would have to be inquiry as to whether, within the family, it is the husband's enjoyments that are equalized and thus maximized at the margin. Or, in his gallant way, does he defer to the preference system of his wife? Or does marriage unite only men and women whose preference schedules are identical? Or does marriage make them identical?

Investigation would turn up a yet more troublesome thing. It

[1]There is a branch of learning—home economics or home science—that does concern itself with such matters. This field is a nearly exclusive preserve of women. It has never been accorded any serious recognition by economists or scholars generally; like physical education or poultry science, it is part of an academic underworld. And home economists or home scientists, in their natural professional enthusiasm for their subject matter and their natural resentment of their poor academic status, have sought to elevate their subject, homemaking, into a thing of unique dignity, profound spiritual reward, infinite social value as well as great nutritional significance. Rarely have they asked whether it cons women into a role that is exceedingly important for economic interest and also highly convenient for the men and institutions they are trained to serve. Some of the best home economists were once students of mine. I thought them superbly competent in their commitment to furthering a housewifely role for women.

JOHN KENNETH GALBRAITH

would be seen that, in the usual case, the place and style of living accord with the preferences and needs of the member of the family who makes the money—in short, the husband. Thus, at least partly his titles: "head of the household," "head of the family." And he would be seen to have a substantial role in decisions on the individual objects of expenditure. But the management of the resulting house, automobile, yard, shopping and social life would be by the wife. It would be seen that this arrangement gives the major decisions concerning consumption extensively to one person and the toil associated with that consumption to another. There would be further question as to whether consumption decisions reflect with any precision or fairness the preferences of the person who has the resulting toil. Would the style of life and consumption be the same if the administration involved were equally shared?

None of these questions get asked, for at precisely the point   27
they obtrude, the accepted economics abruptly sheds its preoccupation with the individual. The separate identities of men and women are merged into the concept of the household. The inner conflicts and compromises of the household are not explored; by nearly universal consent, they are not the province of economics. The household, by a distinctly heroic simplification, is assumed to be the same as an individual. It thinks, acts and arranges its expenditures as would an individual; it is so treated for all purposes of economic analysis.

That, within the household, the administration of consump-   28
tion requires major and often tedious effort, that decisions on consumption are heavily influenced by the member of the household least committed to such tasks, that these arrangements are extremely important if consumption is to expand, are all things that are thus kept out of academic view. Those who study and those who teach are insulated from such adverse thoughts. The concept of the household is an outrageous assault on personality. People are not people; they are parts of a composite or collective that is deemed somehow to reflect the different or conflicting preferences of those who make it up. This is both analytically and ethically indefensible. But for concealing the economic function of women even from women it works.

One notices, at this point, an interesting convergence of eco-   29
nomics with politics. It has long been recognized that women are kept on political leash primarily by urging their higher commitment to the family. Their economic role is also concealed and protected by submerging them in the family or household. There is much, no doubt, to be said for the institution of the family. And it is not surprising that conservatives say so much.

In modern society power rests extensively on persuasion.   30
Such reverse incentives as flogging, though there are law-and-order

circles that seek their revival, are in limbo. So, with increasing afflu-ence, is the threat of starvation. And even affirmative pecuniary re-ward is impaired. For some, at least, enough is enough—the hope for more ceases to drive. In consequence, those who have need for a par-ticular behavior in others resort to persuasion—to instilling the belief that the action they need is reputable, moral, virtuous, socially benef-icent or otherwise good. It follows that what women are persuaded to believe about their social role and, more important, what they are taught to overlook are of prime importance in winning the requisite behavior. They must believe that consumption is happiness and that, however onerous its associated toil, it all adds up to greater happiness for themselves and their families.

If women were to see and understand how they are used, the consequence might be a considerable change in the pattern of their lives, especially in those income brackets where the volume of con-sumption is large. Thus, suburban life sustains an especially large con-sumption of goods, and, in consequence, is especially demanding in the administration required. The claims of roofs, furniture, plumbing, crabgrass, vehicles, recreational equipment and juvenile management are all very great. This explains why unmarried people, regardless of income, favor urban living over the suburbs. If women understood that they are the facilitating instrument of this consumption and were led to reject its administration as a career, there would, one judges, be a general return to a less demanding urban life. 31

More certainly there would be a marked change in the char-acter of social life. Since they are being used to administer consump-tion, women are naturally encouraged to do it well. In consequence, much social activity is, in primary substance, a competitive display of managerial excellence. The cocktail party or dinner party is, essen-tially, a fair, more refined and complex than those at which embroi-dery or livestock are entered in competition but for the same ultimate purpose of displaying and improving the craftsmanship or breed. The cleanliness of the house, the excellence of the garden, the taste, quality and condition of the furnishings and the taste, quality and imagination of the food and intoxicants and the deftness of their service are put on display before the critical eye of those invited to appraise them. Comparisons are made with other exhibitors. Ribbons are not awarded, but the competent administrator is duly proclaimed a good housekeeper, a gracious hostess, a clever manager or, more simply, a really good wife. These competitive social rites and the accompanying titles encourage and confirm women in their role as administrators and thus facilitators of the high levels of consumption on which the high-production economy rests. It would add measurably to economic understanding were they so recognized. But perhaps for some it would detract from their appeal. 32

JOHN KENNETH GALBRAITH

However, the more immediate reward to women from an un- derstanding of their economic role is in liberalizing the opportunity for choice. What is now seen as a moral compulsion—the diligent and informed administration of the family consumption—emerges as a service to economic interests. When so seen, the moral compulsion disappears. Once women see that they serve purposes which are *not* their own, they will see that they can serve purposes which *are* their own.

COMPREHENSION

1. What does Galbraith mean by "convenient social virtue"? How do women enter into this socioeconomic equation?

2. In what ways are the economic lives of women concealed, and for what reasons?

3. What conclusions does the author draw from his analysis?

RHETORIC

1. Why does the author begin his essay with a personal style? What tone is established? What is the impact of this style and tone on the rest of the essay? How would you characterize this later style?

2. Cite the various economic terms that Galbraith uses. Does he employ them concretely or abstractly, and why?

3. Is there a thesis statement in this essay? If so, where is it positioned? If not, why has Galbraith chosen to develop an implied thesis?

4. Explain the cause-effect pattern in this essay. How does the causal chain of economic and social phenomena support Galbraith's thesis?

5. Where does the author use examples? Discuss their relative effectiveness.

6. Which paragraphs constitute the conclusion? How does this conclusion reinforce the argumentative edge of the entire essay?

WRITING

1. Galbraith states, "the concept of household is an outrageous assault on personality." Defend or attack this assertion in a brief essay.

2. Using Galbraith's final paragraph as a focus, write an essay on the new economic status of women.

3. Develop your own analysis of consumption and the economic roles of women.

VIRGINIA WOOLF

Professions for Women

Virginia Woolf (1882–1941), novelist and essayist, was the daughter of Leslie Stephen, a famous critic and writer on economics. An experimental novelist, Woolf attempted to portray consciousness through a poetic, symbolic, and concrete style. Her novels include Jacob's Room *(1922),* Mrs. Dalloway *(1925),* To the Lighthouse *(1927), and* The Waves *(1931). She was also a perceptive reader and critic; her criticism appears in* The Common Reader *(1925) and* The Second Common Reader *(1933). In the following essay, which was delivered originally as a speech to The Women's Service League in 1931, Woolf argues that women must overcome several "angels," or phantoms, in order to succeed in professional careers.*

When your secretary invited me to come here, she told me that your Society is concerned with the employment of women and she suggested that I might tell you something about my own professional experiences. It is true I am a woman; it is true I am employed; but what professional experiences have I had? It is difficult to say. My profession is literature; and in that profession there are fewer experiences for women than in any other, with the exception of the stage—fewer, I mean, that are peculiar to women. For the road was cut many years ago—by Fanny Burney, by Aphra Behn, by Harriet Martineau, by Jane Austen, by George Eliot—many famous women, and many more unknown and forgotten, have been before me, making the path smooth, and regulating my steps. Thus, when I came to write, there were very few material obstacles in my way. Writing was a reputable and harmless occupation. The family peace was not broken by the scratching of a pen. No demand was made upon the family purse. For ten and sixpence one can buy paper enough to write all the plays of Shakespeare—if one has a mind that way. Pianos and models, Paris, Vienna and Berlin, masters and mistresses, are not needed by a writer. The cheapness of writing paper is, of course, the reason why women have succeeded as writers before they have succeeded in the other professions. 1

But to tell you my story—it is a simple one. You have only got to figure to yourselves a girl in a bedroom with a pen in her hand. She had only to move that pen from left to right—from ten o'clock to one. Then it occurred to her to do what is simple and cheap enough after all—to slip a few of those pages into an envelope, fix a penny stamp in the corner, and drop the envelope into the red box at the 2 corner. It was thus that I became a journalist; and my effort was rewarded on the first day of the following month—a very glorious day it was for me—by a letter from an editor containing a cheque for one pound ten shillings and sixpence. But to show you how little I deserve to be called a professional woman, how little I know of the struggles and difficulties of such lives, I have to admit that instead of spending that sum upon bread and butter, rent, shoes and stockings, or butcher's bills, I went out and bought a cat—a beautiful cat, a Persian cat, which very soon involved me in bitter disputes with my neighbours.

What could be easier than to write articles and to buy Persian cats with the profits? But wait a moment. Articles have to be about something. Mine, I seem to remember, was about a novel by a famous man. And while I was writing this review, I discovered that if I were going to review books I should need to do battle with a certain phantom. And the phantom was a woman, and when I came to know her better I called her after the heroine of a famous poem, The Angel in the House. It was she who used to come between me and my paper when I was writing reviews. It was she who bothered me and wasted my time and so tormented me that at last I killed her. You who come of a younger and happier generation may not have heard of her—you may not know what I mean by the Angel in the House. I will describe her as shortly as I can. She was intensely sympathetic. She was immensely charming. She was utterly unselfish. She excelled in the difficult arts of family life. She sacrificed herself daily. If there was chicken, she took the leg; if there was a draught she sat in it—in short she was so constituted that she never had a mind or a wish of her own, but preferred to sympathize always with the minds and wishes of others. Above all—I need not say it—she was pure. Her purity was supposed to be her chief beauty—her blushes, her great grace. In those days—the last of Queen Victoria—every house had its Angel. And when I came to write I encountered her with the very first words. The shadow of her wings fell on my page; I heard the rustling of her skirts in the room. Directly, that is to say, I took my pen in hand to review that novel by a famous man, she slipped behind me and whispered: "My dear, you are a young woman. You are writing about a book that has been written by a man. Be sympathetic; be tender; flatter; deceive; use all the arts and wiles of our sex. Never let anybody guess that you have a mind of your own. Above all, be pure." And she made as if to guide my pen. I now record the one act for which I take some credit to myself, though the credit rightly belongs to some excellent ancestors of mine who left me a certain sum of money—shall we say five hundred pounds a year?—so that it was not necessary for me to depend solely on charm for my living. I turned upon her and caught her by the throat. I did my best to kill her. My excuse, if I were to be had up in a court of law, would be that I acted in self-defense. Had I not killed her she would have killed me. She would have plucked the heart out of my writing. For, as I found, directly I put pen to paper, you cannot review even a novel without having a mind of your own, without expressing what you think to be the truth about human relations, morality, sex. And all these questions, according to the Angel in the House, cannot be dealt with freely and openly by women; they must charm, they must conciliate, they must—to put it bluntly—tell lies if they are to succeed. Thus, whenever I felt the shadow of her wing or the radiance of her halo upon my page, I took up the inkpot and flung it at her. She died hard. Her fictitious nature was of great assistance to her. It is far harder to kill a phantom than a reality. She was always creeping back when I thought I had dispatched her. Though I flatter myself that I killed her in the end, the struggle was severe; it took much time that had better have been spent upon learning Greek grammar; or in roaming the world in search of adventures. But it was a real experience; it was an experience that was bound to befall all women writers at that time. Killing the Angel in the House was part of the occupation of a woman writer.

But to continue my story. The Angel was dead; what then   4
remained? You may say that what remained was a simple and common object—a young woman in a bedroom with an inkpot. In other words, now that she had rid herself of falsehood, that young woman had only to be herself. Ah, but what is "herself"? I mean, what is a woman? I assure you, I do not know. I do not believe that you know. I do not believe that anybody can know until she has expressed herself in all the arts and professions open to human skill. That indeed is one of the reasons why I have come here—out of respect for you, who are in process of showing us by your experiments what a woman is, who are in process of providing us, by your failures and successes, with that extremely important piece of information.

But to continue the story of my professional experiences. I   5
made one pound ten and six by my first review; and I bought a Persian cat with the proceeds. Then I grew ambitious. A Persian cat is all very well, I said; but a Persian cat is not enough. I must have a motor car. And it was thus that I became a novelist—for it is a very strange thing that people will give you a motor car if you will tell them a story. It is a still stranger thing that there is nothing so delightful in the world as telling stories. It is far pleasanter than writing reviews of famous novels. And yet, if I am to obey your secretary and tell you my professional experiences as a novelist, I must tell you about a very strange experience that befell me as a novelist. And to understand it you must try first to imagine a novelist's state of mind. I hope I am not giving away professional secrets if I say that a novelist's chief desire is to be as unconscious as possible. He has to induce in himself a state of perpetual lethargy. He wants life to proceed with the utmost

quiet and regularity. He wants to see the same faces, to read the same books, to do the same things day after day, month after month, while he is writing, so that nothing may break the illusion in which he is living—so that nothing may disturb or disquiet the mysterious nosings about, feelings round, darts, dashes and sudden discoveries of that very shy and illusive spirit, the imagination. I suspect that this state is the same both for men and women. Be that as it may, I want you to imagine me writing a novel in a state of trance. I want you to figure to yourselves a girl sitting with a pen in her hand, which for minutes, and indeed for hours, she never dips into the inkpot. The image that comes to my mind when I think of this girl is the image of a fisherman lying sunk in dreams on the verge of a deep lake with a rod held out over the water. She was letting her imagination sweep unchecked round every rock and cranny of the world that lies submerged in the depths of our unconscious being. Now came the experience, the experience that I believe to be far commoner with women writers than with men. The line raced through the girl's fingers. Her imagination had rushed away. It had sought the pools, the depths, the dark places where the largest fish slumber. And then there was a smash. There was an explosion. There was foam and confusion. The imagination had dashed itself against something hard. The girl was roused from her dream. She was indeed in a state of the most acute and difficult distress. To speak without figure she had thought of something, something about the body, about the passions which it was unfitting for her as a woman to say. Men, her reason told her, would be shocked. The consciousness of what men will say of a woman who speaks the truth about her passions had roused her from her artist's state of unconsciousness. She could write no more. The trance was over. Her imagination could work no longer. This I believe to be a very common experience with women writers—they are impeded by the extreme conventionality of the other sex. For though men sensibly allow themselves great freedom in these respects, I doubt that they realize or can control the extreme severity with which they condemn such freedom in women.

These then were two very genuine experiences of my own. 6 These were two of the adventures of my professional life. The first— killing the Angel in the House—I think I solved. She died. But the second, telling the truth about my own experiences as a body, I do not think I solved. I doubt that any woman has solved it yet. The obstacles against her are still immensely powerful—and yet they are very difficult to define. Outwardly, what is simpler than to write books? Outwardly, what obstacles are there for a woman rather than for a man? Inwardly, I think, the case is very different; she has still many ghosts to fight, many prejudices to overcome. Indeed it will be a long time still, I think, before a woman can sit down to write a book without finding a phantom to be slain, a rock to be dashed against. And if this is so in literature, the freest of all professions for women, how is it in the new professions which you are now for the first time entering?

7

Those are the questions that I should like, had I time, to ask you. And indeed, if I have laid stress upon these professional experiences of mine, it is because I believe that they are, though in different forms, yours also. Even when the path is nominally open—when there is nothing to prevent a woman from being a doctor, a lawyer, a civil servant—there are many phantoms and obstacles, as I believe, looming in her way. To discuss and define them is I think of great value and importance; for thus only can the labour be shared, the difficulties be solved. But besides this, it is necessary also to discuss the ends and the aims for which we are fighting, for which we are doing battle with these formidable obstacles. Those aims cannot be taken for granted; they must be perpetually questioned and examined. The whole position, as I see it—here in this hall surrounded by women practising for the first time in history I know not how many different professions— is one of extraordinary interest and importance. You have won rooms of your own in the house hitherto exclusively owned by men. You are able, though not without great labour and effort, to pay the rent. You are earning your five hundred pounds a year. But this freedom is only a beginning; the room is your own, but it is still bare. It has to be furnished; it has to be decorated; it has to be shared. How are you going to furnish it, how are you going to decorate it? With whom are you going to share it, and upon what terms? These, I think are questions of the utmost importance and interest. For the first time in history you are able to ask for them; for the first time you are able to decide for yourselves what the answers should be. Willingly would I stay and discuss those questions and answers—but not tonight. My time is up; and I must cease.

COMPREHENSION

1. This essay was presented originally as a speech. What internal evidence indicates that it was intended as a talk? How do you respond to it today as a reader?

2. Who or what is the "angel" that Woolf describes in this essay? Why must she kill it? What other obstacles does a professional woman encounter?

3. Paraphrase the last two paragraphs of this essay. What is the essence of Woolf's argument?

RHETORIC

1. There is a significant amount of figurative language in the essay. Locate and explain examples. What does the figurative language contribute to the tone of

the essay? Compare and contrast the figurative language in this essay and in Woolf's "The Death of the Moth."

2. How do we know that Woolf is addressing an audience of women? Why does she pose so many questions, and what does this strategy contribute to the rapport that she wants to establish? Explain the effect of the last two sentences.

3. How does Woolf use analogy to structure part of her argument?

4. Why does Woolf rely on personal narration? How does it affect the logic of her argument?

5. Evaluate Woolf's use of contrast to advance her argument.

6. Where does Woolf place her main proposition? How emphatic is it, and why?

WRITING

1. How effectively does Woolf use her own example as a professional writer to advance a broader proposition concerning all women entering professional life? Answer this question in a brief essay.

2. Explain the value of Woolf's essay for women today.

3. Discusss the problems and obstacles that you anticipate when you enter your chosen career.

4. Compare and contrast the essays by Goodman and Woolf.

RICHARD RODRIGUEZ

Los Pobres

Richard Rodriguez (1944–   ) was born in San Francisco and received degrees from Stanford University and Columbia University. He also did graduate study at the University of California, Berkeley and the Warburg Institute, London. Rodriguez became a nationally known writer with the publication of his autobiography, Hunger of Memory: The Education of Richard Rodriguez *(1982). In it, he describes the struggles of growing up biculturally—feeling alienated from his Spanish-speaking parents yet not wholly comfortable in the dominant culture of the United States. He opposes bilingualism and affirmative action as they are now practiced in the United States, and his stance has caused much controversy in educational and intellectual circles. Rodriguez*

It was at Stanford, one day near the end of my senior year, that a friend told me about a summer construction job he knew was available. I was quickly alert. Desire uncoiled within me. My friend said that he knew I had been looking for summer employment. He knew I needed some money. Almost apologetically he explained: It was something I probably wouldn't be interested in, but a friend of his, a contractor, needed someone for the summer to do menial jobs. There would be lots of shoveling and raking and sweeping. Nothing too hard. But nothing more interesting either. Still, the pay would be good. Did I want it? Or did I know someone who did?   1

I did. Yes, I said, surprised to hear myself say it.   2

In the weeks following, friends cautioned that I had no idea how hard physical labor really is. ("You only *think* you know what it is like to shovel for eight hours straight.") Their objections seemed to me challenges. They resolved the issue. I became happy with my plan. I decided, however, not to tell my parents. I wouldn't tell my mother because I could guess her worried reaction. I would tell my father only after the summer was over, when I could announce that, after all, I did know what "real work" is like.   3

The day I met the contractor (a Princeton graduate, it turned out), he asked me whether I had done any physical labor before. "In high school, during the summer," I lied. And although he seemed to regard me with skepticism, he decided to give me a try. Several days later, expectant, I arrived at my first construction site. I would take off my shirt to the sun. And at last grasp desired sensation. No longer afraid. At last become like a *bracero*. "We need those tree stumps out of here by tomorrow," the contractor said. I started to work.   4

I labored with excitement that first morning—and all the days after. The work was harder that I could have expected. But it was never as tedious as my friends had warned me it would be. There was too much physical pleasure in the labor. Especially early in the day, I would be most alert to the sensations of movement and straining. Beginning around seven each morning (when the air was still damp but the scent of weeds and dry earth anticipated the heat of the sun), I would feel my body resist the first thrusts of the shovel. My arms, tightened by sleep, would gradually loosen; after only several minutes, sweat would gather in beads on my forehead and then—a short while later—I would feel my chest silky with sweat in the breeze. I would return to my work. A nervous spark of pain would   5 fly up my arm and settle to burn like an ember in the thick of my shoulder. An hour, two passed. Three. My whole body would assume regular movements. Even later in the day, my enthusiasm for primitive sensation would survive the heat and the dust and the insects pricking my back. I would strain wildly for sensation as the day came to a close. At three-thirty, quitting time, I would stand upright and slowly let my head fall back, luxuriating in the feeling of tightness relieved.

Some of the men working nearby would watch me and laugh. 6
Two or three of the older men took the trouble to teach me the right way to use a pick, the correct way to shovel. "You're doing it wrong, too fucking hard," one man scolded. Then proceeded to show me— what persons who work with their bodies all their lives quickly learn—the most economical way to use one's body in labor.

"Don't make your back do so much work," he instructed. I 7
stood impatiently listening, half listening, vaguely watching, then noticed his work-thickened fingers clutching the shovel. I was annoyed. I wanted to tell him that I enjoyed shoveling the wrong way. And I didn't want to learn the right way. I wasn't afraid of back pain. I liked the way my body felt sore at the end of the day.

I was about to, but, as it turned out, I didn't say a thing. 8
Rather it was at that moment I realized that I was fooling myself if I expected a few weeks of labor to gain me admission to the world of the laborer. I would not learn in three months what my father had meant by "real work." I was not bound to this job; I could imagine its rapid conclusion. For me the sensations of exertion and fatigue could be savored. For my father or uncle, working at comparable jobs when they were my age, such sensations were to be feared. Fatigue took a different toll on their bodies—and minds.

It was, I know, a simple insight. But it was with this realiza- 9
tion that I took my first step that summer toward realizing something even more important about the "worker." In the company of carpenters, electricians, plumbers, and painters at lunch, I would often sit quietly, observant. I was not shy in such company. I felt easy, pleased by the knowledge that I was casually accepted, my presence taken for granted by men (exotics) who worked with their hands. Some days the younger men would talk and talk about sex, and they would howl at women who drove by in cars. Other days the talk at lunchtime was subdued; men gathered in separate groups. It depended on who was around. There were rough, good-natured workers. Others were quiet. The more I remember that summer, the more I realize that there was no single *type* of worker. I am embarrassed to say I had not expected such diversity. I certainly had not expected to meet, for example, a plumber who was an abstract painter in his off hours and admired the work of Mark Rothko. Nor did I expect to meet so many workers

with college diplomas. (They were the ones who were not surprised that I intended to enter graduate school in the fall.) I suppose what I really want to say here is painfully obvious, but I must say it nevertheless: The men of that summer were middle-class Americans. They certainly didn't constitute an oppressed society. Carefully completing their work sheets; talking about the fortunes of local football teams; planning Las Vegas vacations; comparing the gas mileage of various makes of campers—they were not *los pobres* my mother had spoken about.

On two occasions, the contractor hired a group of Mexican aliens. They were employed to cut down some trees and haul off debris. In all, there were six men of varying age. The youngest in his late twenties; the oldest (his father?) perhaps sixty years old. They came and they left in a single old truck. Anonymous men. They were never introduced to the other men at the site. Immediately upon their arrival, they would follow the contractor's directions, start working— rarely resting—seemingly driven by a fatalistic sense that work which had to be done was best done as quickly as possible. 10

I watched them sometimes. Perhaps they watched me. The only time I saw them pay me much notice was one day at lunchtime when I was laughing with the other men. The Mexicans sat apart when they ate, just as they worked by themselves. Quiet. I rarely heard them say much to each other. All I could hear were their voices calling out sharply to one another, giving directions. Otherwise, when they stood briefly resting, they talked among themselves in voices too hard to overhear. 11

The contractor knew enough Spanish, and the Mexicans—or at least the oldest of them, their spokesman—seemed to know enough English to communicate. But because I was around, the contractor decided one day to make me his translator. (He assumed I could speak Spanish.) I did what I was told. Shyly I went over to tell the Mexicans that the patrón wanted them to do something else before they left for the day. As I started to speak, I was afraid with my old fear that I would be unable to pronounce the Spanish words. But it was a simple instruction I had to convey. I could say it in phrases. 12

The dark sweating faces turned toward me as I spoke. They stopped their work to hear me. Each nodded in response. I stood there. I wanted to say something more. But what could I say in Spanish, even if I could have pronounced the words right? Perhaps I just wanted to engage in small talk, to be assured of their confidence, our familiarity. I thought for a moment to ask them where in Mexico they were from. Something like that. And maybe I wanted to tell them (a lie, if need be) that my parents were from the same part of Mexico. 13

I stood there. 14

Their faces watched me. The eyes of the man directly in front 15

RICHARD RODRIGUEZ

of me moved slowly over my shoulder, and I turned to follow his glance toward *el patrón* some distance away. For a moment I felt swept up by that glance into the Mexicans' company. But then I heard one of them returning to work. And then the others went back to work. I left them without saying anything more.

When they had finished, the contractor went over to pay them 16 in cash. (He later told me that he paid them collectively—"for the job," though he wouldn't tell me their wages. He said something quickly about the good rate of exchange "in their own country.") I can still hear the loudly confident voice he used with the Mexicans. It was the sound of the *gringo* I had heard as a very young boy. And I can still hear the quiet, indistinct sounds of the Mexican, the oldest who replied. At hearing that voice I was sad for the Mexicans. Depressed by their vulnerability. Angry at myself. The adventure of the summer seemed suddenly ludicrous. I would not shorten the distance I felt from *los pobres* with a few weeks of physical labor. I would not become like them. They were different from me. . . .

In the end, my father was right—though perhaps he did not 17 know how right or why—to say that I would never know what real work is. I will never know what he felt at his last factory job. If tomorrow I worked at some kind of factory, it would go differently for me. My long education would favor me. I could act as a public person—able to defend my interests, to unionize, to petition, to speak up—to challenge and demand. (I will never know what real work is.) I will never know what the Mexicans knew, gathering their shovels and ladders and saws.

Their silence stays with me now. The wages those Mexicans 18 received for their labor were only a measure of their disadvantaged condition. Their silence is more telling. They lack a public identity. They remain profoundly alien. Persons apart. People lacking a union obviously, people without grounds. They depend upon the relative good will or fairness of their employers each day. For such people, lacking a better alternative, it is not such an unreasonable risk.

Their silence stays with me. I have taken these many words 19 to describe its impact. Only: the quiet. Something uncanny about it. Its compliance. Vulnerability. Pathos. As I heard their truck rumbling away, I shuddered, my face mirrored with sweat. I had finally come face to face with *los pobres*.

COMPREHENSION

1. How does Rodriguez set the scene for his narrative? What contrasts does he develop in the course of the essay?

2. What are the chief revelations Rodriguez receives from his work experience?

3. Why does Rodriguez focus on the silence of the Mexicans in the final two

LOS POBRES

paragraphs? What is the relationship between this silence and the "real work" his father knows?

RHETORIC

1.   In paragraph 9, Rodriguez puts quotes around "worker"; parentheses around "(exotics)"; and italicizes "*type.*" What is the purpose of each choice of punctuation?

2.   There are several fragments in each of the final two paragraphs. What is the effect of using this sentence structure? Where else are fragments employed in the essay?

3.   Why are paragraphs 2 and 14 so short? How does the length of these paragraphs help delineate Rodriguez's mood?

4.   What sensations does Rodriguez focus on in paragraph 5? Which words contribute most to evoking them?

5.   In what way do the first three paragraphs prepare or fail to prepare you for the narrative that follows?

6.   The opening sentence of paragraph 19 repeats that of paragraph 18. What is the purpose of this repetition?

WRITING

1.   Imagine yourself in the same situation as Rodriguez. Would your presumptions about "hard work" and your co-workers have been the same? Would you be more or less naive than Rodriguez? Explain in a brief essay.

2.   What are the major differences between the Mexican workers and the American workers in the essay? Write an essay focusing on these differences.

3.   Write an essay explaining why Rodriguez feels excluded from each of the two groups.

4.   Have you ever felt like an outsider in a social situation? Describe a time in your life when you were confronted with the desire to be accepted. How were you different from the others? How did you try to transcend this difference?

JOSEPH ADDISON

The Royal Exchange

Joseph Addison (1672–1719) was an essayist, poet, dramatist, statesman, and journalist. As a playwright, he wrote one of the most successful tragedies of the eighteenth century (Cato, in

1713). As a statesman, he served as secretary of state under George I. As an essayist, he wrote with reason and wit in The Tatler *(1709–1711) and* The Spectator *(1711–1712 and 1714). He not only excelled as a statesman and tragedian but also is often considered one of the best English essayists. In this periodical essay, Addison pays tribute to one of Britain's sacred institutions.*

here is no place in the town which I so much love to frequent as the Royal Exchange. It gives me a secret satisfaction, and, in some measure, gratifies my vanity, as I am an Englishman, to see so rich an assembly of countrymen and foreigners consulting together upon the private business of mankind, and making this metropolis a kind of emporium for the whole earth. I must confess I look upon high-change to be a great council, in which all considerable nations have their representatives. Factors in the trading world are what ambassadors are in the politic world; they negotiate affairs, conclude treaties, and maintain a good correspondence between those wealthy societies of men that are divided from one another by seas and oceans, or live on the different extremities of a continent. I have often been pleased to hear disputes adjusted between an inhabitant of Japan and an alderman of London, or to see a subject of the Great Mogul entering into a league with one of the Czar of Muscovy. I am infinitely delighted in mixing with these several ministers of commerce, as they are distinguished by their different walks and different languages: sometimes I am justled among a body of Armenians: sometimes I am lost in a crowd of Jews; and sometimes make one in a group of Dutchmen. I am a Dane, Swede, or Frenchman at different times, or rather fancy myself like the old philosopher, who upon being asked what country-man he was, replied, that he was a citizen of the world. 1

Though I very frequently visit this busy multitude of people, I am known to nobody there but my friend Sir Andrew, who often smiles upon me as he sees me bustling in the crowd, but at the same time connives at my presence without taking any further notice of me. There is indeed a merchant of Egypt, who just knows me by sight, having formerly remitted me some money to Grand Cairo; but as I am not versed in the modern Coptic, our conferences go no further than a bow and a grimace. 2

This grand scene of business gives me an infinite variety of solid and substantial entertainments. As I am a great lover of mankind, my heart naturally overflows with pleasure at the sight of a prosperous and happy multitude, insomuch that at many public solemnities I cannot forbear expressing my joy with tears that have stolen down my cheeks. For this reason I am wonderfully delighted to see 3

THE ROYAL EXCHANGE

331

such a body of men thriving in their own private fortunes, and at the same time promoting the public stock; or in other words, raising estates for their own families, by bringing into their country whatever is wanting, and carrying out of it whatever is superfluous.

Nature seems to have taken a particular care to disseminate 4 her blessings among the different regions of the world, with an eye to this mutual intercourse and traffic among mankind, that the natives of the several parts of the globe might have a kind of dependence upon one another, and be united together by their common interest. Almost every degree produces something peculiar to it. The food often grows in one country, and the sauce in another. The fruits of Portugal are corrected by the products of Barbadoes: the infusion of a China plant sweetened with the pith of an Indian cane. The Philippick Islands give a flavour to our European bowls. The single dress of a woman of quality is often the product of an hundred climates. The muff and the fan come together from the different ends of the earth. The scarf is sent from the torrid zone, and the tippet from beneath the Pole. The brocade petticoat rises out of the mines of Peru, and the diamond necklace out of the bowels of Indostan.

If we consider our own country in its natural prospect, with- 5 out any of the benefits and advantages of commerce, what a barren uncomfortable spot of earth falls to our share! Natural historians tell us that no fruit grows originally among us, besides hips and haws, acorns and pig-nuts, with other delicacies of the like nature; that our climate of itself, and without the assistances of art, can make no further advances towards a plum than to a sloe, and carries an apple to no greater a perfection than a crab: that our melons, our peaches, our figs, our apricots, and cherries, are strangers among us, imported in different ages, and naturalized in our English gardens; and that they would all degenerate and fall away into the trash of our own country, if they were wholly neglected by the planter, and left to the mercy of our sun and soil.

Nor has traffic more enriched our vegetable world than it has 6 improved the whole face of nature among us. Our ships are laden with the harvest of every climate: our tables are stored with spices, and oils, and wines: our rooms are filled with pyramids of China, and adorned with the workmanship of Japan: our morning's-draught comes to us from the remotest corners of the earth: we repair our bodies by the drugs of America, and repose ourselves under Indian canopies. My friend Sir Andrew calls the vineyards of France our gardens; the spice-islands our hot-beds; the Persians our silk-weavers, and the Chinese our potters. Nature indeed furnishes us with the bare necessaries of life, but traffic gives us a great variety of what is useful, and at the same time supplies us with every thing that is convenient and ornamental. Nor is it the least part of this our happiness, that

JOSEPH ADDISON

whilst we enjoy the remotest products of the north and south, we are free from those extremities of weather which give them birth; that our eyes are refreshed with the green fields of Britain, at the same time that our palates are feasted with fruits that rise between the tropics.

For these reasons there are not more useful members in a commonwealth than merchants. They knit mankind together in a mutual intercourse of good offices, distribute the gifts of nature, find work for the poor, add wealth to the rich, and magnificence to the great. Our English merchant converts the tin of his own country into gold, and exchanges his wool for rubies. The Mahometans are clothed in our British manufacture, and the inhabitants of the frozen zone warmed with the fleeces of our sheep. 7

When I have been upon the 'Change, I have often fancied one of our old kings standing in person, where he is represented in effigy, and looking down upon the wealthy concourse of people with which that place is every day filled. In this case, how would he be surprized to hear all the languages of Europe spoken in this little spot of his former dominions, and to see so many private men, who in his time would have been the vassals of some powerful baron, negotiating like princes for greater sums of money than were formerly to be met with in the royal treasury! Trade, without enlarging the British territories, has given us a kind of additional empire: it has multiplied the number of the rich, made our landed estates infinitely more valuable than they were formerly, and added to them an accession of other estates as valuable as the lands themselves. 8

COMPREHENSION

1. Addison seems to have a definite point of view as an Englishman. What is that view?

2. How is Addison's description of himself as a "citizen of the world" and "lover of mankind" reflected in his attitude toward the Royal Exchange?

3. What is Addison's opinion about merchants? About capitalism? About colonialism? About internationalism?

RHETORIC

1. Locate and define these words as they would have been used in Addison's time: *high-change* (paragraph 1); *grimace* (paragraph 2); *Philippick Islands* (paragraph 4); *tippet* (paragraph 4); and *concourse* (paragraph 8). Even though these words are out of date, can they be used in contemporary contexts? Try using them in sentences.

2. What words and phrases in the first paragraph set the tone of the essay? How do sentence balance and parallel structure affect the tone? Find other examples of balance and parallel structure in the essay.

THE ROYAL EXCHANGE

3. Show the structural function of Addison's extended metaphor of the Royal Exchange as a "grand scene of business." To what extent is the Royal Exchange itself a symbol? Explain.

4. What types of illustration does Addison use to advance his thesis?

5. Describe the strength or weakness of Addison's logic in paragraphs 4 to 7.

6. What techniques of development appear in Addison's concluding paragraph?

WRITING

1. Why might Addison be termed a forerunner of today's business booster? What traits does he share with today's apostles of business?

2. Focus on a financial landmark—your local bank, the Stock Exchange, and so forth—and write a speculative essay about it in the manner of Addison.

3. Apply Priestley's observations in "Wrong Ism" to Addison's essay.

LESTER THUROW

Conflicting Theories of the Labor Market

Lester C. Thurow (1938–   ) is an economist, university professor, and author. Born in Montana, he received an M.A. from Oxford in 1962 and a Ph.D. from Harvard in 1964. Dr. Thurow was a member of the President's Council of Economic Advisors. He is a contributing editor to Newsweek *and a member of the editorial board of* The New York Times. *In addition, he is the author of* Zero Sum Society *(1980), an influential book on economics, and of* Dangerous Currents *(1983). In this essay, Thurow discusses the problems and implications of economic theory.*

 ust as archaeologists have two sources of information on ancient civilizations—artifacts and writings—so an observer of economic activity has two sources of information on the labor market: he can examine the observed distribution of wages and employment, or he can turn to the economic literature for a view of how wages and employment are determined. There are problems of a striking mismatch between observed data and theory, but within the theoretical literature is another peculiar phe-

1

LESTER THUROW

nomenon. At least four different theories of the labor market present themselves. Equilibrium price-auction economics, Keynesian macro-economics, monetarists' macro-economics, and labor economics all have different theories to explain what occurs. The theories are mutually inconsistent, but each has its advocates and economic practitioners.

In the standard price-auction model, the labor market is   2
treated as if it were like any other market in which price (wage) is the short-run market-clearing mechanism. Individuals buy and sell skills and raw labor (time) in a bidding framework in which equilibrium prices clear markets leaving no unsatisfied buyers or sellers. Prices clear markets in the short run and provide investment signals in the long run. Cost minimization on the demand side and earnings maximization on the supply side determine shifts in supply-and-demand curves. Investments in skills (human capital) are equivalent to investments in plant and equipment, with the same decision calculus obtaining in both. Individuals invest until the rate of return to both human and physical investments is driven down to the market rate of interest. The marginal productivity theory of distribution applies— every economic actor is paid a wage equal to his marginal revenue product (the extra output that he produces times the price at which that output can be sold). Wages are flexible in the model, and unemployment is impossible.

In sharp contrast, macro-economics of both the Keynesian and   3
monetary variety treat the labor market as a case of fundamental disequilibrium. Disequilibrium must exist, it is reasoned, or unemployment could not exist or persist.

In Keynesian models, money wages are assumed to be rigid   4
downward—the assumption is not explained, but taken as an empirical truth. With wages rigid downward, markets cannot clear in the normal manner. Because flexible wages do not eliminate disequilibria in the labor market, government must intervene to eliminate the disequilibria by manipulating aggregate demand. Specifically, government must intervene to shift the aggregate demand curve for labor so that it crosses the economy's labor-supply curve at full employment.

In the econometric models of Keynesian macro-economics, the   5
demand for labor depends upon total output, not upon the wage rate. Careful calculations are made of the amount of labor that will be absorbed or disgorged when aggregate output goes up or down. Similarly, the equations used to represent the supply of labor depend on long-run demographic trends and job availability, not wages. The labor market, in sum, is a market where fixed-price models apply.

Monetarist macro-economics similarly depends upon assump-   6
tions of rigidity in the labor market. According to the natural rate of unemployment hypothesis, labor demands a specific, rigid collective

real wage gain for each level of unemployment. Labor demands a real wage gain regardless of the experience that may have frustrated it in the past—forever asking for larger and larger nominal wage gains if unemployment is below the natural rate, but forever getting the real wage gain consistent with productivity growth. Just as in Keynesian macro-economics, the rigid demanded real wage gain is an unexplained assumption taken as an empirical truth. No attempt is made here to derive an unalterable demand for a collective real wage gain from the equilibrium price-auction model, because it cannot be done.

The monetarist macro-economic solution is to adjust monetary 7 policies so that the unemployment rate rises or falls to its natural rate. When the natural rate of unemployment is reached, society just lives with both the nominal wage gain and the resulting stable but perhaps high rate of inflation produced by the gap between the nominal wage demands and the economy's rate of productivity growth. If this is not satisfactory, the money supply may be used to push unemployment above its natural rate. If unemployment is pushed above the natural rate, nominal wage demands fall. With lower nominal wage gains and the same rate of growth of productivity, the economy's rate of inflation will fall until it reaches some acceptable level. At that point, monetary policies can be altered to let the unemployment rate drift down to its natural rate. The new induced nominal wage gain then yields a new lower, stable rate of inflation.

No intervention would be necessary except for the fixed-price 8 assumption that labor has a collective real wage gain that it perpetually demands at each level of unemployment. The important point is that both Keynesian and monetary theories of macro-economics leave one wondering about the workings of the equilibrium price-auction model in the labor market. Neither is consistent with it.

In institutional labor economics, inter-skill or inter-industry 9 wage differentials become the focus of analysis. The basic concept here is a wage contour developed by John Dunlop, and the wage relationships various occupations and industries have to one another. The 1974 *Economic Report of the President* states, for example, that 1973 was a year of moderate wage increases because "wages in different industries seemed in good balance." So for this theory, the structure of wages becomes paramount. Except for analysis of how inequities in the structure of wages influence the level of wages, aggregate wages or their rate of increase are ignored. In other words, instead of looking at the determinants of individual productivity, the labor economists' unit of analysis is social or group decision making. In many respects, the thinking here is more closely related to the sociologists' concept of relative deprivation than it is to the equilibrium price-auction model.

Unfortunately, these four theoretical perspectives are often 10

LESTER THUROW

mutually inconsistent. If the price-auction model is correct, the macro-economic problems of unemployment cannot exist, wages are not ex-ogenously set at some rigid money level or some rigid real wage gain, and the labor market is not in perpetual disequilibrium. Conversely, if either the Keynesian or monetarist macro-economic approaches are correct, the conventional model is wrong and economics is left with-out a theory of wage determination. Wages are determined in some unknown manner exogenous to the microeconomic system.

Labor economics, meanwhile, has a theory of the wage dif- 11 ferentials at odds with the price-auction model, but neither does it have a theory to explain the level of wages. The interdependent pref-erences, relative deprivation, norms of social justice, and wage con-tours that labor economists use to determine the structure of wages are thoroughly inconsistent with the postulates of the standard eco-nomic model. Individuals compare themselves to others instead of looking solely at their own productivity and their own wages. A struc-ture of wages set in accordance with the axioms of the marginal-productivity theory cannot conform to a structure set by patterns of interdependent preferences.

Clearly something is wrong with the economics profession 12 when four mutually inconsistent intellectual approaches are needed to explain what happens in one real-world labor market. Various ap-proaches to a phenomenon exist when the moves being made by the players of the game cannot be explained by any one approach. But in this situation, it is not surprising that unexpected results frequently occur in the economy.

The inconsistent approaches and empirical puzzles of the la- 13 bor market have not, however, stimulated the economics profession in general to undertake a re-examination of its basic theories. Mostly the inconsistencies and puzzles have been ignored. Belief in the flex-ible-price world of the equilibrium price-auction market remains un-disturbed as if the observed problems of the labor market did not exist.

COMPREHENSION

1. How does Thurow make his obvious expertise comprehensible to a general audience?

2. What are some of the problems between observed data and economic theory?

3. What does the term *price-auction model* mean?

RHETORIC

1. Use a dictionary to define the following words: *disequilibrium* (paragraph 3), *econometric* (paragraph 5), *differentials* (paragraph 9), *exogenously* (para-graph 10), and *axioms* (paragraph 11).

2. Make a list of the transitional phrases at the start of various paragraphs that contribute to the unity of the essay.

3. What is Thurow's thesis? Where does he state it?

4. Where does the author analyze the shortcomings of each theory?

5. Cite instances where the author uses the pattern of cause and effect.

6. Who is the intended audience for this selection? What does Thurow hope to achieve by writing it?

WRITING

1. Using this article as an indication, how much significance is given to the human dimension in economics? Where does Thurow discuss the costs to actual human beings of various economic theories?

2. Does Thurow believe that a truly effective economic theory can be constructed? What do you suppose would be the basis of such a theory? Do economists presently have the means to construct such a theory? Put your answers in the form of an evaluative essay.

KARL MARX

Bourgeois and Proletarians

Karl Marx (1818–1883), the chief founder of democratic socialism and revolutionary communism, was born in Germany and studied at the Universities of Bonn and Berlin. He met Friedrich Engles, his closest friend and collaborator, in 1843 while living in Paris; he resided in Belgium from 1845 to 1848 and on his return to Germany became spokesperson for radical reform. He (and Engels) wrote The Communist Manifesto *in 1848 on the eve of the revolution in France. After the collapse of the German revolution that same year, Marx fled from Prussia to London, where he spent the rest of his life, often sick and impoverished, in exile. In addition to* The Communist Manifesto, *Marx's major works include* The German Ideology *(1845–1846) and* Das Kapital *(three volumes: 1867, 1885, and 1894). Here is the first chapter of* The Communist Manifesto.

he history of all hitherto existing society is the history of   1
class struggles.

Freeman and slave, patrician and plebeian, lord   2
and serf, guild-master and journeyman, in a word, oppressor and oppressed, stood in constant opposition to one another,
carried on uninterrupted, now hidden, now open fight, a fight that
each time ended, either in a revolutionary re-constitution of society at
large, or in the common ruin of the contending classes.

In the earlier epochs of history we find almost everywhere a   3
complicated arrangement of society into various orders, a manifold
gradation of social rank. In ancient Rome we have patricians, knights,
plebeians, slaves; in the middle ages, feudal lords, vassals, guild-
masters, journeymen, apprentices, serfs; in almost all of these classes,
again, subordinate gradations.

The modern bourgeois society that has sprouted from the   4
ruins of feudal society, has not done away with class antagonisms. It
has but established new classes, new conditions of oppression, new
forms of struggle in place of the old ones.

Our epoch, the epoch of the bourgeoisie, possesses, however,   5
this distinctive feature; it has simplified the class antagonisms. Society
as a whole is more and more splitting up into two great hostile camps,
into two great classes directly facing each other: Bourgeoisie and
Proletariat.

From the serfs of the middle ages sprang the chartered bur-   6
ghers of the earliest towns. From these burgesses the first elements of
the bourgeoisie were developed.

The discovery of America, the rounding of the Cape, opened   7
up fresh ground for the rising bourgeoisie. The East Indian and
Chinese markets, the colonization of America, trade with the colonies,
the increase in the means of exchange and in commodities generally,
gave to commerce, to navigation, to industry, an impulse never before
known, and thereby, to the revolutionary element in the tottering feudal society, a rapid development.

The feudal system of industry, under which industrial pro-   8
duction was monopolized by closed guilds, now no longer sufficed
for the growing wants of the new market. The manufacturing system
took its place. The guild-masters were pushed on one side by the
manufacturing middle-class: division of labor between the different
corporate guilds vanished in the face of division of labor in each single
workshop.

Meantime the markets kept ever growing, the demand ever   9
rising. Even manufacture no longer sufficed. Thereupon, steam and
machinery revolutionized industrial production. The place of manufacture was taken by the giant, Modern Industry, the place of the

industrial middle-class, by industrial millionaires, the leaders of whole industrial armies, the modern bourgeois.

Modern industry has established the world market, for which the discovery of America paved the way. This market has given an immense development to commerce, to navigation, to communication by land. This development has, in its turn, reacted on the extension of industry; and in proportion as industry, commerce, navigation, railways extended, in the same proportion the bourgeoisie developed, increased its capital, and pushed into the background every class handed down from the Middle Ages. 10

We see, therefore, how the modern bourgeoisie is itself the product of a long course of development, of a series of revolutions in the modes of production and of exchange. 11

Each step in the development of the bourgeoisie was accompanied by a corresponding political advance of that class. An oppressed class under the sway of the feudal nobility, an armed and self-governing association in the mediaeval commune, here independent urban republic (as in Italy and Germany), there taxable "third estate" of the monarchy (as in France), afterwards, in the period of manufacture proper, serving either the semi-feudal or the absolute monarchy as a counterpoise against nobility, and, in fact, corner stone of the great monarchies in general, the bourgeoisie has at last, since the establishment of Modern Industry and of the world-market, conquered for itself, in the modern representative State, exclusive political sway. The executive of the modern State is but a committee for managing the common affairs of the whole bourgeoisie. 12

The bourgeoisie, historically, has played a most revolutionary part. 13

The bourgeoisie, wherever it has got the upper hand, has put an end to all feudal, patriarchal, idyllic relations. It has pitilessly torn asunder the motley feudal ties that bound man to his "natural superiors," and has left no other nexus between man and man than naked self-interest, than callous "cash payment." It has drowned the most heavenly ecstasies of religious fervor, of chivalrous enthusiasm, of Philistine sentimentalism, in the icy water of egotistical calculation. It has resolved personal worth into exchange value, and in place of the numberless indefeasible chartered freedoms, has set up that single, unconscionable freedom—Free Trade. In one word, for exploitation, veiled by religious and political illusions, it has substituted naked, shameless, direct, brutal exploitation. 14

The bourgeoisie has stripped of its halo every occupation hitherto honored and looked up to with reverent awe. It has converted the physician, the lawyer, the priest, the poet, the man of science, into its paid wage laborers. 15

KARL MARX

The bourgeoisie has torn away from the family its sentimental   16
veil, and has reduced the family relation to a mere money relation.

The bourgeoisie has disclosed how it came to pass that the   17
brutal display of vigor in the Middle Ages, which reactionists so much
admire, found its fitting complement in the most slothful indolence.
It has been the first to show what man's activity can bring about. It
has accomplished wonders far surpassing Egyptian pyramids, Roman
aqueducts and Gothic cathedrals; it has conducted expeditions that
put in the shade all former Exoduses of nations and crusades.

The bourgeoisie cannot exist without constantly revolution-   18
izing the instruments of production, and thereby the relations of production, and with them the whole relations of society. Conservation
of the old modes of production in unaltered form was, on the contrary,
the first condition of existence for all earlier industrial classes. Constant revolutionizing of production, uninterrupted disturbance of all
social conditions, everlasting uncertainty and agitation distinguish the
bourgeois epoch from all earlier ones. All fixed, fast frozen relations,
with their train of ancient and venerable prejudices and opinions, are
swept away, all new formed ones become antiquated before they can
ossify. All that is solid melts into the air, all that is holy is profaned,
and man is at last compelled to face with sober senses, his real conditions of life, and his relations with his kind.

The need of a constantly expanding market for its products   19
chases the bourgeoisie over the whole surface of the globe. It must
nestle everywhere, settle everywhere, establish connections everywhere.

The bourgeoisie has through its exploitation of the world-   20
market given a cosmopolitan character to production and consumption in every country. To the great chagrin of reactionists, it has drawn
from under the feet of industry the national ground on which it stood.
All old-established national industries have been destroyed or are
daily being destroyed. They are dislodged by new industries, whose
introduction becomes a life and death question for all civilized nations, by industries that no longer work up indigenous raw material,
but raw material drawn from the remotest zones; industries whose
products are consumed, not only at home, but in every quarter of the
globe. In place of the old wants, satisfied by the productions of the
country, we find new wants, requiring for their satisfaction the products of distant lands and climes. In place of the old local and national
seclusion and self-sufficiency, we have intercourse in every direction,
universal interdependence of nations. And as in material, so also in
intellectual production. The intellectual creations of individual nations
become common property. National onesidedness and narrowmind-
edness become more and more impossible, and from the numerous
national local literatures there arises a world-literature.

The bourgeoisie, by the rapid improvement of all instruments 21
of production, by the immensely facilitated means of communication
draws all, even the most barbarian nations into civilization. The cheap
prices of its commodities are the heavy artillery with which it batters
down all Chinese walls, with which it forces the barbarians' intensely
obstinate hatred of foreigners to capitulate. It compels all nations on
pain of extinction, to adopt the bourgeois mode of production; it compels them to introduce what it calls civilization into their midst, *i.e.,*
to become bourgeois themselves. In a word, it creates a world after
its own image.

The bourgeoisie has subjected the country to the rule of the 22
towns. It has created enormous cities, has greatly increased the urban
population as compared with the rural, and has thus rescued a considerable part of the population from the idiocy of rural life. Just as
it has made the country dependent on the towns, so it has made barbarian and semi-barbarian countries dependent on civilized ones, nations of peasants on nations of bourgeois, the East on the West.

The bourgeoisie keeps more and more doing away with the 23
scattered state of the population, of the means of production, and of
property. It has agglomerated population, centralized means of production, and has concentrated property in a few hands. The necessary
consequence of this was political centralization. Independent, or but
loosely connected provinces, with separate interests, laws, governments, and systems of taxation, became lumped together in one nation, with one government, one code of laws, one national class interest, one frontier and one customs tariff.

The bourgeoisie, during its rule of scarce one hundred years, 24
has created more massive and more colossal productive forces than
have all preceding generations together. Subjection of Nature's forces
to man, machinery, application of chemistry to industry and agriculture, steam-navigation, railways, electric telegraphs, clearing of whole
continents for cultivation, canalization of rivers, whole populations
conjured out of the ground—what earlier century had even a presentiment that such productive forces slumbered in the lap of social
labor?

We see then: the means of production and of exchange on 25
whose foundation the bourgeoisie built itself up, were generated in
feudal society. At a certain stage in the deveopment of these means
of production and of exchange, the conditions under which feudal
society produced and exchanged, the feudal organization of agriculture and manufacturing industry, in one word, the feudal relations of
property became no longer compatible with the already developed
productive forces; they became so many fetters. They had to burst
asunder; they were burst asunder.

Into their places stepped free competition, accompanied by 26 social and political constitution adapted to it, and by economical and political sway of the bourgeois class.

A similar movement is going on before our own eyes. Modern 27 bourgeois society with its relations of production, of exchange and of property, a society that has conjured up such gigantic means of production and of exchange, is like the sorcerer, who is no longer able to control the powers of the nether world whom he has called up by his spells. For many a decade past, the history of industry and commerce is but the history of the revolt of modern productive forces against modern conditions of production, against the property relations that are the conditions for the existence of the bourgeoisie and of its rule. It is enough to mention the commercial crises that by their periodical return put on its trail, each time more threateningly, the existence of the entire bourgeois society. In these crises a great part not only of the existing products, but also of the previously created productive forces, are periodically destroyed. In these crises there breaks out an epidemic that, in all earlier epochs, would have seemed an absurdity—the epidemic of overproduction. Society suddenly finds itself put back into a state of momentary barbarism; it appears as if a famine, a universal war of devastation, had cut off the supply of every means of subsistence; industry and commerce seem to be destroyed; and why? Because there is too much civilization, too much means of subsistence, too much industry, too much commerce. The productive forces at the disposal of society no longer tend to further the development of the conditions of the bourgeois property; on the contrary, they have become too powerful for these conditions by which they are fettered, and as soon as they overcome these fetters they bring disorder into the whole of bourgeois society, endanger the existence of bourgeois property. The conditions of bourgeois society are too narrow to comprise the wealth created by them. And how does the bourgeoisie get over these crises? On the one hand by enforced destruction of a mass of productive forces; on the other, by the conquest of new markets, and by the more thorough exploitation of the old ones. That is to say, by paving the way for more extensive and more destructive crises, and by diminishing the means whereby crises are prevented.

The weapons with which the bourgeoisie felled feudalism to 28 the ground are now turned against the bourgeoisie itself.

But not only has the bourgeoisie forged the weapons that 29 bring death to itself; it has also called into existence the men who are to wield those weapons—the modern working-class—the proletarians.

In proportion as the bourgeoisie, *i.e.*, capital, is developed, in 30 the same proportion is the proletariat, the modern working-class, developed, a class of laborers who live only so long as they find work, and who find work only so long as their labor increases capital. These laborers, who must sell themselves piecemeal, are a commodity, like every other article of commerce, and are consequently exposed to all the vicissitudes of competition, to all the fluctuations of the market.

Owing to the extensive use of machinery and to division of labor, the work of the proletarians has lost all individual character, and, consequently, all charm for the workman. He becomes an appendage of the machine, and it is only the most simple, most monotonous and most easily acquired knack that is required of him. Hence, the cost of production of a workman is restricted almost entirely to the means of subsistence that he requires for his maintenance, and for the propagation of his race. But the price of a commodity, and also of labor, is equal to its cost of production. In proportion, therefore, as the repulsiveness of the work increases the wage decreases. Nay more, in proportion as the use of machinery and division of labor increases, in the same proportion the burden of toil increases, whether by prolongation of the working hours, by increase of the work enacted in a given time, or by increased speed of the machinery, etc. 31

Modern industry has converted the little workshop of the patriarchal master into the great factory of the industrial capitalist. Masses of laborers, crowded into factories, are organized like soldiers. As privates of the industrial army they are placed under the command of a perfect hierarchy of officers and sergeants. Not only are they the slaves of the bourgeois class and of the bourgeois state, they are daily and hourly enslaved by the machine, by the overlooker, and above all, by the individual bourgeois manufacturer himself. The more openly this despotism proclaims gain to be its end and aim, the more petty, the more hateful and the more embittering it is. 32

The less the skill and exertion or strength implied in manual labor, in other words, the more modern industry becomes developed, the more is the labor of men superseded by that of women. Differences of age and sex have no longer any distinctive social validity for the working class. All are instruments of labor, more or less expensive to use, according to their age and sex. 33

No sooner is the exploitation of the laborer by the manufacturer, so far at an end, that he receives his wages in cash, than he is set upon by the other portions of the bourgeoisie, the landlord, the shopkeeper, the pawnbroker, etc. 34

The lower strata of the middle class—the small tradespeople, shopkeepers and retired tradesmen generally, the handicraftsmen and peasants—all these sink gradually into the proletariat, partly because their diminutive capital does not suffice for the scale on which Modern Industry is carried on, and is swamped in the competition with the large capitalists, partly because their specialized skill is rendered worthless by new methods of production. Thus the proletariat is recruited from all classes of the population. 35

KARL MARX

The proletariat goes through various states of development.
With its birth begins its struggle with the bourgeoisie. At first the
contest is carried on by individual laborers, then by the workpeople
of a factory, then by the operatives of one trade, in one locality, against
the individual bourgeois who directly exploits them. They direct their
attacks not against the bourgeois conditions of production, but against
the instruments of production themselves; they destroy imported
wares that compete with their labor, they smash to pieces machinery,
they set factories ablaze, they seek to restore by force the vanished
status of the workman of the Middle Ages.

At this stage the laborers still form an incoherent mass scat- 37
tered over the whole country, and broken up by their mutual competition. If anywhere they unite to form more compact bodies, this is
not yet the consequence of their own active union, but of the union
of the bourgeoisie, which class, in order to attain its own political
ends, is compelled to set the whole proletariat in motion, and is moreover yet, for a time, able to do so. At this stage, therefore, the proletarians do not fight their enemies, but the enemies of their enemies,
the remnants of absolute monarchy, the landowners, the non-indus-
trial bourgeois, the petty bourgeoisie. Thus the whole historical movement is concentrated in the hands of the bourgeoisie, every victory so
obtained is a victory for the bourgeoisie.

But with the development of industry the proletariat not only 38
increases in number; it becomes concentrated in greater masses, its
strength grows and it feels that strength more. The various interests
and conditions of life within the ranks of the proletariat are more and
more equalized, in proportion as machinery obliterates all distinctions
of labor, and nearly everywhere reduces wages to the same low level.
The growing competition among the bourgeois, and the resulting
commercial crises, make the wages of the workers even more fluc-
tuating. The unceasing improvement of machinery, ever more rapidly
developing, makes their livelihood more and more precarious; the collisions between individual workmen and individual bourgeois take
more and more the character of collisions between two classes. Thereupon the workers begin to form combinations (Trades' Unions)
against the bourgeois; they club together in order to keep up the rate
of wages; they found permanent associations in order to make provision beforehand for these occasional revolts. Here and there the contest breaks out into riots.

Now and then the workers are victorious, but only for a time. 39
The real fruit of their battle lies not in the immediate result but in the
ever-expanding union of workers. This union is helped on by the improved means of communication that are created by modern industry,
and that places the workers of different localities in contact with one
another. It was just this contact that was needed to centralize the nu-

merous local struggles, all of the same character, into one national struggle between classes. But every class struggle is a political struggle. And that union, to attain which the burghers of the Middle Ages with their miserable highways, required centuries, the modern proletarians, thanks to railways, achieve in a few years.

This organization of the proletarians into a class, and consequently into a political party, is continually being upset again by the competition between the workers themselves. But it ever rises up again, stronger, firmer, mightier. It compels legislative recognition of particular interests of the workers by taking advantage of the divisions among the bourgeoisie itself. Thus the ten hours' bill in England was carried. 40

Altogether collisions between the classes of the old society further, in many ways, the course of development of the proletariat. The bourgeoisie finds itself involved in a constant battle. At first with the aristocracy; later on, with those portions of the bourgeoisie itself whose interests have become antagonistic to the progress of industry; at all times, with the bourgeoisie of foreign countries. In all these battles it sees itself compelled to appeal to the proletariat, to ask for its help, and thus, to drag it into the political arena. The bourgeoisie itself, therefore, supplies the proletariat with its own elements of political and general education; in other words, it furnishes the proletariat with weapons for fighting the bourgeoisie. 41

Further, as we have already seen, entire sections of the ruling class are, by the advance of industry, precipitated into the proletariat, or are at least threatened in their conditions of existence. These also supply the proletariat with fresh elements of enlightenment and progress. 42

Finally, in times when the class-struggle nears the decisive hour, the process of dissolution going on within the ruling class—in fact, within the whole range of an old society—assumes such a violent, glaring character that a small section of the ruling class cuts itself adrift and joins the revolutionary class, the class that holds the future in its hands. Just as, therefore, at an earlier period, a section of the nobility went over to the bourgeoisie, so now a portion of the bourgeoisie goes over to the proletariat, and in particular a portion of the bourgeoisie ideologists, who have raised themselves to the level of comprehending theoretically the historical movements as a whole. 43

Of all the classes that stand face to face with the bourgeoisie to-day the proletariat alone is a really revolutionary class. The other classes decay and finally disappear in the face of modern industry; the proletariat is its special and essential product. 44

The lower middle class, the small manufacturer, the shopkeeper, the artisan, the peasant, all these fight against the bourgeoisie, to save from extinction their existence as fractions of the middle class. 45

KARL MARX

They are therefore not revolutionary, but conservative. Nay more; they are reactionary, for they try to roll back the wheel of history. If by chance they are revolutionary, they are so only in view of their impending transfer into the proletariat; they thus defend not their present, but their future interests; they desert their own standpoint to place themselves at that of the proletariat.

The "dangerous class," the social scum, that passively rotting 46 mass thrown off by the lowest layers of old society, may, here and there, be swept into the movement by a proletarian revolution; its conditions of life, however, prepare it far more for the part of a bribed tool of reactionary intrigue.

In the conditions of the proletariat, those of the old society at 47 large are already virtually swamped. The proletarian is without property; his relation to his wife and children has no longer anything in common with the bourgeois family relations; modern industrial labor, modern subjection to capital, the same in England as in France, in America as in Germany, has stripped him of every trace of national character. Law, morality, religion, are to him so many bourgeois prejudices, behind which lurk in ambush just as many bourgeois interests.

All the preceding classes that got the upper hand sought to 48 fortify their already acquired status by subjecting society at large to their conditions of appropriation. The proletarians cannot become masters of the productive forces of society, except by abolishing their own previous mode of appropriation, and thereby also every other previous mode of appropriation. They have nothing of their own to secure and to fortify; their mission is to destroy all previous securities for and insurances of individual property.

All previous historical movements were movements of mi- 49 norities, or in the interest of minorities. The proletarian movement is the self-conscious, independent movement of the immense majority. The proletariat, the lowest stratum of our present society, cannot stir, cannot raise itself up without the whole superincumbent strata of official society being sprung into the air.

Though not in substance, yet in form, the struggle of the pro- 50 letariat with the bourgeoisie is at first a national struggle. The proletariat of each country must, of course, first of all settle matters with its own bourgeoisie.

In depicting the most general phases of the development of 51 the proletariat, we traced the more or less veiled civil war, raging within existing society, up to the point where that war breaks out into open revolution and where the violent overthrow of the bourgeoisie, lays the foundations for the sway of the proletariat.

Hitherto every form of society has been based, as we have 52 already seen, on the antagonism of oppressing and oppressed classes. But in order to oppress a class, certain conditions must be assured to it under which it can, at least, continue its slavish existence. The serf, in the period of serfdom, raised himself to membership in the commune, just as the petty bourgeois, under the yoke to feudal absolutism, managed to develop into a bourgeois. The modern laborer, on the contrary, instead of rising with the progress of industry, sinks deeper and deeper below the conditions of existence of his own class. He becomes a pauper, and pauperism develops more rapidly than population and wealth. And here it becomes evident that the bourgeoisie is unfit any longer to be the ruling class in society, and to impose its conditions of existence upon society as an over-riding law. It is unfit to rule, because it is incompetent to assure an existence to its slave within his slavery, because it cannot help letting him sink into such a state that it has to feed him, instead of being fed by him. Society can no longer live under this bourgeoisie; in other words, its existence is no longer compatible with society.

The essential condition for the existence, and for the sway of 53 the bourgeois class is the formation and augmentation of capital; the condition for capital is wage labor. Wage labor rests exclusively on competition between the laborers. The advance of industry, whose involuntary promoter is the bourgeoisie, replaces the isolation of the laborers, due to competition, by their involuntary combination, due to association. The development of Modern Industry, therefore, cuts from under its feet the very foundation on which the bourgeoisie produces and appropriates products. What the bourgeoisie therefore produces, above all, are its own grave diggers. Its fall and the victory of the proletariat are equally inevitable.

COMPREHENSION

1. What is Marx's primary intention in this selection? How do you know?

2. On what concept is Marx's economic history predicated? How did bourgeois society come into existence? What are the sins of the bourgeoisie? Why did the modern proletariat arise? How did it develop in relation to the bourgeoisie?

3. Explain the relationship of capital to class struggle.

RHETORIC

1. What extended metaphor does Marx develop to describe the proletariat? Why is it particularly insightful? Cite other instances of figurative language in the essay.

2. Cite examples of words or phrases that Marx uses for both their intellectual and emotive value. What do they contribute to the overall tone of the essay?

3. How does the author develop the main contrast in this essay? What is his central purpose?

4. Demonstrate by reference to various paragraphs the ways in which Marx supports generalizations through the use of specific examples.

5. What are the strengths and weaknesses of this selection as a form of argumentation?

6. Does the last paragraph seem fully justified by the preceding analysis? Explain.

WRITING

1. Do you agree or disagree with Marx's thesis that history is predicated on ecnonomic class struggles? Justify your answer.

2. Compare and contrast various conflicting groups, as you perceive them, in contemporary economic history.

3. Argue for or against Marx's assertion that the revolution of the proletariat against the bourgeoisie and the capitalist system is inevitable.

4. Develop your own "manifesto," outlining the ideal economic system for humanity.

Language, Writing, and Communication

HENRY DAVID THOREAU

On Keeping a Private Journal

Henry David Thoreau (1817–1862), author of the masterpiece Walden *(1854), is one of the most important figures in American thought and literature. A social and political activist, Thoreau opposed the Mexican War, protested slavery, and refused to pay his poll taxes. As a naturalist, he believed in the preeminence of individualism and nature over technology, materialism, and nationalism. In 1845, he went to live at Walden Pond, "living deep and sucking the marrow out of life." Thoreau began writing a journal in 1837, and he used his journals to write his two most famous books,* A Week on the Concord and Merrimack Rivers *(1849) and* Walden. *No wonder that Thoreau, as he explains below at the age of 18, valued journal keeping.*

 s those pieces which the painter sketches for his own 1
amusement in his leisure hours, are often superior to his
most elaborate productions, so it is that ideas often suggest themselves to us spontaneously, as it were, far surpassing in beauty those which arise in the mind upon applying ourselves to any particular subject. Hence, could a machine be invented

350

which would instantaneously arrange on paper each idea as it occurs to us, without any exertion on our part, how extremely useful would it be considered! The relation between this and the practice of keeping a journal is obvious. But yet, the preservation of our scattered thoughts is to be considered an object but of minor importance.

Every one can think, but comparatively few can write, can express their thoughts. Indeed, how often do we hear one complain of his inability to express what he feels! How many have occasion to make the following remark, "I am sensible that I understand this perfectly, but am not able to find words to convey my idea to others."

But if each one would employ a certain portion of each day in looking back upon the time which has passed, and in writing down his thoughts and feelings, in reckoning up his daily gains, that he may be able to detect whatever false coins have crept into his coffers, and, as it were, in settling accounts with his mind, not only would his daily experience be greatly increased, since his feelings and ideas would thus be more clearly defined, but he would be ready to turn over a new leaf, having carefully perused the preceding one, and would not continue to glance carelessly over the same page, without being able to distinguish it from a new one.

Most of us are apt to neglect the study of our own characters, thoughts, and feelings, and for the purpose of forming our own minds, look to others, who should merely be considered as different editions of the same great work. To be sure, it would be well for us to examine the various copies, that we might detect any errors, but yet, it would be foolish for one to borrow a work which he possessed himself, but had not perused.

In fine, if we endeavoured more to improve ourselves by reflection, by making a business of thinking, and giving our thoughts form and expression, we should be led to "read not to contradict and confute, nor to believe and take for granted, nor to find talk and discourse, but to weigh and consider."

COMPREHENSION

1. Does this selection have an explicitly stated thesis? Explain.

2. What reasons does Thoreau give for writing a journal?

3. Why does Thoreau value reflection? How does a journal forward that goal?

RHETORIC

1. There are several metaphors, excluding the extended metaphor in paragraphs 3 and 4. Identify them. What do they have in common?

2. Do you believe that this essay is written in the typical style of a journal? If not, how does it differ? If so, how is it similar?

3. What evidence can you offer that this is an argumentative or persuasive essay?

4. Explain the analogy that introduces the essay. How does this analogy help Thoreau introduce his subject?

5. An extended metaphor is crucial to the development of this essay. Identify the metaphor, and explain how it contributes to the organization of the essay.

6. Divide this essay into two parts. Where did you divide it, and why?

WRITING

1. Do you feel you do your best thinking when you write? What other devices, such as tape recorders, help you think? In an essay, examine the connection between thinking and writing.

2. For the next week, write a daily record of your life in journal form.

3. Write an essay on the value of keeping a private journal.

JOAN DIDION

On Keeping a Notebook

Joan Didion (1934–   ) grew up in California and graduated from the University of California at Berkeley in 1956. She began her career writing for national magazines such as Mademoiselle, Saturday Evening Post, *and* Life. *Didion published her first novel,* Run River, *in 1963. Although she has continued to write novels and has written several screenplays, her most acclaimed work is in nonfiction. This work includes* Slouching Towards Bethlehem *(1968),* The White Album *(1979),* Salvador *(1983),* Democracy *(1984), and* Miami *(1987). Didion is an intensely introspective writer who in her essays attempts to draw significance from the particulars of her own life. In this essay, she describes one of the sources of her work—her own notebooks.*

hat woman Estelle,' " the note reads, " 'is partly the rea-   1
son why George Sharp and I are separated today.' *Dirty crepe-de-Chine wrapper, hotel bar, Wilmington RR, 9:45 a.m. August Monday morning.''*

Since the note is in my notebook, it presumably has some   2
meaning to me. I study it for a long while. At first I have only the

most general notion of what I was doing on an August Monday morning in the bar of the hotel across from the Pennsylvania Railroad station in Wilmington, Delaware (waiting for a train? missing one? 1960? 1961? why Wilmington?), but I do remember being there. The woman in the dirty crepe-de-Chine wrapper had come down from her room for a beer, and the bartender had heard before the reason why George Sharp and she were separated today. "Sure," he said, and went on mopping the floor. "You told me." At the other end of the bar is a girl. She is talking, pointedly, not to the man beside her but to a cat lying in the triangle of sunlight cast through the open door. She is wearing a plaid silk dress from Peck & Peck, and the hem is coming down.

Here is what it is: the girl has been on the Eastern Shore, and now she is going back to the city, leaving the man beside her, and all she can see ahead are the viscous summer sidewalks and the 3 a.m. long-distance calls that will make her lie awake and then sleep drugged through all the steaming mornings left in August (1960? 1961?). Because she must go directly from the train to lunch in New York, she wishes that she had a safety pin for the hem of the plaid silk dress, and she also wishes that she could forget about the hem and the lunch and stay in the cool bar that smells of disinfectant and malt and make friends with the woman in the crepe-de-Chine wrapper. She is afflicted by a little self-pity, and she wants to compare Estelles. That is what that was all about. 3

Why did I write it down? In order to remember, of course, but exactly what was it I wanted to remember? How much of it actually happened? Did any of it? Why do I keep a notebook at all? It is easy to deceive oneself on all those scores. The impulse to write things down is a peculiarly compulsive one, inexplicable to those who do not share it, useful only accidentally, only secondarily, in the way that any compulsion tries to justify itself. I suppose that it begins or does not begin in the cradle. Although I have felt compelled to write things down since I was five years old, I doubt that my daughter ever will, for she is a singularly blessed and accepting child, delighted with life exactly as life presents itself to her, unafraid to go to sleep and unafraid to wake up. Keepers of private notebooks are a different breed altogether, lonely and resistant rearrangers of things, anxious malcontents, children afflicted apparently at birth with some presentiment of loss. 4

My first notebook was a Big Five tablet, given to me by my mother with the sensible suggestion that I stop whining and learn to amuse myself by writing down my thoughts. She returned the tablet to me a few years ago; the first entry is an account of a woman who believed herself to be freezing to death in the Arctic night, only to find, when day broke, that she had stumbled onto the Sahara Desert, 5 where she would die of the heat before lunch. I have no idea what turn of a five-year-old's mind could have prompted so insistently "ironic" and exotic a story, but it does reveal a certain predilection for the extreme which has dogged me into adult life; perhaps if I were analytically inclined I would find it a truer story than any I might have told about Donald Johnson's birthday party or the day my cousin Brenda put Kitty Litter in the aquarium.

So the point of my keeping a notebook has never been, nor is 6 it now, to have an accurate factual record of what I have been doing or thinking. That would be a different impulse entirely, an instinct for reality which I sometimes envy but do not possess. At no point have I ever been able successfully to keep a diary; my approach to daily life ranges from the grossly negligent to the merely absent, and on those few occasions when I have tried dutifully to record a day's events, boredom has so overcome me that the results are mysterious at best. What is this business about "shopping, typing piece, dinner with E, depressed"? Shopping for what? Typing what piece? Who is E? Was this "E" depressed, or was I depressed? Who cares?

In fact I have abandoned altogether that kind of pointless en- 7 try; instead I tell what some would call lies. "That's simply not true," the members of my family frequently tell me when they come up against my memory of a shared event. "The party was *not* for you, the spider was *not* a black widow, *it wasn't that way at all*." Very likely they are right, for not only have I always had trouble distinguishing between what happened and what merely might have happened, but I remain unconvinced that the distinction, for my purposes, matters. The cracked crab that I recall having for lunch the day my father came home from Detroit in 1945 must certainly be embroidery, worked into the day's pattern to lend verisimilitude; I was ten years old and would not now remember the cracked crab. The day's events did not turn on cracked crab. And yet it is precisely that fictitious crab that makes me see the afternoon all over again, a home movie run all too often, the father bearing gifts, the child weeping, an exercise in family love and guilt. Or that is what it was to me. Similarly, perhaps it never did snow that August in Vermont; perhaps there never were flurries in the night wind, and maybe no one else felt the ground hardening and summer already dead even as we pretended to bask in it, but that was how it felt to me, and it might as well have snowed, could have snowed, did snow.

How it felt to me: that is getting closer to the truth about a 8 notebook. I sometimes delude myself about why I keep a notebook, imagine that some thrifty virtue derives from preserving everything observed. See enough and write it down, I tell myself, and then some morning when the world seems drained of wonder, some day when I am only going through the motions of doing what I am supposed to do, which is write—on that bankrupt morning I will simply open my notebook and there it will all be, a forgotten account with accumulated interest, paid passage back to the world out there: dialogue overheard in hotels and elevators and at the hatcheck counter in Pavillon (one middle-aged man shows his hatcheck to another and says, "That's my old football number"); impressions of Bettina Aptheker and Benjamin Sonnenberg and Teddy ("Mr. Acapulco") Stauffer; careful *apercus* about tennis bums and failed fashion models and Greek shipping heiresses, one of whom taught me a significant lesson (a lesson I could have learned from F. Scott Fitzgerald, but perhaps we all must meet the very rich for ourselves) by asking, when I arrived to interview her in her orchid-filled sitting room on the second day of a paralyzing New York blizzard, whether it was snowing outside.

I imagine, in other words, that the notebook is about other 9 people. But of course it is not. I have no real business with what one stranger said to another at the hat-check counter in Pavillon; in fact I suspect that the line "That's my old football number" touched not my own imagination at all, but merely some memory of something once read, probably "The Eighty-Yard Run." Nor is my concern with a woman in a dirty crepe-de-Chine wrapper in a Wilmington bar. My stake is always, of course, in the unmentioned girl in the plaid silk dress. *Remember what it was to be me:* that is always the point.

It is a difficult point to admit. We are brought up in the ethic 10 that others, any others, all others, are by definition more interesting than ourselves; taught to be diffident, just this side of self-effacing. ("You're the least important person in the room and don't forget it," Jessica Mitford's governess would hiss in her ear on the advent of any social occasion; I copied that into my notebook because it is only recently that I have been able to enter a room without hearing some such phrase in my inner ear.) Only the very young and the very old may recount their dreams at breakfast, dwell upon self, interrupt with memories of beach picnics and favorite Liberty lawn dresses and the rainbow trout in a creek near Colorado Springs. The rest of us are expected, rightly, to affect absorption in other people's favorite dresses, other people's trout.

And so we do. But our notebooks give us away, for however 11 dutifully we record what we see around us, the common denominator of all we see is always, transparently, shamelessly, the implacable "I." We are not talking here about the kind of notebook that is patently for public consumption, a structural conceit for binding together a series of graceful *pensées*; we are talking about something private, about bits of the mind's string too short to use, an indiscriminate and erratic assemblage with meaning only for its maker.

And sometimes even the maker has difficulty with the mean- 12 ing. There does not seem to be for example, any point in my knowing for the rest of my life that, during 1964, 720 tons of soot fell on every square mile of New York City, yet there it is in my notebook, labeled "FACT." Nor do I really need to remember that Ambrose Bierce liked to spell Leland Stanford's name "£eland $tanford" or that "smart women almost always wear black in Cuba," a fashion hint without much potential for practical application. And does not the relevance of these notes seem marginal at best?

> In the basement museum of the Inyo County Courthouse in Independence, California, sign pinned to a mandarin coat: "This MANDARIN COAT was often worn by Mrs. Minnie S. Brooks when giving lectures on her TEAPOT COLLECTION." Redhead getting out of car in front of Beverly Wilshire Hotel, chinchilla stole, Vuitton bags with tags reading:
>
> MRS. LOU FOX
> HOTEL SAHARA
> VEGAS

Well, perhaps not entirely marginal. As a matter of fact, Mrs. Minnie S. Brooks and her MANDARIN COAT pull me back into my own childhood, for although I never knew Mrs. Brooks and did not visit Inyo County until I was thirty, I grew up in just such a world, in houses cluttered with Indian relics and bits of gold ore and ambergris and the souvenirs my Aunt Mercy Farnsworth brought back from the Orient. It is a long way from that world to Mrs. Lou Fox's world, where we all live now, and is it not just as well to remember that? Might not Mrs. Minnie S. Brooks help me to remember what I am? Might not Mrs. Lou Fox help me to remember what I am not?

But sometimes the point is harder to discern. What exactly did I have in mind when I noted down that it cost the father of someone I know $650 a month to light the place on the Hudson in which he lived before the Crash? What use was I planning to make of this line by Jimmy Hoffa: "I may have my faults, but being wrong ain't one of them"? And although I think it interesting to know where the girls who travel with the Syndicate have their hair done when they find themselves on the West Coast, will I ever make suitable use of it? Might I not be better off just passing it on to John O'Hara? What is a recipe for sauerkraut doing in my notebook? What kind of magpie keeps this notebook? *"He was born the night the Titanic went down."* That seems a nice enough line, and I even recall who said it, but is it not really a better line in life than it could ever be in fiction?

But of course that is exactly it: not that I should ever use the line, but that I should remember the woman who said it and the afternoon I heard it. We were on her terrace by the sea, and we were finishing the wine left from lunch, trying to get what sun there was,

JOAN DIDION

a California winter sun. The woman whose husband was born the night the *Titanic* went down wanted to rent her house, wanted to go back to her children in Paris. I remember wishing that I could afford the house, which cost $1,000 a month. "Someday you will," she said lazily. "Someday it all comes." There in the sun on her terrace it seemed easy to believe in someday, but later I had a low-grade afternoon hangover and ran over a black snake on the way to the supermarket and was flooded with inexplicable fear when I heard the checkout clerk explaining to the man ahead of me why she was finally divorcing her husband. "He left me no choice," she said over and over as she punched the register. "He has a little seven-month-old baby by her, he left me no choice." I would like to believe that my dread then was for the human condition, but of course it was for me, because I wanted a baby and did not then have one and because I wanted to own the house that cost $1,000 a month to rent and because I had a hangover.

It all comes back. Perhaps it is difficult to see the value in 16
having one's self back in that kind of mood, but I do see it; I think we are well advised to keep on nodding terms with the people we used to be whether we find them attractive company or not. Otherwise they turn up unannounced and surprise us, come hammering on the mind's door at 4 a.m. of a bad night and demand to know who deserted them, who betrayed them, who is going to make amends. We forget all too soon the things we thought we could never forget. We forget the loves and the betrayals alike, forget what we whispered and what we screamed, forget who we were. I have already lost touch with a couple of people I used to be; one of them, a seventeen-year-old, presents little threat, although it would be of some interest to me to know again what it feels like to sit on a river levee drinking vodka-and-orange-juice and listening to Les Paul and Mary Ford and their echoes sing "How High the Moon" on the car radio. (You see I still have the scenes, but I no longer perceive myself among those present, no longer could even improvise the dialogue.) The other one, a twenty-three-year-old, bothers me more. She was always a good deal of trouble, and I suspect she will reappear when I least want to see her, skirts too long, shy to the point of aggravation, always the injured party, full of recriminations and little hurts and stories I do not want to hear again, at once saddening me and angering me with her vulnerability and ignorance, an apparition all the more insistent for being so long banished.

It is a good idea, then, to keep in touch, and I suppose that 17
keeping in touch is what notebooks are all about. And we are all on our own when it comes to keeping those lines open to ourselves: your notebook will never help me, nor mine you. "*So what's new in the whiskey business?*" What could that possibly mean to you? To me it

ON KEEPING A NOTEBOOK

357

means a blonde in a Pucci bathing suit sitting with a couple of fat men by the pool at the Beverly Hills Hotel. Another man approaches, and they all regard one another in silence for a while. "So what's new in the whiskey business?" one of the fat men finally says by way of welcome, and the blonde stands up, arches one foot and dips it in the pool, looking all the while at the cabana where Baby Pignatari is talking on the telephone. That is all there is to that, except that several years later I saw the blonde coming out of Saks Fifth Avenue in New York with her California complexion and a voluminous mink coat. In the harsh wind that day she looked old and irrevocably tired to me, and even the skins in the mink coat were not worked the way they were doing them that year, not the way she would have wanted them done, and there is the point of the story. For a while after that I did not like to look in the mirror, and my eyes would skim the newspapers and pick out only the deaths, the cancer victims, the premature coronaries, the suicides, and I stopped riding the Lexington Avenue IRT because I noticed for the first time that all the strangers I had seen for years—the man with the seeing-eye dog, the spinster who read the classified pages every day, the fat girl who always got off with me at Grand Central—looked older than they once had.

It all comes back. Even that recipe for sauerkraut: even that   18 brings it back. I was on Fire Island when I first made that sauerkraut, and it was raining, and we drank a lot of bourbon and ate the sauerkraut and went to bed at ten, and I listened to the rain and the Atlantic and felt safe. I made the sauerkraut again last night and it did not make me feel any safer, but that is, as they say, another story.

COMPREHENSION

1. Why does Didion mention "keeping" a notebook in her title? How is her essay about keeping rather than writing a notebook?

2. What sort of entries does Didion make in her notebooks? How and why does Didion alter the reality of the events she described in her notebooks?

3. What are the various reasons Didion explores for keeping a notebook? What is her purpose in examining so many possible reasons?

RHETORIC

1. What is the function of the numerous rhetorical questions in the essay?

2. How does the style of Didion's notebooks differ from her regular writing style?

3. How do the introductory quote and other quotes from her notebook help Didion develop the theme of her essay?

4. Repetition is a key device used to unify the essay. Identify examples of important repetitions.

5. Identify topic sentences in the essay. How does Didion prepare us for the thesis through her topic sentences?

6. Analyze causal patterns of development that appear in the essay.

WRITING

1. If you were to keep a notebook, what would you record in it? Why whould you keep it? Write a brief essay on this topic.

2. Write an essay about some events that have occurred in your own past that you feel were significant to your growth.

3. Didion speaks of "lying" or "embroidery" in recounting events. Write an essay about an episode in your life that you like to embellish.

DONALD M. MURRAY

The Maker's Eye: Revising Your Own Manuscripts

Donald M. Murray (1924–   ) was born and raised in Boston. After graduating from Boston University, he worked as a reporter for the Boston Herald, *and he received a Pulitzer Prize in 1954. He later joined* Time *magazine as a contributing editor but turned to teaching, becoming professor of English at the University of New Hampshire. He has published several hundred articles in the* Saturday Evening Post *and the* Reader's Digest. *He has also published several books on writing, including* Writing for Your Readers *(1983),* Read to Write *(1986), and* Write to Learn *(1987). In this essay, Murray explores the often arduous process that goes into the completion of a manuscript and reveals that even the most experienced writers must often grapple with the basics of writing.*

When students complete a first draft, they consider the job   1
of writing done—and their teachers too often agree. When professional writers complete a first draft, they usually feel that they are at the start of the writing process. When a draft is completed, the job of writing can begin.

That difference in attitude is the difference between amateur   2
and professional, inexperience and experience, journeyman and craftsman. Peter F. Drucker, the prolific business writer, calls his first draft

THE MAKER'S EYE: REVISING YOUR OWN MANUSCRIPTS   **359**

"the zero draft"—after that he can start counting. Most writers share the feeling that the first draft, and all of those which follow, are opportunities to discover what they have to say and how best they can say it.

To produce a progression of drafts, each of which says more 3 and says it more clearly, the writer has to develop a special kind of reading skill. In school we are taught to decode what appears on the page as finished writing. Writers, however, face a different category of possibility and responsibility when they read their own drafts. To them the words on the page are never finished. Each can be changed and rearranged, can set off a chain reaction of confusion or clarified meaning. This is a different kind of reading, which is possibly more difficult and certainly more exciting.

Writers must learn to be their own best enemy. They must 4 accept the criticism of others and be suspicious of it; they must accept the praise of others and be even more suspicious of it. Writers cannot depend on others. They must detach themselves from their own pages so that they can apply both their caring and their craft to their own work.

Such detachment is not easy. Science fiction writer Ray Brad- 5 bury supposedly puts each manuscript away for a year to the day and then rereads it as a stranger. Not many writers have the discipline or the time to do this. We must read when our judgment may be at its worst, when we are close to the euphoric moment of creation.

Then the writer, counsels novelist Nancy Hale, "should be 6 critical of everything that seems to him most delightful in his style. He should excise what he most admires, because he wouldn't thus admire it if he weren't . . . in a sense protecting it from criticism." John Ciardi, the poet, adds, "The last act of the writing must be to become one's own reader. It is, I suppose, a schizophrenic process, to begin passionately and to end critically, to begin hot and to end cold; and, more important, to be passion-hot and critic-cold at the same time."

Most people think that the principal problem is that writers 7 are too proud of what they have written. Actually, a greater problem for most professional writers is one shared by the majority of students. They are overly critical, think everything is dreadful, tear up page after page, never complete a draft, see the task as hopeless.

The writer must learn to read critically but constructively, to 8 cut what is bad, to reveal what is good. Eleanor Estes, the children's book author, explains: "The writer must survey his work critically, coolly, as though he were a stranger to it. He must be willing to prune, expertly and hard-heartedly. At the end of each revision, a manuscript may look . . . worked over, torn apart, pinned together, added to, deleted from, words changed and words changed back. Yet the book must maintain its original freshness and spontaneity."

DONALD M. MURRAY

Most readers underestimate the amount of rewriting it usually takes to produce spontaneous reading. This is a great disadvantage to the student writer, who sees only a finished product and never watches the craftsman who takes the necessary step back, studies the work carefully, returns to the task, steps back, returns, steps back, again and again. Anthony Burgess, one of the most prolific writers in the English-speaking world, admits, "I might revise a page twenty times." Roald Dahl, the popular children's writer, states, "By the time I'm nearing the end of a story, the first part will have been reread and altered and corrected at least 150 times. . . . Good writing is essentially rewriting. I am positive of this." 9

Rewriting isn't virtuous. It isn't something that ought to be done. It is simply something that most writers find they have to do to discover what they have to say and how to say it. It is a condition of the writer's life. 10

There are, however, a few writers who do little formal rewriting, primarily because they have the capacity and experience to create and review a large number of invisible drafts in their minds before they approach the page. And some writers slowly produce finished pages, performing all the tasks of revision simultaneously, page by page, rather than draft by draft. But it is still possible to see the sequence followed by most writers most of the time in rereading their own work. 11

Most writers scan their drafts first, reading as quickly as possible to catch the larger problems of subject and form, then move in closer and closer as they read and write, reread and rewrite. 12

The first thing writers look for in their drafts is *information*. They know that a good piece of writing is built from specific, accurate, and interesting information. The writer must have an abundance of information from which to construct a readable piece of writing. 13

Next writers look for *meaning* in the information. The specifics must build to a pattern of significance. Each piece of specific information must carry the reader toward meaning. 14

Writers reading their own drafts are aware of *audience*. They put themselves in the reader's situation and make sure that they deliver information which a reader wants to know or needs to know in a manner which is easily digested. Writers try to be sure that they anticipate and answer the questions a critical reader will ask when reading the piece of writing. 15

Writers make sure that the *form* is appropriate to the subject and the audience. Form, or genre, is the vehicle which carries meaning to the reader, but form cannot be selected until the writer has adequate information to discover its significance and an audience which needs or wants that meaning. 16

Once writers are sure the form is appropriate, they must then 17 look at the *structure*, the order of what they have written. Good writing is built on a solid framework of logic, argument, narrative, or motivation which runs through the entire piece of writing and holds it together. This is the time when many writers find it most effective to outline as a way of visualizing the hidden spine by which the piece of writing is supported.

18 The element on which writers may spend a majority of their time is *development*. Each section of a piece of writing must be adequately developed. It must give readers enough information so that they are satisfied. How much information is enough? That's as difficult as asking how much garlic belongs in a salad. It must be done to taste, but most beginning writers underdevelop, underestimating the reader's hunger for information.

19 As writers solve development problems, they often have to consider questions of *dimension*. There must be a pleasing and effective proportion among all the parts of the piece of writing. There is a continual process of subtracting and adding to keep the piece of writing in balance.

20 Finally, writers have to listen to their own voices. *Voice* is the force which drives a piece of writing forward. It is an expression of the writer's authority and concern. It is what is between the words on the page, what glues the piece of writing together. A good piece of writing is always marked by a consistent, individual voice.

21 As writers read and reread, write and rewrite, they move closer and closer to the page until they are doing line-by-line editing. Writers read their own pages with infinite care. Each sentence, each line, each clause, each phrase, each word, each mark of punctuation, each section of white space between the type has to contribute to the clarification of meaning.

22 Slowly the writer moves from word to word, looking through language to see the subject. As a word is changed, cut, or added, as a construction is rearranged, all the words used before that moment and all those that follow that moment must be considered and reconsidered.

23 Writers often read aloud at this stage of the editing process, muttering or whispering to themselves, calling on the ear's experience with language. Does this sound right—or that? Writers edit, shifting back and forth from eye to page to ear to page. I find I must do this careful editing in short runs, no more than fifteen or twenty minutes at a stretch, or I become too kind with myself. I begin to see what I hope is on the page, not what actually is on the page.

24 This sounds tedious if you haven't done it, but actually it is fun. Making something right is immensely satisfying, for writers begin to learn what they are writing about by writing. Language leads them to meaning, and there is the joy of discovery, of understanding, of

DONALD M. MURRAY

making meaning clear as the writer employs the technical skills of language.

Words have double meanings, even triple and quadruple 25 meanings. Each word has its own potential for connotation and denotation. And when writers rub one word against the other, they are often rewarded with a sudden insight, an unexpected clarification.

The maker's eye moves back and forth from word to phrase 26 to sentence to paragraph to sentence to phrase to word. The maker's eye sees the need for variety and balance, for a firmer structure, for a more appropriate form. It peers into the interior of the paragraph, looking for coherence, unity, and emphasis, which make meaning clear.

I learned something about this process when my first bifocals 27 were prescribed. I had ordered a larger section of the reading portion of the glass because of my work, but even so, I could not contain my eyes within this new limit of vision. And I still find myself taking off my glasses and bending my nose towards the page, for my eyes unconsciously flick back and forth across the page, back to another page, forward to still another, as I try to see each evolving line in relation to every other line.

When does this process end? Most writers agree with the 28 great Russian writer Tolstoy, who said, "I scarcely ever reread my published writings, if by chance I come across a page, it always strikes me: all this must be rewritten; this is how I should have written it."

The maker's eye is never satisfied, for each word has the po- 29 tential to ignite new meaning. This article has been twice written all the way through the writing process, and it was published four years ago. Now it is to be republished in a book. The editors make a few small suggestions, and then I read it with my maker's eye. Now it has been re-edited, re-revised, re-read, re-re-edited, for each piece of writing to the writer is full of potential and alternatives.

A piece of writing is never finished. It is delivered to a dead- 30 line, torn out of the typewriter on demand, sent off with a sense of accomplishment and shame and pride and frustration. If only there were a couple more days, time for just another run at it, perhaps then . . .

COMPREHENSION

1. Is the implied audience for this essay made up of writers? Readers? Students? What attitude does Murray seem to believe his readers have toward writing?

2. Identify the purpose or purposes of the essay.

3. According to Murray, what are the main qualities that distinguish professional writers from student writers? Do they share any problems? Explain.

RHETORIC

1. Murray makes extensive use of the term *maker* for *writer* in the essay. What does this imply about his perception of the professional writer?

2. Review the italicized terms Murray employs in describing the writing process. Do they seem appropriate? Has he left out anything important?

3. What function do the direct quotations serve in the essay?

4. Consider the order of the rewriting steps. Do they seem to follow one another logically? Is there an alternative order that would be just as valid?

5. How does Murray's conclusion reflect his philosophy about writing?

6. In paragraph 18, Murray poses the question, "How much information is enough?" Has Murray provided enough, too little, or too much information on the writing process in this essay?

WRITING

1. What type of writing is Murray referring to in this essay? Is his advice appropriate for all types of writing? Are there any forms of writing that fall outside the purview of this essay? Answer these questions in a brief essay.

2. How would you advise college students to write in order for them to obtain "A" grades? Write an essay describing this process.

3. Many students now use word processors when they write. Write an essay explaining how the use of the word processor facilitates the writing process.

DR. SAMUEL JOHNSON

On the Art of Advertising

Dr. Samuel Johnson (1709–1784) was born in England, the early victim of illness and poverty. He entered Oxford University in 1728 but was forced to withdraw for lack of funds. In 1735, he came to London and began writing essays, poems, and biographies for the Gentleman's Magazine. *He achieved increasing fame through his writings, in particular with the publication of his* Dictionary of the English Language *in 1755. For this work he received the honorary degree from Oxford that became part of his name. Johnson continued to write, publishing* Rasselas *(1759)—a moral romance—and a collection of essays called* The Idler *(1761). He befriended the Scottish lawyer James Boswell,*

*who eventually wrote and published a famous biography of John-
son. Johnson's last work was* Lives of the Poets, *a criticism of
British authors of the preceding 200 years. Although the following essay from a 1759 issue of the* Idler *is over 230 years old,
Johnson's insights and observations are as apt for the world of
advertising as it exists today.*

he practice of appending to the narratives of public 1
transactions more minute and domestic intelligence, and
filling the newspapers with advertisements, has grown
up by slow degrees to its present state.

Genius is shown only by invention. The man who first took 2
advantage of the general curiosity that was excited by a siege or battle,
to betray the readers of news into the knowledge of the shop where
the best puffs and powder were to be sold, was undoubtedly a man
of great sagacity and profound skill in the nature of man. But when
he had once shown the way, it was easy to follow him; and every
man now knows a ready method of informing the public of all that
he desires to buy or sell, whether his wares be material or intellectual;
whether he makes clothes, or teaches the mathematics; whether he be
a tutor that wants a pupil, or a pupil that wants a tutor.

Whatever is common is despised. Advertisements are now so 3
numerous that they are very negligently perused, and it is therefore
become necessary to gain attention by magnificence of promises, and
by eloquence sometimes sublime and sometimes pathetic.

Promise, large promise, is the soul of an advertisement. I re- 4
member a *wash-ball* that had a quality truly wonderful—it gave *an
exquisite edge to the razor.* And there are now to be sold, *for ready money
only,* some *duvets for bed-coverings of down, beyond comparison, superior
to what is called otter-down,* and indeed such, that its *many excellences
cannot be here set forth.* With one excellence we are made acquainted—
it is warmer than four or five blankets, and lighter than one.

There are some, however, that know the prejudice of mankind 5
in favour of modest sincerity. The vender of the *beautifying fluid* sells
a lotion that repels pimples, washes away freckles, smooths the skin,
and plumps the flesh, and yet, with a generous abhorrence of osten-
tation, confesses that it will not *restore the bloom of fifteen to a lady of
fifty.*

The true pathos of advertisements must have sunk deep into 6
the heart of every man that remembers the zeal shown by the seller
of the *anodyne necklace,* for the ease and safety of *poor teething infants,*
and the affection with which he warned every mother that *she would
never forgive herself* if her infant should perish without a necklace.

I cannot but remark to the celebrated author who gave, in his 7
notifications of the camel and dromedary, so many specimens of the

genuine sublime, that there is now arrived another subject yet more worthy of his pen. *A famous Mohawk Indian warrior, who took Dieskaw, the French General prisoner, dressed in the same manner with the native Indians when they go to war, with his face and body painted, with his scalping-knife, tom-axe, and all other implements of war! a sight worthy the curiosity of every true Briton!* This is a very powerful description; but a critic of great refinement would say that it conveys rather *horror* than *terror*. An Indian, dressed as he goes to war, may bring company together; but if he carries the scalping-knife and tom-axe, there are many true Britons that will never be persuaded to see him but through a grate.

It has been remarked by the severer judges that the salutary 8
sorrow of tragic scenes is too soon effaced by the merriment of the epilogue; the same inconvenience arises from the improper disposition of advertisements. The noblest objects may be so associated as to be made ridiculous. The camel and dromedary themselves might have lost much of their dignity between *the true flour of mustard* and the *original Daffy's elixir*; and I could not but feel some indignation when I found this illustrious Indian warrior immediately succeeded by a *fresh parcel of Dublin butter.*

The trade of advertising is now so near to perfection, that it 9
is not easy to propose any improvement. But as every art ought to be exercised in due subordination to the public good, I cannot but propose it as a moral question to these masters of the public ear, Whether they do not sometimes play too wantonly with our passions, as when the registrar of lottery tickets invites us to his shop by an account of the prizes which he sold last year; and whether the advertising controvertists do not indulge asperity of language without any adequate provocation; as in the dispute about *straps for razors*, now happily subsided, and in the altercation which at present subsists concerning *eau de luce?*

In an advertisement it is allowed to every man to speak well 10
of himself, but I know not why he should assume the privilege of censuring his neighbour. He may proclaim his own virtue or skill, but ought not to exclude others from the same pretensions.

Every man that advertises his own excellence should write 11
with some consciousness of a character which dares to call the attention of the public. He should remember that his name is to stand in the same paper with those of the King of Prussia and the Emperor of Germany, and endeavour to make himself worthy of such association.

Some regard is likewise to be paid to posterity. There are men 12
of diligence and curiosity who treasure up the papers of the day merely because others neglect them, and in time they will be scarce. When these collections shall be read in another century, how will

DR. SAMUEL JOHNSON

numberless contradictions be reconciled; and how shall fame be possibly distributed among the tailors and bodice-makers of the present age?

Surely these things deserve consideration. It is enough for me 13 to have hinted my desire that these abuses may be rectified; but such is the state of nature, that what all have the right of doing, many will attempt without sufficient care or due qualifications.

COMPREHENSION

1. Is Johnson using irony in his title by calling advertising an "art"? What does he mean by this? What other examples of irony occur in the essay?

2. What is Johnson's main concern about the influence of advertising? Where in the essay does he enunciate this concern?

3. What is the author's main purpose? Where does he state it?

RHETORIC

1. Study the following sentence from paragraph 2. What aspects of its vocabulary, syntax, or tone "date" the writing style? "But when he had once shown the way, it was easy to follow him; and every man now knows a ready method of informing the public of all that he desires to buy or sell, whether his wares be material or intellectual; whether he makes clothes, or teaches the mathematics; whether he be a tutor that wants a pupil, or a pupil that wants a tutor."

2. How do the following words contribute to the diction of the essay: *sagacity, magnificence, pathos, sublime*, and *altercation*.

3. What seems to be Johnson's tone? What is his particular attitude toward the "art of advertising"? Cite examples to support your view.

4. How does Johnson's introduction prepare you for his essay? Why does it conceal his point of view on the subject?

5. In paragraph 13, Johnson refers to the "abuses" of advertising. What are these abuses? Where in the essay does he begin to enumerate them?

6. What is the function of using italics for many of the words and phrases?

WRITING

1. How apt are Johnson's criticisms of advertising today? Are they any less or more valid than they were in Johnson's time?

2. Select several print advertisements from newspapers and magazines. Write an essay discussing the various techniques the advertiser uses in his or her attempt to persuade the reader.

 ON THE ART OF ADVERTISING

S. I. HAYAKAWA

Words and Children

Samuel Ichize Hayakawa (1906–   ) began his career as a professor of linguistics and was the author of numerous books on languages, such as Language in Thought and Action *(1941),* Our Language and Our World *(1959), and* Symbol, Status, and Personality *(1963). When Hayakawa became president of San Francisco State College, student unrest was at its height. By defending traditional values and, indeed, authority itself, Hayakawa became a national and controversial figure. His notoriety propelled him into the United States Senate. The present essay reflects his original career as a semanticist.*

hose who still believe, after all the writing that semanticists have done, that semantics is a science of words, may be surprised to learn that semantics has the effect—at least, it has had on me and on many others—of reducing rather than increasing one's preoccupation with words. First of all, there is that vast area of nonverbal communication with children that we accomplish through holding, touching, rocking, caressing our children, putting food in their mouths, and all of the little attentions that we give them. These are all communication, and we communicate in this way for a long time before the children even start to talk.

Then, after they start to talk, there is always the problem of interpretation. There is a sense in which small children are recent immigrants in our midst. They have trouble both in understanding and in using the language, and they often make errors. Many people (you can notice this in the supermarkets, especially with parents of two- and three-year-old children) get angry at their children when they don't seem to mind. Anyone standing within earshot of one of these episodes can tell that the child just hasn't understood what the mother said. But the mother feels, "Well, I said it, didn't I? What's wrong with the child that he doesn't understand? It's English, isn't it?" But, as I say, the child is a recent immigrant in our midst and there are things that the child doesn't understand.

There are curious instances. Once, when our daughter was three years old, she found the bath too hot and she said, "Make it warmer." It took me a moment to figure out that she meant, "Bring the water more nearly to the condition we call warm." It makes perfectly good sense looked at that way. Confronted with unusual formulations such as these which children constantly make, many of us react with incredible lack of imagination. Sometimes children are laughed at for making "silly statements," when it only requires understanding their way of abstracting and their way of formulating their abstractions to see that they are not silly at all.

Children are newcomers to the language. Learning a language 4 isn't just learning words; rules of the language are learned at the same time. Prove this? Very simple. Little children use a past tense like "I runned all the way to the park and I swimmed in the pool." "Runned" and "swimmed" are words they did not hear. They made them up by analogy from other past tenses they had heard. This means that they learned not only the vocabulary, they learned the rule for making the past tense—except that the English language doesn't follow its own rules. And when the child proves himself to be more logical than the English language, we take it out on the child—which is nonsense. Children's language should be listened to with great attentiveness and respect.

Again, when our daughter was three years old, I was pound- 5 ing away at my typewriter in my study and she was drawing pictures on the floor when she suddenly said, "I want to go see the popentole."

I kept typing. 6

Then I stopped and said, "What?!" 7

She said, "I want to see the popentole." 8

"Did you say *popentole*?" 9

I just stopped. It was a puzzle to figure out, but I did. In a 10 few seconds I said, "You mean like last Saturday, you want to go to Lincoln Park and see the totem pole?"

She said, "Yes." 11

And what was so warm about this, so wonderful about it, 12 was that having got her point across she played for another twenty minutes singing to herself, happy that she had communicated. I didn't say to her, "Okay, I'll take you next Sunday to see the popentole." The mere fact that she'd made her point and got it registered was a source of satisfaction to her. And I felt very proud of myself at the time for having understood.

One of the things we tend to overlook in our culture is the 13 tremendous value of the acknowledgment of message. Not, "I agree with you" or "I disagree with you" or "That's a wonderful idea" or "That's a silly idea," but just the acknowledgment, "I know exactly what you've said. It goes on the record. You said that." She said, "I want to go see the totem pole." I said, "Okay, you want to go see the totem pole." The acknowledgment of message says in effect, "I know you're around. I know what you're thinking. I acknowledge your presence."

There is also a sense in which a child understands far more 14 than we suspect. Because a child doesn't understand words too well (and also because his nervous system is not yet deadened by years spent as a lawyer, accountant, advertising executive, or professor of philosophy), a child attends not only to what we say but to everything about us as we say it—tone of voice, gesture, facial expression, bodily tensions, and so on. A child attends to a conversation between grown-ups with the same amazing absorption. Indeed, a child listening is, I hope, like a good psychiatrist listening—or like a good semanticist listening—because she watches not only the words but also the non-verbal events to which words bear, in all too many cases, so uncertain a relationship. Therefore a child is in some matters quite difficult to fool, especially on the subject of one's true attitude toward her. For this reason many parents, without knowing it, are to a greater or lesser degree in the situation of the worried mother who said to the psychiatrist to whom she brought her child, "I tell her a dozen times a day that I love her, but the brat still hates me. Why, doctor?"

"Life in a big city is dangerous," a mother once said to me. 15 "You hear so often of children running thoughtlessly out in the street and being struck by passing cars. They will never learn unless you keep telling them and telling them." This is the communication theory that makes otherwise pleasant men and women into nagging parents: You've got to keep telling them; then you've got to remind them; then tell 'em again. Are there no better ways to teach children not to run out into the street? Of course there are. I think it was done in our family without words.

Whenever my wife crossed the street with our boy Alan—he 16 was then about three—she would come to a stop at the curb whether there was any traffic in sight or not, and look up and down the boulevard before crossing. It soon became a habit. One day I absentmindedly started crossing the street without looking up and down—the street was empty. Alan grabbed my coat and pulled me back on the curb to look up and down before we started out again. Children love to know the right way to do things. They learn by imitation far more than by precept.

The uncritical confidence that many people place in words is 17 a matter of constant amazement to me. When we were living in Chicago there was a concrete courtyard behind our apartment house. I heard a great deal of noise and shouting out there one day, and I looked out and saw a father teaching his boy to ride a bicycle. The father was shouting instructions: "Keep your head up. Now push down with your left foot. Now look out, you're running into the wall. Steer away from it. *Steer away from it!* Now push down with your right foot. Don't fall down!" and so on and so on. The poor boy was trying to keep his balance, manage the bicycle, obey his father's instructions all at the same time, and he looked about as totally confused as it is possible for a little boy to get. One thing we learn from general semantics, if we haven't learned it some other way already, is that

S. I. HAYAKAWA

there are limits to what can be accomplished in words. Learning to ride a bicycle is beyond those limits. Having sensed those limits, we become content to let many things take care of themselves without words. All this makes for a quieter household.

The anthropologist Ray Birdwhistell has undertaken a study 18 that he calls "kinesics,"* which is the systematic examination of gesture and body motion in communication; this is a rich area of concern about which many students of human behavior have been much excited. But there is a danger in going too far in this direction—in going overboard to the extent of saying that words are of *no* importance. There are thousands of things children must know and enjoy that it is not possible for them to get *without* words.

The sense of what one misses through the lack of words has 19 been brought home to us by the fact that our second boy, Mark, now twenty-nine, is seriously mentally retarded. At the age of six he was hardly able to talk at all. Now he talks quite a bit, but his speech is very difficult to understand; members of the family can understand it about half the time. He was always able to understand words with direct physical referents—watch, glass of water, orange juice, record-player, television, and so on. But there are certain things that exist only in words, like the concept of the future. I remember the following incident when he was six years old. He came across a candy bar at ten minutes to twelve when lunch was just about to be served. I tried to take it away from him and said, "Look, Mark, you can have it right after lunch. Don't eat it now. You can have it right after lunch." Well, when he was six all he could understand was that it was being taken away from him *now*, and the idea that there was a future in which he'd have it back was something he just couldn't get at the time. Of course, the concept of futurity developed later, but it took him much longer to develop it than it took the other children.

For human beings, the future, which exists *only in language*, is 20 a wonderful dimension in which to live. That is, human beings can readily endure and even enjoy postponement; the anticipation of future pleasures is itself a pleasure. But futurity is something that has no physical referent like "a glass of water." It exists only in language. Mark's frequent frustrations and rage when he was younger were a constant reminder to us that all the warmth and richness of nonverbal communication, all that we could communicate by holding him and feeding him and patting his head and playing on the floor with him, were not enough for the purpose of human interaction. Organized games of any kind all have linguistically formulated rules. Take an organized game like baseball. Can there be a baseball without language? No, there can't. What's the difference between a ball and a

*Ray Birdwhistell, *Kinesics and Context*. Philadelphia: University of Pennsylvania Press, 1970.

strike? There are linguistically formulated rules by which we define the difference. All systematic games, even much simpler games that children play, have to have a language to formulate the rules. An enormous amount of human life is possible only with language, and without it one is very much impoverished.

COMPREHENSION

1. How does the author encourage readers to understand what *semantics* means? Cite examples.

2. Hayakawa says that as a semanticist he has learned that we don't only communicate through words. What other ways of communication does he mention?

3. Hayakawa also points out some of the advantages of language as a communicative skill. What are they?

RHETORIC

1. Hayakawa uses two metaphors to explain a child's relation to language. What are they?

2. Cite examples of Hayakawa's use of scientific jargon. What does this suggest about the audience for which he is writing?

3. Explain how Hayakawa uses process to develop his essay.

4. Hayakawa makes several statements about communication. What are they? How does he use examples to illustrate these points?

5. Where does Hayakawa use personal examples? How do they contribute to the development of the essay?

6. Explain the importance of paragraphs 3, 14, and 18 to the development of the essay.

WRITING

1. Write an essay describing how we use nonverbal forms of communication, such as signals in sports or streetlights. Consider how we communicate through arts such as music, ballet, and painting.

2. Write an essay about the language of children based on your personal experience.

3. Imagine yourself an immigrant or newcomer to a foreign language. In what ways would you be like a child? Describe the situation in an essay.

S. I. HAYAKAWA

The Processing Process

Russell Baker (1925–   ), Pulitzer Prize-winning humorist and journalist, has written a syndicated column called "The Observer" since 1962. His humor runs from allegorical satires on American politics and taste to witty criticisms of current jargon and slang. Baker's columns have been collected in books such as An American in Washington *(1961),* No Cause for Panic *(1964), and* Poor Russell's Almanac *(1972). He has also written a fine autobiography,* Growing Up *(1982). In this essay, Baker satirizes the word processing revolution.*

F or a long time after going into the writing business, I 1 wrote. It was hard to do. That was before the word processor was invented. Whenever all the writers got together, it was whine, whine, whine. How hard writing was. How they wished they had gone into dry cleaning, stonecutting, anything less toilsome than writing.

Then the word processor was invented, and a few pioneers 2 switched from writing to processing words. They came back from the electronic frontier with glowing reports: "Have seen the future and it works." That sort of thing.

I lack the pioneer's courage. It does not run in my family, a 3 family that arrived on the Atlantic beach 300 years ago, moved 50 yards inland for security against high tides, and has scarcely moved since, except to go to the drugstore. Timid genes have made me. I had no stomach for the word processor.

Still, one cannot hold off forever. My family had given up 4 saddle and stirrups for the automobile, hadn't it? Had given up the candle for the kerosene lamp. I, in fact, used the light bulb without the slightest sense of betraying the solid old American values.

And yet. . . . My trade was writing, not processing words. I 5 feared or detested almost all things that had "processing," "process" or "processed" attached to them. Announcements by airplane personnel that I was in a machine engaged in "final landing process" made my blood run cold. Processed words, I feared, would be as bland as processed cheese.

So I resisted, continued to write, played the old fuddy-duddy 6 progress hater when urged to take the easy way and switch to processing words.

When former writers who had turned to processing words 7 spoke of their marvelous new lives, it was the ease they always emphasized.

So easy—the processing process made life so easy (this was 8 what they always said)—so infinitely easier than writing. Only an idiot—and here I caught glances fraught with meaning—only an idiot would continue to suffer the toil of writing when the ease of processing words was available to be wallowed in.

To shorten a tedious story, I capitulated. Of course I had 9 doubts. For all those years I had worked at writing only because it felt so good when you stopped. If processing words was so easy, would there be any incentive left to write?

Why are we moved to act against our best judgment? Because 10 we fear public abuse and ridicule. Thus the once happy cigarette addict is bullied out of his habit by abuse from health fanatics, and the author scratching away happily with his goose quill puts it aside for a typewriter because he fears the contempt of the young phalanxes crying, "Progress!"

My hesitation about processing words was being noticed by 11 aggressive young persons who had processed words from their cradles and thought the spectacle of someone writing was as quaint as a four-child family. I hated being quaint. I switched to processing words, and—man alive! Talk about easy!

It is so easy, not to mention so much fun—listen, folks, I have 12 just switched right here at the start of this very paragraph you are reading—right there I switched from the old typewriter (talk about goose-quill pen days!) to my word processor, which is now clicking away so quietly and causing me so little effort that I don't think I'll ever want to stop this sentence because—well, why should you want to stop a sentence when you're really well launched into the thing— the sentence, I mean—and it's so easy just to keep her rolling right along and never stop since, anyhow, once you do stop, you are going to have to start another sentence, right?—which means coming up with another idea.

What the great thing—really great thing—really and truly 13 great thing is about processing words like this, which I am now doing, is that at the end, when you are finally finished, with the piece terminated and concluded, not to say ended, done and thoroughly completed to your own personal, idiosyncratic, individual, one-of-a-kind, distinctive taste which is unique to you as a human person, male or female, adult or child, regardless of race, creed or color—at the end which I am now approaching on account of exhausting available paper space the processing has been so easy that I am not feeling the least, slightest, smallest or even somewhat minuscule sensation of tired fatigue exhaustion, as was always felt in the old days of writing when the mechanical machines, not to mention goose-quill pens, were so cumbersomely difficult and hard to work that people were constantly forever easing off on them, thus being trapped into the time-

RUSSELL BAKER

wasting thinking process, which just about does it this week, space-wise, folks.

COMPREHENSION

1. This essay is typical of Baker's newspaper columns. How does the author make his subject matter appeal to a varied audience?

2. What does Baker suggest is the main difference between writing and processing words?

3. What is Baker's "best judgment" about writing? Why does he abandon it?

RHETORIC

1. Give a few instances of Baker's use of metaphor.

2. Explain the allusion to "the young phalanxes" (paragraph 10).

3. What does Baker compare writing to? Is this a formal or informal comparison? Explain.

4. What is Baker's purpose in paragraph 3? Where does his Puritanism reveal itself?

5. Why are paragraphs 12 and 13 so much longer and more verbose than the previous paragraphs? What is Baker's purpose in writing this way? Where does he predict the outcome?

6. How is Baker using illustration as a technique in the essay?

WRITING

1. How serious is Baker in this piece? Does he have any real misgivings about word processing? Are his fears legitimate? Explain in a brief essay.

2. How willing are you to step into the unknown? Are you reluctant to abandon familiar customs and beliefs? Do you have a fear of technological innovation? Write an essay on this topic.

3. If you have had experience with word processing, write your own evaluation of it.

MARY McCARTHY

Names

Mary McCarthy (1912–1989) was born in Seattle, Washington, and attended Vassar College; among her friends at Vassar were future poets Elizabeth Bishop and Muriel Rukeyser. Her second

husband, Edmund Wilson, was the first to encourage her to write fiction. A novelist, journalist, essayist, and literary critic, Mc-Carthy is the author of The Company She Keeps *(1942),* The Groves of Academe *(1952),* Memories of a Catholic Girlhood *(1957),* The Group *(1963), and* Vietnam *(1967), among numerous works. Known for her elegant style and sharp comic wit, Mc-Carthy was a foremost—and controversial—literary figure for more than three decades. In the following essay, she reflects with witty and penetrating vigor on the importance of names at Forest Ridge Convent in Seattle, which she attended as a child.*

A nna Lyons, Mary Louise Lyons, Mary von Phul, Emilie von Phul, Eugenia McLellan, Majorie McPhail, Marie-Louise L'Abbé, Mary Danz, Julia Dodge, Mary Fordyce Blake, Janet Preston—these were the names (I can still tell them over like a rosary) of some of the older girls in the convent: the Virtues and Graces. The virtuous ones wore wide blue or green moire goodconduct ribbons, bandoleer-style, across their blue serge uniforms; the beautiful ones wore rouge and powder or at least were reputed to do so. Our class, the eighth grade, wore pink ribbons (I never got one myself) and had names like Patricia ("Pat") Sullivan, Eileen Donohoe, and Joan Kane. We were inelegant even in this respect; the best name we could show, among us, was Phyllis ("Phil") Chatham, who boasted that her father's name, Ralph, was pronounced "Rafe" as in England.

Names had a great importance for us in the convent, and foreign names, French, German, or plain English (which, to us, were foreign, because of their Protestant sound), bloomed like prize roses among a collection of spuds. Irish names were too common in the school to have any prestige either as surnames (Gallagher, Sheehan, Finn, Sullivan, McCarthy) or as Christian names (Kathleen, Eileen). Anything exotic had value: an "olive" complexion, for example. The pet girl of the convent was a fragile Jewish girl named Susie Lowenstein, who had pale red-gold hair and an exquisite retroussé nose, which, if we had had it, might have been called "pug." We liked her name too and the name of a child in the primary grades: Abbie Stuart Baillargeon. My favorite name, on the whole, though, was Emilie von Phul (pronounced "Pool"); her oldest sister, recently graduated, was called Celeste. Another name that appealed to me was Genevieve Albers, Saint Genevieve being the patron saint of Paris who turned back Attila from the gates of the city.

All these names reflected the still-pioneer character of the Pacific Northwest. I had never heard their like in the parochial school in Minneapolis, where "foreign" extraction, in any case, was something to be ashamed of, the whole drive being toward Americaniza-

MARY McCARTHY

tion of first name and surname alike. The exceptions to this were the Irish, who could vaunt such names as Catherine O'Dea and the name of my second cousin, Mary Catherine Anne Rose Violet McCarthy, while an unfortunate German boy named Manfred was made to suffer for his. But that was Minneapolis. In Seattle, and especially in the convent of the Ladies of the Sacred Heart, foreign names suggested not immigration but emigration—distinguished exile. Minneapolis was a granary; Seattle was a port, which had attracted a veritable Foreign Legion of adventurers—soldiers of fortune, younger sons, gamblers, traders, drawn by the fortunes to be made in virgin timber and shipping and by the Alaska Gold Rush. Wars and revolutions had sent the defeated out to Puget Sound, to start a new life; the latest had been the Russian Revolution, which had shipped us, via Harbin, a Russian colony, complete with restaurant, on Queen Anne Hill. The English names in the convent, when they did not testify to direct English origin, as in the case of "Rafe" Chatham, had come to us from the South and represented a kind of internal exile; such girls as Mary Fordyce Blake and Mary McQueen Street (a class ahead of me; her sister was named Francesca) bore their double-barreled first names like titles of aristocracy from the ante-bellum South. Not all our girls, by any means, were Catholic; some of the very prettiest ones—Julia Dodge and Janet Preston, if I remember rightly—were Protestants. The nuns had taught us to behave with special courtesy to these strangers in our midst; and the whole effect was of some superior hostel for refugees of all the lost causes of the past hundred years. Money could not count for much in such an atmosphere; the fathers and grandfathers of many of our "best" girls were ruined men.

Names, often, were freakish in the Pacific Northwest, partic-   4
ularly girls' names. In the Episcopal boarding school I went to later, in Tacoma, there was a girl called De Vere Utter, and there was a girl called Rocena and another called Hermonie. Was Rocena a mistake for Rowena and Hermonie for Hermoine? And was Vere, as we called her, Lady Clara Vere de Vere? Probably. You do not hear names like those often, in any case, east of the Cascade Mountains; they belong to the frontier, where books and libraries were few and memory seems to have been oral, as in the time of Homer.

Names have more significance for Catholics than they do for   5
other people; Christian names are chosen for the spiritual qualities of the saints they are taken from; Protestants used to name their children out of the Old Testament and now they name them out of novels and plays, whose heroes and heroines are perhaps the new patron saints of a secular age. But with Catholics it is different. The saint a child is named for is supposed to serve, literally, as a model or pattern to imitate; your name is your fortune and it tells you what you are or must be. Catholic children ponder their names for a mystic meaning,

 NAMES

like birthstones; my own, I learned, besides belonging to the Virgin and Saint Mary of Egypt, originally meant "bitter" or "star of the sea." My second name, Thérèse, could dedicate me either to Saint Theresa or to the saint called the Little Flower, Soeur Thérèse of Lisieux, on whom God was supposed to have descended in the form of a shower of roses. At Confirmation, I had added a third name (for Catholics then rename themselves, as most nuns do, yet another time, when they take orders); on the advice of a nun, I had taken "Clementina," after Saint Clement, an early pope—a step I soon regretted on account of "My Darling Clementine" and her number nine shoes. By the time I was in the convent, I would no longer tell anyone what my Confirmation name was. The name I had nearly picked was "Agnes," after a little Roman virgin martyr, always shown with a lamb, because of her purity. But Agnes would have been just as bad, I recognized in Forest Ridge Convent—not only because of the possibility of "Aggie," but because it was subtly, indefinably *wrong* in itself. Agnes would have made me look like an ass.

The fear of appearing ridiculous first entered my life, as a 6 governing motive, during my second year in the convent. Up to then, a desire for prominence had decided many of my actions and, in fact, still persisted. But in the eighth grade, I became aware of mockery and perceived that I could not seek prominence without attracting laughter. Other people could, but I couldn't. This laughter was proceeding, not from my classmates, but from the girls of the class just above me, in particular from two boon companions. Elinor Heffernan and Mary Harty, a clownish pair—oddly assorted in size and shape, as teams of clowns generally are, one short, plump, and baby-faced, the other tall, lean, and owlish—who entertained the high-school department by calling attention to the oddities of the younger girls. Nearly every school has such a pair of satirists, whose marks are generally low and who are tolerated just because of their laziness and non-conformity; one of them (in this case, Mary Harty, the plump one) usually appears to be half asleep. Because of their low standing, their indifference to appearances, the sad state of their uniforms, their clowning is taken to be harmless, which, on the whole, it is, their object being not to wound but to divert; such girls are bored in school. We in the eighth grade sat directly in front of the two wits in study hall, so that they had us under close observation; yet at first I was not afraid of them, wanting, if anything, to identify myself with their laughter, to be initiated into the joke. One of their specialties was giving people nicknames, and it was considered an honor to be the first in the eighth grade to be let in by Elinor and Mary on their latest invention. This often happened to me; they would tell me, on the playground, and I would tell the others. As their intermediary, I felt

MARY McCARTHY

myself almost their friend and it did not occur to me that I might be next on their list.

I had achieved prominence not long before by publicly losing   7
my faith and regaining it at the end of a retreat. I believe Elinor and Mary questioned me about this on the playground, during recess, and listened with serious, respectful faces while I told them about my conversations with the Jesuits. Those serious faces ought to have been an omen, but if the two girls used what I had revealed to make fun of me, it must have been behind my back. I never heard any more of it, and yet just at this time I began to feel something, like a cold breath on the nape of my neck, that made me wonder whether the new position I had won for myself in the convent was as secure as I imagined. I would turn around in study hall and find the two girls looking at me with speculation in their eyes.

It was just at this time, too, that I found myself in a perfectly   8
absurd situation, a very private one, which made me live, from month to month, in horror of discovery. I had waked up one morning, in my convent room, to find a few small spots of blood on my sheet; I had somehow scratched a trifling cut on one of my legs and opened it during the night. I wondered what to do about this, for the nuns were fussy about bedmaking, as they were about our white collars and cuffs, and if we had an inspection these spots might count against me. It was best, I decided, to ask the nun on dormitory duty, tall, stout Mother Slattery, for a clean bottom sheet, even though she might scold me for having scratched my leg in my sleep and order me to cut my toenails. You never know what you might be blamed for. But Mother Slattery, when she bustled in to look at the sheet, did not scold me at all; indeed, she hardly seemed to be listening, as I explained to her about the cut. She told me to sit down: she would be back in a minute. "You can be excused from athletics today," she added, closing the door. As I waited, I considered this remark, which seemed to me strangely munificent, in view of the unimportance of the cut. In a moment, she returned, but without the sheet. Instead, she produced out of her big pocket a sort of cloth girdle and a peculiar flannel object which I first took to be a bandage, and I began to protest that I did not need or want a bandage; all I needed was a bottom sheet. "The sheet can wait," said Mother Slattery, succinctly, handing me two large safety pins. It was the pins that abruptly enlightened me; I saw Mother Slattery's mistake, even as she was instructing me as to how this flannel article, which I now understood to be a sanitary napkin, was to be put on.

"Oh no, Mother," I said, feeling somewhat embarrassed. "You   9
don't understand. It's just a little cut, on my leg." But Mother, again, was not listening; she appeared to have grown deaf, as the nuns had

a habit of doing when what you were saying did not fit in with their ideas. And now that I knew what was in her mind, I was conscious of a funny constraint; I did not feel it proper to name a natural process, in so many words, to a nun. It was like trying not to think of their going to the bathroom or trying not to see the straggling irongray hair coming out of their coifs (the common notion that they shaved their heads was false). On the whole, it seemed better just to show her my cut. But when I offered to do so and unfastened my black stocking, she only glanced at my leg, cursorily. "That's only a scratch dear," she said. "Now hurry up and put this on or you'll be late for chapel. Have you any pain?" "No, no, Mother!" I cried. "You don't understand!" "Yes, yes, I understand," she replied soothingly, "and you will too, a little later. Mother Superior will tell you about it some time during the morning. There's nothing to be afraid of. You have become a woman."

"I know all about that," I persisted. "Mother, please listen. I just cut my leg. On the athletic field. Yesterday afternoon." But the more excited I grew, the more soothing, and yet firm, Mother Slattery became. There seemed to be nothing for it but to give up and do as I was bid. I was in the grip of a higher authority, which almost had the power to persuade me that it was right and I was wrong. But of course I was not wrong; that would have been too good to be true. While Mother Slattery waited, just outside my door, I miserably donned the equipment she had given me, for there was no place to hide it, on account of drawer inspection. She led me down the hall to where there was a chute and explained how I was to dispose of the flannel thing, by dropping it down the chute into the laundry. (The convent arrangements were very old-fashioned, dating back, no doubt, to the days of Louis Philippe.)

The Mother Superior, Madame MacIllvra, was a sensible woman, and all through my early morning classes, I was on pins and needles, chafing for the promised interview with her which I trusted would clear things up. *"Ma Mére,"* I would begin, "Mother Slattery thinks . . ." Then I would tell her about the cut and the athletic field. But precisely the same impasse confronted me when I was summoned to her office at recess-time. *I* talked about my cut, and *she* talked about becoming a woman. It was rather like a round, in which she was singing "Scotland's burning, Scotland's burning," and I was singing "Pour on water, pour on water." Neither of us could hear the other, or, rather, I could hear her, but she could not hear me. Owing to our different positions in the convent she was free to interrupt me, whereas I was expected to remain silent until she had finished speaking. When I kept breaking in, she hushed me, gently, and took me on her lap. Exactly like Mother Slattery, she attributed all my references

MARY McCARTHY

to the cut to a blind fear of this new, unexpected reality that had supposedly entered my life. Many young girls, she reassured me, were frightened if they had not been prepared. "And you, Mary, have lost your dear mother, who could have made this easier for you." Rocked on Madame MacIllvra's lap, I felt paralysis overtake me and I lay, mutely listening, against her bosom, my face being tickled by her white, starched, fluted wimple, while she explained to me how babies were born, all of which I had heard before.

There was no use fighting the convent. I had to pretend to have become a woman, just as, not long before, I had had to pretend to get my faith back—for the sake of peace. This pretense was decidedly awkward. For fear of being found out by the lay sisters downstairs in the laundry (no doubt an imaginary contingency, but the convent was so very thorough), I reopened the cut on my leg, so as to draw a little blood to stain the napkins, which were issued me regularly, not only on this occasion, but every twenty-eight days thereafter. Eventually, I abandoned this bloodletting, for fear of lockjaw, and trusted to fate. Yet I was in awful dread of detection; my only hope, as I saw it, was either to be released from the convent or to become a woman in reality, which might take a year at least, since I was only twelve. Getting out of athletics once a month was not sufficient compensation for the farce I was going through. It was not my fault; they had forced me into it; nevertheless, it was I who would look silly—worse than silly; half mad—if the truth ever came to light. 12

I was burdened with this guilt and shame when the nickname finally found me out. "Found me out," in a general sense, for no one ever did learn the particular secret I bore about with me, pinned to the linen band. "We've got a name for you," Elinor and Mary called out to me, one day on the playground. "What is it?" I asked half hoping, half fearing, since not all their sobriquets were unfavorable. "Cye," they answered, looking at each other and laughing. "Si?" I repeated, supposing that it was based on Simple Simon. Did they regard me as a hick? "C.Y.E.," they elucidated, spelling it out in chorus. "The letters stand for something. Can you guess?" I could not and I cannot now. The closest I could come to it in the convent was "Clean Your Ears." Perhaps that was it, though in later life I have wondered whether it did not stand, simply, for "Clever Young Egg" or "Champion Young Eccentric." But in the convent I was certain that it stood for something horrible, something even worse than dirty ears (as far as I knew, my ears were clean), something I could never guess because it represented some aspect of myself that the world could see and I couldn't, like a sign pinned on my back. Everyone in the convent must have known what the letters stood for, but no one would tell me. Elinor and Mary had made them promise. It was like halitosis; 13

not even my best friend, my deskmate, Louise, would tell me, no matter how much I pleaded. Yet everyone assured me that it was "very good," that is, very apt. And it made everyone laugh.

This name reduced all my pretensions and solidified my sense 14 of *wrongness*. Just as I felt I was beginning to belong to the convent, it turned me into an outsider, since I was the only pupil who was not in the know. I liked the convent, but it did not like me, as people say of certain foods that disagree with them. By this, I do not mean that I was actively unpopular, either with the pupils or with the nuns. The Mother Superior cried when I left and predicted that I would be a novelist, which surprised me. And I had finally made friends; even Emilie von Phul smiled upon me softly out of her bright blue eyes from the far end of the study hall. It was just that I did not fit into the convent pattern; the simplest thing I did, like asking for a clean sheet, entrapped me in consequences that I never could have predicted. I was not bad; I did not consciously break the rules; and yet I could never, not even for a week, get a pink ribbon, and this was something I could not understand, because I was trying as hard as I could. It was the same case as with the hated name; the nuns, evidently, saw something about me that was invisible to me.

The oddest part was all that pretending. There I was, a walk- 15 ing mass of lies, pretending to be a Catholic and going to confession while really I had lost my faith, and pretending to have monthly periods by cutting myself with nail scissors; yet all this had come about without my volition and even contrary to it. But the basest pretense I was driven to was the acceptance of the nickname. Yet what else could I do? In the convent, I could not live it down. To all those girls, I had become "Cye McCarthy." That was who I was. That was how I had to identify myself when telephoning my friends during vacations to ask them to the movies: "Hello, this is Cye." I loathed myself when I said it, and yet I succumbed to the name totally, making myself over into a sort of hearty to go with it—the kind of girl I hated. "Cye" was my new patron saint. This false personality stuck to me, like the name, when I entered public high school, the next fall, as a freshman, having finally persuaded my grandparents to take me out of the convent, although they could never get to the bottom of my reasons, since, as I admitted, the nuns were kind, and I had made many nice new friends. What I wanted was a fresh start, a chance to begin life over again, but the first thing I heard in the corridors of the public high school was that name called out to me, like the warmest of welcomes: "Hi, there, Si!" That was the way they thought it was spelled. But this time I was resolute. After the first weeks, I dropped the hearties who called me "Si" and I never heard it again. I got my own name back and sloughed off Clementina and even Therese—the names that did not seem to me any more to be mine but to have been

MARY McCARTHY 8

imposed on me by others. And I preferred to think that Mary meant "bitter" rather than "star of the sea."

COMPREHENSION

1.   According to McCarthy, what was the significance of names in her Catholic convent? What is the relationship of names to culture?

2.   Describe the author's life in the convent school. How does she respond to her nickname? Why does she leave the convent school?

3.   Compare and contrast McCarthy's Catholic education and that of Rodriguez in "Credo."

RHETORIC

1.   Locate "names" in the essay that have unusually vivid connotations for the author. What is the cumulative effect of the listing of so many names on the tone of the essay?

2.   Why does the author use the word *names* at the beginning of paragraphs 1, 2, 3, 4, and 5? How does this one word contribute to the unity of the essay?

3.   Does McCarthy use examples objectively or subjectively in this essay? Explain. Select one paragraph and show how the examples contribute to an understanding of McCarthy's view of the importance of names and "naming" things properly.

4.   How does the author use personal experience as an example? What other types of example does she use?

5.   Where do the patterns of explanation and description blend in this essay?

6.   In what sense is this a definition essay? What is the thesis? What does the last paragraph contribute to the thesis?

WRITING

1.   Why do personal names actually mean certain things? What does your name mean? What does it reveal to you? Prepare an essay on these questions.

2.   Write about your nickname or the nicknames of a group of friends.

3.   Prepare a list of the most popular names for boys and girls in American culture today. Evaluate the importance of names and naming as symbolic acts that tell us about ourselves and our culture.

Notes on Punctuation

Lewis Thomas (1913–   ), physician, educator, and author, was born in New York City. He received a B.S. from Princeton in 1933, an M.D. from Harvard in 1937, and an M.A. from Yale in 1969. In addition to a monthly column in Nature, *Thomas is the author of* Lives of a Cell *(1974), which won the National Book Award;* Medusa and the Snail *(1979); and* The Youngest Science *(1983). Dr. Thomas has also published extensively in scientific and medical journals. Although best known for his ability to explain the life sciences to lay persons, in this essay he takes up the subject of punctuation in a unique and amusing way.*

here are no precise rules about punctuation (Fowler lays out some general advice (as best as he can under the complex circumstances of English prose (he points out, for example, that we possess only four stops (the comma, the semicolon, the colon and the period (the question mark and exclamation point are not, strictly speaking, stops; they are indicators of tone (oddly enough, the Greeks employed the semicolon for their question mark (it produces a strange sensation to read a Greek sentence which is a straightforward question: Why weepest thou; (instead of Why weepest thou? (and, of course, there are parentheses (which are surely a kind of punctuation making this whole matter much more complicated by having to count up the left-handed parentheses in order to be sure of closing with the right number (but if the parentheses were left out, with nothing to work with but the stops, we would have considerably more flexibility in the deploying of layers of meaning than if we tried to separate all the clauses by physical barriers (and in the latter case, while we might have more precision and exactitude for our meaning, we would lose the essential flavor of language, which is its wonderful ambiguity)))))))))))). 1

The commas are the most useful and usable of all the stops. It is highly important to put them in place as you go along. If you try to come back after doing a paragraph and stick them in the various spots that tempt you you will discover that they tend to swarm like minnows into all sorts of crevices whose existence you hadn't realized and before you know it the whole long sentence becomes immobilized and lashed up squirming in commas. Better to use them sparingly, and with affection, precisely when the need for each one arises, nicely, by itself. 2

I have grown fond of semicolons in recent years. The semicolon tells you that there is still some question about the preceding 3 full sentence; something needs to be added; it reminds you sometimes of the Greek usage. It is almost always a greater pleasure to come across a semicolon than a period. The period tells you that that is that; if you didn't get all the meaning you wanted or expected, anyway you got all the writer intended to parcel out and now you have to move along. But with a semicolon there you get a pleasant little feeling of expectancy; there is more to come; read on; it will get clearer.

Colons are a lot less attractive, for several reasons: firstly, they give you the feeling of being rather ordered around, or at least having your nose pointed in a direction you might not be inclined to take if left to yourself, and, secondly, you suspect you're in for one of those sentences that will be labeling the points to be made: firstly, secondly and so forth, with the implication that you haven't sense enough to keep track of a sequence of notions without having them numbered. Also, many writers use this system loosely and incompletely, starting out with number one and number two as though counting off on their fingers but then going on and on without the succession of labels you've been led to expect, leaving you floundering about searching for the ninethly or seventeenthly that ought to be there but isn't. 4

Exclamation points are the most irritating of all. Look! they say, look at what I just said! How amazing is my thought! It is like being forced to watch someone else's small child jumping up and down crazily in the center of the living room shouting to attract attention. If a sentence really has something of importance to say, something quite remarkable, it doesn't need a mark to point it out. And if it is really, after all, a banal sentence needing more zing, the exclamation point simply emphasizes its banality! 5

Quotation marks should be used honestly and sparingly, when there is a genuine quotation at hand, and it is necessary to be very rigorous about the words enclosed by the marks. If something is to be quoted, the *exact* words must be used. If part of it must be left out because of space limitations, it is good manners to insert three dots to indicate the omission, but it is unethical to do this if it means connecting two thoughts which the original author did not intend to have tied together. Above all, quotation marks should not be used for ideas that you'd like to disown, things in the air so to speak. Nor should they be put in place around clichés; if you want to use a cliché you must take full responsibility for it yourself and not try to fob it off on anon., or on society. The most objectionable misuse of quotation marks, but one which illustrates the dangers of misuse in ordinary prose, is seen in advertising, especially in advertisements for small restaurants, for example "just around the corner," or "a good place to eat." No single, identifiable, citable person ever really said, for the record, "just around the corner," much less "a good place to eat," least likely of all for restaurants of the type that use this type of prose. 6

The dash is a handy device, informal and essentially playful, 7
telling you that you're about to take off on a different tack but still in
some way connected with the present course—only you have to remember that the dash is there, and either put a second dash at the
end of the notion to let the reader know that he's back on course, or
else end the sentence, as here, with a period.

The greatest danger in punctuation is for poetry. Here it is 8
necessary to be as economical and parsimonious with commas and
periods as with the words themselves, and any marks that seem to
carry their own subtle meanings, like dashes and little rows of periods,
even semicolons and question marks, should be left out altogether
rather than inserted to clog up the thing with ambiguity. A single
exclamation point in a poem, no matter what else the poem has to
say, is enough to destroy the whole work.

The things I like best in T. S. Eliot's poetry, especially in the 9
Four Quartets, are the semicolons. You cannot hear them, but they are
there, laying out the connections between the images and the ideas.
Sometimes you get a glimpse of a semicolon coming, a few lines farther on, and it is like climbing a steep path through woods and seeing
a wooden bench just at a bend in the road ahead, a place where you
can expect to sit for a moment, catching your breath.

Commas can't do this sort of thing; they can only tell you 10
how the different parts of a complicated thought are to be fitted together, but you can't sit, not even take a breath, just because of a
comma,

COMPREHENSION

1. Does a formal definition of punctuation appear in the essay? Why, or why
not?

2. What is Thomas's purpose in writing "Notes on Punctuation?" What is his
thesis?

3. What is Thomas's favorite form of punctuation? What about it does he like?
What about it does he find irritating?

RHETORIC

1. What stylistic technique does Thomas use to illustrate punctuation? What is
his purpose in doing it this way?

2. Is Thomas's style subjective or objective? Why?

3. Carefully analyze the author's introductory paragraph. How does it set up
the rest of the essay?

4. How does Thomas use classification to develop the essay? What is the basis
of his classification scheme?

LEWIS THOMAS

5. In which paragraphs is illustration used? What is its purpose?

6. What use of transitional devices does Thomas make? Why does he organize his paragraphs in this way?

WRITING

1. Write a brief, amusing essay on your favorite form of punctuation.

2. Compare and contrast the approaches to language taken by Baker and Thomas in their respective essays.

3. In an essay entitled "Language and Evolution," Thomas marvels over the common root for the words *human, humane,* and *humble.* Develop a paper on these related words or any other set of related words that interests you.

GEORGE ORWELL

Politics and the English Language

George Orwell (1903–1950) was the pseudonym of Eric Blair, an English novelist, essayist, and journalist. Orwell served with the Indian Imperial Police from 1922 to 1927 in Burma, fought in the Spanish Civil War, and acquired from his experience a disdain of totalitarian and imperialistic systems. This attitude is reflected in the satiric fable Animal Farm *(1945) and in the bleak, futuristic novel* 1984 *(1949). This essay, one of the more famous of the twentieth century, relates sloppy thinking and writing with political oppression.*

Most people who bother with the matter at all would admit that the English language is in a bad way, but it is generally assumed that we cannot by conscious action do anything about it. Our civilisation is decadent, and our language—so the argument runs—must inevitably share in the general collapse. It follows that any struggle against the abuse of language is a sentimental archaism, like preferring candles to electric light or hansom cabs to aeroplanes. Underneath this lies the half-conscious belief that language is a natural growth and not an instrument which we shape for our own purposes. 1

Now, it is clear that the decline of a language must ultimately have political and economic causes: it is not due simply to the bad 2 influence of this or that individual writer. But an effect can become a cause, reinforcing the original cause and producing the same effect in an intensified form, and so on indefinitely. A man may take to drink because he feels himself to be a failure, and then fail all the more completely because he drinks. It is rather the same thing that is happening to the English language. It becomes ugly and inaccurate because our thoughts are foolish, but the slovenliness of our language makes it easier for us to have foolish thoughts. The point is that the process is reversible. Modern English, especially written English, is full of bad habits which spread by imitation and which can be avoided if one is willing to take the necessary trouble. If one gets rid of these habits one can think more clearly, and to think clearly is a necessary first step towards political regeneration: so that the fight against bad English is not frivolous and is not the exclusive concern of professional writers. I will come back to this presently, and I hope that by that time the meaning of what I have said here will have become clearer. Meanwhile, here are five specimens of the English language as it is now habitually written.

These five passages have not been picked out because they 3 are especially bad—I could have quoted far worse if I had chosen— but because they illustrate various of the mental vices from which we now suffer. They are a little below the average, but are fairly representative samples. I number them so that I can refer back to them when necessary:

1.   I am not, indeed, sure whether it is not true to say the Milton who once seemed not unlike a seventeenth-century Shelley had not become, out of an experience even more bitter in each year, more alien (sic) to the founder of that Jesuit sect which nothing could induce him to tolerate.

Professor Harold Laski (essay in *Freedom of Expression*)

2.   Above all, we cannot play ducks and drakes with a native battery of idioms which prescribes such egregious collocations of vocables as the Basic *put up with* for *tolerate* or *put at a loss* for *bewilder*.

Professor Lancelot Hogben (*Interglossa*)

3.   On the one side we have the free personality: by definition it is not neurotic, for it has neither conflict nor dream. Its desires, such as they are, are transparent, for they are just what institutional approval keeps in the forefront of consciousness; another institutional pattern would alter their number and intensity; there is little in them that is natural, irreducible, or culturally dangerous. But *on the other side*, the social bond itself is nothing but the mutual reflection of these self-secure integrities. Recall the definition of love. Is not this the very

picture of a small academic? Where is there a place in this hall of mirrors for either personality or fraternity?

Essay on psychology in Politics (New York)

4.   All the "best people" from the gentlemen's clubs, and all the frantic Fascist captains, united in common hatred of Socialism and bestial horror of the rising tide of the mass revolutionary movement, have turned to acts of provocation, to foul incendiarism, to medieval legends of poisoned wells, to legalise their own destruction to proletarian organisations, and rouse the agitated petty-bourgeoisie to chauvinistic fervour on behalf of the fight against the revolutionary way out of the crisis.

Communist pamphlet

5.   If a new spirit is to be infused into this old country, there is one thorny and contentious reform which must be tackled, and that is the humanisation and galvanisation of the BBC. Timidity here will bespeak canker and atrophy of the soul. The heart of Britain may be sound and of strong beat, for instance, but the British lion's roar at present is like that of Bottom in Shakespeare's Midsummer Night's Dream—as gentle as any sucking dove. A virile new Britain cannot continue indefinitely to be traduced in the eyes, or rather ears, of the world by the effete languors of Langham Place, brazenly masquerading as "standard English". When the Voice of Britain is heard at nine o'clock, better far and infinitely less ludicrous to hear aitches honestly dropped than the present priggish, inflated, inhibited, schoolma'amish arch braying of blameless bashful mewing maidens!

Letter in Tribune

Each of these passages has faults of its own, but, quite apart from avoidable ugliness, two qualities are common to all of them. The first is staleness of imagery: the other is lack of precision. The writer either has a meaning and cannot express it, or he inadvertently says something else, or he is almost indifferent as to whether his words mean anything or not. This mixture of vagueness and sheer incompetence is the most marked characteristic of modern English prose, and especially of any kind of political writing. As soon as certain topics are raised, the concrete melts into the abstract and no one seems able to think of turns of speech that are not hackneyed: prose consists less and less of words chosen for the sake of their meaning, and more of phrases tacked together like the sections of a prefabricated henhouse. I list below, with notes and examples, various of the tricks by means of which the work of prose construction is habitually dodged:

Dying Metaphors. A newly invented metaphor assists thought by evoking a visual image, while on the other hand a metaphor which is technically "dead" (e.g. *iron resolution*) has in effect reverted to being an ordinary word and can generally be used without loss of vividness. But in between these two classes there is a huge dump of worn-out metaphors which have lost all evocative power and are merely used because they save people the trouble of inventing phrases for themselves. Examples are: *Ring the changes on, take up the cudgels for, toe the line, ride roughshod over, stand shoulder to shoulder with, play into the hands of, no axe to grind, grist to the mill, fishing in troubled waters, rift within the lute, on the order of the day, Achilles' heel, swan song, hotbed.* Many of these are used without knowledge of their meaning (what is a "rift", for instance?), and incompatible metaphors are frequently mixed, a sure sign that the writer is not interested in what he is saying. Some metaphors now current have been twisted out of their original meaning without those who use them even being aware of the fact. For example, *toe the line* is sometimes written *tow the line.* Another example is *the hammer and the anvil*, now always used with the implication that the anvil gets the worst of it. In real life it is always the anvil that breaks the hammer, never the other way about: a writer who stopped to think what he was saying would be aware of this, and would avoid perverting the original phrase.

Operators, or Verbal False Limbs. These save the trouble of picking out   6
appropriate verbs and nouns, and at the same time pad each sentence with extra syllables which give it an appearance of symmetry. Characteristic phrases are: *render inoperative, militate against, prove unacceptable, make contact with, be subjected to, give rise to, give grounds for, have the effect of, play a leading part (rôle) in, make itself felt, take effect, exhibit a tendency to, serve the purpose of,* etc. etc. The keynote is the elimination of simple verbs. Instead of being a single word, such as *break, stop, spoil, mend, kill,* a verb becomes a *phrase*, made up of a noun or adjective tacked on to some general-purposes verb such as *prove, serve, form, play, render.* In addition, the passive voice is wherever possible used in preference to the active, and noun constructions are used instead of gerunds (*by examination of* instead of *by examining*). The range of verbs is further cut down by means of the *-ise* and *de-* formations, and banal statements are given an appearance of profundity by means of the *not un-* formation. Simple conjunctions and prepositions are replaced by such phrases as *with respect to, having regard to, the fact that, by dint of, in view of, in the interests of, on the hypothesis that;* and the ends of sentences are saved from anticlimax by such resounding commonplaces as *greatly to be desired, cannot be left out of account, a development to be expected in the near future, deserving of serious consideration, brought to a satisfactory conclusion,* and so on and so forth.

Pretentious Diction. Words like *phenomenon, element, individual* (as   7

GEORGE ORWELL

noun), *objective, categorical, effective, virtual, basic, primary, promote, constitute, exhibit, exploit, utilise, eliminate, liquidate,* are used to dress up simple statements and give an air of scientific impartiality to biassed judgements. Adjectives like *epoch-making, epic, historic, unforgettable, triumphant, age-old, inevitable, inexorable, veritable,* are used to dignify the sordid processes of international politics, while writing that aims at glorifying war usually takes on an archaic colour, its characteristic words being: *realm, throne, chariot, mailed fist, trident, sword, shield, buckler, banner, jackboot, clarion.* Foreign words and expressions such as *cul de sac, ancien régime, deus ex machina, mutatis mutandis, status quo, Gleichschaltung, Weltanschauung,* are used to give an air of culture and elegance. Except for the useful abbreviations *i.e., e.g.,* and *etc.,* there is no real need for any of the hundreds of foreign phrases now current in English. Bad writers, and especially scientific, political and sociological writers, are nearly always haunted by the notion that Latin or Greek words are grander than Saxon ones, and unnecessary words like *expedite, ameliorate, predict, extraneous, deracinated, clandestine, subaqueous* and hundreds of others constantly gain ground from their Anglo-Saxon opposite numbers.[1] The jargon peculiar to Marxist writing (*hyena, hangman, cannibal, petty bourgeois, these gentry, lacquey, flunkey, mad dog, White Guard,* etc.) consists largely of words and phrases translated from Russian, German or French; but the normal way of coining a new word is to use a Latin or Greek root with the appropriate affix and, where necessary, the *-ise* formation. It is often easier to make up words of this kind (*deregionalise, impermissible, extramarital, non-fragmentatory* and so forth) than to think up the English words that will cover one's meaning. The result, in general, is an increase in slovenliness and vagueness.

Meaningless Words. In certain kinds of writing, particularly in art criticism and literary criticism, it is normal to come across long passages which are almost completely lacking in meaning.[2] Words like *romantic, plastic, values, human, dead, sentimental, natural, vitality,* as used in art criticism, are strictly meaningless, in the sense that they not only do not point to any discoverable object, but are hardly even expected to do so by the reader. When one critic writes, "The outstanding features of Mr X's work is its living quality", while another writes, "The im-

8

---

[1] An interesting illustration of this is the way in which the English flower names which were in use till very recently are being ousted by Greek ones, *snapdragon* becoming *antirrhinum, forget-me-not* becoming *myosotis,* etc. It is hard to see any practical reason for this change of fashion: it is probably due to an instinctive turning-away from the more homely word and a vague feeling that the Greek word is scientific.

[2] Example: "Comfort's catholicity of perception and image, strangely Whitmanesque in range, almost the exact opposite in aesthetic compulsion, continues to evoke that trembling atmospheric accumulative hinting at a cruel, an inexorably serene timelessness ... Wrey Gardiner scores by aiming at simple bullseyes with precision. Only they are not so simple, and through this contented sadness runs more than the surface bitter-sweet of resignation." (*Poetry Quarterly*).

mediately striking thing about Mr X's work is its peculiar deadness", the reader accepts this as a simple difference of opinion. If words like *black* and *white* were involved, instead of the jargon words *dead* and *living*, he would see at once that language was being used in an improper way. Many political words are similarly abused. The word *Fascism* has now no meaning except in so far as it signifies "something not desirable". The words *democracy, socialism, freedom, patriotic, realistic, justice,* have each of them several different meanings which cannot be reconciled with one another. In the case of a word like *democracy*, not only is there no agreed definition, but the attempt to make one is resisted from all sides. It is almost universally felt that when we call a country democratic we are praising it: consequently the defenders of every kind of régime claim that it is a democracy, and fear that they might have to stop using the word if it were tied down to any one meaning. Words of this kind are often used in a consciously dishonest way. That is, the person who uses them has his own private definition, but allows his hearer to think he means something quite different. Statements like *Marshal Pétain was a true patriot, The Soviet press is the freest in the world, The Catholic Church is opposed to persecution,* are almost always made with intent to deceive. Other words used in variable meanings, in most cases more or less dishonestly, are: *class, totalitarian, science, progressive, reactionary, bourgeois, equality.*

Now that I have made this catalogue of swindles and perversions, let me give another example of the kind of writing that they lead to. This time it must of its nature be an imaginary one. I am going to translate a passage of good English into modern English of the worst sort. Here is a well-known verse from *Ecclesiastes*:   9

> I returned, and saw under the sun, that the race is not to the swift, nor the battle to the strong, neither yet bread to the wise, nor yet riches to men of understanding, nor yet favour to men of skill; but time and chance happeneth to them all.

Here it is in modern English: 10

> Objective consideration of contemporary phenomena compels the conclusion that success or failure in competitive activities exhibits no tendency to be commensurate with innate capacity, but that a considerable element of the unpredictable must invariably be taken into account.

This is a parody, but not a very gross one. Exhibit 3, above,   11 for instance, contains several patches of the same kind of English. It will be seen that I have not made a full translation. The beginning and ending of the sentence follow the original meaning fairly closely,

    GEORGE ORWELL

but in the middle the concrete illustrations—race, battle, bread—dissolve into the vague phrase "success or failure in competitive activities". This had to be so, because no modern writer of the kind I am discussing—no one capable of using phrases like "objective consideration of contemporary phenomena"—would ever tabulate his thoughts in that precise and detailed way. The whole tendency of modern prose is away from concreteness. Now analyse these two sentences a little more closely. The first contains 49 words but only 60 syllables, and all its words are those of everyday life. The second contains 38 words of 90 syllables: 18 of its words are from Latin roots, and one from Greek. The first sentence contains six vivid images, and only one phrase ("time and chance") that could be called vague. The second contains not a single fresh, arresting phrase, and in spite of its 90 syllables it gives only a shortened version of the meaning contained in the first. Yet without a doubt it is the second kind of sentence that is gaining ground in modern English. I do not want to exaggerate. This kind of writing is not yet universal, and outcrops of simplicity will occur here and there in the worst-written page. Still, if you or I were told to write a few lines on the uncertainty of human fortunes, we should probably come much nearer to my imaginary sentence than to the one from *Ecclesiastes*.

As I have tried to show, modern writing at its worst does not   12
consist in picking out words for the sake of their meaning and inventing images in order to make the meaning clearer. It consists in gumming together long strips of words which have already been set in order by someone else, and making the results presentable by sheer humbug. The attraction of this way of writing is that it is easy. It is easier—even quicker, once you have the habit—to say *In my opinion it is a not unjustifiable assumption that* than to say *I think*. If you use ready-made phrases, you not only don't have to hunt about for words; you also don't have to bother with the rhythms of your sentences, since these phrases are generally so arranged as to be more or less euphonious. When you are composing in a hurry—when you are dictating to a stenographer, for instance, or making a public speech—it is natural to fall into a pretentious, latinised style. Tags like *a consideration which we should do well to bear in mind* or *a conclusion to which all of us would readily assent* will save many a sentence from coming down with a bump. By using stale metaphors, similes and idioms, you save much mental effort, at the cost of leaving your meaning vague, not only for your reader but for yourself. This is the significance of mixed metaphors. The sole aim of a metaphor is to call up a visual image. When these images clash—as in *The Fascist octopus has sung its swan song, the jackboot is thrown into the melting-pot*—it can be taken as certain that the writer is not seeing a mental image of the objects he is naming; in other words he is not really thinking. Look

again at the examples I gave at the beginning of this essay. Professor Laski (1) uses five negatives in 53 words. One of these is superfluous, making nonsense of the whole passage, and in addition there is the slip *alien* for akin, making further nonsense, and several avoidable pieces of clumsiness which increase the general vagueness. Professor Hogben (2) plays ducks and drakes with a battery which is able to write prescriptions, and, while disapproving of the everyday phrase *put up with*, is unwilling to look *egregious* up in the dictionary and see what it means. (3), if one takes an uncharitable attitude towards it, is simply meaningless: probably one could work out its intended meaning by reading the whole of the article in which it occurs. In (4) the writer knows more or less what he wants to say, but an accumulation of stale phrases chokes him like tea-leaves blocking a sink. In (5) words and meaning have almost parted company. People who write in this manner usually have a general emotional meaning—they dislike one thing and want to express solidarity with another—but they are not interested in the detail of what they are saying. A scrupulous writer, in every sentence that he writes, will ask himself at least four questions, thus: What am I trying to say? What words will express it? What image or idiom will make it clearer? Is this image fresh enough to have an effect? And he will probably ask himself two more: Could I put it more shortly? Have I said anything that is avoidably ugly? But you are not obliged to go to all this trouble. You can shirk it by simply throwing your mind open and letting the ready-made phrases come crowding in. They will construct your sentences for you—even think your thoughts for you, to a certain extent—and at need they will perform the important service of partially concealing your meaning even from yourself. It is at this point that the special connection between politics and the debasement of language becomes clear.

In our time it is broadly true that political writing is bad writing. Where it is not true, it will generally be found that the writer is some kind of rebel, expressing his private opinions, and not a "party line". Orthodoxy, of whatever colour, seems to demand a lifeless, imitative style. The political dialects to be found in pamphlets, leading articles, manifestos, White Papers and the speeches of Under-Secretaries do, of course, vary from party to party, but they are all alike in that one almost never finds in them a fresh, vivid, home-made turn of speech. When one watches some tired hack on the platform mechanically repeating the familiar phrases—*bestial atrocities, iron heel, blood-stained tyranny, free peoples of the world, stand shoulder to shoulder*—one often has a curious feeling that one is not watching a live human being but some kind of dummy: a feeling which suddenly becomes stronger at moments when the light catches the speaker's spectacles and turns them into blank discs which seem to have no eyes behind them. And this is not altogether fanciful. A speaker who uses that

GEORGE ORWELL

kind of phraseology has gone some distance towards turning himself into a machine. The appropriate noises are coming out of his larynx, but his brain is not involved as it would be if he were choosing his words for himself. If the speech he is making is one that he is accustomed to make over and over again, he may be almost unconscious of what he is saying, as one is when one utters the responses in church. And this reduced state of consciousness, if not indispensable, is at any rate favourable to political conformity.

In our time, political speech and writing are largely the de- 14
fence of the indefensible. Things like the continuance of British rule in India, the Russian purges and deportations, the dropping of the atom bombs on Japan, can indeed be defended, but only by arguments which are too brutal for most people to face, and which do not square with the professed aims of political parties. Thus political language has to consist largely of euphemism, question-begging and sheer cloudy vagueness. Defenceless villages are bombarded from the air, the inhabitants driven out into the countryside, the cattle machine-gunned, the huts set on fire with incendiary bullets: this is called *pacification*. Millions of peasants are robbed of their farms and sent trudging along the roads with no more than they can carry: this is called *transfer of population* or *rectification of frontiers*. People are imprisoned for years without trial, or shot in the back of the neck or sent to die of scurvy in Arctic lumber camps: this is called *elimination of unreliable elements*. Such phraseology is needed if one wants to name things without calling up mental pictures of them. Consider for instance some comfortable English professor defending Russian totalitarianism. He cannot say outright, "I believe in killing off your opponents when you can get good results by doing so". Probably, therefore, he will say something like this:

> While freely conceding that the Soviet régime exhibits certain features which the humanitarian may be inclined to deplore, we must, I think, agree that a certain curtailment of the right to political opposition is an unavoidable concomitant of transitional periods, and that the rigours which the Russian people have been called upon to undergo have been amply justified in the sphere of concrete achievement.

The inflated style is itself a kind of euphemism. A mass of 15
Latin words falls upon the facts like soft snow, blurring the outlines and covering up all the details. The great enemy of clear language is insincerity. When there is a gap between one's real and one's declared aims, one turns as it were instinctively to long words and exhausted idioms, like a cuttlefish squirting out ink. In our age there is no such thing as "keeping out of politics". All issues are political issues, and

politics itself is a mass of lies, evasions, folly, hatred and schizophrenia. When the general atmosphere is bad, language must suffer. I should expect to find—this is a guess which I have not sufficient knowledge to verify—that the German, Russian and Italian languages have all deteriorated in the last ten or fifteen years, as a result of dictatorship.

But if thought corrupts language, language can also corrupt 16 thought. A bad usage can spread by tradition and imitation, even among people who should and do know better. The debased language that I have been discussing is in some ways very convenient. Phrases like *a not unjustifiable assumption, leaves much to be desired, would serve no good purpose, a consideration which we should do well to bear in mind*, are a continuous temptation, a packet of aspirins always at one's elbow. Look back through this essay, and for certain you will find that I have again and again committed the very faults I am protesting against. By this morning's post I have received a pamphlet dealing with conditions in Germany. The author tells me that he "felt impelled" to write it. I open it at random, and here is almost the first sentence that I see: "(The Allies) have an opportunity not only of achieving a radical transformation of Germany's social and political structure in such a way as to avoid a nationalistic reaction in Germany itself, but at the same time of laying the foundations of a co-operative and unified Europe." You see, he "feels impelled" to write—feels, presumably, that he has something new to say—and yet his words, like cavalry horses answering the bugle, group themselves automatically into the familiar dreary pattern. This invasion of one's mind by ready-made phrases (*lay the foundations, achieve a radical transformation*) can only be prevented if one is constantly on guard against them, and every such phrase anaesthetises a portion of one's brain.

I said earlier that the decadence of our language is probably 17 curable. Those who deny this would argue, if they produced an argument at all, that language merely reflects existing social conditions, and that we cannot influence its development by any direct tinkering with words and constructions. So far as the general tone or spirit of a language goes, this may be true, but it is not true in detail. Silly words and expressions have often disappeared, not through any evolutionary process but owing to the conscious action of a minority. Two recent examples were *explore every avenue* and *leave no stone unturned*, which were killed by the jeers of a few journalists. There is a long list of fly-blown metaphors which could similarly be got rid of if enough people would interest themselves in the job; and it should also be possible to laugh the *not un-* formation out of existence,[3] to reduce the

---

[3]One can cure oneself of the *not un-* formation by memorising this sentence: *A not unblack dog was chasing a not unsmall rabbit across a not ungreen field.*

GEORGE ORWELL

amount of Latin and Greek in the average sentence, to drive out foreign phrases and strayed scientific words, and, in general, to make
pretentiousness unfashionable. But all these are minor points. The defence of the English language implies more than this, and perhaps it
is best to start by saying what it does *not* imply.

To begin with, it has nothing to do with archaism, with the 18
salvaging of obsolete words and turns of speech, or with the setting-
up of a "standard English" which must never be departed from. On
the contrary, it is especially concerned with the scrapping of every
word or idiom which has outworn its usefulness. It has nothing to do
with correct grammar and syntax, which are of no importance so long
as one makes one's meaning clear, or with the avoidance of Ameri-
canisms, or with having what is called a "good prose style". On the
other hand it is not concerned with fake simplicity and the attempt
to make written English colloquial. Nor does it even imply in every
case preferring the Saxon word to the Latin one, though it does imply
using the fewest and shortest words that will cover one's meaning.
What is above all needed is to let the meaning choose the word, and
not the other way about. In prose, the worst thing one can do with
words is to surrender to them. When you think of a concrete object,
you think wordlessly, and then, if you want to describe the thing you
have been visualising, you probably hunt about till you find the exact
words that seem to fit it. When you think of something abstract you
are more inclined to use words from the start, and unless you make
a conscious effort to prevent it, the existing dialect will come rushing
in and do the job for you, at the expense of blurring or even changing
your meaning. Probably it is better to put off using words as long as
possible and get one's meaning as clear as one can through pictures
or sensations. Afterwards one can choose—not simply *accept*—the
phrases that will best cover the meaning, and then switch around and
decide what impression one's words are likely to make on another
person. This last effort of the mind cuts out all stale or mixed images,
all prefabricated phrases, needless repetitions, and humbug and
vagueness generally. But one can often be in doubt about the effect
of a word or a phrase, and one needs rules that one can rely on when
instinct fails. I think the following rules will cover most cases:

i. Never use a metaphor, simile or other figure of speech which you
are used to seeing in print.

ii. Never use a long word where a short one will do.

iii. If it is possible to cut a word out, always cut it out.

iv. Never use the passive where you can use the active.

POLITICS AND THE ENGLISH LANGUAGE

v. Never use a foreign phrase, a scientific word or a jargon word if you can think of an everyday English equivalent.

vi. Break any of these rules sooner than say anything outright barbarous.

These rules sound elementary, and so they are, but they demand a deep change of attitude in anyone who has grown used to writing in the style now fashionable. One could keep all of them and still write bad English, but one could not write the kind of stuff that I quoted in those five specimens at the beginning of this article.

I have not here been considering the literary use of language,   19 but merely language as an instrument for expressing and not for concealing or preventing thought. Stuart Chase and others have come near to claiming that all abstract words are meaningless, and have used this as a pretext for advocating a kind of political quietism. Since you don't know what Fascism is, how can you struggle against Fascism? One need not swallow such absurdities as this, but one ought to recognise that the present political chaos is connected with the decay of language, and that one can probably bring about some improvement by starting at the verbal end. If you simplify your English, you are freed from the worst follies of orthodoxy. You cannot speak any of the necessary dialects, and when you make a stupid remark its stupidity will be obvious, even to yourself. Political language—and with variations this is true of all political parties, from Conservatives to Anarchists—is designed to make lies sound truthful and murder respectable, and to give an appearance of solidity to pure wind. One cannot change this all in a moment, but one can at least change one's own habits, and from time to time one can even, if one jeers loudly enough, send some worn-out and useless phrase—some *jackboot*, *Achilles' heel, hotbed, melting pot, acid test, veritable inferno* or other lump of verbal refuse—into the dustbin where it belongs.

COMPREHENSION

1. What is Orwell's purpose? For what type of audience is he writing? Where does he summarize his concerns for readers?

2. According to Orwell, "thought corrupts language" and "language can also corrupt thought." Give examples of these assertions in the essay.

3. In what ways does Orwell believe that politics and language are related?

RHETORIC

1. Orwell himself uses similes and metaphors. Locate five of them, and explain their relationship to the author's analysis.

                                   GEORGE ORWELL   8

2. Orwell claims that concrete language is superior to abstract language. Give examples of Orwell's attempt to write concretely.

3. One of the most crucial rhetorical devices in this essay is definition. What important concepts does Orwell define? What methods of definition does he tend to use?

4. Identify an example of hypothetical reasoning in the essay. How does it contribute to the thesis of the essay?

5. After having given five examples of bad English, why does Orwell, in paragraph 9, give another example? How does this example differ from the others? What does it add to the essay?

6. Explain the use of extended analogy in paragraph 13.

WRITING

1. In an analytical essay, assess the state of language in politics today. Cite examples from newspapers and television reports.

2. Apply Orwell's advice on language to either "A Hanging" or "Marrakech."

3. Prepare an essay analyzing the use and abuse of any word that sparks controversy today—for example, *abortion, AIDS,* or *greed.*

JONATHAN SWIFT

The Art of Political Lying

Jonathan Swift (1667–1745) is best known as the author of three satires: A Tale of a Tub *(1704),* Gulliver's Travels *(1726), and* A Modest Proposal *(1729). In these satires, he pricks the balloon of many of his contemporaries' and our own most cherished prejudices, pomposities, and delusions. Swift was also a famous churchman, an eloquent spokesman for Irish rights, and a political journalist. In this essay, he examines a characteristic of politicians that apparently has not changed over the years: lying.*

We are told the devil is the father of lies, and was a liar from the beginning; so that, beyond contradiction, the invention is old: and, which is more, his first Essay of it was purely political, employed in undermining the authority of his prince, and seducing a third part of the subjects from their obedience: for which he was driven down from heaven, where (as Milton expresses it) he had been viceroy of a great western province; and forced to exercise his talent in inferior regions among other fallen spirits, poor or deluded men, whom he still daily tempts to his own sin, and will ever do so, till he be chained in the bottomless pit.

But although the devil be the father of lies, he seems, like other great inventors, to have lost much of his reputation by the continual improvements that have been made upon him.

Who first reduced lying into an art, and adapted it to politics, is not so clear from history, although I have made some diligent inquiries. I shall therefore consider it only according to the modern system, as it has been cultivated these twenty years past in the southern part of our own island.

The poets tell us that, after the giants were overthrown by the gods, the earth in revenge produced her last offspring, which was Fame. And the fable is thus interpreted: that when tumults and seditions are quieted, rumours and false reports are plentifully spread through a nation. So that, by this account, lying is the last relief of a routed, earth-born, rebellious party in a state. But here the moderns have made great additions, applying this art to the gaining of power and preserving it, as well as revenging themselves after they have lost it; as the same instruments are made use of by animals to feed themselves when they are hungry, and to bite those that tread upon them.

But the same genealogy cannot always be admitted for political lying; I shall therefore desire to refine upon it, by adding some circumstances of its birth and parents. A political lie is sometimes born out of a discarded statesman's head, and thence delivered to be nursed and dandled by the rabble. Sometimes it is produced a monster, and licked into shape: at other times it comes into the world completely formed, and is spoiled in the licking. It is often born an infant in the regular way, and requires time to mature it; and often it sees the light in its full growth, but dwindles away by degrees. Sometimes it is of noble birth, and sometimes the spawn of a stockjobber. Here it screams aloud at the opening of the womb, and there it is delivered with a whisper. I know a lie that now disturbs half the kingdom with its noise, [of] which, although too proud and great at present to own its parents, I can remember its whisperhood. To conclude the nativity of this monster; when it comes into the world without a sting it is still-born; and whenever it loses its sting it dies.

No wonder if an infant so miraculous in its birth should be destined for great adventures; and accordingly we see it has been the guardian spirit of a prevailing party for almost twenty years. It can conquer kingdoms without fighting, and sometimes with the loss of a battle. It gives and resumes employments; can sink a mountain to a mole-hill, and raise a mole-hill to a mountain; has presided for many years at committees of elections; can wash a blackmoor white; make

JONATHAN SWIFT

a saint of an atheist, and a patriot of a profligate; can furnish foreign ministers with intelligence, and raise or let fall the credit of the nation. This goddess flies with a huge looking-glass in her hands, to dazzle the crowd, and make them see, according as she turns it, their ruin in their interest, and their interest in their ruin. In this glass you will behold your best friends, clad in coats powdered with *fleurs de lis* and triple crowns; their girdles hung round with chains, and beads, and wooden shoes; and your worst enemies adorned with the ensigns of liberty, property, indulgence, moderation, and a cornucopia in their hands. Her large wings, like those of a flying-fish, are of no use but while they are moist; she therefore dips them in mud, and, soaring aloft, scatters it in the eyes of the multitude, flying with great swiftness; but at every turn is forced to stoop in dirty ways for new supplies.

7   I have been sometimes thinking, if a man had the art of the second sight for seeing lies, as they have in Scotland for seeing spirits, how admirably he might entertain himself in this town, by observing the different shapes, sizes, and colours of those swarms of lies which buzz about the heads of some people, like flies about a horse's ear in summer; or those legions hovering every afternoon in Exchange-alley, enough to darken the air; or over a club of discontented grandees, and thence sent down in cargoes to be scattered at elections.

8   There is one essential point wherein a political liar differs from others of the faculty, that he ought to have but a short memory, which is necessary according to the various occasions he meets with every hour of differing from himself and swearing to both sides of a contradiction, as he finds the persons disposed with whom he has to deal. In describing the virtues and vices of mankind, it is convenient, upon every article, to have some eminent person in our eye, from whom we copy our description. I have strictly observed this rule, and my imagination this minute represents before me a certain great man famous for this talent, to the constant practice of which he owes his twenty years' reputation of the most skilful head in England for the management of nice affairs. The superiority of his genius consists in nothing else but an inexhaustible fund of political lies, which he plentifully distributes every minute he speaks, and by an unparalleled generosity forgets, and consequently contradicts, the next half-hour. He never yet considered whether any proposition were true or false, but whether it were convenient for the present minute or company to affirm or deny it; so that, if you think fit to refine upon him by interpreting everything he says, as we do dreams, by the contrary, you are still to seek, and will find yourself equally deceived whether you believe or not: the only remedy is to suppose that you have heard some inarticulate sounds, without any meaning at all; and besides, that will take off the horror you might be apt to conceive at the oaths where-

THE ART OF POLITICAL LYING

with he perpetually tags both ends of every proposition; although, at the same time, I think he cannot with any justice be taxed with perjury when he invokes God and Christ, because he has often fairly given public notice to the world that he believes in neither.

Some people may think that such an accomplishment as this 9 can be of no great use to the owner, or his party, after it has been often practised and is become notorious; but they are widely mistaken. Few lies carry the inventor's mark, and the most prostitute enemy to truth may spread a thousand without being known for the author: besides, as the vilest writer has his readers, so the greatest liar has his believers; and it often happens that, if a lie be believed only for an hour, it has done its work, and there is no farther occasion for it. Falsehood flies, and truth comes limping after it, so that when men come to be undeceived it is too late; the jest is over, and the tale has had its effect: like a man who has thought of a good repartee when the discourse is changed or the company parted; or like a physician who has found out an infallible medicine after the patient is dead.

Considering that natural disposition in many men to lie, and 10 in multitudes to believe, I have been perplexed what to do with that maxim so frequent in everybody's mouth, that truth will at last prevail. Here has this island of ours, for the greatest part of twenty years, lain under the influence of such counsels and persons, whose principle and interest it was to corrupt our manners, blind our understanding, drain our wealth, and in time destroy our constitution both in church and state, and we at last were brought to the very brink of ruin; yet, by the means of perpetual misrepresentations, have never been able to distinguish between our enemies and friends. We have seen a great part of the nation's money got into the hands of those who, by their birth, education, and merit, could pretend no higher than to wear our liveries; while others, who, by their credit, quality, and fortune, were only able to give reputation and success to the Revolution, were not only laid aside as dangerous and useless, but loaded with the scandal of Jacobites, men of arbitrary principles, and pensioners to France; while truth, who is said to lie in a well, seemed now to be buried there under a heap of stones. But I remember it was a usual complaint among the Whigs, that the bulk of the landed men was not in their interests, which some of the wisest looked on as an ill omen; and we saw it was with the utmost difficulty that they could reserve a majority, while the court and ministry were on their side, till they had learned those admirable expedients for deciding elections and influencing distant boroughs by powerful motives from the city. But all this was more force and constraint, however upheld by most dexterous artifice and management, until the people began to apprehend their properties, their religion, and the monarchy itself in danger; when we saw them greedily laying hold on the first occasion to in-

JONATHAN SWIFT

terpose. But of this mighty change in the dispositions of the people I shall discourse more at large in some following paper: wherein I shall endeavour to undeceive or discover those deluded or deluding persons who hope or pretend it is only a short madness in the vulgar, from which they may soon recover; whereas, I believe it will appear to be very different in its causes, its symptoms, and its consequences; and prove a great example to illustrate the maxim I lately mentioned, that truth (however sometimes late) will at last prevail.

COMPREHENSION

1. According to Swift, what effects can be traced to political lying?

2. Why aren't liars discovered and known to be liars?

3. Compare Orwell's assessment of political language to Swift's.

RHETORIC

1. In paragraphs 8 to 10, Swift uses numerous metaphors and similes. Identify and interpret them, and also explain why Swift uses metaphors and allusive language.

2. How does Swift employ ironic language?

3. Swift employs several extended metaphors, almost fables, to describe liars and lying. Identify these metaphors, and explain how they characterize the liar. What is the effect of using this method of definition?

4. Which paragraphs constitute the introductory part of Swift's essay? What methods of development does he employ here?

5. At what point does Swift divide his essay into two parts? How are these parts different? How are they similar?

6. Swift frequently uses deductive reasoning in this essay. Give examples, and explain how, particularly in paragraphs 8 to 10, deductions further his argument.

WRITING

1. Write an essay on the art of lying as it relates to particular institutions or subjects—college life, business, politics, marriage, or other relevant topics.

2. Examine Swift's use of irony and satire in this essay and his "A Modest Proposal."

3. Study and report on the public life of a contemporary figure, and how he or she used language to lie and deceive.

Literature, Media, and the Arts

JOYCE CAROL OATES

Ernest Hemingway

Joyce Carol Oates (1938–   ) is a poet, novelist, short-story writer, and essayist. She received her B.A. in 1960 from Syracuse University, where she was class valedictorian, and her M.A. in 1961 from the University of Wisconsin. Her first book, By the North Gate *(1963), was a collection of short stories. Since then, Oates's life has been "more or less dedicated to promoting and exploring literature," both as a university professor and the author of many works, including* Wonderland *(1971),* Do with Me What You Will *(1973), and* Solstice *(1985). In this piece, Oates explores the legacy left by one of the twentieth-century's greatest writers.*

early a quarter-century after his violent, self-inflicted   1
death in 1961, Ernest Hemingway remains the most controversial and very likely the most influential of American writers. His influence has been both literary and
personal—and therefore incalculable. The ear, if not the eye, can detect
Hemingwayesque cadences in the elliptical dialogue of Harold Pinter;

the swift, declarative sentences of the young Gabriel Garcia Márquez; the laconic first-person narratives of Albert Camus; the carefully honed, ironic prose of Joan Didion. Norman Mailer, strongly influenced by Hemingway's work in his early career, remains under the not altogether beneficent influence of the man: the Hemingway who believed that *aficion* (passion) justified the expenditure of the self in public.

Like all major artists, Hemingway arouses a diversity of critical responses, ranging from adulation to loathing. But in Hemingway's case the situation is confused by the highly visible presence—one might almost say the embarrassing intrusion—of the writer-as-celebrity, the flamboyant "Papa" Hemingway of the popular media, whose advertisements for himself (as big-game hunter, deep-sea fisherman, grizzled sage, man among men) approached self-parody in the 1950s. (It is interesting to note that the expatriated Hemingway, long a derisory critic of American culture, succumbed to a distinctly American pathology, like Mark Twain and Jack London before him, and more recently Truman Capote: the surrender of the self to the public image, to the inevitable debasement of the self.) Perhaps because media celebrity came early and unbidden to Hemingway—at the age of 18, as a driver for the Red Cross Ambulance Corps, he was wounded in Italy, cited for his extraordinary bravery under fire, and taken up for a time by American wire services and newsreels as a hero—he accepted fame as his due, and believed that, though writing was, in itself, a pure activity, it might also be the means to an end: the enshrinement and immortalization of Ernest Hemingway.

As a consequence, attitudes toward Hemingway's considerable achievement now come sharply conditioned by attitudes toward Hemingway the man: how one feels, for instance, about his highly stylized religion of *machismo* (the glorification of the bullfight as a ritual of beauty, the camaraderie of men who are bonded by their "superiority" not only to women, but to most other men as well); his rites of personal risk and exotic adventure ("It is certainly valuable to a trained writer to crash in an airplane that burns"); the equation of masculinity with greatness in literature.

More than one acquaintance of Hemingway's made the observation that, despite his several wives and liaisons, he seemed to dislike women, and since he rarely wrote of women with sympathy, and virtually never with subtlety and understanding, feminist charges of misogyny are surely justified. (Yet in the context of American literature, this is simply to accuse Hemingway of being a male writer. William Faulkner's more insidious misogyny passes largely unnoted, perhaps because Faulkner's prose is less accessible than Hemingway's and his manner more self-consciously "visionary.") It cannot be surprising that Jewish readers have been disconcerted by the casual anti-

2

3

4

Semitism that pervades his work; or that the sensitive are offended by his fascination with blood sports, like bullfighting and boxing, and that general air of indifference to the suffering of others that seems the more pitiless for being expressed in short, blunt, declarative sentences.

Writers have always admired and learned from Hemingway, as Hemingway in his time admired and learned from any number of other older writers, but critics have been doubtful of his overall worth. Indeed, critical reassessment of Hemingway in the past two or three decades has been so harsh that Malcolm Cowley, in a sympathetic essay titled "Papa and the Parricides," analyzed the phenomenon in terms of Freud's highly speculative "Totem and Taboo"—the notion, never substantiated by anthropologists, that there might exist a primitive rite of murder, dismemberment and devouring of the "primal" father by his own sons. Yet even the most severe critics have granted Hemingway a few classic books—"In Our Time" (1925), "The Sun Also Rises" (1926), "A Farewell to Arms" (1929), "Green Hills of Africa" (1935), the posthumously published "A Moveable Feast" (1964), and a number of masterly short stories.

"The Sun Also Rises," written in Paris and published when Hemingway was 27 years old, immediately established his reputation as one of the most brilliant and original writers of his generation; he was lauded as an unsentimental, if not pitiless, interpreter of post-World War I society. The novel's idle, self-absorbed characters are American and English expatriates in Paris in the early 1920s, veterans in one way or another of the war: the newspaperman-narrator Jake Barnes was wounded on the Italian front and is sexually impotent ("No," Jake says self-mockingly, "I just had an accident"); the woman he loves, Brett Ashley, estranged from an English baronet who became mentally deranged during his service in the Royal Navy, is something of a nymphomaniac-alcoholic ("I've always done just what I wanted," Brett says helplessly to Jake. "I do feel such a bitch").

The novel's title, perfectly chosen, taken from Ecclesiastes ("One generation passeth away, and another cometh; but the earth abideth forever. . . . The sun also ariseth, and the sun goeth down, and hasteth to the place where he arose. . . ."), strikes exactly the right chord of ennui and resignation, and succeeds in lifting Hemingway's story of drifting, alienated, rather superficial men and women to a mythopoeic level. And the novel's other epigraph, long since famous, is Gertrude Stein's: "You are all a lost generation." (In fact, as Hemingway discloses in "A Moveable Feast," Stein appropriated the remark from the manager of a Parisian gas station.)

Reading Hemingway's first novel today, one is likely to be struck by its "modern" sound; the affectless, meiotic prose, confrontations that purposefully eschew emotion, the circular and even des-

JOYCE CAROL OATES

ultory movement of its narrative. The generation of the 1920s was perhaps no more lost than any other postwar generation, but the self-consciousness of being lost, being special, "damned," casually committed to self-destruction (Jake and his friends are virtually all alcoholics or on their way to becoming so), sounds a new note in prose fiction. Jake's impotence is, of course, not accidental. Being estranged from conventional society (that is, one's family back home) and religion (for Jake, Catholicism: a "grand" religion) establishes the primary bond between the novel's characters. Brett says defensively at the novel's end, after she has made a surely minimal gesture of doing good, "It makes one feel rather good deciding not to be a bitch. . . . It's sort of what we have instead of God." As for morality—Jake wonders if it isn't simply what goads a man to feel self-disgust after he has done something shameful.

It seems not to be generally recognized that Hemingway's 9 classic novel owes a good deal to F. Scott Fitzgerald's "The Great Gatsby," which Hemingway read in 1925 and admired greatly. Each novel is narrated by a disaffected young man who observes but does not participate centrally in the action; each novel traces the quixotic love of an outsider for a beautiful if infantile woman; each is an excoriation from within of the "lost generation" and the "fiesta concept of life"—Hemingway's phrase denoting the aristocratic rich "who give each day the quality of a festival and who, when they have passed and taken the nourishment they need, leave everything dead. . . ."

Fitzgerald's Daisy is unhappily married to the wealthy Tom 10 Buchanan, whom Gatsby bravely challenges for her love; Hemingway's Brett intends to marry the drunkard, wealthy-bankrupt Mike Campbell, whom the hapless Robert Cohn fights with his fists. (Cohn knocks the inebriated Campbell down but loses Brett all the same—not to Campbell, but to a 19-year-old bullfighter.) In each novel, men and women set themselves the task of being entertained, absorbed, diverted, not by work (though Jake Barnes is a newspaperman of a literary sort), but primarily by drinking and talking. Hemingway's people in particular are obsessed with various forms of sport—golfing, tennis, swimming, hiking, trout fishing, attending boxing matches and bullfights. And drinking. Only in Malcolm Lowry's "Under the Volcano" are drinks so rigorously catalogued and described—whisky, brandy, champagne, wines of various kinds, absinthe, liqueurs. After a long, drunken sequence, Jake thinks: "Under the wine I lost the disgusted feeling and was happy. It seemed they were all such nice people."

As a story, "The Sun Also Rises" depends primarily upon the 11 reader's acceptance of Jake Barnes as an intelligent and reliable observer, and of Brett in the role of a 34-year-old Circe awash in alcohol

 ERNEST HEMINGWAY

and cheery despair. Though based, like many of Hemingway's characters, on a real person (Lady Twysden, a "legend" in Montparnasse during the time Hemingway and his first wife, Hadley, lived there), Brett is sketchily portrayed; she is "nice," "damned nice," "lovely," "of a very good family," "built with curves like the hull of a racing yacht," but the reader has difficulty envisioning her. Hemingway gives her so little to say that we cannot come to know her. (Whereas Duff Twysden was evidently an artist of some talent and seems to have been an unusually vivacious and intelligent woman.)

Another problematic character is the Jew, Robert Cohn, who [12] evokes everyone's scorn by "behaving badly"—he follows Brett around and intrudes where he isn't wanted. Cohn is so much the scapegoat for the others' cruelty ("That kike!" "He's just so awful!" "Was I rude enough to him?" "He doesn't add much to the gaiety." "[He has] a wonderful quality of bringing out the worst in anybody") that most readers will end up feeling intense sympathy for him. The fact that Cohn cannot drink as heavily as the others, that the bullfight sickens him (especially the disemboweling of the picador's horse), that in this noisy *macho* milieu he finally breaks down and cries—these things seem altogether to his credit; he emerges as the novel's most distinctly drawn character. One waits in vain, however, for Jake Barnes to rise to Nick Carraway's judgment of Jay Gatsby: "You're worth the whole damn bunch put together."

"The Sun Also Rises" is a novel of manners and a homoerotic [13] (though not homosexual) romance, merely in outline a "love story" of unconsummated passion. Like most of Hemingway's books, fiction and nonfiction, it celebrates the mysterious bonds of masculine friendship, sometimes ritualized and sometimes spontaneous. Women are viewed with suspicion and an exaggerated awe that readily turns to contempt. Jake is happiest when he and his friend Bill are away from the company of women altogether and fishing alone in the Rio de la Fabrica valley in Spain. There they achieve a degree of intimacy impossible elsewhere. ("Listen," says Bill. "You're a hell of a good guy, and I'm fonder of you than anybody on earth. I couldn't tell you that in New York. It'd mean I was a faggot.") Of equal importance with male friendship is the worship of the matador, the master of the bull, the only person (in Hemingway's judgment) to live his life to the full.

Aficion means passion and an *aficionado* is one who feels in- [14] tense passion for the bullfight. Says Jake: "Somehow it was taken for granted that an American could not have *aficion*. He might simulate it or confuse it with excitement, but he could not really have it. When they saw that I had *aficion*, and there was no password, no set questions that could bring it out, rather it was sort of oral spiritual examination . . . there was this same embarrassed putting the hand on the shoulder, or a '*Buen hombre.*' But nearly always there was the actual touching." Only at certain rigorously defined moments are men allowed to touch one another, just as, in the ritual of the bullfight (bloody and barbarous to those of us who are not *aficionados*), the tormented bull and the matador "become one" (in Hemingway's repeated phrase) at the moment of the kill. These are quite clearly sacred rites in Hemingway's private cosmology.

If many men are disturbed by Hemingway's code of ethics— as, surely, many women are disturbed by it—it is because Hemingway's exaggerated sense of maleness really excludes most men. The less than exemplary bullfighter is jeered in the ring, even if he has been gored; poor Robert Cohn, whose flaw seems to have been to have felt too deeply and too openly, is ridiculed, broken, and finally banished from the clique. 15

If it seems to us highly unjust that Hemingway's men and women derive their sense of themselves by excluding others and by establishing codes of behavior that enforce these exclusions, it should be recalled that Hemingway prided himself on his ability to write of things as they are, not as they might, or should, be. One can object that he does not rise above his prejudices; he celebrates *aficion* where he finds it, in the postwar malaise of the 1920s and in his own heart. "The Sun Also Rises" remains a distinctly American work, a classic of its time and ours, like its author, controversial and disturbing, but certainly compelling. 16

COMPREHENSION

1.   Explain in your own words the influence that Hemingway has had on modern writing and literature.

2.   Does Oates pursue a single vision of Hemingway in this selection? To what extent are the author's feelings about her subject mixed? How can you tell?

3.   What does Oates admire most about Hemingway? What does she find distasteful? What is her opinion of *The Sun Also Rises*?

RHETORIC

1.   Why does the author use so many parenthetical expressions as a stylistic device? What is the effect?

2.   Explain the significance of the word *afición* in Oates's understanding of Hemingway.

3.   What basic strategies does Oates use to design her introductory paragraph?

4.   Where does Oates use specific examples to structure her paragraphs? Where does she employ an extended example, and what is the effect?

5.   Cite instances of extended definition and of comparison and contrast in this selection. What is the purpose of these rhetorical strategies?

  ERNEST HEMINGWAY

6. What evidence of misogyny does Oates present? How is Hemingway's treatment of women evident in Oates's description of Lady Brett? How important is the issue of misogyny to the development of Oates's thesis?

WRITING

1. There are many critics who say that great writers influence and sometimes even shape the ways we see the world and think about ourselves. There are other critics who maintain that writers merely echo the times in which they live. Based on this examination of Hemingway by Joyce Carol Oates, did Hemingway help shape modern sensibilities, or was he the product of them?

2. Choose a character from a novel, short story, television series, or movie who has had an impact on your life, and discuss the ways in which this person has influenced you. Has this influence been beneficial or harmful? In what ways?

3. For a term project read Hemingway's *The Sun Also Rises* and Fitzgerald's *The Great Gatsby*, and write a comparative essay on them.

SYLVIA PLATH

A Comparison

Sylvia Plath (1932–1963), American poet and novelist, graduated from Smith College and took a master's at Cambridge University. She married the English poet Ted Hughes in 1956. Plath committed suicide at the age of 30. Her best known work is The Bell-Jar *(1963), a highly autobiographical novel about a young woman overwhelmed by crises and suicidal tendencies. Plath's poetry, often reflecting a fascination with suffering, pain, and death, is collected in* The Colossus *(1960),* Ariel *(1965),* Crossing the Water *(1971), and* Winter Trees *(1972). This essay, written in 1962, is an energetic and highly poetic celebration of the artist's craft.*

How I envy the novelist! 1

I imagine him—better say her, for it is the women I look 2 to for . . . a parallel—I imagine her, then, pruning a rose-bush with a large pair of shears, adjusting her spectacles, shuffling about among the teacups, humming, arranging ashtrays or babies, absorbing a slant of light, a fresh edge to the weather, and piercing, with a kind of modest, beautiful X-ray vision, the psychic interiors of her neighbors—her neighbors on trains, in the dentist's waiting room, in the corner teashop. To her, this fortunate one, what is there that *isn't* relevant! Old shoes can be used, doorknobs, air letters, flannel nightgowns, cathedrals, nail varnish, jet planes, rose arbors and budgerigars; little mannerisms—the sucking at a tooth, the tugging at a hemline—any weird or warty or fine or despicable thing. Not to mention emotions, motivations—those rumbling, thunderous shapes. Her business is Time, the way it shoots forward, shunts back, blooms, decays and double-exposes itself. Her business is people in Time. And she, it seems to me, has all the time in the world. She can take a century if she likes, a generation, a whole summer.

I can take about a minute.   3

I'm not talking about epic poems. We all know how long *they*   4
can take. I'm talking about the smallish, unofficial garden-variety poem. How shall I describe it?—a door opens, a door shuts. In between you have had a glimpse: a garden, a person, a rainstorm, a dragonfly, a heart, a city. I think of those round glass Victorian paperweights which I remember, yet can never find—a far cry from the plastic mass-productions which stud the toy counters in Woolworth's. This sort of paperweight is a clear globe, self-complete, very pure, with a forest or village or family group within it. You turn it upside down, then back. It snows. Everything is changed in a minute. It will never be the same in there—not the fir trees, nor the gables, nor the faces.

So a poem takes place.   5

And there is really so little room! So little time! The poet be-   6
comes an expert packer of suitcases:

The apparition of these faces in the crowd;
Petals on a wet black bough.

There it is: the beginning and the end in one breath. How   7
would the novelist manage that? In a paragraph? In a page? Mixing it, perhaps, like paint, with a little water, thinning it, spreading it out.

Now I am being smug, I am finding advantages.   8

If a poem is concentrated, a closed fist, then a novel is relaxed   9
and expansive, an open hand: it has roads, detours, destinations; a heart line, a head line; morals and money come into it. Where the fist excludes and stuns, the open hand can touch and encompass a great deal in its travels.

I have never put a toothbrush in a poem.   10

I do not like to think of all the things, familiar, useful and   11
worthy things, I have never put into a poem. I did, once, put a yew tree in. And that yew tree began, with astounding egotism, to manage and order the whole affair. It was not a yew tree by a church on a road past a house in a town where a certain woman lived . . . and so

  A COMPARISON   411

on, as it might have been in a novel. Oh, no. It stood squarely in the middle of my poem, manipulating its dark shades, the voices in the churchyard, the clouds, the birds, the tender melancholy with which I contemplated it—everything! I couldn't subdue it. And, in the end, my poem was a poem about a yew tree. That yew tree was just too proud to be a passing black mark in a novel.

Perhaps I shall anger some poets by implying that the *poem* 12 is proud. The poem, too, can include everything, they will tell me. And with far more precision and power than those baggy, disheveled and undiscriminate creatures we call novels. Well, I concede these poets their steamshovels and old trousers. I really *don't* think poems should be all that chaste. I would, I think, even concede a toothbrush, if the poem was a real one. But these apparitions, these poetical toothbrushes, are rare. And when they do arrive, they are inclined, like my obstreperous yew tree, to think themselves singled out and rather special.

Not so in novels. 13

There the toothbrush returns to its rack with beautiful promp- 14 titude and is forgot. Time flows, eddies, meanders, and people have leisure to grow and alter before our eyes. The rich junk of life bobs all about us: bureaus, thimbles, cats, the whole much-loved, well-thumbed catalog of the miscellaneous which the novelist wishes us to share. I do not mean that there is no pattern, no discernment, no rigorous ordering here.

I am only suggesting that perhaps the pattern does not insist 15 so much.

The door of the novel, like the door of the poem, also shuts. 16

But not so fast, nor with such manic, unanswerable finality. 17

COMPREHENSION

1. Does this essay have a thesis? Explain.

2. What distinctions does the author draw between the poem and the novel? Why does she envy the novelist? What stated and implied preferences does she have for the poem rather than the novel?

3. Explain the relevance of rosebushes, toothbrushes, and yew trees to Plath's discussion. What is her purpose in incorporating these details into her essay?

RHETORIC

1. The author employs a remarkable variety of poetic techniques in this essay, including metaphors, symbols, allusions, imagery, personification, onomatopoeia, alliteration, consonance, and assonance. Locate and analyze examples of these techniques.

2. Analyze Plath's use of parallelism in paragraphs 2, 4, and 14.

3. Plath uses a series of figurative comparisons to structure the entire essay. Trace and examine the main figurative comparisons that serve to organize the selection.

4. Examine the spatial and rhetorical effects of the numerous one-sentence paragraphs in the essay.

5. What purpose does Plath's method serve in identification and definition of the novelist and poet?

6. Analyze the cumulative use of illustration to achieve emphasis in this essay.

WRITING

1. Comment in a brief essay on Plath's view that the poem, unlike the novel, closes with "manic, unanswerable finality."

2. Write an essay that compares and contrasts—either figuratively or literally—two forms of literature, art, music, or film.

3. Select a poem that you like, and assess it, using Plath's observations on poetry as a guideline.

D. H. LAWRENCE

Why the Novel Matters

David Herbert Lawrence (1885–1930), novelist, essayist, and poet, wrote in the great tradition of English romanticism. He chafed under the conventions of his age and zealously extended the content and style of the English novel. His novels, such as Sons and Lovers *(1913),* The Rainbow *(1915),* Women in Love *(1921),* The Plumed Serpent *(1926), and* Lady Chatterley's Lover *(1928), are famous for their often disquieting depictions of love and ambition in the modern world. Lawrence also wrote criticism: his* Studies in Classic American Literature *(1923) is still a revealing, if idiosyncratic, look at American literature. In the following essay, what matters for Lawrence is not simply the novel, which he treats with energy and enthusiasm, but life itself.*

We have curious ideas of ourselves. We think of ourselves   1
as a body with a spirit in it, or a body with a soul in it,
or a body with a mind in it. *Mens sana in corpore sano.*
The years drink up the wine, and at last throw the bottle
away, the body, of course, being the bottle.

It is a funny sort of superstition. Why should I look at my   2
hand, as it so cleverly writes these words, and decide that it is a mere
nothing compared to the mind that directs it? Is there really any huge
difference between my hand and my brain? Or my mind? My hand
is alive, it flickers with a life of its own. It meets all the strange universe in touch, and learns a vast number of things, and knows a vast
number of things. My hand, as it writes these words, slips gaily along,
jumps like a grasshopper to dot an *i*, feels the table rather cold, gets
a little bored if I write too long, has its own rudiments of thought,
and is just as much *me* as is my brain, my mind, or my soul. Why
should I imagine that there is a *me* which is more *me* than my hand
is? Since my hand is absolutely alive, me alive.

Whereas, of course, as far as I am concerned, my pen isn't   3
alive at all. My pen *isn't me* alive. Me alive ends at my finger-tips.

Whatever is me alive is me. Every tiny bit of my hands is   4
alive, every little freckle and hair and fold of skin. And whatever is
me alive is me. Only my finger-nails, those ten little weapons between
me and an inanimate universe, they cross the mysterious Rubicon
between me alive and things like my pen, which are not alive, in my
own sense.

So, seeing my hand is all alive, and me alive, wherein is it   5
just a bottle, or a jug, or a tin can, or a vessel of clay, or any of the
rest of that nonsense? True, if I cut it it will bleed, like a can of cherries.
But then the skin that is cut, and the veins that bleed, and the bones
that should never be seen, they are all just as alive as the blood that
flows. So the tin can business, or vessel of clay, is just bunk.

And that's what you learn, when you're a novelist. And that's   6
what you are very liable *not* to know, if you're a parson, or a philosopher, or a scientist, or a stupid person. If you're a parson, you
talk about souls in heaven. If you're a novelist, you know that paradise is in the palm of your hand, and on the end of your nose, because
both are alive; and alive, and man alive, which is more than you can
say, for certain, of paradise. Paradise is after life, and I for one am not
keen on anything that is *after* life. If you are a philosopher, you talk
about infinity, and the pure spirit which knows all things. But if you
pick up a novel, you realize immediately that infinity is just a handle
to this self-same jug of a body of mine; while as for knowing, if I find
my finger in fire, I know that fire burns, with a knowledge so emphatic and vital, it leaves Nirvana merely a conjecture. Oh, yes, my
body, me alive, *knows*, and knows intensely. And as for the sum of all
knowledge, it can't be anything more than an accumulation of all the
things I know in the body, and you, dear reader, know in the body.

These damned philosophers, they talk as if they suddenly   7
went off in steam, and were then much more important than they are

when they're in their shirts. It is nonsense. Every man, philosopher included, ends in his own finger-tips. That's the end of his man alive. As for the words and thoughts and sighs and aspirations that fly from him, they are so many tremulations in the ether, and not alive at all. But if the tremulations reach another man alive, he may receive them into his life, and his life may take on a new colour, like a chameleon creeping from a brown rock on to a green leaf. All very well and good. It still doesn't alter the fact that the so-called spirit, the message or teaching of the philosopher or the saint, isn't alive at all, but just a tremulation upon the ether, like a radio message. All this spirit stuff is just tremulations upon the ether into new life, that is because you are man alive, and you take sustenance and stimulation into your alive man in a myriad ways. But to say that the message, or the spirit which is communicated to you, is more important than your living body, is nonsense. You might as well say that the potato at dinner was more important.

Nothing is important but life. And for myself, I can absolutely 8 see life nowhere but in the living. Life with a capital L is only man alive. Even a cabbage in the rain is cabbage alive. All things that are alive are amazing. And all things that are dead are subsidiary to the living. Better a live dog than a dead lion. But better a live lion than a live dog. *C'est la vie!*

It seems impossible to get a saint, or a philosopher, or a sci- 9 entist, to stick to this simple truth. They are all, in a sense, renegades. The saint wishes to offer himself up as spiritual food for the multitude. Even Francis of Assisi turns himself into a sort of angel-cake, of which anyone may take a slice. But an angel-cake is rather less than man alive. And poor St. Francis might well apologize to his body, when he is dying: "Oh, pardon me, my body, the wrong I did you through the years!" It was no wafer, for others to eat.

The philosopher, on the other hand, because he can think, 10 decides that nothing but thoughts matter. It is as if a rabbit, because he can make little pills, should decide that nothing but little pills matter. As for the scientist, he has absolutely no use for me so long as I am man alive. To the scientist, I am dead. He puts under the microscope a bit of dead me, and calls it me. He takes me to pieces, and says first one piece, and then another piece, is me. My heart, my liver, my stomach have all been scientifically me, according to the scientist; and nowadays I am either a brain, or nerves, or glands, or something more up-to-date in the tissue line.

Now I absolutely flatly deny that I am a soul, or a body, or a 11 mind, or an intelligence, or a brain, or a nervous system, or a bunch of glands, or any of the rest of these bits of me. The whole is greater than the part. And therefore, I, who am man alive, am greater than my soul, or spirit, or body, or mind, or consciousness, or anything else that is merely a part of me. I am man, and alive. I am man alive, and as long as I can, I intend to go on being man alive.

For this reason I am a novelist. And being a novelist, I consider myself superior to the saint, the scientist, the philosopher, and the poet, who are all great masters of different bits of man alive, but never get the whole hog. 12

The novel is the one bright book of life. Books are not life. They are only tremulations on the ether. But the novel as a tremulation can make the whole man alive tremble. Which is more than poetry, philosophy, science, or any other book-tremulation can do. 13

The novel is the book of life. In this sense, the Bible is a great confused novel. You may say, it is about God. But it is really about man alive. Adam, Eve, Sarai, Abraham, Isaac, Jacob, Samuel, David, Bath-Sheba, Ruth, Esther, Solomon, Job, Isaiah, Jesus, Mark, Judas, Paul, Peter: what is it but man alive, from start to finish? Man alive, not mere bits. Even the Lord is another man alive, in a burning bush, throwing the tablets of stone at Moses's head. 14

I do hope you begin to get my idea, why the novel is supremely important, as a tremulation on the ether. Plato makes the perfect ideal being tremble in me. But that's only a bit of me. Perfection is only a bit, in the strange make-up of man alive. The Sermon on the Mount makes the selfless spirit of me quiver. But that, too, is only a bit of me. The Ten Commandments set the old Adam shivering in me, warning me that I am a thief and a murderer, unless I watch it. But even the old Adam is only a bit of me. 15

I very much like all these bits of me to be set trembling with life and the wisdom of life. But I do ask that the whole of me shall tremble in its wholeness, some time or other. 16

And this, of course, must happen in me, living. 17

But as far as it can happen from a communication, it can only happen when a whole novel communicates itself to me. The Bible—but *all* the Bible—and Homer, and Shakespeare: these are the supreme old novels. These are all things to all men. Which means that in their wholeness they affect the whole man alive, which is the man himself, beyond any part of him. They set the whole tree trembling with a new access of life, they do not just stimulate growth in one direction. 18

I don't want to grow in any one direction any more. And, if I can help it, I don't want to stimulate anybody else into some particular direction. A particular direction ends in a *cul-de-sac*. We're in a *cul-de-sac* at present. 19

I don't believe in any dazzling revelation, or in any supreme Word. "The grass withereth, the flower fadeth, but the Word of the Lord shall stand for ever." That's the kind of stuff we've drugged ourselves with. As a matter of fact, the grass withereth, but comes up 20

D. H. LAWRENCE

all the greener for that reason, after the rains. The flower fadeth, and therefore the bud opens. But the Word of the Lord, being man-uttered and a mere vibration on the ether, becomes staler and staler, more and more boring, till at last we turn a deaf ear and it ceases to exist, far more finally than any withered grass. It is grass that renews its youth like the eagle, not any Word.

We should ask for no absolutes, or absolute. Once and for all and for ever, let us have done with the ugly imperialism of any absolute. There is no absolute good, there is nothing absolutely right. All things flow and change, and even change is not absolute. The whole is a strange assembly of apparently incongruous parts, slipping past one another.   21

Me, man alive, I am a very curious assembly of incongruous parts. My yea! of today is oddly different from my yea! of yesterday. My tears of tomorrow will have nothing to do with my tears of a year ago. If the one I love remains unchanged and unchanging, I shall cease to love her. It is only because she changes and startles me into change and defies my inertia, and is herself staggered in her inertia by my changing, that I can continue to love her. If she stayed put, I might as well love the pepper-pot.   22

In all this change, I maintain a certain integrity. But woe betide me if I try to put my finger on it. If I say of myself, I am this, I am that!—then, if I stick to it, I turn into a stupid fixed thing like a lamp-post. I shall never know wherein lies my integrity, my individuality, my me. I *can* never know it. It is useless to talk about my ego. That only means that I have made up an *idea* of myself, and that I am trying to cut myself out to pattern. Which is no good. You can cut your cloth to fit your coat, but you can't clip bits off your living body, to trim it down to your idea. True, you can put yourself into ideal corsets. But even in ideal corsets, fashions change.   23

Let us learn from the novel. In the novel, the characters can do nothing but *live*. If they keep on being good, according to pattern, or bad, according to pattern, or even volatile, according to pattern, they cease to live, and the novel falls dead. A character in a novel has got to live, or it is nothing.   24

We, likewise, in life have got to live, or we are nothing.   25

What we mean by living is, of course, just as indescribable as what we mean by *being*. Men get ideas into their heads, of what they mean by Life, and they proceed to cut life out to pattern. Sometimes they go into the desert to seek God, sometimes they go into the desert to seek cash, sometimes it is wine, woman, and song, and again it is water, political reform, and votes. You never know what it will be next: from killing your neighbour with hideous bombs and gas that tears the lungs, to supporting a Foundlings Home and preaching infinite Love, and being co-respondent in a divorce.   26

In all this wild welter, we need some sort of guide. It's no 27
good inventing Thou Shalt Nots!

What then? Turn truly, honourably to the novel, and see 28
wherein you are man alive, and wherein you are dead man in life.
You may love a woman as man alive, and you may be making love
to a woman as sheer dead man in life. You may eat your dinner as
man alive, or as a mere masticating corpse. As man alive you may
have a shot at your enemy. But as a ghastly simulacrum of life you
may be firing bombs into men who are neither your enemies nor your
friends, but just things you are dead to. Which is criminal, when the
things happen to be alive.

To be alive, to be man alive, to be whole man alive: that is 29
the point. And at its best, the novel, and the novel supremely, can
help you. It can help you not to be dead man in life. So much of man
walks about dead and a carcass in the street and house, today: so
much of women is merely dead. Like a pianoforte with half the
notes mute.

But in the novel you can see, plainly, when the man goes 30
dead, the woman goes inert. You can develop an instinct for life, if
you will, instead of a theory of right and wrong, good and bad.

In life, there is right and wrong, good and bad, all the time. 31
But what is right in one case is wrong in another. And in the novel
you see one man becoming a corpse, because of his so-called goodness, another going dead because of his so-called wickedness. Right
and wrong is an instinct: but an instinct of the whole consciousness
in a man, bodily, mental, spiritual at once. And only in the novel are
all things given full play, or at least, they may be given full play, when
we realize that life itself, and not inert safety, is the reason for living.
For out of the full play of all things emerges the only thing that is
anything, the wholeness of a man, the wholeness of a woman, man
alive, and live woman.

COMPREHENSION

1. State Lawrence's thesis in your own words.

2. According to Lawrence, what is the relationship between life and the
novel? Why does the novel matter? Why is the novel "the one bright book of
life"?

3. What contrasts does Lawrence establish between the novelist and the parson, philosopher, and scientist?

RHETORIC

1. Analyze the levels of diction, the very "sound" of Lawrence's prose. Examine the admixture of declarative, interrogative, and exclamatory sentence
structures in the essay. Explain the author's use of fragments, his application of

D. H. LAWRENCE

figurative language, and his use of italics for typographical emphasis. Examine Lawrence's persistent devices of repetition and overstatement in the essay. Evaluate the effect of these numerous strategies on the tone of the essay.

2. What patterns of imagery do you detect in the essay? How do they relate to the thesis?

3. How do the terms "tremulation on the ether" and "bright book of life" serve as structuring principles in the essay?

4. Trace the association of ideas advancing Lawrence's thesis. In the absence of strictly logical development, how unified and coherent is the essay?

5. Analyze patterns of comparison and contrast in the essay. Compare them to the pattern employed by Plath in "A Comparison."

6. Examine the relation of point of view to theme and tone in the essay.

WRITING

1. Do you agree with Lawrence's assertion that the novelist is better equipped than the scientist, philosopher, or theologian to capture the wholeness of life? Explain in an essay.

2. Write a personalized essay on why music matters, why film matters, why drama matters, or a similar subject.

3. Lawrence asserts that the "Bible—and Homer, and Shakespeare" are "supreme old novels." Do you agree or disagree with his position? Answer this question in a brief essay.

RALPH ELLISON

On Becoming a Writer

Ralph Ellison (1914–   ) was born in Oklahoma City and attended Tuskegee Institute. Subsequently he moved to New York, working with the Federal Writers Project and editing Negro Quarterly. *He has taught at numerous colleges, including the University of Chicago and Yale University.* Invisible Man *(1956), Ellison's only novel and a contemporary classic, portrays in vivid and often grotesque detail the crises in the black experience in America. This subject is also the thematic center of Ellison's collection of essays* Shadow and Act *(1964), from which the following selection is taken. In "On Becoming a Writer," Ellison offers*

a highly personalized account of the causal connections between the writer, literature, and American life.

n the beginning writing was far from a serious matter; it was a reflex of reading, an extension of a source of pleasure, escape, and instruction. In fact, I had become curious about writing by way of seeking to understand the aesthetic nature of literary power, the devices through which literature could command my mind and emotions. It was not, then, the *process* of writing which initially claimed my attention, but the finished creations, the artifacts, poems, plays, novels. The act of learning writing technique was, therefore, an amusing investigation of what seemed at best a secondary talent, an exploration, like dabbling in sculpture, of one's potentialities as a "Renaissance Man." This, surely, would seem a most unlikely and even comic concept to introduce here; and yet, it is precisely because I come from where I do (the Oklahoma of the years between World War I and the Great Depression) that I must introduce it, and with a straight face. 1

Anything and everything was to be found in the chaos of Oklahoma; thus the concept of the Renaissance Man has lurked long within the shadow of my past, and I shared it with at least a half dozen of my Negro friends. How we actually acquired it I have never learned, and since there is no true sociology of the dispersion of ideas within the American democracy, I doubt if I ever shall. Perhaps we breathed it in with the air of the Negro community of Oklahoma City, the capital of that state whose Negroes were often charged by exasperated white Texans with not knowing their "place." Perhaps we took it defiantly from one of them. Or perhaps I myself picked it up from some transplanted New Englander whose shoes I had shined of a Saturday afternoon. After all, the most meaningful tips do not always come in the form of money, nor are they intentionally extended. Most likely, however, my friends and I acquired the idea from some book or from some idealistic Negro teacher, some dreamer seeking to function responsibly in an environment which at its most normal took on some of the mixed character of nightmare and of dream. 2

One thing is certain, ours was a chaotic community, still characterized by frontier attitudes and by that strange mixture of the naive and sophisticated, the benign and malignant, which makes the American past so puzzling and its present so confusing; that mixture which often affords the minds of the young who grow up in the far provinces such wide and unstructured latitude, and which encourages the individual's imagination—up to the moment "reality" closes in upon him—to range widely and, sometimes, even to soar. 3

We hear the effects of this in the Southwestern jazz of the thirties, that joint creation of artistically free and exuberantly creative 4

RALPH ELLISON

adventurers, of artists who had stumbled upon the freedom lying within the restrictions of their musical tradition as within the limitations of their social background, and who in their own unconscious way have set an example for any Americans, Negro or white, who would find themselves in the arts. They accepted themselves and the complexity of life as they knew it, they loved their art and through it they celebrated American experience definitively in sound. Whatever others thought or felt, this was their own powerful statement, and only nonmusical assaults upon their artistic integrity—mainly economically inspired changes of fashion—were able to compromise their vision.

Much of so-called Kansas City jazz was actually brought to perfection in Oklahoma by Oklahomans. It is an important circumstance for me as a writer to remember, because while these musicians and their fellows were busy creating out of tradition, imagination, and the sounds and emotions around them, a freer, more complex, and driving form of jazz, my friends and I were exploring an idea of human versatility and possibility which went against the barbs or over the palings of almost every fence which those who controlled social and political power had erected to restrict our roles in the life of the country. Looking back, one might say that the jazzmen, some of whom we idolized, were in their own way better examples for youth to follow than were most judges and ministers, legislators and governors (we were stuck with the notorious Alfalfa Bill Murray). For as we viewed these pillars of society from the confines of our segregated community we almost always saw crooks, clowns, or hypocrites. Even the best were revealed by their attitudes toward us as lacking the respectable qualities to which they pretended and for which they were accepted outside by others, while despite the outlaw nature of their art, the jazzmen were less torn and damaged by the moral compromises and insincerities which have so sickened the life of our country.

Be that as it may, our youthful sense of life, like that of many Negro children (though no one bothers to note it—especially the specialists and "friends of the Negro" who view our Negro-American life as essentially nonhuman) was very much like that of Huckleberry Finn, who is universally so praised and enjoyed for the clarity and courage of his moral vision. Like Huck, we observed, we judged, we imitated and evaded as we could the dullness, corruption, and blindness of "civilization." We were undoubtedly comic because, as the saying goes, we weren't supposed to know what it was all about. But to ourselves we were "boys," members of a wild, free, outlaw tribe which transcended the category of race. Rather we were Americans born into the forty-sixth state, and thus, into the context of Negro-American post-Civil War history, "frontiersmen." And isn't one of the implicit functions of the American frontier to encourage the individual

ON BECOMING A WRITER

421

to a kind of dreamy wakefulness, a state in which he makes—in all ignorance of the accepted limitations of the possible—rash efforts, quixotic gestures, hopeful testings of the complexity of the known and the given?

Spurring us on in our controlled and benign madness was the voracious reading of which most of us were guilty and the vicarious identification and empathetic adventuring which it encouraged. This was due, in part, perhaps to the fact that some of us were fatherless—my own father had died when I was three—but most likely it was because boys are natural romantics. We were seeking examples, patterns to live by, out of a freedom which for all its being ignored by the sociologists and subtle thinkers, was implicit in the Negro situation. Father and mother substitutes also have a role to play in aiding the child to help create himself. Thus we fabricated our own heroes and ideals catch-as-catch can; and with an outrageous and irreverent sense of freedom. Yes, and in complete disregard of ideas of respectability or the surreal incongruity of some of our projections. Gamblers and scholars, jazz musicians and scientists, Negro cowboys and soldiers from the Spanish-American and First World Wars, movie stars and stunt men, figures from the Italian Renaissance and literature, both classical and popular, were combined with the special virtues of some local bootlegger, the eloquence of some Negro preacher, the strength and grace of some local athlete, the ruthlessness of some businessman-physician, the elegance in dress and manners of some headwaiter or hotel doorman.

Looking back through the shadows upon this absurd activity, I realize now that we were projecting archetypes, re-creating folk figures, legendary heroes, monsters even, most of which violated all ideas of social hierarchy and order and all accepted conceptions of the hero handed down by cultural, religious, and racist tradition. But we, remember, were under the intense spell of the early movies, the silents as well as the talkies; and in our community, life was not so tightly structured as it would have been in the traditional South—or even in deceptively "free" Harlem. And our imaginations processed reality and dream, natural man and traditional hero, literature and folklore, like maniacal editors turned loose in some frantic film-cutting room. Remember, too, that being boys, yet in the play-stage of our development, we were dream-serious in our efforts. But serious nevertheless, for *culturally* play is a preparation, and we felt that somehow the human ideal lay in the vague and constantly shifting figures—sometimes comic but always versatile, picaresque, and self-effacingly heroic—which evolved from our wildly improvisatory projections: figures neither white nor black, Christian nor Jewish, but representative of certain desirable essences, of skills and powers, physical, aesthetic, and moral.

RALPH ELLISON

The proper response to these figures was, we felt, to develop ourselves for the performance of many and diverse roles, and the fact that certain definite limitations had been imposed upon our freedom did not lessen our sense of obligation. Not only were we to prepare but we were to perform—not with mere competence but with an almost reckless verve; with, may we say (without evoking the quaint and questionable notion of *négritude*) Negro-American style? Behind each artist there stands a traditional sense of style, a sense of the felt tension indicative of expressive completeness; a mode of humanizing reality and of evoking a feeling of being at home in the world. It is something which the artist shares with the group, and part of our boyish activity expressed a yearning to make any and everything of quality *Negro-American*; to appropriate it, possess it, re-create it in our own group and individual images. 9

And we recognized and were proud of our group's own style where-ever we discerned it, in jazzmen and prizefighters, ballplayers, and tap dancers; in gesture, inflection, intonation, timbre, and phrasing. Indeed, in all those nuances of expression and attitude which reveal a culture. We did not fully understand the cost of that style, but we recognized within it an affirmation of life beyond all question of our difficulties as Negroes. 10

Contrary to the notion currently projected by certain specialists in the "Negro problem" which characterizes the Negro-American as self-hating and defensive, we did not so regard ourselves. We felt, among ourselves at least, that we were supposed to be whoever we would and could be and do anything and everything which other boys did, and do it better. Not defensively, because we were ordered to do so; nor because it was held in the society at large that we were naturally, as Negroes, limited—but because we demanded it of ourselves. Because to measure up to our own standards was the only way of affirming our notion of manhood. 11

Hence it was no more incongruous, as seen from our own particular perspective in this land of incongruities, for young Negro Oklahomans to project themselves as Renaissance men than for white Mississippians to see themselves as ancient Greeks or noblemen out of Sir Walter Scott. Surely our fantasies have caused far less damage to the nation's sense of reality, if for no other reason than that ours were expressive of a more democratic ideal. Remember, too, as William Faulkner made us so vividly aware, that the slaves often took the essence of the aristocratic ideal (as they took Christianity) with far more seriousness than their masters, and that we, thanks to the tight telescoping of American history, were but two generations from that previous condition. Renaissance men, indeed! 12

I managed, by keeping quiet about it, to cling to our boyish ideal during three years in Alabama, and I brought it with me to New 13

 ON BECOMING A WRITER 423

York, where it not only gave silent support to my explorations of what was then an unknown territory, but served to mock and caution me when I became interested in the communist ideal. And when it was suggested that I try my hand at writing it was still with me.

The act of writing requires a constant plunging back into the 14 shadow of the past where time hovers ghostlike. When I began writing in earnest I was forced, thus, to relate myself consciously and imaginatively to my mixed background as American, as Negro-American, and as a Negro from what in its own belated way was a pioneer background. More important, and inseparable from this particular effort, was the necessity of determining my true relationship to that body of American literature to which I was most attracted and through which, aided by what I could learn from the literatures of Europe, I would find my own voice and to which I was challenged, by way of achieving myself, to make some small contribution, and to whose composite picture of reality I was obligated to offer some necessary modifications.

This was no matter of sudden insight but of slow and blun- 15 dering discovery, of a struggle to stare down the deadly and hypnotic temptation to interpret the world and all its devices in terms of race. To avoid this was very important to me, and in light of my background far from simple. Indeed, it was quite complex, involving as it did, a ceaseless questioning of all those formulas which historians, politicians, sociologists, and an older generation of Negro leaders and writers—those of the so-called "Negro Renaissance"—had evolved to describe my group's identity, its predicament, its fate, and its relation to the larger society and the culture which we share.

Here the question of reality and personal identity merge. Yes, 16 and the question of the nature of the reality which underlies American fiction and thus the human truth which gives fiction viability. In this quest, for such it soon became, I learned that nothing could go unchallenged; especially that feverish industry dedicated to telling Negroes who and what they are, and which can usually be counted upon to deprive both humanity and culture of their complexity. I had undergone, not too many months before taking the path which led to writing, the humiliation of being taught in a class in sociology at a Negro college (from Park and Burgess, the leading textbook in the field) that Negroes represented the "lady of the races." This contention the Negro instructor passed blandly along to us without even bothering to wash his hands, much less his teeth. Well, I had no intention of being bound by any such humiliating definition of my relationship to American literature. Not even to those works which depicted Negroes negatively. Negro-Americans have a highly developed ability to abstract desirable qualities from those around them, even from their enemies, and my sense of reality could reject bias while

RALPH ELLISON

appreciating the truth revealed by achieved art. The pleasure which I derived from reading had long been a necessity, and in the *act* of reading, that marvelous collaboration between the writer's artful vision and the reader's sense of life, I had become acquainted with other possible selves; freer, more courageous and ingenuous and, during the course of the narrative at least, even wise.

At the time I was under the influence of Ernest Hemingway, 17 and his description, in *Death in the Afternoon*, of his thinking when he first went to Spain became very important as translated in my own naive fashion. He was trying to write, he tells us,

> and I found the greatest difficulty aside from knowing truly what you really felt, rather than what you were supposed to feel, and had been taught to feel, was to put down what really happened in action; what the actual things were which produced the emotion that you experienced . . .

His statement of moral and aesthetic purpose which followed 18 focused my own search to relate myself to American life through literature. For I found the greatest difficulty for a Negro writer was the problem of revealing what he truly felt, rather than serving up what Negroes were supposed to feel, and were encouraged to feel. And linked to this was the difficulty, based upon our long habit of deception and evasion, of depicting what really happened within our areas of American life, and putting down with honesty and without bowing to ideological expediencies the attitudes and values which give Negro-American life its sense of wholeness and which render it bearable and human and, when measured by our own terms, desirable.

I was forced to this awareness through my struggles with the 19 craft of fiction; yes, and by my attraction (soon rejected) to Marxist political theory, which was my response to the inferior status which society sought to impose upon me (I did not then, now, or ever *consider* myself inferior).

I did not know my true relationship to America—what citizen 20 of the United States really does?—but I did know and accept how I felt inside. And I also knew, thanks to the old Renaissance Man, what I expected of myself in the matter of personal discipline and creative quality. Since by the grace of the past and the examples of manhood picked willy-nilly from the continuing-present of my background, I rejected all negative definitions imposed upon me by others, there was nothing to do but search for those relationships which were fundamental.

In this sense fiction became the agency of my efforts to answer 21 the questions, Who am I, what am I, how did I come to be? What shall I make of the life around me, what celebrate, what reject, how

 ON BECOMING A WRITER

confront the snarl of good and evil which is inevitable? What does American society *mean* when regarded out of my *own* eyes, when informed of my *own* sense of the past and viewed by my *own* complex sense of the present? How, in other words, should I think of myself and my pluralistic sense of the world, how express my vision of the human predicament, without reducing it to a point which would render it sterile before that necessary and tragic—though enhancing—reduction which must occur before the fictive vision can come alive? It is quite possible that much potential fiction by Negro-Americans fails precisely at this point: through the writers' refusal (often through provincialism or lack of courage or through opportunism) to achieve a vision of life and a resourcefulness of craft commensurate with the complexity of their actual situation. Too often they fear to leave the uneasy sanctuary of race to take their chances in the world of art.

COMPREHENSION

1. What is Ellison's purpose in discussing the concept of the "Renaissance Man" throughout the essay?

2. Why did Ellison become a writer? Trace the influences and events in this process.

3. Paraphrase Ellison's commentary on the relationship between the black artist and American society.

RHETORIC

1. Explain in context the following terms and phrases: "the aesthetic nature of literary power" (paragraph 1); "the concept of the Renaissance Man" (paragraph 2); "that joint creation of artistically free and exuberantly creative adventurers" (paragraph 4); "we were projecting archetypes . . ." (paragraph 8); "a traditional sense of style, a sense of the felt tension indicative of expressive completeness" (paragraph 9); and "moral and aesthetic purpose" (paragraph 18). What do these terms have in common?

2. How does the relative difficulty of the syntax in this essay influence the effectiveness of the selection?

3. What do Ellison's use of narrative and first-person point of view contribute to the essay?

4. Where does the author introduce causal analysis? Is he interested in causes, effects, or both? What is the chain of causality? How does he treat primary and secondary causes?

5. Explain the function and purpose of paragraphs 6, 14, and 17.

6. Why is Ellison's concluding paragraph especially significant and successful? What is the purpose of the rhetorical questions?

RALPH ELLISON

WRITING

1. Develop more fully Ellison's observation that reading (and exposure to any form of art) often produces "vicarious identification and empathetic adventuring" (paragraph 7).

2. Write an essay that analyzes the ways in which literature, music, television, and film permit us to relate to some aspect of American life.

3. Ellison implies that appreciating the arts is an act of liberation. Comment on this thesis.

4. How can *you* become the sort of "Renaissance" person Ellison speaks of in his essay? Write an essay describing the characteristics of such an individual.

ALICE WALKER

Saving the Life That Is Your Own: The Importance of Models in the Artist's Life

Alice Walker (1944–   ) was born in Eatonton, Georgia, and now lives in San Francisco and Mendocino County, California. A celebrated poet, short story writer, and novelist, she is the author of Revolutionary Petunias, In Love and Trouble, *and* Meridian, *among other works. Her 1983 novel* The Color Purple *won the American Book Award and the Pulitzer Prize. The following essay, from* In Search of Our Mothers' Gardens *(1983), offers a highly personalized and perceptive analysis of the importance of influence in both art and life.*

 here is a letter Vincent Van Gogh wrote to Emile Bernard that is very meaningful to me. A year before he wrote the letter, Van Gogh had had a fight with his domineering friend Gauguin, left his company, and cut off, in desperation and anguish, his own ear. The letter was written in Saint-Remy, in the South of France, from a mental institution to which Van Gogh had voluntarily committed himself.

I imagine Van Gogh sitting at a rough desk too small for him, looking out at the lovely Southern light, and occasionally glancing

1

2

critically next to him at his own paintings of the landscape he loved so much. The date of the letter is December 1889. Van Gogh wrote:

> However hateful painting may be, and however cumbersome in the times we are living in, if anyone who has chosen this handicraft pursues it zealously, he is a man of duty, sound and faithful.
>
> Society makes our existence wretchedly difficult at times, hence our impotence and the imperfection of our work.
>
> . . . I myself am suffering under an absolute lack of models.
>
> But on the other hand, there are beautiful spots here. I have just done five size 30 canvasses, olive trees. And the reason I am staying on here is that my health is improving a great deal.
>
> What I am doing is hard, dry, but that is because I am trying to gather new strength by doing some rough work, and I'm afraid abstractions would make me soft.

Six months later, Van Gogh—whose health was "improving   3
a great deal"—committed suicide. He had sold one painting during his lifetime. Three times was his work noticed in the press. But these are just details.

The real Vincent Van Gogh is the man who has "just done   4
five size 30 canvasses, olive trees." To me, in context, one of the most moving and revealing descriptions of how a real artist thinks. And the knowledge that when he spoke of "suffering under an absolute lack of models" he spoke of that lack in terms of both the intensity of his commitment and the quality and singularity of his work, which was frequently ridiculed in his day.

The absence of models, in literature as in life, to say nothing   5
of painting, is an occupational hazard for the artist, simply because models in art, in behavior, in growth of spirit and intellect—even if rejected—enrich and enlarge one's view of existence. Deadlier still, to the artist who lacks models, is the curse of ridicule, the bringing to bear on an artist's best work, especially his or her most original, most strikingly deviant, only a fund of ignorance and the presumption that, as an artist's critic, one's judgment is free of the restrictions imposed by prejudice, and is well informed, indeed, about all the art in the world that really matters.

What is always needed in the appreciation of art, or life, is   6
the larger perspective. Connections made, or at least attempted, where none existed before, the straining to encompass in one's glance at the varied world the common thread, the unifying theme through immense diversity, a fearlessness of growth, of search, of looking, that

enlarges the private and the public world. And yet, in our particular society, it is the narrowed and narrowing view of life that often wins.

Recently, I read at a college and was asked by one of the 7 audience what I considered the major difference between the literature written by black and by white Americans. I had not spent a lot of time considering this question, since it is not the difference between them that interests me, but, rather, the way black writers and white writers seem to me to be writing one immense story—the same story, for the most part—with different parts of this immense story coming from a multitude of different perspectives. Until this is generally recognized, literature will always be broken into bits, black and white, and there will always be questions, wanting neat answers, such as this.

Still, I answered that I thought, for the most part, white Amer- 8 ican writers tended to end their books and their characters' lives as if there were no better existence for which to struggle. The gloom of defeat is thick.

By comparison, black writers seem always involved in a moral 9 and/or physical struggle, the result of which is expected to be some kind of larger freedom. Perhaps this is because our literary tradition is based on the slave narratives, where escape for the body and freedom for the soul went together, or perhaps this is because black people have never felt themselves guilty of global, cosmic sins.

This comparison does not hold up in every case, of course, 10 and perhaps does not really hold up at all. I am not a gatherer of statistics, only a curious reader, and this has been my impression from reading many books by black and white writers.

There are, however, two books by American women that il- 11 lustrate what I am talking about: *The Awakening*, by Kate Chopin, and *Their Eyes Were Watching God*, by Zora Neale Hurston.

The plight of Mme Pontellier is quite similar to that of Janie 12 Crawford. Each woman is married to a dull, society-conscious husband and living in a dull, propriety-conscious community. Each woman desires a life of her own and a man who loves her and makes her feel alive. Each woman finds such a man.

Mme Pontellier, overcome by the strictures of society and the 13 existence of her children (along with the cowardice of her lover), kills herself rather than defy the one and abandon the other. Janie Crawford, on the other hand, refuses to allow society to dictate behavior to her, enjoys the love of a much younger, freedom-loving man, and lives to tell others of her experience.

When I mentioned these two books to my audience, I was not 14 surprised to learn that only one person, a young black poet in the first row, had ever heard of *Their Eyes Were Watching God* (*The Awakening* they had fortunately read in their "Women in Literature" class), pri-

 SAVING THE LIFE THAT IS YOUR OWN

marily because it was written by a black woman, whose experience—in love and life—was apparently assumed to be unimportant to the students (and the teachers) of a predominantly white school.

Certainly, as a student, I was not directed toward this book, 15 which would have urged me more toward freedom and experience than toward comfort and security, but was directed instead toward a plethora of books by mainly white male writers who thought most women worthless if they didn't enjoy bullfighting or hadn't volunteered for the trenches in World War I.

Loving both these books, knowing each to be indispensable 16 to my own growth, my own life, I choose the model, the example, of Janie Crawford. And yet this book, as necessary to me and to other women as air and water, is again out of print* But I have distilled as much as I could of its wisdom in this poem about its heroine, Janie Crawford:

> I love the way Janie Crawford
> left her husbands
> the one who wanted to change her
> into a mule
> and the other who tried to interest her
> in being a queen.
> A woman, unless she submits,
> is neither a mule
> nor a queen
> though like a mule she may suffer
> and like a queen pace the floor.

It has been said that someone asked Toni Morrison why she 17 writes the kind of books she writes, and that she replied: Because they are the kind of books I want to read.

This remains my favorite reply to that kind of question. As if 18 anyone reading the magnificent, mysterious *Sula* or the grim, poetic *The Bluest Eye* would require more of a reason for their existence than for the brooding, haunting *Wuthering Heights*, for example, or the melancholy, triumphant *Jane Eyre*. (I am not speaking here of the most famous short line of that book, "Reader, I married him," as the triumph, but, rather, of the triumph of Jane Eyre's control over her own sense of morality and her own stout will, which are but reflections of her creator's, Charlotte Brontë, who no doubt wished to write the sort of books *she* wished to read.)

Flannery O'Connor has written that more and more the seri- 19 ous novelist will write, not what other people want, and certainly not

*Reissued by the University of Illinois Press, 1979.

ALICE WALKER

what other people expect, but whatever interests her or him. And that the direction taken, therefore, will be away from sociology, away from the "writing of explanation," of statistics, and further into mystery, into poetry, and into prophecy. I believe this is true, *fortunately true*; especially for "Third World Writers"; Morrison, Marquez, Ahmadi, Camara Laye make good examples. And not only do I believe it is true for serious writers in general, but I believe, as firmly as did O'Connor, that this is our only hope—in a culture so in love with flash, with trendiness, with superficiality, as ours—of acquiring a sense of essence, of timelessness, and of vision. Therefore, to write the books one wants to read is both to point the direction of vision and, at the same time, to follow it.

When Toni Morrison said she writes the kind of books she wants to read, she was acknowledging the fact that in a society in which "accepted literature" is so often sexist and racist and otherwise irrelevant or offensive to so many lives, she must do the work of two. She must be her own model as well as the artist attending, creating, learning from, realizing the model, which is to say, herself. 20

(It should be remembered that, as a black person, one cannot completely identify with a Jane Eyre, or with her creator, no matter how much one admires them. And certainly, if one allows history to impinge on one's reading pleasure, one must cringe at the thought of how Heathcliff, in the New World far from Wuthering Heights, amassed his Cathy-dazzling fortune.) I have often been asked why, in my own life and work, I have felt such a desperate need to know and assimilate the experiences of earlier black women writers, most of them unheard of by you and by me, until quite recently; why I felt a need to study them and to teach them. 21

I don't recall the exact moment I set out to explore the works of black women, mainly those in the past, and certainly, in the beginning, I had no desire to teach them. Teaching being for me, at that time, less rewarding than star-gazing on a frigid night. My discovery of them—most of them out of print, abandoned, discredited, maligned, nearly lost—came about, as many things of value do, almost by accident. As it turned out—and this should not have surprised me—I found I was in need of something that only one of them could provide. 22

Mindful that throughout my four years at a prestigious black and then a prestigious white college I had heard not one word about early black women writers, one of my first tasks was simply to determine whether they had existed. After this, I could breathe easier, with more assurance about the profession I myself had chosen. 23

But the incident that started my search began several years ago: I sat down at my desk one day, in a room of my own, with key and lock, and began preparations for a story about voodoo, a subject 24 that had always fascinated me. Many of the elements of this story I had gathered from a story my mother several times told me. She had gone, during the Depression, into town to apply for some government surplus food at the local commissary, and had been turned down, in a particularly humiliating way, by the white woman in charge.

My mother always told this story with a most curious expression on her face. She automatically raised her head higher than ever—it was always high—and there was a look of righteousness, a kind of holy *heat* coming from her eyes. She said she had lived to see this same white woman grow old and senile and so badly crippled she had to get about on *two* sticks. 25

To her, this was clearly the working of God, who, as in the old spiritual, "... may not come when you want him, but he's right on time!" To me, hearing the story for about the fiftieth time, something else was discernible: the possibilities of the story, for fiction. 26

What, I asked myself, would have happened if, after the crippled old lady died, it was discovered that someone, my mother perhaps (who would have been mortified at the thought, Christian that she is), had voodooed her? 27

Then, my thoughts sweeping me away into the world of hexes and conjurings of centuries past, I wondered how a larger story could be created out of my mother's story; one that would be true to the magnitude of her humiliation and grief, and to the white woman's lack of sensitivity and compassion. 28

My third quandary was: How could I find out all I needed to know in order to write a story that used *authentic* black witchcraft? 29

Which brings me back, almost, to the day I became really interested in black women writers. I say "almost" because one other thing, from my childhood, made the choice of black magic a logical and irresistible one for my story. Aside from my mother's several stories about root doctors she had heard of or known, there was the story I had often heard about my "crazy" Walker aunt. 30

Many years ago, when my aunt was a meek and obedient girl growing up in a strict, conventionally religious house in the rural South, she had suddenly thrown off her meekness and had run away from home, escorted by a rogue of a man permanently attached elsewhere. 31

When she was returned home by her father, she was declared quite mad. In the backwoods South at the turn of the century, "madness" of this sort was cured not by psychiatry but by powders and by spells. (One can see Scott Joplin's *Treemonisha* to understand the role voodoo played among black people of that period.) My aunt's madness was treated by the community conjurer, who promised, and delivered, the desired results. His treatment was a bag of white powder, bought for fifty cents, and sprinkled on the ground around her 32

ALICE WALKER

house, with some of it sewed, I believe, into the bodice of her night-gown.

So when I sat down to write my story about voodoo, my crazy   33
Walker aunt was definitely on my mind.

But she had experienced her temporary craziness so long ago   34
that her story had all the excitement of a might-have-been. I needed,
instead of family memories, some hard facts about the *craft* of voodoo,
as practiced by Southern blacks in the nineteenth century. (It never
once, fortunately, occurred to me that voodoo was not worthy of the
interest I had in it, or was too ridiculous to study seriously.)

I began reading all I could find on the subject of "The Negro   35
and His Folkways and Superstitions." There were Botkin and Puckett
and others, all white, most racist. How was I to believe anything they
wrote, since at least one of them, Puckett, was capable of wondering,
in his book, if "The Negro" had a large enough brain?

Well, I thought, where are the *black* collectors of folklore?   36
Where is the *black* anthropologist? Where is the *black* person who took
the time to travel the back roads of the South and collect the information I need: how to cure heat trouble, treat dropsy, hex somebody
to death, lock bowels, cause joints to swell, eyes to fall out, and so on.
Where was this black person?

And that is when I first saw, in a *footnote* to the white voices   37
of authority, the name Zora Neale Hurston.

Folklorist, novelist, anthropologist, serious student of voodoo,   38
also all-around black woman, with guts enough to take a slide rule
and measure random black heads in Harlem; not to prove their inferiority, but to prove that whatever their size, shape, or present condition of servitude, those heads contained all the intelligence anyone
could use to get through this world.

Zora Hurston, who went to Barnard to learn how to study   39
what she really wanted to learn: the ways of her own people, and
what ancient rituals, customs, and beliefs had made them unique.

Zora, of the sandy-colored hair and the daredevil eyes, a girl   40
who escaped poverty and parental neglect by hard work and a sharp
eye for the main chance.

Zora, who left the South only to return to look at it again.   41
Who went to root doctors from Florida to Louisiana and said, "Here
I am. I want to learn your trade."

Zora, who had collected all the black folklore I could ever use.   42
That Zora.   43

And having found *that Zora* (like a golden key to a storehouse   44
of varied treasure), I was hooked.

What I had discovered, of course, was a model. A model, who,   45
as it happened, provided more than voodoo for my story, more than
one of the greatest novels America had produced—though, being

America, it did not realize this. She had provided, as if she knew someday I would come along wandering in the wilderness, a nearly complete record of her life. And though her life sprouted an occasional wart, I am eternally grateful for that life, warts and all.

It is not irrelevant, nor is it bragging (except perhaps to gloat a little on the happy relatedness of Zora, my mother and me), to mention here that the story I wrote, called "the Revenge of Hannah Kemhuff," based on my mother's experiences during the Depression, and on Zora Hurston's folklore collection of the 1920s, and on my own response to both out of a contemporary existence, was immediately published and was later selected, by a reputable collector of short stories, as one of the *Best Short Stories of 1974*.   46

I mention it because this story might never have been written, because the very bases of its structure, authentic black folklore, viewed from a black perspective, might have been lost.   47

Had it been lost, my mother's story would have had no historical underpinning, none I could trust, anyway. I would not have written the story, which I enjoyed writing as much as I've enjoyed writing anything in my life, had I not known that Zora had already done a thorough job of preparing the ground over which I was then moving.   48

In that story I gathered up the historical and psychological threads of the life my ancestors lived, and in the writing of it I felt joy and strength and my own continuity. I had that wonderful feeling writers get sometimes, not very often, of being *with* a great many people, ancient spirits, all very happy to see me consulting and acknowledging them, and eager to let me know, through the joy of their presence, that, indeed, I am not alone.   49

To take Toni Morrison's statement further, if that is possible, in my own work I write not only what I want to read—understanding fully and indelibly that if I don't do it no one else is so vitally interested, or capable of doing it to my satisfaction—I write all the things *I should have been able to read*. Consulting, as belatedly discovered models, those writers—most of whom, not surprisingly, are women—who understood that their experience as ordinary human beings was also valuable, and in danger of being misrepresented, distorted, or lost: 50

Zora Hurston—novelist, essayist, anthropologist, autobiographer;

Jean Toomer—novelist, poet, philosopher, visionary, a man who cared what women felt;

Colette—whose crinkly hair enhances her French, part-black face; novelist, playwright, dancer, essayist, newspaperwoman, lover of women, men, small dogs; fortunate not to have been born in America;

Anaïs Nin—recorder of everything, no matter how minute;

Tillie Olson—a writer of such generosity and honesty, she literally saves lives;

Virginia Woolf—who has saved so many of us.

It is, in the end, the saving of lives that we writers are about. 51
Whether we are "minority" writers or "majority." It is simply in our power to do this.

We do it because we care. We care that Vincent Van Gogh 52
mutilated his ear. We care that behind a pile of manure in the yard he destroyed his life. We care that Scott Joplin's music *lives!* We care because we know this: *the life we save is our own.*

COMPREHENSION

1. Explain the significance of Walker's title. How does it serve her purpose and guide readers to her thesis? What is her thesis?

2. According to the author, what is the importance of models in art? What is the relationship of models to life? List the models in Walker's life. Which figures stand out?

3. Paraphrase Walker's remarks on the relationship between black American and white American writing. How do her observations echo Ellison's in "On Becoming a Writer"?

RHETORIC

1. Walker uses many allusions in this essay. Identify as many as you can. What is the allusion in the title? Comment on their general effectiveness.

2. Is the author's style and choice of diction suitable to her subject matter and to her audience? Why, or why not?

3. Why does the author personalize her treatment of the topic? What does she gain? Is there anything lost?

4. Walker employs several unique structuring devices in this essay. Cite at least three, and analyze their utility.

5. Explain Walker's use of examples to reinforce her generalizations and to organize the essay.

6. Which paragraphs constitute Walker's conclusion? What is their effect?

WRITING

1. Discuss the meaning of Walker's remark, "What is always needed in the appreciation of art, or life, is the larger perspective."

2. If you were planning on a career as a writer, artist, actor, or musician, who would your models be, and why?

3. Analyze the various models—personal, cultural, and artistic—in your own life.

4. Explore the types of literature, art, film, and music that you like. How do these varieties of art influence your life?

E. M. FORSTER

Not Looking at Pictures

Edward Morgan Forster (1879–1970), English essayist, novelist, biographer, and literary critic, wrote several notable works of fiction dealing with the constrictive effects of social and national conventions on human relationships. These novels include A Room with a View *(1908),* Howard's End *(1910), and* A Passage to India *(1924). In addition, his lectures on fiction, collected as* Aspects of the Novel *(1927), remain graceful elucidations of the genre. In "Not Looking at Pictures," an essay taken from* Two Cheers for Democracy *(1939), Forster offers a whimsical account of difficulties when trying to evaluate art.*

Pictures are not easy to look at. They generate private 1 fantasies, they furnish material for jokes, they recall scraps of historical knowledge, they show landscapes where one would like to wander and human beings whom one would like to resemble or adore, but looking at them is another matter, yet they must have been painted to be looked at. They were intended to appeal to the eye, but almost as if it were gazing at the sun itself the eye often reacts by closing as soon as it catches sight of them. The mind takes charge instead and goes off on some alien vision. The mind has such a congenial time that it forgets what set it going. Van Gogh and Corot and Michelangelo are three different painters, but if the mind is undisciplined and uncontrolled by the eye, they may all three induce the same mood; we may take just the same course through dreamland or funland from them, each time, and never experience anything new.

I am bad at looking at pictures myself, and the late Roger Fry 2 enjoyed going to a gallery with me now and then, for this very reason. He found it an amusing change to be with someone who scarcely ever saw what the painter had painted. "Tell me, why do you like this, why do you prefer it to that?" he would ask, and listen agape for the

E. M. FORSTER

ridiculous answer. One day we looked at a fifteenth-century Italian predella, where a St. George was engaged in spearing a dragon of the plesiosaurus type. I laughed. "Now, *what* is there funny in this?" pounced Fry. I readily explained. The fun was to be found in the expression upon the dragon's face. The spear had gone through its hooped-up neck once, and now startled it by arriving at a second thickness. "Oh dear, here it comes again, I hoped that was all" it was thinking. Fry laughed too, but not at the misfortunes of the dragon. He was amazed that anyone could go so completely off the lines. There was no harm in it—but really, really! He was even more amazed when our enthusiasms coincided: "I fancy we are talking about different things," he would say, and we always were; I liked the mountain-back because it reminded me of a peacock, he because it had some structural significance, though not as much as the sack of potatoes in the foreground.

Long years of wandering down miles of galleries have convinced me that there must be something rare in those coloured slabs called "pictures," something which I am incapable of detecting for myself, though glimpses of it are to be had through the eyes of others. How much am I missing? And what? And are other modern sightseers in the same fix? Ours is an aural rather than a visual age, we do not get so lost in the concert hall, we seem able to hear music for ourselves, and to hear it as music, but in galleries so many of us go off at once into a laugh or a sigh or an amorous day-dream. In vain does the picture recall us. "What have your obsessions got to do with me?" it complains. "I am neither a theatre of varieties nor a spring-mattress, but paint. Look at my paint." Back we go—the picture kindly standing still meanwhile, and being to that extent more obliging than music—and resume the looking-business. But something is sure to intervene—a tress of hair, the half-open door of a summer-house, a Crivelli dessert, a Bosch fish-and-fiend salad—and to draw us away.

One of the things that helps us keep looking is composition. For many years now I have associated composition with a diagonal line, and when I find such a line I imagine I have gutted the picture's secret. Giorgione's Castelfranco Madonna has such a line in the lance of the warrior-saint, and Titian's Entombment at Venice has a very good one indeed. Five figures contribute to make up the diagonal; beginning high on the left with the statue of Moses, it passes through the heads of the Magdalene, Mary, and the dead Christ, and plunges through the body of Joseph of Arimathea into the ground. Making a right angle to it, flits the winged Genius of Burial. And to the right, apart from it, and perpendicular, balancing the Moses, towers the statue of Faith. Titian's Entombment is one of my easiest pictures. I look at photographs of it intelligently, and encourage the diagonal

NOT LOOKING AT PICTURES

and the pathos to reinforce one another. I see, with more than usual vividness, the grim alcove at the back and the sinister tusked pedestals upon which the two statues stand. Stone shuts in flesh; the whole picture is a tomb. I hear sounds of lamentation, though not to the extent of shattering the general scheme; that is held together by the emphatic diagonal, which no emotion breaks. Titian was a very old man when he achieved this masterpiece; that too I realise, but not immoderately. Composition here really has been a help, and it is a composition which no one can miss: the diagonal slopes as obviously as the band on a threshing-machine, and vibrates with power.

Unfortunately, having no natural esthetic aptitude, I look for diagonals everywhere, and if I cannot find one think the composition must be at fault. It is a word which I have learnt—a solitary word in a foreign language. For instance, I was completely baffled by Velasquez's Las Meninas. Wherever was the diagonal? Then the friend I was with—Charles Mauron, the friend who, after Roger Fry, has helped me with pictures most—set to work on my behalf, and cautiously underlined the themes. There is a wave. There is a half-wave. The wave starts up on the left, with the head of the painter, and curves down and up through the heads of the three girls. The half-wave starts with the head of Isabel de Velasco, and sinks out of the canvas through the dwarfs. Responding to these great curves, or inverting them, are smaller ones on the women's dresses or elsewhere. All these waves are not merely pattern; they are doing other work too—e.g., helping to bring out the effect of depth in the room, and the effect of air. Important too is the pushing forward of objects in the extreme left and right foregrounds, the easel of the painter in the one case, the paws of a placid dog in the other. From these, the composition curves back to the central figure, the lovely child-princess. I put it more crudely than did Charles Mauron, nor do I suppose that his account would have been Velasquez's, or that Velasquez would have given any account at all. But it is an example of the way in which pictures should be tackled for the benefit of us outsiders: coolly and patiently, as if they were designs, so that we are helped at last to the appreciation of something non-mathematical. Here again, as in the case of the Entombment, the composition and the action reinforced one another. I viewed with increasing joy that adorable party, which had been surprised not only by myself but by the King and Queen of Spain. There they were in the looking-glass! Las Meninas has a snapshot quality. The party might have been taken by Philip IV, if Philip IV had had a Kodak. It is all so casual—and yet it is all so elaborate and sophisticated, and I suppose those curves and the rest of it help to bring this out, and to evoke a vanished civilisation.

Besides composition there is colour. I look for that, too, but with even less success. Colour is visible when thrown in my face—

E. M. FORSTER

like the two cherries in the great grey Michael Sweertz group in the National Gallery. But as a rule it is only material for dream.

On the whole, I am improving, and after all these years. I am learning to get myself out of the way a little, and to be more receptive, and my appreciation of pictures does increase. If I can make any progress at all, the average outsider should do better still. A combination of courage and modesty is what he wants. It is so unenterprising to annihilate everything that's made to a green thought, even when the thought is an exquisite one. Not looking at art leads to one goal only. Looking at it leads to so many. 7

COMPREHENSION

1. What is Forster's purpose in writing this essay? What response does he expect of his audience? How do you know?

2. Why does the author declare, "Pictures are not easy to look at"? Why is Forster himself "bad at looking at pictures"?

3. What does the author seem to like about art? Why does he persist in viewing artworks, despite his difficulties?

RHETORIC

1. Identify these allusions in the essay: Van Gogh, Corot, Michelangelo (paragraph 1); Roger Fry (paragraph 2); Crivelli, Bosch (paragraph 3); Giorgione, Titian (paragraph 4); and Velasquez (paragraph 5). What do these allusions tell us about the degree of Forster's expertise?

2. Examine Forster's use of punctuation to establish tone in paragraphs 2 and 3.

3. Analyze the material presented in the introduction and the strategies employed.

4. How does Forster employ illustration to help structure each paragraph in this essay?

5. Explain the author's use of comparison and contrast in this essay. Is the method the same as Plath's in "A Comparison"? Explain.

6. What elements contribute to the gently humorous tone of this essay? Do you detect similar elements in his essay "My Wood"? Explain.

WRITING

1. Forster declares, "Ours is an aural rather than visual age" (paragraph 3). Do you agree or disagree with his assertion, and why?

2. Is it necessary to raise doubts about something seen as positive? Examine this question in an essay, citing specific examples.

 NOT LOOKING AT PICTURES

3. Forster mentions "composition" and "color" as two aspects of art appreciation. Elaborate on these qualities and others in an essay explaining how you evaluate pictures.

4. Analyze a particular work of art based on a museum trip or an illustration.

JOAN DIDION

Georgia O'Keeffe

Joan Didion (1934–   ) grew up in California and graduated from the University of California at Berkeley in 1956. She began writing for national magazines such as Mademoiselle, Saturday Evening Post, *and* Life. *She published her first novel,* Run River, *in 1963. Although she has continued to write novels and has written several screenplays, her most acclaimed work is in nonfiction. This work includes* Slouching Towards Bethlehem *(1968),* The White Album *(1979),* Salvador *(1983),* Democracy *(1984), and* Miami *(1987). "Georgia O'Keeffe" paints a portrait of a highly irreverent and independent woman who challenged the status quo at a time when "the men" were supposed to dictate artistic style.*

Where I was born and where and how I have lived is unimportant," Georgia O'Keeffe told us in the book of paintings and words published in her ninetieth year on earth. She seemed to be advising us to forget the beautiful face in the Stieglitz photographs. She appeared to be dismissing the rather condescending romance that had attached to her by then, the romance of extreme good looks and advanced age and deliberate isolation. "It is what I have done with where I have been that should be of interest." I recall an August afternoon in Chicago in 1973 when I took my daughter, then seven, to see what Georgia O'Keeffe had done with where she had been. One of the vast O'Keeffe "Sky Above Clouds" canvases floated over the back stairs in the Chicago Art Institute that day, dominating what seemed to be several stories of empty light, and my daughter looked at it once, ran to the landing, and kept on looking. "Who drew it," she whispered after a while. I told her. "I need to talk to her," she said finally.

My daughter was making, that day in Chicago, an entirely unconscious but quite basic assumption about people and the work they do. She was assuming that the glory she saw in the work reflected a glory in its maker, that the painting was the painter as the poem is the poet, that every choice one made alone—every word chosen or rejected, every brush stroke laid or not laid down—betrayed one's character. *Style is character.* It seemed to me that afternoon that I had rarely seen so instinctive an application of this familiar principle, and I recall being pleased not only that my daughter responded to style as character but that it was Georgia O'Keeffe's particular style to which she responded: this was a hard woman who had imposed her 192 square feet of clouds on Chicago.

"Hardness" has not been in our century a quality much admired in women, nor in the past twenty years has it even been in official favor for men. When hardness surfaces in the very old we tend to transform it into "crustiness" or eccentricity, some tonic pepperiness to be indulged at a distance. On the evidence of her work and what she has said about it, Georgia O'Keeffe is neither "crusty" nor eccentric. She is simply hard, a straight shooter, a woman clean of received wisdom and open to what she sees. This is a woman who could early on dismiss most of her contemporaries as "dreamy," and would later single out one she liked as "a very poor painter." (And then add, apparently by way of softening the judgment: "I guess he wasn't a painter at all. He had no courage and I believe that to create one's own world in any of the arts takes courage.") This is a woman who in 1939 could advise her admirers that they were missing her point, that their appreciation of her famous flowers was merely sentimental. "When I paint a red hill," she observed coolly in the catalogue for an exhibition that year, "you say it is too bad that I don't always paint flowers. A flower touches almost everyone's heart. A red hill doesn't touch everyone's heart." This is a woman who could describe the genesis of one of her most well-known paintings—the "Cow's Skull: Red, White and Blue" owned by the Metropolitan—as an act of quite deliberate and derisive orneriness. "I thought of the city men I had been seeing in the East," she wrote. "They talked so often of writing the Great American Novel—the Great American Play—the Great American Poetry.... So as I was painting my cow's head on blue I thought to myself, 'I'll make it an American painting. They will not think it great with the red stripes down the sides—Red, White and Blue—but they will notice it.'"

The city men. The men. They. The words crop up again and again as this astonishingly aggressive woman tells us what was on her mind when she was making her astonishingly aggressive paintings. It was those city men who stood accused of sentimentalizing her flowers: "I made you take time to look at what I saw and when you took time to really notice my flower you hung all your associations with flowers on my flower and you write about my flower as if I think and see what you think and see—and I don't." *And I don't.* Imagine those words spoken, and the sound you hear is *don't tread on me.* "The men" believed it impossible to paint New York, so Georgia O'Keeffe painted New York. "The men" didn't think much of her bright color, so she made it brighter. The men yearned toward Europe so she went to Texas, and then New Mexico. The men talked about Cézanne, "long involved remarks about the 'plastic quality' of his form and color," and took one another's long involved remarks, in the view of this angelic rattlesnake in their midst, altogether too seriously. "I can paint one of those dismal-colored paintings like the men," the woman who regarded herself always as an outsider remembers thinking one day in 1922, and she did: a painting of a shed "all low-toned and dreary with the tree beside the door." She called this act of rancor "The Shanty" and hung it in her next show. "The men seemed to approve of it," she reported fifty-four years later, her contempt undimmed. "They seemed to think that maybe I was beginning to paint. That was my only low-toned dismal-colored painting."

Some women fight and others do not. Like so many successful 5 guerrillas in the war between the sexes, Georgia O'Keeffe seems to have been equipped early with an immutable sense of who she was and a fairly clear understanding that she would be required to prove it. On the surface her upbringing was conventional. She was a child on the Wisconsin prairie who played with china dolls and painted watercolors with cloudy skies because sunlight was too hard to paint and, with her brother and sisters, listened every night to her mother read stories of the Wild West, of Texas, of Kit Carson and Billy the Kid. She told adults that she wanted to be an artist and was embarrassed when they asked what kind of artist she wanted to be: she had no idea "what kind." She had no idea what artists did. She had never seen a picture that interested her, other than a pen-and-ink Maid of Athens in one of her mother's books, some Mother Goose illustrations printed on cloth, a tablet cover that showed a little girl with pink roses, and the painting of Arabs on horseback that hung in her grandmother's parlor. At thirteen, in a Dominican convent, she was mortified when the sister corrected her drawing. At Chatham Episcopal Institute in Virginia she painted lilacs and sneaked time alone to walk out to where she could see the line of the Blue Ridge Mountains on the horizon. At the Art Institute in Chicago she was shocked by the presence of live models and wanted to abandon anatomy lessons. At the Art Students League in New York one of her fellow students advised her that, since he would be a great painter and she would end up teaching painting in a girls' school, any work of hers was less important than modeling for him. Another painted over her work to show her how the Impressionists did trees. She had not before heard how the Impressionists did trees and she did not much care.

At twenty-four she left all those opinions behind and went for   6
the first time to live in Texas, where there were no trees to paint and
no one to tell her how not to paint them. In Texas there was only the
horizon she craved. In Texas she had her sister Claudia with her for
a while, and in the late afternoons they would walk away from town
and toward the horizon and watch the evening star come out. "That
evening star fascinated me," she wrote. "It was in some way very
exciting to me. My sister had a gun, and as we walked she would
throw bottles into the air and shoot as many as she could before they
hit the ground. I had nothing but to walk into nowhere and the wide
sunset space with the star. Ten watercolors were made from that star."
In a way one's interest is compelled as much by the sister Claudia
with the gun as by the painter Georgia with the star, but only the
painter left us this shining record. Ten watercolors were made from
that star.

COMPREHENSION

1. Does this essay have an explicit or implied thesis? Explain.

2. What does Didion suggest is O'Keeffe's greatest attribute as an artist? Compare her approach to O'Keeffe to Walker's approach to the artists in her life.

3. Didion refers to specific paintings, museums, and artists in the essay. List them. What assumptions is she making about the cultural and educational background of her reading audience?

RHETORIC

1. What is the purpose of the repetition of the word *men* in paragraph 4? Why is the word italicized and quoted?

2. What do Didion's phrases "ninetieth year on earth" (paragraph 1) and "imposed her 192 square feet of clouds" (paragraph 2) suggest about her attitude toward her subject?

3. Didion begins the essay with a quote from the artist. How does this strategy help set the tone of the essay?

4. In paragraph 3, Didion begins three sentences with the words, "This is a woman . . ."; how do they contribute to the unity and rhetorical effect of the paragraph?

5. Why has Didion included detailed biographical material in paragraph 5? Why has she included this information *after* she discusses O'Keeffe's life as a painter? Which of the facts help us understand O'Keeffe's development as "a woman clean of received wisdom and open to what she sees" (paragraph 3)?

6. Why does Didion's conclusion include a commentary about O'Keeffe's sister? Where and for what purpose does Didion make an implied comparison between O'Keeffe's personality and her sister's habit of firing a gun?

GEORGIA O'KEEFFE   443

PAULINE KAEL

Rocky

Pauline Kael (1919–　　) has been a film critic for McCall's, The New Republic, *and* The New Yorker *and a frequent contributor to other national publications. Perhaps the best known and most controversial film critic in the United States today, Kael is the author of* I Lost It at the Movies *(1965),* Kiss Kiss Bang Bang *(1968),* Going Steady *(1970),* Deeper into the Movies *(1973), and* When the Lights Go Down *(1980). The following review of* Rocky *reflects the energy, brilliance, range, and provocative tone characteristic of Kael's best film interpretation.*

hunky, muscle-bound Sylvester Stallone looks repulsive   1
one moment, noble the next, and sometimes both at
once. In *Rocky*, which he wrote and stars in, he's a thirty-
year-old club fighter who works as a strong-arm man,
collecting money for a loan shark. Rocky never got anywhere, and he
has nothing; he lives in a Philadelphia tenement, and even the name
he fights under—the Italian Stallion—has become a joke. But the
world heavyweight champion, Apollo Creed (Carl Weathers), who's
a smart black jester, like Muhammad Ali, announces that for his Bi-
centennial New Year's fight he'll give an unknown a shot at the title,
and he picks the Italian Stallion for the racial-sexual overtones of the
contest. This small romantic fable is about a palooka gaining his manhood; it's Terry Malloy finally getting his chance to be somebody.
Rocky is a threadbare patchwork of old-movie bits (*On the Waterfront*,

Marty, Somebody Up There Likes Me, Capra's *Meet Joe Doe,* and maybe even a little of Preston Sturges' *Hail the Conquering Hero*), yet it's engaging, and the naïve elements are emotionally effective. John G. Avildsen's directing is his usual strictly-from-hunger approach; he slams through a picture like a poor man's Sidney Lumet. But a more painstaking director would have been too proud to shoot the mildewed ideas and would have tried to throw out as many as possible and to conceal the others—and would probably have wrecked the movie. *Rocky* is shameless, and that's why—on a certain level—it works. What holds it together is innocence.

In his offscreen bravado, Stallone (in Italian *stallone* means stallion) has claimed that he wrote the script in three and a half days, and some professional screenwriters, seeing what a ragtag of a script it is, may think that they could have done it in two and a half. But they wouldn't have been able to believe in what they did, and it wouldn't have got the audience cheering, the way *Rocky* does. The innocence that makes this picture so winning emanates from Sylvester Stallone. It's a street-wise, flowers-blooming-in-the-garbage innocence. Stallone plays a waif, a strong-arm man who doesn't want to hurt anybody, a loner with only his pet turtles to talk to. Yet the character doesn't come across as maudlin. Stallone looks like a big, battered Paul McCartney. There's bullnecked energy in him, smoldering; he has a field of force, like Brando's. And he knows how to use his overripe, cartoon sensuality—the eyelids at half-mast, the sad brown eyes and twisted, hurt mouth. Victor Mature also had this thick sensuality, but the movies used him as if it were simply plushy handsomeness, and so he became ridiculous, until he learned—too late—to act. Stallone is aware that we see him as a hulk, and he plays against this comically and tenderly. In his deep, caveman's voice, he gives the most surprising, sharp, fresh shadings to his lines. He's at his funniest trying to explain to his boss why he didn't break somebody's thumbs, as he'd been told to; he's even funny talking to his turtles. He pulls the whiskers off the film's cliché situations, so that we're constantly charmed by him, waiting for what he'll say next. He's like a child who never ceases to amaze us.

Stallone has the gift of direct communication with the audience. Rocky's naïve observations come from so deep inside him that they have a Lewis Carroll enchantment. His unworldliness makes him seem dumb, but we know better; we understand what he feels at every moment. Rocky is the embodiment of the out-of-fashion pure-at-heart. His macho strut belongs with the ducktails of the fifties—he's a sagging peacock. I'm not sure how much of his archaism is thought out, how much is the accidental result of Stallone's overdeveloped, weight lifter's muscles combined with his simplistic beliefs, but Rocky represents the redemption of an earlier ideal—the man as rock for woman

 ROCKY

to cleave to. Talia Shire plays Adrian, a shy girl with glasses who works in a pet store; she's the Betsy Blair to Stallone's Marty. It's unspeakably musty, but they put it over; her delicacy (that of a button-faced Audrey Hepburn) is the right counterpoint to his primitivism. It's clear that he's drawn to her because she isn't fast or rough and doesn't make fun of him; she doesn't make hostile wisecracks, like the kids in the street. We don't groan at this, because he's such a *tortured* macho nice-guy—he has failed his own high ideals. And who doesn't have a soft spot for the teen-age aspirations congealed inside this thirty-year-old bum?

Stallone is the picture, but the performers who revolve around   4
him are talented. Carl Weathers, a former Oakland Raiders linebacker, is a real find. His Apollo Creed has the flash and ebullience to put the fairy-tale plot in motion; when the champ arrives at the ring dressed as Uncle Sam, no one could enjoy the racial joke as much as he does. Adrian's heavyset brother Paulie is played by Burt Young, who has been turning up in movies more and more frequently in the past three years and still gives the impression that his abilities haven't begun to be tapped. Young, who actually was a professional fighter, has the cracked, mottled voice of someone who's taken a lot of punishment in the sinuses; the resonance is gone. As Mickey, the ancient pug who runs a fighters' gym, Burgess Meredith uses the harsh, racking sound of a man who's been punched too often in the vocal cords. The director overemphasizes Meredith's performance (much as John Schlesinger did in *The Day of the Locust*); Meredith would look better if we were left to discover how good he is for ourselves. I found *Marty* dreary, because the people in it were sapped of energy. But Stallone and Talia Shire and the others here have a restrained force; you feel that they're being pressed down, that they're under a lid. The only one who gets a chance to explode is Paulie, when, in a rage, he wields a baseball bat, and it's a poor scene, out of tune. Yet the actors themselves have so much more to them than they're using that what comes across in their performances is what's under the lid. The actors—and this includes Joe Spinell as Gazzo, Rocky's gangster boss—enable us to feel their reserves of intelligence; they provide tact and taste, which aren't in long supply in an Avildsen film.

Rocky is the kind of movie in which the shots are under-   5
lighted, because the characters are poor and it's wintertime. I was almost never convinced that the camera was in the right place. The shots don't match well, and they're put together jerkily, with cheap romantic music thrown in like cement blocks of lyricism, and sheer noise used to build up excitement at the climactic prizefight, where the camera is so close to the fighters that you can't feel the rhythm of the encounter. And the film doesn't follow through on what it prepares. Early on, we see Rocky with the street-corner kids in his skid-

row neighborhood, but we never get to see how these kids react to his training or to the fight itself. Even the bull mastiff who keeps Rocky company on his early-morning runs is lost track of. I get the feeling that Avildsen is so impatient to finish a film on schedule (or before, as if it were a race) that he hardly bothers to think it out. I hate the way *Rocky* is made, yet better might be worse in this case. Unless a director could take this material and transform it into sentimental urban poetry—a modern equivalent of what Frank Borzage used to do in pictures such as *Man's Castle*, with Spencer Tracy and Loretta Young—we're probably better off with Avildsen's sloppiness than with careful planning; a craftsmanlike *Rocky* would be obsolete, like a TV play of the fifties.

Stallone can certainly write; that is, he can write scenes and dialogue. But as a writer he stays inside the character; we never get a clear outside view of Rocky. For that, Stallone falls back on clichés, on an urban-primitive myth: at the end, Rocky has everything a man needs—his manhood, his woman, maybe even his dog. (If it were rural-primitive, he'd have some land, too.) In a sense, *Rocky* is a piece of innocent art, but its innocence doesn't sit too well. The bad side of *Rocky* is its resemblance to *Marty*—its folklorish, grubby littleness. Unpretentiousness shouldn't be used as a virtue. This warmed-over bum-into-man myth is unworthy of the freak macho force of its star; talking to turtles is too endearing. What separates Stallone from a Brando is that everything Stallone does has one purpose: to make you like him. He may not know how good he could be if he'd stop snuggling into your heart. If not—well, he may be to acting what Mario Lanza was to singing, and that's a form of bumminess.

COMPREHENSION

1.   What does the author like about *Rocky*? What does she dislike about the film?

2.   Examine the value judgments that the author makes about older movies, notably *Marty*; about Stallone and Brando; and about sentimentality in film. Why does she seem to like *Rocky* despite herself?

3.   Reread Oates's essay on Hemingway. In what ways are Stallone and his Rocky creation Hemingway types?

RHETORIC

1.   Locate and discuss examples of figurative language in paragraphs 1 to 3.

2.   List and identify five to ten allusions to film culture (films, actors, directors, etc.). What does Kael presuppose about her audience?

3.   Why is the author's introductory paragraph a model of film criticism? What is her thesis, and where does she place it?

 ROCKY

4. Analyze the overall structure of this essay. What are the focal points of each paragraph? How does Kael handle transitions? Which mode of paragraph development does Kael prefer?

5. How do Kael's descriptive powers reinforce central meanings in the essay?

6. Analyze the relationship of the concluding paragraph to the opening one. What value judgment does she make at the end? How does this affect the tone?

WRITING

1. Kael implies at several points that we like fairy tales—"a Lewis Carroll enchantment"—in films. Do you agree or disagree? What films that you have seen project this fairy tale aura?

2. Write your own review of *Rocky I, Rocky II, Rocky III,* or the entire trilogy.

3. Explore the theme of innocence in American film.

4. Select a film that you like but have mixed feelings about, and evaluate your response to it.

MARYA MANNES

How Do You Know It's Good?

Marya Mannes (1904–   ) has written several novels and some light verse, but she is best known for her essays, which have appeared in Vogue, McCall's, Harper's, *and* The New Republic. *She has collected her essays in* More in Anger *(1958) and in* The New York I Know *(1961). Mannes has also written on such subjects as suicide and euthanasia in* Last Rights *(1974) and television in* Who Owns the Air? *(1960). In this essay from* But Will It Sell? *(1964), she establishes standards for judging excellence in the arts.*

uppose there were no critics to tell us how to react to a   1
picture, a play, or a new composition of music. Suppose we wandered innocent as the dawn into an art exhibition of unsigned paintings. By what standards, by what values would we decide whether they were good or bad, talented or untalented, successes or failures? How can we ever know that what we think is right?

For the last fifteen or twenty years the fashion in criticism or   2

448   MARYA MANNES

appreciation of the arts has been to deny the existence of any valid criteria and to make the words "good" or "bad" irrelevant, immaterial, and inapplicable. There is no such thing, we are told, as a set of standards, first acquired through experience and knowledge and later imposed on the subject under discussion. This has been a popular approach, for it relieves the critic of the responsibility of judgment and the public of the necessity of knowledge. It pleases those resentful of disciplines, it flatters the empty-minded by calling them open-minded, it comforts the confused. Under the banner of democracy and the kind of equality which our forefathers did *not* mean, it says, in effect, "Who are you to tell us what *is* good or bad?" This is the same cry used so long and so effectively by the producers of mass media who insist that it is the public, not they, who decides what it wants to hear and see, and that for a critic to say that *this* program is bad and *this* program is good is purely a reflection of personal taste. Nobody recently has expressed this philosophy more succinctly than Dr. Frank Stanton, the highly intelligent president of CBS television. At a hearing before the Federal Communications Commission, this phrase escaped him under questioning: "One man's mediocrity is another man's good program."

There is no better way of saying "No values are absolute." 3 There is another important aspect to this philosophy of *laissez faire*: It is the fear, in all observers of all forms of art, of guessing wrong. This fear is well come by, for who has not heard of the contemporary outcries against artists who later were called great? Every age has its arbiters who do not grow with their times, who cannot tell evolution from revolution or the difference between frivolous faddism, amateurish experimentation, and profound and necessary change. Who wants to be caught *flagrante delicto* with an error of judgment as serious as this? It is far safer, and certainly easier, to look at a picture or a play or a poem and to say "This is hard to understand, but it may be good," or simply to welcome it as a new form. The word "new"— in our country especially—has magical connotations. What is new must be good; what is old is probably bad. And if a critic can describe the new in language that nobody can understand, he's safer still. If he has mastered the art of saying nothing with exquisite complexity, nobody can quote him later as saying anything.

But all these, I maintain, are forms of abdication from the 4 responsibility of judgment. In creating, the artist commits himself; in appreciating, you have a commitment of your own. For after all, it is the audience which makes the arts. A climate of appreciation is essential to its flowering, and the higher the expectations of the public, the better the performance of the artist. Conversely, only a public ill-served by its critics could have accepted as art and as literature so much in these last years that has been neither. If anything goes, every-

 HOW DO YOU KNOW IT'S GOOD?

thing goes; and at the bottom of the junkpile lie the discarded standards too.

But what are these standards? How do you get them? How do you know they're the right ones? How can you make a clear pattern out of so many intangibles, including that greatest one, the very private I?

Well for one thing, it's fairly obvious that the more you read and see and hear, the more equipped you'll be to practice that art of association which is at the basis of all understanding and judgment. The more you live and the more you look, the more aware you are of a consistent pattern—as universal as the stars, as the tides, as breathing, as night and day—underlying everything. I would call this pattern and this rhythm an order. Not order—*an* order. Within it exists an incredible diversity of forms. Without it lies chaos—the wild cells of destruction—sickness. It is in the end up to you to distinguish between the diversity that is health and the chaos that is sickness, and you can't do this without a process of association that can link a bar of Mozart with the corner of a Vermeer painting, or a Stravinsky score with a Picasso abstraction; or that can relate an aggressive act with a Franz Kline painting and a fit of coughing with a John Cage composition.

There is no accident in the fact that certain expressions of art live for all time and that others die with the moment, and although you may not always define the reasons, you can ask the questions. What does an artist say that is timeless; how does he say it? How much is fashion, how much is merely reflection? Why is Sir Walter Scott so hard to read now, and Jane Austen not? Why is baroque right for one age and too effulgent for another?

Can a standard of craftsmanship apply to art of all ages, or does each have its own, and different, definitions? You may have been aware, inadvertently, that craftsmanship has become a dirty word these years because, again, it implies standards—something done well or done badly. The result of this convenient avoidance is a plentitude of actors who can't project their voices, singers who can't phrase their songs, poets who can't communicate emotion, and writers who have no vocabulary—not to speak of painters who can't draw. The dogma now is that craftsmanship gets in the way of expression. You can do better if you don't know *how* you do it, let alone *what* you're doing.

I think it is time you helped reverse this trend by trying to rediscover craft: the command of the chosen instrument, whether it is a brush, a word, or a voice. When you begin to detect the difference between freedom and sloppiness, between serious experimentation and egotherapy, between skill and slickness, between strength and violence, you are on your way to separating the sheep from the goats, a form of segregation denied us for quite a while. All you need to restore it is a small bundle of standards and a Geiger counter that detects fraud, and we might begin our tour of the arts in an area where both are urgently needed: contemporary painting.

I don't know what's worse: to have to look at acres of bad art to find the little good, or to read what the critics say about it all. In no other field of expression has so much double-talk flourished, so much confusion prevailed, and so much nonsense been circulated: further evidence of the close interdependence between the arts and the critical climate they inhabit. It will be my pleasure to share with you some of this double-talk so typical of our times.

Item one: preface for a catalogue of an abstract painter:

"Time-bound meditation experiencing a life; sincere with plastic piety at the threshold of hallowed arcana; a striving for pure ideation giving shape to inner drive; formalized patterns where neural balances reach a fiction." End of quote. Know what this artist paints like now?

Item two: a review in the *Art News*:

"... a weird and disparate assortment of material, but the monstrosity which bloomed into his most recent cancer of aggregations is present in some form everywhere...." Then, later, "A gluttony of things and processes terminated by a glorious constipation."

Item three, same magazine, review of an artist who welds automobile fragments into abstract shapes:

"Each fragment ... is made an extreme of human exasperation, torn at and fought all the way, and has its rightness of form as if by accident. *Any technique that requires order or discipline would just be the human ego.* No, these must be egoless, uncontrolled, undesigned and different enough to give you a bang—fifty miles an hour around a telephone pole...."

"Any technique that requires order of discipline would just be the human ego." What does he mean—"just be"? What are they really talking about? Is this journalism? Is it criticism? Or is it that other convenient abdication from standards of performance and judgment practiced by so many artists and critics that they, like certain writers who deal only in sickness and depravity, "reflect the chaos about them"? Again, whose chaos? Whose depravity?

I had always thought that the prime function of art was to create order *out* of chaos—again, not the order of neatness or rigidity or convention or artifice, but the order of clarity by which one will and one vision could draw the essential truth out of apparent confusion. I still do. It is not enough to use parts of a car to convey the brutality of the machine. This is as slavishly representative, and just as easy, as arranging dried flowers under glass to convey nature.

Speaking of which, i.e., the use of real materials (burlap, old gloves, bottletops) in lieu of pigment, this is what one critic had to say about an exhibition of Assemblage at the Museum of Modern Art last year:

> Spotted throughout the show are indisputable works of art,   20
> accounting for a quarter or even a half of the total display.
> But the remainder are works of non-art, anti-art, and art sub-
> stitutes that are the aesthetic counterparts of the social defi-
> ciencies that land people in the clink on charges of vagrancy.
> These aesthetic bankrupts ... have no legitimate ideological
> roof over their heads and not the price of a square intellectual
> meal, much less a spiritual sandwich, in their pockets.

I quote these words of John Canaday of *The New York Times*   21
as an example of the kind of criticism which puts responsibility to an
intelligent public above popularity with an intellectual coterie. Canaday has the courage to say what he thinks and the capacity to say it
clearly: two qualities notably absent from his profession.

Next to art, I would say that appreciation and evaluation in   22
the field of music is the most difficult. For it is rarely possible to judge
a new composition at one hearing only. What seems confusing or
fragmented at first might well become clear and organic a third time.
Or it might not. The only salvation here for the listener is, again, an
instinct born of experience and association which allows him to separate intent from accident, design from experimentation, and pretense
from conviction. Much of contemporary music is, like its sister art,
merely a reflection of the composer's own fragmentation: an absorption in self and symbols at the expense of communication with others.
The artist, in short, says to the public: If you don't understand this,
it's because you're dumb. I maintain that you are not. You may have
to go part way or even halfway to meet the artist, but if you must go
the whole way, it's his fault, not yours. Hold fast to that. And remember it too when you read new poetry, that estranged sister of music.

> A multitude of causes, unknown to former times, are now   23
> acting with a combined force to blunt the discriminating pow-
> ers of the mind, and, unfitting it for all voluntary exertion, to
> reduce it to a state of almost savage torpor. The most effective
> of these causes are the great national events which are daily
> taking place and the increasing accumulation of men in cities,
> where the uniformity of their occupations produces a craving
> for extraordinary incident, which the rapid communication of
> intelligence hourly gratifies. To this tendency of life and man-
> ners, the literature and theatrical exhibitions of the country
> have conformed themselves.

MARYA MANNES

This startlingly applicable comment was written in the year 24
1800 by William Wordsworth in the preface to his "Lyrical Ballads";
and it has been cited by Edwin Muir in his recently published book
"The Estate of Poetry." Muir states that poetry's effective range and
influence have diminished alarmingly in the modern world. He believes in the inherent and indestructible qualities of the human mind
and the great and permanent objects that act upon it, and suggests
that the audience will increase when "poetry loses what obscurity is
left in it by attempting greater themes, for great themes have to be
stated clearly." If you keep that firmly in mind and resist, in Muir's
words, "the vast dissemination of secondary objects that isolate us
from the natural world," you have gone a long way toward equipping
yourself for the examination of any work of art.

When you come to theatre, in this extremely hasty tour of the 25
arts, you can approach it on two different levels. You can bring to it
anticipation and innocence, giving yourself up, as it were, to the life
on the stage and reacting to it emotionally, if the play is good, or
listlessly, if the play is boring; a part of the audience organism that
expresses its favor by silence or laughter and its disfavor by coughing
and rustling. Or you can bring to it certain critical faculties that may
heighten, rather than diminish, your enjoyment.

You can ask yourselves whether the actors are truly in their 26
parts or merely projecting themselves; whether the scenery helps or
hurts the mood; whether the playwright is honest with himself, his
characters, and you. Somewhere along the line you can learn to distinguish between the true creative art and the false arbitrary gesture;
between fresh observation and stale cliché; between the avant-garde
play that is pretentious drivel and the avant-garde play that finds new
ways to say old truths.

Purpose and craftsmanship—end and means—these are the 27
keys to your judgment in all the arts. What is this painter trying to
say when he slashes a broad band of black across a white canvas and
lets the edges dribble down? Is it a statement of violence? Is it a self-
portrait? If it is *one* of these, has he made you believe it? Or is this a
gesture of the ego or a form of therapy? If it shocks you, what does
it shock you into?

And what of this tight little painting of bright flowers in a 28
vase? Is the painter saying anything new about flowers? Is it different
from a million other canvases of flowers? Has it any life, any meaning,
beyond its statement? Is there any pleasure in its forms or texture?
The question is not whether a thing is abstract or representational,
whether it is "modern" or conventional. The question, inexorably, is
whether it is good. And this is a decision which only you, on the basis
of instinct, experience, and association, can make for yourself. It takes
independence and courage. It involves, moreover, the risk of wrong

decision and the humility, after the passage of time, of recognizing it as such. As we grow and change and learn, our attitudes can change too, and what we once thought obscure or "difficult" can later emerge as coherent and illuminating. Entrenched prejudices, obdurate opinions are as sterile as no opinions at all.

Yet standards there are, timeless as the universe itself. And when you have committed yourself to them, you have acquired a passport to that elusive but immutable realm of truth. Keep it with you in the forests of bewilderment. And never be afraid to speak up. 29

COMPREHENSION

1. What is the author's thesis? Where does she state it most emphatically?

2. What examples does Mannes provide of the "abdication from the responsibility of judgment" (paragraph 4)?

3. Explain Mannes's criteria or standards for judging excellence in the arts. How would Kael's essay on "Rocky" measure up to these standards?

RHETORIC

1. Account for the author's use of the pronoun *you* in addressing her audience. How does it affect tone, notably at the end of the essay?

2. Explain Mannes's strategy of formulating questions, starting with the title and moving consistently through the essay to the conclusion.

3. Where does the author's introduction end? Analyze the material presented in the introduction and the rhetorical strategies involved. What paragraphs constitute the conclusion of the essay? Describe the nature of the conclusion.

4. Explain the function of paragraphs 5 to 9.

5. How does Mannes employ illustration to structure paragraphs 10 to 26? Analyze the main stages in the organization of this section.

6. Explain the author's use of process and causal analysis in the essay.

WRITING

1. Mannes maintains that standards are absolutely necessary in distinguishing good from bad work in the arts. Do you agree or disagree with her premise, and why? What standards do you employ in determining whether an artistic product is good or bad?

2. Write your own essay entitled "How Do You Know It's Good?" Focus on some aspect of music, art, literature, or film that you know well.

3. Evaluate one literary, artistic, or media work, making clear the standards that you are applying.

Philosophy and Ethics

ROBERT COLES

I Listen to My Parents and I Wonder What They Believe

Robert Coles (1929–   ), author and psychologist, won the Pulitzer Prize for his multivolume work, Children of Crisis, *in which he examines with compassion and intelligence the effects of the controversy over integration on children in the South. Walker Percy has praised Coles because he "spends his time listening to people and trying to understand them." In its final form,* Children of Crisis *has five volumes, and Coles has widened its focus to include the children of the wealthy and poor, the exploited and the exploiters. In collaboration with Jane Coles, he recently completed* Women of Crisis II *(1980). Below, Coles demonstrates his capacity to listen to and to understand children.*

Not so long ago children were looked upon in a sentimental fashion as "angels" or as "innocents." Today, thanks to Freud and his followers, boys and girls are understood to have complicated inner lives; to feel love, hate, envy and rivalry in various and subtle mixtures; to be eager participants in the sexual and emotional politics of the home, neigh-

1

borhood and school. Yet some of us parents still cling to the notion of childhood innocence in another way. We do not see that our children also make ethical decisions every day in their own lives, or realize how attuned they may be to moral currents and issues in the larger society.

In Appalachia I heard a girl of eight whose father owns coal 2 fields (and gas stations, a department store and much timberland) wonder about "life" one day: "I'll be walking to the school bus, and I'll ask myself why there's some who are poor and their daddies can't find a job, and there's some who are lucky like me. Last month there was an explosion in a mine my daddy owns, and everyone became upset. Two miners got killed. My daddy said it was their own fault, because they'll be working and they get careless. When my mother asked if there was anything wrong with the safety down in the mine, he told her no and she shouldn't ask questions like that. Then the Government people came and they said it was the owner's fault—Daddy's. But he has a lawyer and the lawyer is fighting the Government and the union. In school, kids ask me what I think, and I sure do feel sorry for the two miners and so does my mother—I know that. She told me it's just not a fair world and you have to remember that. Of course, there's no one who can be sure there won't be trouble; like my daddy says, the rain falls on the just and the unjust. My brother is only six and he asked Daddy awhile back who are the 'just' and the 'unjust,' and Daddy said there are people who work hard and they live good lives, and there are lazy people and they're always trying to sponge off others. But I guess you have to feel sorry for anyone who has a lot of trouble, because it's poured-down, heavy rain."

Listening, one begins to realize that an elementary-school 3 child is no stranger to moral reflection—and to ethical conflict. This girl was torn between her loyalty to her particular background, its values and assumptions, and to a larger affiliation—her membership in the nation, the world. As a human being whose parents were kind and decent to her, she was inclined to be thoughtful and sensitive with respect to others, no matter what their work or position in society. But her father was among other things a mineowner, and she had already learned to shape her concerns to suit that fact of life. The result: a moral oscillation of sorts, first toward nameless others all over the world and then toward her own family. As the girl put it later, when she was a year older: "You should try to have 'good thoughts' about everyone, the minister says, and our teacher says that too. But you should honor your father and mother most of all; that's why you should find out what they think and then sort of copy them. But sometimes you're not sure if you're on the right track."

Sort of copy them. There could be worse descriptions of how 4 children acquire moral values. In fact, the girl understood how girls and boys all over the world "sort of" develop attitudes of what is right and wrong, ideas of who the just and the unjust are. And they also struggle hard and long, and not always with success, to find out where the "right track" starts and ends. Children need encouragement or assistance as they wage that struggle.

In home after home that I have visited, and in many class- 5 rooms, I have met children who not only are growing emotionally and intellectually but also are trying to make sense of the world morally. That is to say, they are asking themselves and others about issues of fair play, justice, liberty, equality. Those last words are abstractions, of course—the stuff of college term papers. And there are, one has to repeat, those in psychology and psychiatry who would deny elementary-school children access to that "higher level" of moral reflection. But any parent who has listened closely to his or her child knows that girls and boys are capable of wondering about matters of morality, and knows too that often it is their grown-up protectors (parents, relatives, teachers, neighbors) who are made uncomfortable by the so-called "innocent" nature of the questions children may ask or the statements they may make. Often enough the issue is not the moral capacity of children but the default of us parents who fail to respond to inquiries put to us by our daughters and sons—and fail to set moral standards for both ourselves and our children.

Do's and don't's are, of course, pressed upon many of our 6 girls and boys. But a moral education is something more than a series of rules handed down, and in our time one cannot assume that every parent feels able—sure enough of her own or his own actual beliefs and values—to make even an initial explanatory and disciplinary effect toward a moral education. Furthermore, for many of us parents these days it is a child's emotional life that preoccupies us.

In 1963, when I was studying school desegregation in the 7 South, I had extended conversations with Black and white elementary-school children caught up in a dramatic moment of historical change. For longer than I care to remember, I concentrated on possible psychiatric troubles, on how a given child was managing under circumstances of extreme stress, on how I could be of help—with "support," with reassurance, with a helpful psychological observation or interpretation. In many instances I was off the mark. These children weren't "patients"; they weren't even complaining. They were worried, all right, and often enough they had things to say that were substantive—that had to do not so much with troubled emotions as with questions of right and wrong in the real-life dramas taking place in their worlds.

Here is a nine-year-old white boy, the son of ardent segre- 8 gationists, telling me about his sense of what desegregation meant to

 **I LISTEN TO MY PARENTS AND I WONDER WHAT THEY BELIEVE**   **457**

Louisiana in the 1960s: "They told us it wouldn't happen—never. My daddy said none of us white people would go into schools with the colored. But then it did happen, and when I went to school the first day I didn't know what would go on. Would the school stay open or would it close up? We didn't know what to do; the teacher kept telling us that we should be good and obey the law, but my daddy said the law was wrong. Then my mother said she wanted me in school even if there were some colored kids there. She said if we all stayed home she'd be a 'nervous wreck.' So I went.

"After a while I saw that the colored weren't so bad. I saw   9 that there are different kinds of colored people, just like with us whites. There was one of the colored who was nice, a boy who smiled, and he played real good. There was another one, a boy, who wouldn't talk with anyone. I don't know if it's right that we all be in the same school. Maybe it isn't right. My sister is starting school next year, and she says she doesn't care if there's 'mixing of the races.' She says they told her in Sunday school that everyone is a child of God, and then a kid asked if that goes for the colored too and the teacher said yes, she thought so. My daddy said that it's true, God made everyone— but that doesn't mean we all have to be living together under the same roof in the home or the school. But my mother said we'll never know what God wants of us but we have to try to read His mind, and that's why we pray. So when I say my prayers I ask God to tell me what's the right thing to do. In school I try to say hello to the colored, because they're kids, and you can't be mean or you'll be 'doing wrong,' like my grandmother says."

Children aren't usually long-winded in the moral discussions   10 they have with one another or with adults, and in quoting this boy I have pulled together comments he made to me in the course of several days. But everything he said was of interest to me. I was interested in the boy's changing racial attitudes. It was clear he was trying to find a coherent, sensible moral position too. It was also borne in on me that if one spends days, weeks in a given home, it is hard to escape a particular moral climate just as significant as the psychological one.

In many homes parents establish moral assumptions, man-   11 dates, priorities. They teach children what to believe in, what not to believe in. They teach children what is permissible or not permissible—and why. They may summon up the Bible, the flag, history, novels, aphorisms, philosophical or political sayings, personal memories—all in an effort to teach children how to behave, what and whom to respect and for which reasons. Or they may neglect to do so, and in so doing teach their children *that*—a moral abdication, of sorts— and in this way fail their children. Children need and long for words of moral advice, instruction, warning, as much as they need words of affirmation or criticism from their parents about other matters. They

     ROBERT COLES

must learn how to dress and what to wear, how to eat and what to eat; and they must also learn how to behave under X or Y or Z conditions, and why.

All the time, in 20 years of working with poor children and rich children, Black children and white children, children from rural areas and urban areas and in every region of this country, I have heard questions—thoroughly intelligent and discerning questions— about social and historical matters, about personal behavior, and so on. But most striking is the fact that almost all those questions, in one way or another, are moral in nature: Why did the Pilgrims leave England? Why didn't they just stay and agree to do what the king wanted them to do? ... Should you try to share all you've got or should you save a lot for yourself? ... What do you do when you see others fighting—do you try to break up the fight, do you stand by and watch or do you leave as fast as you can? ... Is it right that some people haven't got enough to eat? ... I see other kids cheating and I wish I could copy the answers too; but I won't cheat, though sometimes I feel I'd like to and I get all mixed up. I go home and talk with my parents, and I ask them what should you do if you see kids cheating—pay no attention, or report the kids or do the same thing they are doing?

Those are examples of children's concerns—and surely millions of American parents have heard versions of them. Have the various "experts" on childhood stressed strongly enough the importance of such questions—and the importance of the hunger we all have, no matter what our age or background, to examine what we believe in, are willing to stand up for, and what we are determined to ask, likewise, of our children?

Children not only need our understanding of their complicated emotional lives; they also need a constant regard for the moral issues that come their way as soon as they are old enough to play with others and take part in the politics of the nursery, the back yard and the schoolroom. They need to be told what they must do and what they must not do. They need control over themselves and a sense of what others are entitled to from them—co-operation, thoughtfulness, an attentive ear and eye. They need discipline not only to tame their excesses of emotion but discipline also connected to stated and clarified moral values. They need, in other words, something to believe in that is larger than their own appetites and urges and, yes, bigger than their "psychological drives." They need a larger view of the world, a moral context, as it were—a faith that addresses itself to the meaning of this life we all live and, soon enough, let go of.

Yes, it is time for us parents to begin to look more closely at what ideas our children have about the world; and it would be well to do so before they become teen-agers and young adults and begin to remind us, as often happens, of how little attention we did pay to their moral development. Perhaps a nine-year-old girl from a well-off suburban home in Texas put it better than anyone else I've met:

> I listen to my parents, and I wonder what they believe in more 16
> than anything else. I asked my mom and my daddy once:
> What's the thing that means most to you? They said they
> didn't know but I shouldn't worry my head too hard with
> questions like that. So I asked my best friend, and she said
> she wonders if there's a God and how do you know Him and
> what does He want you to do—I mean, when you're in school
> or out playing with your friends. They talk about God in
> church, but is it only in church that He's there and keeping
> an eye on you? I saw a kid steal in a store, and I know her
> father has a lot of money—because I hear my daddy talk. But
> stealing's wrong. My mother said she's a 'sick girl,' but it's
> still wrong what she did. Don't you think?

There was more—much more—in the course of the months I 17
came to know that child and her parents and their neighbors. But
those observations and questions—a "mere child's"—reminded me
unforgettably of the aching hunger for firm ethical principles that so
many of us feel. Ought we not begin thinking about this need? Ought
we not all be asking ourselves more intently what standards we live
by—and how we can satisfy our children's hunger for moral values?

COMPREHENSION

1. How does the author's title capture the substance of his essay? What is his thesis?

2. According to Coles, why do parents have difficulty explaining ethics to their children? On what aspects of their children's development do they tend to concentrate? Why?

3. There is an implied contrast between mothers' and fathers' attitudes toward morality in Coles's essay. Explain this contrast, and cite examples for your explanation.

RHETORIC

1. What point of view does Coles use here? How does that viewpoint affect the tone of the essay?

2. Compare Coles's sentence structure with the sentence structure of the children he quotes. How do they differ?

3. Does this essay present an inductive or deductive argument? Give evidence for your answer.

ROBERT COLES

4. How does paragraph 13 differ from paragraphs 3, 10, and 17? How do all four paragraphs contribute to the development of the essay?

5. Explain the line of reasoning in the first paragraph. Why does Coles allude to Freud? How is that allusion related to the final sentence of the paragraph?

6. What paragraphs constitute the conclusion of the essay? Why? How do they summarize Coles's argument?

WRITING

1. Coles asserts the need for clear ethical values. How have your parents provided such values? What kind of values will you give your children?

2. Write an essay describing conflict between your parents' ethical views and your own.

3. Gather evidence, based upon conversations, from your friends and relatives about an ethical issue such as poverty, world starvation, abortion, or capital punishment. Incorporate their opinions through direct and indirect quotation into your essay.

4. Compare Coles's observations in this essay with those of DuBois in "On Progress."

EPICURUS

We Should Seek Our Own Pleasure

Epicurus (341–270 B.C.), Greek philosopher, was a contemporary of Aristotle and is best known for asserting that pleasure is the highest good toward which people can strive. Epicurus himself favored a reclusive, moderate life and urged people to practice prudence, justice, and honesty. Although he was a voluminous writer, only a few fragments of his works have survived. One of the more extensive fragments appears below.

 et no one when young delay to study philosophy, nor when he is old grow weary of his study. For no one can come too early or too late to secure the health of his soul. And the man who says that the age for philosophy has either not yet come or has gone by is like the man who says that the age for happiness is not yet come to him, or has passed away. Wherefore both when young and old a man must study philosophy, that as he grows old he may be young in blessings through the grateful recollection of what has been, and that in youth he may be old as well, since he will know no fear of what is to come. We must then meditate on the things that make our happiness, seeing that when that is with us we have all, but when it is absent we do all to win it.

The things which I used unceasingly to commend to you, 2 these do and practise, considering them to be the first principles of the good life. First of all believe that god is a being immortal and blessed, even as the common idea of a god is engraved on men's minds, and do not assign to him anything alien to his immortality or ill-suited to his blessedness: but believe about him everything that can uphold his blessedness and immortality. For gods there are, since the knowledge of them is by clear vision. But they are not such as the many believe them to be: for indeed they do not consistently represent them as they believe them to be. And the impious man is not he who denies the gods of the many, but he who attaches to the gods the beliefs of the many. For the statements of the many about the gods are not conceptions derived from sensation, but false suppositions, according to which the greatest misfortunes befall the wicked and the greatest blessings the good by the gift of the gods. For men being accustomed always to their own virtues welcome those like themselves, but regard all that is not of their nature as alien.

Become accustomed to the belief that death is nothing to us. 3 For all good and evil consists in sensation, but death is deprivation of sensation. And therefore a right understanding that death is nothing to us makes the mortality of life enjoyable, not because it adds to it an infinite span of time, but because it takes away the craving for immortality. For there is nothing terrible in life for the man who has truly comprehended that there is nothing terrible in not living. So that the man speaks but idly who says that he fears death not because it will be painful when it comes, but because it is painful in anticipation. For that which gives no trouble when it comes, is but an empty pain in anticipation. So death, the most terrifying of ills, is nothing to us, since so long as we exist death is not with us; but when death comes, then we do not exist. It does not then concern either the living or the dead, since for the former it is not, and the latter are no more.

But the many at one moment shun death as the greatest of 4 evils, at another yearn for it as a respite from the evils in life. But the wise man neither seeks to escape life nor fears the cessation of life, for neither does life offend him nor does the absence of life seem to be any evil. And just as with food he does not seek simply the larger share and nothing else, but rather the most pleasant, so he seeks to enjoy not the longest period of time, but the most pleasant.

And he who counsels the young man to live well, but the old 5

man to make a good end, is foolish, not merely because of the desirability of life, but also because it is the same training which teaches
to live well and to die well. Yet much worse still is the man who says
it is good not to be born, but

> once born make haste to pass the gates of Death. (Theognis,
> 427)

For if he says this from conviction why does he not pass away out of
life? For it is open to him to do so, if he had firmly made up his mind
to this. But if he speaks in jest, his words are idle among men who
cannot receive them.

We must then bear in mind that the future is neither ours, 6
nor yet wholly not ours, so that we may not altogether expect it as
sure to come, nor abandon hope of it, as if it will certainly not come.

We must consider that of desires some are natural, others 7
vain, and of the natural some are necessary and others merely natural;
and of the necessary some are necessary for happiness, others for the
repose of the body, and others for very life. The right understanding
of these facts enables us to refer all choice and avoidance to the health
of the body and the soul's freedom from disturbance, since this is the
aim of the life of blessedness. For it is to obtain this end that we
always act, namely, to avoid pain and fear. And when this is once
secured for us, all the tempest of the soul is dispersed, since the living
creature has not to wander as though in search of something that is
missing, and to look for some other thing by which he can fulfill the
good of the soul and the good of the body. For it is then that we have
need of pleasure, when we feel pain owing to the absence of pleasure;
but when we do not feel pain, we no longer need pleasure. And for
this cause we call pleasure the beginning and end of the blessed life.
For we recognize pleasure as the first good innate in us, and from
pleasure we begin every act of choice and avoidance, and to pleasure
we return again, using the feeling as the standard by which we judge
every good.

And since pleasure is the first good and natural to us, for this 8
very reason we do not choose every pleasure, but sometimes we pass
over many pleasures, when greater discomfort accrues to us as the
result of them: and similarly we think many pains better than
pleasures, since a greater pleasure comes to us when we have endured
pains for a long time. Every pleasure then because of its natural kin-
ship to us is good, yet not every pleasure is to be chosen: even as
every pain also is an evil, yet not all are always of a nature to be
avoided. Yet by a scale of comparison and by the consideration of
advantages and disadvantages we must form our judgment on all

these matters. For the good on certain occasions we treat as bad, and conversely the bad as good.

And again independence of desire we think a great good— 9 not that we may at all times enjoy but a few things, but that, if we do not possess many, we may enjoy the few in the genuine persuasion that those have the sweetest pleasure in luxury who least need it, and that all that is natural is easy to be obtained, but that which is superfluous is hard. And so plain savours bring us a pleasure equal to a luxurious diet, when all the pain due to want is removed; and bread and water produce the highest pleasure, when one who needs them puts them to his lips. To grow accustomed therefore to simple and not luxurious diet gives us health to the full, and makes a man alert for the needful employments of life, and when after long intervals we approach luxuries, disposes us better towards them, and fits us to be fearless of fortune.

When, therefore, we maintain that pleasure is the end, we do 10 not mean the pleasures of profligates and those that consist in sensuality, as is supposed by some who are either ignorant or disagree with us or do not understand, but freedom from pain in the body and from trouble in the mind. For it is not continuous drinkings and revellings, nor the satisfaction of lusts, nor the enjoyment of fish and other luxuries of the wealthy table, which produce a pleasant life, but sober reasoning, searching out the motives for all choice and avoidance, and banishing mere opinions, to which are due the greatest disturbance of the spirit.

Of all this the beginning and the greatest good is prudence. 11 Wherefore prudence is a more precious thing even than philosophy: for from prudence are sprung all the other virtues, and it teaches us that it is not possible to live pleasantly without living prudently and honourably and justly, nor again, to live a life of prudence, honour, and justice without living pleasantly. For the virtues are by nature bound up with the pleasant life, and the pleasant life is inseparable from them. For indeed who, think you, is a better man than he who holds reverent opinions concerning the gods, and is at all times free from fear of death, and has reasoned out the end ordained by nature? He understands that the limit of good things is easy to fulfill and easy to attain, whereas the course of ills is either short in time or slight in pain: he laughs at destiny, whom some have introduced as the mistress of all things. He thinks that with us lies the chief power in determining events, some of which happen by necessity and some by chance, and some are within our control; for while necessity cannot be called to account, he sees that chance is inconstant, but that which is in our control is subject to no master, and to it are naturally attached praise and blame. For, indeed, it were better to follow the myths about the gods than to become a slave to the destiny of the natural philoso-

EPICURUS

phers: for the former suggests a hope of placating the gods by worship, whereas the latter involves a necessity which knows no placation. As to chance, he does not regard it as a god as most men do (for in god's acts there is no disorder), nor as an uncertain cause of all things: for he does not believe that good and evil are given by chance to man for the framing of a blessed life, but that opportunities for great good and great evil are afforded by it. He therefore thinks it better to be unfortunate in reasonable action than to prosper in unreason. For it is better in a man's actions that what is well chosen should fail, rather than that what is ill chosen should be successful owing to chance.

Meditate therefore on these things and things akin to them night and day by yourself, and with a companion like to yourself, and never shall you be disturbed waking or asleep, but you shall live like a god among men. For a man who lives among immortal blessings is not like to a mortal being. 12

COMPREHENSION

1. What is the author's thesis? Where does he state it?

2. How does Epicurus define *pain, death*, and *pleasure*? Of what kinds of pleasure does Epicurus approve?

3. Why does he believe "independence of desire" is a "great good"?

RHETORIC

1. Examine the tone of the essay. Particularly look for evidence of a hortatory style, and explain its function.

2. What are the connotations of "the many" and "the wise man"? How many people do you think Epicurus believes will profit from his advice?

3. Explain how Epicurus uses classification to order paragraph 7. Are there other examples of classification in this essay? If so, where do they appear?

4. Does Epicurus tend to use deductive or inductive reasoning? Examine particularly paragraph 3 for evidence. Are there other examples elsewhere in the essay of the kind of reasoning that appears in paragraph 3? If so, where?

5. What is the topic sentence in paragraph 11? How important is this sentence to the development of the thesis of the essay?

6. Explain the function of paragraph 10 in the essay. What rhetorical method is Epicurus using here?

WRITING

1. Do you think living according to Epicurus's advice would lead to happiness? What ways of living do you think lead to happiness?

2. Write a paper detailing the three major requirements of the good life for you.

3. Write a paper in which you give advice to readers on dating, education, getting along with your parents, or getting along with friends.

EDITH HAMILTON

Roots of Freedom

Edith Hamilton (1867–1963), teacher, writer, and Grecophile, wrote her first book when she was 63. Her initial career was as headmistress of a private girl's school in Maryland. When she retired, she began to write about ancient civilizations, particularly Greek civilization. In 1930, The Greek Way *was published. In later years, Hamilton also wrote* The Roman Way *(1932) and* The Prophets of Israel *(1936). She retold Greek, Roman, and Norse myths in* Mythology *(1942). At the age of 90, Hamilton visited Greece and was made an honorary citizen. The following essay makes clear why she admired Greek civilization.*

reedom's challenge in the Atomic Age is a sobering topic. We are facing today a strange new world and we are all wondering what we are going to do with it. What are we going to do with one of our most precious possessions, freedom? The world we know, our Western world, began with something as new as the conquest of space. 1

Some 2,500 years ago Greece discovered freedom. Before that there was no freedom. There were great civilizations, splendid empires, but no freedom anywhere. Egypt, Babylon, Nineveh, were all tyrannies, one immensely powerful man ruling over helpless masses. In Greece, in Athens, a little city in a little country, there were no helpless masses, and a time came when the Athenians were led by a great man who did not want to be powerful. Absolute obedience to the ruler was what the leaders of the empires insisted on. Athens said no, there must never be absolute obedience to a man except in war. There must be willing obedience to what is good for all. Pericles, the great Athenian statesman, said: "We are a free government, but we obey the laws, more especially those which protect the oppressed, and the unwritten laws which, if broken, bring shame." 2

Athenians willingly obeyed the written laws which they them- 3 selves passed, and the unwritten, which must be obeyed if free men live together. They must show each other kindness and pity and the many qualities without which life would be intolerable except to a hermit in the desert. The Athenians never thought that a man was free if he could do what he wanted. A man was free if he was self-controlled. To make yourself obey what you approved was freedom. They were saved from looking at their lives as their own private affair. Each one felt responsible for the welfare of Athens, not because it was imposed on him from the outside, but because the city was his pride and his safety. The creed of the first free government in the world was liberty for all men who could control themselves and would take responsibility for the state. This was the conception that underlay the lofty reach of Greek genius.

But discovering freedom is not like discovering atomic bombs. 4 It cannot be discovered once for all. If people do not prize it, and work for it, it will depart. Eternal vigilance is its price. Athens changed. It was a change that took place unnoticed though it was of the utmost importance, a spiritual change which penetrated the whole state. It had been the Athenians' pride and joy to give to their city. That they could get material benefits from her never entered their minds. There had to be a complete change of attitude before they could look at the city as an employer who paid her citizens for doing her work. Now instead of men giving to the state, the state was to give to them. What the people wanted was a government which would provide a comfortable life for them; and with this as the foremost object, ideas of freedom and self-reliance and responsibility were obscured to the point of disappearing. Athens was more and more looked on as a cooperative business possessed of great wealth in which all citizens had a right to share.

She reached the point when the freedom she really wanted 5 was freedom from responsibility. There could be only one result. If men insisted on being free from the burden of self-dependence and responsibility for the common good, they would cease to be free. Responsibility is the price every man must pay for freedom. It is to be had on no other terms. Athens, the Athens of Ancient Greece, refused responsibility; she reached the end of freedom and was never to have it again.

But, "the excellent becomes the permanent," Aristotle said. 6 Athens lost freedom forever, but freedom was not lost forever for the world. A great American statesman, James Madison, in or near the year 1776 A.D. referred to: "The capacity of mankind for self-government." No doubt he had not an idea that he was speaking Greek. Athens was not in the farthest background of his mind, but once a great and good idea has dawned upon man, it is never completely lost. The Atomic Age cannot destroy it. Somehow in this or that man's thought such an idea lives though unconsidered by the world of action. One can never be sure that it is not on the point of breaking out into action only sure that it will do so sometime.

COMPREHENSION

1.   What is the focus of this essay—freedom, Greece, or both? Cite evidence to support your answer.

2.   What were the Greeks' conceptions of freedom? Why, according to Hamilton, did they lose their freedom?

3.   What similarities does Hamilton see between Athens and America?

RHETORIC

1.   Explain the allusions to Pericles in paragraph 2 and James Madison in paragraph 6.

2.   Is Hamilton's tone hopeful or pessimistic? What evidence can you give to support your opinion?

3.   Narrative is an important rhetorical device in this essay. How is chronology developed in this essay? What transition words are used to mark the progress of the narrative? What paragraphs contain elements of narrative?

4.   Where does Hamilton make explicit her comparison between America and Athens? Why does she defer this idea until so late in her essay? What evidence can you find that she intends us to note this comparison before this point?

5.   How much of paragraph 5 is narrative? What other rhetorical methods appear here?

6.   What is the purpose of paragraph 1? How do paragraphs 1 and 6 frame the essay?

WRITING

1.   Do you think our present ideas of freedom and country are similar to those of the early or the late Greeks? What can we do to maintain or improve the situation?

2.   Narrate a personal experience that can illustrate an abstraction such as freedom—for example, tyranny, honesty, or ambition.

3.   Examine the relative health of the concept of freedom in the world today. Develop at least three extended examples to support your thesis.

The Allegory of the Cave

Plato (427?–347 B.C.), pupil and friend of Socrates, was one of the greatest philosophers of the ancient world. Plato's surviving works are all dialogues, many of them purporting to be conversations of Socrates and his disciples. Two key aspects of his philosophy are the dialectical method—represented by the questioning and probing of the particular event to reveal the general truth—and the existence of Forms. Plato's best-known works include Phaedo, Symposium, Phaedrus, *and* Timaeus. *The following selection, from* The Republic, *is an early description of the nature of Forms.*

A nd now, I said, let me show in a figure how far our nature is enlightened or unenlightened: Behold! human beings living in an underground den, which has a mouth open towards the light and reaching all along the den; here they have been from their childhood, and have their legs and necks chained so that they cannot move, and can only see before them, being prevented by the chains from turning round their heads. Above and behind them a fire is blazing at a distance, and between the fire and the prisoners there is a raised way; and you will see, if you look, a low wall built along the way, like the screen which marionette players have in front of them, over which they show the puppets. 1

I see. 2

And do you see, I said, men passing along the wall carrying all sorts of vessels, and statues and figures of animals made of wood and stone and various materials, which appear over the wall? Some of them are talking, others silent. 3

You have shown me a strange image, and they are strange prisoners. 4

Like ourselves, I replied; and they see only their own shadows, or the shadows of one another, which the fire throws on the opposite wall of the cave? 5

True, he said; how could they see anything but the shadows if they were never allowed to move their heads? 6

And of the objects which are being carried in like manner they would only see the shadows? 7

Yes, he said. 8

And if they were able to converse with one another, would they not suppose that they were naming what was actually before them? 9

Very true. 10

And suppose further that the prison had an echo which came   11
from the other side, would they not be sure to fancy when one of the
passers-by spoke that the voice which they heard came from the passing shadow?

No question, he replied.   12

To them, I said, the truth would be literally nothing but the   13
shadows of the images.

That is certain.   14

And now look again, and see what will naturally follow if the   15
prisoners are released and disabused of their error. At first, when any
of them is liberated and compelled suddenly to stand up and turn his
neck round and walk and look towards the light, he will suffer sharp
pains; the glare will distress him and he will be unable to see the
realities of which in his former state he had seen the shadows; and
then conceive some one saying to him, that what he saw before was
an illusion, but that now, when he is approaching nearer to being and
his eye is turned towards more real existence, he has a clearer vision—
what will be his reply? And you may further imagine that his instructor is pointing to the objects as they pass and requiring him to name
them—will he not be perplexed? Will he not fancy that the shadows
which he formerly saw are truer than the objects which are now
shown to him?

Far truer.   16

And if he is compelled to look straight at the light, will he   17
not have a pain in his eyes which will make him turn away to take
refuge in the objects of vision which he can see, and which he will
conceive to be in reality clearer than the things which are now being
shown to him?

True, he said.   18

And suppose once more, that he is reluctantly dragged up a   19
steep and rugged ascent, and held fast until he is forced into the presence of the sun himself, is he not likely to be pained and irritated?
When he approaches the light his eyes will be dazzled and he will
not be able to see anything at all of what are now called realities.

Not all in a moment, he said.   20

He will require to grow accustomed to the sight of the upper   21
world. And first he will see the shadows best, next the reflections of
men and other objects in the water, and then the objects themselves;
then he will gaze upon the light of the moon and the stars and the
spangled heaven; and he will see the sky and the stars by night better
than the sun or the light of the sun by day?

Certainly.   22

Last of all he will be able to see the sun, and not mere reflec-   23
tions of him in the water, but he will see him in his own proper place,
and not in another; and he will contemplate him as he is.

PLATO

Certainly. 24

He will then proceed to argue that this is he who gives the 25
season and the years, and is the guardian of all that is in the visible
world, and in a certain way the cause of all things which he and his
fellows have been accustomed to behold?

Clearly, he said, he would first see the sun and then reason 26
about him.

And when he remembered his old habitation, and the wisdom 27
of the den and his fellow-prisoners, do you not suppose that he would
felicitate himself on the change, and pity them?

Certainly, he would. 28

And if they were in the habit of conferring honors among 29
themselves on those who were quickest to observe the passing shadows and to remark which of them went before, and which followed
after, and which were together; and who were therefore best able to
draw conclusions as to the future, do you think that he would care
for such honors and glories, or envy the possesors of them? Would
he not say with Homer,

Better to be the poor servant of a poor master,

and to endure anything, rather than think as they do and live after
their manner?

Yes, he said, I think that he would rather suffer anything than 30
entertain these false notions and live in this miserable manner.

Imagine once more, I said, such as one coming suddenly out 31
of the sun to be replaced in his old situation; would he not be certain
to have his eyes full of darkness?

To be sure, he said. 32

And if there were a contest, and he had to compete in measur- 33
ing the shadows with the prisoners who had never moved out of the
den, while his sight was still weak, and before his eyes had become
steady (and the time which would be needed to acquire this new habit
of sight might be very considerable) would he not be ridiculous? Men
would say of him that up he went and down he came without his
eyes; and that it was better not even to think of ascending; and if any
one tried to loose another and lead him up to the light, let them only
catch the offender, and they would put him to death.

No question, he said. 34

This entire allegory, I said, you may now append, dear Glau- 35
con, to the previous argument; the prison-house is the world of sight,
the light of fire is the sun, and you will not misapprehend me if you
interpret the journey upwards to be the ascent of the soul into the
intellectual world according to my poor belief, which, at your desire,
I have expressed—whether rightly or wrongly God knows. But,

whether true or false, my opinion is that in the world of knowledge the idea of good appears last of all, and is seen only with an effort; and, when seen, is also inferred to be the universal author of all things beautiful and right, parent of light and of the lord of light in this visible world, and the immediate source of reason and truth in the intellectual; and that this is the power upon which he who would act rationally either in public or private life must have his eye fixed.

I agree, he said, as far as I am able to understand you. 36

Moreover, I said, you must not wonder that those who attain 37 to this beautiful vision are unwilling to descend to human affairs; for their souls are ever hastening into the upper world where they desire to dwell; which desire of their is very natural, if our allegory may be trusted.

Yes, very natural. 38

And is there anything surprising in one who passes from di- 39 vine contemplations to the evil state of man, misbehaving himself in a ridiculous manner; if, while his eyes are blinking and before he has become accustomed to the surrounding darkness, he is compelled to fight in courts of law, or in other places, about the images or the shadows of images of justice, and is endeavouring to meet the conceptions of those who have never yet seen absolute justice?

Anything but surprising, he replied. 40

Any one who has common sense will remember that the be- 41 wilderments of the eyes are of two kinds, and arise from two causes, either from coming out of the light or from going into the light, which is true of the mind's eye, quite as much as of the bodily eye; and he who remembers this when he sees any one whose vision is perplexed and weak, will not be too ready to laugh; he will first ask whether that soul of man has come out of the brighter life, and is unable to see because unaccustomed to the dark, or having turned from darkness to the day is dazzled by excess of light. And he will count the one happy in his condition and state of being, and he will pity the other; or, if he have a mind to laugh at the soul which comes from below into the light, there will be more reason in this than in the laugh which greets him who returns from above out of the light into the den.

That, he said, is a very just distinction. 42

COMPREHENSION

1. What does Plato hope to convey to readers of his allegory?

2. According to Plato, do human beings typically perceive reality? To what does he compare the world?

3. According to Plato, what often happens to people who develop a true idea

of reality? How well do they compete with others? Who is usually considered superior? Why?

RHETORIC

1. Is the conversation portrayed here realistic? How effective is this conversational style at conveying information?

2. How do you interpret such details of this allegory as the chains, the cave, and the fire? What connotations do such symbols have?

3. How does Plato use conversation to develop his argument? What is Glaucon's role in the conversation?

4. Note examples of transition words that mark contrasts between the real and the shadow world. How does Plato use contrast to develop his idea of the true real world?

5. Plato uses syllogistic reasoning to derive human behavior from his allegory. Trace his line of reasoning, noting transitional devices and the development of ideas in paragraphs 5 to 14. Find and describe a similar line of reasoning.

6. In what paragraph does Plato explain his allegory? Why do you think he locates his explanation where he does?

WRITING

1. Are Plato's ideas still influencing contemporary society? How do his ideas affect our evaluation of materialism, sensuality, sex, and love?

2. Write an allegory based upon a sport, business, or space flight to explain how we act in the world.

3. Imagine an encounter between Plato and Epicurus. Report briefly on their conversation.

JOSEPH WOOD KRUTCH

The New Immorality

Joseph Wood Krutch (1893–1970), American journalist, naturalist, and literary critic, is best known for The Desert Year *(1952) and* The Modern Temper *(1956). The following essay, first published in 1960, reflects Krutch's concern for the contemporary condition. In it, he argues against an immoral society and criticizes what he terms "the paradox of our age."*

he provost of one of our largest and most honored institutions told me not long ago that a questionnaire was distributed to his undergraduates and that 40 percent refused to acknowledge that they believed cheating on examinations to be reprehensible.

Recently a report for a New York newspaper stopped six people on the street and asked them if they would consent to take part in a rigged television quiz for money. He reported that five of the six said yes. Yet most of these five, like most of the college cheaters, would probably profess a strong social consciousness. They may cheat, but they vote for foreign aid and for enlightened social measures.

These two examples exhibit a paradox of our age. It is often said, and my observation leads me to believe it true, that our seemingly great growth in social morality has oddly enough taken place in a world where private morality—a sense of the supreme importance of purely personal honor, honesty, and integrity—seems to be declining. Beneficent and benevolent social institutions are administered by men who all too frequently turn out to be accepting "gifts." The world of popular entertainment is rocked by scandals. College students put on their honor, cheat on examinations. Candidates for the Ph.D. hire ghost writers to prepare their theses.

But, one may object, haven't all these things always been true? Is there really any evidence that personal dishonesty is more prevalent than it always was?

I have no way of making a historical measurement. Perhaps these things are not actually more prevalent. What I do know is that there is an increasing tendency to accept and take for granted such personal dishonesty. The bureaucrat and disk jockey say, "Well, yes, I took presents, but I assure you that I made just decisions anyway." The college student caught cheating does not even blush. He shrugs his shoulders and comments: "Everybody does it, and besides, I can't see that it really hurts anybody."

Jonathan Swift once said: "I have never been surprised to find men wicked, but I have often been surprised to find them not ashamed." It is my conviction that though men may be no more wicked then they always have been, they seem less likely to be ashamed. If anybody does it, it must be right. Honest, moral, decent mean only what is usual. This is not really a wicked world, because morality means mores or manners and usual conduct is the only standard.

The second part of the defense, "it really doesn't hurt anybody," is equally revealing. "It doesn't hurt anybody" means it doesn't do that abstraction called society any harm. The harm it did the bribe-taker and the cheater isn't important; it is purely personal.

And personal as opposed to social decency doesn't count for much. Sometimes I am inclined to blame sociology for part of this paradox. Sociology has tended to lay exclusive stress upon social morality, and tended too often to define good and evil as merely the "socially useful" or its reverse.

What social morality and social conscience leave out is the 8 narrower but very significant concept of honor—as opposed to what is sometimes called merely "socially desirable conduct." The man of honor is not content to ask merely whether this or that will hurt society, or whether it is what most people would permit themselves to do. He asks, and he asks first of all, would it hurt him and his self-respect? Would it dishonor him personally?

It was a favorite and no doubt sound argument among early 9 twentieth-century reformers that "playing the game" as the gentleman was supposed to play it was not enough to make a decent society. They were right: it is not enough. But the time has come to add that it is indeed inevitable that the so-called social conscience unsupported by the concept of personal honor will create a corrupt society. But suppose that it doesn't? Suppose that no one except the individual suffers from the fact that he sees nothing wrong in doing what everybody else does? Even so, I still insist that for the individual himself nothing is more important than this personal, interior sense of right and wrong and his determination to follow that rather than to be guided by what everybody does or merely the criterion of "social usefulness." It is impossible for me to imagine a good society composed of men without honor.

We hear it said frequently that what present-day men most 10 desire is security. If that is so, then they have a wrong notion of what the real, the ultimate, security is. No one who is dependent on anything outside himself, upon money, power, fame, or whatnot, is or ever can be secure. Only he who possesses himself and is content with himself is actually secure. Too much is being said about the importance of adjustment and "participation in the group." Even cooperation, to give this thing its most favorable designation, is no more important than the ability to stand alone when the choice must be made between the sacrifice of one's own integrity and adjustment to or participation in group activity.

No matter how bad the world may become, no matter how 11 much the mass man of the future may lose such of the virtues as he still has, one fact remains. If one person alone refuses to go along with him, if one person alone asserts his individual and inner right to believe in and be loyal to what his fellow men seem to have given up, then at least he will still remain what is perhaps the most important part of humanity.

THE NEW IMMORALITY

COMPREHENSION

1.   How do you know that Krutch is writing for a general audience rather than a specialized one?

2.   According to Krutch, what is the paradox of our age? What is unique about this paradox in terms of history?

3.   What are the standard defenses and assumptions concerning the new immorality? How does Krutch respond to them?

RHETORIC

1.   Krutch employs highly connotative language in this essay. What are some of these words? How does the author both control and exploit connotative language in advancing his analysis and argument?

2.   Why is the allusion to Jonathan Swift especially appropriate?

3.   Explain the patterns of development in paragraphs 1 to 4, 5 to 7, and 8 to 11.

4.   Does Krutch present an inductive or deductive argument in this essay? Explain your answer by reference to the text.

5.   In what ways do causal analysis and extended definition enter into the development of the essay?

6.   Analyze the last paragraph of the essay, and evaluate its effectiveness.

WRITING

1.   Do you accept Krutch's premise that a good society depends on people of honor? Why, or why not? Cite examples to support your contention.

2.   Write an analytical essay on cheating on your campus. Is it a problem or not?

3.   Argue for or against the proposition that personal morality in the United States is declining.

MICHAEL NOVAK

Sports: A Sense of Evil

Michael Novak (1933–   ) is a writer, editor, political commentator, and theologian. His interests, though principally in re-

*ligion, also touch upon politics, sports, and popular culture. No-
vak's books include* The Tiber Was Silver *(1961),* The Open
Church *(1964),* The Rise of the Unmeltable Ethnics *(1972), and*
Choosing Our King *(1976). The following essay, which percep-
tively reveals America's schizoid view of sports, appeared in* The
Joy of Sports *(1976).*

he mythic tissue surrounding sports has always sug-   1
gested that sports are "clean" and "All-American." This
mythic world owes much both to Great Britain and to
the Anglo-American spiritual sensitivity. The "fair play"
of the playing fields of Eton, but also the scouting movement, the
Temperance Leagues, the Chatauqua camps, and other American
movements of individualism, self-improvement, and progressive
thinking—these sanctified certain ideal types as truly American, compared to others. In the stories of Frank Merriwell, Garry Grayson, Tom
Swift, and other heroes for red-blooded American boys, the most
highly prized qualities were wit, pluck, clean-living, and implacable
enmity against ever-present "bullies." Sports were imagined to be a
realm of muscular Christianity—of maleness on the one hand and
purity of heart on the other. If in other climes a certain shiftiness,
sensuality, sheer physical aggression, duplicity, and trickiness were
deemed appropriate, the true American hero was pure of heart, candid, straight, true, plucky, modest, and full of boyish charm and
manly courage.

These traditions were not, be it noted, precisely British. The   2
British are an older, wiser culture, given to a certain matter-of-fact
toughness and pragmatic amorality. By contrast, those of the British
who came to New England tended to be enthusiasts, dissidents, saints,
passionately religious. The Anglo-American is quite different from the
Briton: more democratic, more active, rougher, less formal. "Phleg-
matic" would not be an apt description of his national character.
"Moral" would be closer.

In a peculiar way, as a result, the American mythology of   3
sports has moved on two separate levels. On the higher plane march
Frank Merriwell and all the legions of straight-shooters and Christian
athletes, self-effacing, gutsy, and victorious: the clean-living, true-blue
gentlemen athletes. On the lower plane carouse the avaricious, sexy,
aggressive, hedonistic Texans of *North Dallas Forty* and *Semitough*—
the heavy-drinking, womanizing, masculine hell-raisers of the early
days of baseball history, and of today: men like Max McGee, Paul
Hornung, Joe Namath, and the horny hero-villains of contemporary
sports fiction. In Babe Ruth, the high road and the low road ran as
parallel as a modern urban street with elevated highway overhead:

Babe Ruth visiting the orphans in a tuberculosis asylum in the newspaper story, and carousing late at night with the prostitutes in the parlor car, unknown to the public.

The moral pretenses of Anglo-American civilization demand   4
a public standard of rectitude, while permitting a private standard of individual choice. Attacks upon "hypocrisy" are one of the most consistent patterns of our cultural life. "Muckraking" is possible only because the public rectitude is prescriptive rather than descriptive, and the gap between the two is never closed. We are not even sure we want it closed. We hate Puritans. Yet our allergies inflict on us Puritan itches.

Liberal, radical, and (in general) progressive thinkers com-   5
monly undertake a double mission. First, they engage with gusto in the unmasking of hypocrisies. They attempt to reduce the gap between public myth and private practise by a stream of steamy exposés. Thus, they scratch the itch. Second, they hold aloft new standards of moral progress, idealism, and moral striving. "See," they say, "many athletes are horny, vulgar, racist, sexist hedonists. Frankness and candor are required of a truthful generation. Debunk the myths. For our society must *not* be racist, sexist, or nihilist. It must be just, egalitarian, brave, self-sacrificing, generous and truthful. It must live up to its ideals." Our muckrakers are not immoralists. On the contrary, they are busy setting up a new mythology which their children, carrying the endless project forward, will then debunk. Whatever we are allergic to, they inject into the nation's system. Saintly to the bitter end.

But the true practice of sport goes on, beneath the moralistic   6
mythology of virtue and clean-living. Basketball without deception could not survive. Football without aggression, holding, slugging, and other violations—only a few of which the referees actually will censure—could not be played. Baseball without cunning, trickery, and pressing for advantage would scarcely be a contest. Our sports are lively with the sense of evil. The evil in them is, to be certain, ritualized, controlled, and channeled. But it is silly to deny that the disciplines of sport include learning how to cope with the illegal aggressions and unbounded passions of one's opponent and oneself. Sports provide an almost deliberate exercise in pushing the psyche to cheat and take advantage, to be ruthless, cruel, deceitful, vengeful, and aggressive. It is "good sportsmanship" not to let such passions dominate; it is naïve not to see them operate in others and oneself.

In football, defensive players hold, illegally, on almost every   7
play. In basketball, a "non-contact game," the violence under the boards is fierce. In baseball, intimidation by pitchers, baserunners, and defensive players is straightforward and expectable. Morality on the athletic field is not a Pollyanna morality. It is controlled by more rules and referees than is any other part of life. Coaches devise ways to get

around the rules (players change jerseys; feign injuries to stop the clock; call signals to draw the other team offsides, etc.). The many roles of bluff, feint, intimidation and trickery are so important in sports that they are codified and rendered classical. (There are similar codes and classic moves in scholarship, journalism, politics, and every other field.)

Sports, then, are no escape from evil and immorality. They are designed to teach us how to live in a world that is less than moral. That, too, is one of sport's pleasures. To be an American is to be obliged to indulge in certain moral pretenses. The "American way" is to be decent, moral, trustworthy, law-abiding, tolerant, just, egalitarian, and so forth. Which is fairly heavy. To give a fellow an elbow when the referree isn't looking, just before the ball comes off the rim, is profoundly satisfying to the un-American, unregenerate, unsaintly self. 8

It is "good sportsmanship" to see to it that the basic structure and procedures of the contest are fair. A good contest, by its nature, requires fairness. The outcome should hang uncertainly between evenly matched opponents, playing under similar rules. A false conception of good sportsmanship, however, prevents many players from giving themselves fully to the competition. Instead of concentrating on the excellence of their own performance, many amateurs, in particular, begin to worry about the psyche of their opponents; they hold back. They lack the instinct for the jugular. They don't want to "humiliate" their opponents. Their condescension toward the frail ego (as they imagine it) of their opponents prevents them from playing as well as they might. They "let up." When they do, commitment and fire leave the contest. The true morality of sport is absent. 9

It is necessary to be objective about games—to play every one as though it were one's last, seriously, with purpose, at full alert. The point of games is to propel oneself into a more intense mode of being. Not to play hard is to kill time, but not to transcend it. To concentrate on the game is, in a sense, to be indifferent about one's opponent or oneself. It is to refuse to be distracted by wayward passions. If an opponent plays unfairly, the sweetest revenge is not revenge but victory; one avoids striking back in kind in order to concentrate on the one thing necessary: perfect execution. Concentration on the game itself is the best safeguard against indulgence in ugly, errant passions. It is the highest form of sportsmanship. It is not so much a moral as an ontological attitude. One isn't trying to "be good," but to act perfectly. 10

Recently, the moralistic impulse has uncovered homosexuality in sports. Muckrakers have informed us that homosexuals appear in professional sports at about the same frequency as elsewhere in our society. Writers used to leer about fanny-patting, celibate training 11 camps, nudity and team showering, and wrestling matches on the soapy floor. The new muckrakers seem to want to give a double message: "See, the world of sports is corrupt and hollow, a world of fake machismo, infested by gays. But it's all right to be gay, it's great, it's fine." They want it both ways. In the pagan world, in Greece and in Nazi Germany, athleticism and homosexuality went (so to speak) hand-in-hand. As did art and homosexuality. Machismo and homosexuality are not opposites. Sports favors neither one.

Sports are natural religions. All things human are proper to them. In pushing humans to extremities, they push virtues and vices to extremities too. The world of sports is no escape from virtue, excellence, and grace. In sports, we meet our humanity. Assuming one begins with limited hopes, there is more to admire in sports—and in our humanity, and in our nation—than to despise. 12

COMPREHENSION

1. Explain in your own words the "two separate levels" that American sports occupy in our national mythology.

2. Explain what Novak means when he says, "Sports are natural religions."

3. What does Novak mean when he states that hypocrisy and muckraking are American obsessions?

RHETORIC

1. Give examples of Novak's use of philosophical vocabulary.

2. How does the use of slang affect the tone of the essay? How does it complement the use of philosophical terms?

3. How does Novak's comparison in paragraph 2 contribute to the development of the essay?

4. Provide examples of Novak's use of deduction in this essay.

5. Explain the organization of paragraphs 5 and 6. What rhetorical techniques are used in each paragraph? How are the two paragraphs related?

6. Novak uses examples frequently in the essay. Examine their use in paragraphs 1 and 10. How do these kinds of examples differ? How do they contribute to the development of the essay?

WRITING

1. Novak says that the contrast between high and low planes in American sports exists elsewhere. Explain in an essay how the contrast appears in politics, college life, and literature.

2. Write an essay about your own experience as a player or spectator in sports when you confronted the conflict between ideals and reality.

MICHAEL NOVAK

3. Write an essay analyzing other ambiguities in American life, such as the difference between image and reality in regard to politicians, astronauts, or business people.

ALBERT CAMUS

The Myth of Sisyphus

Albert Camus (1913–1960), French author and philosopher, was one of the most important thinkers of the twentieth century. During World War II, he joined the French underground movement against the Germans and was the principal editor of the underground newspaper Combat. *After the war, he became well known for his theories on the absurdity of life. Camus believed that men and women should respond to absurdity with courage and decency, not with despair. His theories are dramatized in* The Stranger *(1942) and in such later works as* The Plague *(1948) and the plays* Caligula *(1944),* State of Siege *(1948), and* The Just Assassins *(1950). Camus was awarded the 1957 Nobel Prize in Literature.* The Myth of Sisyphus *(1942), from which this essay is taken, is often considered the fountain of his absurdist philosophy.*

he gods had condemned Sisyphus to ceaselessly rolling a rock to the top of a mountain, whence the stone would fall back of its own weight. They had thought with some reason that there is no more dreadful punishment than futile and hopeless labor.

If one believes Homer, Sisyphus was the wisest and most prudent of mortals. According to another tradition, however, he was disposed to practice the profession of highwayman. I see no contradiction in this. Opinions differ as to the reasons why he became the futile laborer of the underworld. To begin with, he is accused of a certain levity in regard to the gods. He stole their secrets. Aegina, the daughter of Aesopus, was carried off by Jupiter. The father was shocked by that disappearance and complained to Sisyphus. He, who knew of the abduction, offered to tell about it on condition that Aesopus would give water to the citadel of Corinth. To the celestial thunderbolts he preferred the benediction of water. He was punished for this in the underworld. Homer tells us also that Sisyphus had put Death in chains. Pluto could not endure the sight of his deserted, silent empire.

He dispatched the god of War, who liberated Death from the hands of her conqueror.

It is said also that Sisyphus, being near to death, rashly wanted to test his wife's love. He ordered her to cast his unburied body into the middle of the public square. Sisyphus woke up in the underworld. And there, annoyed by an obedience so contrary to human love, he obtained from Pluto permission to return to earth in order to chastise his wife. But when he had seen again the face of this world, enjoyed water and sun, warm stones and the sea, he no longer wanted to go back to the infernal darkness. Recalls, signs of anger, warnings were of no avail. Many years more he lived facing the curve of the gulf, the sparkling sea, and the smiles of earth. A decree of the gods was necessary. Mercury came and seized the impudent man by the collar and, snatching him from his joys, led him forcibly back to the underworld, where his rock was ready for him.

You have already grasped that Sisyphus is the absurd hero. He *is*, as much through his passions as through his torture. His scorn of the gods, his hatred of death, and his passion for life won him that unspeakable penalty in which the whole being is exerted toward accomplishing nothing. This is the price that must be paid for the passions of this earth. Nothing is told us about Sisyphus in the underworld. Myths are made for the imagination to breathe life into them. As for this myth, one sees merely the whole effort of a body straining to raise the huge stone, to roll it and push it up a slope a hundred times over; one sees the face screwed up, the cheek tight against the stone, the shoulder bracing the claycovered mass, the foot wedging it, the fresh start with arms outstretched, the wholly human security of two earth-clotted hands. At the very end of this long effort measured by skyless space and time without depth, the purpose is achieved. Then Sisyphus watches the stone rush down in a few moments toward that lower world whence he will have to push it up again toward the summit. He goes back down to the plain.

It is during that return, that pause, that Sisyphus interests me. A face that toils so close to stones is already stone itself! I see that man going back down with a heavy yet measured step toward the torment of which he will never know the end. That hour like a breathing-space which returns as surely as his suffering, that is the hour of consciousness. At each of those moments when he leaves the heights and gradually sinks toward the lairs of the gods, he is superior to his fate. He is stronger than his rock.

If this myth is tragic, that is because its hero is conscious. Where would his torture be, indeed, if at every step the hope of succeeding upheld him? The workman of today works every day in his life at the same tasks, and this fate is no less absurd. But it is tragic only at the rare moments when it becomes conscious. Sisyphus, pro-

ALBERT CAMUS

letarian of the gods, powerless and rebellious, knows the whole extent of his wretched condition: it is what he thinks of during his descent. The lucidity that was to constitute his torture at the same time crowns his victory. There is no fate that cannot be surmounted by scorn.

If the descent is thus sometimes performed in sorrow, it can also take place in joy. This word is not too much. Again I fancy Sisyphus returning toward his rock, and the sorrow was in the beginning. When the images of earth cling too tightly to memory, when the call of happiness becomes too insistent, it happens that melancholy rises in man's heart: this is the rock's victory, this is the rock itself. The boundless grief is too heavy to bear. These are our nights of Gethsemane. But crushing truths perish from being acknowledged. Thus, Oedipus at the outset obeys fate without knowing it. But from the moment he knows, his tragedy begins. Yet at the same moment, blind and desperate, he realizes that the only bond linking him to the world is the cool hand of a girl. Then a tremendous remark rings out: "Despite so many ordeals, my advanced age and the nobility of my soul make me conclude that all is well." Sophocles' Oedipus, like Dostoevsky's Kirilov, thus gives the recipe for the absurd victory. Ancient wisdom confirms modern heroism.

One does not discover the absurd without being tempted to write a manual of happiness. "What! by such narrow ways—?" There is but one world, however. Happiness and the absurd are two sons of the same earth. They are inseparable. It would be a mistake to say that happiness necessarily springs from the absurd discovery. It happens as well that the feeling of the absurd springs from happiness. "I conclude that all is well," says Oedipus, and that remark is sacred. It echoes in the wild and limited universe of man. It teaches that all is not, has not been, exhausted. It drives out of this world a god who had come into it with dissatisfaction and a preference for futile sufferings. It makes of fate a human matter, which must be settled among men.

All Sisyphus' silent joy is contained therein. His fate belongs to him. His rock is his thing. Likewise, the absurd man, when he contemplates his torment, silences all the idols. In the universe suddenly restored to its silence, the myriad wondering little voices of the earth rise up. Unconscious, secret calls, invitations from all the faces, they are the necessary reverse and price of victory. There is no sun without shadow, and it is essential to know the night. The absurd man says yes and his effort will henceforth be unceasing. If there is a personal fate, there is no higher destiny, or at least there is but one which he concludes is inevitable and despicable. For the rest, he knows himself to be the master of his days. At that subtle moment when man glances backward over his life, Sisyphus returning toward his rock, in that slight pivoting he contemplates that series of unre-

THE MYTH OF SISYPHUS

lated actions which becomes his fate, created by him, combined under his memory's eye and soon sealed by his death. Thus, convinced of the wholly human origin of all that is human, a blind man eager to see who knows that the night has no end, he is still on the go. The rock is still rolling.

I leave Sisyphus at the foot of the mountain! One always finds 10 one's burden again. But Sisyphus teaches the higher fidelity that negates the gods and raises rocks. He too concludes that all is well. This universe henceforth without a master seems to him neither sterile nor futile. Each atom of that stone, each mineral flake of that night-filled mountain, in itself forms a world. The struggle itself toward the heights is enough to fill a man's heart. One must imagine Sisyphus happy.

COMPREHENSION

1. Explain the author's thesis in this selection.

2. What does Camus mean when he says, "Myths are made for the imagination to breathe life into them" (paragraph 4)?

3. Why does Camus think Sisyphus is such an appropriate symbol of people today?

RHETORIC

1. Explain the style Camus uses to describe Sisyphus in paragraph 4. How does this narration differ in style from the preceding paragraphs?

2. Explore the connotations of such words as *tragic* (paragraph 6), *proletarian* (paragraph 6), *absurd* (paragraph 4), and *myth* (paragraph 4).

3. Why does Camus begin his essay with an analysis of the myth of Sisyphus?

4. Explain the organization of paragraph 4. Why does Camus end the narration where he does? How does this end lead to the next paragraph?

5. How does paragraph 8 differ from the paragraphs before it? How does it affect our sense of Sisyphus?

6. What crucial comparison is made in this essay? In what paragraphs does it appear? What transition words mark the development of the comparison?

WRITING

1. Can you think of any other myths from the ancient world that help to explain our nature? Why do you think myths make such effective symbols of human nature? Write an essay comparing yourself to a Greek hero such as Hercules, Jason, Medea, Odysseus, or Penelope. How do their histories relate to your own?

2. Write your own analysis of absurdity and the conditions of modern life.

ALBERT CAMUS

3. Do you agree with Camus that "the struggle itself toward the heights" is the great pleasure in life—not necessarily reaching the goal? Write an argumentative essay on this topic.

JOAN DIDION

On Morality

Joan Didion (1934–   ) grew up in California and graduated from the University of California at Berkeley in 1956. She began writing for national magazines such as Mademoiselle, Saturday Evening Post, *and* Life. *She published her first novel,* Run River, *in 1963. Although she has continued to write novels and has written several screenplays, her most acclaimed work is in nonfiction. This work includes* Slouching Towards Bethlehem *(1968),* The White Album *(1979),* Salvador *(1983),* Democracy *(1984), and* Miami *(1987). In "On Morality," (1965) Didion finds the issue of morality arising in strange circumstances, and she comes to a personal conclusion on the topic that is at odds with conventional wisdom.*

 s it happens I am in Death Valley, in a room at the Enterprise Motel and Trailer Park, and it is July, and it is hot. In fact it is 119°. I cannot seem to make the air conditioner work, but there is a small refrigerator, and I can wrap ice cubes in a towel and hold them against the small of my back. With the help of the ice cubes I have been trying to think, because *The American Scholar* asked me to, in some abstract way about "morality," a word I distrust more every day, but my mind veers inflexibly toward the particular. 1

Here are some particulars. At midnight last night, on the road in from Las Vegas to Death Valley Junction, a car hit a shoulder and turned over. The driver, very young and apparently drunk, was killed instantly. His girl was found alive but bleeding internally, deep in shock. I talked this afternoon to the nurse who had driven the girl to the nearest doctor, 185 miles across the floor of the Valley and three ranges of lethal mountain road. The nurse explained that her husband, a talc miner, had stayed on the highway with the boy's body until the coroner could get over the mountains from Bishop, at dawn today. "You can't just leave a body on the highway," she said. "It's immoral." 2

 ON MORALITY

485

It was one instance in which I did not distrust the word, because she meant something quite specific. She meant that if a body is
left alone for even a few minutes on the desert, the coyotes close in
and eat the flesh. Whether or not a corpse is torn apart by coyotes
may seem only a sentimental consideration, but of course it is more:
one of the promises we make to one another is that we will try to
retrieve our casualties, try not to abandon our dead to the coyotes. If
we have been taught to keep our promises—if, in the simplest terms,
our upbringing is good enough—we stay with the body, or have bad
dreams.

I am talking, of course, about the kind of social code that is
sometimes called, usually pejoratively, "wagon-train morality." In fact
that is precisely what it is. For better or worse, we are what we learned
as children: my own childhood was illuminated by graphic litanies of
the grief awaiting those who failed in their loyalties to each other. The
Donner-Reed Party, starving in the Sierra snows, all the ephemera of
civilization gone save that one vestigial taboo, the provision that no
one should eat his own blood kin. The Jayhawkers, who quarreled
and separated not far from where I am tonight. Some of them died in
the Funerals and some of them died down near Badwater and most
of the rest of them died in the Panamints. A woman who got through
gave the Valley its name. Some might say that the Jayhawkers were
killed by the desert summer, and the Donner Party by the mountain
winter, by circumstances beyond control; we were taught instead that
they had somewhere abdicated their responsibilities, somehow
breached their primary loyalties, or they would not have found themselves helpless in the mountain winter or the desert summer, would
not have given way to acrimony, would not have deserted one
another, would not have *failed*. In brief, we heard such stories as cau-
tionary tales, and they still suggest the only kind of "morality" that
seems to me to have any but the most potentially mendacious
meaning.

You are quite possibly impatient with me by now; I am talking, you want to say, about a "morality" so primitive that it scarcely
deserves the name, a code that has as its point only survival, not the
attainment of the ideal good. Exactly. Particularly out here tonight, in
this country so ominous and terrible that to live in it is to live with
antimatter, it is difficult to believe that "the good" is a knowable
quantity. Let me tell you what it is like out here tonight. Stories travel
at night on the desert. Someone gets in his pickup and drives a couple
of hundred miles for a beer, and he carries news of what is happening,
back wherever he came from. Then he drives another hundred miles
for another beer, and passes along stories from the last place as well
as from the one before; it is a network kept alive by people whose

instincts tell them that if they do not keep moving at night in the desert they will lose all reason. Here is a story that is going around the desert tonight: over across the Nevada line, sheriff's deputies are diving in some underground pools, trying to retrieve a couple of bodies known to be in the hole. The widow of one of the drowned boys is over there; she is eighteen, and pregnant, and is said not to leave the hole. The divers go down and come up, and she just stands there and stares into the water. They have been diving for ten days but have found no bottom to the caves, no bodies and no trace of them, only the black 90° water going down and down and down, and a single translucent fish, not classified. The story tonight is that one of the divers has been hauled up incoherent, out of his head, shouting— until they got him out of there so that the widow could not hear— about water that got hotter instead of cooler as he went down, about light flickering through the water, about magma, about underground nuclear testing.

That is the tone stories take out here, and there are quite a few of them. And it is more than the stories alone. Across the road at the Faith Community Church a couple of dozen old people, come here to live in trailers and die in the sun, are holding a prayer sing. I cannot hear them and do not want to. What I can hear are occasional coyotes and a constant chorus of "Baby the Rain Must Fall" from the jukebox in the Snake Room next door, and if I were also to hear those dying voices, those Midwestern voices drawn to this lunar country for some unimaginable atavistic rites, *rock of ages cleft for me*, I think I would lose my own reason. Every now and then I imagine I hear a rattlesnake, but my husband says that it is a faucet, a paper rustling, the wind. Then he stands by a window, and plays a flashlight over the dry wash outside.

What does it mean? It means nothing manageable. There is some sinister hysteria in the air out here tonight, some hint of the monstrous perversion to which any human idea can come. "I followed my own conscience." "I did what I thought was right." How many madmen have said it and meant it? How many murderers? Klaus Fuchs said it, and the men who committed the Mountain Meadows Massacre said it, and Alfred Rosenberg said it. And, as we are rotely and rather presumptuously reminded by those who would say it now, Jesus said it. Maybe we have all said it, and maybe we have been wrong. Except on that most primitive level—our loyalties to those we love—what could be more arrogant than to claim the primacy of personal conscience? ("Tell me," a rabbi asked Daniel Bell when he said, as a child, that he did not believe in God. "Do you think God cares?") At least some of the time, the world appears to me as a painting by Hieronymous Bosch; were I to follow my conscience then, it would lead me out onto the desert with Marion Faye, out to where he stood

 ON MORALITY

in *The Deer Park* looking east to Los Alamos and praying, as if for rain, that it would happen: *". . . let it come and clear the rot and the stench and the stink, let it come for all of everywhere, just so it comes and the world stands clear in the white dead dawn."*

Of course you will say that I do not have the right, even if I had the power, to inflict that unreasonable conscience upon you; nor do I want you to inflict your conscience, however reasonable, however enlightened, upon me. ("We must be aware of the dangers which lie in our most generous wishes," Lionel Trilling once wrote. "Some paradox of our nature leads us, when once we have made our fellow men the objects of our enlightened interest, to go on to make them the objects of our pity, then of our wisdom, ultimately of our coercion.") That the ethic of conscience is intrinsically insidious seems scarcely a revelatory point, but it is one raised with increasing infrequency; even those who do raise it tend to *segue* with troubling readiness into the quite contradictory position that the ethic of conscience is dangerous when it is "wrong," and admirable when it is "right." 8

You see I want to be quite obstinate about insisting that we have no way of knowing—beyond that fundamental loyalty to the social code—what is "right" and what is "wrong," what is "good" and what "evil." I dwell so upon this because the most disturbing aspect of "morality" seems to me to be the frequency with which the word now appears; in the press, on television, in the most perfunctory kinds of conversation. Questions of straightforward power (or survival) politics, questions of quite indifferent public policy, questions of almost anything: they are all assigned these factitious moral burdens. There is something facile going on, some self-indulgence at work. Of course we would all like to "believe" in something, like to assuage our private guilts in public causes, like to lose our tiresome selves; like, perhaps, to transform the white flag of defeat at home into the brave white banner of battle away from home. And of course it is all right to do that; that is how, immemorially, things have gotten done. But I think it is all right only so long as we do not delude ourselves about what we are doing, and why. It is all right only so long as we remember that all the *ad hoc* committees, all the picket lines, all the brave signatures in *The New York Times*, all the tools of agitprop straight across the spectrum, do not confer upon anyone any *ipso facto* virtue. It is all right only so long as we recognize that the end may or may not be expedient, may or may not be a good idea, but in any case has nothing to do with "morality." Because when we start deceiving ourselves into thinking not that we want something or need something, not that it is a pragmatic necessity for us to have it, but that it is a *moral imperative* that we have it, then is when we join 9

JOAN DIDION

the fashionable madmen, and then is when the thin whine of hysteria is heard in the land, and then is when we are in bad trouble. And I suspect we are already there.

COMPREHENSION

1. Who is the implied audience of this essay? Where does Didion offer a clue to the nature of this audience?

2. Why is Didion suspicious of the word *morality*? What examples does she provide of this mistrust?

3. Compare Didion's emphasis on the importance of "specificity" in morality with Sartre's idea of action in existentialism (see his essay in the next chapter). What values do the two authors seem to have in common?

RHETORIC

1. Apropos of question 1 in "Comprehension," what specific references does Didion make that indicate her intended audience? How necessary is familiarity with these references to an understanding of her theme?

2. What type of relationship does Didion create between herself and the reader by using the pronoun "you" at the beginning of the second and third sections of the essay?

3. Why does Didion begin her essay with a description of her physical surroundings? How does this strategy complement her general view of the nature of "morality"?

4. Paragraph 7 begins with "What does it mean? It means nothing manageable." How does Didion use example, illustration, and anecdote in the rest of the paragraph to support this "unmanageability"?

5. How does Didion's repetition of the words *what, question,* and *like* contribute to the coherence of paragraph 9?

6. Study the final two sentences of the essay. One is quite long, the other short. What is the effect of this juxtaposition in length? Find other examples of this technique. What similar effects do they create?

WRITING

1. Why does Didion say that "the ethic of conscience is intrinsically insidious" (paragraph 8)? What are your reasons for either agreeing or disagreeing with her?

2. How is morality shaped by the group that adheres to it? Select a group—for example, athletes, criminals, model students—and write an essay describing its

 ON MORALITY

particular morality. What are the group's values? How do its members exhibit these values?

3. Do you have a personal morality? Write an essay describing it, and explain how it helps you to shape your behavior.

4. Examine the ways in which Didion's essay illuminates Coles's "I Listen to My Parents and I Wonder What They Believe."

Religious Thought and Experience

ANNIE DILLARD

A Field of Silence

Annie Dillard (1945–   ) is a poet and essayist. She received her M.A. from Hollins College in Virginia in 1967. Her first book of prose, Pilgrim at Tinker Creek, *won the 1974 Pulitzer Prize. In addition, Dillard has been a columnist for* Living Wilderness *and a contributing editor to* Harpers. *Among her recent work are* Teaching a Stone to Talk *(1982) and* Encounters with Chinese Writers *(1984). In this memoir, written in 1978, she describes a revelatory experience.*

 here is a place called "the farm" where I lived once, in   1
a time that was very lonely. Fortunately I was unconscious of my loneliness then, and felt it only deeply, be-
wildered, in the half-bright way that a puppy feels pain.

I loved the place, and still do. It was an ordinary farm, a calf-   2
raising, haymaking farm, and very beautiful. Its flat, messy pastures
ran along one side of the central portion of a quarter-mile road in the
central part of an island, an island in Puget Sound, so that from the
high end of the road you could look west toward the Pacific, to the

Sound and its hundred islands, and from the other end—and from the farm—you could see east to the water between you and the mainland, and beyond it the mainland's mountains slicked smooth with snow.

I liked the clutter about the place, the way everything blossomed or seeded or rusted; I liked the hundred half-finished projects, the smells and the way the animals always broke loose. It is calming to herd animals. Often a regular rodeo breaks out—two people and a clever cow can kill a morning—but still, it is calming. You laugh for a while, exhausted, and silence is restored; the beasts are back in their pastures, the fences not fixed but disguised as if they were fixed, ensuring the animals' temporary resignation; and a great calm descends, a lack of urgency, a sense of having to invent something to do until the next time you must run and chase cattle.

The farm seemed eternal in the crude way the earth does—extending, that is, a very long time. The farm was as old as earth, always there, as old as the island, the Platonic form of "farm," of human society itself and at large, a piece of land eaten and replenished a billion summers, a piece of land worked on, lived on, grown over, plowed under, and stitched again and again, with fingers or with leaves, in and out and into human life's thin weave. I lived there once.

I lived there once and I have seen, from behind the barn, the long roadside pastures heaped with silence. Behind the rooster, suddenly, I saw the silence heaped on the fields like trays. That day the green hayfields supported silence evenly sown; the fields bent just so under the even pressure of silence, bearing it, even, palming it aloft: cleared fields, part of a land, a planet, they did not buckle beneath the heel of silence, nor split up scattered to bits, but instead lay secret, disguised as time and matter as though that were nothing, ordinary— disguised as fields like those which bear the silence only because they are spread, and the silence spreads over them, great in size.

I do not want, I think, ever to see such a sight again. That there is loneliness here I had granted, in the abstract—but not, I thought, inside the light of God's presence, inside his sanction, and signed by his name.

I lived alone in the farmhouse and rented; the owners, Angus and Lynn, in their twenties, lived in another building just over the yard. I had been reading and restless for two or three days. It was morning. I had just read at breakfast an Updike story, "Packed Dirt, Churchgoing, A Dying Cat, A Traded Car," which moved me. I heard our own farmyard rooster and two or three roosters across the street screeching. I quit the house, hoping at heart to see Lynn or Angus, but immediately to watch our rooster as he crowed.

It was Saturday morning late in the summer, in early September, clear-aired and still. I climbed the barnyard fence between the

ANNIE DILLARD

poultry and the pastures; I watched the red rooster, and the rooster, reptilian, kept one alert and alien eye on me. He pulled his extravagant neck to its maximum length, hauled himself high on his legs, stretched his beak as if he were gagging, screamed, and blinked. It was a ruckus. The din came from everywhere, and only the most rigorous application of reason could persuade me that it proceeded in its entirety from this lone and maniac bird.

After a pause, the roosters across the street would start, answering the proclamation, or cranking out another round, arrhythmically, interrupting. In the same way there is no pattern nor sense to the massed stridulations of cicadas; their skipped beats, enjambments, and failed alterations jangle your spirits, as though each of those thousand insects, each with identical feelings, were stubbornly deaf to the others, and loudly alone.

I shifted along the fence to see if Lynn or Angus was coming or going. To the rooster I said nothing, but only stared. And he stared at me: we were both careful to keep the wooden fence slat from our line of sight, so that this profiled eye and my two eyes could meet. From time to time I looked beyond the pastures to learn if anyone might be seen on the road.

When I was turned away in this manner, the silence gathered and struck me. It bashed me broadside from nowhere, as if I'd been hit by a plank. It dropped from the heavens above me like yard goods; ten acres of fallen, invisible sky choked the fields. The pastures on either side of the road turned green in a surrealistic fashion, monstrous, impeccable, as if they were holding their breath. The roosters stopped. All the things of the world—the fields and the fencing, the road, a parked orange truck—were stricken and self-conscious. A world pressed down on their surfaces, a world battered just within their surfaces, and that real world, so near to emerging, had got stuck.

There was only silence. It was the silence of matter caught in the act and embarrassed. There were no cells moving, and yet there were cells. I could see the shape of the land, how it lay holding silence. Its poise and its stillness were unendurable, like the ring of the silence you hear in your skull when you're little and notice you're living, the ring which resumes later in life when you're sick.

There were flies buzzing over the dirt by the henhouse, moving in circles and buzzing, black dreams in chips off the one long dream, the dream of the regular world. But the silent fields were the real world, eternity's outpost in time, whose look I remembered but never like this, this God-blasted, paralyzed day. I felt myself tall and vertical, in a blue shirt, self-conscious, and wishing to die. I heard the flies again; I looked at the rooster who was frozen looking at me.

Then at last I heard whistling, human whistling far on the air, and I was not able to bear it. I looked around, heartbroken; only at the big yellow Charolais farm far up the road was there motion—a woman, I think, dressed in pink, and pushing a wheelbarrow easily over the grass. It must have been she who was whistling and heaping on top of the silence those hollow notes of song. But the slow sound of the music—the beautiful sound of the music ringing the air like a stone bell—was isolate and detached. The notes spread into the general air and became the weightier part of silence, silence's last straw. The distant woman and her wheelbarrow were flat and detached, like mechanized and pink-painted properties for a stage. I stood in pieces, afraid I was unable to move. Something had unhinged the world. The houses and roadsides and pastures were buckling under the silence. Then a Labrador, black, loped up the distant driveway, fluid and cartoonlike, toward the pink woman. I had to try to turn away. Holiness is a force, and like the others can be resisted. It was given, but I didn't want to see it, God or no God. It was as if God had said, "I am here, but not as you have known me. This is the look of silence, and of loneliness unendurable: it too has always been mine, and now will be yours." I was not ready for a life of sorrow, sorrow deriving from knowledge I could just as well stop at the gate.

I turned away, willful, and the whole show vanished. The 15 realness of things disassembled. The whistling became ordinary, familiar; the air above the fields released its pressure and the fields lay hooded as before. I myself could act. Looking to the rooster I whistled to him myself, softly, and some hens appeared at the chicken house window, greeted the day, and fluttered down.

Several months later, walking past the farm on the way to a 16 volleyball game, I remarked to a friend, by way of information, "There are angels in those fields." Angels! That silence so grave and so stricken, that choked and unbearable green! I have rarely been so surprised at something I've said. Angels! What are angels? I had never thought of angels, in any way at all.

From that time I began to think of angels. I considered that 17 sights such as I had seen of the silence must have been shared by the people who said they saw angels. I began to review the thing I had seen that morning. My impression now of those fields is of thousands of spirits—spirits trapped, perhaps, by my refusal to call them more fully, or by the paralysis of my own spirit at that time—thousands of spirits, angels in fact, almost discernible to the eye, and whirling. If pressed I would say they were three or four feet from the ground. Only their motion was clear (clockwise, if you insist); that, and their beauty unspeakable.

There are angels in those fields, and I presume, in all fields, 18 and everywhere else. I would go to the lions for this conviction, to witness this fact. What all this means about perception, or language, or angels, or my own sanity, I have no idea.

ANNIE DILLARD

COMPREHENSION

1. Why is this selection titled "A Field of Silence"? What does *silence* mean in this context?

2. Trace carefully the sequence of events in nature that unfolds in this essay.

3. Why does Dillard describe the farm as seeming "eternal in the crude way the earth does"? Why is this "Platonic"?

RHETORIC

1. What is the level of language here? Why does Dillard use metaphorical language to such an extent? Cite imagery, similes, and metaphors that you find especially effective.

2. Define the following words: *ruckus* (paragraph 8), *arrhythmically* (paragraph 9), *stridulations* (paragraph 9), *enjambments* (paragraph 9), and *surrealistic* (paragraph 11).

3. What is the thesis of this piece? Where does Dillard reveal it?

4. Why does Dillard go to such lengths to describe the details of the farm? Why is all the description relevant?

5. How does Dillard signal the transition to the world of silence? How long does this last? How does she capture the "something" that "unhinged the world"? Is there a logic or order to this experience? Explain.

6. Where does Dillard describe "the paralysis of my own spirit"? How does that provoke the episode described?

WRITING

1. What will Dillard do as a result of this experience? How will her life be different? Write a short response to this question.

2. Does Dillard experience an objectively real vision of the "silent" world, or is this a product of her own imagination? How can Dillard or anyone test the quality of revelation? Evaluate this topic in an essay.

3. Describe a moment of loneliness or isolation in your life that provided insight into existence or creation.

4. How does Dillard's "sacred" approach to nature resemble that of Momaday in "The Way to Rainy Mountain"? Write a comparative essay on this topic.

The Third Leg of the Table

Martin Buber (1878–1965) was born in Vienna. He taught phi-
losophy and religion at the University of Frankfurt-am-Main until
1933, when he fled the Nazis; from 1933 to 1951, he taught at
the Hebrew University in Jerusalem. Greatly influenced by the
mystical Jewish tradition of Hasidism, as well as existentialism,
Buber's work is important to both secular and religious readers.
Among his works are I and Thou *(1923; 2d ed., 1958),* Jewish
Mysticism and the Legends of Baalshem *(1931),* Moses *(1946),*
and A Believing Humanism *(1967). In this selection, Buber re-*
lates a religious teaching story reflecting his concern about both
the community and the soul.

When Rabbi Yeheskel Landau came to Prague, he spoke   1
to his congregation Sabbath after Sabbath of nothing else
except the bitter need of the destitute in the city. One
had expected to hear from his mouth profound mean-
ings of interpretations and subtle meanings of disputations, but he
only thought of reminding them of the wretched who spread out
unrelieved, unnoticed, in this lane and its surroundings. "Help! Go
there even today in the evening and help!" thus he called ever again.
But the people took it for a sermon and were vexed that it was so
insipid and flat.

Then on a busy market day something wonderful took place.   2
Right through the middle of the tumult came the rabbi and remained
standing in the center of the thickest swarm as though he had wares
to offer for sale and only waited for a favorable moment to commend
them to the crowd. Those who recognized him passed the incomprehensible fact on to others; from everywhere traders and buyers
crowded to that place; they stared at him, but no one dared to question him. Finally there broke from the lips of one who imagined himself intimate with him, "What is our rabbi doing here?"

At once Rabbi Yeheskel began: 3

"If a table has three legs and a piece is broken off of one of
the three legs, what does one do? One supports the leg as well as one
can, and the table stands. But now if still another of the three legs
breaks in two, there is no longer a support. What does one do then?
One shortens the third leg too, and the table stands again.

"Our sages say: 'The world stands on three things: on the   4
teaching, on the service, and on the deeds of love.' When the holiness
is destroyed, then the leg of the service breaks. Then our sages support
it by saying: 'Service with the heart, that is what is meant by prayer.'

But now when the acts of love disappear and the second leg suffers injury, how shall the world still endure? Therefore, I have left the house of teaching and have come to the market place. We must shorten the leg of the teaching in order that the table of the world may again stand firm."

COMPREHENSION

1.   What is Buber's purpose in telling this story? What does Rabbi Landau represent to Buber?

2.   When does this story take place? What clues are there that locate it in time?

3.   Compare Buber's understanding of "holiness" and Dillard's.

RHETORIC

1.   Define the following: *vexed* (paragraph 1), *tumult* (paragraph 2), and *incomprehensible* (paragraph 2).

2.   Is there any figurative language in this essay? Explain.

3.   Is Buber relating a story from his own experience or from tradition? How many levels of narrative are there here?

4.   What is the purpose of the example of the table?

5.   What strategy does Buber use to describe Landau?

6.   How does point of view reinforce the tone of this piece?

WRITING

1.   What responsibility do religious leaders and their congregations have to do service in the community? To what extent have organized religions fulfilled this duty? Answer in a brief essay.

2.   What responsibility do you feel toward the homeless and destitute of our society? How do you meet this responsibility? Is such a duty religious or merely ethical? Write an explanatory essay dealing with these questions.

3.   Is there a necessary conflict between teaching and service? What is your position?

THOMAS MERTON

What Is a Monk?

Thomas Merton (1915–1968) spent most of his life as a Trappist (Cistercian) monk. In addition to his religious duties, Merton had an extensive literary career, producing plays, essays, poems, and translations. Among his works are What Is Contemplation? *(1948),* Emblems of a Season of Fury *(1963), and* Conjectures of a Guilty Bystander *(1966). In this selection, Merton discusses the qualities that make commitment to monasticism possible.*

A monk is a man who has been called by the Holy Spirit to relinquish the cares, desires and ambitions of other men, and devote his entire life to seeking God. The concept is familiar. The reality which the concept signifies is a mystery. For in actual fact, no one on earth knows precisely what it means to "seek God" until he himself has set out to find Him. No man can tell another what his search means unless that other is enlightened, at the same time, by the Spirit speaking within his own heart. In the end, no one can seek God unless he has already begun to find Him. No one can find God without having first been found by Him. A monk is a man who seeks God because he has been found by God.   1

In short, a monk is a "man of God."   2

Since all men were created by God that they might find Him, all men are called in some sense to be "men of God." But not all are called to be monks. A monk is therefore one who is called to give himself exclusively and perfectly to the one thing necessary for all men—the search for God. It is permissible for others to seek God by a road less direct, to lead a good life in the world, to raise a Christian family. The monk puts these things aside, though they may be good. He travels to God by the direct path, *recto tramite*. He withdraws from "the world." He gives himself entirely to prayer, meditation, study, labor, penance, under the eyes of God. The monk is distinguished even from other religious vocations by the fact that he is essentially and exclusively dedicated to seeking God, rather than seeking souls for God.   3

Let us face the fact that the monastic vocation tends to present itself to the modern world as a problem and as a scandal.   4

In a basically religious culture, like that of India, or of Japan, the monk is more or less taken for granted. When all society is oriented beyond the mere transient quest of business and pleasure, no one is surprised that men should devote their lives to an invisible God. In a materialistic culture which is fundamentally irreligious the monk is incomprehensible because he "produces nothing." His life appears to be completely useless. Not even Christians have been exempt from anxiety over this apparent "uselessness" of the monk, and we are familiar with the argument that the monastery is a kind of dynamo which, though it does not "produce" grace, procures this infinitely precious spiritual commodity for the world.   5

The first Fathers of monasticism were concerned with no such arguments, valid though they may be in their proper context. The Fathers did not feel that the search for God was something that needed to be defended. Or rather, they saw that if men did not realize in the first place that God was to be sought, no other defence of monasticism would avail with them. 6

Is God, then, to be sought? 7

The deepest law in man's being is his need for God, for life. God is Life. "In Him was life, and the life was the light of men, and the light shineth in the darkness and the darkness comprehended it not" (John 1:5). The deepest need of our darkness is to comprehend the light which shines in the midst of it. Therefore God has given us, as His first commandment: "Thou shalt love the Lord thy God with thy whole heart, and with thy whole soul and with all thy strength." The monastic life is nothing but the life of those who have taken the first commandment in deadly earnest, and have, in the words of St. Benedict, "preferred nothing to the love of Christ." 8

But Who is God? Where is He? Is Christian monasticism a search for some pure intuition of the Absolute? A cult of the supreme Good? A worship of perfect and changeless Beauty? The very emptiness of such abstractions strikes the heart cold. The Holy One, the Invisible, the Almighty is infinitely greater and more real than any abstraction of man's devising. But He has said: "No one shall see me and live" (Exodus 33:20). Yet the monk persists in crying out with Moses: "Show me Thy face" (Exodus 33:13). 9

The monk, then, is one who is so intent upon the search for God that he is ready to die in order to see Him. That is why the monastic life is a "martyrdom" as well as a "paradise," a life that is at once "angelic" and "crucified." 10

St. Paul resolves the problem: "God who commanded the light to shine out of darkness, hath shined in our hearts to give the light of the knowledge of the glory of God, in the face of Christ Jesus" (2 Corinthians 4:6). 11

The monastic life is the rejection of all that obstructs the spiritual rays of this mysterious light. The monk is one who leaves behind the fictions and illusions of a merely human spirituality in order to plunge himself in the faith of Christ. Faith is the light which illumines him in mystery. Faith is the power which seizes upon the inner depths of his soul and delivers him up to the action of the divine Spirit, the Spirit of liberty, the Spirit of love. Faith takes him, as the power of God took the ancient prophets, and "stands him upon his feet" (Ezekiel 2:2) before the Lord. The monastic life is life in the Spirit of Christ, a life in which the Christian gives himself entirely to the love of God which transforms him in the light of Christ. 12

"The Lord is a Spirit, and where the Spirit of the Lord is, there 13 is liberty. But we all, beholding the glory of the Lord with open face, are transformed into the same image from glory to glory, as by the Spirit of the Lord" (2 Corinthians 3:17–18). What St. Paul has said of the inner life of every Christian becomes in all truth the main objective of the monk, living in his solitary cloister. In seeking Christian perfection the monk seeks the fullness of the Christian life, the complete maturity of Christian faith. For him, "to live is Christ."

In order to be free with the freedom of the children of God, the monk gives up his own will, his power to own property, his love of ease and comfort, his pride, his right to raise a family, his freedom to dispose of his time as he pleases, to go where he likes and to live according to his own judgment. He lives alone, poor, in silence. Why? Because of what he believes. He believes the word of Christ, Who has promised: "There is no man who has left house or parents or brethren or wife or children for the Kingdom of God's sake, who shall not receive much more in this present time, and in the world to come life everlasting" (Luke 18:29–30).

14

COMPREHENSION

1.   What is Merton's purpose in writing this essay? Who is his audience?

2.   What does Merton mean by the phrase "man of God"? How does this apply especially to monks?

3.   Why does Merton say that the monastic vocation presents itself to the world as "a problem and a scandal"? How is this not true in a culture like that of India or Japan?

RHETORIC

1.   How is the word *monastery* "a kind of dynamo"? What is the purpose of Merton's use of the word *commodity* in paragraph 5?

2.   What is the relevance of the biblical allusions and citations in this essay?

3.   How is Merton's introductory paragraph perfect for the type of essay he wants to develop?

4.   List some of Merton's short definitions. Where do they appear? What is their purpose?

5.   How does paragraph 14 formally conclude the essay?

6.   What is an example of a paradox in this selection?

WRITING

1.   Throughout this century, the monastic life has recruited fewer and fewer candidates. Is monasticism still viable in our century? Why, or why not? Write an essay on this issue.

2.   Write an argumentative essay agreeing or disagreeing with Merton's assertion that "merely human spirituality" is nothing but "fictions and illusions."

3.   Write your own brief definition of some religious figure, entitling your selection "What is a _____?" You might want to consider a priest, rabbi, minister, agnostic, ayatollah, or other type.

C. S. LEWIS

The Rival Conceptions of God

Clive Staples Lewis (1898–1963) was born in Belfast, Ireland, but spent the most important years of his life as a lecturer in English at Oxford. His first book, Dymer, *was published in 1926, but it was not until the publication of* The Pilgrim's Regress *in 1933 that he addressed the central work of his life: a passionate defense of the Christian faith. Lewis's immense output embraced science fiction, fantasy, children's books, theology, and literary criticism. Among his best-known works are* The Screwtape Letters *(1950),* The Lion, the Witch, and the Wardrobe *(1950), and* The Chronicles of Narnia *(1956). In this essay, Lewis describes the reasoning that led to his conversion.*

I have been asked to tell you what Christians believe, and   1
I am going to begin by telling you one thing that Christians do not need to believe. If you are a Christian you do not have to believe that all the other religions are simply wrong all through. If you are an atheist you do have to believe that the main point in all the religions of the whole world is simply one huge mistake. If you are a Christian, you are free to think that all these religions, even the queerest ones, contain at least some hint of the truth. When I was an atheist I had to try to persuade myself that most of the human race have always been wrong about the question that mattered to them most; when I became a Christian I was able to take a more liberal view. But, of course, being a Christian does mean thinking that where Christianity differs from other religions, Christianity is right and they are wrong. As in arithmetic—there is only one right answer to a sum, and all other answers are wrong: but some of the wrong answers are much nearer being right than others.

The first big division of humanity is into the majority, who   2
believe in some kind of God or gods, and the minority who do not.

On this point, Christianity lines up with the majority—lines up with ancient Greeks and Romans, modern savages, Stoics, Platonists, Hindus, Mohammedans, etc., against the modern Western European materialist.

Now I go on to the next big division. People who all believe 3 in God can be divided according to the sort of God they believe in. There are two very different ideas on this subject. One of them is the idea that He is beyond good and evil. We humans call one thing good and another thing bad. But according to some people that is merely our human point of view. These people would say that the wiser you become the less you would want to call anything good or bad, and the more clearly you would see that everything is good in one way and bad in another, and that nothing could have been different. Consequently, these people think that long before you got anywhere near the divine point of view the distinction would have disappeared altogether. We call a cancer bad, they would say, because it kills a man; but you might just as well call a successful surgeon bad because he kills a cancer. It all depends on the point of view. The other and opposite idea is that God is quite definitely "good" or "righteous," a God who takes sides, who loves love and hates hatred, who wants us to behave in one way and not in another. The first of these views— the one that thinks God beyond good and evil—is called Pantheism. It was held by the great Prussian philosopher Hegel and, as far as I can understand them, by the Hindus. The other view is held by Jews, Mohammedans and Christians.

And with this big difference between Pantheism and the 4 Christian idea of God, there usually goes another. Pantheists usually believe that God, so to speak, animates the universe as you animate your body: that the universe almost *is* God, so that if it did not exist He would not exist either, and anything you find in the universe is a part of God. The Christian idea is quite different. They think God invented and made the universe—like a man making a picture or composing a tune. A painter is not a picture, and he does not die if his picture is destroyed. You may say, "He's put a lot of himself into it," but you only mean that all its beauty and interest has come out of his head. His skill is not in the picture in the same way that it is in his head, or even in his hands. I expect you see how this difference between Pantheists and Christians hangs together with the other one. If you do not take the distinction between good and bad very seriously, then it is easy to say that anything you find in this world is a part of God. But, of course, if you think some things really bad, and God really good, then you cannot talk like that. You must believe that God is separate from the world and that some of the things we see in it are contrary to His will. Confronted with a cancer or a slum the Pantheist can say, "If you could only see it from the divine point of

C. S. LEWIS

view, you would realize that this also is God." The Christian replies, "Don't talk damned nonsense."* For Christianity is a fighting religion. It thinks God made the world—that space and time, heat and cold, and all the colours and tastes, and all the animals and vegetables, are things that God "made up out of His head" as a man makes up a story. But it also thinks that a great many things have gone wrong with the world that God made and that God insists, and insists very loudly, on our putting them right again.

And, of course, that raises a very big question. If a good God 5 made the world why has it gone wrong? And for many years I simply refused to listen to the Christian answers to this question, because I kept on feeling "whatever you say, and however clever your arguments are, isn't it much simpler and easier to say that the world was not made by any intelligent power? Aren't all your arguments simply a complicated attempt to avoid the obvious?" But then that threw me back into another difficulty.

My argument against God was that the universe seemed so 6 cruel and unjust. But how had I got this idea of *just* and *unjust*? A man does not call a line crooked unless he has some idea of a straight line. What was I comparing this universe with when I called it unjust? If the whole show was bad and senseless from A to Z, so to speak, why did I, who was supposed to be part of the show, find myself in such violent reaction against it? A man feels wet when he falls into water, because man is not a water animal: a fish would not feel wet. Of course I could have given up my idea of justice by saying it was nothing but a private idea of my own. But if I did that, then my argument against God collapsed too—for the argument depended on saying that the world was really unjust, not simply that it did not happen to please my private fancies. Thus in the very act of trying to prove that God did not exist—in other words, that the whole of reality was senseless—I found I was forced to assume that one part of reality—namely my idea of justice—was full of sense. Consequently atheism turns out to be too simple. If the whole universe has no meaning, we should never have found out that it has no meaning: just as, if there were no light in the universe and therefore no creature with eyes, we should never know it was dark. *Dark* would be without meaning.

---

*One listener complained of the word *damned* as frivolous swearing. But I mean exactly what I say— nonsense that is *damned* is under God's curse, and will (apart from God's grace) lead those who believe it to eternal death.

THE RIVAL CONCEPTIONS OF GOD

COMPREHENSION

1. Who is Lewis's audience? What is his purpose? How do you know?

2. Lewis divides humanity into a number of distinct categories. Name them, and discuss his purpose in establishing these categories.

3. What is Lewis's purpose in likening Christianity to arithmetic? In what sense is this apt? Where does he use a similar image?

RHETORIC

1. Look up the following words in paragraph 2 in a dictionary or encyclopedia: *Stoics, Platonists, Hindus,* and *Mohammedans.* What are the major tenets of their beliefs?

2. Explain Lewis's use of the word *damned* (paragraph 4). What is specific about his use of this word? Is it appropriate?

3. How does Lewis develop his argument? What line of reasoning does he follow? What transition markers does Lewis use?

4. How does Lewis use definition to structure certain parts of his argument?

5. In which paragraph is Lewis making what he considers the one irrefutable argument in favor of the existence of God? Is this paragraph coherently reasoned in terms of the whole essay? Explain.

6. Why is Lewis's idea of justice critical to the evaluation of his thought? Is his use of the word *justice* idiosyncratic or objective? How does accepting his definition make an important difference to the response that a reader would give this piece?

WRITING

1. The Western tradition is based, in large part, on the belief that "Christianity is right" and other religions are wrong. Is this belief as strong today as it was in the past? Does it still cohere as an argument?

2. Write an essay describing your religious beliefs and how they originated.

3. Argue for or against atheism.

JOHN DONNE

No Man Is an Island

John Donne (1572–1631), English poet and priest, was a master of wit and devotion. Ben Johnson called him "the first poet in

*the world in some things." Donne's early career was threatened
constantly by poverty, until he became dean of St. Paul's in 1621.
He wrote richly complex poetry and sermons. Most of his works
were published after his death by his son. Collections of his sermons appeared in 1640, 1649, and 1661; a collection of his
poetry appeared in 1633. Donne was a superb inventor of metaphors, as the following essay, called a meditation, indicates.*

Perchance he for whom this bell tolls may be so ill, as that
he knows not it tolls for him; and perchance I may think
myself so much better than I am, as that they who are
about me, and see my state, may have caused it to toll
for me, and I know not that. The church is Catholic, universal, so are
all her actions; all that she does belongs to all. When she baptizes a
child, that action concerns me; for that child is thereby connected to
that body which is my head too, and ingrafted into that body whereof
I am a member. And when she buries a man, that action concerns me:
all mankind is of one author, and is one volume; when one man dies,
one chapter is not torn out of the book, but translated into a better
language; and every chapter must be so translated; God employs several translators; some pieces are translated by age, some by sickness,
some by war, some by justice; but God's hand is in every translation,
and his hand shall bind up all our scattered leaves again for that
library where every book shall lie open to one another. As therefore
the bell that rings to a sermon calls not upon the preacher only, but
upon the congregation to come, so this bell calls us all; but how much
more me, who am brought so near the door by this sickness. There
was a contention as far as a suit (in which both poetry and dignity,
religion and estimation, were mingled), which of the religious orders
should ring to prayers first in the morning; and it was determined,
that they should ring first that rose earliest. If we understand aright
the dignity of this bell that tolls for our evening prayer, we would be
glad to make it ours by rising early, in that application, that it might
be ours as well as his, whose indeed it is. The bell doth toll for him
that thinks it doth; and though it intermit again, yet from that minute
that that occasion wrought upon him, he is united to God. Who casts
not up his eye to the sun when it rises? but who takes off his eye
from a comet when that breaks out? Who bends not his ear to any
bell which upon any occasion rings? but who can remove it from that
bell which is passing a piece of himself out of this world? No man is
an island, entire of itself; every man is a piece of the continent, a part
of the main. If a clod be washed away by the sea, Europe is the less,
as well as if a promontory were, as well as if a manor of thy friend's
or of thine own were: any man's death diminishes me, because I am
involved in mankind, and therefore never send to know for whom

1

the bell tolls; it tolls for thee. Neither can we call this a begging of misery, or a borrowing of misery, as though we were not miserable enough of ourselves, but must fetch in more from the next house, in taking upon us the misery of our neighbors. Truly it were an excusable covetousness if we did, for affliction is a treasure, and scarce any man hath enough of it. No man hath affliction enough that is not matured and ripened by it, and made fit for God by that affliction. If a man carry treasure in bullion, or in a wedge of gold, and have none coined into current money, his treasure will not defray him as he travels. Tribulation is treasure in the nature of it, but it is not current money in the use of it, except we get nearer and nearer our home, heaven, by it. Another man may be sick too, and sick to death, and this affliction may lie in his bowels, as gold in a mine, and be of no use to him; but this bell, that tells me of his affliction, digs out and applies that gold to me: if by this consideration of another's danger I take mine own into contemplation, and so secure myself, by making my recourse to my God, who is our only security.

COMPREHENSION

1. What does Donne mean by the phrase, "No man is an island"?

2. Specify Donne's reasons for being moved by a church's mourning bell. How do his religious beliefs enter into his reasoning?

3. What objection to meditating on death does Donne raise toward the end of his essay? How does he refute these objections?

RHETORIC

1. Give three examples of periodic sentences in this essay. Are such sentences typical of Donne's style? Why?

2. Despite the seriousness of the meditation, Donne puns in this essay. Identify two puns; what are their meanings? How do they affect the seriousness of the meditation?

3. What is the thesis of this meditation? Why does it appear where it does?

4. Donne uses two extended metaphors: the individual is a book and affliction is a treasure. Explain what these metaphors mean and their relation to Donne's thesis.

5. What transitional devices does Donne use to organize and to structure his paragraph?

6. How does Donne use association to develop his essay? How is the meditation genre reflected in the development of ideas in this association?

WRITING

1. In our very different age, should we be moved by the deaths of strangers? If we are, how will that emotion affect our lives?

JOHN DONNE

2.   Take a common sound or sight—one that you hear or see frequently—and write a meditation about it. Relate the event to some crucial religious or moral concern.

3.   Select one aspect of some religious ritual, and explain why it appeals to you.

MARGARET MEAD

New Superstitions for Old

Margaret Mead (1901–1979), famed American anthropologist, was curator of ethnology at the American Museum of Natural History and a professor at Columbia University. Her field expeditions to Samoa, New Guinea, and Bali in the 1920s and 1930s produced several major studies, notably Coming of Age in Samoa *(1928),* Growing Up in New Guinea *(1930), and* Sex and Temperament in Three Primitive Societies *(1935). In this essay, Mead discusses the role that superstition plays in our daily life.*

Once in a while there is a day when everything seems to run smoothly and even the riskiest venture comes out exactly right. You exclaim, "This is my lucky day!" Then as an afterthought you say, "Knock on wood!" Of course, you do not really believe that knocking on wood will ward off danger. Still, boasting about your own good luck gives you a slightly uneasy feeling—and you carry out the little protective ritual. If someone challenged you at that moment, you would probably say, "Oh, that's nothing. Just an old superstition."

But when you come to think about it, what is superstition?

In the contemporary world most people treat old folk beliefs as superstitions—the belief, for instance, that there are lucky and unlucky days or numbers, that future events can be read from omens, that there are protective charms or that what happens can be influenced by casting spells. We have excluded magic from our current world view, for we know that natural events have natural causes.

In a religious context, where truths cannot be demonstrated, we accept them as a matter of faith. Superstitions, however, belong to the category of beliefs, practices and ways of thinking that have been discarded because they are inconsistent with scientific knowledge. It is easy to say that other people are superstitious because they believe what we regard to be untrue. "Superstition" used in that sense is a derogatory term for the beliefs of other people that we do not share. But there is more to it than that. For superstitions lead a kind of half life in a twilight world where, sometimes, we partly suspend our disbelief and act as if magic worked.

Actually, almost every day, even in the most sophisticated home, something is likely to happen that evokes the memory of some old folk belief. The salt spills. A knife falls to the floor. Your nose tickles. Then perhaps, with a slightly embarrassed smile, the person who spilled the salt tosses a pinch over his left shoulder. Or someone recites the old rhyme, "Knife falls, gentleman calls." Or as you rub your nose you think, That means a letter. I wonder who's writing? No one takes these small responses very seriously or gives them more than a passing thought. Sometimes people will preface one of these ritual acts—walking around instead of under a ladder or hastily closing an umbrella that has been opened inside a house—with such remarks as "I remember my great-aunt used to . . ." or "Germans used to say you ought not . . ." And then, having placed the belief at some distance away in time or space, they carry out the ritual. 5

Everyone also remembers a few of the observances of childhood—wishing on the first star; looking at the new moon over the right shoulder; avoiding the cracks in the sidewalk on the way to school while chanting, "Step on a crack, break your mother's back"; wishing on white horses, on loads of hay, on covered bridges, on red cars; saying quickly, "Bread-and-butter" when a post or a tree separated you from the friend you were walking with. The adult may not actually recite the formula "Star light, star bright . . ." and may not quite turn to look at the new moon, but his mood is tempered by a little of the old thrill that came when the observance was still freighted with magic. 6

Superstition can also be used with another meaning. When I discuss the religious beliefs of other peoples, especially primitive peoples, I am often asked, "Do they really have a religion, or is it all just superstition?" The point of contrast here is not between a scientific and a magical view of the world but between the clear, theologically defensible religious beliefs of members of civilized societies and what we regard as the false and childish views of the heathen who "bow down to wood and stone." Within the civilized religions, however, where membership includes believers who are educated and urbane and others who are ignorant and simple, one always finds traditions and practices that the more sophisticated will dismiss offhand as "just superstition" but that guide the steps of those who live by older ways. Mostly these are very ancient beliefs, some handed on from one religion to another and carried from country to country around the world. 7

Very commonly, people associate superstition with the past, 8

MARGARET MEAD

with very old ways of thinking that have been supplanted by modern knowledge. But new superstitions are continually coming into being and flourishing in our society. Listening to mothers in the park in the 1930s, one heard them say, "Now, don't you run out into the sun, or Polio will get you." In the 1940's elderly people explained to one another in tones of resignation, "It was the Virus that got him down." And every year the cosmetics industry offers us new magic—cures for baldness, lotions that will give every woman radiant skin, hair coloring that will restore to the middle-aged the charm and romance of youth—results that are promised if we will just follow the simple directions. Families and individuals also have their cherished, private superstitions. You must leave by the back door when you are going on a journey, or you must wear a green dress when you are taking an examination. It is a kind of joke, of course, but it makes you feel safe.

These old half-beliefs and new half-beliefs reflect the keenness   9
of our wish to have something come true or to prevent something bad from happening. We do not always recognize new superstitions for what they are, and we still follow the old ones because someone's faith long ago matches our contemporary hopes and fears. In the past people "knew" that a black cat crossing one's path was a bad omen, and they turned back home. Today we are fearful of taking a journey and would give anything to turn back—and then we notice a black cat running across the road in front of us.

Child psychologists recognize the value of the toy a child   10
holds in his hand at bedtime. It is different from his thumb, with which he can close himself in from the rest of the world, and it is different from the real world, to which he is learning to relate himself. Psychologists call these toys—these furry animals and old, cozy baby blankets—"transitional objects"; that is, objects that help the child move back and forth between the exactions of everyday life and the world of wish and dream.

Superstitions have some of the qualities of these transitional   11
objects. They help people pass between the areas of life where what happens has to be accepted without proof and the areas where sequences of events are explicable in terms of cause and effect, based on knowledge. Bacteria and viruses that cause sickness have been identified; the cause of symptoms can be diagnosed and a rational course of treatment prescribed. Magical charms no longer are needed to treat the sick; modern medicine has brought the whole sequence of events into the secular world. But people often act as if this change had not taken place. Laymen still treat germs as if they were invisible, malign spirits, and physicians sometimes prescribe antibiotics as if they were magic substances.

Over time, more and more of life has become subject to the   12 controls of knowledge. However, this is never a one-way process. Scientific investigation is continually increasing our knowledge. But if we are to make good use of this knowledge, we must not only rid our minds of old, superseded beliefs and fragments of magical practice, but also recognize new superstitions for what they are. Both are generated by our wishes, our fears and our feeling of helplessness in difficult situations.

Civilized peoples are not alone in having grasped the idea of superstitions—beliefs and practices that are superseded but that still may evoke the different worlds in which we live—the sacred, the secular and the scientific. They allow us to keep a private world also, where, smiling a little, we can banish danger with a gesture and summon luck with a rhyme, make the sun shine in spite of storm clouds, force the stranger to do our bidding, keep an enemy at bay and straighten the paths of those we love. 13

COMPREHENSION

1. Explain in your own words the religious context for this essay.

2. What point is Mead making about superstition in modern life? Where does she state her main idea?

3. Where does Mead define *superstition*? How does it differ from folk beliefs?

RHETORIC

1. Explain what Mead means by "transitional objects." Why does she mention them?

2. Discuss the author's use of the pronouns *we* and *us* in the conclusion. Why does she state the conclusion in personal terms?

3. How does Mead use definition to differentiate *superstition* from *faith*? Explain the logic behind her distinction.

4. How does Mead use classification to describe the "worlds in which we live"? What are these worlds? What examples does she give of superstition in each of these worlds?

5. Look at paragraph 10. What is the purpose of this example? How does it figure in the context of Mead's essay?

6. Discuss the term "theologically defensible" as used in paragraph 7. Does Mead support this concept by example or evidence? Why?

WRITING

1. This article was published in 1966. Have we made any progress toward banishing superstition since then? Will we ever live in a culture free of superstition? Do we want to?

MARGARET MEAD

2. Write an essay about beliefs you once held that you have since abandoned. Why did you abandon them? What was the practical result?

3. Select a saying or phrase based in superstition or folk belief that you or a friend is fond of. Analyze its appeal.

HARVEY COX

Sex and Secularization

Harvey Gallagher Cox (1929–   ) is a theologian. Born in Pennsylvania, he earned a B.A. from the University of Pennsylvania in 1951 and a Ph.D. from Harvard in 1963. Since 1970, he has been the Victor Thomas Professor of Divinity at Harvard. He is the author of The Secular City *(1965),* Feast of Fools *(1969),* The Use and Misuse of People's Religion *(1973), and* Turning East *(1977). Dr. Cox's erudition and his pointedly critical view of modern society are both evident in this selection, which addresses the true meaning of beauty pageants.*

et us begin with Miss America. In the first century B.C.,   1
Lucretius wrote this description of the pageant of Cybele:

Adorned with emblem and crown . . . she is carried in awe-inspiring state. Tight-stretched tambourines and hollow cymbals thunder all round to the stroke of open hands, hollow pipes stir with Phrygian strain. . . . She rides in procession through great cities and mutely enriches mortals with a blessing not expressed in words. They strew all her path with brass and silver, presenting her with bounteous alms, and scatter over her a snow-shower of roses.

Now compare this with the annual twentieth-century Miss   2
America pageant in Atlantic City, New Jersey. Spotlights probe the dimness like votive tapers, banks of flowers exude their varied aromas, the orchestra blends feminine strings and regal trumpets. There is a hushed moment of tortured suspense, a drumroll, then the climax—a young woman with carefully prescribed anatomical proportions and exemplary "personality" parades serenely with scepter and crown to her throne. At TV sets across the nation throats tighten and

eyes moisten. "There she goes, Miss America—" sings the crooner. "There she goes, your ideal." A new queen in America's emerging cult of The Girl has been crowned.

Is it merely illusory or anachronistic to discern in the multiplying pageants of the Miss America, Miss Universe, Miss College Queen type a residuum of the cults of the pre-Christian fertility goddesses? Perhaps, but students of the history of religions have become less prone in recent years to dismiss the possibility that the cultural behavior of modern man may be significantly illuminated by studying it in the perspective of the mythologies of bygone ages. After all, did not Freud initiate a revolution in social science by utilizing the venerable myth of Oedipus to help make sense out of the strange behavior of his Viennese contemporaries? Contemporary man carries with him, like his appendix and his fingernails, vestiges of his tribal and pagan past.

In light of this fertile combination of insights from modern social science and the history of religions, it is no longer possible to see in the Miss America pageant merely an overpublicized prank foisted on us by the advertising industry. It certainly is this, but it is also much more. It represents the mass cultic celebration, complete with a rich variety of ancient ritual embellishments, of the growing place of The Girl in the collective soul of America.

This young woman—though she is no doubt totally ignorant of the fact—symbolizes something beyond herself. She symbolizes The Girl, the primal image, the one behind the many. Just as the Virgin appears in many guises—as our Lady of Lourdes or of Fatima or of Guadalupe—but is always recognizably the Virgin, so with The Girl.

The Girl is also the omnipresent icon of consumer society. Selling beer, she is folksy and jolly. Selling gems, she is chic and distant. But behind her various theophanies she remains recognizably The Girl. In Miss America's glowingly healthy smile, her openly sexual but officially virginal figure, and in the name-brand gadgets around her, she personifies the stunted aspirations and ambivalent fears of her culture. "There she goes, your ideal."

Miss America stands in a long line of queens going back to Isis, Ceres, and Aphrodite. Everything from the elaborate sexual taboos surrounding her person to the symbolic gifts at her coronation hints at her ancient ancestry. But the real proof comes when we find that the function served by The Girl in our culture is just as much a "religious" one as that served by Cybele in hers. The functions are identical—to provide a secure personal "identity" for initiates and to sanctify a particular value structure.

Let us look first at the way in which The Girl confers a kind of identity on her initiates. Simone de Beauvoir says in *The Second Sex*

HARVEY COX

that "no one is *born* a woman." One is merely born a female, and *"becomes* a woman" according to the models and meanings provided by the civilization. During the classical Christian centuries, it might be argued, the Virgin Mary served in part as this model. With the Reformation and especially with the Puritans, the place of Mary within the symbol system of the Protestant countries was reduced or eliminated. There are those who claim that this excision constituted an excess of zeal that greatly impoverished Western culture, an impoverishment from which it has never recovered. Some would even claim that the alleged failure of American novelists to produce a single great heroine (we have no Phaedra, no Anna Karenina) stems from this self-imposed lack of a central feminine ideal.

Without entering into this fascinating discussion, we can certainly be sure that, even within modern American Roman Catholicism, the Virgin Mary provides an identity image for few American girls. Where then do they look for the "model" Simone de Beauvoir convincingly contends they need? For most, the prototype of femininity seen in their mothers, their friends, and in the multitudinous images to which they are exposed on the mass media is what we have called The Girl. 9

In his significant monograph *Identity and the Life Cycle,* Erik Erikson reminds us that the child's identity is not modeled simply on the parent but on the parent's "super-ego." Thus in seeking to forge her own identity the young girl is led beyond her mother to her mother's ideal image, and it is here that what Freud called "the ideologies of the superego . . . the traditions of the race and the people" become formative. It is here also that The Girl functions, conferring identity on those for whom she is—perhaps never completely consciously— the tangible incarnation of womanhood. 10

To describe the mechanics of this complex psychological process by which the fledgling American girl participates in the life of The Girl and thus attains a woman's identity would require a thorough description of American adolescence. There is little doubt, however, that such an analysis would reveal certain striking parallels to the "savage" practices by which initiates in the mystery cults shared in the magical life of their god. 11

For those inured to the process, the tortuous nightly fetish by which the young American female pulls her hair into tight bunches secured by metal clips may bear little resemblance to the incisions made on their arms by certain African tribesmen to make them resemble their totem, the tiger. But to an anthropologist comparing two ways of attempting to resemble the holy one, the only difference might appear to be that with the Africans the torture is over after initiation, while with the American it has to be repeated every night, a luxury only a culture with abundant leisure can afford. 12

In turning now to an examination of the second function of   13
The Girl—supporting and portraying a value system—a comparison
with the role of the Virgin in the twelfth and thirteenth centuries may
be helpful. Just as the Virgin exhibited and sustained the ideals of the
age that fashioned Chartres Cathedral, as Henry Adams saw, so The
Girl symbolizes the values and aspirations of a consumer society. (She
is crowned not in the political capital, remember, but in Atlantic City
or Miami Beach, centers associated with leisure and consumption.)
And she is not entirely incapable of exploitation. If men sometimes
sought to buy with gold the Virgin's blessings on their questionable
causes, so The Girl now dispenses her charismatic favor on watches,
refrigerators, and razor blades—for a price. Though The Girl has built
no cathedrals, without her the colossal edifice of mass persuasion
would crumble. Her sharply stylized face and figure beckon us from
every magazine and TV channel, luring us toward the beatific vision
of a consumer's paradise.

The Girl is *not* the Virgin. In fact she is a kind of anti-   14
Madonna. She reverses most of the values traditionally associated
with the Virgin—poverty, humility, sacrifice. In startling contrast, particularly, to the biblical portrait of Mary in Luke 1:46–55, The Girl has
nothing to do with filling the hungry with "good things," hawking
instead an endless proliferation of trivia on TV spot commercials. The
Girl exalts the mighty, extols the rich, and brings nothing to the hungry but added despair. So The Girl does buttress and bring into personal focus a value system, such as it is. In both social and psychological terms, The Girl, whether or not she is really a goddess,
certainly acts that way.

Perhaps the most ironic element in the rise of the cult of The   15
Girl is that Protestantism has almost completely failed to notice it,
while Roman Catholics have at least given some evidence of sensing
its significance. In some places, for instance, Catholics are forbidden
to participate in beauty pageants, a ruling not entirely inspired by
prudery. It is ironic that Protestants have traditionally been most opposed to lady cults while Catholics have managed to assimilate more
than one at various points in history.

If we are correct in assuming that The Girl *functions* in many   16
ways as a goddess, then the cult of The Girl demands careful Protestant theological criticism. Anything that functions, even in part, as
a god when it is in fact not God, is an idol. When the Reformers and
their Puritan offspring criticized the cult of Mary it was not because
they were anti-feminist. They opposed anything—man, woman, or
beast (or dogma or institution)—that usurped in the slightest the pre-
rogatives that belonged alone to God Almighty. As Max Weber has
insisted, when the prophets of Israel railed against fertility cults, they
had nothing against fertility. It is not against sexuality but against a

HARVEY COX

cult that protest is needed. Not, as it were, against the beauty but against the pageant.

Thus the Protestant objection to the present cult of The Girl   17
must be based on the realization that The Girl is an *idol*. She functions as the source of value, the giver of personal identity. But the values she mediates and the identity she confers are both spurious. Like every idol she is ultimately a creation of our own hands and cannot save us. The values she represents as ultimate satisfactions—mechanical comfort, sexual success, unencumbered leisure—have no ultimacy. They lead only to endless upward mobility, competitive consumption, and anxious cynicism. The devilish social insecurities from which she promises to deliver us are, alas, still there, even after we have purified our breaths, our skins, and our armpits by applying her sacred oils. She is a merciless goddess who draws us farther and farther into the net of accelerated ordeals of obeisance. As the queen of commodities in an expanding economy, the fulfillment she promises must always remain just beyond the tips of our fingers.

Why has Protestantism kept its attention obsessively fastened   18
on the development of Mariolatry in Catholicism and not noticed the sinister rise of this vampirelike cult of The Girl in our society? Unfortunately, it is due to the continuing incapacity of theological critics to recognize the religious significance of cultural phenomena outside the formal religious system itself. But the rise of this new cult reminds us that the work of the reformer is never done. Man's mind is indeed—as Luther said—a factory busy making idols. The Girl is a far more pervasive and destructive influence than the Virgin, and it is to her and her omnipresent altars that we should be directing our criticism.

Besides sanctifying a set of phony values, The Girl compounds   19
her noxiousness by maiming her victims in a Procrustean bed of uniformity. This is the empty "identity" she panders. Take the Miss America pageant, for example. Are these virtually indistinguishable specimens of white, middle-class postadolescence really the best we can do? Do they not mirror the ethos of a mass-production society, in which genuine individualism somehow mars the clean, precision-tooled effect. Like their sisters, the finely calibrated Rockettes, these meticulously measured and pretested "beauties" lined up on the boardwalk bear an ominous similarity to the faceless retinues of goose-steppers and the interchangeable mass exercisers of explicitly totalitarian societies. In short, *who* says this is beauty?

The caricature becomes complete in the Miss Universe contest,   20
when Miss Rhodesia is a blonde, Miss South Africa is white, and Oriental girls with a totally different tradition of feminine beauty are forced to display their thighs and appear in spike heels and Catalina swim suits. Miss Universe is as universal as an American adman's stereotype of what beauty should be.

The truth is that The Girl can*not* bestow the identity she promises. She forces her initiates to torture themselves with starvation diets and beauty-parlor ordeals, but still cannot deliver the satisfactions she holds out. She is young, but what happens when her followers, despite added hours in the boudoir, can no longer appear young? She is happy and smiling and loved. What happens when, despite all the potions and incantations, her disciples still feel the human pangs of rejection and loneliness? Or what about all the girls whose statistics, or "personality" (or color) do not match the authoritative "ideal"?

After all, it is God—not The Girl—who is God. He is the center and source of value. He liberates men and women from the bland uniformity of cultural deities so that they may feast on the luxurious diversity of life He has provided. The identity He confers frees men from all pseudo-identities to be themselves, to fulfill their human destinies regardless of whether their faces or figures match some predetermined abstract "ideal." As His gift, sex is freed from both fertility cults and commercial exploitation to become the thoroughly human thing He intended. And since it is one of the last items we have left that is neither prepackaged nor standardized, let us not sacrifice it too hastily on the omnivorous altar of Cybele.

COMPREHENSION

1. What is Cox saying about the Miss America pageant? What does this event symbolize to him?

2. What does Cox mean when he writes, "The Girl is *not* the Virgin" (paragraph 14)?

3. Why are Protestants especially chastised by Cox? What about the Puritan legacy should make some Protestants particularly antagonistic to the "cult of The Girl"?

RHETORIC

1. Use an encyclopedia or dictionary to define the following: *Cybele* (paragraph 1); *theophanies* (paragraph 6); and *Isis, Ceres,* and *Aphrodite* (paragraph 7). Is Cox being fair in tracing Miss America back to these figures? Explain.

2. Why does Cox use the word *fetish* (paragraph 12)? What is being suggested by the use of this word?

3. What examples of a value system does the author cite to support his claim that "The Girl" is a kind of anti-Madonna? How is Cox contrasting "The Girl" with the Virgin? Cite instances of this comparative pattern of development.

4. What process does Cox define in paragraphs 10 and 11? To what extent is this argument by analogy?

HARVEY COX

5. Explain Cox's functional definition of "The Girl" as a "goddess." Does he mean *goddess* literally or metaphorically? Explain.

6. Where does Cox discuss uniformity? How is this discussion central to his thesis?

WRITING

1. Despite criticism from religious groups, feminists, and social critics, Miss America pageants endure, and so do hundreds of other local and national beauty contests. Why? How do you explain their ability to survive?

2. Do you feel that Americans idealize the physical at the expense of the spiritual? Is there any transcending value to beauty pageants? Write an essay on this topic.

3. Use the essays by Cox and Mead to evaluate their insights into superstition and myth in the modern era.

JEAN-PAUL SARTRE

Existentialism

Jean-Paul Sartre (1905–1980) was born the son of bourgeois French parents. His father died when he was only three, and the boy was raised by his maternal grandfather. While a student, Sartre formed what was to become a lifelong relationship with Simone de Beauvoir, another esteemed French writer. Sartre's first philosophical and fictional works—published in the 1930s— were influenced by the German philosopher Heidegger. His first novels, Nausea *(1938) and* Intimacy *(1939), present a picture of aimless people with stunted emotions who live in a meaningless world. During World War II, Sartre was an advocate for the French Resistance and began to publish plays, the most famous being* No Exit *(1944). With his book* Being and Nothingness, *Sartre became known as the leading proponent of existentialism as well as the paramount French intellectual of his generation. He was offered the Nobel Prize for Literature in 1964, but he declined. The following essay provides a succinct, articulate, often brilliant exposition of the philosophy that he made famous.*

EXISTENTIALISM

517

Man is nothing else but what he makes of himself. Such is 1
the first principle of existentialism. It is also what is
called subjectivity, the name we are labeled with when
charges are brought against us. But what do we mean
by this, if not that man has a greater dignity than a stone or table?
For we mean that man first exists, that is, that man first of all is the
being who hurls himself toward a future and who is conscious of
imagining himself as being in the future. Man is at the start a plan
which is aware of itself, rather than a patch of moss, a piece of garbage, or a cauliflower; nothing exists prior to this plan; there is nothing in heaven; man will be what he will have planned to be. Not what
he will want to be. Because by the word "will" we generally mean a
conscious decision, which is subsequent to what we have already
made of ourselves. I may want to belong to a political party, write a
book, get married, but all that is only a manifestation of an earlier,
more spontaneous choice that is called "will." But if existence really
does precede essence, man is responsible for what he is. Thus, existentialism's first move is to make every man aware of what he is and
to make the full responsibility of his existence rest on him. And when
we say that a man is responsible for himself, we do not only mean
that he is responsible for his own individuality, but that he is responsible for all men.

The word "subjectivism" has two meanings, and our oppo- 2
nents play on the two. Subjectivism means, on the one hand, that an
individual chooses and makes himself; and, on the other, that it is
impossible for man to transcend human subjectivity. The second of
these is the essential meaning of existentialism. When we say that man
chooses his own self, we mean that every one of us does likewise; but
we also mean by that that in making this choice he also chooses all
men. In fact, in creating the man that we want to be, there is not a
single one of our acts which does not at the same time create an image
of man as we think he ought to be. To choose to be this or that is to
affirm at the same time the value of what we choose, because we can
never choose evil. We always choose the good, and nothing can be
good for us without being good for all.

If, on the other hand, existence precedes essence, and if we 3
grant that we exist and fashion our image at one and the same time,
the image is valid for everybody and for our whole age. Thus, our
responsibility is much greater than we might have supposed, because
it involves all mankind. If I am a workingman and choose to join a
Christian trade union rather than be a Communist, and if by being a
member I want to show that the best thing for man is resignation,
that the kingdom of man is not of this world, I am not only involving
my own case—I want to be resigned for everyone. As a result, my
action has involved all humanity. To take a more individual matter,

if I want to marry, to have children, even if this marriage depends solely on my own circumstances or passion or wish, I am involving all humanity in monogamy and not merely myself. Therefore, I am responsible for myself and for everyone else. I am creating a certain image of man of my own choosing. In choosing myself, I choose man.

This helps us understand what the actual content is of such 4 rather grandiloquent words as anguish, forlornness, despair. As you will see, it's all quite simple.

First, what is meant by anguish? The existentialists say at once 5 that man is anguish. What that means is this: the man who involves himself and who realizes that he is not only the person he chooses to be, but also a lawmaker who is, at the same time, choosing all mankind as well as himself, cannot help escape the feeling of his total and deep responsibility. Of course, there are many people who are not anxious; but we claim that they are hiding their anxiety, that they are fleeing from it. Certainly, many people believe that when they do something, they themselves are the only ones involved, and when someone says to them, "What if everyone acted that way?" they shrug their shoulders and answer, "Everyone doesn't act that way." But really, one should always ask himself, "What would happen if everybody looked at things that way?" There is no escaping this disturbing thought except by a kind of double-dealing. A man who lies and makes excuses for himself by saying "not everybody does that," is someone with an uneasy conscience, because the act of lying implies that a universal value is conferred upon the lie.

Anguish is evident even when it conceals itself. This is the 6 anguish that Kierkegaard called the anguish of Abraham. You know the story: an angel has ordered Abraham to sacrifice his son; if it really were an angel who has come and said, "You are Abraham, you shall sacrifice your son," everything would be all right. But everyone might first wonder, "Is it really an angel, and am I really Abraham? What proof do I have?"

There was a madwoman who had hallucinations; someone 7 used to speak to her on the telephone and give her orders. Her doctor asked her, "Who is it who talks to you?" She answered, "He says it's God." What proof did she really have that it was God? If an angel comes to me, what proof is there that it's an angel? And if I hear voices, what proof is there that they come from heaven and not from hell, or from the subconscious, or a pathological condition? What proves that they are addressed to me? What proof is there that I have been appointed to impose my choice and my conception of man on humanity? I'll never find any proof or sign to convince me of that. If a voice addresses me, it is always for me to decide that this is the angel's voice; if I consider that such an act is a good one, it is I who will choose to say that it is good rather than bad.

Now, I'm not being singled out as an Abraham, and yet at 8 every moment I'm obliged to perform exemplary acts. For every man, everything happens as if all mankind had its eyes fixed on him and were guiding itself by what he does. And every man ought to say to himself, "Am I really the kind of man who has the right to act in such a way that humanity might guide itself by my actions?" And if he does not say that to himself, he is masking his anguish.

There is no question here of the kind of anguish which would 9 lead to quietism, to inaction. It is a matter of a simple sort of anguish that anybody who has had responsibilities is familiar with. For example, when a military officer takes the responsibility for an attack and sends a certain number of men to death, he chooses to do so, and in the main he alone makes the choice. Doubtless, orders come from above, but they are too broad; he interprets them, and on this interpretation depend the lives of ten or fourteen or twenty men. In making a decision he cannot help having a certain anguish. All leaders know this anguish. That doesn't keep them from acting; on the contrary, it is the very condition of their action. For it implies that they envisage a number of possibilities, and when they choose one, they realize that it has value only because it is chosen. We shall see that this kind of anguish, which is the kind that existentialism describes, is explained, in addition, by a direct responsibility to the other men whom it involves. It is not a curtain separating us from action, but is part of action itself. .

When we speak of forlornness, a term Heidegger was fond of, 10 we mean only that God does not exist and that we have to face all the consequences of this. This existentialist is strongly opposed to a certain kind of secular ethics which would like to abolish God with the least possible expense. About 1880, some French teachers tried to set up a secular ethics which went something like this: God is a useless and costly hypothesis; we are discarding it; but, meanwhile, in order for there to be an ethics, a society, a civilization, it is essential that certain values be taken seriously and that they be considered as having an *a priori* existence. It must be obligatory, *a priori*, to be honest, not to lie, not to beat your wife, to have children, etc., etc. So we're going to try a little device which will make it possible to show that values exist all the same, inscribed in a heaven of ideas, though otherwise God does not exist. In other words—and this, I believe, is the tendency of everything called reformism in France—nothing will be changed if God does not exist. We shall find ourselves with the same norms of honesty, progress, and humanism, and we shall have made of God an outdated hypothesis which will peacefully die off by itself.

The existentialist, on the contrary, thinks it very distressing 11 that God does not exist, because all possibility of finding values in a heaven of ideas disappears along with Him; there can no longer be

JEAN-PAUL SARTRE

an *a priori* Good, since there is no infinite and perfect consciousness to think it. Nowhere is it written that the Good exists, that we must be honest, that we must not lie; because the fact is we are on a plane where there are only men. Dostoievsky said, "If God didn't exist, everything would be possible." That is the very starting point of existentialism. Indeed, everything is permissible if God does not exist, and as a result man is forlorn, because neither within him nor without does he find anything to cling to. He can't start making excuses for himself.

If existence really does precede essence, there is no explaining things away by reference to a fixed and given human nature. In other words, there is no determinism, man is free, man is freedom. On the other hand, if God does not exist, we find no values or commands to turn to which legitimize our conduct. So, in the bright realm of values, we have no excuse behind us, nor justification before us. We are alone, with no excuses.

That is the idea I shall try to convey when I say that man is condemned to be free. Condemned, because he did not create himself, yet, in other respects is free: because, once thrown into the world, he is responsible for everything he does. The existentialist does not believe in the power of passion. He will never agree that a sweeping passion is a ravaging torrent which fatally leads a man to certain acts and is therefore an excuse. He thinks that man is responsible for his passion.

The existentialist does not think that man is going to help himself by finding in the world some omen by which to orient himself. Because he thinks that man will interpret the omen to suit himself. Therefore, he thinks that man, with no support and no aid, is condemned every moment to invent man. Ponge, in a very fine article, has said, "Man is the future of man." That's exactly it. But if it is taken to mean that this future is recorded in heaven, that God sees it, then it is false, because it would really no longer be a future. If it is taken to mean that, whatever a man may be, there is a future to be forged, a virgin future before him, then this remark is sound. But then we are forlorn.

To give you an example which will enable you to understand forlornness better, I shall cite the case of one of my students who came to see me under the following circumstances: his father was on bad terms with his mother, and, moreover, was inclined to be a collaborationist; his older brother had been killed in the German offensive of 1940, and the young man, with somewhat immature but generous feelings, wanted to avenge him. His mother lived alone with him, very much upset by the half-treason of her husband and the death of her older son; the boy was her only consolation.

The boy was faced with the choice of leaving for England and joining the Free French forces—that is, leaving his mother behind—or remaining with his mother and helping her to carry on. He was fully aware that the woman lived only for him and that his going off—and perhaps his death—would plunge her into despair. He was also aware that every act that he did for his mother's sake was a sure thing, in the sense that it was helping her to carry on, whereas every effort he made toward going off and fighting was an uncertain move which might run aground and prove completely useless; for example, on his way to England he might, while passing through Spain, be detained indefinitely in a Spanish camp; he might reach England or Algiers and be stuck in an office at a desk job. As a result, he was faced with two very different kinds of action: one, concrete, immediate, but concerning only one individual; the other concerned an incomparably vaster group, a national collectivity, but for that very reason was dubious, and might be interrupted en route. And, at the same time, he was wavering between two kinds of ethics. On the one hand, an ethics of sympathy, of personal devotion; on the other, a broader ethics, but one whose efficacy was more dubious. He had to choose between the two.

Who could help him choose? Christian doctrine? No. Christian doctrine says, "Be charitable, love your neighbor, take the more rugged path, etc., etc." But which is the more rugged path? Whom should he love as a brother? The fighting man or his mother? Which does the greater good, the vague act of fighting in a group, or the concrete one of helping a particular human being to go on living? Who can decide *a priori*? Nobody. No book of ethics can tell him. The Kantian ethics says, "Never treat any person as a means, but as an end." Very well, if I stay with my mother, I'll treat her as an end and not as a means; but by virtue of this very fact, I'm running the risk of treating the people around me who are fighting, as means; and, conversely, if I go to join those who are fighting, I'll be treating them as an end, and, by doing that, I run the risk of treating my mother as a means. [17]

If values are vague, and if they are always too broad for the concrete and specific case that we are considering, the only thing left for us is to trust our instincts. That's what this young man tried to do; and when I saw him, he said, "In the end, feeling is what counts. I ought to choose whichever pushes me in one direction. If I feel that I love my mother enough to sacrifice everything else for her—my desire for vengeance, for action, for adventure—then I'll stay with her. If, on the contrary, I feel that my love for my mother isn't enough, I'll leave." [18]

But how is the value of a feeling determined? What gives his feeling for his mother value? Precisely the fact that he remained with her. I may say that I like so-and-so well enough to sacrifice a certain [19]

JEAN-PAUL SARTRE

amount of money for him, but I may say so only if I've done it. I may say "I love my mother well enough to remain with her" if I have remained with her. The only way to determine the value of this affection is, precisely, to perform an act which confirms and defines it. But, since I require this affection to justify my act, I find myself caught in a vicious circle.

On the other hand, Gide has well said that a mock feeling and 20 a true feeling are almost indistinguishable; to decide that I love my mother and will remain with her, or to remain with her by putting on an act, amount somewhat to the same thing. In other words, the feeling is formed by the acts one performs; so, I cannot refer to it in order to act upon it. Which means that I can neither seek within myself the true condition which will impel me to act, nor apply to a system of ethics for concepts which will permit me to act. You will say, "At least, he did go to a teacher for advice." But if you seek advice from a priest, for example, you have chosen this priest; you already knew, more or less, just about what advice he was going to give you. In other words, choosing your adviser is involving yourself. The proof of this is that if you are a Christian, you will say, "Consult a priest." But some priests are collaborating, some are just marking time, some are resisting. Which to choose? If the young man chooses a priest who is resisting or collaborating, he has already decided on the kind of advice he's going to get. Therefore, in coming to see me he knew the answer I was going to give him, and I had only one answer to give: "You're free, choose, that is, invent." No general ethics can show you what is to be done; there are no omens in the world. The Catholics will reply, "But there are." Granted—but, in any case, I myself choose the meaning they have.

When I was a prisoner, I knew a rather remarkable young 21 man who was a Jesuit. He had entered the Jesuit order in the following way: he had had a number of very bad breaks; in childhood, his father died, leaving him in poverty, and he was a scholarship student at a religious institution where he was constantly made to feel that he was being kept out of charity; then, he failed to get any of the honors and distinctions that children like; later on, at about eighteen, he bungled a love affair; finally, at twenty-two, he failed in military training, a childish enough matter, but it was the last straw.

This young fellow might well have felt that he had botched 22 everything. It was a sign of something, but of what? He might have taken refuge in bitterness or despair. But he very wisely looked upon all this as a sign that he was not made for secular triumphs, and that only the triumphs of religion, holiness, and faith were open to him. He saw the hand of God in all this, and so he entered the order. Who can help seeing that he alone decided what the sign meant?

Some other interpretation might have been drawn from this 23

EXISTENTIALISM

series of setbacks; for example, that he might have done better to turn carpenter or revolutionist. Therefore, he is fully responsible for the interpretation. Forlornness implies that we ourselves choose our being. Forlornness and anguish go together.

As for despair, the term has a very simple meaning. It means 24 that we shall confine ourselves to reckoning only with what depends upon our will, or on the ensemble of probabilities which make our action possible. When we want something, we always have to reckon with probabilities. I may be counting on the arrival of a friend. The friend is coming by rail or streetcar; this supposes that the train will arrive on schedule, or that the streetcar will not jump the track. I am left in the realm of possibility; but possibilities are to be reckoned with only to the point where my action comports with the ensemble of these possibilities, and no further. The moment the possibilities I am considering are not rigorously involved by my action, I ought to disengage myself from them, because no God, no scheme, can adapt the world and its possibilities to my will. When Descartes said, "Conquer yourself rather than the world," he meant essentially the same thing.

The Marxists to whom I have spoken reply, "You can rely on 25 the support of others in your action, which obviously has certain limits because you're not going to live forever. That means: rely on both what others are doing elsewhere to help you, in China, in Russia, and what they will do later on, after your death, to carry on the action and lead it to its fulfillment, which will be the revolution. You even *have* to rely upon that, otherwise you're immoral." I reply at once that I will always rely on fellow-fighters insofar as these comrades are involved with me in a common struggle, in the unity of a party or a group in which I can more or less make my weight felt; that is, one whose ranks I am in as a fighter and whose movements I am aware of at every moment. In such a situation, relying on the unity and will of the party is exactly like counting on the fact that the train will arrive on time or that the car won't jump the track. But, given that man is free and that there is no human nature for me to depend on, I cannot count on men whom I do not know by relying on human goodness or man's concern for the good of society. I don't know what will become of the Russian revolution; I may make an example of it to the extent that at the present time it is apparent that the proletariat plays a part in Russia that it plays in no other nation. But I can't swear that this will inevitably lead to a triumph of the proletariat. I've got to limit myself to what I see.

Given that men are free and that tomorrow they will freely 26 decide what man will be, I cannot be sure that, after my death, fellow-fighters will carry on my work to bring it to its maximum perfection. Tomorrow, after my death, some men may decide to set up Fascism, and the others may be cowardly and muddled enough to let them do it. Fascism will then be the human reality, so much the worse for us.

Actually, things will be as man will have decided they are to be. Does that mean that I should abandon myself to quietism? No. First, I should involve myself; then, act on the old saw, "Nothing ventured, nothing gained." Nor does it mean that I shouldn't belong to a party, but rather that I shall have no illusions and shall do what I can. For example, suppose I ask myself, "Will socialization, as such, ever come about?" I know nothing about it. All I know is that I'm going to do everything in my power to bring it about. Beyond that, I can't count on anything. Quietism is the attitude of people who say, "Let others do what I can't do." The doctrine I am presenting is the very opposite of quietism, since it declares, "There is no reality except in action." Moreoever, it goes further, since it adds, "Man is nothing else than his plan; he exists only to the extent that he fulfills himself; he is therefore nothing else than the ensemble of his acts, nothing else than his life." 27

According to this, we can understand why our doctrine horrifies certain people. Because often the only way they can bear their wretchedness is to think, "Circumstances have been against me. What I've been and done doesn't show my true worth. To be sure, I've had no great love, no great friendship, but that's because I haven't met a man or woman who was worthy. The books I've written haven't been very good because I haven't had the proper leisure. I haven't had children to devote myself to because I didn't find a man with whom I could have spent my life. So there remains within me, unused and quite viable, a host of propensities, inclinations, possibilities, that one wouldn't guess from the mere series of things I've done." 28

Now, for the existentialist there is really no love other than one which manifests itself in a person's being in love. There is no genius other than one which is expressed in works of art; the genius of Proust is the sum of Proust's works; the genius of Racine is his series of tragedies. Outside of that, there is nothing. Why say that Racine could have written another tragedy, when he didn't write it? A man is involved in life, leaves his impress on it, and outside of that there is nothing. To be sure, this may seem a harsh thought to someone whose life hasn't been a success. But, on the other hand, it prompts people to understand that reality alone is what counts, that dreams, expectations, and hopes warrant no more than to define a man as a disappointed dream, as miscarried hopes, as vain expectations. In other words, to define him negatively and not positively. However, when we say, "You are nothing else than your life," that does not imply that the artist will be judged solely on the basis of his works of art; a thousand other things will contribute toward summing 29

EXISTENTIALISM

him up. What we mean is that a man is nothing else than a series of undertakings, that he is the sum, the organization, the ensemble of the relationships which make up these undertakings.

When all is said and done, what we are accused of, at bottom, is not our pessimism, but an optimistic toughness. If people throw up to us our works of fiction in which we write about people who are soft, weak, cowardly, and sometimes even downright bad, it's not because these people are soft, weak, cowardly, or bad; because if we were to say, as Zola did, that they are that way because of heredity, the workings of environment, society, because of biological or psychological determinism, people would be reassured. They would say, "Well, that's what we're like, no one can do anything about it." But when the existentialist writes about a coward, he says that this coward is responsible for his cowardice. He's not like that because he has a cowardly heart or lung or brain; he's not like that on account of his physiological make-up; but he's like that because he has made himself a coward by his acts. There's no such thing as a cowardly constitution; there are nervous constitutions; there is poor blood, as the common people say, or strong constitutions. But the man whose blood is poor is not a coward on that account, for what makes cowardice is the act of renouncing or yielding. A constitution is not an act; the coward is defined on the basis of the acts he performs. People feel, in a vague sort of way, that this coward we're talking about is guilty of being a coward, and the thought frightens them. What people would like is that a coward or a hero be born that way. . . . 30

From these few reflections it is evident that nothing is more unjust than the objections that have been raised against us. Existentialism is nothing else than an attempt to draw all the consequences of a coherent atheistic position. It isn't trying to plunge man into despair at all. But if one calls every attitude of unbelief despair, like the Christians, then the word is not being used in its original sense. Existentialism isn't so atheistic that it wears itself out showing that God doesn't exist. Rather, it declares that even if God did exist, that would change nothing. There you've got our point of view. Not that we believe that God exists, but we think that the problem of His existence is not the issue. In this sense existentialism is optimistic, a doctrine of action, and it is plain dishonesty for Christians to make no distinction between their own despair and ours and then to call us despairing. 31

COMPREHENSION

1. What are the basic tenets of the philosophy of existentialism as presented by Sartre?

2. What is Sartre's purpose in writing the essay? Where in the essay does he suggest his purpose?

3. How does Sartre's use of the example of Abraham resemble Camus's handling of the myth of Sisyphus?

RHETORIC

1. Sartre refers to many concepts in his essay, for example, *will, subjectivism, quietism, anguish, forlorness,* and *despair.* How do such terms help to determine the essay's diction?

2. Compare Sartre's tone in this essay to that of Allen in "My Speech to the Graduates." What makes the tone of the former serious and that of the latter humorous?

3. In paragraphs 2 and 3, Sartre discusses the two meanings of the word *subjectivism.* How does he use transitional expressions to facilitate the comparison and contrast of the two meanings?

4. How does Sartre use supporting methods such as definition, example, and illustration to explain the concepts of *anguish, forlorness,* and *despair?*

5. In paragraph 25, Sartre first presents the Marxists' views then refutes them. Why is this an effective method of argument?

6. Throughout the essay, Sartre uses the strategy of asking a question and then answering it. How does this strategy contribute to strengthening the authority of the writer?

WRITING

1. Sartre is one of the twentieth century's most famous philosophers. Does his argument reflect philosophical method as it is described by Tillich in "Theology and Philosophy: An Answer"?

2. If people were to adopt the existential philosophy of life, the world would be a better place. Write an essay arguing for or against this proposition.

3. Write an essay explaining the types of rhetorical strategies that Sartre uses in arguing for the existential view of life.

4. Write an essay explaining why your own life follows or does not follow an existential philosophy.

PAUL TILLICH

Theology and Philosophy: An Answer

Paul Johannes Tillich (1886–1965) was born and educated in Germany. He was an ordained Lutheran minister and a professor of theology and philosophy at the University of Frankfurt. In

1933, he was dismissed from his post at the instigation of the Nazis and came to America, where he spent the remainder of his life teaching at the Union Theological Seminary and later at Harvard and the University of Chicago. Like Martin Buber, Tillich was influenced by existentialism, and his theology reflects the existential belief that no human truth is ultimate. Among his works are The Interpretation of History *(1936),* The Protestant Era *((1948), and* My Search for Absolutes *(1967). Here, Tillich examines the relationship between theology and philosophy.*

hilosophy and theology ask the question of being. But they ask it from different perspectives. Philosophy deals with the structure of being in itself; theology deals with the meaning of being for us. From this difference convergent and divergent trends emerge in the relation of theology and philosophy. 1

The first point of divergence is a difference in the cognitive attitude of the philosopher and the theologian. Although driven by the philosophical *erōs*, the philosopher tries to maintain a detached objectivity toward being and its structures. He tries to exclude the personal, social, and historical conditions which might distort an objective vision of reality. His passion is the passion for a truth which is open to general approach, subject to general criticism, changeable in accordance with every new insight, open and communicable. In all these respects he feels no different from the scientist, historian, psychologist, etc. He collaborates with them. The material for his critical analysis is largely supplied by empirical research. Just as all sciences have their origin in philosophy, so they contribute in turn to philosophy by giving to the philosopher new and exactly defined material far beyond anything he could get from a prescientific approach to reality. Of course, the philosopher, as a philosopher, neither criticizes nor augments the knowledge provided by the sciences. This knowledge forms the basis of his description of the categories, structural laws, and concepts which constitute the structure of being. In this respect the philosopher is as dependent on the scientist as he is dependent on his own prescientific observation of reality—often more dependent. This relation to the sciences (in the broad sense of *Wissenschaften*) strengthens the detached, objective attitude of the philosopher. Even in the intuitive-synthetic side of his procedure he tries to exclude influences which are not purely determined by his object. 2

The theologian, quite differently, is not detached from his object but is involved in it. He looks at his object (which transcends the character of being an object) with passion, fear, and love. This is not the *erōs* of the philosopher or his passion for objective truth; it is the love which accepts saving, and therefore personal, truth. The basic 3 attitude of the theologian is commitment to the content he expounds. Detachment would be a denial of the very nature of this content. The attitude of the theologian is "existential." He is involved—with the whole of his existence, with his finitude and his anxiety, with his self-contradictions and his despair, with the healing forces in him and in his social situation. Every theological statement derives its seriousness from these elements of existence. The theologian, in short, is determined by his faith. Every theology presupposes that the theologian is in the theological circle. This contradicts the open, infinite, and changeable character of philosophical truth. It also differs from the way in which the philosopher is dependent on scientific research. The theologian has no direct relation to the scientist (including the historian, sociologist, psychologist). He deals with him only in so far as philosophical implications are at stake. If he abandons the existential attitude, as some of the "empirical" theologians have done, he is driven to statements the reality of which will not be acknowledged by anybody who does not share the existential presuppositions of the assumedly empirical theologian. Theology is necessarily existential, and no theology can escape the theological circle.

The second point of divergence between the theologian and the philosopher is the difference in their sources. The philosopher looks at the whole of reality to discover within it the structure of reality as a whole. He tries to penetrate into the structures of being by means of the power of his cognitive function and its structures. He assumes—and science continuously confirms this assumption—that there is an identity, or at least an analogy, between objective and subjective reason, between the *logos* of reality as a whole and the *logos* working in him. Therefore, this *logos* is common; every reasonable being participates in it, uses it in asking questions and criticizing the answers received. There is no particular place to discover the structure of being; there is no particular place to stand to discover the categories of experience. The place to look is all places; the place to stand is no place at all; it is pure reason.

The theologian, on the other hand, must look where that which concerns him ultimately is manifest, and he must stand where its manifestation reaches and grasps him. The source of his knowledge is not the universal *logos* but the Logos "who became flesh," that is, the *logos* manifesting itself in a particular historical event. And the medium through which he receives the manifestation of the *logos* is not common rationality but the church, its traditions and its present reality. He speaks in the church about the foundation of the church. And he speaks because he is grasped by the power of this foundation and by the community built upon it. The concrete *logos* which he sees is received through believing commitment and not, like the universal *logos* at which the philosopher looks, through rational detachment.

6

The third point of divergence between philosophy and theology is the difference in their content. Even when they speak about the same object, they speak about something different. The philosopher deals with the categories of being in relation to the material which is structured by them. He deals with causality as it appears in physics or psychology; he analyzes biological or historical time; he discusses astronomical as well as microcosmic space. He describes the epistemological subject and the relation of person and community. He presents the characteristics of life and spirit in their dependence on, and independence of, each other. He defines nature and history in their mutual limits and tries to penetrate into ontology and logic of being and nonbeing. Innumerable other examples could be given. They all reflect the cosmological structure of the philosophical assertions. The theologian, on the other hand, relates the same categories and concepts to the quest for a "new being." His assertions have a soteriological character. He discusses causality in relation to a *prima causa*, the ground of the whole series of causes and effects; he deals with time in relation to eternity, with space in relation to man's existential homelessness. He speaks of the self-estrangement of the subject, about the spiritual center of personal life, and about community as a possible embodiment of the "New Being." He relates the structures of life to the creative ground of life and the structures of spirit to the divine Spirit. He speaks of the participation of nature in the "history of salvation," about the victory of being over nonbeing. Here also the examples could be increased indefinitely; they show the sharp divergence of theology from philosophy with respect to their content.

7

The divergence between philosophy and theology is counterbalanced by an equally obvious convergence. From both sides converging trends are at work. The philosopher, like the theologian, "exists," and he cannot jump over the concreteness of his existence and his implicit theology. He is conditioned by his psychological, sociological and historical situation. And, like every human being, he exists in the power of an ultimate concern, whether or not he is fully conscious of it, whether or not he admits it to himself and to others. There is no reason why even the most scientific philosopher should not admit it, for without an ultimate concern his philosophy would be lacking in passion, seriousness, and creativity. Wherever we look in the history of philosophy, we find ideas and systems which claim to be ultimately relevant for human existence. Occasionally the philosophy of religion openly expresses the ultimate concern behind a system. More often it is the character of the ontological principles, or a special section of a system, such as epistemology, philosophy of nature, politics and ethics, philosophy of history, etc., which is most revealing for the discovery of the ultimate concern and the hidden theology within it. Every creative philosopher is a hidden theologian (some-

PAUL TILLICH

times even a declared theologian). He is a theologian in the degree to which his existential situation and his ultimate concern shape his philosophical vision. He is a theologian in the degree to which his intuition of the universal *logos* of the structure of reality as a whole is formed by a particular *logos* which appears to him on his particular place and reveals to him the meaning of the whole. And he is a theologian in the degree to which the particular *logos* is a matter of active commitment within a special community. There is hardly a historically significant philosopher who does not show these marks of a theologian. But the philosopher does not intend to be a theologian. He wants to serve the universal *logos*. He tries to turn away from his existential situation, including his ultimate concern, toward a place above all particular places, toward pure reality. The conflict between the intention of becoming universal and the destiny of remaining particular characterizes every philosophical existence. It is its burden and its greatness.

The theologian carries an analogous burden. Instead of turning away from his existential situation, including his ultimate concern, he turns toward it. He turns toward it, not in order to make a confession of it, but in order to make clear the universal validity, the *logos* structure, of what concerns him ultimately. And he can do this only in an attitude of detachment from his existential situation and in obedience to the universal *logos*. This obligates him to be critical of every special expression of his ultimate concern. He cannot affirm any tradition and any authority except through a "No" and a "Yes." And it is always possible that he may not be able to go all the way from the "No" to the "Yes." He cannot join the chorus of those who live in unbroken assertions. He must take the risk of being driven beyond the boundary line of the theological circle. Therefore, the pious and powerful in the church are suspicious of him, although they live in dependence upon the work of the former theologians who were in the same situation. Theology, since it serves not only the concrete but also the universal *logos*, can become a stumbling block for the church and a demonic temptation for the theologian. The detachment required in honest theological work can destroy the necessary involvement of faith. This tension is the burden and the greatness of every theological work.

The duality of divergence and convergence in the relation between theology and philosophy leads to the double question: Is there a necessary conflict between the two and is there a possible synthesis between them? Both questions must be answered negatively. Neither is a conflict between theology and philosophy necessary, nor is a synthesis between them possible.

A conflict presupposes a common basis on which to fight. But there is no common basis between theology and philosophy. If the theologian and the philosopher fight, they do so either on a philosophical or on a theological basis. The philosophical basis is the ontological analysis of the structure of being. If the theologian needs this analysis, either he must take it from a philosopher or he must himself become a philosopher. Usually he does both. If he enters the philosophical arena, conflicts as well as alliances with other philosophers are unavoidable. But all this happens on the philosophical level. The theologian has no right whatsoever to argue for a philosophical opinion in the name of his ultimate concern or on the basis of the theological circle. He is obliged to argue for a philosophical decision in the name of the universal *logos* and from the place which is no place: pure reason. It is a disgrace for the theologian and intolerable for the philosopher if in a philosophical discussion the theologian suddenly claims an authority other than pure reason. Conflicts on the philosophical level are conflicts between two philosophers, one of whom happens to be a theologian, but they are not conflicts between theology and philosophy.

Often, however, the conflict is fought on the theological level. 11 The hidden theologian in the philosopher fights with the professed theologian. This situation is more frequent than most philosophers realize. Since they have developed their concepts with the honest intention of obeying the universal *logos,* they are reluctant to recognize the existentially conditioned elements in their systems. They feel that such elements, while they give color and direction to their creative work, diminish its truth value. In such a situation the theologian must break the resistance of the philosopher against a theological analysis of his ideas. He can do this by pointing to the history of philosophy, which discloses that in every significant philosopher existential passion (ultimate concern) and rational power (obedience to the universal *logos*) are united and that the truth value of a philosophy is dependent on the amalgamation of these two elements in every concept. The insight into this situation is, at the same time, an insight into the fact that two philosophers, one of whom happens to be a theologian, can fight with each other and that two theologians, one of whom happens to be a philosopher, can fight with each other; but there is no possible conflict between theology and philosophy because there is no common basis for such a conflict. The philosopher may or may not convince the philosopher-theologian. And the theologian may or may not convert the theologian-philosopher. In no case does the theologian as such stand against the philosopher as such and vice versa.

Thus there is no conflict between theology and philosophy, 12 and there is no synthesis either—for exactly the same reason which insures that there will be no conflict. A common basis is lacking. The idea of a synthesis between theology and philosophy has led to the dream of a "Christian philosophy." The term is ambiguous. It can mean a philosophy whose existential basis is historical Christianity. In this sense all modern philosophy is Christian, even if it is humanistic, atheistic, and intentionally anti-Christian. No philosopher living within Western Christian culture can deny his dependence on it, as no Greek philosopher could have hidden his dependence on an Apollonian-Dionysian culture, even if he was a radical critic of the gods of Homer. The modern vision of reality and its philosophical analysis is different from that of pre-Christian times, whether one is or is not existentially determined by the God of Mount Zion and the Christ of Mount Golgotha. Reality is encountered differently; experience has different dimensions and directions than in the cultural climate of Greece. No one is able to jump out of this "magic" circle. Nietzsche, who tried to do so, announced the coming of the Anti-Christ. But the Anti-Christ is dependent on the Christ against whom he arises. The early Greeks, for whose culture Nietzsche was longing, did not have to fight the Christ; indeed, they unconsciously prepared his coming by elaborating the questions to which he gave the answer and the categories in which the answer could be expressed. Modern philosophy is not pagan. Atheism and anti-Christianity are not pagan. They are anti-Christian in Christian terms. The scars of the Christian tradition cannot be erased; they are a *character indelebilis*. Even the paganism of naziism was not really a relapse to paganism (just as bestiality is not a relapse to the beast).

But the term "Christian philosophy" is often meant in a different sense. It is used to denote a philosophy which does not look at the universal *logos* but at the assumed or actual demands of a Christian theology. This can be done in two ways: either the church authorities or its theological interpreters nominate one of the past philosophers to be their "philosophical saint" or they demand that contemporary philosophers should develop a philosophy under special conditions and with a special aim. In both cases the philosophical *erōs* is killed. If Thomas Aquinas is officially named *the* philosopher of the Roman Catholic church, he has ceased to be for Catholic philosophers a genuine partner in the philosophical dialogue which goes on through the centuries. And if present-day Protestant philosophers are asked to accept the idea of personality as their highest ontological principle because it is the principle most congenial to the spirit of the Reformation, the work of these philosophers is mutilated. There is nothing in heaven and earth, or beyond them, to which the philosopher must subject himself except the universal *logos* of being as it gives itself to him in experience. Therefore, the idea of a "Christian philosophy" in the narrower sense of a philosophy which is intentionally Christian must be rejected. The fact that every modern philosophy has

grown on Christian soil and shows traces of the Christian culture in which it lives has nothing to do with the self-contradicting ideal of a "Christian philosophy."

Christianity does not need a "Christian philosophy" in the   14
narrower sense of the word. The Christian claim that the *logos* who has become concrete in Jesus as the Christ is at the same time the universal *logos* includes the claim that wherever the *logos* is at work it agrees with the Christian message. No philosophy which is obedient to the universal *logos* can contradict the concrete *logos*, the Logos "who became flesh."

COMPREHENSION

1.   Why is this essay titled "Theology and Philosophy: An Answer"? What does it answer?

2.   What is philosophical "truth"? What is theological "truth"? Why is theological "truth" necessarily existential?

3.   What does Tillich mean by the "duality of divergence and convergence" (paragraph 9)?

RHETORIC

1.   Define the following: *logos* (paragraph 4), *epistemological* (paragraph 6), *ontology* (paragraph 6), and *soteriological* (paragraph 6). How important to understanding Tillich's essay is understanding his language?

2.   Look up the word *Wissenschaften* in a German-English dictionary. How does this word mean more than our English word *science*? Why is this broader connotation relevant to Tillich in this essay?

3.   What two definitions of "Christian philosophy" does Tillich give? In what sense does Tillich consider Nietzche a Christian philosopher?

4.   Cite an instance where Tillich contrasts dualities. How does he go beyond comparison and contrast in his resolution of them?

5.   How is Tillich characterizing the different disciplines of theology and philosophy? Briefly list the distinctions that Tillich makes between their methodologies, assumptions, and goals. What does this list tell you about the organization of this essay?

6.   How does Tillich go about framing his proof? What objections could another philosopher or theologian make to Tillich's analysis?

WRITING

1.   Are the questions addressed by Tillich of interest to the average Christian? How is the nature of theological inquiry at odds with "the necessary involvement of faith"? What use does theology have in the life of the average Christian?

2. Write an essay comparing essentialism in philosophy and existentialism in theology. Refer to Sartre's essay for this assignment. Which theory is closer to your approach to discovering the truth? Which theory do you feel yields more reliable results?

3. Review the essays in this section, and outline in an analytical essay some of the main conflicts and issues in religion today.

Mathematics, Science, and Technology

T. H. HUXLEY

We Are All Scientists

Thomas Henry Huxley (1825–1895) was one of the nineteenth century's most brilliant adventurers, educators, polemicists, and scientists. He defended Charles Darwin's theory of evolution to an often hostile English scientific community. He reformed the organization of the English elementary school. He labored incessantly to explain science to Britain's middle and working classes. Most of Huxley's works were republished in his Collected Essays *(nine volumes, 1894–1908). In the following selection, Huxley dispels the popular belief that scientists think differently from the rest of us.*

 he method of scientific investigation is nothing but the expression of the necessary mode of working of the human mind. It is simply the mode at which all phenomena are reasoned about, rendered precise and exact. There is no more difference, between the mental operations of a man of science and those of an ordinary person, than there is between the operations and methods of a baker or of a butcher weighing out his   1 goods in common scales, and the operations of a chemist in performing a difficult and complex analysis by means of his balance and finely graduated weights. It is not that the action of the scales in the one case, and the balance in the other, differ in the principles of their construction or manner of working; but the beam of one is set on an infinitely finer axis than the other, and of course turns by the addition of a much smaller weight.

You will understand this better, perhaps, if I give you some 2 familiar example. You have all heard it repeated, I dare say, that men of science work by means of induction and deduction, and that by the help of these operations, they, in a sort of sense, wring from Nature certain other things, which are called natural laws, and causes, and that out of these, by some cunning skill of their own, they build up hypotheses and theories. And it is imagined by many that the operations of the common mind can be by no means compared with these processes, and that they have to be acquired by a sort of special apprenticeship to the craft. To hear all these large words, you would think that the mind of a man of science must be constituted differently from that of his fellow men; but if you will not be frightened by terms, you will discover that you are quite wrong, and that all these terrible apparatus are being used by yourselves every day and every hour of your lives.

There is a well-known incident in one of Molière's plays, 3 when the author makes the hero express unbounded delight on being told that he had been talking prose during the whole of his life. In the same way I trust that you will take comfort, and be delighted with yourselves, on the discovery that you have been acting on the principles of inductive and deductive philosophy during the same period. Probably there is not one here who has not in the course of the day had occasion to set in motion a complex train of reasoning, of the very same kind, though differing of course in degree, as that which a scientific man goes through in tracing the causes of natural phenomena.

A very trivial circumstance will serve to exemplify this. Sup- 4 pose you go into a fruiterer's shop, wanting an apple—you take up one, and, on biting it, you find it is sour; you look at it, and see that it is hard and green. You take up another one, and that too is hard, green, and sour. The shopman offers you a third; but, before biting it, you examine it, and find that it is hard and green, and you immediately say that you will not have it, as it must be sour, like that you have already tried.

Nothing can be more simple than that, you think; but if you 5 will take the trouble to analyze and trace out into its logical elements what has been done by the mind, you will be greatly surprised. In the first place, you have performed the operation of induction. You found that, in two experiences, hardness and greenness in apples went together with sourness. It was so in the first case, and it was confirmed by the second. True, it is a very small basis, but still it is enough to make an induction from; you generalize the facts, and you expect to find sourness in apples where you get hardness and greenness. You found upon that a general law, that all hard and green apples are sour; and that, so far as it goes, is a perfect induction. Well, having got your natural law in this way, when you are offered another apple which you find is hard and green, you say, "All hard and green apples are sour; this apple is hard and green, therefore this apple is sour." That train of reasoning is what logicians call a syllogism, and has all its various parts and terms—its major premise, its minor premise, and its conclusion. And, by the help of further reasoning, which, if drawn out, would have to be exhibited in two or three other syllogisms, you arrive at your final determination, "I will not have that apple." So that, you see, you have, in the first place, established a law by induction, and upon that you have founded a deduction, and reasoned out the special conclusion of the particular case. Well now, suppose, having got your law, that at some time afterwards, you are discussing the qualities of apples with a friend: you will say to him, "It is a very curious thing but I find that all hard and green apples are sour!" Your friend says to you, "But how do you know that?" You at once reply, "Oh, because I have tried them over and over again, and have always found them to be so." Well, if we were talking science instead of common sense, we should call that an experimental verification. And, if still opposed, you go further, and say, "I have heard from the people in Somersetshire and Devonshire, where a large number of apples are grown, that they have observed the same thing. It is also found to be the case in Normandy, and in North America. In short, I find it to be the universal experience of mankind wherever attention has been directed to the subject." Whereupon, your friend, unless he is a very unreasonable man, agrees with you, and is convinced that you are quite right in the conclusion you have drawn. He believes, although perhaps he does not know he believes it, that the more extensive verifications are—that the more frequently experiments have been made, and results of the same kind arrived at—that the more varied the conditions under which the same results are attained, the more certain is the ultimate conclusion, and he disputes the question no further. He sees that the experiment has been tried under all sorts of conditions, as to time, place, and people; with the same result; and he says with you, therefore, that the law you have laid down must be a good one, and he must believe it.

In science we do the same thing; the philosopher exercises 6 precisely the same faculties, though in a much more delicate manner. In scientific inquiry it becomes a matter of duty to expose a supposed law to every kind of verification, and to take care, moreover, that this

T. H. HUXLEY

is done intentionally, and not left to a mere accident, as in the case of the apples. And in science, as in common life, our confidence in a law is in exact proportion to the absence of variation in the result of our experimental verifications. For instance, if you let go your grasp of an article you may have in your hand, it will immediately fall to the ground. That is a very common verification of one of the best established laws of nature—that of gravitation. The method by which men of science establish the existence of that law is exactly the same as that by which we have established the trivial proposition about the sourness of hard and green apples. But we believe it in such an extensive, thorough, and unhesitating manner because the universal experience of mankind verifies it, and we can verify it ourselves at any time; and that is the strongest possible foundation on which any natural law can rest.

So much, then, by way of proof that the method of establishing laws in science is exactly the same as that pursued in common life. Let us now turn to another matter (though really it is but another phase of the same question), and that is the method by which, from the relations of certain phenomena, we prove that some stand in the position of causes towards the others.

I want to put the case clearly before you, and I will therefore show you what I mean by another familiar example. I will suppose that one of you, on coming down in the morning to the parlor of your house, finds that a teapot and some spoons which had been left in the room on the previous evening are gone—the window is open, and you observe the mark of a dirty hand on the window frame, and perhaps, in addition to that, you notice the impress of a hobnailed shoe on the gravel outside. All these phenomena have struck your attention instantly, and before two seconds have passed you say, "Oh, somebody has broken open the window, entered the room, and run off with the spoons and the teapot!" That speech is out of your mouth in a moment. And you will probably add, "I know he has; I am quite sure of it!" You mean to say exactly what you know; but in reality you are giving expression to what is, in all essential particulars, an hypothesis. You do not *know* it at all; it is nothing but an hypothesis rapidly framed in your own mind. And it is an hypothesis founded on a long train of inductions and deductions.

What are those inductions and deductions, and how have you got at this hypothesis? You have observed, in the first place, that the window is open; but by a train of reasoning involving many inductions and deductions, you have probably arrived long before at the general law—and a very good one it is—the windows do not open of themselves; and you therefore conclude that something has opened the window. A second general law that you have arrived at in the same way is, that teapots and spoons do not go out of a window

7

8

9

spontaneously, and you are satisfied that, as they are not now where you left them, they have been removed. In the third place, you look at the marks on the window sill, and the shoe-marks outside, and you say that in all previous experience the former kind of mark has never been produced by anything else but the hand of a human being; and the same experience shows that no other animal but man at present wears shoes with hobnails in them such as would produce the marks in the gravel. I do not know, even if we could discover any of those "missing links" that are talked about, that they would help us to any other conclusion! At any rate the law which states our present experience is strong enough for my present purpose. You next reach the conclusion that as these kinds of marks have not been left by any other animals than men, or are liable to be formed in any other way than by a man's hand and shoe, the marks in question have been formed by a man in that way. You have, further, a general law, founded on observation and experience, and that, too is, I am sorry to say, a very universal and unimpeachable one—that some men are thieves; and you assume at once from all these premises—and that is what constitutes your hypothesis—that the man who made the marks outside and on the window sill, opened the window, got into the room, and stole your teapot and spoons. You have now arrived at a *vera causa*; you have assumed a cause, which it is plain, is competent to produce all the phenomena you have observed. You can explain all these phenomena only by the hypothesis of a thief. But that is a hypothetical conclusion, of the justice of which you have no absolute proof at all; it is only rendered highly probable by a series of inductive and deductive reasonings.

I suppose your first action, assuming that you are a man of   10
ordinary common sense, and that you have established this hypothesis to your own satisfaction, will very likely be to go off for the police, and set them on the track of the burglar, with the view to the recovery of your property. But just as you are starting with this object, some person comes in, and on learning what you are about, says, "My good friend, you are going on a great deal too fast. How do you know that the man who really made the marks took the spoons? It might have been a monkey that took them and the man may have merely looked in afterwards." You would probably reply, "Well, that is all very well, but you see it is contrary to all experience of the way teapots and spoons are abstracted; so that, at any rate, your hypothesis is less probable than mine." While you are talking the thing over in this way, another friend arrives, one of that good kind of people that I was talking of a little while ago. And he might say, "Oh, my dear sir, you are certainly going on a great deal too fast. You are most presumptuous. You admit that all these occurrences took place when you were fast asleep, at a time when you could not possibly have known any-

T. H. HUXLEY

thing about what was taking place. How do you know that the laws of Nature are not suspended during the night? It may be that there has been some kind of supernatural interference in this case." In point of fact, he declares that your hypothesis is one of which you cannot at all demonstrate the truth, and that you are by no means sure that the laws of Nature are the same when you are asleep as when you are awake.

Well, now, you cannot at the moment answer that kind of reasoning. You feel that your worthy friend has you somewhat at a disadvantage. You will feel perfectly convinced in your own mind, however, that you are quite right, and you say to him, "My good friend, I can only be guided by the natural probabilities of the case, and if you will be kind enough to stand aside and permit me to pass, I will go and fetch the police." Well, we will suppose that your journey is successful, and that by good luck you meet with a policeman; that eventually the burglar is found with your property on his person, and the marks correspond to his hand and to his boots. Probably any jury would consider those facts a very good experimental verification of your hypothesis, touching the cause of the abnormal phenomena observed in your parlor, and would act accordingly.

Now, in this suppositious case, I have taken phenomena of a very common kind, in order that you might see what are the different steps in an ordinary process of reasoning, if you will only take the trouble to analyze it carefully. All the operations I have described, you will see, are involved in the mind of any man of sense in leading him to a conclusion as to the course he should take in order to make good a robbery and punish the offender. I say that you are led, in that case, to your conclusion by exactly the same train of reasoning as that which a man of science pursues when he is endeavoring to discover the origin and laws of the most occult phenomena. The process is, and always must be, the same; and precisely the same mode of reasoning was employed by Newton and Laplace in their endeavors to discover and define the causes of the movements of the heavenly bodies as you, with your own common sense, would employ to detect a burglar. The only difference is that the nature of the inquiry being more abstruse, every step has to be most carefully watched, so that there may not be a single crack or flaw in your hypothesis. A flaw or crack in many of the hypotheses of daily life may be of little or no moment as affecting the general correctness of the conclusions at which we may arrive; but, in a scientific inquiry, a fallacy, a great or small, is always of importance, and is sure to be in the long run constantly productive of mischievous, if not fatal results.

Do not allow yourselves to be misled by the common notion that an hypothesis is untrustworthy simply because it is an hypothesis. It is often urged, in respect to some scientific conclusion, that, after all, it is only an hypothesis. But what more have we to guide us in nine-tenths of the most important affairs of daily life than hypotheses, and often very ill-based ones? So that in science, where the evidence of a hypothesis is subjected to the most rigid examination, we may rightly pursue the same course. You may have hypotheses and hypotheses. A man may say, if he likes, that the moon is made of green cheese: that is an hypothesis. But another man, who has devoted a great deal of time and attention to the subject, and availed himself of the most powerful telescopes and the results of the observations of others, declares that in his opinion it is probably composed of materials very similar to those of which our own earth is made up: and that is also only an hypothesis. But I need not tell you that there is an enormous difference in the value of the two hypotheses. That one which is based on sound scientific knowledge is sure to have a corresponding value; and that which is a mere hasty random guess is likely to have but little value. Every great step in our progress in discovering causes has been made in exactly the same way as that which I have detailed to you. A person observing the occurrence of certain facts and phenomena asks, naturally enough, what process, what kind of operation known to occur in Nature applied to the particular case, will unravel and explain the mystery? Hence you have the scientific hypothesis; and its value will be proportionate to the care and completeness with which its basis has been tested and verified. It is in these matters as in the commonest affairs of practical life: the guess of the fool will be folly, while the guess of the wise man will contain wisdom. In all cases, you see that the value of the result depends on the patience and faithfulness with which the investigator applies to his hypothesis every possible kind of verification.

COMPREHENSION

1. What do you take Huxley's purpose to be in this essay?

2. Describe the process of reasoning that, according to Huxley, people use when they are deciding to eat green apples.

3. Why does Huxley reject the reasoning of "some person" in paragraph 10?

RHETORIC

1. Huxley uses several "large words," particularly in paragraphs 2 and 5. What are these words, and what do they mean?

2. Huxley uses both the second- and first-person pronouns in this essay. How does this affect the tone of the essay?

3. What is the thesis of this essay? Where is it expressed for the first time?

4. How does Huxley use coordinating conjunctions to maintain coherence?

5. Huxley employs two long examples to support and clarify his thesis. Identify these examples, and show how Huxley relates them to his thesis.

6. How does paragraph 2 map out the structure of the essay?

WRITING

1. Do you agree with Huxley's thesis? Why, or why not? Answer in a brief essay.

2. Write a paper using examples to show how you use inductive and deductive reasoning in everyday life.

3. Huxley asserts that "the guess of the fool will be folly, while the guess of the wise man will contain wisdom." Apply this phrase to an event in your own life where your hypothesis either turned out to be foolish or wise.

ALBERT EINSTEIN

The Common Language of Science

Albert Einstein (1879–1955), one of the greatest scientists who ever lived, was born in Germany. Einstein spent the early years of his career working in the Swiss patent office in Bern. In 1905, while working there, he published the first of many papers on the theory of relativity. These papers revolutionized physics. In 1933, with the advent of nazism, Einstein fled to the United States, where he continued his theoretical work and spoke out for peace in the world. His works range from the scientific Relativity: The Special and General Theory *(1918), to the personal* The World as I See It *(1934). In the following essay, Einstein discusses the origin of scientific language.*

he first step towards language was to link acoustically or otherwise commutable signs to sense-impressions. Most likely all sociable animals have arrived at this primitive kind of communication—at least to a certain degree. A higher development is reached when further signs are introduced and understood which establish relations between those other signs designating sense-impression. At this stage it is already possible to report somewhat complex series of impressions; we can say that language has come to existence. If language is to lead at all to understanding, there must be rules concerning the relations between the signs on the one hand and on the other hand there must be a stable correspondence between signs and impressions. In their childhood individuals connected by the same language grasp these rules and relations mainly by intuition. When man becomes conscious of the rules concerning the relations between signs the so-called grammar of language is established.

In an early stage the words may correspond directly to impressions. At a later stage this direct connection is lost insofar as some words convey relations to perceptions only if used in connection with other words (for instance such words as: "is," "or," "thing"). Then word-groups rather than single words refer to perceptions. When language becomes thus partially independent from the background of impressions a greater inner coherence is gained. 2

Only at this further development where frequent use is made of so-called abstract concepts, language becomes an instrument of reasoning in the true sense of the word. But it is also this development which turns language into a dangerous source of error and deception. Everything depends on the degree to which words and word-combinations correspond to the world of impression. 3

What is it that brings about such an intimate connection between language and thinking? Is there no thinking without the use of language, namely in concepts and concept-combinations for which words need not necessarily come to mind? Has not everyone of us struggled for words although the connection between "things" was already clear? 4

We might be inclined to attribute to the act of thinking complete independence from language if the individual formed or were able to form his concepts without the verbal guidance of his environment. Yet most likely the mental shape of an individual, growing up under such conditions, would be very poor. Thus we may conclude that the mental development of the individual and his way of forming concepts depend to a high degree upon language. This makes us realize to what extent the same language means the same mentality. In this sense thinking and language are linked together. 5

What distinguishes the language of science from language as we ordinarily understand the word? How is it that scientific language is international? What science strives for is an utmost acuteness and clarity of concepts as regards their mutual relation and their correspondence to sensory data. As an illustration let us take the language of Euclidian geometry and Algebra. They manipulate with a small number of independently introduced concepts, respectively symbols, such as the integral number, the straight line, the point, as well as with signs which designate the fundamental operations, that is the connections between those fundamental concepts. This is the basis for 6

ALBERT EINSTEIN

the construction, respectively definition of all other statements and concepts. The connection between concepts and statements on the one hand and the sensory data on the other hand is established through acts of counting and measuring whose performance is sufficiently well determined.

The super-national character of scientific concepts and scientific language is due to the fact that they have been set up by the best brains of all countries and all times. In solitude and yet in cooperative effort as regards the final effect they created the spiritual tools for the technical revolutions which have transformed the life of mankind in the last centuries. Their system of concepts have served as a guide in the bewildering chaos of perceptions so that we learned to grasp general truths from particular observations. 7

What hopes and fears does the scientific method imply for mankind? I do not think that this is the right way to put the question. Whatever this tool in the hand of man will produce depends entirely on the nature of the goals alive in this mankind. Once these goals exist, the scientific method furnishes means to realize them. Yet it cannot furnish the very goals. The scientific method itself would not have led anywhere, it would not even have been born without a passionate striving for clear understanding. 8

Perfections of means and confusion of goals seem—in my opinion—to characterize our age. If we desire sincerely and passionately the safety, the welfare and the free development of the talents of all men, we shall not be in want of the means to approach such a state. Even if only a small part of mankind strives for such goals, their superiority will prove itself in the long run. 9

COMPREHENSION

1. According to Einstein, when in the development of language does scientific language appear? How is it different from and similar to nonscientific language?

2. Why does Einstein say that language can "turn" into a dangerous source of error and deception?

3. Compare Einstein's insights into the nature of scientific thinking with Huxley's.

RHETORIC

1. Explain the use of rhetorical questions in this essay.

2. What is the point of view of this essay? How does this viewpoint complement the diction and tone of the essay?

3. What paragraphs use narrative? What words indicate the development of the narrative?

4. Give reasons and evidence for saying this essay uses extended definition.

5. Why is paragraph 6 important to the development of this essay? What rhetorical technique is used here?

6. Explain the relation of paragraphs 8 and 9 to the rest of the essay. What is the topic of paragraph 9?

WRITING

1. If the language of science cannot define goals, what kinds of language can? Can we trust science to solve our problems? Explain in a brief essay.

2. Write an essay distinguishing means from goals in education, religion, or business.

3. Describe a particular kind of language—academic, political, or religious— and explain how it functions in relation to language in general.

LEWIS THOMAS

On Societies as Organisms

Lewis Thomas (1913–   ) is the past president of the Memorial Sloan-Kettering Cancer Center. He first came to public attention when his collection of essays Lives of a Cell *(1974) appeared. Because of his eloquent capacity to extract metaphors from the discoveries of modern biology and because of his optimism, Thomas's essays have attracted a large and enthusiastic following. Another collection of his essays,* The Medusa and the Snail, *was published in 1979. Thomas can discover an almost magical value in the most humble activities, as the essay below demonstrates.*

Viewed from a suitable height, the aggregating clusters of   1
medical scientists in the bright sunlight of the boardwalk at Atlantic City, swarmed there from everywhere for the annual meetings, have the look of assemblages of social insects. There is the same vibrating, ionic movement, interrupted by the darting back and forth of jerky individuals to touch antennae and exchange small bits of information; periodically, the mass casts out, like a trout-line, a long single file unerringly toward Child's. If the boards were not fastened down, it would not be a surprise to see them put together a nest of sorts.

It is permissible to say this sort of thing about humans. They do resemble, in their most compulsively social behavior, ants at a distance. It is, however, quite bad form in biological circles to put it the other way round, to imply that the operation of insect societies has any relation at all to human affairs. The writers of books on insect behavior generally take pains, in their prefaces, to caution that insects are like creatures from another planet, that their behavior is absolutely foreign, totally unhuman, unearthly, almost unbiological. They are more like perfectly tooled but crazy little machines, and we violate science when we try to read human meanings in their arrangements.

It is hard for a bystander not to do so. Ants are so much like human beings as to be an embarrassment. They farm fungi, raise aphids as livestock, launch armies into wars, use chemical sprays to alarm and confuse enemies, capture slaves. The families of weaver ants engage in child labor, holding their larvae like shuttles to spin out the thread that sews the leaves together for their fungus gardens. They exchange information ceaselessly. They do everything but watch television.

What makes us most uncomfortable is that they, and the bees and termites and social wasps, seem to live two kinds of lives: they are individuals, going about the day's business without much evidence of thought for tomorrow, and they are at the same time component parts, cellular elements, in the huge, writhing, ruminating organism of the Hill, the nest, the hive. It is because of this aspect, I think, that we most wish for them to be something foreign. We do not like the notion that there can be collective societies with the capacity to behave like organisms. If such things exist, they can have nothing to do with us.

Still, there it is. A solitary ant, afield, cannot be considered to have much of anything on his mind; indeed, with only a few neurons strung together by fibers, he can't be imagined to have a mind at all, much less a thought. He is more like a ganglion on legs. Four ants together, or ten, encircling a dead moth on a path, begin to look more like an idea. They fumble and shove, gradually moving the food toward the Hill, but as though by blind chance. It is only when you watch the dense mass of thousands of ants, crowded together around the Hill, blackening the ground, that you begin to see the whole beast, and now you observe it thinking, planning, calculating. It is an intelligence, a kind of live computer, with crawling bits for its wits.

At a stage in the construction, twigs of certain size are needed, and all the members forage obsessively for twigs of just this size. Later, when outer walls are to be finished, thatched, the size must change, and as though given new orders by telephone, all the workers shift the search to the new twigs. If you disturb the arrangement of a part of the Hill, hundreds of ants will set it vibrating, shifting, until it is put right again. Distant sources of food are somehow sensed, and long lines, like tentacles, reach out over the ground, up over walls, behind boulders, to fetch it in.

Termites are even more extraordinary in the way they seem   7
to accumulate intelligence as they gather together. Two or three termites in a chamber will begin to pick up pellets and move them from place to place, but nothing comes of it; nothing is built. As more join in, they seem to reach a critical mass, a quorum, and the thinking begins. They place pellets atop pellets, then throw up columns and beautiful, curving, symmetrical arches, and the crystalline architecture of vaulted chambers is created. It is not known how they communicate with each other, how the chains of termites building one column know when to turn toward the crew on the adjacent column, or how, when the time comes, they manage the flawless joining of the arches. The stimuli that set them off at the outset, building collectively instead of shifting things about, may be pheromones released when they reach committee size. They react as if alarmed. They become agitated, excited, and then they begin working, like artists.

.   Bees live lives of organisms, tissues, cells, organelles, all at the   8
same time. The single bee, out of the hive retrieving sugar (instructed by the dancer: "south-southeast for seven hundred meters, clover—mind you make corrections for the sundrift") is still as much a part of the hive as if attached by a filament. Building the hive, the workers have the look of embryonic cells organizing a developing tissue; from a distance they are like the viruses inside of a cell, running off row after row of symmetrical polygons as though laying down crystals. When the time for swarming comes, and the old queen prepares to leave with her part of the population, it is as though the hive were involved in mitosis. There is an agitated moving of bees back and forth, like granules in cell sap. They distribute themselves in almost precisely equal parts, half to the departing queen, half to the new one. Thus, like an egg, the great, hairy, black and golden creature splits in two, each with an equal share of the family genome.

The phenomenon of separate animals joining up to form an   9
organism is not unique in insects. Slime-mold cells do it all the time, of course, in each life cycle. At first they are single amebocytes swimming around, eating bacteria, aloof from each other, untouching, voting straight Republican. Then, a bell sounds, and acrasin is released by special cells toward which the others converge in stellate ranks, touch, fuse together, and construct the slug, solid as a trout. A splendid stalk is raised, with a fruiting body on top, and out of this comes the next generation of amebocytes, ready to swim across the same moist ground, solitary and ambitious.

Herring and other fish in schools are at times so closely in-   10
tegrated, their actions so coordinated, that they seem to be function-

ally a great multi-fish organism. Flocking birds, especially the seabirds nesting on the slopes of offshore islands in Newfoundland, are similarly attached, connected, synchronized.

Although we are by all odds the most social of all social animals—more interdependent, more attached to each other, more inseparable in our behavior than bees—we do not often feel our conjoined intelligence. Perhaps, however, we are linked in circuits for the storage, processing, and retrieval of information, since this appears to be the most basic and universal of all human enterprises. It may be our biological function to build a certain kind of Hill. We have access to all the information of the biosphere, arriving as elementary units in the stream of solar photons. When we have learned how these are rearranged against randomness, to make, say, springtails, quantum mechanics, and the late quartets, we may have a clearer notion how to proceed. The circuitry seems to be there, even if the current is not always on.

The system of communications used in science should provide a neat, workable model for studying mechanisms of information-building in human society. Ziman, in a recent *Nature* essay, points out, "the invention of a mechanism for the systematic publication of *fragments* of scientific work may well have been the key event in the history of modern science." He continues:

> A regular journal carries from one research worker to another the various ... observations which are of common interest. ... A typical scientific paper has never pretended to be more than another little piece in a larger jigsaw—not significant in itself but as an element in a grander scheme. *This technique, of soliciting many modest contributions to the store of human knowledge, has been the secret of Western science since the seventeenth century, for it achieves a corporate, collective power that is far greater than any one individual can exert.* [italics mine]

With some alteration of terms, some toning down, the passage could describe the building of a termite nest.

It is fascinating that the word "explore" does not apply to the searching aspect of the activity, but has its origins in the sounds we make while engaged in it. We like to think of exploring in science as a lonely, meditative business, and so it is in the first stages, but always, sooner or later, before the enterprise reaches completion, as we explore, we call to each other, communicate, publish, send letters to the editor, present papers, cry out on finding.

COMPREHENSION

1. In this essay does Thomas write for a specialized or general audience? Explain your answer.

2. Describe the insects that Thomas says have humanlike behavior. What is his thesis?

3. Why do writers of books about insects avoid using personification in their descriptions? Why does Thomas purposely use it?

RHETORIC

1. Thomas tends to use words that are not generally used; therefore, define *genome, ionic, amebocytes, mitosis, acrasin, ganglion, stellate,* and *organism.*

2. Thomas uses metaphors frequently and imaginatively. List seven metaphors in the essay, and describe how they are used. Compare his use of metaphor to that of Virginia Woolf in "The Death of the Moth."

3. Paragraph 4 is crucial to the organization of the essay. What two methods of classification does it introduce?

4. What is the difference between solitary and collective behavior among the social insects? Thomas compares this behavior to certain kinds of human behavior. What are the details of this comparison?

5. What is the etymology of the word *explore* according to your dictionary? How does Thomas use this etymology?

6. Thomas extends his discussion in paragraph 9 beyond insects. What effect does he achieve by doing this?

WRITING

1. Do you find it reassuring or disturbing to compare human behavior to insect behavior? Do you find it difficult to consider human society an organism? Why do you think Thomas finds this encouraging?

2. Divide human behavior into groups (school, sports, business), and compare solitary and collective behavior within one or more groups.

3. Write an essay comparing your pet's behavior to human behavior.

4. Thomas has complained about "how awful the prose is in scientific papers." Evaluate the author's own prose in this essay. Argue for or against its effectiveness.

LEWIS THOMAS

How Natural Is Natural?

Loren Eiseley (1907–1977) was an educator, anthropologist, poet, and author. He is best known for his books The Immense Journey *(1957),* Darwin's Century *(1958),* The Firmament of Time *(1960), and* The Night Country *(1971). His books wonderfully combine poetic imagination with scientific objectivity. In the following essay, Eiseley shows his capacity for seeing profoundly into the most common scenes.*

I n the more obscure scientific circles which I frequent there is a legend circulating about a late distinguished scientist who, in his declining years, persisted in wearing enormous padded boots much too large for him. He had developed, it seems, what to his fellows was a wholly irrational fear of falling through the interstices of that largely empty molecular space which common men in their folly speak of as the world. A stroll across his living-room floor had become, for him, something as dizzily horrendous as the activities of a window washer on the Empire State Building. Indeed, with equal reason he could have passed a ghostly hand through his own ribs.

The quivering network of his nerves, the awe-inspiring movement of his thought had become a vague cloud of electrons interspersed with the light-year distances that obtain between us and the farther galaxies. This was the natural world which he had helped to create, and in which, at last, he had found himself a lonely and imprisoned occupant. All around him the ignorant rushed on their way over the illusion of substantial floors, leaping, though they did not see it, from particle to particle, over a bottomless abyss. There was even a question as to the reality of the particles which bore them up. It did not, however, keep insubstantial newspapers from being sold, or insubstantial love from being made.

Not long ago I became aware of another world perhaps equally natural and real, which man is beginning to forget. My thinking began in New England under a boat dock. The lake I speak of has been pre-empted and civilized by man. All day long in the vacation season high-speed motorboats, driven with the reckless abandon common to the young Apollos of our society, speed back and forth, carrying loads of equally attractive girls. The shores echo to the roar of powerful motors and the delighted screams of young Americans with uncounted horsepower surging under their hands. In truth, as I sat there under the boat dock, I had some desire to swim or to canoe in the older ways of the great forest which once lay about this region.

Either notion would have been folly. I would have been gaily chopped to ribbons by teen-age youngsters whose eyes were always immutably fixed on the far horizons of space, or upon the dials which indicated the speed of their passing. There was another world, I was to discover, along the lake shallows and under the boat dock, where the motors could not come.

As I sat there one sunny morning when the water was peculiarly translucent, I saw a dark shadow moving swiftly over the bottom. It was the first sign of life I had seen in this lake, whose shores seemed to yield little but washed-in beer cans. By and by the gliding shadow ceased to scurry from stone to stone over the bottom. Unexpectedly, it headed almost directly for me. A furry nose with gray whiskers broke the surface. Below the whiskers green water foliage trailed out in an inverted V as long as his body. A muskrat still lived in the lake. He was bringing in his breakfast. 4

I sat very still in the strips of sunlight under the pier. To my surprise the muskrat came almost to my feet with his little breakfast of greens. He was young, and it rapidly became obvious to me that he was laboring under an illusion of his own, and that he thought animals and men were still living in the Garden of Eden. He gave me a friendly glance from time to time as he nibbled his greens. Once, even, he went out into the lake again and returned to my feet with more greens. He had not, it seemed, heard very much about men. I shuddered. Only the evening before I had heard a man describe with triumphant enthusiasm how he had killed a rat in the garden because the creature had dared to nibble his petunias. He had even showed me the murder weapon, a sharp-edged brick. 5

On this pleasant shore a war existed and would go on until nothing remained but man. Yet this creature with the gray, appealing face wanted very little: a strip of shore to coast up and down, sunlight and moonlight, some weeds from the deep water. He was an edge-of-the-world dweller, caught between a vanishing forest and a deep lake preempted by unpredictable machines full of chopping blades. He eyed me nearsightedly, a green leaf posed in his mouth. Plainly he had come with some poorly instructed memory about the lion and the lamb. 6

"You had better run away now," I said softly, making no movement in the shafts of light. "You are in the wrong universe and must not make this mistake again. I am really a very terrible and cunning beast. I can throw stones." With this I dropped a little pebble at his feet. 7

He looked at me half blindly, with eyes much better adjusted to the wavering shadows of his lake bottom than to sight in the open air. He made almost as if to take the pebble up into his forepaws. Then a thought seemed to cross his mind—a thought perhaps tele- 8

LOREN EISELEY

pathically received, as Freud once hinted, in the dark world below and before man, a whisper of ancient disaster heard in the depths of a burrow. Perhaps after all this was not Eden. His nose twitched carefully; he edged toward the water.

As he vanished in an oncoming wave, there went with him a 9
natural world, distinct from the world of girls and motorboats, distinct from the world of the professor holding to reality by some great snowshoe effort in his study. My muskrat's shore-line universe was edged with the dark wall of hills on one side and the waspish drone of motors farther out, but it was a world of sunlight he had taken down into the water weeds. It hovered there, waiting for my disappearance. I walked away, obscurely pleased that darkness had not gained on life by any act of mine. In so many worlds, I thought, how natural is "natural"—and is there anything we can call a natural world at all?

COMPREHENSION

1. State in your own words the thesis of this essay.

2. Describe the three "worlds" mentioned in this essay by Eiseley.

3. Why is Eiseley surprised that a muskrat still lives in the lake? Cite specific details that might threaten a muskrat in the lake's world.

RHETORIC

1. The phrases "sunlight world" and "darkness" (paragraph 9) are meant to be taken figuratively. What do they mean?

2. Explain the allusions to "Apollos" (paragraph 3); "the Garden of Eden" (paragraph 5); and Freud (paragraph 8).

3. Explain the relation between paragraphs 1 to 2 and 3 to 9. What rhetorical technique do both groups use?

4. How does Eiseley use narration and description in his essay? Cite examples of both.

5. What details does Eiseley use in contrasting the muskrat's world to the typical American's world?

6. Analyze the way Eiseley develops his concluding paragraph.

WRITING

1. Why does Eiseley despair at the disappearance of the other world? Why should we protect wildlife and wilderness if it means limiting our own growth?

2. Write an essay in which you contrast aspects of the natural world with the artificial world. Use details to support your contrast. For example, you can de-

scribe the life of a bird in the city, of a raccoon in the suburbs, or a deer or bear in a state park.

3. Both Eiseley and E. B. White (in "Once More to the Lake") focus on specific bodies of water in order to develop insights into human nature and the natural world. Explain their purpose and how they develop it in a comparative essay.

4. Analyze the writing styles of Eiseley and Thomas. Examine sentence structure, descriptive techniques, use of evidence, and figurative language.

RACHEL CARSON

The Changing Year

Rachel Carson (1907–1964) could write with eloquence and sensitivity even as she presented the reader with a rigorous, often demanding, scientific scrutiny of nature. Carson's most famous works are The Sea Around Us *(1951) and* The Silent Spring *(1962). The former book won her the National Book Award. The latter, an early study of the danger of pesticides to our environment, influenced President John Kennedy to appoint a commission to study her allegations. The following essay, a chapter from* The Sea Around Us, *illustrates her knowledge as a scientist and her skill as a writer.*

Thus with the year seasons return.

MILTON

or the sea as a whole, the alternation of day and night, the passage of the seasons, the procession of the years, are lost in its vastness, obliterated in its own changeless eternity. But the surface waters are different. The face of the sea is always changing. Crossed by colors, lights, and moving shadows, sparkling in the sun, mysterious in the twilight, its aspects and its moods vary hour by hour. The surface waters move with the tides, stir to the breath of the winds, and rise and fall to the endless, hurrying forms of the waves. Most of all, they change with the advance of the seasons. Spring moves over the temperate lands of our Northern Hemisphere in a tide of new life, of pushing green shoots and unfolding buds, all its mysteries and meanings symbolized in the northward migration of the birds, the awakening of sluggish amphibian life as the chorus of frogs rises again from the wet lands, the

1

different sound of the wind which stirs the young leaves where a month ago it rattled the bare branches. These things we associate with the land, and it is easy to suppose that at sea there could be no such feeling of advancing spring. But the signs are there, and seen with understanding eye, they bring the same magical sense of awakening.

In the sea, as on land, spring is a time for the renewal of life. 2 During the long months of winter in the temperate zones the surface waters have been absorbing the cold. Now the heavy water begins to sink, slipping down and displacing the warmer layers below. Rich stores of minerals have been accumulating on the floor of the continental shelf—some freighted down the rivers from the lands; some derived from sea creatures that have died and whose remains have drifted down to the bottom; some from the shells that once encased a diatom, the streaming protoplasm of a radiolarian, or the transparent tissues of a pteropod. Nothing is wasted in the sea; every particle of material is used over and over again, first by one creature, then by another. And when in spring the waters are deeply stirred, the warm bottom water brings to the surface a rich supply of minerals, ready for use by new forms of life.

Just as land plants depend on minerals in the soil for their 3 growth, every marine plant, even the smallest, is dependent upon the nutrient salts or minerals in the sea water. Diatoms must have silica, the element of which their fragile shells are fashioned. For these and all other microplants, phosphorus is an indispensable mineral. Some of these elements are in short supply and in winter may be reduced below the minimum necessary for growth. The diatom population must tide itself over this season as best it can. It faces a stark problem of survival, with no opportunity to increase, a problem of keeping alive the spark of life by forming tough protective spores against the stringency of winter, a matter of existing in a dormant state in which no demands shall be made on an environment that already withholds all but the most meager necessities of life. So the diatoms hold their place in the winter sea, like seeds of wheat in a field under snow and ice, the seeds from which the spring growth will come.

These, then, are the elements of the vernal blooming of the 4 sea: the "seeds" of the dormant plants, the fertilizing chemicals, the warmth of the spring sun.

In a sudden awakening, incredible in its swiftness, the sim- 5 plest plants of the sea begin to multiply. Their increase is of astronomical proportions. The spring sea belongs at first to the diatoms and to all the other microscopic plant life of the plankton. In the fierce intensity of their growth they cover vast areas of ocean with a living blanket of their cells. Mile after mile of water may appear red or brown or green, the whole surface taking on the color of the infinitesimal grains of pigment contained in each of the plant cells.

 THE CHANGING YEAR

The plants have undisputed sway in the sea for only a short 6
time. Almost at once their own burst of multiplication is matched by
a similar increase in the small animals of the plankton. It is the spawning time of the copepod and the glassworm, the pelagic shrimp and
the winged snail. Hungry swarms of these little beasts of the plankton
roam through the waters, feeding on the abundant plants and themselves falling prey to larger creatures. Now in the spring the surface
waters become a vast nursery. From the hills and valleys of the continent's edge lying far below, and from the scattered shoals and banks,
the eggs or young of many of the bottom animals rise to the surface
of the sea. Even those which, in their maturity, will sink down to a
sedentary life on the bottom, spend the first weeks of life as freely
swimming hunters of the plankton. So as spring progresses new
batches of larvae rise into the surface each day, the young of fishes
and crabs and mussels and tube worms, mingling for a time with the
regular members of the plankton.

Under the steady and voracious grazing, the grasslands of the 7
surface are soon depleted. The diatoms become more and more scarce,
and with them the other simple plants. Still there are brief explosions
of one or another form, when in a sudden orgy of cell division it
comes to claim whole areas of the sea for its own. So, for a time each
spring, the waters may become blotched with brown, jellylike masses,
and the fishermen's nets come up dripping a brown slime and containing no fish, for the herring have turned away from these waters
as though in loathing of the viscid, foul-smelling algae. But in less
time than passes between the full moon and the new, the spring flowering of Phaeocystis is past and the waters have cleared again.

In the spring the sea is filled with migrating fishes, some of 8
them bound for the mouths of great rivers, which they will ascend to
deposit their spawn. Such are the spring-run chinooks coming in from
the deep Pacific feeding grounds to breast the rolling flood of the
Columbia, the shad moving in to the Chesapeake and the Hudson
and the Connecticut, the alewives seeking a hundred coastal streams
of New England, the salmon feeling their way to the Penobscot and
the Kennebec. For months or years these fish have known only the
vast spaces of the ocean. Now the spring sea and the maturing of their
own bodies lead them back to the rivers of their birth.

Other mysterious comings and goings are linked with the ad- 9
vance of the year. Capelin gather in the deep, cold water of the Barents
Sea, their shoals followed and preyed upon by flocks of auks, fulmars,
and kittiwakes. Cod approach the banks of Lofoten, and gather off
the shores of Iceland. Birds whose winter feeding territory may have
encompassed the whole Atlantic or the whole Pacific converge upon
some small island, the entire breeding population arriving within the
space of a few days. Whales suddenly appear off the slopes of the

coastal banks where the swarms of shrimplike krill are spawning, the whales having come from no one knows where, by no one knows what route.

With the subsiding of the diatoms and the completed spawn- 10 ing of many of the plankton animals and most of the fish, life in the surface waters slackens to the slower pace of midsummer. Along the meeting places of the currents the pale moon jelly Aurelia gathers in thousands, forming sinuous lines or windrows across miles of sea, and the birds see their pale forms shimmering deep down in the green water. By midsummer the large red jellyfish Cyanea may have grown from the size of a thimble to that of an umbrella. The great jellyfish moves through the sea with rhythmic pulsations, trailing long tenta- cles and as likely as not shepherding a little group of young cod or haddock, which find shelter under its bell and travel with it.

A hard, brilliant, coruscating phosphorescence often illumi- 11 nates the summer sea. In waters where the protozoa Noctiluca is abundant it is the chief source of this summer luminescence, causing fishes, squids, or dolphins to fill the water with racing flames and to clothe themselves in a ghostly radiance. Or again the summer sea may glitter with a thousand thousand moving pinpricks of light, like an immense swarm of fireflies moving through a dark wood. Such an effect is produced by a shoal of the brilliantly phosphorescent shrimp Meganyctiphanes, a creature of cold and darkness and of the places where icy water rolls upward from the depths and bubbles with white ripplings at the surface.

Out over the plankton meadows of the North Atlantic the dry 12 twitter of the phalaropes, small brown birds, wheeling and turning, dipping and rising, is heard for the first time since early spring. The phalaropes have nested on the arctic tundras, reared their young, and now the first of them are returning to the sea. Most of them will continue south over the open water far from land, crossing the equator into the South Atlantic. Here they will follow where the great whales lead, for where the whales are, there also are the swarms of plankton on which these strange little birds grow fat.

As the fall advances, there are other movements, some in the 13 surface, some hidden in the green depths, that betoken the end of summer. In the fog-covered waters of Bering Sea, down through the treacherous passes between the islands of the Aleutian chain and southward into the open Pacific, the herds of fur seals are moving. Left behind are two small islands, treeless bits of volcanic soil thrust up into the waters of Bering Sea. The islands are silent now, but for the several months of summer they resounded with the roar of mil- lions of seals come ashore to bear and rear their young—all the fur seals of the eastern Pacific crowded into a few square miles of bare rock and crumbling soil. Now once more the seals turn south, to roam down along the sheer underwater cliffs of the continent's edge, where the rocky foundations fall away steeply into the deep sea. Here, in a blackness more absolute than that of arctic winter, the seals will find rich feeding as they swim down to prey on the fishes of this region of darkness.

Autumn comes to the sea with a fresh blaze of phosphores- 14 cence, when every wave crest is aflame. Here and there the whole surface may glow with sheets of cold fire, while below schools of fish pour through the water like molten metal. Often the autumnal phosphorescence is caused by a fall flowering of the dinoflagellates, multiplying furiously in a short-lived repetition of their vernal blooming.

Sometimes the meaning of the glowing water is ominous. Off 15 the Pacific coast of North America, it may mean that the sea is filled with the dinoflagellate Gonyaulax, a minute plant that contains a poison of strange and terrible virulence. About four days after Gonyaulax comes to dominate the coastal plankton, some of the fishes and shellfish in the vicinity become toxic. This is because, in their normal feeding, they have strained the poisonous plankton out of the water. Mussels accumulate the Gonyaulax toxins in their livers, and the toxins react on the human nervous system with an effect similar to that of strychnine. Because of these facts, it is generally understood along the Pacific coast that it is unwise to eat shellfish taken from coasts exposed to the open sea where Gonyaulax may be abundant, in summer or early fall. For generations before the white men came, the Indians knew this. As soon as the red streaks appeared in the sea and the waves began to flicker at night with the mysterious blue-green fires, the tribal leaders forbade the taking of mussels until these warning signals should have passed. They even set guards at intervals along the beaches to warn inlanders who might come down for shellfish and be unable to read the language of the sea.

But usually the blaze and glitter of the sea, whatever its mean- 16 ing for those who produce it, implies no menace to man. Seen from the deck of a vessel in open ocean, a tiny, man-made observation point in the vast world of sea and sky, it has an eerie and unearthly quality. Man, in his vanity, subconsciously attributes a human origin to any light not of moon or stars or sun. Lights on the shore, lights moving over the water, mean lights kindled and controlled by other men, serving purposes understandable to the human mind. Yet here are lights that flash and fade away, lights that come and go for reasons meaningless to man, lights that have been doing this very thing over the eons of time in which there were no men to stir in vague disquiet.

On such a night of phosphorescent display Charles Darwin 17 stood on the deck of the *Beagle* as she plowed southward through the Atlantic off the coast of Brazil.

RACHEL CARSON

The sea from its extreme luminousness presented a wonderful and most beautiful appearance [he wrote in his diary]. Every part of the water which by day is seen as foam, glowed with a pale light. The vessel drove before her bows two billows of liquid phosphorus, and in her wake was a milky train. As far as the eye reached the crest of every wave was bright; and from the reflected light, the sky just above the horizon was not so utterly dark as the rest of the Heavens. It was impossible to behold this plain of matter, as it were melted and consuming by heat, without being reminded of Milton's description of the regions of Chaos and Anarchy.*

Like the blazing colors of the autumn leaves before they 18 wither and fall, the autumnal phosphorescence betokens the approach of winter. After their brief renewal of life the flagellates and the other minute algae dwindle away to a scattered few; so do the shrimps and the copepods, the glassworms and the comb jellies. The larvae of the bottom fauna have long since completed their development and drifted away to take up whatever existence is their lot. Even the roving fish schools have deserted the surface waters and have migrated into warmer latitudes or have found equivalent warmth in the deep, quiet waters along the edge of the continental shelf. There the torpor of semi-hibernation descends upon them and will possess them during the months of winter.

The surface waters now become the plaything of the winter 19 gales. As the winds build up the giant storm waves and roar along their crests, lashing the water into foam and flying spray, it seems that life must forever have deserted this place.

For the mood of the winter sea, read Joseph Conrad's descrip- 20 tion:

The greyness of the whole immense surface, the wind furrows upon the faces of the waves, the great masses of foam, tossed about and waving, like matted white locks, give to the sea in a gale an appearance of hoary age, lustreless, dull, without gleams, as though it had been created before light itself.**

But the symbols of hope are not lacking even in the grayness 21 and bleakness of the winter sea. On land we know that the apparent lifelessness of winter is an illusion. Look closely at the bare branches

*From *Charles Darwin's Diary of the Voyage of H.M.S. Beagle*, edited by Nora Barlow, 1934 edition, Cambridge University Press, p. 107.
**From *The Mirror of the Sea*, Kent edition, 1925, Doubleday-Page, p. 71.

 THE CHANGING YEAR

of a tree, on which not the palest gleam of green can be discerned. Yet, spaced along each branch are the leaf buds, all the spring's magic of swelling green concealed and safely preserved under the insulating, overlapping layers. Pick off a piece of the rough bark of the trunk; there you will find hibernating insects. Dig down through the snow into the earth. There are the eggs of next summer's grasshoppers; there are the dormant seeds from which will come the grass, the herb, the oak tree.

So, too, the lifelessness, the hopelessness, the despair of the winter sea are an illusion. Everywhere are the assurances that the cycle has come to the full, containing the means of its own renewal. There is the promise of a new spring in the very iciness of the winter sea, in the chilling of the water, which must, before many weeks, become so heavy that it will plunge downward, precipitating the overturn that is the first act in the drama of spring. There is the promise of new life in the small plantlike things that cling to the rocks of the underlying bottom, the almost formless polyps from which, in spring, a new generation of jellyfish will bud off and rise into the surface waters. There is unconscious purpose in the sluggish forms of the copepods hibernating on the bottom, safe from the surface storms, life sustained in their tiny bodies by the extra store of fat with which they went into this winter sleep. 22

Already, from the gray shapes of cod that have moved, unseen by man, through the cold sea to their spawning places, the glassy globules of eggs are rising into the surface waters. Even in the harsh world of the winter sea, these eggs will begin the swift divisions by which a granule of protoplasm becomes a living fishlet. 23

Most of all, perhaps, there is assurance in the fine dust of life that remains in the surface waters, the invisible spores of the diatoms, needing only the touch of warming sun and fertilizing chemicals to repeat the magic of spring. 24

COMPREHENSION

1. What is the author's main purpose? Support your answer with evidence from the essay.

2. What kinds of sea life appear in each season?

3. In her description, Carson indirectly describes the aquatic food chain. Explain this.

RHETORIC

1. Carson frequently uses metaphors in this essay. Many of them concern human feelings, agriculture, and commerce. Identify them, and explain their utility to the essay. Explain also the allusions to Joseph Conrad and Charles Darwin in paragraphs 17 and 20. Why are allusions to them especially appropriate?

2. Identify unfamiliar animals and places in the essay. What effect does Carson achieve by listing the names of unfamiliar creatures and places? Does she demand more of her audience than Eiseley? Explain.

3. How does Carson develop her introductory paragraph?

4. In Carson's description of the cycle of the seasons, time is a crucial structural device. Identify temporal transitional devices in this essay.

5. How does the image of time presented in the essay contribute to Carson's conclusion?

6. How does Carson use analogies to explain the seasons?

WRITING

1. Because the life of the sea has been deeply threatened by pollution in recent years, can you share Carson's view of the cycle of life in the sea? What can we do to protect the sea? Explain in an essay.

2. Our lives are full of cycles. Write an essay describing one of the following cycles: a college semester, a sports year, or a television season.

3. Select your favorite season, and in a process essay trace its natural rhythms.

BERTRAND RUSSELL

The Study of Mathematics

Bertrand Arthur William Russell (1872–1970) was one of the great philosophers, mathematicians, liberal political theorists, and authors of the twentieth century. His works are legion. From the early Principles of Mathematics *(1903) to his* An Inquiry into Meaning and Truth *(1940) and finally to his three-volume* Autobiography *(1967–1969), Russell demonstrated his multivarious talents as a writer and thinker. He was awarded the Nobel Prize in Literature in 1950. One aspect of Russell's career—his desire to explain science to lay people—is represented in the following essay.*

 n regard to every form of human activity it is necessary   1
that the question should be asked from time to time,
What is its purpose and ideal? In what way does it contribute to the beauty of human existence? As respects
those pursuits which contribute only remotely, by providing the
mechanism of life, it is well to be reminded that not the mere fact of

living is to be desired, but the art of living in the contemplation of great things. Still more in regard to those avocations which have no end outside themselves, which are to be justified, if at all, as actually adding to the sum of the world's permanent possessions, it is necessary to keep alive a knowledge of their aims, a clear prefiguring vision of the temple in which creative imagination is to be embodied.

Although tradition has decreed that the great bulk of educated men shall know at least the elements of the subject [of mathematics], the reasons for which the tradition arose are forgotten, buried beneath a great rubbish-heap of pedantries and trivialities. To those who inquire as to the purpose of mathematics, the usual answer will be that it facilitates the making of machines, the travelling from place to place, and the victory over foreign nations, whether in war or commerce. If it be objected that these ends—all of which are of doubtful value—are not furthered by the merely elementary study imposed upon those who do not become expert mathematicians, the reply, it is true, will probably be that mathematics trains the reasoning faculties. Yet the very men who make this reply are, for the most part, unwilling to abandon the teaching of definite fallacies, known to be such, and instinctively rejected by the unsophisticated mind of every intelligent learner. And the reasoning faculty itself is generally conceived, by those who urge its cultivation, as merely a means for the avoidance of pitfalls and a help in the discovery of rules for the guidance of practical life. All these are undeniably important achievements to the credit of mathematics; yet it is none of these that entitles mathematics to a place in every liberal education. 2

Mathematics, rightly viewed, possesses not only truth, but supreme beauty—a beauty cold and austere, like that of sculpture, without appeal to any part of our weaker nature, without the gorgeous trappings of painting or music, yet sublimely pure, and capable of a stern perfection such as only the greatest art can show. The true spirit of delight, the exaltation, the sense of being more than man, which is the touchstone of the highest excellence, is to be found in mathematics as surely as in poetry. What is best in mathematics deserves not merely to be learnt as a task, but to be assimilated as a part of daily thought, and brought again and again before the mind with ever-renewed encouragement. Real life is, to most men, a long second-best, a perpetual compromise between the ideal and the possible; but the world of pure reason knows no compromise, no practical limitations, no barrier to the creative activity embodying in splendid edifices the passionate aspiration after the perfect from which all great work springs. Remote from human passions, remote even from the pitiful facts of nature, the generations have gradually created an ordered cosmos, where pure thought can dwell as in its natural home, and 3 where one, at least, of our nobler impulses can escape from the dreary exile of the actual world.

So little, however, have mathematicians aimed at beauty, that hardly anything in their work has had this conscious purpose. Much, owing to irrepressible instincts, which were better than avowed beliefs, has been moulded by an unconscious taste; but much also has been spoilt by false notions of what was fitting. The characteristic excellence of mathematics is only to be found where the reasoning is rigidly logical: the rules of logic are to mathematics what those of structure are to architecture. In the most beautiful work, a chain of argument is presented in which every link is important on its own account, in which there is an air of ease and lucidity throughout, and the premises achieve more than would have been thought possible, by means which appear natural and inevitable. Literature embodies what is general in particular circumstances whose universal significance shines through their individual dress; but mathematics endeavours to present whatever is most general in its purity, without any irrelevant trappings.

COMPREHENSION

1.   What is Russell's thesis?

2.   In this essay, Russell compares and contrasts several disciplines or vocations to mathematics. Of which one does he approve? Of which ones does he disapprove?

3.   According to Russell, what are the reasons for studying mathematics?

RHETORIC

1.   Identify examples of connotative language in this essay.

2.   How many specific details appear in this essay? How does this affect the style of the essay?

3.   Describe the structure of this four-paragraph essay.

4.   Why does Russell compare mathematics to the arts? How is mathematics superior?

5.   What assumptions about the world of nature and human beings and of the mind underlie the essay?

6.   In paragraph 4, what method of definition does Russell use?

WRITING

1.   How would you define *beauty,* as Russell uses the word? Does your own idea of beauty differ from Russell's? How is mathematics "beautiful"? Write a brief essay on this topic.

2. Imitate the structure of this essay to organize your definition of engineering, literature, or medicine. Use specific details and examples from the field to clarify your extended definition.

3. Write your own personal essay entitled "My Study of Mathematics."

RICHARD SELZER

Letter to a Young Surgeon

Richard Selzer (1928–   ) is a surgeon with a full-time practice in New Haven, Connecticut, who began writing several hours each night after already establishing a successful medical career. His first book of essays, Mortal Lessons *(1974), established him as a prominent essayist specializing in the world of medicine and surgery. Selzer employs his elegant prose style in describing the often tragic, unpleasant, and painful world of medical patients. He is a contributor to popular magazines, and his essays have been collected in several books, among them* Confessions of a Knife *(1979) and* Letters to a Young Doctor *(1982). The following essay demonstrates Selzer's experience and expertise as a surgeon as well as his unique ability to describe the world of medicine in poetic and graceful terms.*

t this, the start of your surgical internship, it is well that you be told how to behave in an operating room. You cannot observe decorum unless you first know what decorum is. Say that you have already changed into a scrub suit, donned cap, mask and shoe covers. You have scrubbed your hands and been helped into your gown and gloves. Now stand out of the way. Eventually, your presence will be noticed by the surgeon, who will motion you to take up a position at the table. Surgery is not one of the polite arts, as are Quilting and Illuminating Manuscripts. Decorum in the operating room does not include doffing your cap in the presence of nurses. Even the old-time surgeons knew this and operated without removing their hats.

The first rule of conversation in the operating room is silence. It is a rule to be broken freely by the Master, for he is engaged in the art of teaching. The forceful passage of bacteria through a face mask during speech increases the contamination of the wound and therefore the possibility of infection in that wound. It is a risk that must be taken. By the surgeon, wittingly, and by the patient, unbeknownst. Say what you will about a person's keeping control over his own destiny, there are some things that cannot be helped. Being made use of for teaching purposes in the operating room is one of them. It is an inevitable, admirable and noble circumstance. Besides, I have placated Fate too long to believe that She would bring on wound infection as the complication of such a high enterprise.

Observe the least movement of the surgeon's hands. See how $\quad$ 3 he holds out his hand to receive the scalpel. See how the handle of it rides between his thumb and fingertips. The scalpel is the subtlest of the instruments, transmitting the nervous current in the surgeon's arm to the body of the patient. Too timidly applied, and it turns flabby, lifeless; too much pressure and it turns vicious. See how the surgeon applies the blade to the skin—holding it straight in its saddle lest he undercut and one edge of the incision be thinner than the other edge. The application of knife to flesh proclaims the master and exposes the novice. See the surgeon advancing his hand blindly into the abdomen as though it were a hollow in a tree. He is wary, yet needing to know. Will it be something soft and dead? Or a sudden pain in his bitten finger!

The point of the knife is called the *tang*, from the Latin word $\quad$ 4 for *touch*. The sharp curving edge is the *belly* of the blade. The tang is for assassins, the belly for surgeons. Enough! You will not hold this knife for a long time. Do not be impatient for it. Nor reckon the time. Ripen only. Over the course of your training you will be given ever more elaborate tasks to perform. But for now, you must watch and wait. Excessive ego, arrogance and self-concern in an intern are out of place, as they preclude love for the patient on the table. There is no room for clever disobedience here. For the knife is like fire. The small child yearns to do what his father does, and he steals matches from the man's pocket. The fire he lights in his hiding place is beautiful to him; he toasts marshmallows in it. But he is just as likely to be burned. And reverence for the teacher is essential to the accumulation of knowledge. Even a bad surgeon will teach if only by the opportunity to see what not to do.

You will quickly come to detect the difference between a true $\quad$ 5 surgeon and a mere product of the system. Democracy is not the best of all social philosophies in the selection of doctors for training in surgery. Anyone who so desires, and who is able to excel academically and who is willing to undergo the harsh training, can become a surgeon whether or not he is fit for the craft either manually or by temperament. If we continue to award licenses to the incompetent and the ill-suited, we shall be like those countries where work is given over not to those who can do it best, but to those who need it. That offers irritation enough in train stations; think of the result in airplane cockpits or operating rooms. Ponder long and hard upon this point. The mere decision to be a surgeon will not magically confer upon you the dexterity, compassion and calmness to do it.

Even on your first day in the operating room, you must look ahead to your last. An old surgeon who has lost his touch is like an old lion whose claws have become blunted, but not the desire to use them. Knowing when to quit and retire from the consuming passion of your life is instinctive. It takes courage to do it. But do it you must. No consideration of money, power, fame or fear of boredom may give you the slightest pause in laying down your scalpel when the first flagging of energy, bravery or confidence appears. To withdraw gracefully is to withdraw in a state of grace. To persist is to fumble your way to injury and ignominy.

Do not be dismayed by the letting of blood, for it is blood that animates this work, distinguishes it from its father, Anatomy. Red is the color in which the interior of the body is painted. If an operation be thought of as a painting in progress, and blood red the color of the brush, it must be suitably restrained and attract no undue attention; yet any insufficiency of it will increase the perishability of the canvas. Surgeons are of differing stripes. There are those who are slow and methodical, obsessive beyond all reason. These tortoises operate in a field as bloodless as a cadaver. Every speck of tissue in its proper place, every nerve traced out and brushed clean so that a Japanese artist could render it down to the dendrites. Should the contents of a single capillary be inadvertently shed, the whole procedure comes to a halt while Mr. Clean irrigates and suctions and mops and clamps and ties until once again the operative field looks like Holland at tulip time. Such a surgeon tells time not by the clock but by the calendar. For this, he is ideally equipped with an iron urinary bladder which he has disciplined to contract no more than once a day. To the drop-in observer, the work of such a surgeon is faultless. He gasps in admiration at the still life on the table. Should the same observer leave and return three hours later, nothing will have changed. Only a few more millimeters of perfection.

Then there are the swashbucklers who crash through the underbrush waving a machete, letting tube and ovary fall where they may. This surgeon is equipped with gills so that he can breathe under blood. You do not set foot in his room without a slicker and boots. Seasoned nurses quake at the sight of those arms, elbow-deep and *working*. It is said that one such surgeon entertained the other guests at a department Christmas party by splenectomizing a cat in thirty seconds from skin to skin.

Then there are the rest of us who are neither too timid nor too brash. We are just right. And now I shall tell you a secret. To be a good surgeon does not require immense technical facility. Compared

RICHARD SELZER

to a violinist it is nothing. The Japanese artist, for one, is skillful at double brushing, by which technique he lays on color with one brush and shades it off with another, both brushes being held at the same time and in the same hand, albeit with different fingers. Come to think of it, a surgeon, like a Japanese artist, ought to begin his training at the age of three, learning to hold four or five instruments at a time in the hand while suturing with a needle and thread held in the teeth. By the age of five he would be able to dismantle and reconstruct an entire human body from calvarium to calcaneus unassisted and in the time it would take one of us to recite the Hippocratic Oath. A more obvious advantage of this baby surgeon would be his size. In times of difficulty he could be lowered whole into the abdomen. There, he would swim about, repair the works, then give three tugs on a rope and ... Presto! Another gallbladder bites the dust.

In the absence of any such prodigies, each of you who is full-grown must learn to exist in two states—Littleness and Bigness. In your littleness you descend for hours each day through a cleft in the body into a tiny space that is both your workshop and your temple. Your attention in Lilliput is total and undistracted. Every artery is a river to be forded or dammed, each organ a mountain to be skirted or moved. At last, the work having been done, you ascend. You blink and look about at the vast space peopled by giants and massive furniture. Take a deep breath ... and you are Big. Such instantaneous hypertrophy is the process by which a surgeon reenters the outside world. Any breakdown in this resonance between the sizes causes the surgeon to live in a Renaissance painting where the depth perception is so bad.

Nor ought it to offend you that, a tumor having been successfully removed, and the danger to the patient having been circumvented, the very team of surgeons that only moments before had been a model of discipline and deportment comes loose at the seams and begins to wobble. Jokes are told, there is laughter, a hectic gaiety prevails. This is in no way to be taken as a sign of irreverence or callousness. When the men of the Kalahari return from the hunt with a haunch of zebra, the first thing everybody does is break out in a dance. It is a rite of thanksgiving. There will be food. They have made it safely home.

Man is the only animal capable of tying a square knot. During the course of an operation you may be asked by the surgeon to tie a knot. As drawing and coloring are the language of art, incising, suturing and knot tying are the grammar of surgery. A facility in knot tying is gained only by tying ten thousand of them. When the operation is completed, take home with you a package of leftover sutures. Light a fire in the fireplace and sit with your lover on a rug in front of the fire. Invite her to hold up her index finger, gently crooked in a gesture of beckoning. Using her finger as a strut, tie one of the threads about it in a square knot. Do this one hundred times. Now make a hundred grannies. Only then may you permit yourself to make love to her. This method of learning will not only enable you to master the art of knot tying, both grannies and square, it will bind you, however insecurely, to the one you love.

To do surgery without a sense of awe is to be a dandy—all 13 style and no purpose. No part of the operation is too lowly, too menial. Even when suturing the skin at the end of a major abdominal procedure, you must operate with piety, as though you were embellishing a holy reliquary. The suturing of the skin usually falls to the lot of the beginning surgeon, the sights of the Assistant Residents and Residents having been firmly set upon more biliary, more gastric glories. In surgery, the love of inconsiderable things must govern your life—ingrown toenails, thrombosed hemorrhoids, warts. Never disdain the common ordinary ailment in favor of the exotic or rare. To the patient every one of his ailments is unique. One is not to be amused or captivated by disease. Only to a woodpecker is a wormy tree more fascinating than one uninhabited. There is only absorption in your patient's plight. To this purpose, willingly accept the smells and extrusions of the sick. To be spattered with the phlegm, vomitus and blood of suffering is to be badged with the highest office.

The sutured skin is all of his operation that the patient will 14 see. It is your signature left upon his body for the rest of his life. For the patient, it is the emblem of his suffering, a reminder of his mortality. Years later, he will idly run his fingers along the length of the scar, and he will hush and remember. The good surgeon knows this. And so he does not overlap the edges of the skin, makes no dog-ears at the corners. He does not tie the sutures too tightly lest there be a row of permanent crosshatches. (It is not your purpose to construct a ladder upon which a touring louse could climb from pubis to navel and back.) The good surgeon does not pinch the skin with forceps. He leaves the proper distance between the sutures. He removes the sutures at the earliest possible date, and he uses sutures of the finest thread. All these things he does and does not do out of reverence for his craft and love for his patient. The surgeon who does otherwise ought to keep his hands in his pockets. At the end of the operation, cholecystectomy, say, the surgeon may ask you to slit open the gallbladder so that everyone in the room might examine the stones. Perform even this cutting with reverence as though the organ were still within the patient's body. You cut, and notice how the amber bile runs out, leaving a residue of stones. Faceted, shiny, they glisten. Almost at once, these wrested dewy stones surrender their warmth and

RICHARD SELZER

moisture; they grow drab and dull. The descent from jewel to pebble takes place before your eyes.

Deep down, I keep the vanity that surgery is the red flower 15 that blooms among the leaves and thorns that are the rest of Medicine. It is Surgery that, long after it has passed into obsolescence, will be remembered as the glory of Medicine. Then men shall gather in mead halls and sing of that ancient time when surgeons, like gods, walked among the human race. Go ahead. Revel in your Specialty; it is your divinity.

It is quest and dream as well. 16

The incision has been made. One expects mauve doves and 17 colored moths to cloud out of the belly in celebration of the longed-for coming. Soon the surgeon is greeted by the eager blood kneeling and offering its services. Tongues of it lap at his feet; flames and plumes hold themselves aloft to light his way. And he follows this guide that flows just ahead of him through rifts, along the edges of cliffs, picking and winding, leaping across chasms, at last finding itself and pooling to wait for him. But the blood cannot wait a moment too long lest it become a blob of coagulum, something annulled by its own puddling. The surgeon rides the patient, as though he were riding a burro down into a canyon. This body is beautiful to him, and he to it—he whom the patient encloses in the fist of his flesh. For months, ever since the first wild mitosis, the organs had huddled like shipwrecks. When would he come? Will he never come? And suddenly, into the sick cellar—fingers of light! The body lies stupefied at the moment of encounter. The cool air stirs the buried flesh. Even the torpid intestine shifts its slow coils to make way.

Now the surgeon must take care. The fatal glissade, once be- 18 gun, is not to be stopped. Does this world, too, he wonders, roll within the precincts of mercy? The questing dreamer leans into the patient to catch the subtlest sounds. He hears the harmonies of their two bloods, his and the patient's. They sing of death and the beauty of the rose. He hears the playing together of their two breaths. If Pythagoras is right, there is no silence in the universe. Even the stars make music as they move.

Only do not succumb to self-love. I know a surgeon who, 19 having left the room, is certain, beyond peradventure of doubt, that his disembodied radiance lingers on. And there are surgeons of such aristocratic posture that one refrains only with difficulty from slipping them into the nobility. As though they had risen from Mister to Doctor to Professor, then on to Baron, Count, Archduke, then further, to Apostle, Saint. I could go further.

Such arrogance can carry over to the work itself. There was a 20 surgeon in New Haven, Dr. Truffle, who had a penchant for long midline incisions—from sternum to pubis—no matter the need for exposure. Somewhere along the way, this surgeon had become annoyed by the presence of the navel, which, he decided, interrupted the pure line of his slice. Day in, day out, it must be gone around, either to the right or to the left. Soon, what was at first an annoyance became a hated impediment that must be got rid of. Mere circumvention was not enough. And so, one day, having arrived at the midpoint of his downstroke, this surgeon paused to cut out the navel with a neat ellipse of skin before continuing on down to the pubis. Such an elliptical incision when sutured at the close of the operation forms the continuous straight line without which this surgeon could not live. Once having cut out a navel (the first incidental umbilectomy, I suppose, was the hardest) and seeing the simple undeviate line of his closure, he vowed never again to leave a navel behind. Since he was otherwise a good surgeon, and very successful, it was not long before there were thousands of New Haveners walking around minus their belly buttons. Not that this interfered with any but the most uncommon of activities, but to those of us who examined them postoperatively, these abdomens had a blind, bland look. Years later I would happen upon one of these bellies and know at once the author of the incision upon it. Ah, I would say, Dr. Truffle has been here.

It is so difficult for a surgeon to remain "unconscious," retaining the clarity of vision of childhood, to know and be secure in his ability, yet be unaware of his talents. It is almost impossible. There are all too many people around him paying obeisance, pandering, catering, beaming, lusting. Yet he must try.   21

It is not enough to love your work. Love of work is a kind of self-indulgence. You must go beyond that. Better to perform endlessly, repetitiously, faithfully, the simplest acts, like trimming the toenails of an old man. By so doing, you will not say *Here I Am*, but *Here It Is*. You will not announce your love but will store it up in the bodies of your patients to carry with them wherever they go.   22

Many times over, you will hear otherwise sensible people say, "You have golden hands," or, "Thanks to you and God, I have recovered." (Notice the order in which the credit is given.) Such ill-directed praise has no significance. It is the patient's disguised expression of relief at having come through, avoided death. It is a private utterance, having nothing to do with you. Still, such words are enough to turn a surgeon's head, if any more turning were needed.   23

Avoid these blandishments at all cost. You are in service to your patients, and a servant should know his place. The world is topsy-turvy in which a master worships his servant. You are a kindly, firm, experienced servant, but a servant still. If any patient of mine were to attempt to bathe my feet, I'd kick over his basin, suspecting that he possessed not so much a genuine sentiment as a conventional   24 one. It is beneath your dignity to serve as an object of veneration or as the foil in an act of contrition. To any such effusion a simple "Thank you" will do. The rest is pride, and everyone knoweth before *what* that goeth.

Alexander the Great had a slave whose sole responsibility was   25
to whisper "Remember, you are mortal" when he grew too arrogant. Perhaps every surgeon should be assigned such a deflator. The surgeon is the mere instrument which the patient takes in his hand to heal himself. An operation, then, is a time of revelation, both physical and spiritual, when, for a little while, the secrets of the body are set forth to be seen, to be touched, and the surgeon himself is laid open to Grace.

An operation is a reenactment of the story of Jonah and the   26
Whale. In surgery, the patient is the whale who swallows up the surgeon. Unlike Jonah, however, the surgeon does not cry out *non serviam*, but willingly descends into the sick body in order to cut out of it the part that threatens to kill it. In an operation where the patient is restored to health, the surgeon is spewed out of the whale's body, and both he and his patient are healed. In an operation where the patient dies on the table, the surgeon, although he is rescued from the whale and the sea of blood, is not fully healed, but will bear the scars of his sojourn in the belly of the patient for the rest of his life.

COMPREHENSION

1. How do you know that this is not a true letter? Why has Selzer titled it a "letter"?

2. Assuming one did not know the author is a surgeon, what gives the "voice" of the essay its authority?

3. Summarize the advice that Selzer offers the young surgeon. What does he mean when he states, "Revel in your Specialty; it is your divinity" (paragraph 15)?

RHETORIC

1. With paragraph 3, there begins extensive use of the imperative. How does it impact on the tone of the essay? What relationship does it establish between the writer and the implied reader?

2. How does Selzer make effective use of figurative language in paragraphs 7, 8, and 10?

3. Paragraphs 7, 8, and 9 employ classification. What is Selzer classifying? What transitional device does Selzer use to unify these three paragraphs?

4. Why is there a break after paragraph 11? How does the beginning of paragraph 12 shift the focus of the essay?

5. What is the central image of paragraph 17? How do the various elements in the paragraph contribute to creating the image?

6. In the concluding paragraph, Selzer states, "An operation is a reenactment of the story of Jonah and the Whale." What other paragraphs in the essay reflect this analogy?

WRITING

1. In paragraph 15, Selzer suggests that surgeons are "like gods." Does the profession of surgery warrant this analogy? Why, or why not?

2. Develop a theme that makes a comparison between a profession and something else, for example, "Basketball players are like ballet dancers," "Novelists are like gods," or "Teachers are like parents." Write an essay based on the comparison you have chosen.

3. Write a "letter" to a novice college student. Instruct the student in what to expect and how to behave in college.

J. B. S. HALDANE

On Being the Right Size

John Burdon Saunderson Haldane (1892–1964) was a geneticist, biologist, and writer of science books for the lay reader. His best-known work is Animal Biology *(1972), written in collaboration with John S. Huxley. He also wrote* Adventures of a Biologist *(1940) and* Everything Has a History *(1951), a collection of essays. Haldane was famous for his ability to explain the abstract, often abstruse, ideas of modern science with concrete examples. "On Being the Right Size," which mixes mathematics and physics with insects and elephants, exemplifies Haldane's skill.*

 he most obvious differences between different animals are differences of size, but for some reason the zoologists have paid singularly little attention to them. In a large textbook of zoology before me I find no indication that the eagle is larger than the sparrow, or the hippopotamus bigger than the hare, though some grudging admissions are made in the case of the mouse and the whale. But yet it is easy to show that a hare could not be as large as a hippopotamus, or a whale as small as a herring.

1

For every type of animal there is a most convenient size, and a large change in size inevitably carries with it a change of form.

Let us take the most obvious of possible cases, and consider $\quad$ 2 a giant man sixty feet high—about the height of Giant Pope and Giant Pagan in the illustrated *Pilgrim's Progress* of my childhood. These monsters were not only ten times as high as Christian, but ten times as wide and ten times as thick, so that their total weight was a thousand times his, or about eighty to ninety tons. Unfortunately the cross sections of their bones were only a hundred times those of Christian, so that every square inch of giant bone had to support ten times the weight borne by a square inch of human bone. As the human thighbone breaks under about ten times the human weight, Pope and Pagan would have broken their thighs every time they took a step. This was doubtless why they were sitting down in the picture I remember. But it lessens one's respect for Christian and Jack the Giant Killer.

To turn to zoology, suppose that a gazelle, a graceful little $\quad$ 3 creature with long thin legs, is to become large, it will break its bones unless it does one of two things. It may make its legs short and thick, like the rhinoceros, so that every pound of weight has still about the same area of bone to support it. Or it can compress its body and stretch out its legs obliquely to gain stability, like the giraffe. I mention these two beasts because they happen to belong to the same order as the gazelle, and both are quite successful mechanically, being remarkably fast runners.

Gravity, a mere nuisance to Christian, was a terror to Pope, $\quad$ 4 Pagan, and Despair. To the mouse and any smaller animal it presents practically no dangers. You can drop a mouse down a thousand-yard mine shaft; and, on arriving at the bottom, it gets a slight shock and walks away, provided that the ground is fairly soft. A rat is killed, a man is broken, a horse splashes. For the resistance presented to movement by the air is proportional to the surface of the moving object. Divide an animal's length, breadth, and height each by ten; its weight is reduced to a thousandth, but its surface only to a hundredth. So the resistance to falling in the case of the small animal is relatively ten times greater than the driving force.

An insect, therefore, is not afraid of gravity; it can fall without $\quad$ 5 danger, and can cling to the ceiling with remarkably little trouble. It can go in for elegant and fantastic forms of support like that of the daddy-longlegs. But there is a force which is as formidable to an insect as gravitation to a mammal. This is surface tension. A man coming out of a bath carries with him a film of water of about one-fiftieth of an inch in thickness. This weighs roughly a pound. A wet mouse has to carry about its own weight of water. A wet fly has to lift many times its own weight and, as everyone knows, a fly once wetted by water or any other liquid is in a very serious position indeed. An

ON BEING THE RIGHT SIZE

insect going for a drink is in as great danger as a man leaning out over a precipice in search of food. If it once falls into the grip of the surface tension of the water—that is to say, gets wet—it is likely to remain so until it drowns. A few insects, such as waterbeetles, contrive to be unwettable; the majority keep well away from their drink by means of a long proboscis.

Of course tall land animals have other difficulties. They have 6 to pump their blood to greater heights than a man, and therefore, require a larger blood pressure and tougher blood-vessels. A great many men die from burst arteries, especially in the brain, and this danger is presumably still greater for an elephant or a giraffe. But animals of all kinds find difficulties in size for the following reason. A typical small animal, say a microscopic worm or rotifer, has a smooth skin through which all the oxygen it requires can soak in, a straight gut with sufficient surface to absorb its food, and a single kidney. Increase its dimensions tenfold in every direction, and its weight is increased a thousand times, so that if it is to use its muscles as efficiently as its miniature counterpart, it will need a thousand times as much food and oxygen per day and will excrete a thousand times as much of waste products.

Now if its shape is unaltered its surface will be increased only 7 a hundredfold, and ten times as much oxygen must enter per minute through each square millimetre of skin, ten times as much food through each square millimetre of intestine. When a limit is reached to their absorptive powers their surface has to be increased by some special device. For example, a part of the skin may be drawn out into tufts to make gills or pushed in to make lungs, thus increasing the oxygen-absorbing surface in proportion to the animal's bulk. A man, for example, has a hundred square yards of lung. Similarly, the gut, instead of being smooth and straight, becomes coiled and develops a velvety surface, and other organs increase in complication. The higher animals are not larger than the lower because they are more compli-cated. They are more complicated because they are larger. Just the same is true of plants. The simplest plants, such as the green algae growing in stagnant water or on the bark of trees, are mere round cells. The higher plants increase their surface by putting out leaves and roots. Comparative anatomy is largely the story of the struggle to increase surface in proportion to volume.

Some of the methods of increasing the surface are useful up 8 to a point, but not capable of a very wide adaptation. For example, while vertebrates carry the oxygen from the gills or lungs all over the body in the blood, insects take air directly to every part of their body by tiny blind tubes called tracheae which open to the surface at many different points. Now, although by their breathing movements they can renew the air in the outer part of the tracheal system, the oxygen

J. B. S. HALDANE

has to penetrate the finer branches by means of diffusion. Gases can diffuse easily through very small distances, not many times larger than the average length travelled by a gas molecule between collisions with other molecules. But when such vast journeys—from the point of view of a molecule—as a quarter of an inch have to be made, the process becomes slow. So the portions of an insect's body more than a quarter of an inch from the air would always be short of oxygen. In consequence hardly any insects are much more than half an inch thick. Land crabs are built on the same general plan as insects, but are much clumsier. Yet like ourselves they carry oxygen around in their blood, and are therefore able to grow far larger than any insects. If the insects had hit on a plan for driving air through their tissues instead of letting it soak in, they might well have become as large as lobsters, though other considerations would have prevented them from becoming as large as man.

Exactly the same difficulties attach to flying. It is an elementary principle of aeronautics that the minimum speed needed to keep an aeroplane of a given shape in the air varies as the square root of its length. If its linear dimensions are increased four times, it must fly twice as fast. Now the power needed for the minimum speed increases more rapidly than the weight of the machine. So the larger aeroplane, which weighs sixty-four times as much as the smaller, needs one hundred and twenty-eight times its horsepower to keep up. Applying the same principle to the birds, we find that the limit to their size is soon reached. An angel whose muscles developed no more power weight for weight than those of an eagle or a pigeon would require a breast projecting for about four feet to house the muscles engaged in working its wings, while to economize its weight, its legs would have to be reduced to mere stilts. Actually a large bird such as an eagle or kite does not keep in the air mainly by moving its wings. It is generally to be seen soaring, that is to say balanced on a rising column of air. And even soaring becomes more and more difficult with increasing size. Were this not the case eagles might be as large as tigers and as formidable to man as hostile aeroplanes.

But it is time that we pass to some of the advantages of size. One of the most obvious is that it enables one to keep warm. All warm-blooded animals at rest lose the same amount of heat from a unit area of skin, for which purpose they need a food-supply proportional to their surface and not to their weight. Five thousand mice weigh as much as a man. Their combined surface and food or oxygen consumption are about seventeen times a man's. In fact a mouse eats about one quarter its own weight of food every day, which is mainly used in keeping it warm. For the same reason small animals cannot live in cold countries. In the arctic regions there are no reptiles or amphibians, and no small mammals. The smallest mammal in Spitz-

ON BEING THE RIGHT SIZE

bergen is the fox. The small birds fly away in winter, while the insects die, though their eggs can survive six months or more of frost. The most successful mammals are bears, seals, and walruses.

Similarly, the eye is a rather inefficient organ until it reaches a large size. The back of the human eye on which an image of the outside world is thrown, and which corresponds to the film of a camera, is composed of a mosaic of "rod and cones" whose diameter is little more than a length of an average light wave. Each eye has about a half a million, and for two objects to be distinguishable their images must fall on separate rods or cones. It is obvious that with fewer but larger rods and cones we should see less distinctly. If they were twice as broad two points would have to be twice as far apart before we could distinguish them at a given distance. But if their size were diminished and their number increased we should see no better. For it is impossible to form a definite image smaller than a wave-length of light. Hence a mouse's eye is not a small-scale model of a human eye. Its rods and cones are not much smaller than ours, and therefore there are far fewer of them. A mouse could not distinguish one human face from another six feet away. In order that they should be of any use at all the eyes of small animals have to be much larger in proportion to their bodies than our own. Large animals on the other hand only require relatively small eyes, and those of the whale and elephant are little larger than our own.

For rather more recondite reasons the same general principle holds true of the brain. If we compare the brain-weights of a set of very similar animals such as the cat, cheetah, leopard, and tiger, we find that as we quadruple the body-weight the brain-weight is only doubled. The larger animal with proportionately larger bones can economize on brain, eyes, and certain other organs.

Such are a very few of the considerations which show that for every type of animal there is an optimum size. Yet although Galileo demonstrated the contrary more than three hundred years ago, people still believe that if a flea were as large as a man it could jump a thousand feet into the air. As a matter of fact the height to which an animal can jump is more nearly independent of its size than proportional to it. A flea can jump about two feet, a man about five. To jump a given height, if we neglect the resistance of the air, requires an expenditure of energy proportional to the jumper's weight. But if the jumping muscles form a constant fraction of the animal's body, the energy developed per ounce of muscle is independent of the size, provided it can be developed quickly enough in the small animal. As a matter of fact an insect's muscles, although they can contract more quickly than our own, appear to be less efficient; as otherwise a flea or grasshopper could rise six feet into the air.

J. B. S. HALDANE

COMPREHENSION

1. According to Haldane, how do people adapt to the problems of their size?

2. What are the effects of size on insects and mice?

3. Explain Haldane's thesis in your own words.

RHETORIC

1. Cite examples of personification in the essay. Why does Haldane use them?

2. Haldane is an adept practitioner of parallel structure. Cite examples of parallel structure in paragraphs 4 and 5.

3. Describe the simple dichotomy Haldane uses to organize his essay.

4. Because Haldane is describing neither a scene nor an event, he can use neither temporal nor spatial transitional devices to make his essay coherent. Identify the transitional devices he employs.

5. Many of Haldane's explanations involve mathematical formulas. Give specific examples of how he helps his reader understand his math.

6. Where does Haldane use hypothetical examples? Why are they effective?

WRITING

1. Based on Haldane's discussion of size, speculate on how the size of a country, of a business, of a family, or of a college might have limits.

2. Write an essay on the effect of size on a human institution.

3. Although explaining mathematical and physical laws is difficult, Haldane is successful. Write an essay in which you try to explain a physical law.

STEPHEN JAY GOULD

Darwin at Sea

Stephen Jay Gould (1941–   ), an acclaimed contemporary science writer, teaches biology, geology, and the history of science at Harvard University. He writes a monthly column, "This View of Life," for Natural History, *and he is the author of* Ever Since Darwin *(1977),* Ontogeny and Phylogeny *(1977), and* The Panda's Thumb *(1980). In this essay, which appeared originally in the September 1983 issue of* Natural History, *the author offers*

a revisionist interpretation of Darwin's discovery of evolution, the nature of scientific procedure, and the basis of scientific creativity.

harles Darwin and Abraham Lincoln were born on the same day—February 12, 1809. They are also linked in another curious way—for both must simultaneously play, and for similar reasons, the role of man and legend. In a nation too young to have mythic heroes, men and women must substitute. Hence we have Honest Abe, who frees the slaves from a pure sense of the burning injustice of it all, and who, as a young man, trudges for miles to return a few cents to a woman he has inadvertently short-changed. We may have a national or psychological need for such a Lincoln, but it also behooves historians to rescue the real, and wondrously complex, man from this factually inaccurate role. Likewise, science has no gods, and ancient sages are in strict short supply. Thus, historical figures again form the stuff of necessary legends. The apple beans Newton; Galileo drops his missiles from the Leaning Tower; and Darwin, alone at sea, transforms the intellectual world in splendid mental isolation. 1

The myth of the *Beagle*—that Darwin became an evolutionist by simple, unbiased observation of an entire world laid out before him during a five-year circumnavigation of the globe—fits all our romantic criteria for the best of legends: a young man, freed from the trammels of English society and its constraining presuppositions, face to face with nature, parrying his fresh and formidable mind with all the challenges provided by plants and animals and rocks throughout the world. He leaves England in 1831, planning to become a country parson upon his return. He lands in 1836, having seen evolution in the raw, understanding (albeit dimly) its implications and committed to a scientific life as revolutionary thinker. The chief catalyst: the Galápagos Islands. The main actors: tortoises, mockingbirds, and above all, the thirteen species of Darwin's finches that form the finest evolutionary laboratory offered to us anywhere in nature. 2

We may need such legends for that peculiar genre of literature known as the textbook. But it also behooves historians to rescue human beings from the legends in science—if only so that we may understand the process of scientific thought aright. Darwin, to begin, did not become an evolutionist until several months after his return to London—probably not until March 1837 (the *Beagle* docked in October 1836). He did not appreciate the evolutionary significance of the Galápagos while he was there, and he originally misunderstood the finches so thoroughly that he was barely able to reconstruct the story later from his sadly inadequate records. The legend of the finches may persist, but it has been splendidly debunked in two recent articles by 3

STEPHEN JAY GOULD

historian of science Frank Sulloway. His arguments form the basis of this essay. (For full details, see F. Sulloway, "Darwin and His Finches: The Evolution of a Legend," *Journal of the History of Biology*, Spring 1982, pp. 1-53; and "Darwin's Conversion: The Beagle Voyage and Its Aftermath," same journal, Fall 1982, pp. 325-96.)

The thirteen species of Darwin's finches form a closely knit genealogical group of widely divergent adaptations—a classic case of adaptive radiation into a series of roles and niches that would be filled by members of several bird families in more conventional, and crowded, continental situations. We get our major clues about the adaptive strategies of these species from the shapes of their bills. Three species of ground finches have large, medium, and small beaks, while a fourth has a sharp, pointed bill. All are adapted to eating differing seeds of appropriate size and hardness. Two species feed on cactus and another on mangroves. Four inhabit trees—of these, one is a vegetarian, while the other three eat large, medium, and small insects, respectively. A twelfth species closely resembles warblers in form and habits; while the thirteenth, the most curious of all, uses twigs and cactus spines as tools to extract insects from crevices in tree trunks. 4

The fine work of the great British ornithologist David Lack has taught us that the thirteen species evolved and became more distinct through a four-stage process of colonization, isolation and speciation, reinvasion, and perfecting of adaptation in competition. Lack also gave the birds their felicitous name of "Darwin's finches," in his 1947 book of the same title. But, contrary to anachronistic legend, this classic description of speciation is not a story that Darwin ever knew. 5

Darwin visited the Galápagos in September and October 1835, landing on only four of the islands. At sea, sometime during the middle of 1836, he penned a famous statement in his *Ornithological Notes*, a major source for the legend that his Galápagos experiences directly converted him to evolution and that the finches were instrumental in this process: 6

> When I recollect, the fact from the form of the body, shape of scales and general size, the Spaniards can at once pronounce, from which Island any Tortoise may have been brought. When I see these Islands in sight of each other, and possessed of but a scanty stock of animals, tenanted by these birds, but slightly differing in structure and filling the same place in Nature, I must suspect that they are only varieties. The only fact of a similar kind of which I am aware, is the constant asserted difference—between the wolf-like Fox of East and West Falkland Islds.—If there is the slightest foundation for these remarks the zoology of Archipelagos—will be well

DARWIN AT SEA

worth examining; for such facts would undermine the stability of Species.

First of all, the "birds" of this passage are Galápagos mock- 7 ingbirds, not finches. Darwin did not notice that three of the four islands he visited contained distinctly different mockingbirds. At face value, this statement seems to display a strong bias for evolution; it certainly raises the possibility. But a familiarity with nineteenth-century zoological terminology suggests an alternate interpretation. All creationists admitted that species often differentiated into mildly distinct forms in situations, as on island chains and archipelagoes, where populations could become isolated in differing circumstances of ecology and climate. These local races were called varieties, and they did not threaten the created and immutable character of a species' essence. Darwin is actually saying in this famous statement that either the tortoises and mockingbirds are merely varieties—in which case they do not threaten his creationist views—or they have become separate species, in which case they do. He briefly considered evolution by admitting the second possibility, but he ultimately rejected it while still at sea by tentatively deciding (incorrectly, for the mockingbirds at least) that the island forms were only varieties. Darwin's memories as an old man confirm this view that he only briefly flirted with, and then rejected, evolution while on the *Beagle*. He wrote to the German naturalist Otto Zacharias in 1877: "When I was on board the *Beagle* I believed in the permanence of species, but, as far as I can remember, vague doubts occasionally flitted across my mind."

A second statement, taken in conjunction with a misreading 8 of the *Ornithological Notes*, might also be considered as a confirmation that Darwin became an evolutionist at sea in 1836. He wrote in his pocket journal: "In July opened first notebook on 'Transmutation of Species'—Had been greatly struck from about Month of previous March on character of S. American fossils—and species on Galapagos Archipelago. These facts origin (especially latter) of all my views." We know that he started the first Transmutation notebook in July 1837, and we might therefore interpret the "previous March" as 1836, about the time that he penned the *Ornithological Notes* at sea. But the previous March might as well be 1837 when, as we shall soon see, he was in London learning from specialists at the Zoological Society about the true character of his Galápagos collections—a set of phenomena that he had failed to observe during his own visit.

What, then, did Darwin see on the Galápagos, and what did 9 he miss? Three groups of animals have come down through history as the most famous evolutionary laboratories of the Galápagos: mockingbirds, tortoises, and finches. Only for the mockingbirds did Darwin make the key observation that underlies the evolutionary tale later supplied (although, as we have seen, Darwin first explicitly rejected the evolutionary reading for a different interpretation). In short, he noticed that varying forms (later recognized as true species, although Darwin originally labeled them varieties) inhabited the different islands he visited. He landed first at Chatham Island, then at Charles, and he realized that he could distinguish the Charles Island mockingbird from the form he had previously collected at Chatham. Thus, he collected more mockingbirds wherever he landed and he carefully kept the separate island collections well labeled and distinct. He could not distinguish the Albermarle mockingbird, on the third island he visited, from the Chatham form, but the James Island bird represented a third, distinct variety (as he interpreted it).

Galápagos tortoises are all of one species, but virtually each 10
island has its own recognizable subspecies. These span an impressive range of form, from smooth, dome-shaped carapaces to the peculiar saddlebacks, with a pronounced hump in the carapace just above the head. Darwin missed this story completely. He never even noted the saddlebacks. His concept of this species virtually guaranteed that he would not be able to make the key observation.

Nicholas Lawson, the vice-governor, told Darwin that "the 11
tortoises differed from the different islands, and that he could with certainty tell from which island any one was brought" (although distinctions abound, this statement is overly optimistic and modern experts cannot always distinguish each island). But Darwin, by his own admission, made little of this information, writing in the 1845 edition of the *Beagle Voyage*:

> I did not for some time pay sufficient attention to this statement, and I had already partially mingled together the collections from two of the islands. I never dreamed that islands, about fifty or sixty miles apart, and most of them in sight of each other, formed of precisely the same rocks, placed under quite similar climate, rising to a nearly equal height, would have been differently tenanted.

As the result of an error in classification widely current at the 12
time, Darwin was ill-disposed to consider the differences between islands as evolutionarily (or even taxonomically) meaningful. Darwin accepted the general view that the Galápagos tortoise was not taxonomically distinct but was the same creature as *Testudo indicus*, the giant land tortoise of the Aldabra Islands in the Indian Ocean. It had only recently been brought, so the false story continued, to the Galápagos by buccaneers. Hence, differences among islands, if they existed at all, could only represent immediate and superficial varietal distinctions inspired by harsh climates at the time of introduction. Moreover,

Darwin never saw live saddleback tortoises. He only observed living tortoises on James and Chatham islands, and both contain nearly indistinguishable versions of the dome-shaped form.

Still, Darwin cannot be entirely excused from a charge of some 13 carelessness in observation. He did have an opportunity to observe the saddleback form but either failed to do so or recorded no impression. The Charles Island race was extinct when Darwin landed, but carapaces were abundant at the settlement there, where they were commonly used as flowerpots. Moreover, Darwin showed singularly little interest in preserving specimens for comparison among islands, a sure sign that he did not regard Lawson's statement as significant (much to his later regret). Captain Fitzroy took thirty large Chatham tortoises on board to beef up the *Beagle's* supply of fresh meat during the long Pacific crossing. Sulloway remarks:

> But Darwin and the other crew members gradually ate their way through the evidence that eventually, in the form of hearsay, was to revolutionize the biological sciences. Regrettably, not one of the thirty Chatham Island carapaces reached England, having all been thrown overboard with the other inedible remains.

Darwin's reaction to the Galápagos finches was even more 14 replete with error and misunderstanding. Again, he showed no appreciation of the importance of differences between islands. In fact, he didn't even bother to record or label the islands from which he had procured his specimens. Only three of his thirty-one finches are identified by island in the *Ornithological Notes*, all members of a highly distinctive species that Darwin remembered seeing only on James Island. He later wrote with regret in the *Voyage of the Beagle*: "Unfortunately most of the specimens of the finch tribe were mingled together." Secondly, he failed completely to collect any finches on one of the islands he visited—Albemarle. True, he was there for only part of a day, but his own diary records an abundance of easily collectable finches at a spring they visited near Bank's Cove: "To our disappointment the little pits in the Sandstone contained scarcely a gallon of water and that not good. It was however sufficient to draw together all the little birds in the country; Doves and Finches swarmed around its margin."

Third, with the exception of cactus and warbler finches, Dar- 15 win failed to observe any distinction in diet among the species and believed erroneously that they all ate the same kinds of food. Thus, he could not have reconstructed our modern story, even if he had been inclined to evolutionary views.

Fourth, Darwin's entire style of collection on the Galápagos 16

STEPHEN JAY GOULD

strongly reflected his creationist presuppositions. Evolutionists see variation as fundamental, as the raw material of evolutionary change. Species can only be well characterized by collecting many specimens and defining the spectrum of variation. Creationists believe that each species is endowed with a fixed essence. Variation is a mere nuisance, a confusing array of environmentally induced departures from an ideal form. Creationists tend to gather a limited number of specimens from each species and to concentrate on procuring individuals closest to the essential form. Darwin collected very few specimens, generally only a male and female of each species. In all, he procured but thirty-one finches from the Galápagos. By contrast, a 1905-06 California Academy of Sciences expedition, sent out to study evolution explicitly, brought back more than 8,000 specimens.

Fifth, and most importantly, the finches tell no evolutionary 17 tale unless you recognize that, despite their outward differences in form and behavior, all form a tightly knit genealogical group. But Darwin, while on the Galápagos, was fooled by the stunning diversity and failed to recognize Darwin's finches as a taxonomic entity. He referred the cactus finch to a family of birds that includes orioles and meadowlarks, and he misclassified the warbler finch as either a wren or warbler. Those that he recognized as finches, he divided into two distantly related groups within the family. Sulloway remarks: "As for Darwin's supposed insight into evolution by adaptive radiation while he was still in the Galápagos, the more the various species of finch exhibited this remarkable phenomenon, the more Darwin mistook them at the time for the forms they were mimicking."

The theoretical source of Darwin's error lies in a fairly arcane 18 principle of the creationist style of taxonomy that he followed. If animals are created according to a rational and general plan in the Deity's mind, then certain "key" characters might be clues to taxonomic structure at different levels. For example, variation in such "superficial" characters as size and shape might define different species, while variation in such "fundamental" traits as the form of essential organs might record the more important differences between genera and families. Ideally, a hierarchy of key characters should define taxonomic levels. Darwin tried to follow such a system in his preliminary *Beagle* classifications. Species within a bird genus should differ in plumage, while genera should be separated by such characters as the form of the beak. Darwin's finches are all similar in plumage, but differ greatly in their styles of feeding and, consequently, in the shapes of their beaks. By Darwin's creationist key character hierarchy, they belonged to different genera or families.

The key character hierarchy makes no sense in an evolution- 19 ary context. Characters that define genera in one situation might vary widely among species within another group. Bills may define feeding

 DARWIN AT SEA

types, and feeding types may usually distinguish genera on continents. But if only one kind of small bird manages to reach an oceanic archipelago and then radiates, in the absence of competitors, into a wide range of niches and feeding types, then this usual criterion for genera will now differ among closely related species. In the blooming and buzzing confusion of evolution, as opposed to the order of a creator's mind, it all depends upon what part of the body becomes subject to adaptive modification. Behavior and plumage in one place; feeding and beak shape in another. There is no such thing as an invariably "specific" or "generic" character.

In summary, then, Darwin entered and left the Galápagos as 20 a creationist, and his style of collection throughout the visit reflected his theoretical stance. Several months later, compiling his notes at sea during the long hours of a Pacific crossing, he briefly flirted with evolution while thinking about tortoises and mockingbirds, not finches. But he rejected this heresy and docked in England, October 2, 1836, still a creationist although with nascent doubts.

This retelling of the finch story should be welcome because it 21 squares so much better than the legend with Darwin's use of the Galápagos finches throughout his later writing. He never mentioned them in any of the four *Transmutation Notebooks*, which he kept from 1837 to 1839 and which form the foundation for his later work. They receive only passing notice in the first (1839) edition of the *Voyage of the Beagle*. To be sure, the second edition (1845) does contain this prophetic statement, written after Darwin had learned that the finches form a closely knit genealogical group.

> Seeing this gradation and diversity of structure in one small, intimately related group of birds, one might really fancy that from an original paucity of birds in this archipelago, one species had been taken and modified for different ends.

But if the finches made such a belated impression, the impact 22 didn't seem to last. Darwin's finches are not mentioned at all in the *Origin of Species* (1859); the ornithological star of that great book is the domesticated pigeon. Sulloway concludes, rightly I think:

> Contrary to the legend, Darwin's finches do not appear to have inspired his earliest theoretical views on evolution, even after he finally became an evolutionist in 1837; rather it was his evolutionary views that allowed him, retrospectively, to understand the complex case of the finches.

Darwin returned to England in 1836 as an ambitious young 23 man, anxious to make his mark in science; his later, courtly modesty as an old man should not be allowed to mask this youthful vigor. He knew that the key to his reputation lay in the valuable specimens he had collected on the *Beagle*, and thus he made determined and successful efforts to farm them out to the best specialists and to procure funds for publication of the results. In March 1837 he moved to London to be near the various experts who were studying his specimens. He began a series of meetings with these men, finally learned the true character of his material, and emerged within a month or two as an evolutionist.

He wrote, in the famous entry in his pocket journal cited earlier, that the character of South American fossils and species of the Galápagos had been the primary catalysts of his evolutionary conversion. Richard Owen, Britain's most eminent vertebrate paleontologist, had agreed to study the fossils and informed Darwin that they represented different, usually larger versions of distinctive animals that still inhabit South America. Darwin recognized that the best interpretation of this "law of succession" cast the ancient forms as evolutionary ancestors of altered modern animals. 24

The famous ornithologist John Gould (no relation) had taken charge of the *Beagle*'s birds. Darwin met with him toward the middle of March and learned that the three forms of mockingbirds were clearly distinct at the species level, not mere and superficial varieties of a single, created form. Darwin had already proclaimed that such a conclusion (which he had previously rejected) "would undermine the stability of species." Moreover, Gould informed him that twenty-five of his twenty-six Galápagos land birds were new species, but clearly allied to related forms on the South American mainland. Darwin integrated this spatial information with the temporal data that Owen had supplied, and he wavered further toward evolution. The distinct Galápagos birds must be evolutionary descendants of mainland colonists from South America. Darwin was now fully primed for an evolutionary reading of the finches, and Gould's correction of Darwin's errors furnished this piece of the puzzle as well (although it never drove Gould himself to adopt evolutionary views). 25

Although a creationist in taxonomy, Gould saw right away that bills could not be used as a key character to separate genera of Galápagos finches. He recognized that these birds were not, as Darwin had thought, a heterogeneous assemblage of divergent finches with an unrelated warbler and oriole thrown in, but a peculiar group of thirteen closely related species, which he placed in a single genus with three subgenera. "The bill appears to form only a secondary character," Gould proclaimed. Darwin finally had the basis of an evolutionary story. 26

Darwin was exhilarated as he converted to evolution and prepared to reread his entire voyage in this new light. But he was also 27 acutely embarrassed because he now realized that his failure to separate finches by islands, no particular problem in a creationist context, had been a serious and lamentable lapse. He couldn't do much with his own collection, beyond calling upon a faulty and fading memory; but fortunately, three of his shipmates had also collected finches—and since they (ironically) had not collected with any particular theory in mind that suggested an irrelevancy for locality data, they had recorded the islands of collection. As a further irony, one of these collections had been made by Captain Fitzroy himself, later Darwin's implacable foe and the man who stalked around the British Association meeting where Huxley creamed Wilberforce, holding a Bible above his head and exclaiming, "the Book, the Book." (Fitzroy's collection included twenty-one finches, all labeled by island. Darwin also had access to the smaller collections of his servant Syms Covington and of Harry Fuller, who had spent a week collecting with him on James Island.)

Darwin therefore tried to reconstruct the localities of his own 28 specimens by comparing them with the accurately labeled collections of his shipmates and, unfortunately as it turned out, by assuming that the finch story would resemble that of the mockingbirds—with certain species confined to definite islands. But since most of the finch species inhabit several islands, this procedure led to a large number of errors. Sulloway reports that substantial doubt still exists about the accuracy of locality information for eight of fifteen among Darwin's "type" (or name bearing) specimens of finches. No wonder he was never able to make a clear and coherent story of Darwin's finches. No wonder, perhaps, that they never even appeared in the *Origin of Species*.

Why, in conclusion, is this correction of the finch legend of 29 any great importance? Are the two stories really all that different? Darwin, in either case, was greatly influenced by evidence from the Galápagos. In the first, and false, version he sees it for himself while on the visit. In the second, modified account he requires a nudge (and some substantial corrections) from his friends when he returns to London.

I find a world of difference between the tales for what they 30 imply about the nature of creativity. The first (false) version upholds the romantic and empirical view that genius attains its status from an ability to see nature through eyes unclouded by the prejudices of surrounding culture and philosophical presupposition. The idea that such a thing is even possible has nurtured most legends in the history of science and purveys seriously false views about the process of scientific thought. Human beings cannot escape their presuppositions and see "purely"; Darwin functioned as an active creationist all through the *Beagle* voyage. Creativity is not an escape from culture but a unique use of its opportunities combined with a clever end run around its constraints. Scientific accomplishment is also a community activity, not a hermit's achievement. Where would Darwin have been in 1837 without Gould, Owen, and the active scientific life of London and Cambridge?

Once we abandon the alluring, but fallacious, image of Darwin winning his intellectual battle utterly alone at sea, we can ask the really interesting question that begins to probe Darwin's particular genius. Gould was the expert. Gould saw the story right. Gould, a staunch creationist in taxonomy, nonetheless recognized that he had to abandon beaks as key characters. Darwin was able to accomplish none of this. But Darwin, not Gould, saw that all the pieces required a stunningly new explanation—evolution—to make a coherent story. The amateur triumphed when the stakes were highest, while the professional got the details right and missed the organizing theme. 31

Darwin functioned this way all his life. Somehow, as an amateur, he could cut through older patterns of thought to glimpse new modes of explanation that might better fit an emerging, detailed story constructed by experts who, somehow, could not take the big and final step. But Darwin worked with his culture and with his colleagues. Science is a collective endeavor, but some individuals operate with an enlarged vision—and we would like to know how and why. This is one of the hardest questions we can ask, and I propose no general solution. But we do need to clear away heroic legends before we can begin. 32

COMPREHENSION

1.   State, in your own words, the thesis of this essay.

2.   Summarize the "myth" and "reality" of Darwin's trip to the Galápagos. How did he hit on the idea of evolution? Where did he go badly astray? What, according to Gould, apparently saved this "amateur"?

3.   What is the difference, as seen in Gould's account, between the way the creationist and the evolutionist view variation? How do these differing views affect collection of specimens?

RHETORIC

1.   Using context clues, a dictionary, or scientific textbooks, explain the following terms: *adaptation, adaptive radiation, species* (paragraph 4); *colonization, isolation and speciation, reinvasion* (paragraph 5); *ecology* (paragraph 7); *classification, taxonomically* (paragraph 12); *variation* (paragraph 16); *genus* (paragraph 18); and *vertebrate paleontologist* (paragraph 24). To what branch of science do most of these terms refer? How does the use of these terms affect the tone of the essay? What do they presuppose of the essay's audience?

2.   How does Gould's word choice reflect style and tone? Does the language tend to be general or specific, abstract or concrete?

 DARWIN AT SEA

3. What paragraphs constitute Gould's introduction? What is the thesis? Identify three unique aspects of this introduction. What paragraph comprise the ending? What conclusions does the author draw from the evidence?

4. What varieties of evidence does Gould use? Why is the cumulative weight of this evidence especially effective?

5. Does Gould use inductive or deductive reasoning in this essay? Explain.

6. This essay is rich in a variety of major rhetorical strategies. Identify five of them, and point out notably successful examples of the method.

WRITING

1. Gould declares, "Creativity is not an escape from culture but a unique use of its opportunities combined with a clever end run around its constraints" (paragraph 30). Do you agree with this definition or a more "romantic" one? Explain.

2. Gould accumulates different kinds of evidence to relate particular causes by a specific effect. Write an essay on some topic in science in which you cite evidence you have gathered to relate causes and effects.

3. Research a notable man or woman of science, and write a paper on the myths and realities surrounding the scientist's theories.

4. Write a brief biography of a scientist, focusing on the time in that individual's life when a key creative moment led to a notable discovery.

5. Define the nature of scientific creativity. Evaluate whether scientific creativity differs from other forms of creativity.

13

Civilization

OLIVER GOLDSMITH

National Prejudices

Oliver Goldsmith (1730–1774), the son of an Anglican curate, was an Anglo-Irish essayist, poet, novelist, dramatist, and journalist. His reputation as an enduring figure in English literature is based on his novel, The Vicar of Wakefield *(1766); his play* She Stoops to Conquer *(1773); his major peom,* The Deserted Village *(1770); and the essays and satiric letters collected in* The Bee *(1759) and* The Citizen of the World *(1762). In this essay, Goldsmith argues quietly for a new type of citizen who can transcend the xenophobia governing national behavior.*

 s I am one of that sauntering tribe of mortals, who spend the greatest part of their time in taverns, coffee houses, and other places of public resort, I have thereby an opportunity of observing an infinite variety of characters, which, to a person of a contemplative turn, is a much higher entertainment than a view of all the curiosities of art or nature. In one of these, my late rambles, I accidentally fell into the company of half a dozen gentlemen, who were engaged in a warm dispute about some

1

political affair; the decision of which, as they were equally divided in their sentiments, they thought proper to refer to me, which naturally drew me in for a share of the conversation.

Amongst a multiplicity of other topics, we took occasion to   2
talk of the different characters of the several nations of Europe; when one of the gentlemen, cocking his hat, and assuming such an air of importance as if he had possessed all the merit of the English nation in his own person, declared that the Dutch were a parcel of avaricious wretches; the French a set of flattering scycophants; that the Germans were drunken sots, and beastly gluttons; and the Spaniards proud, haughty, and surly tyrants; but that in bravery, generosity, clemency, and in every other virtue, the English excelled all the rest of the world.

This very learned and judicious remark was received with a   3
general smile of approbation by all the company—all, I mean, but your humble servant; who, endeavoring to keep my gravity as well as I could, and reclining my head upon my arm, continued for some time in a posture of affected thoughtfulness, as if I had been musing on something else, and did not seem to attend to the subject of con-versation; hoping by these means to avoid the disagreeable necessity of explaining myself, and thereby depriving the gentleman of his im-aginary happiness.

But my pseudo-patriot had no mind to let me escape so easily.   4
Not satisfied that his opinion should pass without contradiction, he was determined to have it ratified by the suffrage of every one in the company; for which purpose addressing himself to me with an air of inexpressible confidence, he asked me if I was not of the same way of thinking. As I am never forward in giving my opinion, especially when I have reason to believe that it will not be agreeable; so, when I am obliged to give it, I always hold it for a maxim to speak my real sentiments. I therefore told him that, for my own part, I should not have ventured to talk in such a peremptory strain, unless I had made the tour of Europe, and examined the manners of these several nations with great care and accuracy: that, perhaps, a more impartial judge would not scruple to affirm that the Dutch were more frugal and industrious, the French more temperate and polite, the Germans more hardy and patient of labour and fatigue, and the Spaniards more staid and sedate, than the English; who, though undoubtedly brave and generous, were at the same time rash, headstrong, and impetuous; too apt to be elated with prosperity, and to despond in adversity.

I could easily perceive that all the company began to regard   5
me with a jealous eye before I had finished my answer, which I had no sooner done, that the patriotic gentleman observed, with a con-temptuous sneer, that he was greatly surprised how some people could have the conscience to live in a country which they did not love, and to enjoy the protection of a government, to which in their

OLIVER GOLDSMITH

hearts they were inveterate enemies. Finding that by this modest declaration of my sentiments I had forfeited the good opinion of my companions, and given them occasion to call my political principles in question, and well knowing that it was in vain to argue with men who were so very full of themselves, I threw down my reckoning and retired to my own lodgings, reflecting on the absurd and ridiculous nature of national prejudice and prepossession.

Among all the famous sayings of antiquity, there is none that 6 does greater honour to the author, or affords greater pleasure to the reader (at least if he be a person of a generous and benevolent heart), than that of the philosopher, who, being asked what "countryman he was," replied, that he was, "a citizen of the world."—How few are there to be found in modern times who can say the same, or whose conduct is consistent with such a profession!—We are now become so much Englishmen, Frenchmen, Dutchmen, Spaniards, or Germans, that we are no longer citizens of the world; so much the natives of one particular spot, or members of one petty society, that we no longer consider ourselves as the general inhabitants of the globe, or members of that grand society which comprehends the whole human kind.

Did these prejudices prevail only among the meanest and low- 7 est of the people, perhaps they might be excused, as they have few, if any, opportunities of correcting them by reading, travelling, or conversing with foreigners; but the misfortune is, that they infect the minds, and influence the conduct, even of our gentlemen; of those, I mean, who have every title to this appellation but an exemption from prejudice, which however, in my opinion, ought to be regarded as the characteristical mark of a gentleman; for let a man's birth be ever so high, his station ever so exalted, or his fortune ever so large, yet if he is not free from national and other prejudices, I should make bold to tell him, that he had a low and vulgar mind, and had no just claim to the character of a gentleman. And in fact, you will always find that those are most apt to boast of national merit, who have little or no merit of their own to depend on; than which, to be sure, nothing is more natural: the slender vine twists around the sturdy oak, for no other reason in the world but because it has not strength sufficient to support itself.

Should it be alleged in defense of national prejudice, that it is 8 the natural and necessary growth of love to our country, and that therefore the former cannot be destroyed without hurting the latter, I answer, that this is a gross fallacy and delusion. That it is the growth of love to our country, I will allow; but that it is the natural and necessary growth of it, I absolutely deny. Superstition and enthusiasm too are the growth of religion; but who ever took it in his head to affirm that they are the necessary growth of this noble principle? They are, if you will, the bastard sprouts of this heavenly plant, but not its natural and genuine branches, and may safely enough be lopped off, without doing any harm to the parent stock; nay, perhaps, till once they are lopped off, this goodly tree can never flourish in perfect health and vigour.

Is it not very possible that I may love my own country, without hating the natives of other countries? that I may exert the most heroic bravery, the most undaunted resolution, in defending its laws and liberty, without despising all the rest of the world as cowards and poltroons? Most certainly it is; and if it were not—But why need I suppose what is absolutely impossible?—But if it were not, I must own, I should prefer the title of the ancient philosopher, viz. a citizen of the world, to that of an Englishman, a Frenchman, a European, or to any other appellation whatever. 9

COMPREHENSION

1. Why does Goldsmith maintain that he is "a citizen of the world"? According to the author, could such an individual also be a patriot? Explain.

2. What connection does Goldsmith establish between national prejudices and the conduct of gentlemen? Why does he allude to the manners of gentlemen?

3. Compare and contrast Goldsmith's observations with those of Priestley in "Wrong Ism."

RHETORIC

1. Locate in the essay examples of the familiar style in writing. What is the relationship between this style and the tone and substance of the essay?

2. Explain the metaphors at the end of paragraphs 7 and 8.

3. What is the relevance of the introductory narrative, with its description of characters, to the author's declaration of thesis? Where does the author state his proposition concerning national prejudices?

4. Analyze the function of classification and contrast in paragraphs 2 to 5. How does the entire essay serve as a pattern of definition?

5. Examine the pattern of reasoning involved in the author's presentation of his argument in the essay, notably in paragraphs 6 to 8. What appeals to emotion and to reason does he make?

6. Assess the rhetorical effectiveness of Goldsmith's concluding paragraph.

WRITING

1. Why has it been difficult to eliminate the problem that Goldsmith posed in 1765? Are we better able today to function as citizens of the world? In what ways? What role does the United Nations play in this issue? What factors contribute to a new world citizenry? Explore these questions in an essay.

2. Write an argumentative essay on the desirability of world government or on the need to be a citizen of the world.

3. Write a paper on contemporary national prejudices—from the viewpoint of an ingenious foreigner.

JOHN STEINBECK

Americans and the Land

John Steinbeck (1902–1968) was born in California, the setting for some of his best fiction. Steinbeck's fiction of the 1930s, including The Pastures of Heaven *(1932),* Tortilla Flat *(1935),* In Dubious Battle *(1936),* Of Mice and Men *(1937), and the Pulitzer Prize-winning epic* The Grapes of Wrath *(1939), offers one of the best imaginative presentations of the American Depression. Steinbeck won the Nobel Prize in Literature in 1962 for "realistic and imaginative writings, distinguished as they are by a sympathetic humor and a social perception." In this section from* America and Americans *(1966), Steinbeck offers a probing, critical appraisal of American social development.*

 have often wondered at the savagery and thoughtlessness with which our early settlers approached this rich continent. They came at it as though it were an enemy, which of course it was. They burned the forests and changed the rainfall; they swept the buffalo from the plains, blasted the streams, set fire to the grass, and ran a reckless scythe through the virgin and noble timber. Perhaps they felt that it was limitless and could never be exhausted and that a man could move on to new wonders endlessly. Certainly there are many examples to the contrary, but to a large extent the early people pillaged the country as though they hated it, as though they held it temporarily and might be driven off at any time.

This tendency toward irresponsibility persists in very many of us today; our rivers are poisoned by reckless dumping of sewage and toxic industrial wastes, the air of our cities is filthy and dangerous to breathe from the belching of uncontrolled products from combustion of coal, coke, oil, and gasoline. Our towns are girdled with wreckage and the debris of our toys—our automobiles and our packaged pleasures. Through uninhibited spraying against one enemy we have

 AMERICANS AND THE LAND

destroyed the natural balances our survival requires. All these evils can and must be overcome if America and Americans are to survive; but many of us still conduct ourselves as our ancestors did, stealing from the future for our clear and present profit.

Since the river-polluters and the air-poisoners are not criminal   3
or even bad people, we must presume that they are heirs to the early conviction that sky and water are unowned and that they are limitless. In the light of our practices here at home it is very interesting to me to read of the care taken with the carriers of our probes into space to make utterly sure that they are free of pollution of any kind. We would not think of doing to the moon what we do every day to our own dear country.

When the first settlers came to America and dug in on the   4
coast, they huddled in defending villages hemmed in by the sea on one side and by endless forests on the other, by Red Indians and, most frightening, the mystery of an unknown land extending nobody knew how far. And for a time very few cared or dared to find out. Our first Americans organized themselves and lived in a state of military alertness; every community built its blockhouse for defense. By law the men went armed and were required to keep their weapons ready and available. Many of them wore armor, made here or imported; on the East Coast, they wore the cuirass and helmet, and the Spaniards on the West Coast wore both steel armor and heavy leather to turn arrows.

On the East Coast, and particularly in New England, the colo-   5
nists farmed meager lands close to their communities and to safety. Every man was permanently on duty for the defense of his family and his village; even the hunting parties went into the forest in force, rather like raiders than hunters, and their subsequent quarrels with the Indians, resulting in forays and even massacres, remind us that the danger was very real. A man took his gun along when he worked the land, and the women stayed close to their thick-walled houses and listened day and night for the signal of alarm. The towns they settled were permanent, and most of them exist today with their records of Indian raids, of slaughter, of scalpings, and of punitive counter-raids. The military leader of the community became the chief authority in time of trouble, and it was a long time before danger receded and the mystery could be explored.

After a time, however, brave and forest-wise men drifted   6
westward to hunt, to trap, and eventually to bargain for the furs which were the first precious negotiable wealth America produced for trade and export. Then trading posts were set up as centers of collection and the exploring men moved up and down the rivers and crossed the mountains, made friends for mutual profit with the Indians, learned the wilderness techniques, so that these explorer-trad-

JOHN STEINBECK

ers soon dressed, ate, and generally acted like the indigenous people around them. Suspicion lasted a long time, and was fed by clashes sometimes amounting to full-fledged warfare; but by now these Americans attacked and defended as the Indians did.

For a goodly time the Americans were travelers, moving about the country collecting its valuables, but with little idea of permanence; their roots and their hearts were in the towns and the growing cities along the eastern edge. The few who stayed, who lived among the Indians, adopted their customs and some took Indian wives and were regarded as strange and somehow treasonable creatures. As for their half-breed children, while the tribe sometimes adopted them they were unacceptable as equals in the eastern settlements. 7

Then the trickle of immigrants became a stream, and the population began to move westward—not to grab and leave but to settle and live, they thought. The newcomers were of peasant stock, and they had their roots in a Europe where they had been landless, for the possession of land was the requirement and the proof of a higher social class than they had known. In America they found beautiful and boundless land for the taking—and they took it. 8

It is little wonder that they went land-mad, because there was so much of it. They cut and burned the forests to make room for crops; they abandoned their knowledge of kindness to the land in order to maintain its usefulness. When they had cropped out a piece they moved on, raping the country like invaders. The topsoil, held by roots and freshened by leaf-fall, was left helpless to the spring freshets, stripped and eroded with the naked bones of clay and rock exposed. The destruction of the forests changed the rainfall, for the searching clouds could find no green and beckoning woods to draw them on and milk them. The merciless nineteenth century was like a hostile expedition for loot that seemed limitless. Uncountable buffalo were killed, stripped of their hides, and left to rot, a reservoir of permanent food supply eliminated. More than that, the land of the Great Plains was robbed of the manure of the herds. Then the plows went in and ripped off the protection of the buffalo grass and opened the helpless soil to quick water and slow drought and the mischievous winds that roamed through the Great Central Plains. There has always been more than enough desert in America; the new settlers, like overindulged children, created even more. 9

The railroads brought new hordes of land-crazy people, and the new Americans moved like locusts across the continent until the western sea put a boundary to their movements. Coal and copper and gold drew them on; they savaged the land, gold-dredged the rivers to skeletons of pebbles and debris. An aroused and fearful government made laws for the distribution of public lands—a quarter sec- 10

 AMERICANS AND THE LAND

tion, one hundred and sixty acres, per person—and a claim had to be proved and improved; but there were ways of getting around this, and legally. My own grandfather proved out a quarter section for himself, one for his wife, one for each of his children, and, I suspect, acreage for children he hoped and expected to have. Marginal lands, of course, suitable only for grazing, went in larger pieces. One of the largest land-holding families in California took its richest holdings by a trick: By law a man could take up all the swamp or water-covered land he wanted. The founder of this great holding mounted a scow on wheels and drove his horses over thousands of acres of the best bottom land, then reported that he had explored it in a boat, which was true, and confirmed his title. I need not mention his name; his descendants will remember.

Another joker with a name still remembered in the West 11 worked out a scheme copied many times in after years. Proving a quarter section required a year of residence and some kind of improvement—a fence, a shack—but once the land was proved the owner was free to sell it. This particular princely character went to the stews and skid rows of the towns and found a small army of hopeless alcoholics who lived for whiskey and nothing else. He put these men on land he wanted to own, grubstaked them and kept them in cheap liquor until the acreage was proved, then went through the motions of buying it from his protégés and moved them and their one-room shacks on sled runners to new quarter sections. Bums of strong constitution might prove out five or six homesteads for this acquisitive hero before they died of drunkenness.

It was full late when we began to realize that the continent 12 did not stretch out to infinity; that there were limits to the indignities to which we could subject it. Engines and heavy mechanical equipment were allowing us to ravage it even more effectively than we had with fire, dynamite, and gang plows. Conservation came to us slowly, and much of it hasn't arrived yet. Having killed the whales and wiped out the sea otters and most of the beavers, the market hunters went to work on game birds; ducks and quail were decimated, and the passenger pigeon eliminated. In my youth I remember seeing a market hunter's gun, a three-gauge shotgun bolted to a frame and loaded to the muzzle with shingle nails. Aimed at a lake and the trigger pulled with a string, it slaughtered every living thing on the lake. The Pacific Coast pilchards were once the raw material for a great and continuing industry. We hunted them with aircraft far at sea until they were gone and the canneries had to be closed. In some of the valleys of the West, where the climate makes several crops a year available, which the water supply will not justify, wells were driven deeper and deeper for irrigation, so that in one great valley a million acre feet more of water was taken out than rain and melting snow could replace, and

JOHN STEINBECK

the water table went down and a few more years may give us a new desert.

The great redwood forests of the western mountains early at- 13 tracted attention. These ancient trees, which once grew everywhere, now exist only where the last Ice Age did not wipe them out. And they were found to have value. The Sempervirens and the Gigantea, the two remaining species, make soft, straight-grained timber. They are easy to split into planks, shakes, fenceposts, and railroad ties, and they have a unique virtue: they resist decay, both wet and dry rot, and an inherent acid in them repels termites. The loggers went through the great groves like a barrage, toppling the trees—some of which were two thousand years old—and leaving no maidens, no seedlings or saplings on the denuded hills.

Quite a few years ago when I was living in my little town on 14 the coast of California a stranger came in and bought a small valley where the Sempervirens redwoods grew, some of them three hundred feet high. We used to walk among these trees, and the light colored as though the great glass of the Cathedral at Chartres had strained and sanctified the sunlight. The emotion we felt in this grove was one of awe and humility and joy; and then one day it was gone, slaughtered, and the sad wreckage of boughs and broken saplings left like nonsensical spoilage of the battle-ruined countryside. And I remember that after our rage there was sadness, and when we passed the man who had done this we looked away, because we were ashamed for him.

From early times we were impressed and awed by the fan- 15 tastic accidents of nature, like the Grand Canyon and Yosemite and Yellowstone Park. The Indians had revered them as holy places, visited by the gods, and all of us came to have somewhat the same feeling about them. Thus we set aside many areas of astonishment as publicly owned parks; and though this may to a certain extent have been because there was no other way to use them as the feeling of preciousness of the things we had been destroying grew in Americans, more and more areas were set aside as national and state parks, to be looked at but not injured. Many people loved and were in awe of the redwoods; societies and individuals bought groves of these wonderful trees and presented them to the state for preservation.

No longer do we Americans want to destroy wantonly, but 16 our new-found sources of power—to take the burden of work from our shoulders, to warm us, and cool us, and give us light, to transport us quickly, and to make the things we use and wear and eat—these power sources spew pollution on our country, so that the rivers and streams are becoming poisonous and lifeless. The birds die for the lack of food; a noxious cloud hangs over our cities that burns our lungs and reddens our eyes. Our ability to conserve has not grown with our power to create, but this slow and sullen poisoning is no longer ignored or justified. Almost daily, the pressure of outrage among Americans grows. We are no longer content to destroy our beloved country. We are slow to learn; but we learn. When a super-highway was proposed in California which would trample the red-wood trees in its path, an outcry arose all over the land, so strident and fierce that the plan was put aside. And we no longer believe that a man, by owning a piece of America, is free to outrage it.

But we are an exuberant people, careless and destructive as 17 active children. We make strong and potent tools and then have to use them to prove that they exist. Under the pressure of war we finally made the atom bomb, and for reasons which seemed justifiable at the time we dropped it on two Japanese cities—and I think we finally frightened ourselves. In such things, one must consult himself because there is no other point of reference. I did not know about the bomb, and certainly I had nothing to do with its use, but I am horrified and ashamed; and nearly everyone I know feels the same thing. And those who loudly and angrily justify Hiroshima and Nagasaki—why, they must be the most ashamed of all.

COMPREHENSION

1. What is Steinbeck's purpose in writing this essay? State, in your own words, his thesis.

2. According to Steinbeck, how did the American attitude toward the land evolve?

3. Does Steinbeck think that the American attitude toward the land can be changed? Cite evidence from the essay to support your answer.

RHETORIC

1. Analyze Steinbeck's use of figurative language in paragraphs 1, 2, 9, and 14.

2. Locate images and vocabulary relating to "rape" and destruction in the es-say. What is the relevance of this motif to the development of Steinbeck's thesis?

3. How does Steinbeck use examples in paragraphs 1 and 2 to establish the subject and thesis of his essay?

4. Analyze the relationship between the patterns of description and example in the essay. What types of illustration does Steinbeck employ? How does he achieve concreteness through examples? Where does he employ extended ex-ample? Does he use examples subjectively or objectively? Explain.

5. How does Steinbeck employ process analysis to highlight his thesis?

6. Explain the relationship between paragraph 16 and paragraph 17 in the essay.

1. Compare and contrast Steinbeck's essay with "Wasteland" by Marya Mannes.

2. Write an essay entitled "Americans and the Land," using examples to support your thesis.

3. Write an essay on the relationship between ecology and the state of civilization.

JAMES BALDWIN

Stranger in the Village

James Baldwin (1924–1988), a major American essayist, novelist, short story writer, and playwright, was born and grew up in Harlem. He won a Eugene Saxon Fellowship and lived in Europe from 1948 to 1956. Always an activist in civil rights causes, Baldwin focused in his essays and fiction on the black search for identity in modern America and on the myth of white superiority. Among his principal works are Go Tell It on the Mountain *(1953)*, Notes of a Native Son *(1955)*, Giovanni's Room *(1958)*, Nobody Knows My Name *(1960)*, Another Country *(1962), and* If Beale Street Could Talk *(1975). One of the finest contemporary essayists, Baldwin has a rare talent for portraying the deepest concerns about civilization in an intensely personal style, as the following essay indicates.*

From all available evidence no black man had ever set foot in this tiny Swiss village before I came. I was told before arriving that I would probably be a "sight" for the village; I took this to mean that people of my complexion were rarely seen in Switzerland, and also that city people are always something of a "sight" outside of the city. It did not occur to me—possibly because I am an American—that there could be people anywhere who had never seen a Negro. 1

It is a fact that cannot be explained on the basis of the inaccessibility of the village. The village is very high, but it is only four hours from Milan and three hours from Lausanne. It is true that it is virtually unknown. Few people making plans for a holiday would elect to come here. On the other hand, the villagers are able, presumably, to come and go as they please—which they do: to another town 2 at the foot of the mountain, with a population of approximately five thousand, the nearest place to see a movie or go to the bank. In the village there is no movie house, no bank, no library, no theater; very few radios, one jeep, one station wagon; and, at the moment, one typewriter, mine, an invention which the woman next door to me here had never seen. There are about six hundred people living here, all Catholic—I conclude this from the fact that the Catholic church is open all year round, whereas the Protestant chapel, set off on a hill a little removed from the village, is open only in the summertime when the tourists arrive. There are four or five hotels, all closed now, and four or five *bistros*, of which, however, only two do any business during the winter. These two do not do a great deal, for life in the village seems to end around nine or ten o'clock. There are a few stores, butcher, baker, *épicerie*, a hardware store, and a money-changer—who cannot change travelers' checks, but must send them down to the bank, an operation which takes two or three days. There is something called the *Ballet Haus*, closed in the winter and used for God knows what, certainly not ballet, during the summer. There seems to be only one schoolhouse in the village, and this for the quite young children; I suppose this to mean that their older brothers and sisters at some point descend from these mountains in order to complete their education—possibly, again, to the town just below. The landscape is absolutely forbidding, mountains towering on all four sides, ice and snow as far as the eye can reach. In this white wilderness, men and women and children move all day, carrying washing, wood, buckets of milk or water, sometimes skiing on Sunday afternoons. All week long boys and young men are to be seen shoveling snow off the rooftops, or dragging wood down from the forest in sleds.

The village's only real attraction, which explains the tourist season, is the hot spring water. A disquietingly high proportion of these tourists are cripples, or semi-cripples, who come year after year—from other parts of Switzerland, usually—to take the waters. This lends the village, at the height of the season, a rather terrifying air of sanctity, as though it were a lesser Lourdes. There is often something beautiful, there is always something awful, in the spectacle of a person who has lost one of his faculties, a faculty he never questioned until it was gone, and who struggles to recover it. Yet people remain people, on crutches or indeed on deathbeds; and wherever I passed, the first summer I was here, among the native villagers or among the lame, a wind passed with me—of astonishment, curiosity, amusement, and outrage. The first summer I stayed two weeks and never intended to return. But I did return in the winter, to work; the village offers, obviously, no distractions whatever and has the further advantage of being extremely cheap. Now it is winter again, a year later, and I am here again. Everyone in the village knows my name, though they scarcely ever use it, knows that I come from America—though, this, apparently they will never really believe: black men come from Africa—and everyone knows that I am the friend of the son of a woman who was born here, and that I am staying in their chalet. But I remain as much a stranger today as I was the first day I arrived, and the children shout *Neger! Neger!* as I walk along the streets.

It must be admitted that in the beginning I was far too 4 shocked to have any real reaction. In so far as I reacted at all, I reacted by trying to be pleasant—it being a great part of the American Negro's education (long before he goes to school) that he must make people "like" him. This smile-and-the-world-smiles-with-you routine worked about as well in this situation as it had in the situation for which it was designed, which is to say that it did not work at all. No one, after all, can be liked whose human weight and complexity cannot be, or has not been, admitted. My smile was simply another unheard-of phenomenon which allowed them to see my teeth—they did not, really, see my smile and I began to think that, should I take to snarling, no one would notice any difference. All of the physical characteristics of the Negro which had caused me, in America, a very different and almost forgotten pain were nothing less than miraculous—or infernal—in the eyes of the village people. Some thought my hair was the color of tar, that it had the texture of wire, or the texture of cotton. It was jocularly suggested that I might let it all grow long and make myself a winter coat. If I sat in the sun for more than five minutes some daring creature was certain to come along and gingerly put his fingers on my hair, as though he were afraid of an electric shock, or put his hand on my hand, astonished that the color did not rub off. In all of this, in which it must be conceded there was the charm of genuine wonder and in which there was certainly no element of intentional unkindness, there was yet no suggestion that I was human: I was simply a living wonder.

I knew that they did not mean to be unkind, and I know it 5 now; it is necessary, nevertheless, for me to repeat this to myself each time I walk out of the chalet. The children who shout *Neger!* have no way of knowing the echoes this sound raises in me. They are brimming with good humor and the more daring swell with pride when I stop to speak with them. Just the same, there are days when I cannot pause and smile, when I have no heart to play with them; when, indeed, I mutter sourly to myself, exactly as I muttered on the streets of a city these children have never seen, when I was no bigger than these children are now: *Your* mother *was a nigger.* Joyce is right about history being a nightmare—but it may be the nightmare from which no one *can* awaken. People are trapped in history and history is trapped in them.

There is a custom in the village—I am told it is repeated in 6 many villages—of "buying" African natives for the purpose of converting them to Christianity. There stands in the church all year round a small box with a slot for money, decorated with a black figurine, and into this box the villagers drop their francs. During the *carnaval* which precedes Lent, two village children have their faces blackened—out of which bloodless darkness their blue eyes shine like ice—and fantastic horsehair wigs are placed on their blond heads; thus disguised, they solicit among the villagers for money for the missionaries in Africa. Between the box in the church and the blackened children, the village "bought" last year six or eight African natives. This was reported to me with pride by the wife of one of the *bistro* owners and I was careful to express astonishment and pleasure at the solicitude shown by the village for the souls of black folk. The *bistro* owner's wife beamed with a pleasure far more genuine than my own and seemed to feel that I might now breathe more easily concerning the souls of at least six of my kinsmen.

I tried not to think of these so lately baptized kinsmen, of the price paid for them, or the peculiar price they themselves would pay, and said nothing about my father, who having taken his own conversion too literally never, at bottom, forgave the white world (which he described as heathen) for having saddled him with a Christ in whom, to judge at least from their treatment of him, they themselves no longer believed. I thought of white men arriving for the first time in an African village, strangers there, as I am a stranger here, and tried to imagine the astounded populace touching their hair and marveling at the color of their skin. But there is a great difference between being the first white man to be seen by Africans and being the first black man to be seen by whites. The white man takes the astonishment as tribute, for he arrives to conquer and to convert the natives, whose inferiority in relation to himself is not even to be questioned; whereas I, without a thought of conquest, find myself among a people whose culture controls me, has even, in a sense, created me, people who have cost me more in anguish and rage than they will ever know, who yet do not even know of my existence. The astonishment with which I might have greeted them, should they have stumbled into my African village a few hundred years ago, might have rejoiced their hearts. But the astonishment with which they greet me today can only poison mine.

And this is so despite everything I may do to feel differently, despite my friendly conversations with the *bistro* owner's wife, despite their three-year-old son who has at last become my friend, despite the *saluts* and *bonsoirs* which I exchange with people as I walk, despite the fact that I know that no individual can be taken to task for what history is doing, or has done. I say that the culture of these people controls me—but they can scarcely be held responsible for European

JAMES BALDWIN

culture. America comes out of Europe, but these people have never seen America nor have most of them seen more of Europe than the hamlet at the foot of their mountain. Yet they move with an authority which I shall never have; and they regard me, quite rightly, not only as a stranger in their village but as a suspect latecomer, bearing no credentials, to everything they have—however unconsciously—inherited.

For this village, even were it incomparably more remote and incredibly more primitive, is the West, the West onto which I have been so strangely grafted. These people cannot be, from the point of view of power, strangers anywhere in the world; they have made the modern world, in effect, even if they do not know it. The most illiterate among them is related, in a way that I am not, to Dante, Shakespeare, Michelangelo, Aeschylus, Da Vinci, Rembrandt, and Racine; the cathedral at Chartres says something to them which it cannot say to me, as indeed would New York's Empire State Building, should anyone here ever see it. Out of their hymns and dances come Beethoven and Bach. Go back a few centuries and they are in their full glory—but I am in Africa, watching the conquerors arrive. 9

The rage of the disesteemed is personally fruitless, but it is also absolutely inevitable; this rage, so generally discounted, so little understood even among the people whose daily bread it is, is one of the things that makes history. Rage can only with difficulty, and never entirely, be brought under the domination of the intelligence and is therefore not susceptible to any arguments whatever. This is a fact which ordinary representatives of the *Herrenvolk*, having never felt this rage and being unable to imagine it, quite fail to understand. Also, rage cannot be hidden, it can only be dissembled. This dissembling deludes the thoughtless, and strengthens rage and adds, to rage, contempt. There are, no doubt, as many ways of coping with the resulting complex of tensions as there are black men in the world, but no black man can hope ever to be entirely liberated from this internal warfare—rage, dissembling, and contempt having inevitably accompanied his first realization of the power of white men. What is crucial here is that, since white men represent in the black man's world so heavy a weight, white men have for black men a reality which is far from being reciprocal; and hence all black men have toward all white men an attitude which is designed, really, either to rob the white man of the jewel of his naïveté, or else to make it cost him dear. 10

The black man insists, by whatever means he finds at his disposal, that the white man cease to regard him as an exotic rarity and recognize him as a human being. This is a very charged and difficult moment, for there is a great deal of will power involved in the white man's naïveté. Most people are not naturally reflective any more than they are naturally malicious, and the white man prefers to keep the 11 black man at a certain human remove because it is easier for him thus to preserve his simplicity and avoid being called to account for crimes committed by his forefathers, or his neighbors. He is inescapably aware, nevertheless, that he is in a better position in the world than black men are, nor can he quite put to death the suspicion that he is hated by black men therefore. He does not wish to be hated, neither does he wish to change places, and at this point in his uneasiness he can scarcely avoid having recourse to those legends which white men have created about black men, the most usual effect of which is that the white man finds himself enmeshed, so to speak, in his own language which describes hell, as well as the attributes which lead one to hell, as being as black as night.

Every legend, moreover, contains its residuum of truth, and 12 the root function of language is to control the universe by describing it. It is of quite considerable significance that black men remain, in the imagination, and in overwhelming numbers in fact, beyond the disciplines of salvation; and this despite the fact the West has been "buying" African natives for centuries. There is, I should hazard, an instantaneous necessity to be divorced from this so visibly unsaved stranger, in whose heart, moreover, one cannot guess what dreams of vengeance are being nourished; and, at the same time, there are few things on earth more attractive than the idea of the unspeakable liberty which is allowed the unredeemed. When, beneath the black mask, a human being begins to make himself felt one cannot escape a certain awful wonder as to what kind of human being it is. What one's imagination makes of other people is dictated, of course, by the laws of one's own personality and it is one of the ironies of black-white relations that, by means of what the white man imagines the black man to be, the black man is enabled to know who the white man is.

I have said, for example, that I am as much a stranger in this 13 village today as I was the first summer I arrived, but this is not quite true. The villagers wonder less about the texture of my hair than they did then, and wonder rather more about me. And the fact that their wonder now exists on another level is reflected in their attitudes and in their eyes. There are the children who make those delightful, hilarious, sometimes astonishingly grave overtures of friendship in the unpredictable fashion of children; other children, having been taught that the devil is a black man, scream in genuine anguish as I approach. Some of the older women never pass without a friendly greeting, never pass, indeed, if it seems that they will be able to engage me in conversation; other women look down or look away or rather contemptuously smirk. Some of the men drink with me and suggest that I learn how to ski—partly, I gather, because they cannot imagine what I would look like on skis—and want to know if I am married, and ask questions about my *métier*. But some of the men have accused *le*

JAMES BALDWIN

sale négre—behind my back—of stealing wood and there is already in the eyes of some of them that peculiar, intent, paranoiac malevolence which one sometimes surprises in the eyes of American white men when, out walking with their Sunday girl, they see a Negro male approach.

There is a dreadful abyss between the streets of this village and the streets of the city in which I was born, between the children who shout *Neger!* today and those who shouted *Nigger!* yesterday—the abyss is experience, the American experience. The syllable hurled behind me today expresses, above all, wonder: I am a stranger here. But I am not a stranger in America and the same syllable riding on the American air expresses the war my presence has occasioned in the American soul. 14

For this village brings home to me this fact: that there was a day, and not really a very distant day, when Americans were scarcely Americans at all but discontented Europeans, facing a great unconquered continent and strolling, say, into a marketplace and seeing black men for the first time. The shock this spectacle afforded is suggested, surely, by the promptness with which they decided that these black men were not really men but cattle. It is true that the necessity on the part of the settlers of the New World of reconciling their moral assumptions with the fact—and the necessity—of slavery enhanced immensely the charm of this idea, and it is also true that this idea expresses, with a truly American bluntness, the attitude which to varying extents all masters have had toward all slaves. 15

But between all former slaves and slave-owners and the drama which begins for Americans over three hundred years ago at Jamestown, there are at least two differences to be observed. The American Negro slave could not suppose, for one thing, as slaves in past epochs had supposed and often done, that he would ever be able to wrest the power from his master's hands. This was a supposition which the modern era, which was to bring about such vast changes in the aims and dimensions of power, put to death; it only begins, in unprecedented fashion, and with dreadful implications, to be resurrected today. But even had this supposition persisted with undiminished force, the American Negro slave could not have used it to lend his condition dignity, for the reason that this supposition rests on another: that the slave in exile yet remains related to his past, has some means—if only in memory—of revering and sustaining the forms of his former life, is able, in short, to maintain his identity. 16

This was not the case with the American Negro slave. He is unique among the black men of the world in that his past was taken from him, almost literally, at one blow. One wonders what on earth the first slave found to say to the first dark child he bore. I am told that there are Haitians able to trace their ancestry back to African 17 kings, but any American Negro wishing to go back so far will find his journey through time abruptly arrested by the signature on the bill of sale which served as the entrance paper for his ancestor. At the time—to say nothing of the circumstances—of the enslavement of the captive black man who was to become the American Negro, there was not the remotest possibility that he would ever take power from his master's hands. There was no reason to suppose that his situation would ever change, nor was there, shortly, anything to indicate that his situation had ever been different. It was his necessity, in the words of E. Franklin Frazier, to find a "motive for living under American culture or die." The identity of the American Negro comes out of this extreme situation, and the evolution of this identity was a source of the most intolerable anxiety in the minds and the lives of his masters.

For the history of the American Negro is unique also in this: 18 that the question of his humanity, and of his rights therefore as a human being, became a burning one for several generations of Americans, so burning a question that it ultimately became one of those used to divide the nation. It is out of this argument that the venom of the epithet *Nigger!* is derived. It is an argument which Europe has never had, and hence Europe quite sincerely fails to understand how or why the argument arose in the first place, why its effects are so frequently disastrous and always so unpredictable, why it refuses until today to be entirely settled. Europe's black possessions remained—and do remain—in Europe's colonies, at which remove they represented no threat whatever to European identity. If they posed any problem at all for the European conscience, it was a problem which remained comfortingly abstract: in effect, the black man, *as a man*, did not exist for Europe. But in America, even as a slave, he was an inescapable part of the general social fabric and no American could escape having an attitude toward him. Americans attempt until today to make an abstraction of the Negro, but the very nature of these abstractions reveals the tremendous effects the presence of the Negro has had on the American character.

When one considers the history of the Negro in America it is 19 of the greatest importance to recognize that the moral beliefs of a person, or a people, are never really as tenuous as life—which is not moral—very often causes them to appear; these create for them a frame of reference and a necessary hope, the hope being that when life has done its worst they will be enabled to rise above themselves and to triumph over life. Life would scarcely be bearable if this hope did not exist. Again, even when the worst has been said, to betray a belief is not by any means to have put oneself beyond its power; the betrayal of a belief is not the same thing as ceasing to believe. If this were not so there would be no moral standards in the world at all. Yet one must also recognize that morality is based on ideas and that all ideas are dangerous—dangerous because ideas can only lead to action and where the action leads no man can say. And dangerous in this respect: that confronted with the impossibility of becoming free of them, one can be driven to the most inhuman excesses. The ideas on which American beliefs are based are not, though Americans often seem to think so, ideas which originated in America. They came out of Europe. And the establishment of democracy on the American continent was scarcely as radical a break with the past as was the necessity, which Americans faced, of broadening this concept to include black men.

This was, literally, a hard necessity. It was impossible, for one thing, for Americans to abandon their beliefs, not only because these beliefs alone seemed able to justify the sacrifices they had endured and the blood that they had spilled, but also because these beliefs afforded them their only bulwark against a moral chaos as absolute as the physical chaos of the continent it was their destiny to conquer. But in the situation in which Americans found themselves, these beliefs threatened an idea which, whether or not one likes to think so, is the very warp and woof of the heritage of the West, the idea of white supremacy. 20

Americans have made themselves notorious by the shrillness and the brutality with which they have insisted on this idea, but they did not invent it; and it has escaped the world's notice that those very excesses of which Americans have been guilty imply a certain, unprecedented uneasiness over the idea's life and power, if not, indeed, the idea's validity. The idea of white supremacy rests simply on the fact that white men are the creators of civilization (the present civilization, which is the only one that matters; all previous civilizations are simply "contributions" to our own) and are therefore civilization's guardians and defenders. Thus it was impossible for Americans to accept the black man as one of themselves, for to do so was to jeopardize their status as white men. But not so to accept him was to deny his human reality, his human weight and complexity, and the strain of denying the overwhelmingly undeniable forced Americans into rationalizations so fantastic that they approached the pathological. 21

At the root of the American Negro problem is the necessity of the American white man to find a way of living with the Negro in order to be able to live with himself. And the history of this problem can be reduced to the means used by Americans—lynch law and law, segregation and legal acceptance, terrorization and concession—either to come to terms with this necessity, or to find a way around it, or (most usually) to find a way of doing both these things at once. The resulting spectacle, at once foolish and dreadful, led someone to make the quite accurate observation that "the Negro-in-America is a form of insanity which overtakes white men." 22

In this long battle, a battle by no means finished, the unfore- 23

STRANGER IN THE VILLAGE

seeable effects of which will be felt by many future generations, the white man's motive was the protection of his identity; the black man was motivated by the need to establish an identity. And despite the terrorization which the Negro in America endured and endures sporadically until today, despite the cruel and totally inescapable ambivalence of his status in his country, the battle for his identity has long ago been won. He is not a visitor to the West, but a citizen there, an American; as American as the Americans who despise him, the Americans who fear him, the Americans who love him—the Americans who became less than themselves, or rose to be greater than themselves by virtue of the fact that the challenge he represented was inescapable. He is perhaps the only black man in the world whose relationship to white men is more terrible, more subtle, and more meaningful than the relationship of bitter possessed to uncertain possessor. His survival depended, and his development depends, on his ability to turn his peculiar status in the Western world to his own advantage and, it may be, to the very great advantage of that world. It remains for him to fashion out of his experience that which will give him sustenance, and a voice.

The cathedral at Chartres, I have said, says something to the 24 people of this village which it cannot say to me; but it is important to understand that this cathedral says something to me which it cannot say to them. Perhaps they are struck by the power of the spires, the glory of the windows; but they have known God, after all, longer than I have known him, and in a different way, and I am terrified by the slippery bottomless well to be found in the crypt, down which heretics were hurled to death, and by the obscene, inescapable gargoyles jutting out of the stone and seeming to say that God and the devil can never be divorced. I doubt that the villagers think of the devil when they face a cathedral because they have never been identified with the devil. But I must accept the status which myth, if nothing else, gives me in the West before I can hope to change the myth.

Yet, if the American Negro has arrived at his identity by vir- 25 tue of the absoluteness of his estrangement from his past, American white men still nourish the illusion that there is some means of recovering the European innocence, of returning to a state in which black men do not exist. This is one of the greatest errors Americans can make. The identity they fought so hard to protect has, by virtue of that battle, undergone a change: Americans are as unlike any other white people in the world as it is possible to be. I do not think, for example, that it is too much to suggest that the American vision of the world—which allows so little reality, generally speaking, for any of the darker forces in human life, which tends until today to paint moral issues in glaring black and white—owes a great deal to the battle waged by Americans to maintain between themselves and black

JAMES BALDWIN

men a human separation which could not be bridged. It is only now beginning to be borne in on us—very faintly, it must be admitted, very slowly, and very much against our will—that this vision of the world is dangerously inaccurate, and perfectly useless. For it protects our moral high-mindedness at the terrible expense of weakening our grasp of reality. People who shut their eyes to reality simply invite their own destruction, and anyone who insists on remaining in a state of innocence long after that innocence is dead turns himself into a monster.

26   The time has come to realize that the interracial drama acted out on the American continent has not only created a new black man, it has created a new white man, too. No road whatever will lead Americans back to the simplicity of this European village where white men still have the luxury of looking on me as a stranger. I am not, really, a stranger any longer for any American alive. One of the things that distinguishes Americans from other people is that no other people has ever been so deeply involved in the lives of black men, and vice versa. This fact faced, with all its implications, it can be seen that the history of the American Negro problem is not merely shameful, it is also something of an achievement. For even when the worst has been said, it must also be added that the perpetual challenge posed by this problem was always, somehow, perpetually met. It is precisely this black-white experience which may prove of indispensable value to us in the world we face today. This world is white no longer, and it will never be white again.

COMPREHENSION

1. According to Baldwin, what distinguishes Americans from other people? What is his purpose in highlighting these differences?

2. What connections between Europe, Africa, and America emerge from this essay? What is the relevance of the Swiss village to this frame of reference?

3. In the context of the essay, explain what Baldwin means by his statement, "People are trapped in history and history is trapped in them" (paragraph 5).

RHETORIC

1. Analyze the effect of Baldwin's repetition of "there is" and "there are" constructions in paragraph 2. What does the parallelism at the start of paragraph 8 accomplish? Locate other examples of parallelism in the essay.

2. Analyze the figure of speech "wind" in paragraph 3 and its relation to the rest of the essay.

3. Where in the essay is Baldwin's complex thesis condensed for the reader? What does this placement of thesis reveal about the logical method of development in the essay?

 STRANGER IN THE VILLAGE

4. How does Baldwin create this introduction? What is the focus? What key motifs does the author present that will inform the rest of the essay? What is the relationship of paragraph 5 to paragraph 6?

5. What paragraphs constitute the second section of the essay? What example serves to unify this section? What major shift in emphasis occurs in the third part of the essay? Explain the cathedral of Chartres as a controlling motif between these two sections.

6. What comparisons and contrasts help to structure and unify the essay?

WRITING

1. Examine the paradox implicit in Baldwin's statement in the last paragraph that the American Negro problem is "something of an achievement."

2. Write an essay on civilization based on the last sentence in Baldwin's essay: "This world is white no longer, and it will never be white again."

3. Describe a time when you felt yourself a "stranger" in a certain culture.

4. In a comparative essay, analyze "Stranger in the Village" and Wright's "The Psychological Reactions of Oppressed Peoples."

WOODY ALLEN

My Speech to the Graduates

Allen Stewart Konigsberg (1935–   ), legally renamed Heywood Allen and known popularly as Woody Allen, is a comedian, actor, director, and writer for television, film, drama, and such national publications as Playboy, New Yorker, *and* Esquire. *His notable screenplays include* What's New, Pussycat? *(1965),* Bananas *(1970),* Play It Again, Sam *(1972),* Sleeper *(1973), and* Annie Hall *(1977), a film that won the Academy Award, with Allen also taking honors for best director and, with Marshall Brickman, for best original screenplay. Allen's books, filled with the same comic genius as his best films, include* Getting Even *(1971),* Without Feathers *(1975), and* Side Effects *(1980). This essay is a parody of one graduation ritual as well as a satire on present civilization.*

ore than any other time in history, mankind faces a crossroads. One path leads to despair and utter hopelessness. The other, to total extinction. Let us pray we have the wisdom to choose correctly. I speak, by the way, not with any sense of futility, but with a panicky conviction of the absolute meaninglessness of existence which could easily be misinterpreted as pessimism. It is not. It is merely a healthy concern for the predicament of modern man. (Modern man is here defined as any person born after Nietzche's edict that "God is dead," but before the hit recording "I Wanna Hold Your Hand.") This "predicament" can be stated in one of two ways, though certain linguistic philosophers prefer to reduce it to a mathematical equation where it can be easily solved and even carried around in the wallet.

Put in its simplest form, the problem is: How is it possible to find meaning in a finite world given my waist and shirt size? This is a very difficult question when we realize that science has failed us. True, it has conquered many diseases, broken the genetic code, and even placed human beings on the moon, and yet when a man of 80 is left in a room with two 18-year-old cocktail waitresses nothing happens. Because the real problems never change. After all, can the human soul be glimpsed through a microscope? Maybe—but you'd definitely need one of those very good ones with two eyepieces. We know that the most advanced computer in the world does not have a brain as sophisticated as that of an ant. True, we could say that of many of our relatives but we only have to put up with them at weddings or special occasions. Science is something we depend on all the time. If I develop a pain in the chest I must take an X-ray. But what if the radiation from the X-ray causes me deeper problems? Before I know it, I'm in for surgery. Naturally, while they're giving me oxygen an intern decides to light up a cigarette. The next thing you know I'm rocketing over the World Trade Center in bedclothes. Is this science? True, science has taught us how to pasteurize cheese. And true, this can be fun in mixed company—but what of the H-bomb? Have you ever seen what happens when one of those things falls off a desk accidentally? And where is science when one ponders the eternal riddles? How did the cosmos originate? How long has it been around? Did matter begin with an explosion or by the word of God? And if by the latter, could He not have begun it just two weeks earlier to take advantage of some of the warmer weather? Exactly what do we mean when we say man is mortal? Obviously it's not a compliment.

Religion, too, has unfortunately let us down. Miguel de Unamuno writes blithely of the "eternal persistence of consciousness," but that is no easy feat. Particularly when reading Thackeray. I often think how comforting life must have been for early man because he believed in a powerful, benevolent Creator who looked after all things. Imagine his disappointment when he saw his wife putting on weight. Contemporary man, of course, has no such peace of mind. He finds himself in the midst of a crisis of faith. He is what we fashionably call "alienated." He has seen the ravages of war, he has known natural catastrophes, he has been to singles bars. My good friend Jacques Monod spoke often of the randomness of the cosmos. He believed everything in existence occurred by pure chance with the possible exception of his breakfast, which he felt certain was made by his housekeeper. Naturally belief in a divine intelligence inspires tranquillity. But this does not free us from our human responsibilities. Am I my brother's keeper? Yes. Interestingly, in my case I share that honor with the Prospect Park Zoo. Feeling godless then, what we have done is made technology God. And yet can technology really be the answer when a brand new Buick, driven by my close associate, Nat Persky, winds up in the window of Chicken Delight causing hundreds of customers to scatter? My toaster has never once worked properly in four years. I follow the instructions and push two slices of bread down in the slots and seconds later they rifle upward. Once they broke the nose of a woman I loved very dearly. Are we counting on nuts and bolts and electricity to solve our problems? Yes, the telephone is a good thing—and the refrigerator—and the air conditioner. But not every air conditioner. Not my sister Henny's, for instance. Hers makes a loud noise and still doesn't cool. When the man comes over to fix it, it gets worse. Either that or he tells her she needs a new one. When she complains, he says not to bother him. This man is truly alienated. Not only is he alienated but he can't stop smiling.

The trouble is, our leaders have not adequately prepared us 4 for a mechanized society. Unfortunately our politicians are either incompetent or corrupt. Sometimes both on the same day. The Government is unresponsive to the needs of the little man. Under five-seven, it is impossible to get your Congressman on the phone. I am not denying that democracy is still the finest form of government. In a democracy at least, civil liberties are upheld. No citizen can be wantonly tortured, imprisoned, or made to sit through certain Broadway shows. And yet this is a far cry from what goes on in the Soviet Union. Under their form of totalitarianism, a person merely caught whistling is sentenced to 30 years in a labor camp. If, after 15 years, he still will not stop whistling they shoot him. Along with this brutal fascism we find its handmaiden, terrorism. At no other time in history has man been so afraid to cut into his veal chop for fear that it will explode. Violence breeds more violence and it is predicted that by 1990 kidnapping will be the dominant mode of social interaction. Overpopulation will exacerbate problems to the breaking point. Figures tell us there are already more people on earth than we need to move even the heaviest piano. If we do not call a halt to breeding, by the year 2000 there will

WOODY ALLEN

be no room to serve dinner unless one is willing to set the table on the heads of strangers. Then they must not move for an hour while we eat. Of course energy will be in short supply and each car owner will be allowed only enough gasoline to back up a few inches.

Instead of facing these challenges we turn to distractions like drugs and sex. We live in far too permissive a society. Never before has pornography been this rampant. And those films are lit so badly! We are a people who lack defined goals. We have never learned to love. We lack leaders and coherent programs. We have no spiritual center. We are adrift in the cosmos wreaking monstrous violence on one another out of frustration and pain. Fortunately, we have not lost our sense of proportion. Summing up, it is clear the future holds great opportunities. It also holds pitfalls. The trick will be to avoid the pitfalls, seize the opportunities, and get back home by six o'clock.

COMPREHENSION

1. For what purpose does Allen adopt a comic tone? How does this tone serve his audience?

2. Explain the author's comic attitude toward science, religion, and politics. What specific subjects does he ridicule?

3. Beneath the surface of comedy in the essay, we can infer that Allen is concerned with the modern "predicament." Cite examples to support this judgment.

RHETORIC

1. What purpose does the author's allusion to Nietzsche, Unamuno, and Monod serve?

2. Does the author use understatement or overstatement in his ironic language? Explain by reference to the essay.

3. What is the relationship of the title to the substance of the essay? Does the author, in his introduction, give any appearance of writing seriously? How does the introduction echo standard speeches to graduates? How does Allen approach such standard speeches?

4. What role does logic, either inductive or deductive, play within the pattern of the essay?

5. In what manner does the pattern of cause and effect heighten the irony in the essay?

6. Examine the substance and structure of Allen's "summing up" in the last paragraph.

WRITING

1. Does Allen's variety of humor seem too slapstick or strained? Explain in a brief essay.

 MY SPEECH TO THE GRADUATES

2. Write your own comic speech to the graduates.

3. Satirize one aspect of contemporary college life.

MARTIN LUTHER KING, JR.

The World House

Martin Luther King, Jr. (1929–1968) was born in Atlanta, Georgia and earned degrees from Morehouse College, Crozer Theological Seminary, Boston University, and Chicago Theological Seminary. As Baptist clergyman, civil rights leader, founder and president of the Southern Christian Leadership Council, and in 1964 Nobel Peace Prize winner, King was a celebrated advocate of nonviolent resistance to achieve equality and racial integration in the world. King was a gifted orator and a highly persuasive writer. His books include Letter from Birmingham City Jail *(1963),* Why We Can't Wait *(1964),* Stride Toward Freedom *(1958),* Strength to Love *(1963), and* Where Do We Go from Here: Chaos or Community? *(1967), a book published shortly before Reverend King was assassinated on April 4, 1968, in Memphis, Tennessee. In "The World House," a section from his last book, King uses analogy to promote his long-standing vision of a peaceful and united world civilization.*

Some years ago a famous novelist died. Among his papers was found a list of suggested plots for future stories, the most prominently underscored being this one: "A widely separated family inherits a house in which they have to live together." This is the great new problem of mankind. We have inherited a large house, a great "world house" in which we have to live together—black and white, Easterner and Westerner, Gentile and Jew, Catholic and Protestant, Moslem and Hindu—a family unduly separated in ideas, culture and interest, who, because we can never again live apart, must learn somehow to live with each other in peace.

However deeply American Negroes are caught in the struggle to be at last at home in our homeland of the United States, we cannot ignore the larger world house in which we are also dwellers. Equality with whites will not solve the problems of either whites or Negroes if it means equality in a world society stricken by poverty and in a universe doomed to extinction by war.

All inhabitants of the globe are now neighbors. This world-wide neighborhood has been brought into being largely as a result of the modern scientific and technological revolutions. The world of to-day is vastly different from the world of just one hundred years ago. A century ago Thomas Edison had not yet invented the incandescent lamp to bring light to many dark places of the earth. The Wright brothers had not yet invented that fascinating mechanical bird that would spread its gigantic wings across the skies and soon dwarf distance and place time in the service of man. Einstein had not yet challenged an axiom and the theory of relativity had not yet been posited.

Human beings, searching a century ago as now for better understanding, had no television, no radios, no telephones and no motion pictures through which to communicate. Medical science had not yet discovered the wonder drugs to end many dread plagues and diseases. One hundred years ago military men had not yet developed the terrifying weapons of warfare that we know today—not the bomber, an airborne fortress raining down death; nor napalm, that burner of all things and flesh in its path. A century ago there were no skyscraping buildings to kiss the stars and no gargantuan bridges to span the waters. Science had not yet peered into the unfathomable ranges of interstellar space, nor had it penetrated oceanic depths. All these new inventions, these new ideas, these sometimes fascinating and sometimes frightening developments came later. Most of them have come within the past sixty years, sometimes with agonizing slowness, more characteristically with bewildering speed, but always with enormous significance for our future.

The years ahead will see a continuation of the same dramatic developments. Physical science will carve new highways through the stratosphere. In a few years astronauts and cosmonauts will probably walk comfortably across the uncertain pathways of the moon. In two or three years it will be possible, because of the new supersonic jets, to fly from New York to London in two and one-half hours. In the years ahead medical science will greatly prolong the lives of men by finding a cure for cancer and deadly heart ailments. Automation and cybernation will make it possible for working people to have un-dreamed-of amounts of leisure time. All this is a dazzling picture of the furniture, the workshop, the spacious rooms, the new decorations and the architectural pattern of the large world house in which we are living.

Along with the scientific and technological revolution, we have also witnessed a world-wide freedom revolution over the last few decades. The present upsurge of the Negro people of the United States grows out a a deep and passionate determination to make freedom and equality a reality "here" and "now." In one sense the civil rights movement in the United States is a special American phenomenon which must be understood in the light of American history and dealt with in terms of the American situation. But on another and more important level, what is happening in the United States today is a significant part of a world development.

We live in a day, said the philosopher Alfred North Whitehead, "when civilization is shifting its basic outlook; a major turning point in history where the pre-suppositions on which society is structured are being analyzed, sharply challenged, and profoundly changed." What we are seeing now is a freedom explosion, the realization of "an idea whose time has come," to use Victor Hugo's phrase. The deep rumbling of discontent that we hear today is the thunder of disinherited masses, rising from dungeons of oppression to the bright hills of freedom. In one majestic chorus the rising masses are singing, in the words of our freedom song, "Ain't gonna let nobody turn us around." All over the world like a fever, freedom is spreading in the widest liberation movement in history. The great masses of people are determined to end the exploitation of their races and lands. They are awake and moving toward their goal like a tidal wave. You can hear them rumbling in every village street, on the docks, in the houses, among the students, in the churches and at political meetings. For several centuries the direction of history flowed from the nations and societies of Western Europe out into the rest of the world in "conquests" of various sorts. That period, the era of colonialism, is at an end. East is moving West. The earth is being redistributed. Yes, we are "shifting our basic outlooks." 7

These developments should not surprise any student of history. Oppressed people cannot remain oppressed forever. The yearning for freedom evenutally manifests itself. The Bible tells the thrilling story of how Moses stood in Pharaoh's court centuries ago and cried, "Let my people go." This was an opening chapter in a continuing story. The present struggle in the United States is a later chapter in the same story. Something within has reminded the Negro of his birthright of freedom, and something without has reminded him that it can be gained. Consciously or unconsciously, he has been caught up by the spirit of the times, and with his black brothers of Africa and his brown and yellow brothers in Asia, South America and the Caribbean, the United States Negro is moving with a sense of great urgency toward the promised land of racial justice. 8

Nothing could be more tragic than for men to live in these revolutionary times and fail to achieve the new attitudes and the new mental outlooks that the new situation demands. In Washington Irving's familiar story of Rip Van Winkle, the one thing that we usually remember is that Rip slept twenty years. There is another important 9

MARTIN LUTHER KING, JR.

point, however, that is almost always overlooked. It was the sign on the inn in the little town on the Hudson from which Rip departed and scaled the mountain for his long sleep. When he went up, the sign had a picture of King George III of England. When he came down, twenty years later, the sign had a picture of George Washington. As he looked at the picture of the first President of the United States, Rip was confused, flustered and lost. He knew not who Washington was. The most striking thing about this story is not that Rip slept twenty years, but that he slept through a revolution that would alter the course of human history.

10 One of the great liabilities of history is that all too many people fail to remain awake through great periods of social change. Every society has its protectors of the status quo and its fraternities of the indifferent who are notorious for sleeping through revolutions. But today our very survival depends on our ability to stay awake, to adjust to new ideas, to remain vigilant and to face the challenge of change. The large house in which we live demands that we transform this world-wide neighborhood into a world-wide brotherhood. Together we must learn to live as brothers or together we will be forced to perish as fools.

11 We must work passionately and indefatigably to bridge the gulf between our scientific progress and our moral progress. One of the great problems of mankind is that we suffer from a poverty of the spirit which stands in glaring contrast to our scientific and technological abundance. The richer we have become materially, the poorer we have become morally and spiritually.

12 Every man lives in two realms, the internal and the external. The internal is that realm of spiritual ends expressed in art, literature, morals and religion. The external is that complex of devices, techniques, mechanisms and instrumentalities by means of which we live. Our problem today is that we have allowed the internal to become lost in the external. We have allowed the means by which we live to outdistance the ends for which we live. So much of modern life can be summarized in that suggestive phrase of Thoreau: "Improved means to an unimproved end." This is the serious predicament, the deep and haunting problem, confronting modern man. Enlarged material powers spell enlarged peril if there is not proportionate growth of the soul. When the external of man's nature subjugates the internal, dark storm clouds begin to form.

13 Western civilization is particularly vulnerable at this moment, for our material abundance has brought us neither peace of mind nor serenity of spirit. An Asian writer has portrayed our dilemma in candid terms:

You call your thousand material devices "labor-saving ma-

THE WORLD HOUSE

617

chinery," yet you are forever "busy." With the multiplying of your machinery you grow increasingly fatigued, anxious, nervous, dissatisfied. Whatever you have, you want more; and wherever you are you want to go somewhere else . . . your devices are neither time-saving nor soul-saving machinery. They are so many sharp spurs which urge you on to invent more machinery and to do more business.[1]

This tells us something about our civilization that cannot be cast aside as a prejudiced charge by an Eastern thinker who is jealous of Western prosperity. We cannot escape the indictment.

This does not mean that we must turn back the clock of scientific progress. No one can overlook the wonders that science has wrought for our lives. The automobile will not abdicate in favor of the horse and buggy, or the train in favor of the stagecoach, or the tractor in favor of the hand plow, or the scientific method in favor of ignorance and superstition. But our moral and spiritual "lag" must be redeemed. When scientific power outruns moral power, we end up with guided missiles and misguided men. When we foolishly minimize the internal of our lives and maximize the external, we sign the warrant for our own day of doom.   14

Our hope for creative living in this world house that we have inherited lies in our ability to re-establish the moral ends of our lives in personal character and social justice. Without this spiritual and moral reawakening we shall destroy ourselves in the misuse of our own instruments.   15

COMPREHENSION

1. What does the author mean by the concept of a "world house"? How is the modern era drawing the peoples of the world together? How does King explain the dangers confronting the world house? What is his proposal for "creative living"?

2. According to King, what are the two "realms" that we live in? How are these realms reflected in the content of this selection?

3. Explain the connection that King draws between oppression, freedom, and revolution.

RHETORIC

1. King, a compelling preacher and speaker (see his "I Have a Dream" speech, delivered in 1963 at the end of the March on Washington, a contemporary classic), often injected his prose with biblical and oratorical rhythms. Find three

[1] Abraham Mitrie Rihbany, *Wise Men from the East and from the West*, Houghton, Mifflin, 1922.

MARTIN LUTHER KING, JR.

examples of rhythmical, carefully balanced cadences in this essay, and explain their effect. Compare these rhythms with those in "I Have a Dream."

2.   A second characteristic of King's oratorical and literary style is his fondness for figurative language. Locate and identify five examples of figurative language.

3.   What is King's thesis? How does the key rhetorical strategy of analogy help to advance it? What minor analogies exist in the essay?

4.   Describe King's relationship with his reading audience. Identify words and phrases that clarify this relationship. Why, for example, does the author use the pronoun *we*?

5.   How do the first and last paragraphs serve as a frame for this selection? How effective are they, and why?

6.   What argumentative and persuasive techniques do you detect in this essay. How does King use illustration, comparison, and contrast to advance his proposition?

WRITING

1.   Comment on the relevance of King's analogy to the 1990s.

2.   Write a paper on "the world house," using contemporary events, quotations from authorities, and your own ideas about today's conflicts to frame the analogy.

3.   Using Whitehead's quotation (paragraph 7) as a guide, develop an argumentative essay on whether we are at a turning point in civilization.

EDITH HAMILTON

The Lessons of the Past

Edith Hamilton (1867–1963), teacher, writer, and Grecophile, wrote her first book when she was 63. Her initial career was as headmistress of a private girl's school in Maryland. When she retired, she began to write about ancient civilizations, particularly Greek civilization. In 1930, The Greek Way *was published. In later years, Hamilton also wrote* The Roman Way *(1932) and* The Prophets of Israel *(1936). She retold Greek, Roman, and Norse myths in* Mythology *(1942). At the age of 90, Hamilton visited Greece and was made an honorary citizen. This essay focuses on Greek civilization in order to illuminate the problems confronting the modern era.*

s there an ever-present past? Are there permanent truths which are forever important for the present? Today we are facing a future more strange and untried than any other generation has faced. The new world Columbus opened seems small indeed beside the illimitable distances of space before us, and the possibilities of destruction are immeasurably greater than ever. In such a position can we afford to spend time on the past? That is the question I am often asked. Am I urging the study of the Greeks and Romans and their civilizations for the atomic age?

Yes; that is just what I am doing. I urge it without qualifications. We have a great civilization to save—or to lose. The greatest civilization before ours was the Greek. They challenge us and we need the challenge. They, too, lived in a dangerous world. They were a little, highly civilized people, the only civilized people in the west, surrounded by barbarous tribes and with the greatest Asiatic power, Persia, always threatening them. In the end they succumbed, but the reason they did was not that the enemies outside were so strong, but that their own strength, their spiritual strength, had given way. While they had it they kept Greece unconquered and they left behind a record in art and thought which in all the centuries of human effort since has not been surpassed.

The point which I want to make is not that their taste was superior to ours, not that the Parthenon was their idea of church architecture nor that Sophocles was the great drawing card in the theaters, nor any of the familiar comparisons between fifth-century Athens and twentieth-century America, but that Socrates found on every street corner and in every Athenian equivalent of the baseball field people who were caught up by his questions into the world of thought. To be able to be caught up into the world of thought—that is to be educated.

How is that great aim to be reached? For years we have eagerly discussed ways and means of education, and the discussion still goes on. William James once said that there were two subjects which if mentioned made other conversation stop and directed all eyes to the speaker. Religion was one and education the other. Today Russia seems to come first, but education is still emphatically the second. In spite of all the articles we read and all the speeches we listen to about it, we want to know more; we feel deeply its importance.

There is today a clearly visible trend toward making it the aim of education to defeat the Russians. That would be a sure way to defeat education. Genuine education is possible only when people realize that it has to do with persons, not with movements.

When I read educational articles it often seems to me that this important side of the matter, the purely personal side, is not emphasized enough; that fact that it is so much more agreeable and inter-

EDITH HAMILTON

esting to be an educated person than not. The sheer pleasure of being educated does not seem to be stressed. Once long ago I was talking with Prof. Basil L. Gildersleeve of Johns Hopkins University, the greatest Greek scholar our country has produced. He was an old man and he had been honored everywhere, in Europe as well as in America. He was just back from a celebration held for him in Oxford. I asked him what compliment received in his long life had pleased him most. The question amused him and he laughed over it, but he thought too. Finally he said, "I believe it was when one of my students said, 'Professor, you have so much fun with your own mind.'" Robert Louis Stevenson said that a man ought to be able to spend two or three hours waiting for a train at a little country station when he was all alone and had nothing to read, and not be bored for a moment.

What is the education which can do this? What is the furniture 7 which makes the only place belonging absolutely to each one of us, the world within, a place where we like to go? I wish I could answer that question. I wish I could produce a perfect decorator's design warranted to make any interior lovely and interesting and stimulating; but even if I could, sooner or later we would certainly try different designs. My point is only that while we must and should change the furniture, we ought to throw away old furniture very cautiously. It may turn out to be irreplaceable. A great deal was thrown away in the last generation or so, long enough ago to show some of the results. Furniture which had for centuries been foremost, we lightly, in a few years, discarded. The classics almost vanished from our field of education. That was a great change. Along with it came another. There is a marked difference between the writers of the past and the writers of today who have been educated without benefit of Greek and Latin. Is this a matter of cause and effect? People will decide for themselves, but I do not think anyone will question the statement that clear thinking is not the characteristic which distinguishes our literature today. We are more and more caught up by the unintelligible. People like it. This argues an inability to think, or, almost as bad, a disinclination to think.

Neither disposition marked the Greeks. They had a passion 8 for thinking things out, and they loved unclouded clarity of statement as well as of thought. The Romans did, too, in their degree. They were able to put an idea into an astonishingly small number of words without losing a particle of intelligibility. It is only of late, with a generation which has never had to deal with a Latin sentence, that we are being submerged in a flood of words, words, words. It has been said that Lincoln at Gettysburg today would have begun in some such fashion as this: "Eight and seven-tenths decades ago the pioneer workers in this continental area implemented a new group based on an ideology of free boundaries and initial equality," and might easily

 THE LESSONS OF THE PAST

have ended, "That political supervison of the integrated units, for the integrated units, by the integrated units, shall not become null and void on the superficial area of this planet." Along with the banishment of the classics, gobbledegook has come upon us—and the appalling size of the Congressional Record, and the overburdened mail service.

Just what the teaching in the schools was which laid the foundation of the Greek civilization we do not know in detail; the result we do know. Greek children were taught, Plato said, to "love what is beautiful and hate what is ugly." When they grew up their very pots and pans had to be pleasant to look at. It was part of their training to hate clumsiness and awkwardness; they loved grace and practiced it. "Our children," Plato said, "will be influenced for good by every sight and sound of beauty, breathing in, as it were, a pure breeze blowing to them from a good land." 9

All the same, the Athenians were not, as they showed Socrates when he talked to them, preoccupied with enjoying lovely things. The children were taught to think. Plato demanded a stiff examination, especially in mathematics, for entrance to his Academy. The Athenians were a thinking people. Today the scientists are bearing away the prize for thought. Well, a Greek said that the earth went around the sun, sixteen centuries before Copernicus thought of it. A Greek said if you sailed out of Spain and kept to one latitude, you would come at last to land, seventeen hundred years before Columbus did it. Darwin said, "We are mere schoolboys in scientific thinking compared to old Aristotle." And the Greeks did not have a great legacy from the past as our scientists have; they thought science out from the beginning. 10

The same is true of politics. They thought that out, too, from the beginning, and they gave all the boys a training to fit them to be thinking citizens of a free state that had come into being through thought. 11

Basic to all the Greek achievement was freedom. The Athenians were the only free people in the world. In the great empires of antiquity—Egypt, Babylon, Assyria, Persia—splendid though they were, with riches beyond reckoning and immense power, freedom was unknown. The idea of it never dawned in any of them. It was born in Greece, a poor little country, but with it able to remain unconquered no matter what manpower and what wealth were arrayed against her. At Marathon and at Salamis overwhelming numbers of Persians had been defeated by small Greek forces. It has been proved that one free man was superior to many submissively obedient subjects of a tyrant. Athens was the leader in that amazing victory, and to the Athenians freedom was their dearest possession. Demosthenes said that they would not think it worth their while to live if they could 12 not do so as free men, and years later a great teacher said, "Athenians, if you deprive them of their liberty, will die."

Athens was not only the first democracy in the world, it was also at its height an almost perfect democracy—that is, for men. There was no part in it for women or foreigners or slaves, but as far as the men were concerned it was more democratic than we are. The governing body was the Assembly, of which all citizens over eighteen were members. The Council of Five Hundred which prepared business for the Assembly and, if requested, carried out what had been decided there, was made up of citizens who were chosen by lot. The same was true of the juries. Minor officials also were chosen by lot. The chief magistrates and the highest officers in the army were elected by the Assembly. Pericles was a general, very popular, who acted for a long time as if he were head of the state, but he had to be elected every year. Freedom of speech was the right the Athenians prized most and there has never been another state as free in that respect. When toward the end of the terrible Peloponnesian War the victorious Spartans were advancing upon Athens, Aristophanes caricatured in the theater the leading Athenian generals and showed them up as cowards, and even then as the Assembly opened, the herald asked, "Does anyone wish to speak?" 13

There was complete political equality. It was a government of the people, by the people, for the people. An unregenerate old aristocrat in the early fourth century, B.C., writes: "If you *must* have a democracy, Athens is the perfect example. I object to it because it is based on the welfare of the lower, not the better, classes. In Athens the people who row the vessels and do the work have the advantage. It is their prosperity that is important." All the same, making the city beautiful was important too, as were also the great performances in the theater. If, as Plato says, the Assembly was chiefly made up of cobblers and carpenters and smiths and farmers and retail-business men, they approved the construction of the Parthenon and the other buildings on the Acropolis, and they crowded the theater when the great tragedies were played. Not only did all free men share in the government; the love of the beautiful and the desire to have a part in creating it were shared by the many, not by a mere chosen few. That has happened in no state except Athens. 14

But those free Greeks owned slaves. What kind of freedom was that? The question would have been incomprehensible to the ancient world. There had always been slaves; they were a first necessity. The way of life everywhere was based upon them. They were taken for granted; no one ever gave them a thought. The very best Greek minds, the thinkers who discovered freedom and the solar system, had never an idea that slavery was evil. It is true that the greatest 15

THE LESSONS OF THE PAST

thinker of them all, Plato, was made uncomfortable by it. He said that slaves were often good, trustworthy, doing more for a man than his own family would, but he did not follow his thought through. The glory of being the first one to condemn it belongs to a man of the generation before Plato, the poet Euripides. He called it, "That thing of evil," and in several of his tragedies showed its evil for all to see. A few centuries later the great Greek school of the Stoics denounced it. Greece first saw it for what it is. But the world went on in the same way. The Bible accepts it without comment. Two thousand years after the Stoics, less than a hundred years ago, the American Republic accepted it.

Athens treated her slaves well. A visitor to the city in the early fourth century, B.C., wrote: "It is illegal here to deal a slave a blow. In the street he won't step aside to let you pass. Indeed you can't tell a slave by his dress; he looks like all the rest. They can go to the theater too. Really, the Athenians have established a kind of equality between slaves and free men." They were never a possible source of danger to the state as they were in Rome. There were no terrible slave wars and uprisings in Athens. In Rome, crucifixion was called "the slave's punishment." The Athenians did not practice crucifixion, and had no so-called slave's punishment. They were not afraid of their slaves. 16

In Athens' great prime Athenians were free. No one told them what they must do or what they should think—no church or political party or powerful private interests or labor unions. Greek schools had no donors of endowments they must pay attention to, no government financial backing which must be made secure by acting as the government wanted. To be sure, the result was that they had to take full responsibility, but that is always the price for full freedom. The Athenians were a strong people, they could pay the price. They were a thinking people; they knew what freedom means. They knew—not that they were free because their country was free, but that their country was free because they were free. 17

A reflective Roman traveling in Greece in the second century A.D. said, "None ever throve under democracy save the Athenians; *they* had sane self-control and were law-abiding." He spoke truly. That is what Athenian education aimed at, to produce men who would be able to maintain a self-governed state because they were themselves self-governed, self-controlled, self-reliant. Plato speaks of "the education in excellence which makes men long to be perfect citizens, knowing both how to rule and be ruled." "We are a free democracy," Pericles said. "We do not allow absorption in our own affairs to interfere with participation in the city's; we yield to none in independence of spirit and complete self-reliance, but we regard him who holds 18

EDITH HAMILTON

aloof from public affairs as useless." They called the useless man a "private" citizen, *idiotes,* from which our word "idiot" comes.

They had risen to freedom and to ennoblement from what 19
Gilbert Murray calls "effortless barbarism"; they saw it all around
them; they hated its filth and fierceness; nothing effortless was among
the good things they wanted. Plato said, "Hard is the good," and a
poet hundreds of years before Plato said,

> Before the gates of Excellence the high gods have placed
> sweat.
> Long is the road thereto and steep and rough at the first,
> But when the height is won, then is there ease.

When or why the Greeks set themselves to travel on that road 20
we do not know, but it led them away from habits and customs accepted everywhere that keep men down to barbaric filth and fierceness. It led them far. One example is enough to show the way they
took. It was the custom—during how many millenniums, who can
say—for a victor to erect a trophy, a monument of his victory. In
Egypt, where stone was plentiful, it would be a slab engraved with
his glories. Farther east, where the sand took over, it might be a great
heap of severed heads, quite permanent objects; bones last a long time.
But in Greece, though a man could erect a trophy, it must be made
of wood and it could never be repaired. Even as the victor set it up
he would see in his mind how soon it would decay and sink into ruin,
and there it must be left. The Greeks in their onward pressing along
the steep and rough road had learned a great deal. They knew the
victor might be the vanquished next time. There should be no permanent records of the manifestly impermanent. They had learned a
great deal.

An old Greek inscription states that the aim of mankind 21
should be "to tame the savageness of man and make gentle the life
of the world." Aristotle said that the city was built first for safety, but
then that men might discover the good life and lead it. So the
Athenians did according to Pericles. Pericles said that Athens stood
for freedom and for thought and for beauty, but in the Greek way,
within limits, without exaggeration. The Athenians loved beauty, he
said, but with simplicity; they did not like the extravagances of luxury.
They loved the things of the mind, but they did not shrink from hardship. Thought did not cause them to hesitate, it clarified the road to
action. If they had riches they did not make a show of them, and no
one was ashamed of being poor if he was useful. They were free because of willing obedience to law, not only the written, but still more
the unwritten, kindness and compassion and unselfishness and the

THE LESSONS OF THE PAST

many qualities which cannot be enforced, which depend on a man's free choice, but without which men cannot live together.

If ever there is to be a truly good and great and enduring republic it must be along these lines. We need the challenge of the city that thought them out, wherein for centuries one genius after another grew up. Geniuses are not produced by spending money. We need the challenge of the way the Greeks were educated. They fixed their eyes on the individual. We contemplate millions. What we have undertaken in this matter of education has dawned upon us only lately. We are trying to do what has never been attempted before, never in the history of the world—educate all the young in a nation of 170 millions; a magnificent idea, but we are beginning to realize what are the problems and what may be the results of mass production of education. So far, we do not seem appalled at the prospect of exactly the same kind of education being applied to all the school children from the Atlantic to the Pacific, but there is an uneasiness in the air, a realization that the individual is growing less easy to find; an idea, perhaps, of what standardization might become when the units are not machines, but human beings. 22

Here is where we can go back to the Greeks with profit. The Athenians in their dangerous world needed to be a nation of independent men who could take responsibility, and they taught their children accordingly. They thought about every body. Someday he would be a citizen of Athens, responsible for her safety and her glory, "each one," Pericles said, "fitted to meet life's chances and changes with the utmost versatility and grace." To them education was by its very nature an individual matter. To be properly educated a boy had to be taught music; he learned to play a musical instrument. He had to learn poetry, a great deal of it, and recite it—and there were a number of musical instruments and many poets; though, to be sure, Homer was the great textbook. 23

That kind of education is not geared to mass production. It does not produce people who instinctively go the same way. That is how Athenian children lived and learned while our millions learn the same lessons and spend hours before television sets looking at exactly the same thing at exactly the same time. For one reason and another we are more and more ignoring differences, if not trying to obliterate them. We seem headed toward a standardization of the mind, what Goethe called "the deadly commonplace that fetters us all." That was not the Greek way. 24

The picture of the Age of Pericles drawn by the historian Thucydides, one of the greatest historians the world has known, is of a state made up of people who are self-reliant individuals, not echoes or copies, who want to be let alone to do their own work, but who 25

EDITH HAMILTON

are also closely bound together by a great aim, the commonweal, each one so in love with his country—Pericles' own words—that he wants most of all to use himself in her service. Only an ideal? Ideals have enormous power. They stamp an age. They lift life up when they are lofty; they drag down and make decadent when they are low—and then, by that strange fact, the survival of the fittest, those that are low fade away and are forgotten. The Greek ideals have had a power of persistent life for twenty-five hundred years.

Is it rational that now when the young people may have to face problems harder than we face, is it reasonable that with the atomic age before them, at this time we are giving up the study of how the Greeks and Romans prevailed magnificently in a barbaric world; the study, too, of how that triumph ended, how a slackness and softness finally came over them to their ruin? In the end, more than they wanted freedom, they wanted security, a comfortable life, and they lost all—security and comfort and freedom. 26

Is not that a challenge to us? Is it not true that into our education have come a slackness and softness? Is hard effort prominent? The world of thought can be entered in no other way. Are we not growing slack and soft in our political life? When the Athenians finally wanted not to give to the state, but the state to give to them, when the freedom they wished most for was freedom from responsibility, then Athens ceased to be free and was never free again. Is not that a challenge? 27

Cicero said, "To be ignorant of the past is to remain a child." Santayana said, "A nation that does not know history is fated to repeat it." The Greeks can help us, help us as no other people can, to see how freedom is won and how it is lost. Above all, to see in clearest light what freedom is. The first nation in the world to be free sends a ringing call down through the centuries to all who would be free. Greece rose to the very height, not because she was big, she was very small; not because she was rich, she was very poor; not even because she was wonderfully gifted. So doubtless were others in the great empires of the ancient world who have gone their way leaving little for us. She rose because there was in the Greeks the greatest spirit that moves in humanity, the spirit that sets men free. 28

Plato put into words what the spirit is. "Freedom," he says, "is no matter of laws and constitutions; only he is free who realizes the divine order within himself, the true standard by which a man can steer and measure himself." True standards, ideals that lift life up, marked the way of the Greeks. Therefore their light has never been extinguished. 29

"The time for extracting a lesson from history is ever at hand for them who are wise." Demosthenes. 30

COMPREHENSION

1. State, in your own words, the thesis of this essay.

2. According to Hamilton, what is the relationship between Greek civilization and the quality of American education?

3. How does the author seek to justify Greek democracy, even though, as she admits, slaves, women, and foreigners were not free or equal? List the qualities and cherished goals of Greek citizens that, according to Hamilton, made them free.

RHETORIC

1. Explain the analogy in paragraph 7.

2. Analyze the elements of style in paragraph 28.

3. How does the first paragraph prepare for the author's thesis.

4. How does the author order her main topics in the essay?

5. What causal patterns of development appear in the essay? Where is comparison and contrast used as a rhetorical strategy? How does she use rhetorical questions as an argumentative tactic?

6. Explain the significance of definition as a pattern of development in Hamilton's essay.

WRITING

1. Speaking of the Greeks, Hamilton writes: "In the end, more than they wanted freedom, they wanted security, a comfortable life, and they lost it all—security and comfort and freedom" (paragraph 26). What is the relevance of Hamilton's observation to the state of modern American civilization? In this connection, do you believe that there is an ever-present past? Explain in an essay.

2. Write an essay on the lessons that modern nations can learn from the past.

3. Define freedom in terms of the American experience.

4. Analyze the state of freedom in the modern world. Cite specific examples to support your views.

Reflections on the Human Condition

Margaret Mead (1901–1979), famed American anthropologist, was curator of ethnology at the American Museum of Natural History and a professor at Columbia University. Her field expeditions to Samoa, New Guinea, and Bali in the 1920s and 1930s produced several major studies, notably Coming of Age in Samoa *(1928),* Growing Up in New Guinea *(1930), and* Sex and Temperament in Three Primitive Societies *(1963). In this essay, Mead reflects on the meaning of the changes she has witnessed in her life.*

I turned twenty in December 1921. I was halfway through college and still uncertain about which of the human sciences I would specialize in, but I was fairly sure that I would reject my other alternatives: painting and politics. My father was an economist who had worked on the quantity theory of money; my mother was a sociologist who did some of the first work on the assimilation of immigrants into the United States. I knew about the comparative study of cultures; I knew that all human groups had the same kinds of varying capacities; I knew how economic institutions changed; and I knew about the consequences of the United States Senate's failure to honor the promises that President Woodrow Wilson had made on our behalf.

Although the hopes engendered by World War I were still with us, I also knew that the seeds of World War II were already being sown because of the failure of the United States and Russia to join the League of Nations. Those of us who were aware of what this meant knew that however much our lives were in our own hands, another world war might indeed destroy civilization. We had not yet come to fear the destruction of all life on this planet nor the possible destruction of the planet itself, but we were acutely aware that civilization had been built laboriously over centuries by human beings and that it was within the power of human beings to destroy it. The English comment about World War I, "The lamps are going out all over Europe; we shall not see them lit again in our lifetime," echoed in our minds.

To us, "civilization" meant Europe and Europe's offspring. Although we knew that the great Asian countries had ancient and impressive traditions and that Japan had entered the war as one of the modern nations, civilization as a concept was actually confined to the Graeco-Roman tradition in government and the Hellenic, Judeo-

Christian tradition in religion, philosophy, and science. "Democracy" covered a wide range of hopes: freedom from tyranny, freedom from slavery, freedom of thought and enquiry, freedom of religion, and freedom of opportunity for all. But we actually did not yet think of the world as a whole. There was the European tradition, of which Americans were a part; there was the tradition of freedom from tyrannical monarchical and colonial regimes, which the countries of South America shared with those of North America; and there was the belief that the overthrow of the Czar in the Russian Revolution was a harbinger of freedom for the Russian people. Germany was to become democratic; battleships were to be sunk; and the warring world was to disarm.

There were many things that we did not understand. Malthu- 4 sianism was not popular, nor had the Depression ushered in the practices of burning crops and slaughtering little pigs. There had been famines, but during and after World War I, the American people had responded to calls for help. Without war it seemed that supplies of food could be plentiful. I had no sense yet that the resources of the earth were so limited and so distributed that the question of how they were to be used would be a crucial one. Nor did I have any idea of the changes that would be wrought by the introduction of automation.

The possibilities of new resource uses with automation were 5 not realized until about 1930, when Howard Scott, who founded the very premature and prophetic movement called Technocracy, began to talk about joining together in economically viable units regions— in North and South America, China and India, Europe and Northern Asia—having resources and technical knowledge. The various kinds of socialist utopias, including guild socialism, were components in our thinking about the future of the world. We had no hint yet that the labor theory of value would have to be replaced by kilocalories, which combined energy (human and resource-based) and our assessments of our capacity to produce food or control the rate of growth.

For myself, I had a sense of an open future, that I would be 6 free to pick a career, marry or not marry, have children or not have children, be a politician, a painter, writer, or social scientist. Many of the old debates that had agitated my grandparents' and my parents' generations seemed to be over: the battle between science and religion; the acceptance of Freud's documentation of the importance of the unconscious, especially in creative activities; the right of women to vote, to organize, to participate in political life, to work as the intellectual equals of men in a new atmosphere of freedom, to combine a career and marriage, or to choose either one. I combined a sense of the possibility of developing an increasingly more just world with plenty for all with the sense that a second world war was nevertheless hanging over us. The young people five to ten years my senior were already being spoken of as "the lost generation." For my college generation, the expectation of another world war meant a shortened time perspective within which to do what needed to be done, rather than a profound pessimism.

As a girl I had read various books on utopias and counter-utopias and science fiction dealing with prophecies of the twenty-first century: *Caesar's Column*, in which the author Ignatius Donnelly invented airplanes but not automobiles; *The British Barbarians* by Grant Allen, where the disillusioned time traveler returned to the twenty-first century disgusted with the provincialism of nineteenth-century British natives; H. G. Wells' *War of the Worlds* and Sir Arthur Conan Doyle's *The Lost World*; Jules Verne's *Twenty Thousand Leagues Under the Sea* and *Around the World in Eighty Days*, with their precursors of modern technology; Jack London's *Before Adam*, with its first speculations of the way in which man's membership within biological orders and families would later have great significance; and *Erewhon* by Samuel Butler, in which criminals were treated as sick and deserving of sympathy, and the sick treated as criminals. Among the poets, there were the usual prescient whisperings of later disaster. The American poet Edna St. Vincent Millay had published in 1921 "The Blue-Flag in the Bog" with its picture of a world destroyed: 7

God had called us and we came;
  Our loved Earth to ashes left;
Heaven was a neighbor's house,
  Open flung to us, bereft.

Weary wings that rise and fall
  All day long above the fire!—
Red with heat was every wall,
  Rough with heat was every wire—
But the earth forevermore
  Is a place where nothing grows,—
Dawn will come, and no bud break;
  Evening, and no blossom close.

The science fiction writers and the poets were slowly building up the consciousness with which, twenty-four years later, I could understand that the discovery of the atom bomb meant the end of the world in which I had been reared, that not one line of a book that I was writing on the post-World War II world could now stand. I tore the manuscript up and threw it all away. But in 1921 the specter of a future that would be less bearable than the present and the fear of new forms of tyranny that would replace the old monarchical forms that had been our shorthand for tyranny then, were not yet with us. 8

The word "international" was the word we knew. Ideas like 9
One World of the early 1940s and Planet Earth of the 1960s were not
yet born. The map in my mind at that time was shaped like a globe,
old style, not like Buckminster Fuller's map, which really shows how
the land masses are related. There were vast spaces on my map about
which I knew almost nothing. Africa was an unknown continent, fit-
fully illuminated by books like *Batouala* or plays like *The Emperor Jones*,
by the influences of African wood sculpture on European art. India
was a place where Gandhi was trying to restore to themselves a people who had been grievously exploited by a colonial regime; China
was a vast and different civilization so far away that one knew hardly
anything about it. I knew that there had been pre-Columbian high
civilizations in Mexico and in South America and that these civilizations had developed independently along quite different lines from
the rest of the world. But these, too, had been destroyed by invading
Europeans on horseback. In 1921 Mexico was a scene of revolutions
against dictators who somehow belied the democratic processes that
were supposed to accompany representative government.

Of the various groups of primitive peoples who lived in re- 10
mote jungles and forests and on the islands of the South Seas, whose
study was to become my principal task for the next forty years, I knew
very little beyond current claims: by missionaries, that these people
needed to be rescued from their heathen ways; by artists, that the
clothes the missionaries brought spoiled the islanders as subjects for
aesthetic appreciation and gave them new diseases; and by anti-
imperialists and socialists, that these primitive people were being exploited. Imperialism was represented in my mind by Kipling's tales
and poetry and by Thorstein Veblen's *Imperial Germany and the Industrial Revolution,* the coming economic world by Maynard Keynes's *Economic Consequences of the Peace.*

If I try to reconstruct what I believed then to be the quality 11
of life for which all human beings should strive and what I believed
were the necessary steps toward attaining it, I find that peace came
first (obviously, since war destroyed lives, towns, the countryside,
hope), and after that came economic justice, a resolute willingness to
revise our social system so that everyone could have the necessities
of life. I would not have been able to list these necessities as food,
housing, education, medical care, etc. I do not think that I had any
concept of the possibility of eradicating the great scourges of the
world—tuberculosis, for example. My friends were still being sent to
sanatoriums for many years' "curing." I knew that there were terrible
plagues that attacked everyone, native and foreigner, and that these
diseases (cholera in India, for example) had something to do with
hygiene and poverty. But the vision of a world freed from these great
scourges was as far from my mind as was the idea that there could

MARGARET MEAD

be too many people in the world—too many hungry people, too many unschooled people, too many people who lived under tyrannical political regimes, too many people who toiled under terrible conditions in mines and factories, too many women veiled and housebound, too many children forced to engage in child labor.

Yes, I knew these were conditions that required enormous efforts—possibly revolution, possibly reform—to correct. But I myself hoped to have six children in an era when childbearing was not very popular with the intellectual middle class, many of whom had no children or only one. I wanted to have six children because I enjoyed children, and having children and a life of responsible usefulness seemed to fit together. In those days I expected to live in a country parsonage and work in local communities. I ended up with only one child (who has one child), and I now work, not in a country parsonage, but in the World Council of Churches programs in church and society, and theology and science. And my present community is the world. 12

Today we associate improvement in the quality of life with radical changes in our cities, new designs that will correct the terrible urban sprawl that the automobile has made possible and bring people back together again into multigeneration, multiracial, multiclass, multi-occupational communities—not households but communities— where people can know and trust their neighbors, and into a living style where much of the natural world of farm and wilderness is within walking distance of the very young and the very old. When I was twenty-one, the present urban style, which so many people now feel has always been with us, was still in the future. There was still good public transportation; even in the big cities people lived in neighborhoods. Only a few grandparents, affluent and footloose, went to Florida or California. The word "baby-sitting" had not been invented, but there were families who had no kin or neighbors to help. In college I organized my friends into baby-sitting groups, because I thought it was bad for us to spend so many months without contact with children. But the dreadful loneliness of the isolated nuclear family of today, isolated in transient slums, isolated in developments, isolated in suburbs, had not yet become a way of life for a large proportion—and the style-setting section—of the population. 13

My mother was interested in cooperative laundries, more cooperative relations between households, and in ways of giving domestic servants dignity. But the world of today—the world in which it is taken for granted that each couple will live wherever they can find housing they can afford, within driving distance of the husband's job, or both their jobs, and will expect no help from anyone; the world in which gadgets replace helping hands, where telephone conversations with distant mothers take the place of visits over the back fence, 14 where driving substitutes for bicycling, walking, and riding street-cars—was only foreshadowed. Today we know that in order to restore a human quality to living, town and country roads and transportation systems must all be redesigned, not to conform to the old image but nonetheless in a way that will recreate some of the values that were destroyed with the development of our automobile-based society.

In 1921 I knew a good deal about racial and social injustice, [15] and I knew how precious basic dignity and opportunity were to the minorities—Negroes, European and Asian immigrants, Jews, and Catholics—who were often accorded neither dignity nor opportunity. Since then I have lived through the period in the United States when we fought for the integration of individual members of minorities as students, physicians, lawyers, travelers, property owners. And we have seen the rise and fall of totalitarian terrors—massacre and genocide—of newly liberated countries emulating their former colonial conquerers in savagery and racial prejudice. But here, I do not think that my perceptions have changed very much. For the quality of life that we want for all cannot be attained until no human beings are demeaned or denied dignity or an equal chance for a livelihood because of race or color, nationality, or ideology of their parents. People of every physique must have a world to live in where they can find beautiful both their own parents and very different peoples' parents.

I believe I was fully conscious of the way in which the culture [16] in which one was born and reared, one's class position, whether one was rich or poor, determined whether genius was to flower or not. I was fully conscious that there is a wide range of intelligence in every human group, and that, to date, civilizations have wasted large numbers of their gifted. I would have phrased this thought then in the words of Thomas Gray's "Elegy Written in a Country Churchyard":

> Perhaps in this neglected spot is laid
> Some heart once pregnant with celestial fire;
> Hands, that the rod of empire might have sway'd,
> Or waked to extasy the living lyre.
>
> But Knowledge to their eyes her ample page
> Rich with the spoils of time, did ne'er unroll;
> Chill Penury repress'd their noble rage,
> And froze the genial current of the soul.
>
> Full many a gem of purest ray serene
> The dark unfathom'd caves of ocean bear:
> Full many a flower is born to blush unseen,
> And waste its sweetness on the desert air.

But in my youth I was not as conscious of how much the   17
quality of a culture depended not only on the way it provided for
expression of the gifted but also the way it treated its crippled and
unfortunate. I think if someone had made the point then and had
suggested a program on birth defects like that of the American March
of Dimes today, with half the funds going to research to prevent the
birth defects in the future and half to care for those who are born
defective today, I would have understood it. But no one did. And no
one had yet formulated the idea of the interrelationship between the
climate of opinion in a society and what changes the members of that
society can make. That was in the future, too.

These are the issues that concern us today: the prevention of   18
war; the protection of the environment; the balancing of population
and resources; the management of energy so that we will neither ex-
haust our resources with unbridled growth nor contaminate the environment; the distribution of resources among nations and groups
who have been differently dowered in the past by nature and history;
the humanization of technology so that technology can be used for
human ends and not primarily for profit or for power; the replanning
of towns and cities so that neighborhoods can again be a microcosm
of three-generational wholeness of life; the creation of transcendental
values that will no longer set members of one religion against another,
or of one ideology against another, so that all human beings can move
in new ways without being traitors to the old. Of these, only the need
to prevent war was as clear to me then as it is now.

Perhaps most important of all, I did not have any doubt then   19
that the world was changing, that change was in the very air we
breathed, absolutely unpreventable and absolutely necessary. I think
this too is part of the quality of life, that human beings must have a
chance to learn to cherish the past, act in the present, and leave the
future open.

COMPREHENSION

1. What is Mead's purpose in writing this selection? What response does she
wish to elicit from her readers?

2. In what sense is this piece about Mead's education? How well did her upbringing prepare her to live in the twentieth century?

3. Explain, in your own words, what Mead means by "civilization."

RHETORIC

1. Use a dictionary to define the following: *Malthusianism* (paragraph 4),
Technocracy (paragraph 5), *eradicating* (paragraph 11), *scourges* (paragraph 11),
and *dowered* (paragraph 18). What is unusual about Mead's use of *dowered* in
the context of the sentence.

2.   Explain the connotations that Mead brings to the word *civilization*. How does her use of the term change throughout the essay?

3.   Why does Mead structure her essay chronologically? How would it be a different essay without narration?

4.   How does the author employ comparative methods to structure her essay?

5.   Explain the relationship between paragraphs 7 and 11.

6.   What relationship does the conclusion bear to the whole essay? How does Mead's tripartite prescription inform the content of the entire work?

WRITING
1.   After reading this piece, do you feel optimistic or pessimistic about the future? Can we "learn to cherish the past, act in the present, and leave the future open"?

2.   Write an essay that predicts changes in your own future. What will the world be like in twenty years? How accurate do you think your forecast will be? Why?

3.   In a narrative essay, trace your own education to date, focusing on what you have learned about various civilizations and "the human condition."

HENRY ADAMS

The Dynamo and the Virgin

Henry Adams (1838–1918), American historian and author, the descendant of the United States presidents John Adams and John Quincy Adams, was one of the most important observers of the rapidly accelerating forces shaping modern life at the start of the twentieth century. A critic of the modernist impulse toward disunity, he investigated in two of his later books, Mont-Saint-Michel and Chartres *(1905) and* The Education of Henry Adams *(1907), the uses of power in relationship to society. In this famous chapter from* The Education, *Adams contrasts medieval civilization, with its achievement of order, and the modern age, which lacks the center that he so earnestly sought throughout his adult life.*

HENRY ADAMS

Until the Great Exposition of 1900 closed its doors in November, Adams haunted it, aching to absorb knowledge, and helpless to find it. He would have liked to know how much of it could have been grasped by the best-informed man in the world. While he was thus meditating chaos, Langley came by, and showed it to him. At Langley's behest, the Exhibition dropped its superfluous rags and stripped itself to the skin, for Langley knew what to study, and why, and how; while Adams might as well have stood outside in the night, staring at the Milky Way. Yet Langley said nothing new, and taught nothing that one might not have learned from Lord Bacon, three hundred years before; but though one should have known the "Advancement of Science" as well as one knew the "Comedy of Errors," the literary knowledge counted for nothing until some teacher should show how to apply it. Bacon took a vast deal of trouble in teaching King James I and his subjects, American or other, towards the year 1620, that true science was the development or economy of forces; yet an elderly American in 1900 knew neither the formula nor the forces; or even so much as to say to himself that his historical business in the exposition concerned only the economies or developments of force since 1893, when he began the study at Chicago. 1

Nothing in education is so astonishing as the amount of ignorance it accumulates in the form of inert facts. Adams had looked at most of the accumulations of art in the storehouses called Art Museums; yet he did not know how to look at the art exhibits of 1900. He had studied Karl Marx and his doctrines of history with profound attention, yet he could not apply them at Paris. Langley, with the ease of a great master of experiment, threw out of the field every exhibit that did not reveal a new application of force, and naturally threw out, to begin with, almost the whole art exhibit. Equally, he ignored almost the whole industrial exhibit. He led his pupil directly to the forces. His chief interest was in new motors to make his airship feasible, and he taught Adams the astonishing complexities of the new Daimler motor, and of the automobile, which, since 1893, had become a nightmare at a hundred kilometres an hour, almost as destructive as the electric train which was only ten years older; and threatening to become as terrible as the locomotive steam-engine itself, which was almost exactly Adams's own age. 2

Then he showed his scholar the great hall of dynamos, and explained how little he knew about electricity or force of any kind, even of his own special sun, which spouted heat in inconceivable volume, but which, as far as he knew, might spout less or more, at any time, for all the certainty he felt in it. To him, the dynamo itself was but an ingenious channel for conveying somewhere the heat latent in a few tons of poor coal hidden in a dirty engine-house carefully kept 3 out of sight; but to Adams the dynamo became a symbol of infinity. As he grew accustomed to the great gallery of machines, he began to feel the forty-foot dynamos as a moral force, much as the early Christians felt the Cross. The planet itself seemed less impressive, in its old-fashioned, deliberate, annual or daily revolution, than this huge wheel, revolving within arm's-length at some vertiginous speed, and barely murmuring—scarcely humming an audible warning to stand a hair's-breadth further for respect of power—while it would not wake the baby lying close against its frame. Before the end, one began to pray to it; inherited instinct taught the natural expression of man before silent and infinite force. Among the thousand symbols of ultimate energy, the dynamo was not so human as some, but it was the most expressive.

Yet the dynamo, next to the steam-engine, was the most familiar of exhibits. For Adams's objects its value lay chiefly in its occult mechanism. Between the dynamo in the gallery of machines and the engine-house outside, the break of continuity amounted to abysmal fracture for a historian's objects. No more relation could he discover between the steam and the electric current than between the Cross and the cathedral. The forces were interchangeable if not reversible, but he could see only an absolute *fiat* in electricity as in faith. Langley could not help him. Indeed, Langley seemed to be worried by the same trouble, for he constantly repeated that the new forces were anarchical, and specially that he was not responsible for the new rays, that were little short of parricidal in their wicked spirit towards science. His own rays, with which he had doubled the solar spectrum, were altogether harmless and beneficent; but Radium denied its God—or, what was to Langley the same thing, denied the truths of his Science. The force was wholly new. 4

A historian who asked only to learn enough to be as futile as Langley or Kelvin, made rapid progress under this teaching, and mixed himself up in the tangle of ideas until he achieved a sort of Paradise of ignorance vastly consoling to his fatigued senses. He wrapped himself in vibrations and rays which were new, and he would have hugged Marconi and Branly had he met them, as he hugged the dynamo; while he lost his arithmetic in trying to figure out the equation between the discoveries and the economies of force. The economies, like the discoveries, were absolute, supersensual, occult; incapable of expression in horse-power. What mathematical equivalent could he suggest as the value of a Branly coherer? Frozen air, or the electric furnace, had some scale of measurement, no doubt, if somebody could invent a thermometer adequate to the purpose; but X-rays had played no part whatever in man's consciousness, and the atom itself had figured only as a fiction of thought. In these seven years man had translated himself into a new universe which had no 5

HENRY ADAMS

common scale of measurement with the old. He had entered a super-sensual world, in which he could measure nothing except by chance collisions of movements imperceptible to his senses, perhaps even imperceptible to his instruments, but perceptible to each other, and so to some known ray at the end of the scale. Langley seemed prepared for anything, even for an indeterminable number of universes interfused—physics stark mad in metaphysics.

Historians undertake to arrange sequences—called stories, or 6 histories—assuming in silence a relation of cause and effect. These assumptions, hidden in the depths of dusty libraries, have been astounding, but commonly unconscious and childlike; so much so, that if any captious critic were to drag them to light, historians would probably reply, with one voice, that they had never supposed themselves required to know what they were talking about. Adams, for one, had toiled in vain to find out what he meant. He had even published a dozen volumes of American history for no other purpose than to satisfy himself whether, by the severest process of stating, with the least possible comment, such facts as seemed sure, in such order as seemed rigorously consequent, he could fix for a familiar moment a necessary sequence of human movement. The result had satisfied him as little as at Harvard College. Where he saw sequence, other men saw something quite different, and no one saw the same unit of measure. He cared little about his experiments and less about his statesmen, who seemed to him quite as ignorant as himself and, as a rule, no more honest; but he insisted on a relation of sequence, and if he could not reach it by one method, he would try as many methods as science knew. Satisfied that the sequence of men led to nothing and that the sequence of their society could lead no further, while the mere sequence of time was artificial, and the sequence of thought was chaos, he turned at last to the sequence of force; and thus it happened that, after ten years' pursuit, he found himself lying in the Gallery of Machines at the Great Exposition of 1900, his historical neck broken by the sudden irruption of forces totally new.

Since no one else showed much concern, an elderly person 7 without other cares had no need to betray alarm. The year 1900 was not the first to upset schoolmasters. Copernicus and Galileo had broken many professorial necks about 1600; Columbus had stood the world on its head toward 1500; but the nearest approach to the revolution of 1900 was that of 310, when Constantine set up the Cross. The rays that Langley disowned, as well as those which he fathered, were occult, supersensual, irrational; they were a revelation of mysterious energy like that of the Cross; they were what, in terms of mediaeval science, were called immediate modes of the divine substance.

The historian was thus reduced to his last resources. Clearly 8 if he was bound to reduce all these forces to a common value, this common value could have no measure but that of their attraction on his own mind. He must treat them as they had been felt; as convertible, reversible, interchangeable attractions on thought. He made up his mind to venture it; he would risk translating rays into faith. Such a reversible process would vastly amuse a chemist, but the chemist could not deny that he, or some of his fellow physicists, could feel the force of both. When Adams was a boy in Boston, the best chemist in the place had probably never heard of Venus except by way of scandal, or of the Virgin except as idolatry; neither had he heard of dynamos or automobiles or radium; yet his mind was ready to feel the force of all, though the rays were unborn and the women were dead.

Here opened another totally new education, which promised 9 to be by far the most hazardous of all. The knife-edge along which he must crawl, like Sir Lancelot in the twelfth century, divided two kingdoms of force which had nothing in common but attraction. They were as different as a magnet is from gravitation, supposing one knew what a magnet was, or gravitation, or love. The force of the Virgin was still felt at Lourdes, and seemed to be as potent as X-rays: but in America neither Venus nor Virgin ever had value as force—at most as sentiment. No American had ever been truly afraid of either.

This problem in dynamics gravely perplexed an American his- 10 torian. The Woman had once been supreme; in France she still seemed potent, not merely as a sentiment, but as a force. Why was she unknown in America? For evidently America was ashamed of her, and she was ashamed of herself, otherwise they would not have strewn fig-leaves so profusely all over her. When she was a true force, she was ignorant of fig-leaves, but the monthly-magazine-made American female had not a feature that would have been recognized by Adam. The trait was notorious, and often humorous, but any one brought up among Puritans knew that sex was sin. In any previous age, sex was strength. Neither art nor beauty was needed. Every one, even among Puritans, knew that neither Diana of the Ephesians nor any of the Oriental goddesses was worshipped for her beauty. She was goddess because of her force; she was the animated dynamo; she was reproduction—the greatest and most mysterious of all energies; all she needed was to be fecund. Singularly enough, not one of Adams's many schools of education had ever drawn his attention to the opening lines of Lucretius, though they were perhaps the finest in all Latin literature, where the poet invoked Venus exactly as Dante invoked the Virgin:—

"Quae quoniam rerum naturam *sola* gubernas."

HENRY ADAMS

The Venus of Epicurean philosophy survived in the Virgin of the Schools:—

"Donna, sei tanto grande, e tanto vali,
Che qual vuol grazia, e a te non ricorre,
Sua disianza vuol volar senz' ali."

All this was to American thought as though it had never existed. The true American knew something of the facts, but nothing of the feelings; he read the letter, but he never felt the law. Before this historical chasm, a mind like that of Adams felt itself helpless; he turned from the Virgin to the Dynamo as though he were a Branly coherer. On one side, at the Louvre and at Chartres, as he knew by the record of work actually done and still before his eyes, was the highest energy ever known to man, the creator of four-fifths of his noblest art, exercising vastly more attraction over the human mind than all the steam-engines and dynamos ever dreamed of; and yet this energy was unknown to the American mind. An American Virgin would never dare command; an American Venus would never dare exist.

The question, which to any plain American of the nineteenth century seemed as remote as it did to Adams, drew him almost violently to study, once it was posed; and on this point Langleys were as useless as though they were Herbert Spencers or dynamos. The idea survived only as art. There one turned as naturally as though the artist were himself a woman. Adams began to ponder, asking himself whether he knew of any American artist who had ever insisted on the power of sex, as every classic had always done; but he could think only of Walt Whitman; Bret Harte, as far as the magazines would let him venture; and one or two painters, for the flesh-tones. All the rest had used sex for sentiment, never for force; to them, Eve was a tender flower, and Herodias an unfeminine horror. American art, like the American language and American education, was as far as possible sexless. Society regarded this victory over sex as its greatest triumph, and the historian readily admitted it, since the moral issue, for the moment, did not concern one who was studying the relations of unmoral force. He cared nothing for the sex of the dynamo until he could measure its energy.

Vaguely seeking a clue, he wandered through the art exhibit, and, in his stroll, stopped almost every day before St. Gaudens' General Sherman, which had been given the central post of honor. St. Gaudens himself was in Paris, putting on the work his usual interminable last touches, and listening to the usual contradictory suggestions of brother sculptors. Of all the American artists who gave to American art whatever life it breathed in the seventies, St. Gaudens was perhaps the most sympathetic, but certainly the most inarticulate.

THE DYNAMO AND THE VIRGIN

General Grant or Don Cameron had scarcely less instinct of rhetoric than he. All the others—the Hunts, Richardson, John La Farge, Stanford White—were exuberant; only St. Gaudens could never discuss or dilate on an emotion, or suggest artistic arguments for giving to his work the forms that he felt. He never laid down the law, or affected the despot, or became brutalized like Whistler by the brutalities of his world. He required no incense; he was no egoist; his simplicity of thought was excessive; he could not imitate, or give any form but his own to the creations of his hand. No one felt more strongly than he the strength of other men, but the idea that they could affect him never stirred an image in his mind.

This summer his health was poor and his spirits were low. 13 For such a temper, Adams was not the best companion, since his own gaiety was not *folle*; but he risked going now and then to the studio on Mont Parnasse to draw him out for a stroll in the Bois de Boulogne, or dinner as pleased his moods, and in return St. Gaudens sometimes let Adams go about in his company.

Once St. Gaudens took him down to Amiens, with a party of 14 Frenchmen, to see the cathedral. Not until they found themselves actually studying the sculpture of the western portal, did it dawn on Adams's mind that, for his purposes, St. Gaudens on that spot had more interest to him than the cathedral itself. Great men before great monuments express great truths, provided they are not taken too solemnly. Adams never tired of quoting the supreme phrase of his idol Gibbon, before the Gothic cathedrals: "I darted a contemptuous look on the stately monuments of superstition." Even in the footnotes of his history, Gibbon had never inserted a bit of humor more human than this, and one would have paid largely for a photograph of the fat little historian, on the background of Notre Dame of Amiens, trying to persuade his readers—perhaps himself—that he was darting a contemptuous look on the stately monument, for which he felt in fact the respect which every man of his vast study and active mind always feels before objects worthy of it; but besides the humor, one felt also the relation. Gibbon ignored the Virgin, because in 1789 religious monuments were out of fashion. In 1900 his remark sounded fresh and simple as the green fields to ears that had heard a hundred years of other remarks, mostly no more fresh and certainly less simple. Without malice, one might find it more instructive than a whole lecture of Ruskin. One sees what one brings, and at that moment Gibbon brought the French Revolution. Ruskin brought reaction against the Revolution. St. Gaudens had passed beyond all. He liked the stately monuments much more than he liked Gibbon or Ruskin; he loved their dignity; their unity; their scale; their lines; their lights and shadows; their decorative sculpture; but he was even less conscious than they of the force that created it all—the Virgin, the Woman—by whose genius "the stately monuments of superstition" were built, through which she was expressed. He would have seen more meaning in Isis with the cow's horns, at Edfoo, who expressed the same thought. The art remained, but the energy was lost even upon the artist.

Yet in mind and person St. Gaudens was a survival of the 15 1500's; he bore the stamp of the Renaissance, and should have carried an image of the Virgin round his neck, or stuck in his hat, like Louis XI. In mere time he was a lost soul that had strayed by chance into the twentieth century, and forgotten where it came from. He writhed and cursed at his ignorance, much as Adams did at his own, but in the opposite sense. St. Gaudens was a child of Benvenuto Cellini, smothered in an American cradle. Adams was a quintessence of Boston, devoured by curiosity to think like Benvenuto. St. Gaudens's art was starved from birth, and Adams's instinct was blighted from babyhood. Each had but half of a nature, and when they came together before the Virgin of Amiens they ought both to have felt in her the force that made them one; but it was not so. To Adams she became more than ever a channel of force; to St. Gaudens she remained as before a channel of taste.

For a symbol of power, St. Gaudens instinctively preferred the 16 horse, as was plain in his horse and Victory of the Sherman monument. Doubtless Sherman also felt it so. The attitude was so American that, for at least forty years, Adams had never realized that any other could be in sound taste. How many years had he taken to admit a notion of what Michael Angelo and Rubens were driving at? He could not say; but he knew that only since 1895 had he begun to feel the Virgin or Venus as force, and not everywhere even so. At Chartres— perhaps at Lourdes—possibly at Cnidos if one could still find there the divinely naked Aphrodite of Praxiteles—but otherwise one must look for force to the goddesses of Indian mythology. The idea died out long ago in the German and English stock. St. Gaudens at Amiens was hardly less sensitive to the force of the female energy than Matthew Arnold at the Grande Chartreuse. Neither of them felt goddesses as power—only as reflected emotion, human expression, beauty, purity, taste, scarcely even as sympathy. They felt a railway train as power; yet they, and all other artists, constantly complained that the power embodied in a railway train could never be embodied in art. All the steam in the world could not, like the Virgin, build Chartres.

Yet in mechanics, whatever the mechanicians might think, 17 both energies acted as interchangeable forces on man, and by action on man all known force may be measured. Indeed, few men of science measure force in any other way. After once admitting that a straight line was the shortest distance between two points, no serious mathematician cared to deny anything that suited his convenience, and rejected no symbol, unproved or unproveable, that helped him to ac-

 THE DYNAMO AND THE VIRGIN

complish work. The symbol was force, as a compass needle or a triangle was force, as the mechanist might prove by losing it, and nothing could be gained by ignoring their value. Symbol or energy, the Virgin had acted as the greatest force the Western world ever felt, and had drawn man's activities to herself more strongly than any other power, natural or supernatural, had ever done; the historian's business was to follow the track of the energy; to find where it came from and where it went to; its complex source and shifting channels; its values, equivalents, conversions. It could scarcely be more complex than radium; it could hardly be deflected, diverted, polarized, absorbed more perplexingly than other radiant matter. Adams knew nothing about any of them, but as a mathematical problem of influence on human progress, though all were occult, all reacted on his mind, and he rather inclined to think the Virgin easiest to handle.

The pursuit turned out to be long and tortuous, leading at last   18
into the vast forests of scholastic science. From Zeno to Descartes, hand in hand with Thomas Aquinas, Montaigne, and Pascal, one stumbled as stupidly as though one were still a German student of 1860. Only with the instinct of despair could one force one's self into this old thicket of ignorance after having been repulsed at a score of entrances more promising and more popular. Thus far, no path had led anywhere, unless perhaps to an exceedingly modest living. Forty-five years of study had proved to be quite futile for the pursuit of power; one controlled no more force in 1900 than in 1850, although the amount of force controlled by society had enormously increased. The secret of education still hid itself somewhere behind ignorance, and one fumbled over it as feebly as ever. In such labyrinths, the staff is a force almost more necessary than the legs; the pen becomes a sort of blind-man's dog, to keep him from falling into the gutters. The pen works for itself, and acts like a hand, modelling the plastic material over and over again to the form that suits it best. The form is never arbitrary, but is a sort of growth like crystallization, as any artist knows too well; for often the pencil or pen runs into side-paths and shapelessness, loses its relations, stops or is bogged. Then it has to return on its trail, and recover, if it can, its line of force. The result of a year's work depends more on what is struck out than on what is left in; on the sequence of the main lines of thought, than on their play or variety. Compelled once more to lean heavily on this support, Adams covered more thousands of pages with figures as formal as though they were algebra, laboriously striking out, altering, burning, experimenting, until the year had expired, the Exposition had long been closed, and winter drawing to its end, before he sailed from Cherbourg, on January 19, 1901, for home.

COMPREHENSION

1. What did Adams find out from his inquiry into "the dynamo" and "the Virgin"?

2. Explain Adams's philosophy of history and his attitude toward civilization. Why does he prefer medieval to modern times?

3. What does the author say about the process of his own education?

RHETORIC

1. Adams develops many striking figures of speech to illuminate and reinforce abstract concepts and propositions in this essay. Locate examples of this inter-relation of figurative and abstract language.

2. Identify the allusions to Langley (paragraph 1), Daimler (paragraph 2), Marconi and Branly (paragraph 5), and St. Gaudens (paragraph 12). What is the purpose of these allusions? What set of allusions is juxtaposed against them?

3. Explain the way the twin symbols of the Virgin and the dynamo create meaning, coherence, and unity in Adams's essay. What subject links these twin symbols? How do they dictate patterns of comparison and contrast?

4. Why does Adams, writing his autobiography, refer to himself in the third person? What is the effect? How does this strategy reinforce the overall tone of the essay?

5. Analyze the author's presentation of causal analysis in the essay.

6. Why does Adams emphasize St. Gaudens in paragraphs 12 through 16? How does this section prepare for the concluding two paragraphs?

WRITING

1. Comment on Adams's declaration, "Nothing in education is so astonishing as the amount of ignorance it accumulates in the form of inert facts" (paragraph 2).

2. Write an essay investigating what you have learned about civilization from the process of your education.

3. Analyze the role of education in dealing with the forces of modern civilization.

4. Compare and contrast the narratives of Adams and Mead in this chapter.

Glossary
of Terms

Abstract/concrete patterns of language reflect an author's word choice. Abstract words (for example, *wisdom, power, beauty*) refer to general ideas, qualities, or conditions. Concrete words name material objects and items associated with the five senses—words like *rock, pizza,* and *basketball.* Both abstract and concrete language are useful in communicating ideas. Generally you should not be too abstract in writing. It is best to employ concrete words, naming things that can be seen, touched, smelled, heard, or tasted in order to support generalizations, topic sentences, or more abstract ideas.

Acronym is a word formed from the first or first few letters of several words, as in OPEC (Organization of Petroleum Exporting Countries).

Action in narrative writing is the sequence of happenings or events. This movement of events may occupy just a few minutes or extend over a period of years or centuries.

Alliteration is the repetition of initial consonant sounds in words placed closely next to each other, as in "what a *t*ale of *t*error now their *t*urbulency *t*ells." Prose that is highly rhythmical or "poetic" often makes use of this method.

Allusion is a literary, biographical, or historical reference, whether real or imaginary. It is a "figure of speech" (a fresh, useful comparison) employed to illuminate an idea. A writer's prose style can be made richer through this economical method of evoking an idea or emotion, as in E. M. Forster's biblical allusion in this sentence: "Property produces men of weight, and it was a man of weight who failed to get into the Kingdom of Heaven."

Analogy is a form of comparison that uses a clear illustration to explain a difficult idea or function. It is unlike a formal comparison in that its subjects of comparison are from different categories or areas. For example, an analogy likening "division of labor" to the activity of bees in a hive makes the first concept more concrete by showing it to the reader through the figurative comparison with the bees. Analogy in exposition can involve a few sentences, a paragraph or set of paragraphs, or an entire essay. Analogies can also be used in argumentation to heighten an appeal to emotion, but they cannot actually *prove* anything.

Analysis is a method of exposition in which a subject is broken up into its parts so as to explain their nature, function, proportion, or relationship. Analysis thus explores connections and processes within the context of a given subject. (See *Causal analysis* and *Process analysis*.)

Anecdote is a brief, engaging account of some happening, often historical, biographical, or personal. As a technique in writing, anecdote is especially effective in creating interesting essay introductions and also in illuminating abstract concepts in the body of the essay.

Antecedent in grammar refers to the word, phrase, or clause to which a pronoun refers. In writing, antecedent also refers to any happening or thing that is prior to another, or to anything that logically precedes a subject.

Antithesis is the balancing of one idea or term against another for emphasis.

Antonym is a word whose meaning is opposite to that of another word.

Aphorism is a short, pointed statement expressing a general truism or idea in an original or imaginative way. Marshall McLuhan's statement that "the medium is the message" is a well-known contemporary aphorism.

Archaic language is vocabulary or usage that belongs to an early period and is old-fashioned today. A word like *thee* for *you* would be an archaism still in use in certain situations.

Archetypes are special images or symbols that, according to Carl Jung, appeal to the total racial or cultural understanding of a people. Such images or symbols as the mother archetype, the cowboy in American film, a sacred mountain, or spring as a time of renewal tend to trigger the "collective unconscious" of the human race.

Argumentation is a formal variety of writing that offers reasons for or against something. Its goal is to persuade or convince the reader through logical reasoning and carefully controlled emotional appeal. Argumentation as a formal mode of writing contains many properties that distinguish it from exposition. (See *Assumption, Deduction, Evidence, Induction, Logic, Persuasion, Proposition,* and *Refutation*.)

Assonance defined generally is likeness or rough similarity of sound. Its specific definition is a partial rhyme in which the stressed vowel sounds are alike but the consonant sounds are unlike, as in *late* and *make*. Although more common to poetry, assonance can also be detected in highly rhythmic prose.

Assumption in argumentation is anything taken for granted or presumed to be accepted by the audience and therefore unstated. Assumptions in argumentative writing can be dangerous because the audience might not always accept the idea implicit in them. (See *Begging the question*.)

Audience is that readership toward which an author directs his or her essay. In composing essays, writers must acknowledge the nature of their expected readers—whether specialized or general, minimally educated or highly educated, sympathetic or unsympathetic toward the writer's opinions, and so forth. Failure to focus on the writer's true audience can lead to confusions in language and usage, presentation of inappropriate content, and failure to appeal to the expected reader.

Balance in sentence structure refers to the assignment of equal treatment in the arrangement of coordinate ideas. It is often used to heighten a contrast of ideas.

Begging the question is an error or fallacy in reasoning and argumentation in which the writer assumes as a truth something for which evidence or proof is actually needed.

Causal analysis is a form of writing that examines causes and effects of events or conditions as they relate to a specific subject. Writers can investigate the causes of a particular effect or the effects of a particular cause or combine both methods. Basically, however, causal analysis looks for connections between things and reasons behind them.

Characterization especially in narrative or descriptive writing is the creation of people involved in the action. Authors use techniques of dialogue, description, reportage, and observation in attempting to present vivid and distinctive characters.

Chronology or chronological order is the arrangement of events in the order in which they happened. Chronological order can be used in such diverse narrative situations as history, biography, scientific process, and personal account. Essays that are ordered by chronology move from one step or point to the next in time.

Cinematic technique in narration, description, and occasionally exposition is the conscious application of film art to the development of the contemporary essay. Modern writers often are aware of such film techniques as montage (the process of cutting and arranging film so that short scenes are presented in rapid succession), zoom (intense enlargement of subject), and various forms of juxtaposition, using these methods to enhance the quality of their essays.

Classification is a form of exposition in which the writer divides a subject into categories and then groups elements in each of those categories according to their relationships to each other. Thus a writer using classification takes a topic, divides it into several major groups, and then often subdivides these groups, moving always from larger categories to smaller ones.

Cliché is an expression that once was fresh and original but has lost much of its vitality through overuse. Because terms like "as quick as a wink" and "blew her stack" are trite or common today, they should be avoided in writing.

Climactic ordering is the arrangement of a paragraph or essay so that the most important items are saved for last. The effect is to build slowly through a sequence of events or ideas to the most critical part of the composition.

Coherence is a quality in effective writing that results from the careful ordering of each sentence in a paragraph and each paragraph in the essay. If an essay is coherent, each part will grow naturally and logically from those parts that come before it. Following careful chronological, logical, spatial, or sequential order is the most natural way to achieve coherence in writing. The main devices used in achieving coherence are transitions, which help to connect one thought with another.

Colloquial language is conversational language used in certain types of informal and narrative writing but rarely in essays, business writing, or research writing. Expressions like "cool," "pal," or "I can dig it" often have a place in conversational settings. However, they should be used sparingly in essay writing for special effects.

Comparison and contrast as an essay pattern treats similarities and differences between two subjects. Any useful comparison involves two items from the same class. Moreover, there must be a clear reason for the comparison or contrast. Finally, there must be a balanced treatment of the various comparative or contrasting points between the two subjects.

Conclusions are the endings of essays. Without a conclusion, an essay would be incomplete, leaving the reader with the feeling that something important has been left out. There are numerous strategies for conclusions available to writers: summarizing main points in the essay, restating the main idea, using an effective quotation to bring the essay to an end, offering the reader the climax to a series of events, returning to the beginning and echoing it, offering a solution to a problem, emphasizing the topic's significance, or setting a new frame of reference by generalizing from the main thesis. A conclusion should end the essay in a clear, convincing, or emphatic way.

Concrete (See *Abstract/concrete*.)

Conflict in narrative writing is the clash or opposition of events, characters, or ideas that makes the resolution of action necessary.

Connotation and denotation are terms specifying the way a word has meaning. Connotation refers to the "shades of meaning" that a word might have because of various emotional associations it calls up for writers and readers alike. Words like *patriotism, pig,* and *rose* have strong connotative overtones to them. Denotation refers to the "dictionary" definition of a word—its exact meaning. Good writers understand the connotative and denotative value of words and must control the shades of meaning that many words possess.

Context is the situation surrounding a word, group of words, or sentence. Often the elements coming before or after a certain confusing or difficult construction will provide insight into the meaning or importance of that item.

Coordination in sentence structure refers to the grammatical arrangement of parts of the same order or equality in rank.

Declarative sentences make a statement or assertion.

Deduction is a form of logic that begins with a generally stated truth or principle and then offers details, examples, and reasoning to support the generalization. In other words, deduction is based on reasoning from a known principle to an unknown principle, from the general to the specific, or from a premise to a logical conclusion. (See *Syllogism.*)

Definition in exposition is the extension of a word's meaning through a paragraph or an entire essay. As an extended method of explaining a word, this type of definition relies on other rhetorical methods, including detail, illustration, comparison and contrast, and anecdote.

Denotation (See *Connotation.*)

Description in the prose essay is a variety of writing that uses details of sight, sound, color, smell, taste, and touch to create a word picture and to explain or illustrate an idea.

Development refers to the way a paragraph or essay elaborates or builds upon a topic or theme. Typical development proceeds either from general illustrations to specific ones or from one generalization to another. (See *Horizontal/vertical.*)

Dialogue is the reproduction of speech or conversation between two or more persons in writing. Dialogue can add concreteness and vividness to an essay and can also help to reveal character. A writer who reproduces dialogue in an essay must use it for a purpose and not simply as a decorative device.

Diction is the manner of expression in words, choice of words, or wording. Writers must choose vocabulary carefully and precisely to communicate a message and also to address an intended audience effectively; this is good diction.

Digression is a temporary departure from the main subject in writing. Any digression in the essay must serve a purpose or be intended for a specific effect.

Discourse (Forms of) relates conventionally to the main categories of writing—narration, description, exposition, and argumentation. In practice, these forms of discourse often blend or overlap. Essayists seek the ideal fusion of forms of discourse in the treatment of their subject.

Division is that aspect of classification in which the writer divides some large subject into categories. Division helps writers to split large and potentially complicated subjects into parts for orderly presentation and discussion.

Dominant impression in description is the main impression or effect that writers attempt to create for their subject. It arises from an author's focus on a single subject and from the feelings the writer brings to that subject.

Editorialize is to express personal opinions about the subject of the essay. An editorial tone can have a useful effect in writing, but at other times an author might want to reduce editorializing in favor of a better balanced or more objective tone.

Effect is a term used in causal analysis to describe the outcome or expected result of a chain of happenings.

Emphasis indicates the placement of the most important ideas in key positions in the essay. As a major principle, emphasis relates to phrases, sentences, paragraphs—the construction of the entire essay. Emphasis can be achieved by repetition, subordination, careful positioning of thesis and topic sentences, climactic ordering, comparison and contrast, and a variety of other methods.

Episodic relates to that variety of narrative writing that develops through a series of incidents or events.

Essay is the name given to a short prose work on a limited topic. Essays take many forms, ranging from personal narratives to critical or argumentative treatments of a subject. Normally an essay will convey the writer's personal ideas about the subject.

Etymology is the origin and development of a word—tracing a word back as far as possible.

Evidence is material offered to support an argument or a proposition. Typical forms of evidence are facts, details, and expert testimony.

Example is a method of exposition in which the writer offers illustrations in order to explain a generalization or a whole thesis. (See *Illustration*.)

Exclamatory sentences in writing express surprise or strong emotion.

Expert testimony as employed in argumentative essays and in expository essays is the use of statements by authorities to support a writer's position or idea. This method often requires careful quotation and acknowledgment of sources.

Exposition is a major form of discourse that informs or explains. Exposition is the form of expression required in much college writing, for it provides facts and information, clarifies ideas, and establishes meaning. The primary methods of exposition are illustration, comparison and contrast, analogy, definition, classification, causal analysis, and process analysis (see entries).

Extended metaphor is a figurative comparison that is used to structure a significant part of the composition or the whole essay. (See *Figurative language* and *Metaphor*.)

Fable is a form of narrative containing a moral that normally appears clearly at the end.

Fallacy in argumentation is an error in logic or the reasoning process. Fallacies occur because of vague development of ideas, lack of awareness on the part of writers of the requirements of logical reasoning, or faulty assumptions about the proposition.

Figurative language, as opposed to literal language, is a special approach to writing that departs from what is typically a concrete, straightforward style. It is the use of vivid, imaginative statements to illuminate or illustrate an idea. Figurative language adds freshness, meaning, and originality to a writer's style. Major figures of speech include allusion, hyperbole, metaphor, personification, and simile (see entries).

Flashback is a narrative technique in which the writer begins at some point in the action and then moves into the past in order to provide crucial information about characters and events.

Foreshadowing is a technique that indicates beforehand what is to occur at a later point in the essay.

Frame in narration and description is the use of a key object or pattern—typically at the start and end of the essay—that serves as a border or structure to contain the substance of the composition.

Generalization is a broad idea or statement. All generalizations require particulars and illustrations to support them.

General/specific words are the basis of writing, although it is wise in college composition to keep vocabulary as specific as possible. General words refer to broad categories and groups, whereas specific words capture with force and clarity the nature of a term. General words refer to large classes, concepts, groups, and emotions; specific words are more particular in providing meanings. The distinction between general and specific language is always a matter of degree.

Genre is a type or form of literature—for example, short fiction, novel, poetry, drama.

Grammatical structure is a systematic description of language as it relates to the grammatical nature of a sentence.

Horizontal/vertical paragraph and essay development refers to the basic way a writer moves either from one generalization to another in a carefully related series of generalizations (horizontal) or from a generalization to a series of specific supporting examples (vertical).

Hortatory style is a variety of writing designed to encourage, give advice, or urge to good deeds.

Hyperbole is a form of figurative language that uses exaggeration to overstate a position.

Hypothesis is an unproven theory or proposition that is tentatively accepted to explain certain facts. A working hypothesis provides the basis for further investigation or argumentation.

Hypothetical examples are illustrations in the form of assumptions that are based on the hypothesis. As such, they are conditional rather than absolute or certain facts.

Identification as a method of exposition refers to focusing on the main subject of the essay. It involves the clear location of the subject within the context or situation of the composition.

Idiomatic language is the language or dialect of a people, region, or class— the individual nature of a language.

Ignoring the question in argumentation is a fallacy that involves the avoidance of the main issue by developing an entirely different one.

Illustration is the use of one or more examples to support an idea. Illustration permits the writer to support a generalization through particulars or specifics.

Imagery is clear, vivid description that appeals to our sense of sight, smell, touch, sound, or taste. Much imagery exists for its own sake, adding descriptive flavor to an essay. However, imagery (especially when it involves a larger pattern) can also add meaning to an essay.

Induction is a method of logic consisting of the presentation of a series of facts, pieces of information, or instances in order to formulate or build a likely generalization. The key is to provide prior examples before reaching a logical conclusion. Consequently, as a pattern of organization in essay writing, the inductive method requires the careful presentation of relevant data and information before the conclusion is reached at the end of the paper.

Inference involves arriving at a decision or opinion by reasoning from known facts or evidence.

Interrogative sentences are sentences that ask or pose a question.

Introduction is the beginning or opening of an essay. The introduction should alert the reader to the subject by identifying it, set the limits of the essay, and indicate what the thesis (or main idea) will be. Moreover, it should arouse the reader's interest in the subject. Among the devices available in the creation of good introductions are making a simple statement of thesis; giving a clear, vivid description of an important setting; posing a question or series of questions; referring to a relevant historical event; telling an anecdote; using comparison and contrast to frame the subject; using several examples to reinforce the statement of the subject; and presenting a personal attitude about a controversial issue.

Irony is the use of language to suggest the opposite of what is stated. Writers use irony to reveal unpleasant or troublesome realities that exist in life or to poke fun at human weaknesses and foolish attitudes. In an essay there may be verbal irony, in which the author says one thing but means another, or situational irony, in which the result of a sequence of ideas or events is the opposite of what normally would be expected. A key to the identification of irony in an essay is our ability to detect where the author is stating the opposite of what he or she actually believes.

Issue is the main question upon which an entire argument rests. It is the idea that the writer attempts to prove.

Jargon is the use of special words associated with a specific area of knowledge or a particular profession. Writers who employ jargon either assume that readers know specialized terms or take care to define terms for the benefit of the audience.

Juxtaposition as a technique in writing or essay organization is the placing of elements—either similar or contrasting—close together; positioning them side by side in order to illuminate the subject.

Levels of language refer to the kinds of language used in speaking and writing. Basically there are three main levels of language—formal, informal, and colloquial. Formal English, used in writing or speech, is the type of English employed to address special groups and professional people. Informal English is the sort of writing found in newspapers, magazines, books, and essays. It is popular English for an educated audience but still more formal than conversational English. Finally, colloquial English is spoken (and occasionally written) English used in conversations with friends, employees, and peer group members; it is characterized by the use of slang, idioms, ordinary language, and loose sentence structure.

Linear order in paragraph development means the clear line of movement from one point to another.

Listing is a simple technique of illustration in which facts or examples are used in order to support a topic or generalization.

Logic as applied to essay writing is correct reasoning based on induction or deduction. The logical basis of an essay must offer reasonable criteria or principles of thought, present these principles in an orderly manner, avoid faults in reasoning, and result in a complete and satisfactory outcome in the reasoning process.

Metaphor is a type of figurative language in which an item from one category is compared briefly and imaginatively with an item from another area. Writers use such implied comparisons to assign meaning in a fresh, vivid, and concrete way.

Metonymy is a figure of language in which a thing is not designated by its own name but by another associated with or suggested by it, as in "The Supreme Court has decided" (meaning that the judges of the Supreme Court have decided).

Mood is the creation of atmosphere in descriptive writing.

Motif in an essay is any series of components that can be detected as a pattern.

For example, a particular detail, idea, or image can be elaborated upon or designed so as to form a pattern or motif in the essay.

Myth in literature is a traditional story or series of events explaining some basic phenomenon of nature; the origin of humanity; or the customs, institutions, and religious rites of a people. Myth often relates to the exploits of gods, goddesses, and heroes.

Narration as a form of essay writing is the presentation of a story in order to illustrate an idea.

Non sequitur in argumentation is a conclusion or inference that does not follow from the premises or evidence on which it is based. The *non sequitur* thus is a type of logical fallacy.

Objective/subjective writing refers to the attitude that writers take toward their subject. When writers are objective, they try not to report their personal feelings about the subject; they attempt to be detached, impersonal, and unbiased. Conversely, subjective writing reveals an author's personal attitudes and emotions. For many varieties of college writing, such as business or laboratory reports, term papers, and literary analyses, it is best to be as objective as possible. But for many personal essays in composition courses, the subjective touch is fine. In the hands of skilled writers, the objective and subjective tones often blend.

Onomatopoeia is the formation of a word by imitating the natural sound associated with the object or action, as in *buzz* or *click*.

Order is the arrangement of information or materials in an essay. The most common ordering techniques are *chronological order* (time in sequence); *spatial order* (the arrangement of descriptive details); *process order* (a step-by-step approach to an activity); *deductive order* (a thesis followed by information to support it); and *inductive order* (evidence and examples first, followed by the thesis in the form of a conclusion). Some rhetorical patterns such as comparison and contrast, classification, and argumentation require other ordering methods. Writers should select those ordering principles that permit them to present materials clearly.

Overstatement is an extravagant or exaggerated claim or statement.

Paradox is a statement that seems to be contradictory but actually contains an element of truth.

Paragraph is a unit in an essay that serves to present and examine one aspect of a topic. Composed normally of a group of sentences (one-sentence paragraphs can be used for emphasis or special effect), the paragraph elaborates an idea within the larger framework of the essay and the thesis unifying it.

Parallelism is a variety of sentence structure in which there is "balance" or coordination in the presentation of elements. "I came, I saw, I conquered" is a standard example of parallelism, presenting both pronouns and verbs in a coordinated manner. Parallelism can appear in a sentence, a group of sentences, or an entire paragraph.

Paraphrase as a literary method is the process of rewording the thought or meaning expressed in something that has been said or written before.

Parenthetical refers to giving qualifying information or explanation. This information normally is marked off or placed within parentheses.

Parody is ridiculing the language or style of another writer or composer. In parody, a serious subject tends to be treated in a nonsensical manner.

Periphrasis is the use of many words where one or a few would do; it is a roundabout way of speaking or writing.

Persona is the role or characterization that writers occasionally create for themselves in a personal narrative.

Personification is giving an object, thing, or idea lifelike or human characteristics, as in the common reference to a car as "she." Like all forms of figurative language, personification adds freshness to description and makes ideas vivid by setting up striking comparisons.

Persuasion is the form of discourse, related to argumentation, that attempts basically to move a person to action or to influence an audience toward a particular belief.

Point of view is the angle from which a writer tells a story. Many personal and informal essays take the *first-person* (or "I") point of view, which is natural and fitting for essays in which the author wants to speak in a familiar way to the reader. On the other hand, the *third-person* point of view ("he," "she," "it," "they") distances the reader somewhat from the writer. The third-person point of view is useful in essays in which the writers are not talking exclusively about themselves but about other people, ideas, and events.

Post hoc, ergo, propter hoc in logic is the fallacy of thinking that a happening that follows another must be its results. It arises from a confusion about the logical causal relationship.

Process analysis is a pattern of writing that explains in a step-by-step way how something is done, how it is put together, how it works, or how it occurs. The subject can be a mechanical device, a product, an idea, a natural phenomenon, or a historical sequence. However, in all varieties of process analysis, the writer traces all important steps, from beginning to end.

Progression is the forward movement or succession of acts, events, or ideas presented in an essay.

Proportion refers to the relative emphasis and length given to an event, idea, time, or topic within the whole essay. Basically, in terms of proportion the writer gives more emphasis to a major element than to a minor one.

Proposition is the main point of an argumentative essay—the statement to be defended, proven, or upheld. It is like a *thesis* (see entry) except that it presents an idea that is debatable or can be disputed. The *major proposition* is the main argumentative point; *minor propositions* are the reasons given to support or prove the issue.

Purpose is what the writer wants to accomplish in an essay. Writers having a clear purpose will know the proper style, language, tone, and materials to utilize in designing an effective essay.

Refutation in argumentation is a method by which you recognize and deal effectively with the arguments of your opponents. Your own argument will be stronger if you refute—prove false or wrong—all opposing arguments.

Repetition is a simple method of achieving emphasis by repeating a word, phrase, or idea.

Rhetoric is the art of using words effectively in speaking or writing. It is also the art of literary composition, particularly in prose, including both figures of speech and such strategies as comparison and contrast, definition, and analysis.

Rhetorical question is a question asked only to emphasize a point, introduce a topic, or provoke thought, but not to elicit an answer.

Rhythm in prose writing is a regular recurrence of elements or features in sentences, creating a patterned emphasis, balance, or contrast.

Sarcasm is a sneering or taunting attitude in writing, designed to hurt by evaluating or critcizing. Basically, sarcasm is a heavy-handed form of irony (see entry). Writers should try to avoid sarcastic writing and to use more acceptable varieties of irony and satire to criticize their subject.

Satire is the humorous or critical treatment of a subject in order to expose the subject's vices, follies, stupidities, and so forth. The *intention* of such satire is to reform by exposing the subject to comedy or ridicule.

Sensory language is language that appeals to any of the five senses—sight, sound, touch, taste, or feel.

Sentimentality in prose writing is the excessive display of emotion, whether intended or unintended. Because sentimentality can distort the true nature of a situation or idea, writers should use it cautiously, or not at all.

Series as a technique in prose is the presentation of several items, often concrete details or similar parts of grammar such as verbs or adjectives, in rapid sequence.

Setting in narrative and descriptive writing is the time, place, environment, background, or surroundings established by an author.

Simile is a figurative comparison using "like" or "as."

Slang is a kind of language that uses racy or colorful expressions associated more often with speech than with writing. It is colloquial English and should be used in essay writing only to reproduce dialogue or to create a special effect.

Spatial order in descriptive writing is the careful arrangement of details or materials in space—for example, from left to right, top to bottom, or near to far.

Specific words (See *General/specific words.*)

Statistics are facts or data of a numerical kind, assembled and tabulated to present significant information about a given subject. As a technique of illustration, statistics can be useful in analysis and argumentation.

Style is the specific or characteristic manner of expression, execution, construction, or design of an author. As a manner or mode of expression in language, it is the unique way each writer handles ideas. There are numerous stylistic categories—literary, formal, argumentative, satiric—but ultimately no two writers have the same style.

Subjective (See *Objective/subjective.*)

Subordination in sentence structure is the placing of a relatively less important idea in an inferior grammatical position to the main idea. It is the designation of a minor clause that is dependent upon a major clause.

Syllogism is an argument or form of reasoning in which two statements or premises are made and a logical conclusion drawn from them. As such, it is a form of deductive logic—reasoning from the general to the particular. The *major premise* presents a quality of class ("All writers are mortal."). The *minor premise* states that a particular subject is a member of that class ("Ernest Hemingway was a writer."). The conclusion states that the qualities of the class and the member of the class are the same ("Hemingway was mortal.").

Symbol is something—normally a concrete image—that exists in itself but also stands for something else or has greater meaning. As a variety of figurative language, the symbol can be a strong feature in an essay, operating to add depth of meaning and even to unify the composition.

Synonym is a word that means roughly the same as another word. In practice, few words are exactly alike in meaning. Careful writers use synonyms to vary word choice without ever moving too far from the shade of meaning intended.

Theme is the central idea in an essay; it is also termed the *thesis*. Everything in an essay should support the theme in one way or another.

Thesis is the main idea in an essay. The *thesis sentence,* appearing early in the essay (normally somewhere in the first paragraph) serves to convey the main idea to the reader in a clear and emphatic manner.

Tone is the writer's attitude toward his or her subject or material. An essay writer's tone may be objective, subjective, comic, ironic, nostalgic, critical, or a reflection of numerous other attitudes. Tone is the "voice" that writers give to an essay.

Topic sentence is the main idea that a paragraph develops. Not all paragraphs contain topic sentences; often the topic is implied.

Transition is the linking of ideas in sentences, paragraphs, and larger segments of an essay in order to achieve *coherence* (see entry). Among the most common techniques to achieve smooth transitions are: (1) repeating a key word or phrase; (2) using a pronoun to refer back to a key word or phrase; (3) relying on traditional connectives such as *thus, however, moreover, for example, therefore, finally,* and *in conclusion;* (4) using parallel structure (see *Parallelism*); and (5) creating a sentence or paragraph that serves as a bridge from one part of an essay to another. Transition is best achieved when a writer presents ideas and details carefully and in logical order.

Understatement is a method of making a weaker statement than is warranted by truth, accuracy, or importance.

Unity is a feature in an essay whereby all material relates to a central concept and contributes to the meaning of the whole. To achieve a unified effect in an essay, the writer must design an effective introduction and conclusion, maintain consistent tone or point of view, develop middle paragraphs in a coherent manner, and above all stick to the subject, never permitting unimportant or irrelevant elements to enter.

Usage is the way in which a word, phrase, or sentence is used to express a particular idea; it is the customary manner of using a given language in speaking or writing.

Vertical (See *Horizontal/vertical.*)

Acknowledgments

in Contrasts" from *The American Story*, edited by Earl Schenk Miers, Channel Press, 1956. Reprinted by permission of U.S. Capitol Historical Society.

Robert Coles, "I Listen to My Parents and I Wonder What They Believe." Appeared in *Redbook* magazine, February, 1980. Reprinted by permission of the author.

Harvey Cox, "Sex and Secularization" from *The Secular City*. Copyright © 1965 by Harvey Cox. Reprinted by permission of Macmillan Publishing Company.

Harry Crews, "Why I Live Where I Live." Copyright © 1980 by Harry Crews. Reprinted by permission of John Hawkins & Associates, Inc.

Joan Didion, "Georgia O'Keeffe" from *The White Album*. Copyright © 1968, 1976, 1979, 1989 by Joan Didion. Reprinted by permission of Farrar, Straus & Giroux, Inc. "On Keeping a Notebook" from *Slouching Towards Bethlehem*. Copyright © 1966, 1968 by Joan Didion. Reprinted by permission of Farrar, Straus & Giroux, Inc. "On Morality" from *Slouching Towards Bethlehem*. Copyright © 1965, 1968 by Joan Didion. Reprinted by permission of Farrar, Straus & Giroux, Inc.

Annie Dillard, "A Field of Silence." Copyright © 1978 by Annie Dillard. Reprinted by permission of the author and her agent, Blanche C. Gregory, Inc. "An American Childhood" from *An American Childhoood*. Copyright © 1987 by Annie Dillard. Reprinted by permission of Harper & Row, Publishers, Inc.

Gretel Ehrlich, "Wyoming: The Solace of Open Spaces" from *The Solace of Open Spaces*. Copyright © 1985 by Gretel Ehrlich. Reprinted by permission of Viking Penguin, Inc.

Albert Einstein, "The Common Language of Science" from *Out of My Later Years*. Copyright © 1973 by The Estate of Albert Einstein. Published by arrangement with Carol Publishing Group.

Loren Eiseley, "How Natural Is Natural?" from *The Firmament of Time*. Copyright © 1960 by Loren Eiseley.

Copyright © 1960 by The Trustees of The University of Pennsylvania. Reprinted by permission of Atheneum Publishers, an imprint of Macmillan Publishing Company

Ralph Ellison, "On Becoming a Writer" from *Shadow and Act*. Copyright © 1964 by Ralph Ellison. Reprinted by permission of Random House, Inc.

Frances Fitzgerald, "America Revised" from *America Revised*. Copyright © 1979 by Frances Fitzgerald. First appeared in *The New Yorker*. Reprinted by permission of Little, Brown and Company.

E. M. Forster, "My Wood" from *Abinger Harvest*. Copyright 1936 and renewed 1964 by Edward Morgan Forster. Reprinted by permission of Harcourt Brace Jovanovich, Inc. "Not Looking at Pictures" from *Two Cheers For Democracy*. Copyright 1951 by E. M. Forster and renewed 1979 by Donald Parry. Reprinted by permission of Harcourt Brace Jovanovich, Inc.

Sigmund Freud, "Libidinal Types" from *International Journal of Psycho-Analysis*, 13:277-280. Copyright © 1932 Institute of Psycho-Analysis. Reprinted by permission of the International Journal of Psycho-Analysis and A. W. Freud et al.

John Kenneth Galbraith, "The Higher Economic Status of Women" from *Annals of an Abiding Liberal*. Copyright © 1979 by John Kenneth Galbraith. Reprinted by permission of Houghton Mifflin Company.

Ellen Goodman, "Bamama Goes to College." © 1980, The Boston Globe Newspaper Company/Washington Post Writers Group. Reprinted by permission. "Being a Secretary Can Be Hazardous to Your Health" from *At Large*. Copyright © 1981 by The Washington Post Company. Reprinted by permission of Summit Books, a division of Simon & Schuster, Inc.

Stephen Jay Gould, "Darwin at Sea" from *Natural History*, vol. 92, no. 9. Copyright by the American Museum of Natural History, 1983. Reprinted by permission of *Natural History*.

J.B.S. Haldane, "On Being the Right Size" from *Possible Worlds*. Copyright

1928 by Harper & Row, Publishers, Inc. Renewed 1965 by J.B.S. Haldane. Reprinted by permission of Harper & Row, Publishers, Inc., the author's estate, and Chatto and Windus.

Edith Hamilton, "The Lessons of the Past." Reprinted by permission of John D. Gray, Esq., Executor of the Estate of Doris Fielding Reid. "Roots of Freedom" from *The Ever-Present Past.* Copyright © 1964 by W. W. Norton & Company, Inc. Reprinted by permission of W. W. Norton & Company, Inc.

Vaclav Havel, "The Revolution Has Just Begun." Copyright 1990 The Time Inc. Magazine Company. Reprinted by permission.

S. I. Hayakawa, "Words and Children" from *Through the Communication Barrier.* Reprinted by permission of the author.

Langston Hughes, "Salvation" from *The Big Sea.* Copyright 1940 by Langston Hughes. Copyright renewed © 1968 by Arna Bontemps and George Houston Bass. Reprinted by permission of Hill and Wang, a division of Farrar, Straus & Giroux, Inc.

Pauline Kael, "Rocky" from *When the Lights Go Down.* Copyright © 1980 by Pauline Kael. Reprinted by permission of Henry Holt and Company, Inc.

Rosabeth Moss Kanter, "The 'Roast Pig' Problem" from *The Changemasters.* Copyright © 1983 by Rosabeth Moss Kanter. Reprinted by permission of Simon & Schuster, Inc.

Alfred Kazin, "The Kitchen," excerpt from "The Kitchen" in *A Walker in the City.* Copyright 1951 and renewed 1979 by Alfred Kazin. Reprinted by permission of Harcourt Brace Jovanovich, Inc.

Martin Luther King, Jr., "I Have a Dream." Copyright © 1963 by Martin Luther King, Jr. Reprinted by permission of Joan Daves. "The World House" from *Where Do We Go From Here: Chaos or Community?* Copyright © 1967 by Martin Luther King, Jr. Reprinted by permission of Harper & Row, Publishers, Inc.

Maxine Hong Kingston, "The Woman Warrior" from *The Woman Warrior: Memoirs of a Girlhood Among Ghosts.* Copyright © 1975, 1976 by Maxine Hong Kingston. Reprinted by permission of Alfred A. Knopf, Inc.

Joseph Wood Krutch, "The New Immorality" from *Saturday Review* magazine, July 30, 1960. Reprinted by permission.

Elizabeth Kübler-Ross, "The Emotional Quadrant" from *On Death and Dying.* Copyright © 1969 by Elizabeth Kübler-Ross. Reprinted by permission of Macmillan Publishing Company.

D. H. Lawrence, "Why the Novel Matters" from *Phoenix: The Posthumous Papers of D. H. Lawrence* by D. H. Lawrence, edited by Edward McDonald. Copyright 1936 by Frieda Lawrence. Copyright renewed © 1964 by the Estate of Frieda Lawrence. Reprinted by permission of Viking Penguin, Inc.

Mary Leakey, "Footprints in the Ashes of Time" from *National Geographic Magazine,* April, 1979. © 1979 National Geographic Magazine. Reprinted by permission of Dr. Mary Leakey.

C. S. Lewis, "The Rival Conceptions of God" from *Mere Christianity.* Copyright © 1942, 1945, 1952. Reprinted by permission of William Collins Sons & Company, Ltd.

Barry Lopez, "Perimeter," an essay from *Desert Notes: Reflections in the Eye of a Raven.* Copyright © 1976 by Barry Holstun Lopez. Reprinted by permission of Andrews & McMeel, Inc.

Marya Mannes, "How Do You Know It's Good?" from *Glamour* magazine, November 1962, copyright © 1962 by Marya Mannes. Reprinted by permission of David J. Blow. "Wasteland" from *More in Anger.* J. B. Lippincott Co., 1958, © 1958 by Marya Mannes. Reprinted by permission of David J. Blow.

Mary McCarthy, "Names" from *Memories of a Catholic Girlhood.* Copyright © 1957, 1985 by Mary McCarthy. Reprinted by permission of Harcourt Brace Jovanovich, Inc.

Carson McCullers, "Home for Christmas" from *The Mortgaged Heart.* Copyright 1940, 1941, 1942, 1945, 1953, 1956, © 1959, 1963, 1967, 1971 by Floria V. Lasky, Executrix of the Estate of Carson McCullers. Copyright 1936, 1952, © 1955, 1957, 1963 by Carson McCullers. Reprinted by permission of Houghton Mifflin Company.

John McPhee, "Travels in Georgia" from *Pieces of the Frame*. Copyright © 1963, 1969, 1970, 1971, 1972, 1973, 1974, 1975 by John McPhee. Reprinted by permission of Farrar, Straus & Giroux, Inc.

Margaret Mead, "New Superstitions for Old" from *A Way of Seeing*. Copyright © 1962, 1970 by Margaret Mead. Reprinted by permission of William Morrow & Company. "Reflections on the Human Condition" from *Voices For Life*, edited by Dom Moraes. Reprinted by permission of The United Nations Population Fund.

Thomas Merton, "What Is a Monk?" from *The Silent Life*. Copyright © 1957 by The Abbey of Our Lady of Gethsemani. Copyright renewed © 1985 by the Trustees of the Thomas Merton Legacy Trust. Reprinted by permission of Farrar, Straus & Giroux, Inc.

Ann Grace Mojtabai, "Polygamy." Copyright © 1980 by The New York Times Company. Reprinted by permission.

N. Scott Momaday, "The Way to Rainy Mountain" from *The Way To Rainy Mountain*. © 1969 by the University of New Mexico Press. First published in *The Reporter*, 26 January 1967. Reprinted by permission of the University of New Mexico Press.

Donald M. Murray, "The Maker's Eye: Revising Your Own Manuscript" from *The Writer* magazine, October, 1973. Copyright © 1973 by Donald M. Murray. Reprinted by permission of the author and Roberta Pryor, Inc.

Vladimir Nabokov, "Philistines and Philistinism" from *Lectures on Russian Literature*. Copyright © 1981 by the Estate of Vladimir Nabokov. Reprinted by permission of Harcourt Brace Jovanovich, Inc.

Pablo Neruda, "The Odors of Homecoming" from *Passions and Impressions* by Pablo Neruda. English translation copyright © 1980, 1981, 1983 by Farrar, Straus & Giroux, Inc. Reprinted by permission.

Anais Nin, "Notes on Feminism" from *The Massachusetts Review*. © 1972 The Massachusetts Review, Inc. Reprinted by permission.

Michael Novak, "Sports: A Sense of Evil" from *The Joy of Sports*. Copyright © 1976 by Michael Novak. Reprinted by permission of The Sterling Lord Agency, Inc.

Joyce Carol Oates, "Ernest Hemingway" from *(Woman) Writer: Essays* (Dutton, 1988). Copyright © 1984 by The Ontario Review, Inc. Reprinted by permission of the author.

George Orwell, "Marrakech" from *Such, Such Were the Joys*. Copyright 1952 and renewed 1980 by Sonia Brownell Orwell. Reprinted by permission of Harcourt Brace Jovanovich, Inc., the estate of the late Sonia Brownell Orwell and Secker & Warburg. "Politics and the English Language" from *Shooting an Elephant and Other Essays*. Copyright 1946 by Sonia Brownell Orwell and renewed 1974 by Sonia Orwell. Reprinted by permission of Harcourt Brace Jovanovich, Inc., the estate of the late Sonia Brownell Orwell and Secker & Warburg. "Shooting an Elephant" from *Shooting an Elephant and Other Essays*. Copyright 1950 by Sonia Brownell Orwell and renewed 1978 by Sonia Pitt-Rivers. Reprinted by permission of Harcourt Brace Jovanovich, Inc., the estate of the late Sonia Brownell Orwell and Secker & Warburg.

Noel Perrin, "Falling for Apples" from *Second Person Rural*. Copyright © 1980 by Noel Perrin. Reprinted by permission of David R. Godine, Publisher.

Sylvia Plath, "A Comparison" from *Johnny Panic and the Bible of Dreams*. Copyright © 1962 by Sylvia Plath, © 1962, 1977 by Ted Hughes. Reprinted by permission of Harper & Row, Publishers, Inc. and of Olywn Hughes Literary Agency.

J. B. Priestley, "Wrong Ism" from *Essays of Five Decades*. Copyright © 1966 by J. B. Priestley. Reprinted by permis-

sion of the Peters Fraser & Dunlop
Group Ltd.

Santha Rama Rau, "By Any Other
Name" from *Gifts of Passage*. Copy-
right 1951 by Vasanthi Rama Rau
Bowers. Originally appeared in *The
New Yorker*. Reprinted by permission
of Harper & Row, Publishers, Inc.

Adrienne Rich, "The Anger of a Child"
from *OF WOMAN BORN, Motherhood
as Experience and Institution*. Copyright
© 1976 by W. W. Norton & Company.
Reprinted by permission of W. W.
Norton & Company, Inc.

Richard Rodriguez, "Credo" and "Los
Pobres" from *Hunger of Memory*.
Copyright © 1982 by Richard Rodri-
guez. Reprinted by permission of
David R. Godine, Publisher.

Bertrand Russell, "Knowledge and Wis-
dom" from *Portraits From Memory*.
Copyright © 1951, 1952, 1953, 1956 by
Bertrand Russell. Reprinted by kind
permission of Unwin Hyman Ltd.
"The Study of Mathematics" from
Mysticism and Logic. Copyright 1929
by Allen & Unwin, Ltd. Reprinted by
kind permission of Unwin Hyman
Ltd.

Jean-Paul Sartre, "Existentialism" from
Existentialism by Jean-Paul Sartre,
translated by Hazel E. Barnes. Copyright © 1956 The Philosophical Library. Reprinted by permission of The
Philosophical Library, a division of
Allied Books.

Richard Selzer, "Letter to a Young Surgeon" from *Letters to a Young Doctor*.
Copyright © 1982 by David Goldman
and Janet Selzer, Trustees. Reprinted
by permission of Simon & Schuster,
Inc.

Isaac Bashevis Singer, "Why the Geese
Shrieked" from *A Day of Pleasure*.
Copyright © 1963, 1965, 1966, 1969 by
Isaac Bashevis Singer. Reprinted by
permission of Farrar, Straus & Giroux,
Inc.

Adam Smith, "You Keep Bringing Up
Exogenous Variables" from *Paper
Money*. Copyright © 1981 by George J.
W. Goodman. Reprinted by permis-
sion of Summit Books, a division of
Simon & Schuster, Inc.

John Steinbeck, "Americans and the
Land" from *America and Americans*.
Copyright © 1966 by John Steinbeck.
Reprinted by permission of Viking
Penguin Inc.

Gloria Steinem, "Erotica and Pornography" from *Outrageous Acts and Everyday Rebellions*. Copyright © 1983 by
Gloria Steinem, © 1984 by East Toledo
Productions, Inc. Reprinted by permission of Henry Holt and Company,
Inc.

Dylan Thomas, "A Visit to Grandpa's"
from *Portrait of the Artist as a Young
Dog*. Copyright © 1940 by New Directions Publishing Corporation. Reprinted by permission of New Directions Publishing Corporation.

Lewis Thomas, "Notes on Punctuation"
from *The Medusa and the Snail*. Copyright © 1979 by Lewis Thomas.
Reprinted by permission of Viking
Penguin, Inc. "On Societies as Organisms" from *The Lives of a Cell*. Copyright © 1971 by the Massachusetts
Medical Society. Reprinted by permission of Viking Penguin, Inc.

Lester Thurow, "Conflicting Theories of
the Labor Market" from *Dangerous
Currents*. Copyright © 1983 by Lester
C. Thurow. Reprinted by permission
of Random House, Inc.

Paul Tillich, "Theology and Philosophy:
An Answer" from *Systematic Philosophy*, The University of Chicago Press,
1973. Copyright © 1967 by The University of Chicago Press. Reprinted by
permission.

Barbara Tuchman, "An Inquiry into the
Persistence of Unwisdom in Government" from *Esquire* magazine, May
1980. Copyright © 1980 by Barbara
Tuchman. Reprinted by permission of
Russell & Volkening, as agents for the
author.

Mark Twain, "The Mesmerizer" from
Mark Twain in Eruption by Mark
Twain, edited by Bernard DeVoto.
Copyright 1922 by Harper & Row,
Publishers, Inc., renewed 1940 by The
Mark Twain Company. Reprinted by
permission of Harper & Row, Publish-
ers, Inc.

Alice Walker, "Saving the Life that is

Your Own: The Importance of Models in the Artist's Life" from *In Search of Our Mothers' Gardens: Womanist Prose*. Copyright © 1976 by Alice Walker. Reprinted by permission of Harcourt Brace Jovanovich, Inc.

Eudora Welty, "One Writer's Beginnings" from *One Writer's Beginnings*. Copyright © 1983, 1984 by Eudora Welty. Reprinted by permission of Harvard University Press, Cambridge, Mass.

E. B. White, "Education" from *One Man's Meat*. Copyright 1939, 1967 by E. B. White. Reprinted by permission of Harper & Row, Publishers, Inc. "Once More to The Lake" from *Essays of E. B. White*. Copyright 1941, 1969 by E. B. White. Reprinted by permission of Harper & Row, Publishers, Inc.

Virginia Woolf, "The Death of the Moth" and "Professions for Women" from *The Death of the Moth and Other Essays*. Copyright 1942 by Harcourt Brace Jovanovich, Inc. and renewed 1970 by Marjorie T. Parsons, Executrix. Reprinted by permission of the publisher.

Richard Wright, "The Library Card" from *Black Boy*. Copyright 1937, 1942, 1944, 1945 by Richard Wright. Reprinted by permission of Harper & Row, Publishers, Inc. "The Psychological Reactions of Oppressed People" from *White Man, Listen!* Copyright © 1957 by Richard Wright. Reprinted by permission of John Hawkins & Associates, Inc.

INDEX